KU-711-076

Sulu Sea

Kuda

Kota Belud

6 *Gunung Kinabalu* ▲ (4,101m)

Kota Kinabalu

○ Sandakan

Beaufort

LABUAN

○ Keningau

Kinabatangan

Lahad Datu

7

SABAH

Muara

BANDAR SERI BEGAWAN

Limbang

Kuala Belait

4

5 *Ulu Temburong National Park*

BRUNEI

Limbang

○ Semporna

○ Tawau

Nunukan

Miah onal Park

8 ♦ *Sipadan Island Marine Reserve*

Celebes Sea

Bario ○

MALAYSIA

○ Tarakan

aga

Tanjungselor ○

Tanjung Redeb ○

Sangkulirang ○

Long Iram ○

KALIMANTAN

Tenggarong ○

○ Samarinda

INDONESIA

○ Balikpapan

SOUTH SULAWESI

Tanahgrogot ○

alangkaraya

○ Tanjung

Amuntai

Banjarmasin

9

Martapura

Pagatan

Pulau Sipadan
The marine reserve off Sabah has achieved legendary status among snorkellers and divers all over the world.

Footprint **Borneo**

James Alexander, Joshua Eliot and Dinah Gardner
1st edition

*"The river meandered, grew broader and more shallow, and then entered
a very long straight reach. A paradise was disclosed. An inland kingdom,
secluded almost beyond reach, of padi fields and banana trees, palms
and coconuts, lay in its own wide valley, surrounded by jungle hills; a huge
longhouse, its atap roof blending into the landscape, was set back from the
left bank of the river, about three miles off; some forest giants had been left
standing here and there, and on one of these a pair of Brahminy kites were
sitting, the birds of Singalong Burong, King of the Gods."*

Redmond O'Hanlon, *Into the Heart of Borneo* (1985)

Borneo Highlights

❶ Kuching
City of sampans, shophouses and colonial splendour

❷ Sungai Rejang
Malaysia's longest river; tiny craft bump through rapids to reach forest longhouses

❸ Niah National Park
Prehistoric cave paintings and millions of bats

❹ Kampong Ayer
Brunei's massive water village: houses on stilts and wonky walkways

❺ Ulu Temburong National Park
The jewel in the crown of Brunei's ecotourism push

❻ Gunung Kinabalu
Borneo's tallest peak and most magnificent sight

❼ Sungai Kinabatangan
The river is an ideal environment for spotting Borneo's wildlife

❽ Sipadan
Amorous turtles delight snorkellers at this world-class diving site

❾ Banjarmasin
'Venice of the Orient': floating markets, teashops and macaque monkeys

❿ Tanjung Puting National Park
Wild orang-utans, proboscis monkeys, crocodiles, lizards, birds and more

N

0 km   50
0 miles   50

South China Sea

Bintulu

SARAWA

Sibu

Kapit

Rej

❶ Kuching

Bandar
Sri Aman

Singkawang

Semitau

Ngabang

Sanggau

Sintang

Pontianak

Nangah Pinoh

Sukadana

Kendawangan

Pangkalanbun

❿ ◆ Tanjung Puting National Park

Samp

Java Sea

A foot in the door

Straddling the equator and dominated by luxuriant rainforests, Borneo is the third largest island in the world, its territory apportioned unevenly between the countries of Malaysia, Indonesia and Brunei. It was during the dynasty of 'white rajahs', who ruled Sarawak from 1841 to 1941, that the island acquired its reputation as the archetypal primeval wilderness – a land of strange creatures and fearsome headhunters. Since then, Borneo has become a byword for adventure travel and journeys into the unknown. Thankfully, the gruesome ritual of headhunting has long gone out of fashion, but the image of a little-known tropical wilderness still has currency today. Borneo's virgin forests are now acknowledged as the most biodiverse habitats on Earth – places that still hold many secrets from modern science (only recently, a mysterious furry carnivore was photographed in remote Kalimantan).

As can only be expected, 21st-century Borneo is a fast-changing place. Logging has decimated a good deal of the island's coastal rainforests, as have oil palm plantations – and this trend is bound to continue in coming years, particularly in light of depleting oil reserves. But conflicting forces are at work on the island, and not all of them are bad news for the environment. Ecotourism in particular is set to play an important role in the island's economy, with the Malaysian states of Sarawak and Sabah leading the way. Despite the fast pace of change, indigenous culture remains ingrained in the various lifestyles of Borneo's inhabitants. Beyond the Malay-dominated towns and cities (characterized by the call of the muezzin and the trappings of oil wealth), life still revolves around the longhouse and the river. For the visitor, it is the legendary hospitality of Borneo's tribal peoples, as much as the magnificent rainforests themselves, that make the island such a magical place to encounter.

6

1 *Danum Valley is home to some of Sabah's rarest animals, including the sunbear.* ▸▸ See page 227.

2 *Big, brash Kiarong Mosque, built to commemorate the sultan's Silver Jubilee, has no less than 29 gilded cupolas.* ▸▸ See page 261.

3 *Known as 'man of the jungle', the oran-utan, Asia's only great ape, is endemic to the tropical forests of Sumatra and Borneo.* ▸▸ See page 331.

4 *Lack of roads often means rivers are the only viable way of getting around. If there is no regular boat, you can charter a local longboat, although this can be expensive.* ▸▸ See page 29.

5 *Locals gather to buy and sell their produce at the local* tamu *(market); the word comes from the Malay word* tetamu, *to meet.* ▸▸ See page 201.

6 *Beaches are often lined with stretches of casuarina forest, while mangroves occupy tidal mud flats around sheltered bays and estuaries.* ▸▸ See page 330.

7 *Kuching, capital of Sarawak, is a great starting point to explore Borneo.* ▸▸ See page 86.

8 *The seas off Borneo, the third largest island in the world, offer some of the most varied diving on the planet.* ▸▸ See page 40.

9 *The designs and patterns used in Iban textiles sometimes represent mythical deities, which are believed to protect individuals from harm.* ▸▸ See page 327.

10 *There is a large Chinese population in Sarawak, and Chinese culture dominates the south side of Kuching.* ▸▸ See page 86.

12 *Women and children return from the diamond mines near Martapura, in Kalimantan.* ▸▸ See page 291.

12 *According to the Kadazan people, the summit of Gunung Kinabalu is home to the spirits of the dead.* ▸▸ See page 207.

Rice

Rice, which is farmed by the Kadazan people, is not only the main ingredient in Sahaban cuisine, but is also used to make the fiery rice wine, tapai.

Contents

Essentials

⁑ Footprint features

Planning your trip

Where to go

The Malaysian states of Sarawak and Sabah are by far the most visited regions of Borneo and – along with Brunei – they are the island's most accessible entry points. Kalimantan, despite covering approximately two-thirds of the Borneo land mass, is less frequented by tourists, and trips deep into its interior are about as adventurous as 'adventure' travel can get. Rivers, rather than roads, are the main arteries in Borneo and, even today, river travel forms the principle means of getting about the island. Borneo can accommodate trips of anything from a couple of days to a month, or more; if you intend to head upriver independently and stay in longhouses, the longer you have the better. Crossing international borders within Borneo is a fairly straightforward process, particularly if you are travelling between Malaysia and Brunei, or vice versa, but you should allow time within your itinerary for immigration and custom formalities. ▸▸ *For further details, see Visas and immigration, page 19, and Getting around, page 29.*

Stopover
If you are just passing through, the tiny sultanate of Brunei makes a good stopover. Allow a day for the sights around the capital, Bandar Seri Begawan, including a tour of the water village and a proboscis monkey river safari. Then, head for the Ulu Temburong National Park, with its excellent (if daunting) canopy walkway. Longer stays in Brunei could take in Tasek Merimbun (Brunei's largest lake) or longboat journeys upriver to Iban longhouses.

Two weeks
Two weeks will fly by in Borneo. The two most popular options for a fortnight would be either to speed about Sarawak and Sabah, taking in the major highlights – say, Kuching, Bako National Park, the Rejang River and Gunung Mulu National Park (in Sarawak); followed by Mount Kinabalu, Sepilok, the Turtle Islands and the Kinabatangan Wetlands (in Sabah) – or to stick to one state and explore it in more depth (a week, perhaps, in the tranquil Kelabit Highlands and another in the Kuching area; or a week at a beach resort in Sabah, combined with the climb up Mount Kinabalu). A few days in Brunei could also be incorporated, especially if this is your point of entry to Borneo. Alternatively, a fortnight would allow sufficient time to explore one of the interior regions of Kalimantan.

Four to six weeks
With plenty of time on your hands, you could take in all the major sites of Borneo. Even so, there's only so much jungle trekking and river travel one can endure, so you'll probably want to be choosy about where you go, pinpointing a specific area to explore in detail. In six weeks, you'll be able to cover most of the suggestions detailed below, though, to avoid burnout, it's best to pick and choose between the national parks. And bear in mind that journeys deep into the jungle or upriver can be expensive. You might begin in Kuching, administrative capital of Sarawak, using this attractive riverine city as a base for forays deeper into the state. Destinations not to be missed in the region include Bako National Park, on the tip of the Santubong Peninsula; the Sarawak Cultural Village; the Semenggoh Wildlife Rehabilitation Centre; and Gunung Gading, where giant rafflesia flowers bloom. Also, head up the Batang Ai River to stay at a series of Iban longhouses. The mighty Batang Rejang River runs through the heart of Sarawak, and a journey upriver is a great way to get a feel for

the state, passing Iban, Kenyah and Kayan longhouses along the way. You might make a brief visit to the Melanau heartland, Mukah, before heading along the coast to the magnificent Niah Caves. Inland from here is the Gunung Mulu National Park, one of Sarawak's highlights and home to the world's largest cave. The Kelabit Highlands, meanwhile, offer a laid-back retreat high in the jungled mountains of Sarawak. From here, move on to Sabah via Brunei, stopping for a few days in the Brunei capital, with a river trip in search of proboscis monkeys. Then, press on to Kota Kinabalu, capital of Sabah, and prepare for the ascent of Mount Kinabalu. Afterwards, rest your limbs at the Poring Hot Springs, or jump on a launch to the islands of the Tungku Abdul Rahman National Park. Then, cross the state to Sandakan, your base for a trip to the idyllic Turtle Islands National Park and to the Sepilok Orang-Utan Rehabilitation Centre. Next, head for the Kinabatangan Wetlands for your best chance of spotting wild elephants, orang-utans and proboscis monkeys. If you've got the time and money, spend a few days in the remarkable Danum Valley Conservation Area, rich in wildlife. Divers will head straight for Semporna to catch a launch out to Pulau Sipadan, reckoned by some to be the best dive site in the world. From here, adventurous travellers may decide to head across the border into Kalimantan. The east coast city of Samarinda is the launch-pad for trips up the Mahakam River, which winds almost as far as the Sarawak border. Allow at least a week to get the most of a tour upriver. Alternatively strike out north for the Kutai National Park. Then move on to Bandjarmasin in the south, a city dominated by its waterways (and Borneo's largest conurbation). Close by are the Cempeka diamond fields, while further afield, in Kalteng province, is Kalimantan's best known national park, the Tanjung Puting National Park – home to a concentration of wild orang-utans. West Kalimantan attracts few tourists, though die-hard travellers might like to venture up the Kapuas River, Borneo's longest.

When to go

Climate
When planning a trip to Borneo, always take into account the rainy season. The worst rains are usually from November to February and some roads are impassable in these months. However, the main highways are usually open all year round. Travelling during the wet season can also have advantages: hotel prices are generally negotiable and resorts that may be excessively crowded at peak times of year can be wonderfully quiet. Conversely, in the dry season some rivers become unnavigable. In recent years, the onset of the wet and dry seasons in Borneo has become less predictable; environmentalists ascribe this to deforestation and/or global warming.

Festivals and events
Note that in Sabah and Sarawak, school holidays run from mid- to late February, mid-May to early June, mid- to late August and late November to early January. During these periods it is advisable to book hotels in advance. Room rates also increase significantly during these holiday periods. During Ramadan travel can be more difficult and many restaurants close during daylight hours. After dusk many Muslims break their fast at stalls which do a roaring trade, although generally Ramadan is not a period when Muslims eat out, but instead dine at home.

A great time to visit Brunei is the week of the Sultan's birthday celebrations in mid-July. The event is celebrated across the country with parties and fireworks, and this is the only time of year when the palace grounds are opened to the public. ▸▸ *For further details, see Festivals and events, page 36.*

Tour operators

For regional tour operators, such as **Borneo Eco Tours**, www.borneoecotours.com, refer to the Activities and tours listings in the guide.

UK

Audley Travel, 6 Willows Gate, Stratton Audley, Oxfordshire, OX27 9AU, T01869-276200, www.audleytravel.com.

Eastern Oriental Express, Sea Containers House, 20 Upper Ground, London, SE1 9PF, T020-78055100, www.orient-express trains.com. Offices worldwide. Luxury train trips in Thailand, Malaysia and Singapore.

Exodus, Grange Mills, Weir Rd, London, SW12 0NE, T020-86755550, www.exodus.co.uk. Wide range of trips in Southeast Asia. The Borneo Explorer tour includes river journeys and the caves at the Niah National Park.

Explore Worldwide, 1 Frederick St, Aldershot, Hampshire, GU11 1LQ, T01252-760100, www.explore.co.uk. Arranges small group tours (average 16 people) with many different types of trip offered, including cultural excursions, adventure holidays and natural history tours.

Kuoni Travel, Kuoni House, Dorking, Surrey, T01306-747002, www.kuoni.co.uk. Consistently high-quality tour operator that organizes trips all over Southeast Asia.

Magic of the Orient, 14 Frederick Place, Clifton, Bristol BS8 1AS, T0117-3116050, www.magicoftheorient.com. Knowledgeable staff specializing in tailor-made holidays to Southeast Asia and the Far East.

realworld-travel, The Foundry, 156 Blackfriars Road, London, SE1 8E, T0870-7364757, www.4real.co.uk. Everything from self-drive tours to beaches and rainforest treks.

Regaldive, 58 Lancaster Way, Ely, Cambridgeshire, CB6 3NW, T0870-2201777, www.regal-diving.co.uk. Diving tours around Sipadan and Mabul islands on the southeast coast of Sabah.

Silk Steps, Deep Meadow, Edington, Bridgewater, TA7 9JH, T01278 722460, www.silksteps.co.uk. Tours to Borneo.

Trans Indus, Northumberland House, 11 The Pavement, Popes Lane, Ealing, London W5 4NG, T020-85662729, www.transindus.co.uk. Specializes in tailor-made tours.

Travel Mood, 214 Edgware Rd, London W2 1DH; 1 Brunswick Ct, Bridge St, Leeds, LS2 7QU; 16 Reform St, Dundee, DD1 1RG, T0870-5001002, www.travelmood.com. 21 years' experience in tailor-made travel to the Far East and specialists in adventure and activity travel.

Trekforce Expeditions, Naldred Farm Offices, Borde Hill Lane, Haywards Heath, West Sussex, RH16 1XR, T01444-474123, www.trekforce. org.uk. A UK-based charity offering programmes consisting of sustainable projects, language, teaching and cultural experiences.

USA

Asian Pacific Adventures, T1-800-8251680, www.asianpacificadventures.com. Small group, tailor-made and family adventure tours to Borneo and throughout Asia.

Australia
Intrepid Travel, 11 Spring St, Fitzroy, Victori
T1300-360887, www.intrepidtravel.com.au.
Australian company with agents all over the

world. Dozens of different tours of Malaysia,
including some that also take in
neighbouring countries like Thailand.

Finding out more

Useful websites

www.aseansec.org Homepage of the
Asean Secretariat, the Southeast Asian
regional organization of which Singapore is
a founder member. Lots of government
statistics, acronyms, etc.
www.asiainfo-by-cj.com A good and
informative non-commercial website on
Southeast Asia.
www.brunei.gov.bn The government of
Brunei's official website.
headlines.yahoo.com/full_coverage/world/
malaysia/ An excellent news site for
Malaysian current affairs.
www.indonesia-tourism.com The official
tourism website for Indonesia.
www.journeymalaysia.com A great
web resource that covers the majority of
Malaysia's tourist sites in an entertaining
and factual way. You can also book tours.
www.jungle-drum.com An expat
perspective on Brunei for visitors and people
living there.
www.malaysiamydestination.com The
website for Tourism Malaysia.
www.sabahtourism.com A nicely designed
but hard to navigate site about Sabah by the
state's tourism board.
www.sabahtravelguide.com A great travel
site with links to the official tourist board.
There are interactive maps, tour agents,

up-to-date descriptions of destinations,
good travel advice and travel features.
www.sarawaktourism.com A newly
spruced-up site with heaps of information
on the state.
www.tourismbrunei.com Brunei's official
tourism site.
www.virtualtourist.com A good website
with content by other travellers. Put in your
destination and find information on hotels,
restaurants, things to see and even tourist
traps and places to avoid.

Tourist boards

Sarawak and Sabah (Malaysia)
Australia, Level 2, 171 Clarence St, Sydney,
NSW 2000, T02-92994441, mtpb.sydney@
tourism.gov.my; 56 William St, Perth, WA
6000, T08-9481 0400, mtpb.perth@
tourism.gov.my.
Canada, 1590-1111 W Georgia St,
Vancouver, BC, V6E 4M3, T1-604-689 8899,
mtpb.vancouver@tourism.gov.my.
France, 29 rue des Pyramides, 75001 Paris,
T01-4297 4171, mtpb.paris@tourism.gov.my.
Germany, Rossmarkt 11, Frankfurt Am
Main, D-60311, T069-283782,
mtpb.frankfurt@tourism.gov.my.
Italy, Via Priviata della Passarella, No 4, 20122
Milan, T02-796702.

Essentials Planning your trip

Indonesia, Jl HR Rasuna Said, Kav.x/6, No 1-3, Kuningan, Jakarta Selatan 12950, T021-522 0765 (ext 3030), www.tourism.gov.my.
Japan, 5F Chiyoda Bldg, 1-6-4 Yurakucho Chiyoda-ku, Tokyo 100, T03-3501 8691, mtpb.tokyo@tourism.gov.my.
Singapore, 01-01B/C/D, 80 Robinson Rd, Singapore 068898, T6532 6321, mtpb.singapore@tourism.gov.my.
South Africa, 1st Floor, 5 Commerce Sq, 39 Rivonia Rd, Sándhurst, T011-2680292, mtpb.johannesburg@tourism.gov.my

Sweden, Klarabergsgatan 35, 2tr Box 131, 10122 Stockholm, T08-249900 mtpb.stockholm@tourism.gov.my.
UK, 57 Trafalgar Sq, London, WC2N 5DU, T020-7930 7932, mtpb.london@tourism.gov.my.
USA, 120 East 56th St, Suite 810, New York 10022, T1-212-745 1114, mtpb.ny@tourism.gov.my.

Brunei and Kalimantan
For tourist information, contact the relevant embassy in your country (see page 20) or refer to the official tourism websites (see above).

Language

Bahasa Melayu (the Malay language, normally just shortened to bahasa) is the national language in Sarawak, Sabah and Brunei. It is very similar to Bahasa Indonesia, which evolved from Malay. All communities, Malay, Chinese and Indian, as well as tribal groups in Sabah and Sarawak, speak Malay, as most are schooled in the Malay medium. Nearly everyone in Malaysia speaks some English, except in remoter rural areas. In Brunei, English is widely spoken, too, and is taught in schools. Chinese is also spoken, mainly Hokkien but also Cantonese, Hakka and Mandarin.

The best way to take a crash course in Malay is to buy a 'teach-yourself' book; there are several on the market, but one of the best ones is *Everyday Malay* by Thomas G Oey (Periplus Language Books, 1995), which is widely available. A Malay/English dictionary or phrase book is a useful companion too; these are also readily available in bookshops.

The national language in Kalimantan is **Bahasa Indonesia**. English is the most common foreign language. Bahasa Indonesia is a relatively easy language to learn, and visitors may have a small but functional vocabulary after just a few weeks. Unlike Thai, it is not tonal and is grammatically very straightforward. However, this does not mean it is an easy language to speak well. There are many cheap, pocket-sized Indonesian-English dictionaries available in Indonesia. They are fine for the odd request for a towel or a slightly cleaner room, but anyone wishing to learn more will find them disappointing. For visitors interested in studying Bahasa Indonesia in more depth, the Cornell course, though expensive, is recommended.

Basic grammar and pronunciation The basic grammar of both languages is very simple: there are no tenses, genders or articles and the structure of sentences is straightforward. Pronunciation is not difficult either as there is a close relationship between the letter as it is written and the sound. Stress is usually placed on the second syllable of a word. **a** is pronounced as *ah* in an open syllable, or as in *but* for a closed syllable; **e** is pronounced as in *open* or *bed*; **i** is pronounced as in *feel*; **o** is pronounced as in *all*; **u** is pronounced as in *foot*. The letter **c** is pronounced *ch* as in *change* or *chat*. The **r** is rolled. ►► *For further information, see Useful words and phrases, page 334.*

Disabled travellers

For travel to this area, it would be best to contact a specialist travel agent or organization dealing with travellers with special needs. In the UK, contact **RADAR** (The Royal Association for Disability and Rehabilitation) ① *12 City Forum, 250 City Road,*

London, EC1V 8AF, T020-72503222, www.radar.org.uk. In North America, contact the
Society for Accessible Travel & Hospitality (SATH) ① *Suite 610, 347 5th Avenue, New
York, NY 10016, T1-212-447 7284.*

Sabah and Sarawak Disabled travellers are not well catered for in Malaysia.
Pavements are treacherous for those in wheelchairs, crossing roads is a hazard, and
public transport is not well adapted for those with disabilities. This is surprising for a
country which in so many other ways presents itself as cutting edge. But it is not
impossible for disabled people to travel in Malaysia. For those who can afford to stay in
the more expensive hotels, the assistance of hotel staff makes life a great deal easier,
and there are also lifts and other amenities. Even those staying in budget
accommodation will find that local people are very helpful.

Brunei Facilities for disabled travellers are better than those across the border in
Malaysia, though they are still limited by Western standards. Contact **Brunei Tourism**
for specifics. The top hotels – the **Empire** and the **Sheraton** – have pretty good
facilities for disabled travellers.

Kalimantan Indonesia has almost no infrastructure to enable disabled people to
travel easily. Pavements are frequently very high, uneven and ridden with holes and
missing slabs. Buildings, including shops and museums, are frequently reached via
steps with no ramps for wheelchair access. Public transport is frequently cramped and
overcrowded. However, some of the Western-owned hotels at the top end of the market
do go out of their way to provide wheelchair access and facilities for disabled visitors.

Gay and lesbian travellers

Sabah and Sarawak Malaysia – officially at least – is not particularly accepting of what
might be regarded as alternative lifestyles, and homosexuality remains a crime. (Bear in
mind that even Malaysia's former deputy prime minister, Anwar Ibrahim, was charged
with sodomy in 1999.) However there is a bubbling gay scene in KL and, to a lesser extent,
in Kota Kinabalu and Kuching. There are two good websites for gay and lesbian travellers
to the region: www.fridae.com, which has city listings, features on local gay and lesbian
issues, an events page and a personals section with a search by region; and
www.utopia-asia.com/tipsmala.htm, which provides a listing of gay clubs, bars, discos,
gyms and meeting spots. However, the site's homepage states: "Gay life in Malaysia is
blossoming. However, Muslims, both Malay and visitors, are subject to antiquated
religious laws which punish gay or lesbian sexual activity with flogging and male
transvestism with imprisonment. Police may arrest and harass any gay person (Muslim or
non-Muslim) in a public place (ie cruise spots), so discretion is advised." Other websites
are http://members.tripod.com/gaycapitalkl/ for KL and www.geocities.com/swkgay
scene/ for Sarawak.

Brunei As is the case in Malaysia, Brunei is not a good place to be gay – at least not
officially: homosexual sex is illegal and punishable with jail sentences and fines. In
reality, things are more easygoing, although it's best not to flaunt your sexuality. The
www.utopia-asia.com website provides more information.

Kalimantan Indonesia is surprisingly tolerant of homosexuality given that it goes
against the tenets of both Islam and traditional indigenous religions. Homosexuality is
not illegal; the age of consent is 16 years for men and women. Indonesian men are
generally affectionate in public, which allows foreign gay men to blend in more easily.

Student travellers

Anyone in full-time education is entitled to an International Student Identity Card (ISIC). These are issued by student travel offices and travel agencies across the world and offer special rates on all forms of transport and other concessions and services. The ISIC head office is **ISIC Association** ⓘ *Box 9048, 1000 Copenhagen, Denmark, T+45 33939303.* Students can benefit from discounts on some entrance charges and special deals on transport. However, there is no institutionalized system of discounts for students.

Travelling with children

Travelling with children in this part of the world is an awful lot easier – and safer – than in many other so-called 'developing' countries. Food hygiene is good, bottled water is sold almost everywhere, public transport is cheap (including taxis) and ubiquitous, most museums and other attractions provide good discounts for children, powdered milk and baby food (as well as all the other baby/child paraphernalia), including disposable nappies, are widely sold, and high chairs are available in most restaurants.

Naturally, taking a child to a 'developing' country is not something to be taken on lightly; travelling is slower and more expensive and there are additional health risks for the child or baby. But it can be a most rewarding experience. Children are excellent passports into a local culture. You will also receive the best service and help from officials and members of the public when in difficulty.

❧ *In Brunei, be sure to pay a visit to the Jerudong Playground, a theme park without the queues.*

Children in Borneo are given 24-hour attention by parents, grandparents and siblings. They are rarely left to cry and are carried for most of the first eight months of their lives since crawling is considered animal-like. A non-Asian child is still something of a novelty and parents may find their child frequently taken off their hands, even mobbed in more remote areas. This can either be a great relief (at mealtimes, for instance) or most alarming.

The advice given in the health section (see page 44) on food and drink should be applied even more stringently where young children are concerned. Be aware that some expensive hotels may have squalid cooking conditions; the cheapest street stall can be more hygienic. Where possible, try to watch the food being prepared. Stir-fried vegetables and rice or noodles are the best bet; meat and fish may have been pre-cooked and then left out before being re-heated. Various fruits can be bought very cheaply right across Southeast Asia: papaya, banana and avocado are all excellent sources of nutrition, and can be self-peeled ensuring cleanliness. Bottled water and fizzy drinks are also sold widely. If your child is at the 'grab everything and put it in mouth' stage, a damp cloth and some disinfectant are useful. Frequent wiping of hands and tabletops can help to minimize the chance of infection.

At the hottest time of year, air conditioning may be essential for a baby or young child's comfort when sleeping. This rules out many of the cheaper hotels, but air-conditioned accommodation is available in all but the most out-of-the-way spots. Guesthouses probably won't have cots but more expensive hotels should be able to provide them (it is worth emailing or phoning to check). When the child is bathing, be aware that the water could carry parasites, so avoid letting him or her drink it.

Public transport may be a problem; trains are fine but long bus journeys are restrictive and uncomfortable. Hiring a car is undoubtedly the most convenient way to see a country with a small child. Back seatbelts are fitted in more recent models and it is possible to buy child-seats in capital cities or rent them from larger car hire outfits.

Checklist Pack your own standard baby/child equipment and include baby wipes; child paracetamol; disinfectant; first-aid kit; immersion element for boiling water; oral rehydration salts (such as **Dioralyte**); sarong or backpack for carrying child; **Sudocreme** (or similar); high-factor sunblock; sunhat; thermometer; powdered or instant food.

Women travellers

Unaccompanied women often attract unwarranted attention. Most male attention is bravado and there have been few serious incidents involving foreign female tourists (or male, for that matter). However, women should be sensitive to the fact that all three countries in Borneo are predominantly Muslim and should dress appropriately, avoiding short skirts and singlets. In beach resorts clothing conventions are more relaxed but topless bathing remains unacceptable to most Muslims. If swimming outside beach resort areas bear in mind that local women usually bathe fully clothed, so stripping off and running into the sea with nothing more than a bikini may raise one or two eyebrows. When travelling, it is best to keep to public transport and to travel during the day. Hitching is not advisable for women travelling on their own.

Working in Borneo

For a website listing jobs and working opportunities in Malaysia and Indonesia, as well as tips (and links) for anyone thinking of working there, see www.escapeartist.com/as/pac.htm. The Malaysian government recently began an incentive programme for foreigners to move or retire to the country called, *Malaysia: My Second Home*. This scheme offers a renewable five-year multiple-entry visa called a Social Visit Pass. The catch is you need to have RM150,000 banked in Malaysia and a minimum of RM7000 monthly income. If you are retired, you only need one of these. Apply through Malaysian embassies or Tourism Malaysia offices. The **Ministry of Human Resources** (MOHR) provides the official view of labour law and practice in Malaysia, details of which can be found on its website, www.mohr.gov.my/.

Before you travel

Visas and immigration

Malaysia No visa is required for a stay of up to three months in Malaysia (provided it is not for the purpose of working) for citizens of the United Kingdom, the United States, Australia, New Zealand, Canada, Ireland and the majority of other European countries. If you intend to stay in the country for longer, two-month extensions are usually easy to get from immigration offices. Note that Israeli passport holders are not allowed to enter Malaysia.

Visitor passes issued for entry into Peninsular Malaysia are not automatically valid for entry into the states of **Sabah** and **Sarawak**. (The reason for this anomaly is that Sabah and Sarawak maintain control over immigration and even Malaysian visitors from the 'mainland' are required to obtain a travel permit to come here.) On entry into these states from Peninsular Malaysia, visitors will have to go through immigration and receive a new stamp in their passport, usually valid for one month. If you want to stay for longer, then you must ask the official. Apply to the immigration offices in Kota Kinabalu and Kuching for a one-month extension; two extensions are usually granted with little fuss. There are certain areas of East

Malaysia where entry permits are necessary – for example for Bario and the Kelabit Highlands in Sarawak; these can be obtained from the residents' offices (see appropriate sections).

Brunei All visitors to Brunei must have valid passports, onward tickets and sufficient funds to support themselves while in the country (though the latter is rarely checked). Visitors from the UK, Germany, New Zealand, Malaysia and Singapore do not need a visa for visits of up to 30 days. US nationals can stay for up to three months without visas. Visitors from Belgium, Denmark, France, Luxembourg, the Netherlands, Norway, Spain, Sweden, Switzerland, Japan, the Maldives, the Philippines, South Korea and Thailand do not need visas for visits of up to 14 days. Australian passport holders are issued visas on arrival at Brunei International Airport for stays of up to 14 days. All other nationals must obtain visas prior to arrival from diplomatic missions abroad. These visas are normally valid for 14 days, but can easily be extended. For all visitors, getting permission to extend your stay is usually a formality; apply at the **Immigration Department** ① *Jl Menteri, Bandar Seri Begawan*.

Kalimantan (Indonesia) All visitors to Indonesia must possess passports valid for at least six months from their date of arrival in Indonesia and, in theory, they should have proof of onward travel. Many visitors find that immigration officials are happy if there's some indication that sufficient funds (for example traveller's cheques) are available to purchase a return flight. Visas are not required for nationals of ASEAN countries (Brunei, Laos, Malaysia, Myanmar, Philippines, Singapore, Thailand and Vietnam), Argentina, Australia, Austria, Belgium, Brazil, Canada, Chile, Denmark, Egypt, Finland, France, Germany, Greece, Iceland, Ireland, Italy, Japan, Kuwait, Liechtenstein, Luxembourg, Malta, Mexico, Morocco, the Netherlands, New Zealand, Norway, Saudi Arabia, South Korea, Spain, Sweden, Switzerland, Taiwan, Turkey, UAE, UK, USA and Venezuela. These tourists may stay for a maximum of two months (non-extendable) but they are only permitted to enter and exit Kalimantan through one of the so-called 'Gateway' airports of Balikpapan and Pontianak or via the land crossing from Tebedu (Sarawak) to Entikong. If entering or leaving through any other city, a visa is required. Visas are also required by nationals of all countries not listed above. They can be obtained from any Indonesian embassy or consulate and are valid for one month only (extension possible at an immigration office). Two passport photographs and a small fee are required, plus a confirmed onward flight.

Embassies and consulates

Malaysia

Australia, Malaysian High Commission, 7 Perth Av, Yarralumla, Canberra, ACT 2600, T02-6273 1543.

Brunei, Malaysian High Commission, 61 Simpang 336, Jl Kebangsaan BA 1211 kg. Sungai Akar, PO Box 2826, Bandar Seri Begawan BS8675, T238 1095.

Canada, Malaysian High Commission, 60 Boteler St, Ottawa, Ontario KN 8Y7, T1-613-241 5182.

France, Malaysian Embassy, 2 bis rue Benouville, Paris, T01-4553 1185.

Germany, Malaysian Embassy, Klingelhoefer St 6, D-10785 Berlin, T030-885 7490.

Italy, Malaysian Embassy, Via Nomentana 297, 00162 Rome, T06-841 5764.

Japan, Malaysian Embassy, 20-16, Nanpeidai-Machi, Shibuya-ku, Tokyo 150, T03-3476 3840.

New Zealand, Malaysian High Commission, 10 Washington Av, Brooklyn, Wellington, T04-385 2439.

Spain, Malaysian Embassy, Paseo de La Castellano 91-50, Centro 23, 28046 Madrid, T091-555 0684.

Sweden, Malaysian Embassy, Karlavagen 37, PO Box 26053, 10041 Stockholm, T08-791 7960.

Switzerland, Malaysian Embassy, Jungfraustrasse 1, CH-3005 Berne, T031-350 4700.

UK, Malaysian High Commission, 45 Belgrave Sq, London, SW1X 8QT, T020-7235 8033.
USA, Malaysian Embassy, 3516 International Court, NW, Washington DC 20008, T1-202-572 9700.

Brunei
Australia, 10 Beale Crescent, Deakin, Canberra, ACT 2606, T02-6285 4500.
Belgium, 238 Av Franklin Roosevelt 1050, Brussels, T02-675 0878.
Canada, 395 Laurier Av East, Ottawa, Ontario K1N 6R4, T1-613-234 5656.
France, 7 rue de Presbourg, 75116 Paris, T01-5364 6760.
Germany, Zentralverband des Deutschen Baugewerbes, 1st Floor, Kronenstrasse 55-58, 10117 Berlin-Mitte, T030-2060 7600.
Japan, 5-2 Kitashinagawa 6-Chome, Sinagawa-ku, Tokyo 141, T03-3447 7997.
Malaysia, 19 Menara Tan & Tan, Jl Tun Razak, 50400 Kuala Lumpur, T03-2161 2800.

Singapore, 325 Tanglin Rd, Singapore 24795, T733 9055.
Switzerland, Block F/G, 20 Route de Pre Bois, 1215 Geneva 15, T022-929 8240.

Indonesia
Australia, 8 Darwin Av, Yarralumla, Canberra, ACT 2600, T02-6250 8600.
Canada, 287 MacLaren St, Ottawa, Ontario, K2P 0L9, T1-613-236 7403.
Germany, Esplanade 7-9, 13187 Berlin, T030- 445 9210.
Japan, Higashi Gotanda 5-2-9, Shinagawa-ku, Tokyo, T03-3441 4201.
New Zealand, 70 Glen Rd, Kelburn, Wellington, T04-475 8697.
UK, 38 Grosvenor Sq, London W1K 2HW, T020-7499 7661.
USA, 2020 Massachussetts Av, NW Washington, DC 20036, T1-202-775 5200.

Essentials Before you travel

Customs

Malaysia Duty-free allowance is 200 cigarettes, 50 cigars or 250g of tobacco and one litre of liquor or wine. Cameras, watches, pens, lighters, cosmetics, perfumes and portable radio/cassette players are also duty-free in Malaysia. Visitors bringing in dutiable goods, such as video equipment, may have to pay a refundable deposit for temporary importation. It is advisable to carry receipt of purchases to avoid this problem. Export permits are required for gold, platinum, precious stones and jewellery (except reasonable personal effects). Export permits are also required for antiques (from the Director General of Museums, Muzium Negara, Kuala Lumpur).

Brunei Duty-free allowance for those over 17 is 200 cigarettes or 250g of tobacco, 60ml of perfume and 250ml eau de toilette. Non-Muslims are allowed two bottles of liquor and 12 cans of beer for personal consumption. All alcohol must be declared on arrival. Trafficking illegal drugs carries the death penalty in Brunei.

Indonesia Two litres of alcohol, 200 cigarettes or 50 cigars or 100g of tobacco, plus a reasonable amount of perfume. A limit of 50,000 Rp can be carried in or out of the country. There are no restrictions on the import or export of foreign currency, either cash or traveller's cheques, and of some electrical goods.

Vaccinations

A certificate of vaccination for yellow fever is necessary for those coming from endemic zones, except children under one year of age. ➤ *For further details, see also Health, page 44.*

What to take

Travellers usually take too much with them. There is a tendency, rather than to take inappropriate articles of clothing, to take too many of the same article. When packing, remember that most items are available in Borneo's main towns and cities – often at a lower price than in Western countries – and that laundry services are cheap and rapid, so there is no need to arrive loaded down with supplies. You may wish to pack your favourite brand of sun cream or insect repellent, for instance, but even these will be fairly easy to track down in the major department stores, particularly in Brunei, where large shops are as sophisticated as their counterparts in the West. Of course, if you're heading to more remote areas, you will need to stock up in advance, as items may be unavailable or in short supply in local towns and villages.

The following lists provide an idea of what to take with you on a trip to Borneo: bumbag, first-aid kit, insect repellent, international driving licence, passports (valid for at least six months), photocopies of essential documents, spare passport photographs, sun protection, sunglasses, Swiss Army knife, torch, umbrella, phrase book. Those intending to stay in budget accommodation might also include: cotton sheet sleeping bag, money belt, padlock (for room and pack), soap, student card, towel, travel wash. For women travellers: a supply of tampons (although these are available in most towns), a wedding ring for single female travellers who might want to help ward off the attentions of amorous admirers. There is a good smattering of camping grounds in Sabah and Sarawak. If intending to camp, then all the usual equipment is necessary: a tent, stove, cooking utensils, sleeping bag, etc.

Money

Currency
Malaysia The unit of currency is the **Malaysian dollar** or **ringgit** (RM), which is divided into 100 cents or sen. Bank notes come in denominations of RM1, 5, 10, 20, 50, 100, 500 and 1000. Coins are issued in 1, 5, 10, 20 and 50 sen. The ringgit is one of the world's few currencies still pegged to the US dollar at a rate of RM3.80 = US$1.

Brunei The official currency is the **Brunei dollar** (B$), which is interchangeable with the Singapore dollar. Notes are available in denominations of B$1, B$5, B$10, B$50, B$100, B$1000 and B$10,000 (about US$6000!). There are 1, 5, 10, 20 and 50 cent coins. The exchange rate in January 2006 was approximately B$1.70 = US$1.

Indonesia The unit of currency in Indonesia is the **rupiah** (Rp), which is divided into 100 sen. Denominations are 100 Rp, 500 Rp, 1000 Rp, 5000 Rp, 10,000 Rp, 20,000 Rp and 50,000 Rp. Coins are minted in 25 Rp, 50 Rp, 100 Rp and 500 Rp denominations. The exchange rate in January 2006 was 9470 Rp = US$1.

Exchange
Sarawak and Sabah Most of the bigger hotels, restaurants and shops accept international credit cards, including American Express, BankAmericard, Diners, MasterCard and Visa. Visa and MasterCard are the most widely accepted. Cash advances can be issued against credit cards in most banks, although some banks limit the amount that can be drawn. A passport is usually required for over-the-counter transactions. It is also possible to draw cash from ATMs, using a credit or debit card, if you have a PIN number. **Maybank** will accept both Visa and MasterCard at its ATMs; cards with the Cirrus mark will also be accepted at most banks' ATMs. Traveller's cheques can be exchanged at banks and money changers and in some big hotels (often guests only). Money changers often offer the best rates, but it is worth shopping around. Banks charge commission on traveller's cheques. Those from all major issuing companies and denominated in just about any major currency are widely accepted. But, as elsewhere, US dollars are probably best.

Brunei Banks charge a commission of B$10-15 for exchanging cash or traveller's cheques. Money changers often don't charge a set commission at all, but their rates won't be quite so good. ATMs are widespread in Brunei and many accept debit cards (with Maestro), as well as credit cards. Depending on who you bank with, withdrawing money on your debit card is often free (there are plenty of HSBC ATMs around, for instance). Most hotels and many shops and establishments accept credit cards, too.

Kalimantan Banks and money changers outside main centres tend to give poor rates; shop around as there can be great variations between exchange rates. In more out-of-the-way places it is worth making sure that you have a stock of smaller notes and coins, as it can be hard to break larger bills. Major credit cards are accepted in larger hotels, airline offices, department stores and some restaurants, although this method of payment is often subject to a 3% surcharge. Visa and MasterCard are the most widely accepted. Banks in larger towns have ATMs which provide credit card advances. Traveller's cheques can usually be changed in larger towns and tourist destinations. The US dollar is the most readily acceptable currency, both for traveller's cheques (especially American Express) and cash. Money changers often give better rates than banks but will occasionally charge a commission – check beforehand. If changing cash, note that banks like bills in pristine condition. Thomas Cook cheques are not always accepted by banks in provincial towns. Hotels will sometimes change traveller's cheques but rates vary a great deal, from competitive to appalling.

Cost of travelling

It is best not to calculate your budget simply by multiplying the number of days you intend to stay by the figures given below: a couple of days' diving or the need to hire a guide on a trek, for example, would throw such careful calculations right out.

Sarawak and Sabah Because the ringgit has been held down at a lower-than-market exchange rate tied to the US dollar, Malaysia is relatively cheap for overseas visitors. A slump in the tourist industry sparked by 'international terrorism' and the fear of bird flu and, previously, Sars means hotels and restaurants have kept their prices down. It is possible to travel on a relatively tight budget, and getting by on US$15-20 (RM60-80) per day – including accommodation, meals and transport – is certainly possible, if you stay in the bottom-end guesthouses, eat at stalls or in hawker centres and travel on public transport. Cheaper guesthouses charge around RM20-40 a night for two (US$5-10). Dorm beds are less common these days, but are available in big towns for around RM10-20 (US$3). It is usually possible to find a simple air-conditioned room for RM40-80 (US$10-20). A room in a top-quality, international-class hotel will cost RM300-500 (US$80-130), and in a tourist-class hotel (with air conditioning, room service, restaurant and probably a swimming pool), RM100-150 (US$26-40). Eating out is also comparatively cheap: a good curry can cost as little as RM2-4 (US$0.50-1). Finally, overland travel is a bargain and the bus network is not only extremely good, but fares are very good value.

Brunei Per capita, Brunei is one of the wealthiest countries in the developing world, with a GDP not far off that of Singapore. This means that everything, from hotel rates to groceries and transport, is more expensive than in the rest of Borneo. Unless you hire a car, you may have to rely on taxis (the bus network is skimpy at best) and these are not cheap. By Western standards, however, Brunei is not particularly expensive. And, when it comes to local food at market stalls or in *kedai kopi* (traditional coffeeshops), the prices are only marginally higher than those across the border.

Kalimantan Visitors staying in first-class hotels and eating in hotel restaurants will probably spend over 300,000 Rp (US$32) a day. Tourists staying in cheaper air-conditioned accommodation and eating in local restaurants will probably spend about 150,000 Rp (US$16) a day. A backpacker, staying in fan-cooled guesthouses and eating cheaply, might expect to be able to live on 30,000 Rp (US$3) a day. A meal should cost 5000 to 10,000 representative in a simple *warung*, about 10,000 to 20,000 Rp in a local restaurant, and 20,000 Rp or more in a swish hotel coffee shop.

Note Owing to the volatility of the domestic currency and rapid inflation, prices in Indonesia are highly unstable. There is every chance that you will find that the prices quoted here may have increased, sometimes markedly.

Getting there

Air

Royal Brunei Airlines ⓘ *49 Cromwell Rd, London, SW7 2ED, T020-7584 6660, www.bruneiair.com*, is the only airline that flies direct to Borneo from the UK; daily flights between **London Heathrow** and Bandar Seri take 16 hours, including a brief stop in Dubai for refuelling, and cost in the region of £450-650. **Royal Brunei Airlines** ⓘ *BT Tower, 1 Market Square, Sydney NSW 2000, T02-8267 5300*, also flies direct to/from Australia and New Zealand, with three flights per week to and from **Sydney**, **Perth**, **Brisbane**, **Darwin** and **Auckland**. Malaysia Airlines (MAS; www.malaysiaairlines.com) flies from Sydney and Perth to Kuching (Sarawak). There are no direct flights to Borneo from the **USA** and **Canada**.

A popular alternative to one of these direct flights is to fly to **Kuala Lumpur** or **Singapore** and then transfer flights for the remainder of the journey. Around 40 international carriers serve Kuala Lumpur and Singapore. Direct flights from **Europe** leave from London Heathrow (12½ hours), Manchester, Amsterdam, Frankfurt, Paris, Rome, Vienna and Zurich. From other cities a change of plane is often necessary en route. From **North America**, there are flights from Los Angeles (20 hours) via Tokyo and Canada. From **Australasia**, you can fly direct from **Sydney, Melbourne, Brisbane, Darwin, Cairns, Perth** and **Auckland** (flight times range between five and nine hours). From other cities a change of plane is often necessary en route. There are also flights to Kuala Lumpur and Singapore from all regional centres in Southeast Asia.

Connecting flights from Kuala Lumpur and Singapore go to: **Bandar Seri Begawan** (Brunei); **Kuching** and **Sibu** (Sarawak); **Kota Kinabalu** and **Pulau Labuan** (Sabah). The main airlines serving these destinations are **Air Asia** (a budget airline; www.airasia.com), **Malaysian Airlines (MAS)**, **Royal Brunei Airlines** and **Singapore Airlines** (www.singaporeair.co.uk). **Silk Air** (www.silkair.com) has a flight from Singapore to **Balikpapan** (Kalimantan). There are also flights to Borneo from other Southeast Asian hubs, including **Johor Bahru** (JHB) with **Air Asia** and MAS; **Bangkok** (BKK) to Kota Kinabalu or Bandar Seri Begawan, and **Jakarta** (JKT) to Balikpapan, Banjarmasin or Pontianak with **Garuda Indonesia** (www.garuda-indonesia.com).

Flight agents

North America

Air Brokers International, 323 Geary St, Suite 411, San Francisco, CA94102, T1-800-883 3273, www.airbrokers.com. Consolidator and specialist on RTW and Circle Pacific tickets.

UK and Ireland

STA Travel, 86 Old Brompton Rd, London, SW7 3LH, T020-7437 6262, www.statravel.co.uk. Other branches across the UK. Specialists in low-cost student/youth flights and tours, student IDs and insurance.

Trailfinders, 194 Kensington High St, London, W8 7RG, T020-79383939. www.trailfinders.com.

Discount Airfares Worldwide On-Line, www.etn.nl/discount.htm. A hub of consolidator and discount agent links.

International Travel Network/Airlines of the Web, www.itn.net/airlines. Online air travel information and reservations.

STA Travel, 5900 Wilshire Blvd, Suite 2110, Los Angeles, CA 90036, T1-800-777 0112, www.sta-travel.com. Branches across US.
Travel CUTS, 187 College St, Toronto, Ontario, M5T 1P7, T1-800-667 2887, www.travelcuts.com. Specialist in student discount fares, IDs and other travel services. Branches in other Canadian cities.
Travelocity, www.travelocity.com. Online consolidator.

Australia and New Zealand
Flight Centres, 82 Elizabeth St, Sydney, T133133, T1-300- 733 867, www.flightcentre.com.au; 205 Queen St, Auckland, T09-309 6171. Other branches.
STA Travel, 702 Harris St, Ultimo, Sydney, and 256 Flinders St, Melbourne, T1-300-360960, www.statravelaus.com.au; 10 High St, Auckland, T09-366 6673. Also in major towns and university campuses.
Travel.com.au, 80 Clarence St, Sydney, T02-929 01500.

Sea

Passenger ships and cruise liners run between Port Klang, west of Kuala Lumpur, Georgetown (Penang), Singapore, Kuantan, Kuching and Kota Kinabalu. Deluxe cabins are available. Schedules change annually; contact **Tourism Malaysia** for bookings, see page 54. There is also a regular ferry service between Sandakan in Sabah and Zamboanga in the southern Philippines.

Touching down

Airport information

The majority of visitors will be touching down at one of three international airports: Kuala Lumpur, Singapore or Brunei.

Kuala Lumpur

The new **Kuala Lumpur International Airport** (KLIA; www.klia.com.my) is at Sepang, 72 km from the city. Glitzy and high-tech, reflecting Malaysia's 2020 vision, it has loads of restaurants, shops, banks and such like. A helpful **Tourism Malaysia** desk dishes out lots of pamphlets on KL and beyond. The old airport at Subang (sounding confusingly similar to Sepang), 24 km southwest of KL, is now closed, but discussions are underway to open it as a budget airline airport.

Airport departure tax is RM10 for domestic flights and RM45 for international, but this is almost always included in the ticket price. ►► *For further information see Ins and outs, page 53, and Transport, page 66.*

Singapore

Singapore's **Changi Airport** (SIN; www.changi.airport.com) – regularly voted the world's leading or favourite airport – is at the extreme eastern tip of the island, about 20 km from town. There are two terminals, divided between airlines (all clearly indicated). A third terminal is currently under construction but will not be completed until early 2008. The airport's stress-free terminals belie its status as one of the world's most hectic transit hubs. It processes around 26 million passengers a year – around seven times more than the population of Singapore. About 80% of Singapore's tourists arrive by air and it takes only 20 minutes from touchdown to baggage claim – characteristically called 'accelerated passenger through flow'.

Changi's facilities are excellent and include banks, hotel reservations and **Singapore Tourist Board** desks, a medical centre, business centre, children's

Touching down

Country codes Sabah and Sarawak (Malaysia) +60; **Brunei** +673; **Kalimantan** (Indonesia) +62.
Emergencies Sabah and Sarawak: Ambulance, police or fire, T999. **Brunei**: Ambulance T991; Police T993; Fire T995. **Kalimantan**: Ambulance T110; Police T113; Fire T118.
Business hours Sabah and Sarawak: Government offices Mon-Thu 0800-1245, 1400-1615, Fri 0800-1200, 1430-1615, Sat 0800-1245. Note that offices and banks are shut on the 1st and 3rd Sat of every month.

Brunei Mon-Fri 0900-1500, Sat 0900-1100 (banks), though most shopping malls are open daily 1000-2130.
Official language Bahasa Melayu (Malay) in Sarawak, Sabah and Brunei; Bahasa Indonesia in Kalimantan.
Official time Eight hours ahead of GMT.
Voltage 220-240 volts, 50 cycle AC. Some hotels supply adaptors.
Weights and measures Metric, although road distances are marked in both kilometres and miles.

Essentials Touching down

discovery corner, free internet centre, day rooms, restaurants, left-luggage facilities, mail and telecommunications desks, shopping arcades, supermarkets, sports facilities (health centre and swimming pool), hairdresser, nature trails in seven different themed gardens, a movie theatre and accommodation. Everything is clearly signposted in English and the two terminals are connected by a monorail. There is an excellent canteen/food centre in Terminal 2, reached via the multi-deck car park. A tourist information pack is available just after Immigration, near the Customs Hall.
▸▸ *For further information see Ins and outs, page 68, and Transport, page 82.*

Airport tax, payable on departure, is S$21 for all flights to all countries (but many tickets already have this included in their price). A PSC (Passenger Service Charge) coupon can be purchased at most hotels, travel agencies and airline offices in town before departure, which saves time at the airport. The 5% **Goods and Sales tax** (GST) is refundable at the airport for goods bought (over US$300) with appropriate receipts.

Brunei

Brunei International Airport (BWN; www.brunet.bn/gov/dca/fids/) is small, quiet and pleasant with minimal (but adequate) facilities, all of which are located in Departures, on the first floor. There are two banks and a currency exchange/information booth, all subject to standard opening hours. A separate ATM machine, which takes all major cards (including Maestro debit cards), is operational 24 hours daily. There are showers and inexpensive day rooms, which charge an hourly (or eight-hourly) rate. There's a car-hire booth in arrivals, and airport taxis line up outside, with set fares to each hotel.
▸▸ *For further information see Ins and outs, page 254, and Transport, page 274.*

There is an **airport tax** of B$5 for Singapore and Malaysia, B$12 for all other destinations. There is no sales tax in Brunei.

Local customs and laws

Conduct As elsewhere in Southeast Asia, in Borneo 'losing face' brings shame. Even when bargaining, using a loud voice or wild gesticulations will be taken to signify anger and, hence, 'loss of face'. By the same token, the person you shout at will also feel loss of face, particularly if it happens in public. In Muslim company it is impolite to touch others with the left hand or with other objects – even loose change. You should also not use your left hand to pick up or pass food. Men shake hands in Malaysia but it is not usual for a man to shake a woman's hand except in Kuala Lumpur. Indeed, excessive personal contact should be avoided. However, Indonesians of the same sex tend to be more affectionate – holding hands, for example. Using the index finger to point at people, even at objects, is regarded as insulting. The thumb or whole hand should be used to indicate something, or to wave down a taxi. Before entering a private home, remember to remove your shoes; it is also usual to take a small gift for the host, which is not opened until after the visitor has left.

Dress Clothes are light, cool and casual most of the time, but also fairly smart. Some establishments, mainly exclusive restaurants, require a long-sleeved shirt with tie or local batik shirt and do not allow shorts in the evening. For jungle treks, a waterproof is advisable, as are canvas jungle boots, which dry faster than leather. Dress codes are important to observe from the point of view cultural and religious sensitivities. Women should be particularly careful not to offend. Dress modestly and avoid shorts, short skirts and sleeveless dresses or shirts (except at recognised beach resorts). Public nudity and topless bathing are not acceptable. Remove shoes before entering mosques and temples; in mosques, women should cover their heads, shoulders and legs and men should wear long trousers.

Prohibitions The trafficking of illegal drugs into Malaysia and Brunei carries the death penalty. In Indonesia, for trafficking even modest quantities, you can expect a lengthy jail term at least. Brunei is a 'dry' country: sale of alcohol is banned, while consumption is prohibited for Muslims. Non-Muslims may consume alchohol that has been declared at Customs (two bottles of liquor or 12 cans of beer; see page 21), but not in public. Certain restaurants will allow non-Muslims to bring their own alcohol to drink with the meal but always check in advance.

Punctuality *Jam karet* or 'rubber time' is a peculiarly Indonesian phenomenon. Patience and a cool head are very important; appointments rarely take place at the time arranged.

Tipping Tipping is unusual in Malaysia, as a service charge of 10% is automatically added to restaurant and hotel bills, plus a 5% government tax (indicated by the + and ++ signs). Nor is tipping expected in smaller restaurants where a service charge is not automatically added to the bill. For personal services, porterage for example, a modest tip may be appropriate. In Indonesia, a 10% service charge is added to bills at more expensive hotels (in addition to tax of 11%). Porters expect to be tipped about 500 Rp a bag. In more expensive restaurants, where no service is charged, a tip of 5-10% is sometimes appropriate. Taxi drivers (in larger towns) appreciate a small tip (200-300 Rp).

Responsible tourism

"Tourism is like fire. It can either cook your food or burn your house down". This sums up the ambivalent attitude that many people have regarding the effects of tourism. It is a major foreign exchange earner and the world's largest single industry; yet many people in receiving countries would rather that tourists stayed home. Tourism is seen to be the cause of polluted beaches, rising prices, loose morals, consumerism, and much else besides.

Most international tourists come from a handful of wealthy countries. This is why many see tourism as the new 'imperialism', imposing alien cultures and ideals on

⁑ How big is your footprint?

- Learn about the country you're visiting.
- Start enjoying your travels before you leave by tapping into as many sources of information as you can.
- Think about where your money goes – be fair and realistic about how cheaply you travel. Try and put money into local people's hands; drink local beer or fruit juice rather than imported brands and stay in locally-owned accommodation.
- Open your mind to new cultures and traditions. It can transform your holiday experience and you'll earn respect and be more readily welcomed by local people.
- Think about what happens to your rubbish – take biodegradable products and a water filter bottle. Be sensitive to limited resources like water, fuel and electricity.
- Help preserve local wildlife and habitats by respecting rules and regulations, such as sticking to footpaths, not standing on coral and not buying products made from endangered plants or animals.
- Use your guidebook as a starting point, not the only source of information. Talk to local people, then *discover your own adventure!*
- Don't treat people as part of the landscape, they may not want their picture taken. Put yourself in their shoes, ask first and respect their wishes.

Taken from the Tourism Concern website (www.tourismconcern.org.uk), which provides further elaboration of the points noted here.

sensitive and less-modernized peoples. The problem, however, is that discussions of the effects of tourism tend to degenerate into simplifications – culminating in the drawing up of a checklist of 'positive' and 'negative' effects. Although such tables may be useful in highlighting problem areas, they also do a disservice by reducing a complex issue to a simple set of rather one-dimensional 'costs' and 'benefits'. Different destinations will be affected in different ways; these effects are likely to vary over time; and different groups living in a particular destination will feel the effects of tourism in different ways and to varying degrees. At no time or place can tourism (or any other influence) be categorized as uniformly 'good' or 'bad'.

Ironically, 'travellers' or 'backpackers' sometimes find it difficult to consider themselves as tourists at all. This, of course, is hubris built upon the notion that the traveller is an 'independent' explorer somehow beyond the bounds of the industry. Anna Borzello in an article entitled 'The myth of the traveller' in the journal *Tourism in Focus* (No 19, 1994) writes that, "Independent travellers cannot acknowledge – without shattering their self-image – that to many local people they are simply a good source of income ..[not] inheritors of Livingstone, [but] bearers of urgently needed money." Although she does, in writing this, grossly underestimate the ability of travellers to see beyond their thongs and friendship bracelets, she does have a point when she suggests that it is important for travellers honestly to appraise their role as tourists, because, "Not only are independent travellers often frustrated by the gap between the way they see themselves and the way they are treated, but unless they acknowledge that they are part of the tourist industry they will not take responsibility for the damaging effects of their tourism."

For suggestions on how to minimize your impact on the country you're visiting and its people, see How big is your footprint?, page 28. You could also contact the UK-based charity **Tourism Concern** ① *Stapleton House, 277-281 Holloway Rd, London N7 8HN, www.tourismconcern.org.uk*, and subscribe to their magazine, *In Focus*.

Getting around

Owing to Borneo's inadequate road network, flying is by far the easiest way to travel around the island, with frequent and inexpensive flights between the main towns. Speed ferries also skirt the island, passing immigration points either en route, or at the departure and arrival points. The cheapest (and slowest) means of travelling on Borneo is by bus. When travelling around the island, remember that Sarawak has its own immigration rules (independent to those of Malaysia), with visitors receiving a one-month entry stamp, which needs to be renewed in Kuching for longer stays.

Air

Malaysian Airlines (**MAS**; www.malaysia-airlines.com.my) and the budget airline, **AirAsia** (www.airasia.com) both have extensive flight networks in Borneo. Flying is relatively inexpensive but flights get very booked up on public holidays (see page 36). **MAS** serves Kota Kinabalu, Kudat, Pulau Labuan, Lahad Datu, Sandakan, Semporna and Tawau (Sabah); Bario, Belaga, Bintulu, Kuching, Lawas, Limbang, Marudi, Miri, Mulu and Sibu (Sarawak); Bandar Seri (Brunei); Pontianak (Kalimantan). Non-Malaysian passport holders who have flown in to or out of Malaysia with **Malaysian Airlines** are eligible for the *Discover Malaysia Pass*. The pass, which must be purchased within 14 days of arrival, costs US$199 and entitles the holder to five internal flights within 28 days, including one return trip between Peninsular Malaysia and East Malaysia (Sabah and Sarawak). Local **MAS** offices are listed under each town. **AirAsia** serves Kota Kinabalu, Kuala Terengganu, Kuching, Pulau Labuan, Miri, Sandakan, Sibu and Tawau. In addition, **Royal Brunei Airlines** flies from Bandar Seri to Kuching, Kota Kinabalu and Balikpapan (Kalimantan), although note that it usually cheaper to fly from Malaysian Borneo into Brunei rather than vice versa.

Rail

Trains are not a feasible way of getting around Borneo as the infrastructure is virtually non-existent and the rolling stock very old. In the state of Sabah, however, there is one railway line, which passes through the spectacular **Padas River Gorge** (see page 203).

River and sea

There are speedy ferry services to Brunei each day from Limbang and Lawas (Sarawak) and from Pulau Labuan, which in turn has an onward service to Kota Kinabalu in Sabah. Tawau, in Sabah, is the main crossing point between Malaysian and Indonesian Borneo, with daily ferries leaving for Nunakan and Tarakan.

There are excellent coastal and upriver express boat services in Sarawak and Sabah, where local water transport comes into its own, as lack of roads makes it the only viable means of communication. Express boat services are also the primary means of travelling around Kalimantan. If there is no regular boat, it is nearly always possible to charter a local longboat, although this can be expensive. In the dry season the upper reaches of many rivers are unnavigable except by smaller boats. In times of heavy rain, logs and branch debris can make rivers unsafe.

Road

Travel around Borneo is not always easy, as the road network is limited and some routes are not in a good state of repair. The highway between KK and Sandakan, for example, is sometimes blocked by mud slides after heavy rain. In many areas, air or water transport may be the only options.

It is possible to cross overland from Sarawak and Sabah to Kalimantan and Brunei. The main crossing point into Kalimantan is in the west, between Kuching (Sarawak) and Pontianak (Kalimantan), with frequent buses between these two towns. From Miri (Sarawak) there are regular buses to Kuala Belait and Bandar Seri Begawan (Brunei), with an immigration post on either side of the border where passengers disembark briefly for customs formalities. Less regular bus services run between Sipitang (Sabah) to Bangar (Brunei), from where there is a ferry service to the capital.

Bus

Air-conditioned buses connect major towns; seats can be reserved and prices are reasonable, although they vary according to whether the bus is express or regular, and between companies. (Be warned that the air conditioning can be very cold.) In larger towns there may be a number of bus stops and some private companies may operate directly from their own offices. Beyond the main towns, buses are less reliable and road conditions are poorer. Bus routes, journey times and fares are listed in individual towns under 'Transport'.

> ‼ *During the school holiday period, it can be difficult to get bus tickets and it is worth booking ahead.*

Car hire

Visitors can hire a car provided they are in possession of an international driving licence, are over 23 and not older than 65, and have at least one year's driving experience. In Sabah and Sarawak, car hire costs from RM100 to RM250 per day approximately depending on the model and the company. 4WD vehicles are expensive but they are readily available and are de rigeur in Sabah. Cheaper weekly and monthly rates and special deals may be available.

Driving is on the left; give way to drivers on the right. The wearing of seat belts is compulsory for front-seat passengers and the driver. Most road signs are international but note that '*awas*' means caution.

Hitchhiking

It is easy for foreigners to hitch in Borneo, as long as they look reasonably presentable. However, hitching is not advisable for women travelling alone.

Taxi

There are two types of taxi in Borneo – local and 'out-station' – or long distance. Local taxis are fairly cheap in Sabah, Sarawak and Kalimantan, but it is rare to find a taxi with a meter, so you will need your bargaining skills. Taxis in Brunei are metered.

Out-station taxis connect towns and cities. They operate on a shared-cost basis: as soon as the full complement of four passengers turns up, the taxi sets off. Alternatively, it is possible to charter the whole taxi for the price of four single fares. Taxi stands are usually next door to major bus stations. If shared, taxi fares usually cost about twice as much as bus fares, but they are much faster. For groups travelling

Maps

Country maps Bartholomew Singapore and Malaysia (1:150,000); Nelles Malaysia (1:1,500,000); Nelles Indonesia (1:4,000,000). Decent maps of Brunei are more or less impossible to obtain.

Locally available maps Maps are widely available in Malaysia and Singapore. The Malaysian tourist board produces good maps of Kuala Lumpur and a series of not-so-good state maps. The Sabah and Sarawak tourist boards also publish reasonable maps.

Map shops In the UK, the best selection is available from **Stanfords** ① *12-14 Long Acre, London WC2E 9LP, T020-78361321*; also recommended is **McCarta** ① *15 Highbury Place, London N15 1QP, T020-73541616*.

Sleeping

Sarawak and Sabah

Room rates are subject to 5-10% tax. Many of the major international chains have hotels, such as **Hilton**, **Holiday Inn** and **Hyatt**. Room rates in the big hotels have been fairly stable for the last few years. The number of four- and five-star hotel rooms has also multiplied and this, combined with a weak ringgit and generally depressed economy, has helped to keep prices stable. By world standards, even the most expensive hotels are good value for money. It is also worth noting that in tourist resorts, many hotels have two, sometimes three, room tariffs: one for weekdays, one for weekends and, sometimes, a third for holiday periods. Room rates can vary substantially between these periods.

It is often possible to stay with families in Malay kampongs (villages) as part of the so-called homestay programme (contact the local tourist office or travel agent for more information) or in longhouses, where rates are at the discretion of the visitor (see page 114). For accommodation in national parks (see relevant chapters), it is necessary to book in advance.

Youth hostels are only available in KL and Kota Kinabalu. There are not many campsites, either, but 'wild camping' is easy. In Sabah, you can camp exactly where you want to be, for example at Tunkul Abdul Rahman Marine Park.

Brunei

Brunei has a real dearth of places to stay – though, given its size and population, this should come as no particular surprise – and accommodation is significantly more expensive than in neighbouring Sarawak, Sabah and, especially, Kalimantan. Most of the hotels are functional, business-oriented places, and there are virtually no budget options, apart from the youth hostel in Bandar Seri Begawan and the indigenous longhouses, some of which offer homestay programmes. At the top end, Brunei boasts the impressive, six-star **Empire Hotel and Country Club** (see page 269), one of the world's flashiest hotels. With relatively small visitor numbers, there should never be a problem finding a room, whatever your budget. What's more, the top-end hotels frequently offer excellent promotions.

✱ Hotel prices and facilities

LL US$200 and above and **L** US$130-200 Luxury: most hotels in this bracket are confined to Brunei and Singapore.

AL US$90-130 International class: impeccable service, beautifully appointed, offering an array of facilities and business services.

A US$40-90 First class: good range of services and facilities, sometimes including a swimming pool, gym and maybe a spa. Very competitively priced, given standards of service.

B US$20-40 Tourist class: hotels in this category provide a basic range of services and facilities including a coffee shop and/or simple restaurant and all rooms should have a/c.

C US$10-20 Economy: while there are some excellent economy hotels in this category, few provide much in the way of services. Guests will usually have the option of a/c or fan-cooled rooms and a choice of attached/shared bathrooms. In Sarawak and Sabah, backpacker hostels fall into this category, and usually offer good travel advice, laundry service, breakfast facilities and maybe a common fridge and kitchen and are suitable for families on a budget.

D US$5-10 Budget: most hotels in this class are located in town centres; they are often noisy and many are pretty scruffy joints with not much in the way of service or facilities. At the upper end, rooms have a/c and attached bathrooms; cheaper rooms have fans and communal bathrooms. Some fine old tumbledown colonial relics in this range offer good value for money. Youth hostels fall into this price range.

E US$2.50-5 Lodging house/guesthouse/hostel: for this price range you are looking at a simple room with shared bathroom and fan. Some backpacker places will have simple rooms and dorms in this category.

F under US$2.50 In this price category you'll get a space in a dorm at a bottom-of-the-range hostel, or a simple A-frame near the beach, if you're lucky. In Kalimantan you'll get a fan-cooled room, often with shared *mandi* and Asian 'squat' toilet. Toilet paper and towels are unlikely to be provided, although bed linen will be. Places in this category vary a great deal, and can change very rapidly. Other travellers are the best source of up-to-the-minute reviews.

Kalimantan

Tourist and business centres usually have a good range of accommodation for all budgets. However, visitors venturing off the beaten track may find hotels restricted to dingy, over-priced places catering for local businessmen and officials.

Terminology can be confusing: a *losmen* is a cheaper hotel; a *wisma* is a guesthouse. **Note** The government has introduced a ruling requiring all tourist accommodation to have Indonesian names rather than use Western words, so be prepared for hotel name changes.

The 'star' system used in Indonesia can give a rough guide to the price of the establishment. The *melati* (flower) system is for cheaper hotels; while the *bintang* (star) system is for more expensive hotels. All hotels are required to display their room rates on a price list, with rooms on higher floors usually cheaper. Hotels in the middle and lower price categories often provide breakfast in the room rate. In the more out-of-the-way places or in hotels geared to Indonesians, this is usually fried rice or something similar. In the more expensive hotels, service charge (10%) and government tax (11%) are added onto the bill; they are usually excluded from the advertised room rate, which tends to be quoted in US dollars. During the off-season, hotels in tourist destinations may halve their room rates, so it is always worth bargaining or asking whether there is a 'special' price.

Baths and showers are not a feature of many cheaper *losmen*, instead a *mandi* – a water tank and ladle – is used. Water is ladled from the tank and splashed over the head. Some bathrooms will also have a shower attachment, occasionally with hot water although more often not. The traditional Asian toilet is of the squat variety. Water scooped from a *mandi*, or a large water jar, is used to 'flush' the bowl. In cheaper accommodation you are expected to bring your own towels, soap and toilet paper, and the bed may only have a bottom sheet and pillow (so bring your own top sheet if you want to keep the mosquitoes at bay).

Camping is not common and, even in national parks, camping facilities are poor and limited.

Eating

Sarawak and Sabah

Malaysians love their food and the dishes of the three main communities, Malay, Chinese and Indian, comprise a hugely varied national menu. Even within each ethnic cuisine, there is a vast choice; for example, there is north Indian food, south Indian food and Indian Muslim food. Malaysia also has great seafood, which the Chinese do best. You'll also find various tribal specialities. For non-meat-eaters, there are numerous Chinese and Malay vegetarian dishes, although it is not unusual to find slivers of meat even when a vegetable dish is specifically requested. ▸▸ *For further details, see the Food glossary, page 338.*

The best **Malay** food is usually found at stalls in hawker centres. The staple diet is rice and curry, which is rich and creamy due to the use of coconut milk. Herbs and spices include chillis, ginger, turmeric, coriander, lemongrass, anise, cloves, cumin, caraway and cinnamon.

Cantonese and **Hainanese** cooking are the most prevalent Chinese cuisines in Malaysia. Some of the more common Malaysian-Chinese dishes are Hainanese chicken rice (rice cooked in chicken stock and served with steamed or roast chicken), *char kway teow* (Teochew-style fried noodles, with eggs, cockles and chilli paste), or *luak* (Hokkien oyster omelette), *dim sum* (steamed dumplings and patties) and *yong tow foo* (beancurd and vegetables stuffed with fish). Good Chinese food is available in restaurants, coffee shops and from hawker stalls.

Indian cooking can be divided into three schools: northern and southern (neither eat beef) and Muslim (no pork). Northern dishes tend to be more subtly spiced, use more meat and are served with breads. Southern dishes use fiery spices, emphasize vegetables and are served with rice. The best known north Indian food is tandoori, which is served with delicious fresh naan breads, baked in ovens on-site. Other pancakes include *roti, thosai* and *chapati*. Malaysia's famous *mamak* men are Indian Muslims who are highly skilled at making everything from *teh tarik* (see Drink below) to rotis.

⁑ For restaurant price codes, see box, page 34, or the inside front cover. For health matters relating to food, see page 44. For food glossaries see page 338.

The Kadazan form the largest ethnic group in Sabah and their **Sabahan** food, tends to use mango and can be on the sour side.

♣ Restaurant price codes explained

♦♦♦	Expensive	US$10 and above
♦♦	Mid-range	US$3.50-10
♦	Cheap	under US$3.50

Prices refer to a two-course meal (starter plus main course) without a drink for one person, unless otherwise stated.

Drink Soft drinks, mineral water and freshly squeezed fruit drinks are available. Anchor and Tiger beer are widely sold and are cheapest at the hawker stalls (RM5-7 per bottle). A beer will cost RM8-15 per bottle in coffee shops. Malaysian-brewed Guinness is popular, mainly because the Chinese believe it has medicinal qualities. Malaysians like strong coffee and unless you specify *kurang manis* (less sugar), *tak mahu manis* (no sugar) or *kopi kosong* (black, no sugar), it will come with lashings of condensed milk.

One of the most interesting cultural refinements of the Indian Muslim community is the *mamak* man, who is famed for *teh tarik* (pulled tea), which is thrown across a distance of about a metre, from one cup to another, with no spillages. The idea is to cool it down for customers but it has become an art form; *mamak* men appear to cultivate the nonchalant look when pouring. Malaysian satirist Kit Lee says a tea-stall *mamak* "could 'pull' tea in free fall without spilling a drop – while balancing a *beedi* on his lower lip and making a statement on Economic Determinism".

Eating out The cheapest places to eat are in hawker centres and roadside stalls (often concentrated in or close to night markets) where it is possible to eat well for just RM3-4. Stalls may serve Malay, Indian or Chinese dishes and, even, some food which approximates to 'Western'. Next in the sequence of sophistication and price come the ubiquitous *kedai kopi* (coffee shops), where a meal will cost upwards of RM5. Usually run by Chinese or Indian families, rather than Malay, they open at around 0900 and close in the early evening; some open at dawn to serve dim sum to people on their way to work; they are also the only coffee shops where it is possible to track down a cold beer. Malay-run *kedai kopi* are good for lunch with their *nasi campur* spreads. Hotel restaurants regularly lay on buffet spreads, which are good value at about RM20-30, often much cheaper than the price of a room would suggest.

> ♣ *Many restaurants charge an extra 15% service and tax. During Ramadan many restaurants close during daylight hours.*

Brunei

The variety and quality of food in Brunei is outstanding, with a medley of restaurants, market stalls and food courts offering a wide range of cuisines, from Malay, Chinese and Indian, to Indonesian, Japanese and European. Because of Brunei's relative wealth, there isn't the same density of street food as elsewhere in Borneo. Nevertheless, the informal local restaurants and food courts are still the best places to sample good local cuisine (at great prices).

Drink Brunei is a 'dry' country: sale of alcohol is banned, while consumption is prohibited for Muslims. Certain restaurants will allow non-Muslims to bring their own alcohol to drink with the meal. Always check in advance.

Indonesians will eat rice – or *nasi* (milled, cooked rice) – at least three times a day. Breakfast often consists of left-over rice, stir-fried and served up as *nasi goreng*. Mid-morning snacks are often sticky rice cakes or *pisang goreng* (fried bananas). Rice is the staple for lunch, served up with two or three meat and vegetable dishes and followed by fresh fruit. The main meal is supper, which is served quite early and again consists of rice, this time accompanied by as many as five or six other dishes. *Sate/satay* (grilled skewers of meat), *soto* (a nourishing soup) or *bakmi* (noodles, a dish of Chinese origin) may be served first.

Foodstalls, or *warung* as they are known, may be temporary structures or more permanent buildings, with simple tables and benches. In the larger cities, there may be an area of *warung*, all under one roof. Night markets or *pasar malam* are usually better for eating than day markets.

Feast days, such as Lebaran marking the end of Ramadan, are a cause for great celebration and traditional dishes are served. *Lontong* or *ketupat* are made at this time. They are both versions of boiled rice – simmered in a small container or bag, so that as it cooks, the rice is compressed to make a solid block.

In addition to rice, there are a number of other common ingredients used across the country. Coconut milk, ginger, chilli peppers and peanuts are used nationwide, while dried salted fish and soybeans are important sources of protein.

Drink Although Indonesia is a predominantly Muslim country, alcoholic drinks are widely available. The two most popular beers – light lagers – are the locally brewed Anker and Bintang brands. Imported spirits are usually only sold in the more expensive restaurants and hotels. There are, however, a number of local brews including *brem* (rice wine), *arak* (rice whisky) and *tuak* (palm wine).

Water must be boiled before it is safe to drink. Hotels and most restaurants, as a matter of course, should boil the water they offer customers. Ask for *air minum*, literally 'drinking water'. Bottled water is cheap. Over the last few years, 'mineral water' – of which the most famous is **Aqua** (*aqua* has become the generic word for mineral water) – has become increasingly popular. There have been some reports of empty mineral water bottles being refilled with tap water, so always check the seal before accepting a bottle.

Western bottled and canned drinks are widely available in Indonesia and are comparatively cheap to buy. Alternatively, most restaurants will serve *air jeruk* – citrus fruit juices – with or without ice (*es*). Ice in many places is fine but in cheaper restaurants and away from tourist areas, many people recommend taking drinks without ice. The milk of a fresh coconut is a good thirst-quencher and a good source of potassium and glucose. Fresh, strong coffee (*kopi*) is usually served sweet (*kopi manis*) and black; if you want to have it without sugar, you should ask for it '*tidak pakai gula*'. Tea (*teh*), usually weak, is obtainable almost everywhere. Hot ginger tea is a refreshing alternative.

Shopping

Except in the larger fixed-price stores, bargaining (with good humour) is expected; start bargaining at 50-60% lower than the asking price. Do not expect to achieve instant results; if you walk away from the shop, you will almost certainly be followed, with a lower offer. If the salesperson agrees to your price, you should really feel obliged to purchase – it is considered very ill mannered to agree on a price and then not buy the article.

Sarawak and Sabah

The traditional handicraft industry is flourishing in Sarawak (see page 168). Kuching, the state capital, is full of handicraft and antique shops selling tribal pieces collected from upriver; those going upriver themselves can often find items being sold in towns and even longhouses en route. Typical handicrafts include woodcarvings, *pua kumbu* (rust-coloured tie-dye blankets), beadwork and basketry (see page 107).

Larger urban areas may have a Chinatown (with a few curio shops and a *pasar malam*, or night market) and an Indian quarter; these are the best places to buy sarongs, longis, dotis and saris (mostly imported from India) as well as other textiles. Malay handicrafts are usually only found in markets or government craft centres. The island of Labuan has duty-free shopping, although the choice is limited.

Brunei

Compared to Malaysia, Brunei is not up to much when it comes to shopping; the range of goods on offer is limited and the prices much higher. That said, you'll have no trouble finding international branded and luxury items.

Kalimantan

Indonesia offers a wealth of distinctive handicrafts and other products. Best buys include textiles (batik and ikat), silverwork, woodcarving, puppets, paintings, ceramics and local black opals. Early-morning purchases may well be cheaper, as salespeople often believe the first sale augers well for the rest of the day.

Entertainment

Firstly, it should be said that Borneo is most certainly not Ibiza. Kuching and Kota Kinabalu have a fair sprinkling of discos and clubs but these are usually in the glitzier hotels and so are all very sanitized. Larger towns in Sabah and Sarawak have a choice of cinemas, showing Hollywood movies, along with local films, Bollywood blockbusters and films from Japan, Hong Kong and Korea. Note that Bollywood movies and local films are unlikely to have English sub-titles. In a dry country like Brunei, you might expect there to be some form of replacement entertainment. But, no, come evening time, everything quietens down yet another gear. The centre of Bandar Seri Begawan itself is more or less deserted after dark. The suburb of Gadong is probably the busiest place in the evenings, its lively *pasar malam* churning out local food until late at night to an endless stream of Bruneians, who turn up in their 4WDs, pick up their food, then drive home to eat it. If there were tables and chairs laid out at the night market, it might become Brunei's prime hang-out; but then, that wouldn't be in the spirit of things.

Festivals and events

Islam is the dominant religion on Borneo. The timing of Islamic festivals is an art rather than a science and is calculated on the basis of local sightings of various phases of the moon. Muslim festivals move forward by around nine or 10 days each year. To check out the exact dates of local festivals, see www.tourism.gov.my, or www.holidayfestival.com. Chinese, Indian (Hindu) and some Christian holidays are also movable. To make things even more exciting, each state has its own public holidays when shops close and banks pull down their shutters. This makes calculating public holidays in advance a bit of a quagmire of lunar events, assorted kings' birthdays and tribal festivals.

Islamic festivals

Maal Hijrah (**Awal Muharram**) (public holiday in Malaysia, Brunei and Indonesia) marks the 1st day of the Muslim calendar and celebrates the Prophet Muhammad's journey from Mecca to Medina on the lunar equivalent of 16 Jul, AD 622. Religious discussions and lectures commemorate the event.

Maulidur Rasul (public holiday in Malaysia) /**Maulud Nabi** (public holiday in Brunei) /**Garebeg Maulad** (public holiday in Indonesia) commemorates Prophet Muhammad's birthday in AD 571. Koran recitals and processions in most Malaysian towns; public gatherings and coloured lights in BSB. Celebrations in Indonesia begin a week before and last a month, with *selamatans* in homes, mosques and schools.

Israk Mekraj (public holiday in Brunei)/ **Al Miraj/Isra Miraj Nabi Muhammed** (public holiday in Indonesia) celebrates the Prophet's journey to Jerusalem, led by the archangel Gabriel, and his ascension through the 7 heavens. He speaks with God and returns to earth the same night, with instructions, which include the 5 daily prayers.

Awal Ramadan (public holiday in Brunei) is the 1st day of Ramadan, a month of fasting for all Muslims. During this month Muslims abstain from all food and drink (as well as smoking) from sunrise to sundown – if they are very strict, Muslims do not even swallow their own saliva during daylight hours. The only people exempt from fasting are the elderly as well as women who are pregnant or are menstruating.

Nuzul Al-Quran (public holiday in Brunei), Anniversary of the Revelation of the Koran. Includes various religious observances, climaxing in a Koran-reading competition.

Hari Raya Puasa/Hari Raya Aidil Fitri /**Lebaran/Eid** (public holiday in Malaysia, Brunei and Indonesia) celebrates the end of Ramadan, the Islamic fasting month, with prayers and celebrations. In order for Hari Raya to be declared, the new moon of Syawal has to be sighted; if it is not, fasting continues for another day. It is the most important time of the year for Muslim families to get together. This is not a good time to travel; trains, planes and buses are booked up weeks in advance and hotels are also often full. Malays living in

towns and cities return home to their village, where it is 'open house' for relatives and friends, and special local delicacies are served. Hari Raya is also enthusiastically celebrated by Indian Muslims in Malaysia. In Brunei, families keep themselves to themselves on the 1st day but on the 2nd, they throw their doors open. Everyone dresses up in their best; men wear a length of *tenunan* around their waist, a cloth woven with gold thread.

Hari Raya Qurban (public holiday in Malaysia)/**Hari Raya Haji** (public holiday in Brunei)/**Idhul Adha** (public holiday in Indonesia). Held on the 10th day of Zulhijgah, the 12th month of the Islamic calendar, this is the 'festival of the sacrifice' and commemorates the willingness of Abraham to sacrifice his son. The festival marks the return of pilgrims from the Haj to Mecca. The Haj is one of the 5 keystones of Islam. In the morning, prayers are offered and later, families hold 'open house'. Those who can afford it sacrifice goats or cows to be distributed to the poor. Muslim men who have been on the Haj wear a white skull-hat. Many Malays have the title Haji in their name, meaning they have made the pilgrimage to Mecca.

Unlike in neighbouring Islamic states, the cost of a trip to Mecca is affordable by many in Brunei, so there is a large population of Hajis. Every year 4000 Bruneians go on the Haj. If any pilgrim has difficulty making ends meet, the Ministry of Religious Affairs will provide a generous subsidy.

Sarawak and Sabah

Schools in Sabah and Sarawak have 5 breaks through the year, that generally fall in the months of Jan (1 wk), Mar (2 wks), May (3 wks), Aug (1 wk), and October (4 wks). State holidays, which can last several days, may disrupt travel itineraries, so confirm your travel plans in advance. In addition, note that many government offices (including some tourism offices) are closed on the 1st and 3rd Sat of each month.

Besides those festivals celebrated throughout the country – including Chinese New Year, Christmas and Hari Raya – Sabah

Essentials Festivals & events

and Sarawak have their own festivals. Exact dates can be procured from the tourist offices in the capitals.

1 Jan New Year's Day (public holiday).

Jan Thaipusam (movable) is celebrated by many Hindus throughout Malaysia in honour of their deity Lord Subramanian (also known as Lord Muruga), who represents virtue, bravery, youth and power. Held during full moon in the month of Thai, it is a day of penance and thanksgiving.

Jan/Feb Chinese New Year (movable; public holiday) a 15-day lunar festival. Chinatown streets are crowded for weeks with shoppers buying traditional oranges which signify luck. Lion, unicorn or dragon dances welcome in the New Year and, unlike in Singapore, thousands of firecrackers are ignited to ward off evil spirits. Chap Goh Mei is the 15th day of the Chinese New Year and brings celebrations to a close. The Chinese believe that in order to find good husbands, girls should throw oranges into the river/sea on this day. In Sarawak the festival is known as **Guan Hsiao Cheih** (Lantern Festival).

1 Feb Federal Territory Day (state holiday in KL and Pulau Labuan).

Mar/Apr Easter (movable). Good Fri is a public holiday in Sabah and Sarawak.

1 May Labour Day (public holiday). **Kurah Aran** is celebrated by the Bidayuh tribe in Sarawak (see page 160) after the paddy harvest is over.

May Kadazan Harvest Festival or **Tadau Keamatan** (movable; state holiday in Sabah and Labuan) marks the end of the rice harvest in Sabah; the *magavau* ritual is performed to nurse the spirit back to health in readiness for the next planting season. Celebrated with feasting, *tapai* (rice wine) drinking, dancing and general merry-making. There are also agricultural shows, buffalo races, cultural performances and traditional games. The traditional *sumazal* dance is one of the highlights of the festivities.

May Wesak Day (movable; public holiday except Labuan), the most important day in the Buddhist calendar, celebrates the Buddha's birth, death and enlightenment. Temples throughout the country are packed with devotees offering incense, joss-sticks and prayers. Lectures on Buddhism and special exhibitions are held.

May/Jun Gawai Dayak (movable; state holiday in Sarawak) is the major festival of the year for the Iban of Sarawak; longhouses party continuously for a week. The Gawai celebrates the end of the rice harvest and welcomes the new planting season. The main ritual is called *magavau* and nurses the spirit of the grain back to health in advance of the planting season. Like the Kadazan harvest festival in Sabah (see above), visitors are welcome to join in, but in Sarawak, the harvest festival is much more traditional. Urban residents return to their rural roots for a major binge. On the 1st day of celebrations everyone dresses up in traditional costumes, singing, dancing and drinking *tuak* rice wine until they drop.

Jun Dragon Boat Festival (movable) honours the suicide of an ancient Chinese poet hero, Qu Yuan. He tried to press for political reform by drowning himself in the Mi Luo River as a protest against corruption. In an attempt to save him fishermen played drums and threw rice dumplings to try and distract vultures. His death is commemorated with dragon boat races and the enthusiastic consumption of rice dumplings.

Jun Gawai Batu (Sarawak) is a whetstone feast held by Iban farmers.

3 Jun Official birthday of HM the Yang di-Pertuan Agong (public holiday).

Aug Mooncake or Lantern Festival (movable). This Chinese festival marks the overthrow of the Mongol Dynasty in China; celebrated, as the name suggests, with the exchange and eating of mooncakes. According to Chinese legend secret messages of revolt were carried inside these cakes and led to the uprising. In the evening, children light festive lanterns while women pray to the Goddess of the Moon.

31 Aug Hari Kebangsaan/National Day (public holiday) commemorates Malaysian independence (*merdeka*) in 1957. In Sarawak it is celebrated in a different divisional capital each year.

Aug/Sep Festival of the Hungry Ghosts (movable) on the 7th moon in the Chinese lunar calendar, souls in purgatory are believed to return to earth to feast. Food is offered to these wandering spirits. Altars are set up in the streets and candles with faces are burned on them.

14 Sep Governor of Sarawak's birthday (state holiday in Sarawak).
16 Sep Governor of Sabah's birthday (state holiday in Sabah).
Oct Festival of the Nine Emperor Gods or Kiew Ong Yeah (movable) marks the return of the spirits of the 9 emperor gods to earth. Devotees visit temples dedicated to the nine gods. A strip of yellow cotton is often bought from the temple and worn on the right wrist as a sign of devotion. The ceremonies usually culminate with a fire-walking ritual.
Oct/Nov Deepvali (movable; public holiday except Sarawak and Labuan), the Hindu festival of lights commemorates the victory of light over darkness and good over evil: the triumphant return of Rama after his defeat of the evil Ravanna in the Hindu epic, the Ramayana. Every Hindu home is brightly lit and decorated for the occasion.
Nov/Dec Gawai Antu/Gawai Nyunkup /Rugan (Sarawak) is an Iban tribute to departed spirits. In simple terms, it is a party to mark the end of mourning for anyone whose relative had died in the previous six months.
25 Dec Christmas Day (public holiday). Christmas in Malaysia is a commercial spectacle these days with fairy lights and decorations and tropical Santa Clauses – although it does not compare with celebrations in Singapore. Midnight mass is the main Christmas service held in churches.

Other tribal festivals (gawai) in Sarawak include Gawai Burung, which honours the Iban war god, Singallang Burong; Gawai Mpijong Jaran Rantau, celebrated by the Bidayuh before grass cutting in new paddy fields; Gawai Bineh, celebrated by the Iban after harvest to welcome back the spirits of the paddy from the fields; and Gawai Sawa, celebrated by the Bidayuh to offer thanksgiving for the last year and to make the next year a plentiful one.

Brunei

1 Jan New Year's Day (public holiday).
Jan/Feb Chinese New Year (public holiday), a 15-day lunar festival.
23 Feb Hari Kebangsaan Negara Brunei Darussalam/National Day (public holiday) processions parades and firework displays are held in BSB.

31 May Armed Forces Day (public holiday), celebrated by the Royal Brunei Armed Forces who parade their equipment around town.
15 Jul Sultan's Birthday (public holiday) is celebrated until the end of the 2nd week in Aug. There's a procession, with lanterns and fireworks and a traditional boat race in BSB.
25 Dec Christmas Day.

Kalimantan

1 Jan Tahun Baru/New Year's Day (public holiday). New Year's Eve is celebrated with street carnivals, shows, fireworks and all-night festivities. In Christian areas, festivities are more exuberant, people visit each other on New Year's Day and attend church services.
Jan/Feb Imlek/Chinese New Year (movable) is not an official holiday but many Chinese shops and businesses close for at least 2 days.
Mar Nyepi/Hindu New Year (movable; public holiday)
Mar/Apr Wafat Isa Al-Masih/Good Friday (movable; public holiday).
21 Apr Kartini Day. A ceremony held by women to mark the birthday of Raden Ajeng Kartini, born in 1879 and proclaimed as a pioneer of women's emancipation. The festival is rather like mothers' day, in that women are supposed to be pampered by their husbands and children, although it is women's organizations like the Dharma Wanita who get most excited. Women wear national dress.
May Waisak Day (movable; public holiday). Marks the birth and death of the historic Buddha; at Candi Mendut, a procession of monks carrying flowers, candles and images of the Buddha walk to Borobudur.
May Kenaikan Isa Al-Masih or Ascension Day (movable; public holiday).
17 Aug Independence Day (public holiday). This is the most important national holiday, celebrated with processions, dancing and other merry-making. Festivities continue for a month.
1 Oct Hari Pancasila, commemorates the Five Basic Principles of Pancasila.
5 Oct Armed Forces Day. The anniversary of the founding of the Indonesian Armed Forces, with parades and demonstrations.
25-26 Dec Christmas (public holiday). Celebrated by Christians.

Sport and activities

Birdwatching

Borneo is home to hundreds of birds, including many migratory species, and there are great facilities for birdwatchers. Popular areas are Bako, Similajau, Lambir Hill and Gunung Mulu national parks in Sarawak; Tempasuk River, Kinabalu Park, Kinabatangan Riverine Forest area, Lahad Dat and Layang Layang Island in Sabah; Ulu Temburong in Brunei, and Tanjung Putting and Kutai national parks in Kalimantan. For organized birdwatching holidays, see www.birdtours.co.uk.

Cookery courses

For those wishing to learn more about Malaysian cuisine, several state tourist boards offer short courses. Enquire at **Tourism Malaysia** information centres. A wide variety of Malaysian cookery books is available at leading bookshops.

Diving

Borneo's underwater life is as diverse as anywhere in the world. There are immaculate corals, enormous whalesharks and schools of hammerheads as well as shallow waters, rich in tiny and rare marine creatures. The island is the third largest in the world and its land mass is ringed by the South China, Sulu, Celebes and Java seas. Together they create some of the most varied diving on the planet.

Sarawak and Sabah
The state of Sabah is *the* destination for those who come to Borneo for no other reason than to submerge. Sabah's coastal and offshore reefs are washed by currents that create favourable conditions and better visibility than its more southerly neighbour, Sarawak, whose shallow, somewhat murky waters attract less marine life. The island of Labuan, which sits between the two states, has also gained a moderate dive reputation due to four well-known wrecks. Sea and wind conditions vary, so diving can be challenging but there are many places that are suitable for novices. The principal resorts are:

Sipadan The most famous of Borneo's dive destinations, this tiny spit of land sits off the eastern tip of Borneo on the Litigan Reefs. It is an all-out magnet for divers. The walls off the island drop to well over 600 m and this unique geography has created a spectacular marine environment. If you are looking for big stuff, this is the place. Turtles are everywhere, so prolific and curious that they will follow you around on a dive. Sharks are easy to spot: white tips snooze on sandy shelves and hammerheads are frequently sighted. On Barracuda Point, huge schools of barracuda just hang about. There are plenty of small and colourful creatures to see as well. Dive conditions are variable, currents can be strong and dives are done as drifts. Contact **Sipadan Water Village Resort** ① *PO Box No 62156, 91031 Tawau, Sabah, T089-752996, www.sipadan-village.com.my.*

Mabul Sipadan's nearest neighbour is best known as a special place for spotting small creatures. The island is quite large compared to both Sipadan and nearby Kapalai, with a village and several resorts, including **Sipadan-Mabul Resort**ⓘ *PO Box 15571, 88864 Kota Kinabalu, Sabah, T088-230006, www.sipadan-mabul.com.my.* Offshore there is an oil rig: frankly, it's one of the ugliest things you will ever see, until you get beneath it and discover it's also one of the best muck dives in the region, with more unusual creatures than you ever thought you'd see in one small area. Shore dives are equally spectacular, with seahorses, frogfish and ghost pipefish. Conditions are mostly easy, although occasional currents can restrict dives choices.

Kapalai Although charted on maps, there is only a sand bar remaining from what was once a small island, a short motor from Sipadan. The flat topography extends underwater, yet visibility is reasonable as the reef mounds are washed daily by gentle tides. Corals tend to be low lying to the contours of the landscape and are a great haven for masses of sea creatures. Leaffish, hawkfish and frogfish appear on virtually every dive. The **Sipadan Kapalai Resort**ⓘ *484 Bandar Sabindo, 91021 Tawau, Sabah, T089-765200, www.sipadan-kapalai.com,* is a water village perched on stilts over an aquarium-like lagoon and the dive from the jetty is spectacular – resident mating mandarin fish, blue-ringed octopus, batfish and even baby nurse sharks reside within a couple of fin strokes. Diving is year-round and suitable for everyone.

Lankayan An hour or so by boat from Sandakan into the Sulu Sea, idyllic Lankayan is ringed by an iridescent white beach and covered in a labyrinth of unruly jungle. The reefs surrounding the island are gently shelving, flat plateaus. A recent survey confirmed high biodiversity but visibility can be low at times, due to the proximity of the mainland and the high concentration of plankton. Diving here is about looking for the animals that thrive in these nutrient-rich conditions. There are plenty, including rare rhinopias and occasional whalesharks. Several shipwrecks ensure good variety, including one straight off the jetty. **Lankayan Island Resort** ⓘ *484 Bandar Sabindo, 91021 Tawau, Sabah, T089-765200, www.lankayan-island.com,* is open all year, with mostly easy conditions, which makes it a great place for trainees or new divers.

Layang Layang An hour north of Kota Kinabalu, Layang Layang is a tiny, man-made island sitting on a stunning lagoon. Around the edge of the lagoon is a large atoll whose steep-sided walls drop off to unimaginable depths. Strong currents drag nutrients across the reefs, which, in turn, ensures prolific hard coral growth and creates a haven for masses of pelagic life. However, most people come for the curious hammerhead phenomena every Easter, when large schools swarm around Layang then head off again a few weeks later. **Layang Layang Island Resort**ⓘ *A-0-3 Block A, Megan Phileo Av II,12, Jl Yap Kwan Seng, 50450 Kuala Lumpur, T03-21622877, www.layanglayang.com,* is open March to September.

Pulau Labuan This Malay Federal Territory is 8 km off the west coast of Sabah and short a hop from Brunei. The marine park off Labuan's south coast consists of three small islands with pretty beaches, ringed by some shallow reefs that are suitable for snorkelling. However, the real draw is the cluster of accessible wrecks. A couple – the American and Australian wrecks – date from the Second World War, while the Blue Water and Cement wrecks are more recent. This last is suitable for beginners, but the others require more advanced diving experience. Fish and coral growth on the structures are both reasonable, which is a good thing as the local reefs suffer from sediments and low visibility. The best dive season is between May and September.

Miri The coastal region off northern Sarawak has a growing dive reputation but is sadly affected by both the weather and the coastal marine environment. Miri sits on the mouth of a river which extends seawards as a flat plateau, never dropping far beyond 15 m. The areas can be awash with sediment, caused by both man-made and natural erosion. But arrive on a clear day, when there has been little rain, and the diving can be very good. Further offshore there are some dive sites that reach 30 m and several oil rigs make great artificial reefs, attracting pelagics like barracuda and turtles. The reefs here are 'undiscovered' but whether you enjoy the diving will depend much on the visibility. Contact **Tropical Dives Miri** ① *1 Lobby Arcade, Jln Temenggong Datuk Oyang Lawai, 98000 Miri, T085-414300, www.seridanmulu.com.*

Brunei

The incredibly wealthy, oil rich Sultanate of Brunei is better known for its wealthy capital backed by untouched rainforest than its underwater realm and there is good reason for that. Like Labuan Island just north and Miri to the south, the waters here are never very clear, having been affected by erosion, shipping and industry. Until recently, there wasn't even a dive centre. However, with the establishment of the PADI-affiliated **Scuba Tech Dive Centre** ① *Empire Hotel and Country Club, Jerudong BG3122, Negara Brunei Darussalam, T673-2418888, www.theempirehotel.com*, and access to offshore reefs and the Labuan wrecks (see above), diving here has the potential to develop.

Kalimantan

Comprising over two-thirds of Borneo, Kalimantan has much less of a reputation for diving than Sabah and Sarawak. This is simply because there is no easy way to reach the small resorts that hover off the northeast coast. Not far from the Sabah border are Sangalaki, Derawan and Kakaban, amongst others, and the diving here can be as thrilling and rewarding as the resorts around Sipadan.

Sangalaki This small lush island is surrounded by a shallow lagoon that extends someway offshore and is completed by a series of patch reefs. This is a protected marine park and as such, the reefs are in good condition. The smaller reefs are rich with all sorts of marine creatures but what attracts most divers are regular sightings of two much bigger animals: manta rays and turtles. There are several manta cleaning stations just north of the island and encounters are year round. Green turtles also use Sangalaki's lovely beach for nesting. Contact **Sangalaki Dive Lodge** ① *PO Box 16360, 88000 Kota Kinabalu, Sabah, T088-242336, www.sangalaki.net.*

Derawan and Kakaban Both these islands are less than an hour from Sangalaki and can be easily reached on a day trip. Derawan also has a resort with a lovely house reef, an excellent jetty dive and several wall dives, a feature not found further south. Kakaban, however, has one of the most unusual features both in the region and on the planet. When geological forces pushed the atoll upwards, Kakaban's lagoon became landlocked, leaving a completely enclosed, brackish lake. The species that have developed here are unique and include masses of jellyfish that have evolved without the capacity to sting as they have no predators. There is no accommodation on Kakaban but the best diving and facilities can all be accessed from Sangalaki.

Diving practicalities

Diving seasons and conditions It is hard to be general about seasons across Borneo. Although it is warm and humid all year round, each state is governed by different wind patterns and currents. No matter what time of year you visit, or what area, the water is invariably warm. Temperatures hover between 25°C and 29°C but may occasionally drop as low as 23°C.

Equipment A 3 mm wetsuit is as much as you are likely to need, unless you plan to do more than three dives a day. Almost every dive centre will rent good quality equipment but bringing your own will considerably reduce costs. Prior to departure, check baggage allowance with the airlines and see if you can come to some arrangement for extra weight.

Dive facilities While there are highly professional dive operations in Sabah and Kalimantan, the unpredictable nature of the diving in Brunei, Labuan and Sarawak means that the industry is less developed. Always check a company's qualifications and affiliations to governing bodies like PADI, NAUI, CMAS and BSAC. It's always worth asking around if you're unsure of what's on offer.

Dive health If you plan to dive make sure that you are fit do so. Check that any dive company you use is reputable and has appropriate certification from BSAC or the **Professional Association of Diving Instructors** (PADI) ① *Unit 7, St Philips Central, Albert Rd, St Philips, Bristol, BS2 0TD, T0117-3007234, www.padi.com.* Should you become victim to a suspected decompression attack, immediately contact the 24-hr **Malaysian Diving Emergency Hotline**, T05-930 4114, for advice. Recompression facilities are available at the **Labuan Recompression Chamber** ① *Labuan Pejabat Selam, Markas Wilayah Laut Dua, 87007, Labuan, T087-412122,* operated by the Malaysian Navy, and at **Naval Medicine and Hyperbaric Centre** ① *36 Admiralty Rd, West Singapore 759960, T750 5544.* Note that air evacuation services, if available, are extremely expensive and hyperbaric chambers can charge up to US$800 per hour.

Dive insurance Good dive insurance is imperative. It is inexpensive and well worth it in case of a problem. Many general travel insurance policies do not cover diving. Contact **DAN** (the **Divers Alert Network**) ① *www.diversalertnetwork.org,* **DAN Europe** ① *www.daneurope.org,* or **DAN South East Asia Pacific** ① *www.danseap.org,* for more information. If you have no insurance you can join online.

Trekking and climbing

There are numerous opportunities for climbing in Sarawak and Sabah. Most national parks offer hiking trails, but the best are in the Niah, Gunung Mulu and Gunung Kinabalu national parks. Climbing Mount Kinabalu in Sabah, to be at the summit for sunrise, is one of the most popular hikes.

Water rafting

Wild or whitewater rafting is not a well established activity in Borneo, although there are some good spots to take to the swirl. Tour operators can organize rafting on the Padas (Grade 3) and the Kiulu (Grade 2) rivers in Sabah.

Health

Before you go

Ideally, you should see your GP/practice nurse or travel clinic at least six weeks before your departure for general advice on travel risks, malaria and recommended vaccinations. Your local pharmacist can also be a good source of readily accessible advice. Make sure you have travel insurance, get a dental check (especially if you are going to be away for more than a month), know your own blood group and if you suffer a long-term condition such as diabetes or epilepsy make sure someone knows or that you have a Medic Alert bracelet/necklace with this information on it.

Recommended vaccinations

Vaccinations for tuberculosis, hepatitis B, rabies and Japanese B encephalitis are commonly recommended for Borneo. The final decision, however, should be based on a consultation with your GP or travel clinic. You should also confirm your primary courses and boosters are up to date (diphtheria, tetanus, poliomyelitis, hepatitis A, typhoid). A yellow fever certificate is required by visitors over one year old, who are coming from or have recently passed through an infected area.

A-Z of health risks

AIDS/HIV

The main risk to travellers is from casual sex. The same precautions should be taken as when encountering any sexually transmitted disease (see Sexual health below). HIV can be passed via unsterile needles which have been previously used to inject an HIV-positive patient, but the risk of this is very small indeed. It would, however, be sensible to check that needles have been properly sterilized or disposable needles are used. The chance of picking up Hepatitis B in this way is more of a danger. The risk of receiving a blood transfusion with blood infected with the HIV virus is greater than from dirty needles because of the amount of fluid exchanged. Supplies of blood for transfusion are supposed to be screened for HIV in all reputable hospitals so the risk should be small. The only way to be sure if you feel you have been put at risk is to have a blood test for HIV antibodies on your return to a place where there are reliable laboratory facilities. However the test does not become positive for many weeks.

Altitude sickness

Acute mountain sickness can strike from about 3000 m upwards and in general is more likely to affect those who ascend rapidly (for example, by plane) and those who over-exert themselves. Acute mountain sickness takes a few hours or days to come on and presents with headache, lassitude, dizziness, loss of appetite, nausea and vomiting. Insomnia is common and often associated with a suffocating feeling when lying down in bed. You may notice that your breathing tends to wax and wane at night and your face is puffy in the mornings – this is all part of the syndrome. If the symptoms are mild, the treatment is rest and painkillers (preferably not aspirin-based) for the headaches. Should the symptoms be severe and prolonged it is best to descend to a lower altitude immediately and reascend, if necessary, slowly and in stages. The symptoms disappear very quickly – even after a few hundred metres of descent.

The best way of preventing acute mountain sickness is a relatively slow ascent.
When trekking to high altitude, some time spent walking at medium altitude, getting fit and acclimatizing is beneficial. The avoidance of alcohol, cigarettes and heavy food will go a long way towards preventing acute mountain sickness.

Bites and stings

This is a very rare event indeed for travellers, but if you are unlucky (or careless) enough to be bitten by a venomous snake, spider, scorpion or sea creature, try to identify the culprit, without putting yourself in further danger (do not try to catch a live snake).

Snake bites in particular are very frightening, but in fact rarely poisonous – even venomous snakes sometimes bite without injecting venom. Victims should be taken to a hospital or a doctor without delay. It is not advised for travellers to carry snake bite antivenom as it can do more harm than good in inexperienced hands. Reassure and comfort the victim frequently. Immobilize the limb with a bandage or a splint and get the patient to lie still. Do not slash the bite area and try to suck out the poison. This also does more harm than good. You should apply a tourniquet in these circumstances, but only if you know how to. Do not attempt this if you are not experienced.

Certain tropical fish inject venom into bathers' feet when trodden on, which can be exceptionally painful. Wear plastic shoes if such creatures are reported. The pain can be relieved by immersing the foot in hot water (as hot as you can bear) for as long as the pain persists.

Dengue fever

This is a viral disease spread by mosquitoes that tend to bite during the day. The symptoms are fever and often intense joint pains; some people also develop a rash. Symptoms last about a week but it can take a few weeks to recover fully. Dengue can be difficult to distinguish from malaria as both diseases tend to occur in the same countries. There are no effective vaccines or antiviral drugs though, fortunately, travellers rarely develop the more severe forms of the disease (these can prove fatal). Rest, plenty of fluids and paracetamol (not aspirin) is the recommended treatment.

Diarrhoea and intestinal upset

Diarrhoea can refer either to loose stools or an increased frequency of bowel movement, both of which can be a nuisance. Symptoms should be relatively short lived but if they persist beyond two weeks specialist medical attention should be sought. Also seek medical help if there is blood in the stools and/or fever.

Adults can use an antidiarrhoeal medication such as loperamide to control the symptoms but only for up to 24 hours. In addition keep well hydrated by drinking plenty of fluids and eat bland foods. Oral rehydration sachets taken after each loose stool are a useful way to keep well hydrated. These should always be used when treating children and the elderly.

Bacterial travellers' diarrhoea is the most common form. **Ciproxin (Ciprofloxacin)** is a useful antibiotic and can be obtained by private prescription in the UK. You need to take one 500 mg tablet when the diarrhoea starts. If there are no signs of improvement after 24 hours the diarrhoea is likely to be viral and not bacterial. If it is due to other organisms such as those causing giardia or amoebic dysentery, different antibiotics will be required.

The standard advice is to be careful with water and ice for drinking. Ask yourself where the water came from. If you have any doubts then boil it or filter and treat it. There are many filter/treatment devices now available on the market. Food can also transmit disease. Be wary of salads (what were they washed in, who handled them), re-heated foods or food that has been left out in the sun having been cooked earlier in the day. There is a simple adage that says wash it, peel it, boil it or forget it. Also be wary of unpasteurised dairy products as these can transmit a range of diseases.

Hepatitis

Hepatitis means inflammation of the liver. Viral causes of the disease can be acquired anywhere in the world. The most obvious symptom is a yellowing of your skin or the whites of your eyes. However, prior to this all that you may notice is itching and tiredness. Pre-travel hepatitis A vaccine is the best bet. Hepatitis B (for which there is a vaccine) is spread through blood and unprotected sexual intercourse, both of which can be avoided.

Japanese B encephalitis

This is a viral disease of the brain spread by mosquitoes. It is very rare in travellers but those visiting rural areas, especially in Indonesia, during the wet season may be advised to have the vaccine.

Malaria

Malaria is present in Malaysia and Indonesia. It can start as something just resembling an attack of flu but can cause death within 24 hours. You may feel tired, lethargic, headachy, feverish; or more seriously, develop fits, followed by coma and then death. Have a low index of suspicion because it is very easy to write off vague symptoms, which may actually be malaria. If you have a temperature, visit a doctor as soon as you can and ask for a malaria test. On your return home, if you suffer any of these symptoms, have a test as soon as possible. Even if a previous test proved negative, this could save your life.

Treatment is with drugs and may be oral or into a vein depending on the seriousness of the infection. Remember **ABCD: Awareness** (of whether the disease is present in the area you are travelling in), **Bite avoidance**, **Chemoprohylaxis**, **Diagnosis**.

To prevent mosquito bites wear clothes that cover arms and legs, use effective insect repellents in areas with known risks of insect-spread disease and use a mosquito net treated with an insecticide. Repellents containing 30-50% DEET (Di-ethyltoluamide) are recommended when visiting malaria-endemic areas; lemon eucalyptus (**Mosiguard**) is a reasonable alternative. The key advice is to guard against contracting malaria by taking the correct anti-malarials and finishing the recommended course. If you are a popular target for insect bites or develop lumps quite soon after being bitten use antihistamine tablets and apply a cream such as hydrocortisone.

Remember that it is risky to buy medicine, and in particular anti-malarials, in some developing countries. These may be sub-standard or part of a trade in counterfeit drugs.

Rabies

Rabies is a problem in both Malaysia and Indonesia so be aware of the dangers of the bite from any animal. Rabies vaccination before travel can be considered but if bitten always seek urgent medical attention – whether or not you have been previously vaccinated – after first cleaning the wound and treating with an iodine base disinfectant or alcohol.

Sexual health

The range of visible and invisible diseases is awesome. Unprotected sex can spread HIV, Hepatitis B and C, gonorrhea (green discharge), chlamydia (nothing to see but may cause painful urination and later female infertility), painful recurrent herpes, syphilis and warts, just to name a few. You can cut down the risk by using condoms or a femidom but the best prevention is to avoid sex altogether.

Sun and heat

Take good heed of advice regarding protection against the sun. Overexposure can lead to sunburn and, in the longer term, skin cancers and premature skin aging. The best advice is simply to avoid exposure to the sun by covering exposed skin, wearing a hat and staying out of the sun if possible, particularly between late morning and early afternoon. Apply a high-factor sunscreen (greater than SPF15) and also make sure it screens against UVB. A further danger in tropical climates is heat exhaustion or, more seriously, heatstroke. This can be avoided by good hydration, which means drinking water past the point of simply quenching thirst. Also when first exposed to tropical heat take time to acclimatize by avoiding strenuous activity in the middle of the day. If you cannot avoid heavy exercise it is also a good idea to increase salt intake.

Typhoid

A disease spread by the insanitary preparation of food. A number of new vaccines against this condition are now available; the older TAB and monovalent typhoid vaccines are being phased out. The newer, for example Typhim Vi, cause less side effects, but are more expensive. For those who do not like injections, there are now oral vaccines.

Water

There are a number of ways of purifying water. Dirty water should first be strained through a filter bag and then boiled or treated. Bring water to a rolling boil for several minutes. There are sterilizing methods that can be used and products generally contain chlorine (eg **Puritabs**) or iodine (eg **Pota Aqua**) compounds. There are a number of water sterilizers now on the market available in personal and expedition size. Make sure you take the spare parts or spare chemicals with you and do not believe everything the manufacturers say.

Other diseases and risks

There are a range of other insect-borne diseases that are quite rare in travellers but worth finding out about. Examples are filiariasis, typhus, sleeping sickness, river blindness and leishmaniasis. Fresh water can also be a source of diseases such as leptospirosis (present in Malaysia) so it is worth investigating before bathing in lakes and streams.

Further information

Websites
Fit for Travel (UK), www.fitfortravel.scot.nhs.uk. This site from Scotland provides a quick A-Z of vaccine and travel health advice requirements for each country.
Foreign and Commonwealth Office (FCO; UK), www.fco.gov.uk.
National Travel Health Network and Centre (NaTHNaC), www.nathnac.org/.

World Health Organisation (WHO), www.who.int.

Books
Dawood, R (ed), *Travellers' Health* (Oxford University Press).
Warrell, David and Anderson, Sarah (eds). *Expedition Medicine* (Royal Geographic Society).

Keeping in touch

Communications

Internet

Sarawak and Sabah Malaysia is one of the most gung-ho places on the planet when it comes to information technology and the internet. In line with this, internet cafés have sprung up all over the place and every town, however small, down-at-heel and apparently forgotten by the wider world will have, at the very least, a place offering internet services. Rates are cheap too: RM2.50 per hour at the bottom end, with most places charging around RM3-5 per hour and some hotels charging up to RM10 per hour. Generally, internet cafés geared to tourists are more expensive than those serving the local market, where teenage boys spend hours playing online games.

Brunei As you might expect, there are plenty of internet cafés in Brunei, too, and all the top-end and most of the mid-range hotels offer internet access. For those travelling with laptops, a dial-up internet service is provided by BruNet; visit www.brunet.bn to subscribe.

Kalimantan Email has caught on fast in Indonesia, and any town of any size has its cyber café.

Post

Sarawak and Sabah Malaysia's post is cheap and reasonably reliable, although incoming and outgoing parcels should be registered. To send postcards and aerograms overseas costs RM0.50, while letters cost RM0.90 (up to 10 g) or RM1.40 (up to 20 g). Post office opening hours are Monday to Saturday 0830-1700 (closed the first Saturday of every month). Fax services are available in most state capitals. Poste restante, available at general post offices in major cities, is reliable; make sure your surname is capitalized and underlined. Most post offices provide a packing service for a reasonable fee (around RM5). You can also buy **AirAsia** tickets at post offices.

Brunei Post offices are open Monday to Thursday and Saturday 0745-1630, Friday 0800-1100 and 1400-1600. Most hotels provide postal services at reception. The cost of a stamp for a postcard to Europe is approximately 50 cents.

Kalimantan The postal service is relatively reliable, though important mail should be registered. Every town and tourist centre has either a *kantor pos* (post office) or postal agent, where you can buy stamps and post letters and parcels. In many cases poste restante services are also available; make sure your surname is capitalized and underlined. *Kantor pos* are open Monday to Saturday 0800-1400; postal agents have much longer hours, often until 2200 daily.

Telephone

Sarawak and Sabah There are public telephone booths in most towns; telephones take RM0.10 and RM0.20 coins. Card phones are now widespread and they make good sense if phoning abroad. (*iTalk* offers the best IDD rate). Cards come in denominations from RM20 to RM100 and are available from airports, petrol stations, most outlets of 7-eleven and also from magazine stalls on the street. International direct calls can be made from any telephone with an IDD (international direct dialling) facility, including most **Kedai Telekom** booths in major towns.

⁞ Telephone information

Telephone numbers in this guide are shown as they should be dialled long distance WITHIN the country. If phoning from abroad, dial your country's international access code, the country code for Malaysia, Singapore, Brunei or Indonesia, followed by the area code (minus the initial zero) and then the number.

International country codes Malaysia: +60; Singapore: +65; Brunei: +673; Indonesia: +62.

Operator Malaysia: T101; Singapore: T100; Brunei: T113; Indonesia: T100/101.

Directory enquries Malaysia: T102/103; Singapore: T100; Brunei: T0213; Indonesia: T108/106.

IDD access codes Malaysia: 00; Singapore: 020 for calls to Malaysia (no country code required) or 00 for calls to other countries; Brunei: 00; Indonesia: 001/008.

International assistance Malaysia: T108; Singapore: T104; Brunei: T113; Indonesia: T102.

You can use your mobile phone in Malaysia if you have a GSM model, but the service will be expensive. A better idea is to get a pre-paid SIM card when you arrive; these are available from most mobile phone shops.

Brunei There are no area codes in Brunei. With a *Hallo Kad* phonecard (widely available, including at the airport) you can make international calls from any phone. You can also make international calls from your room in many of the hotels. Coin phones take 10 and 20 cent pieces.

Kalimantan Indonesia has a comprehensive telecommunications network. Every town has its communication centre – **Warpostel** – where you can make local and international calls. Most Warpostels open early in the morning and operate until around midnight. International calls have a cheap rate between midnight and 0800, and all Saturday and Sunday; otherwise calls are expensive. There is a wide network of card phones and coin phones (taking 50 Rp and 100 Rp coins) in main towns and cities, in hotels, shopping centres and street corners. Phone cards (*Kartu telepon*) are sold in Warpostels, supermarkets and a wide range of shops.

Media

Newspapers
Sarawak and Sabah The main English-language newspapers are the *Sabah Daily News* and the *Sarawak Tribune*. *The Sun* is a free English-language daily found in train stations and shopping centres but is generally packed with ads and little else. The English-language dailies are government owned and this is reflected in their content, which tends to be relentlessly pro-government. *Aliran Monthly* (www.aliran.com) is a high-brow but fascinating publication offering current affairs analysis from a non-government perspective. *The Rocket* is the Democratic Action Party's opposition newspaper, and also presents an alternative perspective. International editions of leading foreign newspapers and news magazines can be obtained at main news-stands and book stalls, although some of these are not cleared through customs until mid-afternoon.

Brunei There are two daily newspapers in Brunei: the *Borneo Bulletin* (English) and the *Media Permata* (Malay), which cover both local and international news.

Kalimantan English-language newspapers are the *Indonesia Times* and the *Indonesia Observer/Sunday Observer*. One of the outcomes of Indonesia's halting progress towards democratization, is the emergence of a much more independent and combative press. Of the international newspapers available, *The Asian Wall Street Journal* and the *International Herald Tribune* can be purchased in major cities and tourist destinations; so too can the *Singapore Straits Times*. Among English-language magazines, the Hong Kong-based *Far Eastern Economic Review*, which is well informed and provides the most comprehensive regional coverage.

Radio

Sarawak and Sabah There are six government radio stations which broadcast in various languages including English. **Radio 1** broadcasts in Bahasa Melayu; **Radio 2** is a music station; **Radio 3** is Malay; **Radio 4** is in English; **Radio 5**, Chinese; **Radio 6**, Tamil. The **BBC World Service** can be picked up on short-wave; the main frequencies are (in kHz): 11750, 9740, 6195 and 3915.

Brunei More likely than not, during your first taxi ride in Brunei you'll be confronted with the surreal sound of London's **Capital Radio** ringing loud and clear across the airwaves. It's the most popular radio station in Brunei. **Capital Gold** is also broadcast live in Brunei.

Kalimantan **Republik Indonesia** (RRI) broadcasts throughout the country. News and commentary in English is broadcast for about an hour a day. Short-wave radios will pick up **Voice of America**, the **BBC World Service** and **Australian Broadcasting**.

Television

Sarawak and Sabah RTM1 and RTM2 are operated by Radio Television Malaysia, the government-run broadcasting station. Apart from locally produced programmes, some American and British series are shown. Programmes for all channels are listed in daily newspapers. Satellite TV only recently arrived in Malaysia. Many hotels carry the ASTRO service which offers HBO, STAR movies, ESPN, CNN, BBC, Discovery and MTV as well as a host of Chinese channels.

Brunei The national television network transmits local programmes and Malaysian TV. Satellite television is widespread in Brunei (even remote longhouses have dishes) and virtually all hotels provide a wide range of channels including CNN and BBC.

Kalimantan Indonesia has put satellites into geostationary orbit so that television pictures can be received anywhere in the archipelago. The vast 'parabolas' outside many houses, including shacks which may not even have piped water, testifies to the power of television and the priorities of many Indonesian households. **Televisi Republik Indonesia** (TVRI) is the government-run channel. There are also four private stations – although these rigorously toe the government line when it comes to reporting news. Hotels also usually receive satellite TV and if they have a significant foreign clientele they may well tune into English-language channels. CNN, BBC, Star, Television Australia, Malaysian, Philippine and Thai television can all be received in Indonesia.

Kuala Lumpur & Singapore

⁑ Footprint features

Introduction

Kuala Lumpur and Singapore serve as gateways to Borneo and for many people this provides a good opportunity to stop over for a few days in either of these cities.

In recent decades, Malaysia's capital, Kuala Lumpur, has transformed itself from a scruffy, polluted metropolis into one of Asia's great cities, hot on the heels of Singapore. The mighty Petronas Towers (which for a time held the record as tallest buildings in the world) are fitting symbols of the new KL, a cosmopolitan place where East and West blend on every corner. Highlights include a trip up to the Skybridge on the Petronas Towers; the green, rolling Lake Gardens with its huge bird park; several good museums, including the Islamic Arts Museum; the wonderful blend of colonial and modern architecture; and, of course, the limitless shopping and dining opportunities.

Singapore is often unfairly slated as dull and sterile. Granted, the country's unprecedented climb to prosperity has been achieved at a cost – its populace straight-jacketed by what Western commentators would describe as Draconian social policies. But with a more vocal younger generation coming to the fore, things are set to change. Meanwhile, the arts scene has blossomed in recent years, with a commendable line-up of new museums and galleries and a stunning new arts centre on Marina Bay (Singapore's answer to the Sydney Opera House). Singapore's principle lure remains its cuisine – this is a city fully deserving of the designation 'Culinary Capital of Asia' – but there are plenty of other worthy diversions. Don't miss Raffles, the new Esplanade, the Asian Civilisations Museum, the immaculate Botanical Gardens, Chinatown and (for the kids) Sentosa.

Kuala Lumpur

In the space of a century, Kuala Lumpur grew from a trading post and tin-mining shanty town into a colonial capital. Today, it is a modern, cosmopolitan business hub and centre of government. The economic boom that started in the late 1980s has caused a building bonanza that has rivalled Singapore's. In downtown Kuala Lumpur, old and new are juxtaposed. The jungled backdrop of the Supreme Court's copper-topped clock tower has been replaced by scores of stylish, high-rise office blocks, dominated by the soaring, angular-roofed Maybank headquarters. The Victorian, Moorish and Moghul-style buildings, the Art Deco central market, and the Chinese shophouses stand in marked contrast to these impressive skyscrapers. The Petronas Twin Towers offer the most impressive addition to the modern skyline; part of the Kuala Lumpur City Centre (KLCC) development, this is the second tallest building in the world. ⏵ *For Sleeping, Eating and other listings, see pages 61-67.*

Ins and outs ⏵ *Population: 1,500,000.*

Getting there As befitting Malaysia's capital, Kuala Lumpur (KL) is well linked both to other areas of Malaysia and to the wider world. The international airport at Sepang provides a slick point of entry to the country. Domestic air connections (including to Sabah and Sarawak) also pass through Sepang.

Public buses into the city are available one floor down from the arrivals concourse. From KLIA express coaches operate every 30 minutes to hotels in KL, RM25 one-way. From KLIA the first coach leaves at 0500 and the last departure at 2230. The journey takes around one hour. The coach first goes to Hentian Duta bus station, and then passengers change to a shuttle bus for hotel connection. Take the clearly marked signs from the arrivals hall.

The **KLIA Ekspres** train runs from 0500 until midnight between the airport and KL Sentral train station in the centre of the city. From here you will need to take a taxi to your hotel. The non-stop journey takes around half hour and there's a train at least every 20 minutes (35RM one way). Alternatively you can take the KLIA transit which takes around 35 minutes to make the same journey, but still costs RM35. It stops at three intermediate stations and leaves between 0550 and 0100. If your plane arrives outside these hours you will have to either take a taxi into KL or hire a car (most major rental companies have counters open 24 hours).

❗ For a good map of the Integrated Urban Transportation system go to www.kiat.net/malaysia/KL/transit.html. The map is up to date, the text is not.

For a **taxi** expect to pay around RM60-80 (after midnight a taxi to the centre will cost RM86.10). They operate on a coupon system; make sure you pick up one from the taxi counter at the exit in arrivals (near Door 3); touts charge more than double the official rate. Many hotels provide a pick-up service, but make sure they are aware of your arrival details; there is a hotel pick-up office just outside the terminal exit. Major car rental companies have desks in the arrivals concourse.⏵ *See also Airport information, page 25, and Transport, page 66.*

Getting around Kuala Lumpur is not the easiest city to navigate, with its sights spread thinly over a wide area. Pedestrians have not been very high on the list of priorities for Malaysian urban planners, with many roads, especially outside the city centre, built without pavements, making walking both hazardous and difficult. In addition, with the exception of the area around Central Market, Chinatown and Dayabumi, distances between sights are too great to cover comfortably on foot, both because of the lack of pavements and because of heavy pollution and the hot and humid climate. Kuala Lumpur's bus system is labyrinthine and congested streets mean that travelling by taxi can make for a tedious wait in a traffic jam. Try to insist that taxi drivers use their meters, although do not be surprised if they refuse. The two **Light Rail Transit (LRT)**, the **Monorail** and the **KMT Komuter** rail lines are undoubtedly the least hassle and provide a great elevated and air-conditioned view of the city.

Orientation The colonial core is around the Padang and down Jalan Raja and Jalan Tun Perak. East of the Padang, straight over the bridge on Lebuh Pasar Besar, is the main commercial area, occupied by banks and finance companies. To the southeast of Merdeka Square is KL's vibrant Chinatown.

The streets to the north of the Padang – the cricket pitch in front of the old Selangor Club, next to Merdeka Square – are central shopping streets with modern department stores and smaller shops.

To find a distinctively Malay area, it is necessary to venture further out, along Jalan Raja Muda Musa to Kampong Baru, to the northeast. To the south of Kampong Baru, on the opposite side of the Klang River, is Jalan Ampang, once KL's 'millionaires' row', where tin magnates, or *towkays*, and sultans first built their homes. The road is now mainly occupied by embassies and high commissions. To the southeast of Jalan Ampang is KL's so-called Golden Triangle, to which the modern central business district has migrated. In recent years the city's residential districts have been expanding out towards the jungled hills surrounding the KL basin, at the far end of Ampang, past the zoo to the north, and to Bangsar, to the southwest. KL has become a city of condominiums, which have sprung up everywhere from the centre of town to these outlying suburbs. Greater KL sprawls out into the Klang Valley, once plantation country and now home to the industrial satellites of Petaling Jaya and Shah Alam.

The most recent – and grandiose – development is Putrajaya, Malaysia's new administrative capital, which has been hacked out of plantations 35 km south of KL.

Best time to visit The weather in KL is hot and humid all year round with temperatures rarely straying far below 20°C or much above 30°C. There is no rainy season per se, although you can get rainstorms throughout the year. Try to to be here for one of the festivals (see page 36), particularly the Thaipusam Festival (see page 38), one of the most colourful and shocking. To access an up-to-date weather report, call T1052.

Tourist information Malaysian Tourism Centre (MTC) ① *109 Jl Ampang, T03-21633664, daily 0700-2400*, is located in an opulent mansion formerly belonging to a Malaysian planter and tin miner. It provides information on all 13 states, as well as money-changing facilities, an express bus-ticketing counter, reservations for package holidays, a souvenir shop, Malay restaurant, cultural shows every Tuesday, Thursday, Saturday and Sunday at 1500 (RM5) and demonstrations of traditional handicrafts and 15-minute-long audio-visual shows. There is a Visitor Services Centre on Level 3 of the airport's main terminal building. **Tourism Malaysia** ① *Level 2, Putra World Trade Centre, 45 Jl Tun Ismail, T03-26158188, www.tourismmalaysia.gov.my, Mon-Fri 0900-1800*. Other useful contacts are **KL Tourist Police** ① *T03-21496593*, and **Wildlife and National Parks Department** ① *Km 10, Jl Cheras, T03-90752872, F3-90752873*.

Many companies offer city tours, usually of around three hours, which include visits to Chinatown, the National Museum, the Railway Station, Thean Hou Temple, Masjid Negara (the National Mosque), the Padang area and Masjid Jamek – most of which cost about RM30. City night tours take in Chinatown, the Sri Mahmariamman Temple and a cultural show (RM60). Other tours visit sights close to the city such as Batu Caves, a batik factory and the Selangor Pewter Complex (RM30), as well as day trips to Melaka, Port Dickson, Fraser's Hill, Genting Highlands and Pulau Ketam (RM40-80). Helicopter tours are also available.

24 hours in Kuala Lumpur

Begin the day by heading to the Petronas Twin Towers. Queue for a free ticket to the skybridge (closed Mondays) to survey the city from above. Head back to earth, pick up a copy of the *New Straits Times* and enjoying a leisurely coffee before making a foray for the classic Malay breakfast: *nasi lemak* – rice cooked in coconut milk served with prawn sembal, *ikan bilis* (rather like anchovies), hard boiled egg, cucumber and peanuts.

Make your way to Chinatown and discover two facets of Malaysia's cultural heritage: the Sri Mahamariamman Temple and the Chan See Shu Yuen Temple. For the sake of cultural balance make your way to the Masjid Negara National Mosque, stopping en route at the art deco Central Market to browse handicrafts and souvenirs.

At midday engage with a dim sum buffet lunch which you can work off with a walk in the 90-ha Lake Gardens before looking around the Islamic Arts Museum near its southern tips. By mid-afternoon shake off the past and witness Malaysia's tryst with modernity.

Start the evening with a mouth-tingling cold beer at the **Coliseum Café** before heading back to Chinatown around 1930 when the copy-watch sellers and all sorts of other hawkers emerge from their work load.

For dinner, sample another slice of this culinary melting pot in the unique Nyonya cuisine of the Straits Malays. See listings page 78.

While KL is not Ibiza there is still a reasonably hot stock of bars and clubs on Jl Pinang and Jl P Ramlee, and a less touristy congregation in Bangsar Baru to the west of the city centre and near the university of Malaya. If your stomach grumbles after midnight, 24-hour *mamak* canteens are plentiful in Bangsar.

Lie on your bed and reflect on what's in your stomach or in your head: Indian, French, Taoist, Hindu, Chinese, Malay, Muslim and Western. Quite a cultural score for one day.

Sights

Kuala Lumpur is a bit of a sprawl of a city. The big shopping malls, trendy restaurants and bars are clustered around The Golden Triangle and the KLCC. Here too are the Petronas Towers, once the tallest in the world, and the KL Tower, another mighty spike on the landscape. The ethnic neighbourhoods lie southwest of here – there's Chinatown, a web of bustling streets filled with temples, funeral stores, restaurants and shophouses, and Little India, packed with stores selling Bollywood CDs, saris and spices. Also here is the colonial core where the remnants of the British empire ring Merdeka Square. You can escape from the hustle a few streets southwest of here in the Lake Gardens which house the fine Islamic Arts Museum and a bird and orchid park.

Colonial core and Little India

Behind the Masjid Jamek mosque, from the corner of Jalan Tuanku Abdul Rahman and Jalan Raja Laut, are the colonial-built public buildings, distinguished by their grand, Moorish architecture. The **Sultan Abdul Samad Building**, with its distinctive clock tower and bulbous copper domes, houses the Supreme Court. To the south of here is another Moorish building, the excellent **Textile Museum** ① *26 Jl Sultan Hishamuddin, daily 0930-1800, free.*

The Sultan Abdul Samad Building faces on to the **Padang** on the opposite side of the road, next to **Merdeka Square**. The old Selangor Club cricket pitch is the venue for

Independence Day celebrations. The centrepiece of Merdeka Square is the tallest flagpole in the world (100 m high) and the huge Malaysian flag that flies from the top can be seen across half the city, particularly at night when it is floodlit.

The very British mock-Tudor **Royal Selangor Club** fronts the Padang and was the centre of colonial society after its construction in 1890. Much of the building was damaged by a fire in the late 1960s and the north wing was built in 1970. The Selangor Club is still a gathering place for KL's VIPs. It has one of the finest colonial saloons, filled with trophies and pictures of cricket teams. The famous Long Bar (known as 'The Dog') – which contains a fascinating collection of old photographs of KL – is still an exclusively male preserve.

North of the mosque, back towards the Padang, is the 35-storey, marble **Dayabumi Complex**. Located on Jalan Raya, it is one of KL's most striking modern landmarks. It was designed by local architect Datuk Nik Mohamed, and introduces contemporary Islamic achitecture to the skyscraper era. The government office-cum-shopping centre used to house Petronas, the secretive national oil company, which has since moved to the even more grandiose Petronas Twin Towers (see page 60).

On the opposite bank to the Dayabumi Complex is the **Central Market** ① *www.centralmarket.com.my*, a former wet market built in 1928 in Art Deco-style, tempered with 'local Baroque' trimmings. In the early 1980s it was revamped to become a focus for KL's artistic community and a handicraft centre – KL's version of London's Covent Garden or San Francisco's Fisherman's Wharf. It is a warren of boutiques, handicraft and souvenir stalls – some with their wares laid out on the wet market's original marble slabs. On the second level of the market are several restaurants and a small hawker centre.

The fairy-tale Moorish-style **Railway Station** on Jalan Sultan Hishamuddin is now the **Heritage Station Hotel** and has been replaced by the new Sentral Station a few streets further south).

To the northwest of the old railway station is the **Masjid Negara** (the National Mosque) ① *Sat-Thu 0900-1800, Fri 1445-1800; Muslims can visit the mosque from 0630-2200; women must use a separate entrance*, the modern spiritual centre of KL's Malay population and the symbol of Islam for the whole country. Completed in 1965, it occupies a 5-ha site at the end of Jalan Hishamuddin. Close to the National Mosque is the **Museum of Islamic Arts Malaysia** ① *Jl Lembah Perdana, T603 2274 2020, www.iamm.org.my, Tue-Sun, 1000-1800, closed Mon, RM8*, which provides a fascinating collection of textiles and metalware and is a wonderful oasis of calm in the midst of the city.

Little India's streets – Jalan Masjid India and nearby lanes – echo to the sounds of Bollywood CDs and hawker cries. There are stalls and stores selling garish gold, saris, fabrics, great *kurta* (pyjama smocks), traditional medicines, flowers and spices. It is also a good place to eat cheap Indian snacks and sip on sweet lassis. Although the streets are fairly scruffy, the smells and colours make up for its lack of gloss.

At the muddy confluence of the Klang and Gombak rivers where KL's founders stepped ashore, stands the **Masjid Jamek** ① *daily 0900-1100, 1400-1600*, formerly the National Mosque (main entrance on Jalan Tun Perak). Built in 1909 by English architect, AB Hubbock, the design was based on that of a Moghul mosque in North India. The mosque has a walled courtyard (*sahn*) and a three-domed prayer hall. It is striking with its striped white and salmon-coloured brickwork and domed minarets, cupolas and arches. Surrounded by coconut palms, the mosque is an oasis of peace in the middle of modern KL, as is apparent by the number of Malays who sleep through the heat of the lunchtime rush hour on the prayer hall's cool marbled floors.

No women are allowed in the mosque at prayer time.

Chinatown

Southeast of the Central Market lies Chinatown, roughly bounded by Jalan Tun HS Lee (Jalan Bandar), Jalan Petaling and Jalan Sultan, a mixture of crumbling shophouses, market stalls, coffee shops and restaurants. This quarter wakes up during late afternoon, after about 1630, and in the evening, when its streets become the centre of frenetic trading and haggling. Jalan Petaling and parts of Jalan Sultan are transformed into an open-air night market, *pasar malam*, and food stalls selling Chinese, Indian and Malay delicacies, fruit stalls, copy watch stalls, pirate DVDs, leather bag stalls and all manner of impromptu boutiques line the streets. Jalan Hang Lekir, which straddles the gap between Jalan Sultan and Jalan Petaling, is full of popular Chinese restaurants with their tables set up on the pavement. Off the north side of Jalan Hang Lekir, there is a lively covered fruit and vegetable market in two intersecting arcades.

The extravagantly decorated **Sri Mahamariamman Temple** is south of Jalan Hang Lekir, tucked away on Jalan Tun HS Lee (Jalan Bandar). Incorporating gold, precious stones and Spanish and Italian tiles, it was founded in 1873 by Tamils from southern India who had come to Malaya as contract labourers to work in the rubber plantations or on the roads and railways. Its construction was funded by the wealthy Chettiar money-lending caste, and it was rebuilt on its present site in 1985. It has a silver chariot dedicated to Lord Murugan (Subramaniam), which is taken in procession to the Batu Caves (see page 61) during the Thaipusam Festival, when Hindu devotees converge on the temple. Large numbers flock to the temple to participate in the ritual; this is usually preceded by about half-an-hour's chanting, which itself is accompanied by music.

⏺ In testament to Malaysia's sometimes muddled ethnic and religious mix, it is not uncommon to find Chinese devotees joining in the Thaipusam Festival.

There are two prominent Chinese temples in the Chinatown area. The elaborate **Chan See Shu Yuen Temple**, at the southernmost end of Jalan Petaling, was built in 1906 and has a typical open courtyard and symmetrical pavilions. Paintings, woodcarvings and ceramic sculptures decorate the façade. It serves both as a place of worship and as a community centre. The older **Sze Ya Temple**, close to the central market on Lebuh Pudu, off Jalan Cheng Lock, was built in the 1880s on land donated by Yap Ah Loy. He also funded the temple's construction and a photograph of him sits on one of the altars. Ancestor worship is more usually confined to the numerous ornate clan houses (*kongsis*); a typical one is the **Chan Kongsi** on Jalan Maharajalela, near the Chan See Shu Yuen Temple.

Lake Gardens and around

Overlooking Jalan Damansara, near the southern tip of the Lake Gardens, is the **Muzium Negara** ⓘ *T03-22826255, daily 0900-1800, RM2*, with its traditional Minangkabau-style roof and two large murals of Italian glass mosaic on either side of the main entrance. They depict the main historical episodes and cultural activities of Malaysia. The museum was opened in 1963 and, set on three floors, provides an excellent introduction to Malaysia's history, geography, natural history and culture.

Close to the museum is the south entrance to the 90-ha Lake Gardens (**Taman Tasek Perdana**). Pedal boats can be hired on the main lake, Tasek Perdana, at the weekend. The gardens also house a **Hibiscus Garden** (Taman Bunga Raya), with over 500 species; an **Orchid Garden** (Taman Bunga Orkid), which has over 800 species and is transformed into an orchid market at weekends; as well as children's playgrounds, picnic areas, restaurants and cafés, and a small deer park. At the north end of the Lake Gardens is the **National Monument**. Located at the far side of Jalan Parlimen, this 15-m-tall memorial provides a good view of Parliament House. Below the monument is a **sculpture garden** with exhibits from all the Association of South East Asian (ASEAN) countries.

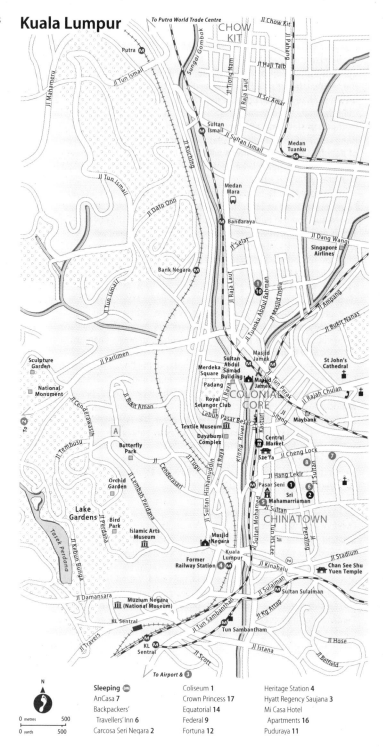

Sleeping
AnCasa **7**
Backpackers'
  Travellers' Inn **6**
Carcosa Seri Negara **2**

Coliseum **1**
Crown Princess **17**
Equatorial **14**
Federal **9**
Fortuna **12**

Heritage Station **4**
Hyatt Regency Saujana **3**
Mi Casa Hotel
  Apartments **16**
Puduraya **11**

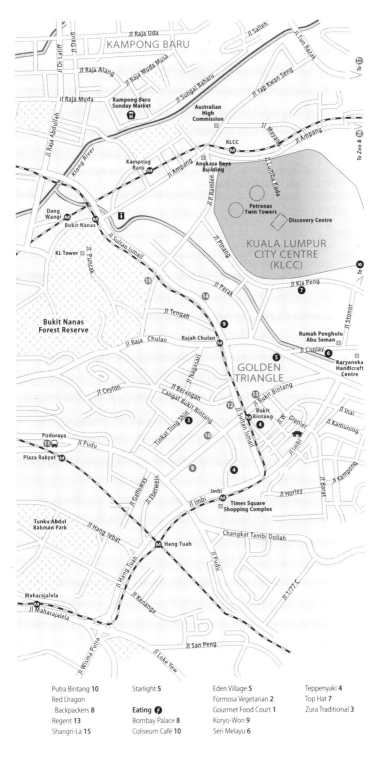

Putra Bintang 10
Red Dragon
  Backpackers 8
Regent 13
Shangri-La 15

Starlight 5

Eating ⓕ
Bombay Palace 8
Coliseum Café 10

Eden Village 5
Formosa Vegetarian 2
Gourmet Food Court 1
Koryo-Won 9
Seri Melayu 6

Teppenyaki 4
Top Hat 7
Zura Traditional 3

The showpiece of the Lake Gardens is the **Bird Park (Taman Burung)** ⓘ *daily 0900-1830, RM22, children RM15*. Opened in 1991 in an effort to outdo neighbouring Singapore's famous Jurong Bird Park (see page 76), this aviary is twice the size of Jurong and is billed as the world's largest covered bird park, and houses more than 2000 birds from 200 species, ranging from ducks to hornbills. Spread out over 20 ha of landscaped gardens, most of the birds are free and very accustomed to being around people.

The **Butterfly Park (Taman Rama-rama)** ⓘ *daily 0900-1800, adult RM10, child RM3*, is a five-minute drive from the main entrance to the Lake Gardens, coming in from Jalan Parlimen. It is a miniature jungle, which is home to almost 8000 butterflies, from 150 species. There are also small mammals, amphibians and reptiles, and rare tropical insects in the park. There is an insect museum and souvenir shop on the site.

To get to the Lake Gardens, take bus 21C or 48C from behind Kotaraya Plaza, or bus 18 or 21A from Chow Kit; get off at the old railway station. Taxis away from the park can be difficult to find – it may be worth either chartering one to wait for you or booking one in advance.

Kuala Lumpur City Centre (KLCC)

The old Selangor Turf Club racecourse, which lies to the southeast of this intersection, has been the focus of extraordinary redevelopment in the guise of the Kuala Lumpur City Centre (KLCC), www.klcc.com.my, a 'city within a city'. High-rise development came late to KL but has rapidly gained a foothold. The city's offices, hotels and shopping complexes are mostly concentrated in the Golden Triangle, on the east side of the city. The complex is one of the largest real estate developments in the world, covering a 40-ha site and including the Petronas Towers, see below.

The **Petronas Twin Towers** were designed by American architect Cesar Pelli and the surrounding park by the Brazilian landscape artist Roberto Marx Burle. The sky bridge, which links the two towers on the 41st floor, is open to the public Tuesday to Sunday 0830 to 1700. Visitors must queue for a ticket which gives free access to the bridge and some stunning views. Only a limited number of people are allowed up every day, so it is advisable to get there before 0900. The **Discovery Centre** ⓘ *Level 4, Suria KLCC Petrosains, T03-23318181, Mon-Thu 0930-1730, Fri 1330-1730, Sat and Sun 0930-1830, RM12, children RM7*, which is really a petroleum promotion exercise, has rides and hands-on computer games all glorifying this industry but is actually a great place for children.

Menara KL and the Bukit Nanas Forest Reserve

ⓘ *T03-20205448, for reservations, T03-20205055, www.menarakl.com.my, daily 1000-2200, RM15, children RM9; there is no public transport, so take a taxi or walk from one of the nearby roads.*

Near the intersection of Jalan Ampang and Jalan Sultan Ismail atop Bukit Nanas stands the Menara KL (**KL Tower**). This 421-m-high tower is the second tallest telecommunications tower in Asia and the fourth tallest in the world (the viewing tower stands at 276 m). Characteristically, the tower is the brain-child of former Prime Minister Dr Mahathir Mohammed. There are 22 levels and 2058 stairs, so the lift is recommended! At ground level there are several shops and fast-food restaurants and a mini amphitheatre. Above the viewing platform is the **Seri Angkasa** revolving restaurant. It has excellent Malay cuisine and revolves once every 60 minutes, so diners get to see the whole city between hors d'oeuvre and ice cream.

Combine a visit to the tower with a walk in the surrounding Bukit Nanas Forest Reserve ⓘ *free*, a beautiful 11-ha area of woodland in the centre of the city with marked trails. KL is perhaps the only city with a patch of rainforest at its heart. There are a couple of entrances into this reserve and various tracks running through it – you can get onto one of these tracks from the road going up to KL Tower. There are also

signposts. Butterflies, monkeys, squirrels and birds live in the forest. There are
warnings about dangerous snakes.

The Golden Triangle

The **Rumah Penghulu Abu Seman** ① *Jl Stonor, T03-21627459 for information on
exhibitions, Mon-Fri 1000-1600*, otherwise known as the **Heritage Centre of the Badan
Warisan Malaysia**, is to be found in a mock-Tudor building off Jalan Conloy, on the
northern edge of the Golden Triangle. In the garden is a reconstructed headman's
house made of timber – it displays detailed carvings and is furnished in the style of a
1930s house. Just to the east of the Heritage Centre is the **Komplex Budaya Kraf**, a local
handicraft centre offering visitors the chance to dabble in batik or watch artists at work.

One of the newest shopping plazas in the Golden Triangle is **Times Square** on Jalan
Imbi, which features a roller coaster, an Imax cinema, and hotel complex as well as the
usual retail and dining suspects.

The **Karyaneka Handicraft Centre** (Kompleks Seni Budaya) ① *Jl Conlay, daily
0900-1800*, to the east of the city centre, is popular with tour groups. There is a
small museum illustrating the batik, weaving and pottery processes. Craft
demonstrations are held from 1000 to 1800, and there are crafts on sale from each
of the 13 states of Malaysia. To get there, take a minibus or **Intrakota** No 40 from
Jalan Tuanku Abdul Rahman.

Around Kuala Lumpur

The most popular day trip from KL is the **Batu Caves** ① *13 km north of KL, open until
about 2100, RM1*, around half an hour's drive north (one hour by public bus) and a fun
day out. This series of caverns, whose entrances are wreathed in mist, is reached by a
sweat-inducing flight of steps with colourful Hindu paraphernalia everywhere. To get
there take a taxi or else bus 11 or 11D from near Central Market or taxi; the caves are a
short walk off the main road. This system of caverns, set high in a massive limestone
outcrop, was 'discovered' by American naturalist William Hornaby in the 1880s. In 1891
Hindu priests set up a shrine in the main cave dedicated to Lord Subramaniam and it
has now become the biggest Indian pilgrimage centre in Malaysia during the annual
Thaipusam Festival (see page 38), when over 800,000 Hindus congregate here. The
main cave is reached by a steep flight of 272 steps. Coloured lights provide illumination
for the fantasy features and formations of the karst limestone cavern. There are a
number of other, less spectacular caves in the outcrop, including the **Museum Cave** (at
ground level) displaying elaborate sculptures of Hindu mythology. During the Second
World War, the Japanese Imperial Army used some of the caves as factories for the
manufacture of ammunition and as arms dumps; the concrete foundations for the
machinery can be seen at the foot of the cliffs.

● Sleeping

Most top hotels are between Jl Sultan Ismail
and Jl P Ramlee, in KL's Golden Triangle.
South of Jl Raja Chulan, in the Bukit Bintang
area, south of the Golden Triangle, there is
another concentration of big hotels. There
are also lots of cheap hotels in the Golden
Triangle, particularly along Jl Bukit Bintang,
convenient for upmarket restaurants, bars
and shopping, while the Chinatown area is
home to rock bottom budget places which
are looking the worst for wear.

Many of the cheaper hotels are around
Jl Tuanku Abdul Rahman, Jl Masjid India
and Jl Raja Laut, all of which are within
easy walking distance of the colonial core
of KL (although these tend to be quite
sleazy and run down), northeast of the
Padang. Some top hotels drastically
reduce their room rates during weekdays.

Colonial core and Little India *p55, map p58*

C **Coliseum**, 100 Jl Tuanku Abdul Rahman, T03-26926270. Fans or a/c, restaurant, colonial hotel. If arriving outside hours, knock on one of the side doors. Large, simply furnished rooms, a famous bar and restaurant (see page 64) and friendly staff. No attached bathrooms. Rooms facing main street are very noisy. For those on a budget who want a taste of the 1920s, it is certainly worth a try.

Chinatown *p57, map p58*

A **AnCasa Hotel**, Jl Cheng Lock, situated next to the Puduraya bus station, T03-20266060, F20313350. International hotel. Well-furnished, clean a/c rooms with televisions, internet access, minibar and in-room safe. Restaurant and bar. Breakfast included. Walking tours of KL available. Recommended.

B **Puduraya**, 4th floor, Puduraya Bus Station, Jl Pudu, T03-20721000, F20705567. A/c, restaurant, breakfast included, clean, spacious rooms, some with spectacular views overlooking the city centre. Residents have access to on-site health club. Very convenient for bus station.

B-E **Heritage Station**, Banguanan Stesen Keretapi, Jl Sultan Hishamuddin, T03-22721688, www.heritagehotelmalaysia.com. Part of the magnificent Moorish-style railway station. After its redevelopment it managed to retain some of its colonial splendour, but disappointingly the standard rooms have been furnished in a contemporary style. It's more of a faded elegance these days, with cranky lifts, saggy floors and lukewarm food. But unbeatable for atmosphere and location. Also backpacker dorms available in a/c rooms with their own bathroom.

C **Red Dragon Backpackers**, 83 Jl Sultan, T03-20706000, F3-20701707. Converted from the old Rex cinema and newly opened at the end of 2004. Big complex of nondescript a/c doubles and dorm rooms, all with shared bathrooms. Many of the rooms have no windows. Backpacker-friendly café downstairs with book exchange and beer. Good place for breakfast.

C **Starlight**, 90-92 Jl Hang Kasturi, T03-20789811. A/c, spacious rooms with (basic) en suite facilities. Excellent staff. Well situated for Central Market, Chinatown, bus stations, eateries, shops, places of interest. Being opposite the Klang bus station, it can be noisy. Recommended.

C-D **Backpackers' Travellers' Inn**, 2nd Floor, 60 Jl Sultan (opposite Furama Hotel), T03-2382473. Some a/c, centrally and conveniently located in Chinatown next to excellent stalls/restaurants, popular and professionally run. Rooms are small but generally clean, ranging from non-a/c dorm rooms to a/c rooms with attached showers. Left luggage, washing and cooking facilities also available, as well as book exchange, video, television and laundry. Recommended.

Lake Gardens and around *p57, map p58*

L **Carcosa Seri Negara**, Taman Tasek Perdana, T03-22821888, F3-22826868. A/c, restaurant, pool. Former residence of the British High Commissioner and built in 1896, it is now a luxury hotel, where Queen Elizabeth II stayed when she visited Malaysia during the Commonwealth Conference in 1989 and where other important dignitaries, presidents and prime ministers are pampered on state visits. Situated in a relatively secluded wooded hillside and overlooking the Lake Gardens. Recommended.

KLCC *p60, map p58*

L-AL **MiCasa Hotel Apartments**, 368b Jl Tun Razak, T03-2618833, micasa@po.jaring.my. A/c, restaurant, pool, shopping arcade, hair salon, dentist and doctor, children's pool, jacuzzi, tennis, squash, gym, sauna, children's playhouse, business centre and is first rate, especially for longer stays. It has 240 suites, which include fully equipped kitchen with utensils and sitting room. There's also an Italian restaurant and tapas bar. Recommended.

AL **Crown Princess**, City Sq Centre, Jl Tun Razak, T03-21625522, www.crownprincess. com.my. A/c, on the 10th floor is a pool and a restaurant, good for 'high tea' buffet. The **Taj Indian** restaurant is on the 11th floor, as is the lobby lounge with baby grand piano and cafés. There is also a business centre, adjacent shopping centre with 168 shops, opulent decor and over 500 spacious rooms with panoramic views. Recommended.

AL **Shangri-La**, 11 Jl Sultan Ismail, T03-20322388, www.shangri-la.com. A/c, Chinese, Japanese and French restaurants,

small, rather old-fashioned pool, health club, sauna, jacuzzi, tennis. With its grand marble lobby and 720 rooms, the 'Shang' has remained KL's ritziest hotel despite the arrival of swish upstart competition. It plays host to political leaders and assorted royalty for dinner. The best feature is its ground floor **Gourmet Corner** deli, which stocks a great variety of European food. Recommended.
AL-A Equatorial, Jl Sultan Ismail, T03-21617777, www.equatorial.com. A/c, restaurant (excellent Cantonese), pool, one of KL's earlier international hotels, the **Equatorial** has had several revamps over the years, its 1960s-style coffee shop has metamorphosed into one of the best hotel coffee shops in town, open 24 hrs (see Eating, below), with an international news agency in the basement, the hotel is the favoured repose of visiting journalists. Choose a room at the back to reduce disturbance by traffic noise, 2 no-smoking floors.

The Golden Triangle p61, map p58
L Regent, 160 Jl Bukit Bintang, T03-21418000, www.regenthotels.com. A/c, Western, Cantonese and Japanese restaurants, beautiful pool, gym with Roman baths, children's pool, a/c squash courts, health club, business centre (open until 2400), the ultimate hotel in KL – it won the 'Best Hotel in Malaysia' award the year it opened in 1990. All suites have butler service and the rooms and bathrooms are lavishly appointed, the enormous lobby is designed around a pool of cascading water. Recommended.
L-AL Federal, 35 Jl Bukit Bintang, T03-21489166, www.federalhotel.com.my. A/c, Indian restaurant, revolving restaurant, ice-cream bar, cafés, bowling, shopping arcade, business centre, pool. When it opened in the early 1960s it was the pride of KL: its **Mandarin Palace** restaurant was once rated as the most elegant restaurant in the Far East, and is still good, but does not compare with the world-class glitz that KL has attracted of late.
B Fortuna, 87 Jl Berangan, T03-21419111, fortuna@tm.net.my. A/c, coffee house with live band, health centre, just off Bukit Bintang, tucked away and slightly quieter than most, behind **McDonalds**, good value for money. Recommended.

C-D Putra Bintang, 72 Jl Bukit Bintag, T03-21419228, F3-21429678. Gleaming new and efficient. Basic rooms with a/c, attached shower and shiny tiles. Popular. 24-hour internet room downstairs. If it's clean you're after, this is a good budget choice. Best to book ahead.

Airport
AL Hyatt Regency Saujana Hotel & Country Club, 2 km off Sultan Abdul Aziz Shah Airport Highway, Petaling Jaya , T03-78461234, http://saujana.regency.hyatt.com. 5 mins from the airport and 2 mins from the golf course (it has 2 18-hole championship courses), low-rise hotel set in landscaped gardens, it is a particularly convenient stop-over for early-morning flights. Provides shuttle service to and from airport.

☻ Eating

Many of KL's big hotels in the **Jl Sultan Ismail/Bukit Bintang** areas serve excellent-value buffet lunches. Recently, **Cangkat Bukit Bintang** and **Tingkat Tong Shin**, a couple of streets sprouting west from Jl Bukit Bintang have emerged as trendy eating areas.
Food stalls The best area for food stalls is **Chow Kit**. On Jl Raja Muda Abdul Aziz there is a food court with great Indian and Afghan food. **Jl Haji Hussien** has a picturesque collection of superb food stalls. Walk up Jl Haji Hussien and turn right. The food court on the top floor of The Mall, built like rows of old Chinese shophouses, is run-down but has an attractive ambience. The Indian, Malay and Chinese food is all good, but the majority of these eating places close by 2000. It's cheap too – tandoori chicken, naan, dal and drink, all for just RM8. **Jl Raja Alang** and **Jl Raja Bot** stalls, off Jl Tuanku Abdul Rahman, are mostly Malay. Next to Keramat supermarket there is a South Indian stall with good mutton soup. In the alleyway between Keramat supermarket and the Pakistani mosque there are lots of good food stalls during the day. **Kampong Baru** and **Kampong Datok Keramat** are Malay communities. On the riverfront behind Jl Mesjid India are good Indian and Malay night stalls. **Jalan Masjid India**, **Little India**, has many good Indian and Malay foodstalls. **Lorong Raja Muda Food Centre**, off Jl Raja Muda, on the edge of Kampong Baru, has

mainly Malay food. **Sunday Market**, Kampong Baru (main market actually takes place on Sat night), has many Malay hawker stalls.

Colonial core and Little India *p55, map p58*

¶¶ **Coliseum Café**, 100 Jl Tuanku Abdul Rahman (Batu Rd), next door to the old Coliseum Theatre, long-famed for its sizzling lamb and beef steaks, Hainanese (Chinese) food and Western-style (mild) curries, all served by frantic waiters in buttoned-up white suits. During the Communist Emergency, planters were said to come here for gin and curry, handing their guns in to be kept behind the bar; it is easy to believe it. Recommended.

Chinatown *p57, map p58*

¶ **Formosa Vegetarian**, 48 Jl Sultan. Mammoth menu of fake meats and fish, beancurds and other creative veggie dishes. Recommended.

¶ **The 'Gourmet Food Court'**, Jl Petaling, opposite **The Swiss Inn**, has a great vegetarian counter with a dozen choices of tasty vegetables and beancurd to pile on rice. Best cheap breakfast in Chinatown. Recommended.

Lake Gardens and around *p57, map p58*

¶¶¶ **Carcosa Seri Negara**, Persiaran Mahameru, Taman Tasek Perdana (Lake Gardens), T03-22821888 (reservations). Daily 1530-1800. Built in 1896 to house the British Administrator for the Federated Malay States, **Carcosa** offers English-style high tea (recommended) in a sumptuous, colonial setting, expensive Italian lunches and dinners are also served in the Mahsuri dining hall on fine china plates with solid silver cutlery.

¶¶ **Seri Melayu**, 1 Jl Conlay, T03-21451833. Open 1100-1500, 1900-2300 (reservations recommended for groups of 4 or more – although it seats 500!). One of the best Malay restaurants in town in traditional Minangkabau-style building, the brain-child of former Malaysian prime minister, Dr Mahatir Mohamad, and has a beautifully designed interior in the style of Negeri Sembilan palace. Don't be put off by cultural shows or the big groups – the food is superb and amazing in its variety,

including regional specialities; it's very popular with locals too. Individual dishes are expensive, the buffet is the best bet (choice of more than 50 dishes), with promotions featuring cuisine from different states each month. Those arriving in shorts will be given a sarong to wear. Recommended.

KLCC *p60, map p58*

¶¶¶ **Ciao**, 428 Jl Tun Razak, T03-9854827. Tue-Sun 1200-1430, 1900-2230. Authentic tasty Italian food served in a beautifully renovated bungalow. Recommended.

¶¶ **Bangles**, 270 Jl Ampang, T03-45324100. This is reckoned to be among the best North Indian tandoori restaurants in KL. It's often necessary to book in the evenings. Recommended.

¶¶ **Bombay Palace**, 388 Jl Tun Razak, next to US Embassy, T03-21454241. 1200-1500, 1830-2300. Good-quality North Indian food in tasteful surroundings with staff in traditional Indian uniform, menu includes vegetarian section. Tourism award winners for several years.

¶¶ **Top Hat** , 7 Jl Kia Peng, T03-22413611. 1200-1500, 1900-2400. Good Eastern Nyonya set menu, some Western dishes such as chicken pie. Set in a 1930s colonial bungalow, just south of KLCC. Recommended.

The Golden Triangle *p61, map p58*

¶¶¶ **Lai Ching Yuen**, Regent Hotel, Jl Bukit Bintang, T03-21418000. Set in a mock Chinese pavilion, holder of 4 Malaysian Tourism Gold Awards for consistently fine cuisine, popular with Chinese gourmets, luxury table settings, revolving solid granite table centres.

¶¶¶ **Zipangu**, Shangri-La Hotel, 11 Jl Sultan Ismail, T03-20322388. Regular winner of best restaurant, with a small Japanese garden. Limited menu but highly regarded.

¶¶ **Eden Village**, 260 Jl Raja Chulan. Wide-ranging menu, but probably best known for seafood. Resembles a glitzy Minangkabau palace with garden behind. Cultural Malay, Chinese and Indian dances every night (less touristy outlet in PJ 25-31 Jl 5322/23, Damansara Jaya).

¶¶ **Marco Polo**, Wisma Lim Foo Yong, 86 Jl Raja Chulan, T03-21425595. 1200-1500, 1900-2300. Extensive menu, barbecue roast suckling pig recommended, 1970s-style decor, very busy at lunchtimes.

Koryo-Won, Kompleks Antarabangsa, Jl Sultan Ismail, T03-21482322. Excellent Korean barbecues, particularly when washed down with Jung Jong rice wine. Recommended.

Zura Traditional, 19 Tingkat Tong Shin (just behind Jl Bukit Bintang), T03-21486466. Arty eatery serving traditional Peranakan cuisine. The spicy coconut fish comes recommended.

Sri Thai, 42 Jl Sultan Ismail, T03-21429915. Well-established eatery near Jl Bukit Bintang, although it's looking a bit faded now. It's lasted 25 years in a city where a restaurant's expected life span is often very short, so it must be doing something right.

Lodge Coffee Shop, Jl Sultan Ismail. Good value for money, particularly local dishes – *nasi goreng*, curries and buffets. Recommended.

Teppanyaki, 2nd Floor, Sungai Wang Plaza, Jl Bukit Bintang and Lot 10, Jl Sultan Ismail, basement. Excellent Japanese fast food, set meal for RM10.

Teahouses

Try out the traditional Chinese teahouse opposite **Sungai Wang Hotel** on Jl Bukit Bintang.

Bars and clubs

Kuala Lumpur now has a vibrant bar scene. Several streets have emerged over the past 5 years or so as hip scenes to be seen in. The **Golden Triangle** is a good place to find bars and clubs – the main bar and club street being **Jl P Ramlee**, but a few bars have begun setting up pumps in **Cangkat Bukit Bintang**, and this area is slated to grow more nightspots. **Bangsar** and **Desi Sri Hartamas** are 2 areas just outside the centre of KL which have developed into popular night-time spots. Bars, restaurants, coffee shops and *mamaks* stand side by side in a network of streets in these 2 areas. Most stay open until the early hours of the morning.

The Metro section in *The Star* (Malaysia's most widely read English-language daily) is devoted to what's on and where. Also check out freebie magazines such as *Juice* (available in bars and clubs) or *KL lifestyle*, *KLUE* and *KL Vision* (usually free in hotels, if not they are

available in newsagents for about RM5).

Zouk, 113 Jl Ampang. Perhaps KL's newest and trendiest nightclub following in the footsteps of Singapore's **Zouk**. A glowing domed exterior, with changing hue encapsulates the groovy interior. Hosts occasional gay parties. Attracts international DJs such as **Tiesto** and has a great chillout bar, **Velvet Underground**. Recommended.

Entertainment

Cultural shows

Central Market, T03-22746542. During the weekends at 1945, performances of Bangsawan (Malay Traditional Theatre), Nadagam (Indian Traditional Theatre) and Chinese Opera all take place.

Temple of Fine Arts, 116 Jl Berhala, Brickfields, T03-22743709. This organization, set up in Malaysia to preserve and promote Indian culture, stages cultural shows every month with dinner, music and dancing. The temple organizes an annual Festival of Arts (call for details), which involves a week-long stage production featuring traditional and modern Indian dance (free, since "the Temple believes art has no price"). It also runs classes in classical and folk dancing, and in playing traditional musical instruments.

Shopping

Many of the handicrafts are imported from Indonesia. The areas to look for Chinese arts and handicrafts are along **Jl Tuanku Abdul Rahman** and in the centre of **Bangsar**. **Jl Masjid India**, running parallel with Jl Tuanku Abdul Rahman, is treasure trove of all things Indian, from saris to sandlewood oil, from bangles to brass incense burners. For clothes, shoes, bags and textiles try **Jl Sultan** and **Jl Tun HS Lee**, close to Klang bus station. In Petaling St, Chinatown, you can barter for Chinese lanterns, paintings, incense holders, etc.

Batik Corner, Lot L1.13, Weld Shopping Centre, 76 Jl Raja Chulan, excellent selection of sarong lengths and ready-mades in batiks from all over Malaysia and Indonesia.

Central Market, Jl Hang Kasturi, a purpose-built area with 2 floors of boutiques and stalls selling just about every conceivable craft – pewter, jewellery, jade, wood and ceramics for a start. Stalls of note include one that sells all kinds of moulds and cutters for baking, a wonderful spice stall, another one for nuts and a third for dried fruits. Downstairs are hand-painted silk batik scarves downstairs, many shops sell batik in sarong lengths.

Evolution, G24, Citypoint, Dayabumi Complex, Jl Sultan Hishamuddin, T03-2913711. Fashionable range of ready-mades and other batik gift ideas by designer Peter Hoe.

Faruzzi Weld Shopping Centre, Jl Raja Chulan (also at 42B Jl Nirwana, just off Jl Tun Ismail), exclusive and original batiks. Recommended.

Kampong Baru Sunday Market (Pasar Minggu), off Jl Raja Muda Musa (a large Malay enclave at the north end of KL). This open-air market comes alive on Sat nights. Malays know it as the Sun market as their Sun starts at dusk on Sat (so don't go on the wrong night), when a variety of stalls selling batik sarongs, bamboo birdcages and traditional handicrafts compete with dozens of food stalls. However, the Pasar Minggu has largely been superseded by Central Market as a place to buy handicrafts.

Jalan Melayu is another interesting area for browsing – Indian shops filled with silk saris and brass pots and Malay shops specializing in Islamic paraphernalia such as songkok (velvet Malay hats) and prayer rugs as well as herbal medicines and oils.

Jalan Tuanku Abdul Rahman (Batu Rd) was KL's best shopping street for decades and is transformed into a pedestrian mall and night market every Sat between 1700 and 2200.

Pertama Shopping Complex, Jl Abdul Tunku Abdul Rahman. In the Chow Kit area near the Bandaraya LRT station, one of the older complexes and a great place for bargain hunters. It has a wide range of mid-budget products from souvenirs to fashion and a basement bazaar, as well as photographic and electronic goods. KL's original department store.

⊖ Transport

Air

KL's international airport is at Sepang (T03-8776 2000), 72 km south of the city. The **KLIA Ekspres** train (T03-22678000, www.KLIAekspres.com) runs 0500-2400 between the airport and **KL Sentral** train station in the city centre, 30 mins, every 20 mins, 35RM one way. Alternatively, you can take the **KLIA Transit**, 35 mins, RM35. It stops at 3 intermediate stations and leaves between 0550 and 0100. If using the KLIA Ekspres you can check your luggage in at KL Sentral for outgoing flights.

The **KLIA Ekspres Coach Service** (T03-6203 3064) provides an efficient service from Sepang International Airport into the city centre to Hentian Duta (near the Tun Razak Hockey Stadium), 1 hr, every 30 mins from 0500 to 2230, RM25, with a RM1 shuttle bus service from Hentian Duta to major hotels.

Bargain hard for a **taxi** to the city. For a taxi from the city to KL Airport expect to pay around RM70-90 when you buy a coupon, 1 hr. Hotels can arrange a good fare in the RM60 range. Make sure the taxi fare includes the motorway toll for either direction.

Bus

Intrakota has taken over most routes now but it's not an easy system to grasp. An **Intrakota** bus map should be available free from City Hall.

Car

Car-hire firms have desks at the airport terminal. Arrange hotel pick-up service in advance or at the office outside the terminal.

Taxi

KL is one of the cheaper cities in Southeast Asia for taxis and there are stands all over town, but you can hail a taxi pretty much anywhere you like. Most are a/c and metered, but it is a challenge sometimes to get the driver to use the meter: RM2 for the first 1 km and RM0.10 for every 200 m thereafter. Extra charges apply between 2400 and 0600 (50% surcharge), for each extra passenger in excess of 2, as well as RM1 for luggage in the boot. Waiting charges are RM2 for the first 2 mins, RM0.10 for every subsequent 45 secs. During rush hours, shift change (around 1500) or if it's raining, it can be very difficult to persuade taxis to travel to the centre of town; negotiate a price (locals claim that waving a RM10 bill helps) or jump in and feign ignorance. For 24-hr taxi service try the following: **Comfort**, T03-80242727; **KL Taxi**, T03-92214241; **Teletaxi**, T03-92211011.

Train

Within the city there are 5 rail systems: 2 **LRT** lines, the Putra (pink) and Star (yellow and light green); 2 **KTM Komuter** lines (blue and red), and the new **monorail** (light blue). Trains leave every 5-15 mins, and tickets cost upwards of RM1.20. Going from one line to the other often means coming out of the station and crossing a road. All lines except the **Star LRT** go through KL Sentral. The trains are a great way to see the city as they mostly run on elevated rails, 10 m above street level.

❶ Directory

Banks Money changers are in all the big shopping centres and along the main shopping streets and they generally give better rates than banks. Most branches of the leading Malaysian and foreign banks have foreign exchange desks, although some (for example **Bank Bumiputra**) impose limits on charge card cash advances.There are bank ATMs everywhere that will provide Ringgit for cards with Cirrus, Visa, MasterCard, Maestro or Plus. **American Express**, 18th Floor, The Weld (near KL Tower), Jl Raja Chulan, T03-20500000. **Embassies and consulates** Australia, 6 Jl Yap Kwan Seng, T03-21465555. Canada, 7th Floor, Plaza MBS,

172 Jl Ampang, T03-21612155. **Denmark**, 22nd Floor, Bangunan Angkasa Raya, 123 Jl Ampang, T03-20322001. **France**, 192 Jl Ampang, T03-21620671. **Germany**, 3 Jl U Thant, T03-21480073. **Netherlands**, 4 Jl Mesra (off Jl Damai), T03-21610148. **New Zealand**, 191 Jl Ampang, T03-20782533. **Norway**, 11th Floor, Bangunan Angkasa Raya, Jl Ampang, T03-21485317. **Sweden**, 6th Floor, Angkasa Raya Bldg, 123 Jl Ampang, T03-21485433. **UK**, 185 Jl Ampang, T03-21482122. **USA**, 376 Jl Tun Razak, T03-21685000. **Emergencies** Fire T994. Police/ambulance T999. **Internet** There are internet cafés everywhere, many of them are open 24 hrs. There are dozens along Jl Bukit Bintang and a few around Chinatown. The Chinatown internet venues are often packed with gaming schoolboys which can make it very noisy. Many backpacker places will offer internet. Expect to pay upward of 3RM per hr. For a classier surf, buy a coffee at **Hotel Equatorial's Etoile Bistro**, and you get 30 mins' free broadband access. **Medical services** Casualty wards are open 24 hrs. **Assunta Hospital**, Petaling Jaya, T03-77823433. **Damai Service Hospital**, 115-119 Jl Ipoh, T03-40434900. **Pudu Specialist Centre**, Jl Baba, T03- 21429146. **Tung Shin Hospital**, 102 Jl Pudu, T03-20721655.

Singapore

To some, Singapore has all the ambience of a supermarket checkout lane and has even been described as a Californian resort-town run by Mormons. It has frequently been dubbed sterile and dull – a report in The Economist *judged Singapore to be the most boring city in the world – and for those who fail to venture beyond the plazas that line Orchard Road, or spend their 3½ days on coach trips to the ersatz cultural extravaganzas, this is not surprising. But there is a cultural and architectural heritage in Singapore beyond the one which the government tries so hard to manufacture. Despite its brash consumerism and toy-town mentality, Singapore is certainly not without its charm. It is difficult to fathom, especially from afar, but beneath its slick veneer of westernized modernity, many argue that its heart and soul are Asian. Behind the computers, hi-tech industries, marble, steel and smoked-glass tower blocks, highways and shopping centres is a society ingrained with conservative Confucian values. For those stopping over in Singapore for just a few days, there are several key sights that should not be missed. Many who visit, however, consider that it is far more important to enjoy the food. The island has an unparalleled variety of restaurants to suit every palate and wallet. Hawker centres in particular are a highly recommended part of the Singapore epicurean experience – they are inexpensive, and many are open into the early hours.* ▸▸ *For Sleeping, Eating and other listings, see pages 76-82.*

Ins and outs

Getting there

Almost all visitors arrive at Singapore's Changi Airport (see page 25). Hotels will only meet guests with a previous arrangement; some charge, but others offer the service free. The car pick-up area is outside the arrivals halls of both terminals. A number of **buses** run between the airport and nearby bus interchanges. Bus 36 loops along Orchard Road passing many of the major hotels including the YMCA. The service runs from 0600 until 2300; fare is less than S$2. An **airport shuttle** runs between 0600 and midnight, every 15 minutes and every 30 minutes (0600-1800), adults S$7, children S$5; booking counters are in arrivals halls. These minibuses will drop off at any destination within the central business district. If you are in a group of three or four, it is probably cheaper to take a taxi.

The airport is now connected to the **MRT underground line**. Trains to the centre of Singapore take approximately 30 minutes. The fare is S$1.40. Trains runs every 12 minutes between 0530 and 2320.

Taxis queue up outside the arrival halls. They are metered but there is an airport surcharge of S$3, which increases to S$5 on Fri, Sat and Sun and after 1700. A trip to the centre of town should cost about S$20 including the surcharge. ►► *For further information, see Airport information, page 25, and Transport, page 82.*

Getting around

Situated to the north of the Singapore River, the colonial core is bordered to the northeast by Rochor Road and Rochor Canal Road, to the northwest by Selegie Road and Canning Hill, and to the southeast by the sea. The area is small enough to walk around – just. To walk from the Singapore Art Museum in the far northwest corner of this area to the mouth of the Singapore River shouldn't take more than 30 minutes. You may want to take a cab to get over to Fort Canning Park if it is a particularly hot and humid day. The river itself is lined with restaurants, bars and leafy walkways. For fun day trips head north of the city for Jurong Bird Park, the zoo, the night safari and Japanese gardens. South, Sentosa Island is linked to the mainland by a cable car and offers beaches, an oceanarium, a fun park and a trapeze.

The island's public transport system is cheap and painless. Buses go almost everywhere and the **Mass Rapid Transit (MRT)** underground railway provides an efficient subterranean back-up. A useful guide to Singapore's transport system is the pocket-sized *TransitLink Guide* (S$3.50), listing all bus and MRT routes and stops, available at news outlets, bookshops and MRT stations, as well as at many hotels. ►► *For further information, see Transport, page 82.*

Best time to visit

There is no best season to visit Singapore and it is hot throughout the year. It gets even stickier before the monsoon breaks in November, while the hottest months are July and August. The wettest months are November, December and January, during the period of the northeast monsoon, when it is also coolest – but even 'cool' days are hot by most temperate people's standards. As one would expect, the hottest time of day is early afternoon when the average temperature is around 30°C, but even during the coolest time of the day, just before dawn, the temperature is still nearly 24°C.

Tourist information

Singapore Tourism Board ⓘ *Tourism Court, 1 Orchard Spring Lane, T1800-7362000 (24-hour and toll-free in Singapore), www.visitsingapore.com, daily 0800-2230. Other offices at: Liang Court Shopping Centre, 177 River Valley Rd, Level 1, T6336*

⚇ 24 hours in Singapore

Breakfast at one of the streetside cafés or hawker centres along Orchard Road. After fueling, pick from a selection of Singapore's finest malls here to window shop, or spend money – Tanglin Shopping Mall is famous for Persian carpets, Forum has a giant toy store, while Palais Renaissance crackles with designer labels.

End your shopping spree with a gentle walk around the Botanic Gardens. Hop across the river to Chinatown for a tour of the city state's backbone Chinese community – there are traditional medicine shops, funeral stores and streets of shuttered traders' homes, now beautifully restored. On nearby Neil Road, you can enjoy a delicate Chinese brew at the Tea Chapter.

It's a few stops on the MRT line to Little India, whose muddle of streets are packed with astrologers, tailors, spice sellers, gaudy jewellers, stalls of sequinned fabrics, thumping Bollywood DVD stores and vendors of Hindu paraphernalia.

A few streets east and you are in the very un-Singapore market warren of Bugis Street – the place to buy pirated goods, bling bling, T-shirts and snacks.

As dusk falls head to the Singapore River, and enjoy dinner and a cocktail at one of the waterside restaurants.

Dinner does not spell the end of the night, however. Take a taxi to Singapore's Night Safari for a tour of the zoo in the dark – the lions will roar and the bats will flap.

The city has tried hard to pump life into its party scene, to some success. If you feel like dancing and you have the cash, head to **Zouk**, **Liquid** or **Centro** – all very cool clubs that attract international DJs.

On your way home, chat to your taxi driver, who, in perfect Singlish will no doubt extol the virtues of his clean, ordered city.

2888, daily 1030-2200; Plaza Singapura, 68 Orchard Rd Level 1, T6332 9298, daily 1000-2200. Changi Airport, arrivals halls 1 and 2, daily 0600-0200; The Galleria at Suntec City Mall, T6333 3825, daily 1000-1800 and The InnCrowd Backpacker's Hostel, 73 Dunlop St, Little India, T6296 4280, daily 1000-2200. It produces a good free official guide called Visitor's Guide to Singapore and is a good sources of brochures and maps. Complaints can also be registered at these offices. The 24-hour Touristline gives automated information in English, Mandarin, Japanese and German. **Indonesian Tourist Board** ⓘ T6737 7422. **Malaysian Tourist Board** ⓘ Ocean Building, 11 Collyer Quay, T6532 6351.

Sights

Singapore is a city state with a land area of just under 650 sq km and, as public transport is impeccably quick and efficient, nowhere is exactly 'off the beaten track'.

Singapore is a great place to bring young children. It is clean, safe and efficient, there are good hospitals, you can drink the water, drivers take notice of pedestrian crossings – all in all it is a child-friendly and parent-soothing place to visit. There are also a multitude of places to see.

Colonial core

The **Padang** ('playing field' in Malay) is at the centre of the colonial area. Many of the great events in Singapore's short history have been played out within sight or sound of the Padang. It was close to here that Stamford Raffles first set foot on the island on the

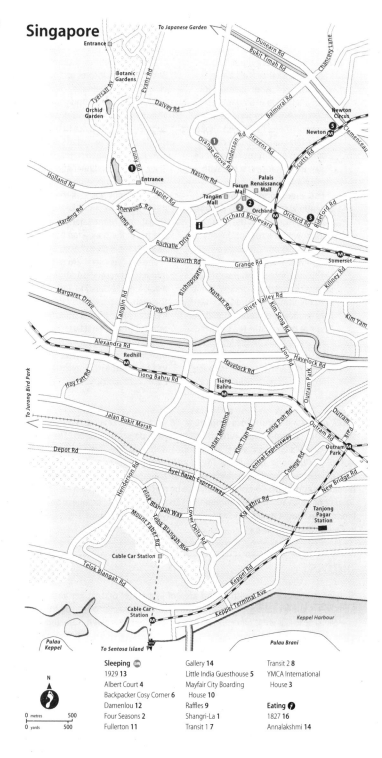

Sleeping

1929 **13**
Albert Court **4**
Backpacker Cosy Corner **6**
Damenlou **12**
Four Seasons **2**
Fullerton **11**
Gallery **14**
Little India Guesthouse **5**
Mayfair City Boarding
 House **10**
Raffles **9**
Shangri-La **1**
Transit 1 **7**
Transit 2 **8**
YMCA International
 House **3**

Eating

1827 **16**
Annalakshmi **14**

N

0 metres   500
0 yards   500

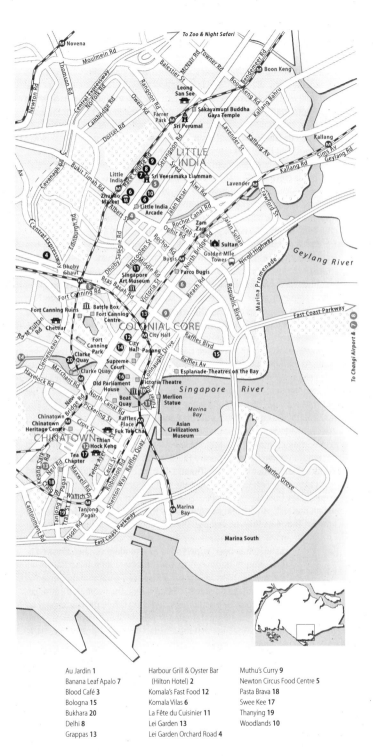

Kuala Lumpur & Singapore Singapore

To Changi Airport &

Au Jardin **1**	Harbour Grill & Oyster Bar	Muthu's Curry **9**
Banana Leaf Apalo **7**	(Hilton Hotel) **2**	Newton Circus Food Centre **5**
Blood Café **3**	Komala's Fast Food **12**	Pasta Brava **18**
Bologna **15**	Komala Vilas **6**	Swee Kee **17**
Bukhara **20**	La Fête du Cuisinier **11**	Thanying **19**
Delhi **8**	Lei Garden **13**	Woodlands **10**
Grappas **13**	Lei Garden Orchard Road **4**	

morning of 28 January 1819, where the Japanese surrendered to Lord Louis Mountbatten on 12 September 1945, and where Lee Kuan Yew, the first Prime Minister of the city state, declared the country independent in 1959.

Flanking the Padang are the houses of justice and government: the domed **Supreme Court** (formerly the Hotel de l'Europe) and the City Hall. The neoclassical **City Hall** was built with Indian convict labour for a trifling S$2 million and was finished in 1929. Hearings usually start at 1000 and the public are allowed to sit at the back and hear cases in session; you can enter via the lower entrance at the front.

The revamped **Raffles Hotel** – with its 875 designer-uniformed staff (a ratio of two staff to every guest) and 104 suites (each fitted with Persian carpets), eight restaurants, a culinary academy, five bars, playhouse and custom-built, leather-upholstered cabs, is the jewel in the crown of Singapore's tourist industry. In true Singapore style, it manages to boast a 5000-sq-m shopping arcade and there's even a **museum** ⓘ *daily 1000-1900, free,* of rafflesian memorabilia on the third floor. Raffles Hotel's original (but restored) billiard table still stands in the Billiard Room. The **Palm Court** is still there and so is the **Tiffin Room**, which still serves tiffin (a snack/lunch).

West of **Raffles Hotel** is **Fort Canning Park**, which, over the last few years, has evolved into something a little more ambitious than just a park. The **Battle Box** ⓘ *daily 1000-1800, last admission 1700, S$8, children S$5,* opened in 1997, is a museum contained within the bunker where General Percival directed the unsuccessful campaign against the invading Japanese in 1942. Visitors are first shown a 15-minute video recounting the events that led up to the capture of Singapore. They are then led into the Malaya Command headquarters – the Battle Box – where the events of the final historic day, 15 February 1942, are re-enacted. Visitors are given earphones and are then taken from the radio room, to the cipher rooms and on to the command room, before arriving at the bunker where Percival gathered his senior commanders for their final, fateful, meeting. It is very well done with a good commentary, figures and film. The bunker is also air conditioned, a big plus after the hot walk up. Dhoby Ghaut is the nearest MRT.

Above the Battle Box are the **ruins of Fort Canning**: the Gothic gateway, derelict guardhouse and earthworks are all that remain of a fort which once covered 3 ha. There are now some 40 modern sculptures here. Below the sculpture garden to the south is the renovated **Fort Canning Centre** (built 1926), which is the home venue of **Theatre Works** and the **Singapore Dance Theatre**. In front of Fort Canning Centre is an old Christian cemetery – **Fort Green** – where the first settlers, including the architect George Coleman, are buried.

Below Canning Hill, on Clemenceau Avenue, is the Hindu **Chettiar Temple**, also known as the **Sri Thandayuthapani Temple**. The original temple on this site was built in the 19th century by wealthy Chettiar Indians (money-lending caste). It has been superseded by a modern version, finished in 1984, and is dedicated to Lord Subramaniam (also known as Lord Muruga). The ceiling has 48 painted-glass panels, angled to reflect sunset and sunrise. Its gopuram, the five-tiered entrance, aisles, columns and hall all sport rich sculptures depicting Hindu deities, carved by sculptors trained in Madras. This Hindu temple is the richest in Singapore – some argue, in all of Southeast Asia. It is here that the spectacular Kavadi procession of the Thaipusam Festival culminates (see page 38).

Many Hindu temples close in the heat of the day, so are best seen before 1100 or after 1500.

Singapore River and the City

The mouth of the river is marked by the bizarre symbol of Singapore – the grotesque **Merlion statue** , half lion, half mermaid. The financial heart of the city is just south of here – tall towers cast shadows on streets which on weekdays are a frenzy of suited traders, bankers and office workers. The most pleasant area by far is along the river which offers peaceful walks along its banks. The riverside is punctuated with pockets of restaurants and bars making it a lively place at night. The Merlion is best viewed from the Padang side of the river. It is inspired by the two ancient (Sanskrit) names for the island: *Singa Pura* meaning 'lion city', and *Temasek* meaning 'sea-town'.

On the north side of the river, opposite the Merlion and looking like a pair of giant metal durians, is the **Esplanade-Theatres on the Bay** ⓘ *www.esplanade.com*, the centre of Singapore's performing arts scene, completed in 2002. Within the complex there's a 1800-seater concert hall, a 2000-seat theatre, and various outdoor performing spaces and, of course, a shopping plaza. To get there, walk through the underground CityLink Mall (from City Hall MRT). Between High Street and Singapore River are a number of architectural legacies from the colonial period: **Old Parliament House**, the **Victoria Theatre** and **Empress Place**, now the second wing of the **Asian Civilisations Museum** ⓘ *Mon 1300-1900, Tue-Sun 0900-1900, Fri 0900-2100, S$5, Fri free admission 1900-2100*. As its name suggests, the focus of the museum is Asian culture and civilization – 5000 years of it. The 10 galleries explore religion, art, architecture, textiles, writing and ceramics from China to West Asia. In front of the theatre is the original **statue of Sir Thomas Stamford Raffles**, sculpted in bronze by Thomas Woolner in 1887. The first branch of the **Asian Civilisations Museum** ⓘ *www.nhb.gov.sg /ACM/acm.shtml, same hours, S$3, free admission Fri 1900-2100, free guided tours in English, Mon 1400, Tue-Fri 1100 and 1400, and additional 1530 tour at the weekends*, is on Armenian Street, close to Stamford Road, and is well worth a visit. The museum is set on three floors. On the first floor is an outstanding collection of Peranakan pieces, displaying the exquisite level of workmanship in jewellery, beadwork and ceramics achieved by Singapore's original 'Baba' Chinese. Some of the pieces are on loan, while the museum gradually builds up its own collection. On the floor above is a display of calligraphy and its accoutrements. Along with the permanent collection, there are travelling exhibitions, which are often excellent.

Along the south bank of the river, facing Empress Place, is **Boat Quay** – commercially speaking, one of the most successful restoration projects of the Urban Redevelopment Authority (URA). The strip now provides a great choice of drinking holes and restaurants for Singapore's upwardly mobile young, expats and tourists, although the area's hipness has faded in recent years and is predominantly patronized by tourists only. Further upriver, **Clarke Quay** has also been renovated and is lined with swanky shops, bars and restaurants which are particularly popular with the large expat crowd. A good way of seeing the sights along Singapore River is on a **bumboat cruise** ⓘ *0900-2300, S$12, children S$6, 30 mins*, which can be taken from Clarke Quay or Boat Quay. A **river taxi** ⓘ *S$1 morning and S$3 afternoon*, also operates from here.

Chinatown

Encompassing Smith, Temple, Pagoda, Trengganu and Sago streets, this was the area that Raffles marked out for the Chinese *kampong* and it became the hub of the Chinese community. Renovation by the URA has meant that these streets still retain their characteristic baroque-style shophouses, with weathered shutters and ornamentation. A good example is the **Thong Chai Medical Institute** on Eu Tong Sen Street, at the corner of Merchant Road. In **Sago Street** (or 'death house alley' as it was known in Cantonese, after its hospices for the dying), **Temple Street** and **Smith Street**, there are shops making paper houses and cars, designed to improve the quality of the afterlife for dead relatives. The English probably gave Sago Street its name in the early 19th century, as Singapore became a centre of high-quality sago production for export to India and Europe. There are also a number of **Chinese medicine shops** in this area – for example, **Kwang Onn Herbal**, 14 Trengganu Street, and others on Sago Street. On show are antlers and horns, dried frogs and flying lizards, trays of mushrooms and fungi, baskets of dried seahorses and octopus, sharks' fins and ginseng. For anyone looking for a full range of Chinese products – from silk camisoles, to herbal medicines, to beaded bags and Chinese tea – a good bet is to visit the **Yue Hwa Chinese Emporium** on the corner of Eu Tong Sen and Upper Cross streets.

As if to illustrate Singapore's reputation as a racial and religious melting pot, the Hindu **Sri Mariamman Temple** is situated nearby at 244 South Bridge Road. The building is dedicated to Sri Mariamman, a manifestation of Siva's wife Parvati. The temple is the site of the annual Thimithi Festival, which takes place at the end of October or the beginning of November.

Also located on Pagoda Street is the new **Chinatown Heritage Centre** ⓘ *www.chinatownheritage.com.sg, Mon-Thu 0900-1800, Fri-Sun 0900-2100, S$8.80, children S$5.30*, which is well worth a visit. The centre evocatively captures the lives of early Chinese settlers with mock ups of boats, coffee houses, opium dens, and squalid housing through the ages including kitchens, bedrooms, and even a prostitute's boudoir.

Telok Ayer Street is full of shophouses and fascinating temples of different religions and was once one of the most important in Singapore. The city's oldest Chinese temple, the Taoist **Thian Hock Keng** temple, or Temple of Heavenly Happiness, is a gem (notwithstanding the naff fibreglass wishing well in one corner). A little way north of Thian Hock Keng is another much smaller Chinese temple, the **Fuk Tak Chai Temple** ⓘ *76 Telok Ayer St, daily 1000-2200, free*, one of the oldest of Singapore's temples, restored in 1998 and now a museum. It's a little oasis of calm amidst the frenetic life of the city and holds a limited display of exhibits, including some Peranakan jewellery, Chinese stone inscriptions, a pair of porcelain pillows, a model of a Chinese junk and an excellent 'diorama' of Telok Ayer Street, as it must have been in the mid-1850s.

One of Chinatown's more interesting places to visit is the **Tea Chapter** ⓘ *9 Neil Rd, www.tea-chapter.com.sg/, daily 1100-2300*, where visitors are introduced to the intricacies of tea tasting in elegant surroundings. You will be invited to remove your shoes and can choose either to sit in one of their special rooms or upstairs on the floor. All in all it's a soothing experience.

Orchard Road and Botanic Gardens

Orchard Road is a long curl of air-conditioned malls, the spine of modern-day Singapore and home to its national pastime – shopping. This glass-fronted materialism is nicely juxtaposed at its western edge with the Botanic Gardens, an elegant park planted with rubber trees, hundreds of orchids, and popular with joggers and stretching tai chi practitioners. There are 3 MRT stations on, or close to, Orchard Road: Dhoby Ghaut, at the eastern end, Somerset, on Somerset Road, and Orchard station, which is at the intersection of Orchard Road and Scotts Road. To walk Orchard Road from end to end is quite a slog – from Dhoby Ghaut to the northwestern end of Orchard Road past Scotts Road is around 2.5 km.

At the western end of Orchard Road, on Cluny Road, not far from Tanglin, are the **Botanic Gardens** ⓘ *T6471 9933, daily 0500-2400, free*. The gardens contain almost 500,000 species of plants and trees from around the world in its 47 ha of landscaped parkland, primary jungle, lawns and lakes. Every morning and evening the park fills with joggers and Tai Chi fanatics. During the day, wedding parties pose for pictures among the foliage. The bandstand in the centre is used for live music performances at the weekends. A map can be acquired from the Ranger's office, five minutes' walk into the garden. Lots of buses run past the Botanic Gardens including Nos 7, 77, 105, 106, 123 and 174 (alight at the junction of Cluny and Napier roads, next to Gleneagles Hospital). The Botanic Gardens also house the **National Orchid Garden** ⓘ *daily 0830-1900, last ticket sales at 1800, S$5, children S$1*, where 700 species and 2100 hybrids of Singapore's favourite flower are lovingly cultivated. It is billed as the 'Largest Orchid Showcase in the World'. The closest entrance to the Botanic Gardens for the Orchid Garden is on Tyersall Avenue.

Little India

The city's South Asian community has its roots in the grid of streets branching off Serangoon Road. Tourist-spruced handicraft shops are packed into the Little India Arcade opposite the more gritty wet market of the Tekka Centre. The best Indian restaurants lie shoulder to shoulder along Race Course Road, while a bit of exploring will unearth theatres, a Bengali temple and a hand-operated spice mill. Little India **MRT** station on the Northeast line has an exit that opens onto the Tekka Centre market.

The lively **Zhujiao** (or Tekka Centre) **Market**, on the corner of Buffalo and Serangoon roads, is an entertaining spot to wander. Spices can be ground to your own requirements. Upstairs there is a maze of shops and stalls; the wet market is beyond the hawker centre, travelling west along Buffalo Road. Opposite the market on Serangoon Road is the **Little India Arcade**, another Urban Redevelopment Authority (URA) project. This collection of handicraft shops is a great place to pick up Indian knick-knacks: leather sandals and bags, spices and curry powders, incense, saris and other printed textiles. There is also a food court. The closely packed shops in the surrounding network of streets house astrologers, framers, tailors, spice merchants, jewellers and pumping Bollywood DVD and Hindi CD shops. Walking up Serangoon Road, take a right at Cuff Road to see Little India's last **spice mill** ① *closed 1300-1400*, at work in a blue and mustard yellow shophouse, owned by P Govindasamai Pillai. It's hard to miss the chugging of the mill, let alone the rich smells of the spices.

The **Sri Veeramaka-liamman Temple** ① *Serangoon Rd, closed 1230-1600*, is dedicated to Kali, the ferocious incarnation of Siva's wife. Worshippers and visitors should walk clockwise around the temple hall and, for good luck, an odd number of times. The principal black image of Kali in the temple hall (clasping her club of destruction) is flanked by her sons, Ganesha and Murugan.

Further up Serangoon Road is another Indian temple, **Sri Perumal** ① *daily 0630-1200, 1800-2100*, with its high goporum sculptured with five manifestations of Vishnu. For the best experience of all, visit during the two-day festival of **Thaipusam** – generally held in January – which celebrates the birthday of Murugan, one of Kali's sons.

Further north is the **Buddhist Sakayamuni Buddha Gaya Temple** (Temple of One Thousand Lights) ① *366 Race Course Rd (parallel to Serangoon Rd), daily 0730-1645; remove shoes before entering*. Across the road is the Chinese Mahayana Buddhist **Leong San See Temple** (Dragon Mountain Temple) with its carved entrance (where you don't have to remove your shoes).

Arab Street

The smallest of Singapore's ethnic quarters, Arab Street is a pedestrianized tourist market strip with shops hawking all manner of Middle Eastern and Islamic goods – prayer rugs, Egyptian perfume bottles, baskets, rattan, silk, velvets and jewellery. There are also great Middle Eastern canteens and the imposing golden-domed **Sultan Mosque** ① *North Bridge Rd, 0900-1300, 1400-1600*, which attracts thousands of the faithful every Friday. Remember to dress modestly. In the maze of side streets around the Sultan Mosque, there is a colourful jumble of Malay, Indonesian and Middle Eastern merchandise. Excellent selections of batik (which is sold in sarong lengths of just over 2 m) jostle for space with silk and Indian textiles (especially along Arab Street), wickerware, jewellery, perfumes and religious paraphernalia. **Bugis Street** is southwest of Arab Street, right across the road from the Bugis Street MRT station. It is packed with stalls selling cheap T-shirts, copy watches and handicrafts – like a street market you might see in Thailand or Malaysia, but something that seems rather out of place in modern-day Singapore. The whole street has been re-created from a road that was demolished to make way for the MRT in the mid-1980s.

Jurong Bird Park

ⓘ *T6265 0022, www.birdpark.com.sg, daily 0900-1800, S$14, S$7 children under 12; a S$30 all-in-one ticket allows entrance to Jurong Bird Park, Singapore Zoo and the Night Safari.*

Situated on Jalan Ahmad Ibrahim, Jurong Bird Park is a beautifully kept 20-ha haven for more than 8000 birds of 600 species from all over the world, including a large collection of Southeast Asian birds. Highlights include the world's largest collection of Southeast Asian hornbills and South American toucans and an entertaining air-conditioned penguin corner, complete with snow. Another main attraction is one of the largest walk-in aviaries in the world, with a 30-m-high man-made waterfall and 1500 birds. There are bird shows throughout the day (the birds of prey show – at 1000 and 1600 – is particularly good). Take MRT westbound to Boon Lay then SBS bus 194 or 251 from Boon Lay MRT interchange. There is a monorail service (S$4, children S$2) round the park for those who find the heat too much.

Singapore Zoo and Night Safari

ⓘ *80 Mandai Lake Rd, T62693411, www.zoo.com.sg. Zoo: daily 0830-1800, S$14, children S$7. Night Safari: 1930-2400, S$18, children S$12 (tram ride is an extra S$6, children S$3. For the all-in-one ticket, see Jurong Bird Park, above; combined Zoo and Night Safari ticket, S$24, children S$12. Take the MRT to Ang Mo Kio and then bus No 138 from the station. A taxi from the city will cost around S$15-20 and takes 30 mins.*

These zoological gardens have one of the world's few open zoos – with moats replacing bars – making it also one of the most attractive zoos, with animals in environments vaguely reminiscent of their habitats. It contains over 170 species of animals (about 2000 actual animals), some of them rare – like the dinosauric Komodo dragons and the golden lion tamarin – as well as many endangered species from Asia, such as the Sumatran tiger and the clouded leopard. The pygmy hippos are relatively recent newcomers; they live in glass-fronted enclosures (as do the polar bears), so visitors can watch their underwater exploits. Animals are sponsored by companies; Tiger beer, for example, sponsors the tigers and Qantas the kangaroos. There are animal shows throughout the day carrying a strong ecological message: elephants (1130 and 1530) and sealions (1430, extra show at 1700 at weekends). Animal feeding times are provided upon arrival. There are tram tours for those too weary to walk (S$4 and S$2), with recorded commentaries, and several restaurants. Overall, it is a well-managed and informative zoo and well worth the trip out there.

The unique Night Safari, next to the zoo, has been cunningly converted into a series of habitats, populated with wildlife from the Indo-Malayan, Indian, Himalayan and African zoogeographical regions. The park supports 1200 animals belonging to 110 species, including the tiger, Indian lion, great Indian rhinoceros, fishing cat, Malayan tapir, Asian elephant, bongo, striped hyena, Cape buffalo and giraffe. Visitors can either hop on a tram to be taken on a 40-minute guided safari through the jungle, or they can walk along three short trails at their own pace – or they can do both. The whole affair is extremely well conceived and managed, and the experience is rewardingly authentic. Children especially, love the experience.

● Sleeping

Many of Singapore's upmarket hotels are concentrated in the main shopping and business areas, including Orchard and Scotts roads, and near Raffles City and the Marina complexes. Discounts are almost always on offer and few people pay the full rate. Enquire at the airport hotel desk on arrival whether there are any special offers. 'Budget' hotels are scarce though there are a few cheaper places to stay and dorm beds can be found for S$12 or so. Most budget accommodation is concentrated in the Little India and Arab St areas to the north of town.

Tipping is virtually non-existent; only tip for special personal services. Most hotels and restaurants add 10% service charge and 5% government tax to bills.

Colonial core *p69, map p70*
LL Raffles, 1 Beach Rd, T6337 1886, www.raffleshotel.com. Singapore's most famous hotel and, despite criticisms, it is still a great place to stay – if you can afford it. There are 9 restaurants and a Culinary Academy, 5 bars and 70 shops. The 103 suites have been immaculately refurbished, with wooden floors, high ceilings, stylish colonial furniture and plenty of space. Bathrooms are the ultimate in luxury and the other facilities are excellent – a peaceful rooftop pool with jacuzzis (although the gym is small), both 24 hr. Very exclusive. Highly recommended.
L-AL The Gallery, 76 Robertson Quay, T6849 8686, www.galleryhotel.com.sg. Marketed as the 'First hip hotel in Singapore', this Philip Starck-styled hotel provides 222 minimalist rooms, divided between 3 ultra-modern blocks. Brightly coloured cushions provide some light relief from the austerity in the standard rooms (showers only in these rooms). There is free internet access in all rooms, and 'smart wired rooms' have their lighting and air-conditioning controlled with sensors, offering such features as guiding lights to the bathroom at night without having to press a switch. The 5th-floor pool is certainly different, with glass on all sides. A thoroughly funky choice. The hotel has chillout lounges and bars including the very popular 4000-sq-ft **Liquid Room** club.
C Mayfair City Boarding House, 40 Armenian St, T9001 2526. Great location facing the Asian Civilisations Museum in the heart of Singapore. Rooms are nothing glam, but are large and serviceable with attached bathrooms. Singles, doubles and triples available. Backpacker friendly with an information board and cheery staff. All rooms have windows, and the ones in the front have good views of leafy Armenian St. Recommended.

Chinatown *p73, map p70*
L Fullerton, 1 Fullerton Sq, T6733 8388, www.fullertonhotel.com. Great position at the head of the Singapore River, this is Singapore's 5-star newcomer. It has 399 rooms in Phillipe Starck style, very functional and well equipped. The restaurants are excellent: the Chinese **Jade**; international **Town Club**; and seafood **Post Bar**. The infinity swimming pool is stunning with views over the Singapore River, with the CBD on one side and Boat Quay on the other.
A Hotel 1929, 50 Keong Saik Rd, Chinatown, T6347 1929, www.hotel1929.com. Singapore's newest funky boutique hotel. The owners have used their own collection of retro and designer furniture for this quirkily restored shophouse. The 32 rooms are small, but so chic that size does not matter for once. There's no pool or gym, but a small jacuzzi, free internet and in-room safes. Recommended.
A-B Damenlou, 12 Ann Siang Rd, Chinatown, T6221 1900, yokewong12@hotmail.com. Marked by a quaint entrance, this small establishment remains a great place to stay for budget travellers. A/c, attached bathroom, TV, minibar; cheaper rooms are very small but neat and clean, and well presented. Very friendly management and located in an attractive street of shophouses, 1st-floor Cantonese restaurant. Recommended.

Orchard Road and Botanic Gardens
p74, map p70
LL Four Seasons, 190 Orchard Blvd, T6734 1110, www.fourseasons.com. Hard to beat, this intimate hotel of 254 rooms (and more than 300 staff) provides exceptional personal service. Rooms are elegantly decorated in traditional European style, with feather pillows, writing desk, multi-disc player, and spacious bathrooms. The hotel has a unique Asian art collection, with attractive artwork in all the rooms. There are 2 pools and the only a/c tennis courts in Singapore, a golf simulator and a well-equipped health and fitness centre, with attendants on hand all day. Restaurants include Cantonese and contemporary American cuisine, with lunchtime buffet. Although, primarily a business hotel, children are well catered for. Recommended.
LL Shangri-La, 22 Orange Grove Rd, T6737 3644, www.shangri-la.com. This is one of Singapore's finest hotels, set in a beautifully maintained, spacious landscaped garden. There are more than 700 rooms, recently very stylishly refurbished; those in the refined and relaxed **Valley Wing** are superior

and the service is exceptional. The excellent leisure facilities include a spacious pool area surrounded by greenery and waterfalls, jacuzzi, indoor pool, good fitness centre, squash and tennis courts, and a 3-hole pitch and putt golf course. Possibly the best conference facilities in town. There are 3 good restaurants: **Shang Palace** for dim sum, the Japanese **Nadamon** and the outstanding **Blu**, a Californian-French restaurant on the top floor. Winner of Singapore Tourism Board's award for best hotel year after year. Recommended.

B YMCA International House, 1 Orchard Rd, T6336 6000, www.ymca.org.sg. Facilities are well above the usual YMCA standards, a/c, restaurant, rooftop pool, squash courts, badminton, billiards and fitness centre. Grotty from the outside, but it is very clean and efficient. Good value for this location, S$29 for 4 bed a/c dorm. Non members pay a small fee of S$3.15 for the first night. Recommended.

Little India *p75, map p70*
AL Albert Court, 180 Albert St, Little India, T6339 3939, www.albertcourt.com.sg. An unusually designed hotel (a mixture of Western and Peranakan), lying behind a courtyard of renovated shophouses. This is an intimate place built to high specifications, with attractive extras. Ask for a room with big windows. Right next to a good range of restaurants in Albert Court. Recommended.
C Little India Guesthouse, 3 Veerasamy Rd, T62942866, www.singapore-guesthouse.com. Some a/c, no private bathrooms, but spotless male/female shower areas and fairly clean rooms. No food served here, but plenty on the street. Good location in the heart of Little India and all in an attractive salmon-pink shophouse. Recommended.

Arab Street *p75, map p70*
C-D Backpacker Cosy Corner, 2/F, 490 North Bridge Rd, T6224 6859. A newly renovated guesthouse above a series of Muslim and Indian restaurants on North Bridge Rd, just south of Liang Seah St. After its spruce up this place is a good backpacker choice with clean, simple rooms and dorms with shared bathrooms only and nice touches like free internet and breakfast.

Airport
B Transit Hotel 1, Level 3 Changi Airport Terminal 1, T6542 5538, www.airport-hotel.com.sg. Short-stay rate quoted (6 hrs). A good place to take a break if you are stuck at Changi for an extended period and no need to clear immigration.
B Transit Hotel 2, departure/transit lounge south, Changi Airport Terminal 2, T6542 8122, www.airport-hotel.com.sg. Excellent hotel on the airport property, short-stay rate quoted (6 hrs). Booking is recommended. It also provides a 'freshen up' service including showers, sauna and gym from S$8.40.

● Eating

Eating is the national pastime in Singapore and has acquired the status of a refined art. The island is a tropical paradise for epicureans of every persuasion and budget. Fish-head curry must surely qualify as the national dish, but you can sample 10 Chinese cuisines, North and South Indian, Malay and Nonya (Straits Chinese) food, plus Indonesian, Vietnamese, Thai, Japanese, Korean, French, Italian (and other European), Russian, Mexican, Polynesian and Scottish. There's a very respectable selection of Western food at the top end of the market, a few good places in the middle bracket, and swelling ranks of cheaper fast food restaurants and an explosion of pizza outlets.

Among the best places to eat are **Chinatown**, **Little India** and **Arab St**. The last couple of years has seen a burgeoning of restaurants along **Club St**; all are top-end eateries, catering for city business people.

For North Indian cuisine, the best option is to the southern end of **Race Course Rd**, where there are 6 good restaurants in a row, all competing for business, including the **Banana Leaf Apolo**, **Delhi** and, most famous of all, **Muthu's**. Some of the best vegetarian restaurants – South Indian particularly – are found on the other side of **Serangoon Rd**, along Upper Dickson Rd. **Arab St** is the best area for Muslim food of all descriptions – Malay, Indonesian, Indian or Arabic. Try **New Bugis St** for simple open-air fare and jugs of cold beer.

Colonial core *p69, map p70*

¶¶¶ 1827, Old Parliament House, 1 Parliament Lane, T63371871. Elegant Thai restaurant on the ground floor of the beautifully renovated Parliament House. Great ambience.

¶¶¶ Annalakshmi, 02-10 Excelsior Hotel and Shopping Centre, 5 Coleman St, T6339 9993. North and South Indian vegetarian cuisine. Staffed by women volunteers, profits go to the Kalamandhir Indian cultural group. The health drinks are excellent – especially *Mango Tharang* (mango juice, honey and ginger) and *Annalakshmi Special* (fruit juices, yoghurt, honey and ginger). The restaurant, which sprawls out onto the veranda overlooking the tennis courts, closes at 2130. Recommended.

¶¶¶ Grappas, CHIJMES, Gallery Floor, 30 Victoria St, T6334 9928. Large Italian restaurant in this trendy courtyard. Extensive menu, with mostly pasta and risotto dishes as well as some meat entrées; booking advisable. Recommended.

¶¶¶ Lei Garden, Gallery Floor, CHIJMES, 30 Victoria St, T6339 3822. A menu which is said to comprise 2000 dishes. Outstanding Cantonese food: silver codfish, emperor's chicken and such regulars as dim sum and Peking duck. Dignatories, royalty and film stars dine here. Tasteful decor and a 2-tier aquarium displaying the day's offerings. Despite seating for 250, you need to book in advance. Worth every penny. Recommended.

¶¶¶ Raffles Grill, Raffles Hotel, 1 Beach Rd (main building, lobby), T6412 1185. Excellent French cuisine in an elegant colonial setting, with silver-plate settings, chandeliers and reproduction Chippendale furniture.

¶¶¶ Ristorante Bologna, Marina Mandarin Hotel, 6 Raffles Blvd, Marina Sq, T6845 1113. Award-winning Italian restaurant. House specialities include spaghetti alla marinara and baked pigeon. Diners lounge amidst sophisticated decor whilst wandering minstrels strum.

¶¶ Bukhara, Block 3C, River Valley Rd, Clarke Quay, T6338 1411. This award-winning restaurant dishes up West Asian cuisine. Its creamy chicken kebab is recommended. The menu derives from food typically eaten by nomads – meat barbecued over a clay oven.

¶ Komala's Fast Food, Upper Dickson Rd. South Indian delicacies including *thalis*, *masala dosas* and *idlis* are served in an a/c restaurant. Very popular and recommended.

Chinatown *p73, map p70*

¶¶¶ Thanying, Amara Hotel, T6227 7856. Provides the best Thai food in town with an extensive menu and superb food (the 15 female chefs are all said to have trained in the royal household in Bangkok). Booking necessary. Recommended.

¶¶ Pasta Brava, 11 Craig Rd, Tanjong Pagar. Tastiest Italian in town in an equally tasty shophouse conversion; fairly expensive, but good choice of genuine Italian fare. Recommended.

¶¶ Swee Kee, 12 Ann Siang Rd, T6222 8926. This 1st-floor Chinese restaurant has acquired some degree of local renown due to the owner Tang Kwong Swee – known to his friends as 'Fish-head' – having run the same place for 60 years (although the location has changed). Recommended are the deep-fried chicken, Hainanese style, fish-head noodle soup and prawns in magi sauce; very popular.

Orchard Road and Botanic Gardens
p74, map p70

¶¶¶ Au Jardin, EJH Corner House, Singapore Botanic Gardens Visitors' Centre, 1 Cluny Rd, T6466 8812. Situated in the former garden director's black and white bungalow, with only 12 tables, this French restaurant is elegant and sophisticated, with a menu which is changed weekly. Booking essential.

¶¶¶ Blu, Shangri-La Hotel, 22 Orange Grove Rd, T6213 4598. Situated on the 24th floor, Blu provides stunning views, great service and excellent Californian food. Recommended.

¶¶¶ Harbour Grill and Oyster Bar, Hilton Hotel, 581 Orchard Rd, T6730 3393. Contemporary surroundings with nautical theme, serving international food. Delicacies include caviar and smoked salmon; monthly guest chef. Impeccable service.

¶¶ Blood Café, 290 Orchard Rd, Paragon, T6735 6765. Funky café with style and fashion magazines to browse through. ProjectShock BloodBrothers clothes shop on the 2nd floor. Relaxing place, with an inventive menu featuring couscous, roasted vegetables and chunky sandwiches. Hip and healthy. Good veggie choices. Recommended.

¶¶ Lei Garden, Orchard Shopping Centre, 321 Orchard Rd, T6734 3988, and **Orchard Plaza**, 150 Orchard Rd, T6738 2448. The famous Cantonese restaurant (see page 79). Book in advance. Recommended.

Little India *p75, map p70*

¶¶¶ La Fête du Cuisinier, 161 Middle Rd, T63330917, on the corner of Waterloo St and Middle Rd. A surprising location for one of the more sophisticated restaurants in town. Exquisite French Creole cuisine – a lavish menu of foie gras, oysters and crab (and that's only the starters). Attractive setting, elaborate French decor in Marie Antoinette style.

¶¶ Banana Leaf Apolo, 56-58 Race Course Rd. North Indian food, a popular fish-head curry spot, a/c and more sophisticated than the name might imply – although the food is still served on banana leaves. Recommended.

¶¶ Delhi, Race Course Rd. North Indian food including chicken tikka, various tandooris, as well as creamy Kashmiri concoctions. Popular and award-winning restaurant.

¶¶ Komala Vilas, 76-78 Serangoon Rd, T6293 6980, and 12 Buffalo Rd. South Indian *thalis* and *masala dosas*, bustling café, with a little more room upstairs. Recommended.

¶¶ Muthu's Curry, corner of Rotan Lane and Race Course Rd, T6293 7029. North Indian food, reckoned by connoisseurs to be among the best banana leaf restaurants in town; Muthu's fish-heads are famous. Recommended.

¶ Woodlands, 12 Upper Dickson Rd (off Serangoon Rd), T6297 1594. *Thalis*, *masala dosa* and vegetarian curries, good and cheap. Recommended.

Arab Street *p75, map p70*

¶ Zam Zam Restaurant, junction of Arab St and North Bridge Rd. Muslim Malay-Indian dishes served in busy and chaotic coffee shop. Very popular and recommended for a taste of the other Singapore – spicy meats, chargrilled seafood, creamy curries.

Eslewhere

¶¶¶ Long Beach Seafood, 31 Marina Park, Marina South, T6323 2222. One of the island's most famous seafood restaurants, specializing in pepper and chilli-crabs, drunken prawns and baby squid cooked in honey.

Hawker centres and food courts

Food courts are the modern, a/c, sanitized version of Singapore's old hawker centres. Hawker centres are found beneath HDB blocks and in some specially allocated areas in the city; food courts are usually in the basement of shopping plazas. Customers claim a table, then graze their way down the rows of Chinese, Malay and Indian stalls. It is not necessary to eat from the stall you are sitting next to.

Lau Pa Sat Festival Market (formerly the **Telok Ayer Food Centre**), Raffles Quay end of Shenton Way in the old Victorian market. Good range of food on offer: Chinese, Indian, Nonya, Korean, Penang, ice creams, fruit drinks – best in the evening when Boon Tat St is closed off and satay stalls serve up cheap, tasty sticks of chicken, beef, mutton or prawns washed down with jugs of Tiger beer.

Newton Circus, Scotts Rd, north of Orchard Rd. Despite threats of closure by the government, this huge food centre of over 100 stalls is still surviving and dishing up some of the best food of its kind. Open later than others so very popular with tourists.

Lavender Food Square, Lavender Rd, north of Little India. One of the best hawker centres in town.

Zhujiao or Kandang Kerbau (KK) Food Centre, corner of Buffalo and Serangoon roads. Wide range of dishes, and the best place for Indian Muslim food: curries, *rotis*, *dosai* and *murtabak* are hard to beat (beer can be bought from the Chinese stalls on the other side).

Cafés and bakeries

Zhong Guo Hua Tuo Guan, 52 Queen St (name above the tea house is in Chinese characters), just by the Albert and Waterloo streets roadside market. A traditional Chinese tea house with quite a few outlets, including this atmospheric one. It sells Hua Tuo's ancient recipes, helpful for 'relieving of heatiness' and 'inhibiting the growth of tumor cells,' amongst other things. Very friendly proprietress will introduce you to wild ginseng and *showfrog* or *longan* (a fruit like a lychee) herbal jelly, and tell you why you will feel better (that's if you can get any of the concoctions down!).

❶ Bars and clubs

There are lots of bars on **Boat** and **Clarke** quays; those at the former are wilder and less packaged, although the last few years has seen a slight deterioration in quality as locals have moved on and tourists have become the dominant clientele. One of the more dramatic changes over the past couple of years is the development along the riverfront westwards. Both **Robertson's Walk** and **The Quayside** are gradually filling up with shops and restaurants, and the nearby **Mohammed Sultan Rd** has become an extremely popular watering hole; the entire street is lined with bars and clubs. The west side is a row of restored shophouses, whilst the east is a modern high-rise block.

There are several quiet bars on **Duxton Hill**, Chinatown, in a pleasant area of restored shophouses – a retreat from the hustle and bustle of Boat Quay or the city. **Duxton Rd** and **Tanjong Pagar Rd** also have a dozen or so bars in restored shophouses.

Peranakan Place just off Hollywood Rd is home to a string of funky New York-style bars carved out of restored shophouses. You are looking at S$15 a pint, these places are not cheap, but they are very stylish, albeit for poseurs.

There are several options in the famous **Raffles Hotel**, Beach Rd, including **Bar and Billiard Room**, which is lavishly furnished with teak tables, oriental carpets and 2 original billiard tables; **The Long Bar**, home of the Singapore Sling, originally concocted by bartender Ngiam Tong Boon in 1915, now on 2 levels and extremely popular with tourists and locals; gratuitous, tiny, dancing mechanical *punkah-wallahs* sway out of sync to the cover band; and **Writers' Bar**, (just off the main lobby), in honour of the likes of Somerset Maugham, Rudyard Kipling, Joseph Conrad, Noel Coward and Herman Hesse, who are said either to have wined, dined or stayed at the hotel. Bar research (ie bookcases and mementoes) indicates that other literary luminaries from James A Michener to Noel Barber and the great Arthur Hailey are also said to have sipped Tigers at the bar.

The Dubliner, Winsland Conservation House, 165 Penang Rd, T67352220. Irish pub set inside a beautifully restored colonial house. Very friendly, good hearty Irish food as well as the compulsory pints of Guinness and Kilkenny. Recommended.

Harry's Bar, 28 Boat Quay. Large bar with seating outside overlooking the river, popular with City boys, serves pricey food on the 1st floor, jazz band.

Liquid Room, Gallery Ev@son, 76 Robertson Quay. Hi-tech disco on 2 floors, with different music on each: the **Sound Bar**, daily 1900-0300, and the **Liquid Room**, 2230-0300. Happy hour is from 1900-2100.

Number 5, 5 Emerald Hill. Happy hours 1200-2100 Mon-Sat, 1700-2100 Sun, at the top of the pedestrianized section of Emerald Hill, retro-chic restored shophouse bar and restaurant (upstairs), popular with young expats and Chuppies (Chinese yuppies), great music. Recommended.

Trader Vics, 5th Floor, **New Otani Hotel**, River Valley Rd. Hawaii 5-0 decor and Chin-Ho's favourite cocktails – try a few goblets of Tikki Puka Puka for something violently different.

Velvet Underground, 17 Jiak Kim St (off Kim Seng Rd), next door to **Zouk** and under the same management. Small nightclub, Tue-Sat 2100-0300, cover S$25, free for women on Wed nights. Recommended. Often has gay or lesbian parties.

Zouk, 17 Jiak Kim St, opposite the **Concorde Hotel**. Huge quirky club, with a fun design. Described as the place for hard clubbing.

O Shopping

Singaporeans have taken shopping to their hearts and to new heights. While the city is not the bargain basement place it was, it is still a great place to browse and buy with care.

It doesn't take long to get the feel of where you can bargain and where you cannot. Department stores are fixed price, but most smaller outfits – even those in smart shopping complexes – can sometimes be talked into discounts – 20-30% can be knocked off the asking price, sometimes more.

Probably the best area for window shopping is around **Scotts Rd** and **Orchard Rd**, where many of the big complexes and department stores are located. This area comes alive after dark and most shops stay open late. The towering **Raffles City**

● *The Singapore Sling is the island's best-known cocktail. It was invented in the Raffles Hotel in*
● *1915 and contains a blend of gin, cherry brandy, sugar, lemon juice and angostura bitters.*

Complex, **Parco** at Bugis Junction, **Suntec City** and **Marina Sq** are the other main shopping centres. Serangoon Rd (or **Little India**), **Arab St** and **Chinatown** offer a more exotic shopping experience.

⊖ Transport

Air
For details of Changi International Airport, see Touching down, page 25.

Car
Car hire desks are in Terminals 2's arrival hall 0700-2300; **Avis** T6542 8855, **Hertz** T6542 5300. To book limousine service from your hotel, call **Avis**, T6737 1668, **City Cab**, T6454 2222, **Comfort**, T6552 1111, **TIBS**, T6555 8888, or **Hertz**, T1800-7344646.

Bus
SBS (Singapore Bus Service) and TIBS (Trans-Island Bus Services) are both efficient, convenient and cheap. Fares range from 70¢ (non a/c) to S$1.70, and buses run daily 0600-2400. The sightseeing **Singapore Explorer** trolley, T6339 6833, travels all day between Orchard Rd, the river, Chinatown, Raffles Hotel, Boat Quay, Clarke Quay and Suntec City. Some hotels sell tickets, or else buy from the driver; S$9, children S$7, for unlimited rides throughout the day.

Mass Rapid Transit (MRT)
Singapore has one of the most technologically advanced, user-friendly light railway systems in the world. Trains run 0600-2400, every 2½-8 mins (depending on the time of day). Fare stages are posted in station concourses, and tickets dispensed, with change, from the vending machines. Fares range from 80¢ to S$1.80.

Taxis
Singapore's taxis provide excellent value for money and are definitely the best way to get around. All are metered, a/c and accept credit or debit cards. They can be hailed anywhere but it's best to go to a taxi stand or about 50 m from traffic lights. There are stands outside most main shopping centres and hotels. Drivers are impeccably polite and will even round down fares to the nearest dollar. Unlike most of the rest of Asia,

language is not a barrier to communication. Taxis displaying red destination labels on their dashboards are going home and are only required to take passengers in the direction they are going. For taxi services ring: **Comfort**, T6552 1111; **City Cab**, T6552 2222; **TIBS**, T6555 8888.

❶ Directory

Embassies and consulates Australia (High Commission), 25 Napier Rd, T6836 4100. Austria, 600 North Bridge Rd, T6396 6350. Belgium, 8 Shenton Way, 1401 Temasek Tower, T6220 7677. Canada (High Commission), 1400 Fuji Xerox Towers, 80 Anson Rd, T6325 3200. Denmark, 1301 United Sq, 101 Thomson Rd T63555010. France, 101-103 Cluny Park Rd T68807800. Germany, 1200 Singapore Land Tower, 50 Raffles Place, T65336002. Israel, 24 Stevens Close, T62350966. Italy, 101 Thomson Road, No 27-02 United Sq, T62506022. Japan, 16 Nassim Rd, T62358855. Malaysia (High Commission), 30 Hill St, T6235 0111. Netherlands, 1301 Liat Towers, 541 Orchard Rd, T6737 1155. New Zealand (High Commission), 391A Orchard Rd, T6235 9966. Norway, 1401 Hong Leong Building, 16 Raffles Quay, T6220 7122. South Africa (High Commission), 15th Floor, Odeon Towers, 331 North Bridge Road, T6339 3319. Spain, 3900 Suntec Tower One, 7 Temasek Boulevard, T6333 3035. Sweden, 111 Somerset Rd, T6415 9720. Thailand, 370 Orchard Rd, T6737 2158. UK (High Commission), 100 Tanglin Rd, T6424 4270. USA, 27 Napier Rd, T6476 9100. **Medical services** Alexandra, 378 Alexandra Rd, T6475 5222. East Shore, 321 Joo Chiat Pl, T6344 7588. Gleneagles, 6A Napier Rd, T6473 7222. Mount Alvernia, 820 Thomson Rd, T2534818. Mount Elizabeth, 3 Mount Elizabeth, T6737 2666. National University, 5 Lower Kent Ridge Rd, T6779 5555. Singapore General, Outram Rd, T6222 3322. Traveller's Health and Vaccination Clinic, Tan Tock Seng Hospital Medical Centre, Level 1, 11 Jl Tan Tock Seng, T6357 2222, www.ttsh.com.sg.
Telephone There are no area codes in Singapore; all standard-tariff numbers have 8 digits. Dial T020, plus the area code (minus the initial zero) to call a city or town in Malaysia (see also page 49).

Sarawak

❖ Footprint features

Introduction

Sarawak, the 'land of the hornbill', is the largest state in Malaysia, covering an area of nearly 125,000 sq km in northwest Borneo and with a population of a little more than two million. Sarawak has a swampy coastal plain, a hinterland of undulating foothills and an interior of steep-sided, jungle-covered mountains. The lowlands and plains are dissected by a network of broad rivers which are the main arteries of communication and where the majority of the population is settled.

In the mid-19th century, Charles Darwin described Sarawak as "one great wild, untidy, luxuriant hothouse, made by nature for herself". Sarawak is Malaysia's great natural storehouse, where little more than half a century ago great swathes of forest were largely unexplored and where tribal groups, collectively known as the Dayaks, would venture downriver from the heartlands of the state to exchange forest products of hornbill ivory and precious woods. Today the Dayaks have been gradually incorporated into the mainstream and the market economy has infiltrated the lives of the great majority of the population. But much remains unchanged. The forests, although much reduced by a rapacious logging industry, are still some of the most species-rich on the globe; more than two-thirds of Sarawak's land area, roughly equivalent to that of England and Scotland combined, is still covered in jungle, although this is diminishing.

Sarawak

★ **Don't miss ...**

1   **Sarawak Museum** Wince at the display
    of *palang* – a Dayak bamboo tool for piercing
    the glans of the penis – in Kuching, page 88.

2   **Bako National Park** Get nose to nose with the
    proboscis monkey; it's one of the best places
    in Sarawak for seeing them, page 99.

3   **Kuching waterfront** Amble along the
    promenade, snacking on *ais cream goreng*
    (fried ice cream), page 105.

4   **Longhouse stay** Secure an overnight
    invitation to an Iban, Bidayuh or Orang Ulu
    village, page 114.

5   **Sungai Rejang** Ride the rapids on a boat
    trip to Kapit or Belaga, page 120.

6   **Caving** Become a spelunker and admire
    the prehistoric cave art in Niah National Park,
    page 131.

7   **Pinnacles** Trek to Mulu's forest of razor-
    sharp limestone needles on Fire Mountain;
    it's a challenging hike, page 148.

Map of Sarawak showing locations including Bandar Seri Begawan, Brunei, Gunung Mulu National Park, Miri, Niah National Park, Bintulu, Belaga, Kapit, Sibu, Kuching, and the South China Sea, with numbered "Don't miss" markers 1–7 and Indonesia (Kalimantan) to the south.

Kuching and around

▶▶ Colour map 1, C2. Population: around 425,000.

Because of Kuching's relative isolation and the fact that it was not bombed during the
Second World War, Sarawak's state capital has retained much of its 19th-century
dignity and charm, despite the increasing number of modern high-rise buildings.
Chinese shophouses still line many of the narrow streets. Kuching is a great starting
point to explore the state and there are many sights within its compact centre,
including the renowned Sarawak Museum and the Petra Jaya State Mosque.

   Within easy reach is the Semenggoh Orang-Utan Sanctuary and the national parks
of Gunung Gading, Kubah and Tanjung Datu National Park. North of Kuching is the
Damai Peninsula and Bako National Park on the Muara Tebas Peninsula. ▶▶ For
Sleeping, Eating and other listings, see pages 101-111.

Ins and outs

Getting there
There are daily connections with KL and also regular flights to other destinations in
Borneo and the rest of Malaysia. International connections are limited to Bandar Seri
Begawan (Brunei), Singapore, Hong Kong (via Kota Kinabalu), and Perth. The airport
is 10 km south of Kuching. A taxi from the airport is paid for by a fixed-price coupon
(RM17.50) to the city centre. There are several out-of-town bus companies and they
provide services to destinations in the vicinity. Interior towns are sometimes difficult
to access by road. There is also a bus service to Pontianak in Kalimantan (10 hours)
and to Brunei, via Miri. Express boats serve Sibu and Sarikei. ▶▶ For further details, see
Transport page 110.

Getting around
The central portion of the city, which is the most interesting, can be negotiated on foot.
Sampans (perahu tambang), provide cross-river transport and operate as river taxis.
There are two city bus companies that provide a cheap and fairly efficient service. Taxis
are found outside many of the larger hotels and at designated taxi stands. There are
several international as well as local self-drive car hire firms in Sarawak.

Best time to visit
Kuching is hot and humid year-round. While heavy showers can happen at any time,
they are more likely during the rainy season (November to February), which could
make trekking difficult. May and June are also the months for Gawai Dayak (see page
38) a kind of harvest festival – a time for feasting and partying.

Tourist information
Sarawak Tourism Board ⓘ Visitors' Information Centre, Jl Tun Abang Haji Openg,
T082-410944, www.sarawaktourism.com, Mon-Fri 0800-1800, 1st and 3rd Sat of the
month 0800-1500 (2nd and 4th Sat 0800-1600), is housed in the beautiful Old
Courthouse Complex. It has a good stock of maps and pamphlets. The smaller branch
office of the **Sarawak Tourism Association** ⓘ Waterfront, Main Bazaar, T082-240620,
F082-427151, Mon-Thu 0800- 1245, 1400-1645, Fri 0800-1130, 1430-1645, Sat
0800-1245 (closed 1st and 3rd Sat of the month), has infinitely more helpful and
courteous staff. There is a desk at **Kuching International Airport** ⓘ T082-450944,
which is good for information on bus routes, approved travel agents and itineraries.
Tourism Malaysia ⓘ Bangunan Rugayah, Jl Song Thian Cheok, T082-246575,

The state and national tourism organizations are both well informed and helpful; they can offer advice on itineraries and travel agents and have up-to-date information on facilities in national parks.

National parks information

For information and advance accommodation booking for the national parks of Bako, Gunung Gading, Kubah and Matang Wildlife Centres, contact the **National Parks and Wildlife Booking Office** ⓘ *Tourist Information Centre in the Old Courthouse, Jl Tun Haji Openg, To82-248088, Fo82-248087; you can also book through www.forestry.sarawak.gov.my, click on 'online services', and then 'booking of national park'; also npbooking@sarawak.net.gov.my.*

History

Shortly after dawn on 15 August 1839 British explorer James Brooke sailed round a bend in the Sarawak River and, from the deck of his schooner, *The Royalist*, had his first view of Kuching. According to the historian Robert Payne, he saw "...a very small town of brown huts and longhouses made of wood or the hard stems of the nipah palm, sitting in brown squalor on the edge of mudflats." The settlement, 32 km upriver from the sea, had been established less than a decade earlier by Brunei chiefs who had come to oversee the mining of antimony in the Sarawak River valley. The antimony – used as an alloy to harden other metals, particularly pewter – was exported to Singapore where the tin-plate industry was developing.

By the time James Brooke had become Rajah in 1841, the town had a population of local Malays, Dayaks and Cantonese, Hokkien and Teochew traders. Chinatown dominated the south side of the river while the Malay kampongs were strung out along the riverbanks to the west. A few Indian traders also set up in the bazaar, among the Chinese shophouses. Under Charles Brooke, the second of the White Rajahs, Kuching began to flourish; he commissioned most of the town's main public buildings. Brooke's wife, Ranee Margaret, wrote: "The little town looked so neat and fresh and prosperous under the careful jurisdiction of the Rajah and his officers, that it reminded me of a box of painted toys kept scrupulously clean by a child."

Background

Sarawak's capital is divided by the Sarawak River; the south is a commercial and residential area, dominated by Chinese, while the north shore is predominantly Malay in character with the old kampong houses lining the river. The **Astana**, **Fort Margherita** and the **Petra Jaya area**, with its modern government offices, are also on the north side of the river. The two parts of the city are very different in character and even have separate mayors. Kuching's cosmopolitan make-up is immediately evident from its religious architecture: Chinese and Hindu temples, the imposing state mosque and Protestant and Roman Catholic churches.

Of all the cities in Malaysia, Kuching has been the worst affected by the smog – euphemistically known as 'the haze' – that periodically engulfs large areas of Borneo and the Indonesian island of Sumatra, largely blamed on slash and burn deforestation in Kalimantan. This was most severe in mid-1997, but occurs to some extent every year. At the peak of the 'emergency' – for that is what it became – in late September 1997, Kuching came to a stop. It was too dangerous to drive and, seemingly, too dangerous to breathe. People were urged to remain indoors. Schools, government offices and factories closed. The port and airport were also closed. Tourism traffic dropped to virtually zero and for 10 days the city stopped. At one point there was even discussion of evacuating the population of the State of Sarawak. People began to buy up necessities and the prices of some commodities rose 500%.

Sights

Sarawak Museum

ⓘ *Daily 0900-1700, closed on first day of public holidays, free. There is a library and a bookshop attached to the museum as well as a giftshop, the Curio Shoppe, all proceeds of which go to charity. Permits to visit the Niah's Painted Cave can be obtained, free of charge, from the curator's office.*

Kuching's biggest attraction is this internationally renowned museum, housed in two sections on both sides of Jalan Tun Haji Openg. The old building to the east of the main road is a copy of a Normandy town hall, designed by Charles Brooke's French valet. The Rajah was encouraged to build the museum by the naturalist Alfred Russel Wallace, who spent over two years in Sarawak, where he wrote his first paper on natural selection. The museum was opened in 1891, extended in 1911, and the 'new' wing built in 1983. Its best known curators have been naturalist Eric Mjoberg, who made the first ascent of Sarawak's highest peak – Gunung Murudi (see page 150) – in 1922, and ethnologist and explorer Tom Harrisson, whose archaeological work at Niah made world headlines in 1957. The museum overlooks pleasant botanical gardens and the Heroes Memorial, built to commemorate the dead of the Second World War, the Communist insurgency and the confrontation with Indonesia. Across the road, and linked by a footbridge, is the Dewan Tun Abdul Razak building, a newer extension of the museum.

The museum has a strong ethnographic section, although some of its displays have been superseded by the **Cultural Village** (see page 97), Sarawak's 'living museum'. The old museum's ethnographic section includes a full-scale model of an Iban longhouse, a reproduction of a Penan hut and a selection of Kayan and Kenyah woodcarvings. There is also an impressive collection of Iban war totems (*kenyalang*) and carved Melanau sickness images (*blum*), used in healing ceremonies. The museum's assortment of traditional daggers (*kris*) is the best in Malaysia. The Chinese and Islamic ceramics include 17th-20th century Chinese jars, which are treasured heirlooms in Sarawak (see page 93).

‡ *Check the website www.museum.sarawak. gov.my for information on Sarawak's museums.*

The natural science collection, covering the flora and fauna of Sarawak, is also noteworthy. The new Tun Abdul Razak ethnological and historical collection includes prehistoric artefacts from the Niah Caves, Asia's most important archaeological site (see page 131); there is even a replica of Niah's Painted Cave – without the smell of guano.

Sarawak Islamic Museum

ⓘ *Jl P Ramlee, Sat-Thu 0900-1700, closed Fri.*

Not far from the Sarawak Museum, this collection is housed in the restored Maderasah Melayu Building, an elegant, single-storey colonial edifice. As its name suggests, the museum is devoted to Islamic artefacts from all the ASEAN countries, with the collection of manuscripts, costumes, jewellery, weaponry, furniture, coinage, textiles and ceramics spread over seven galleries, each with a different theme, and set around a central courtyard.

Waterfront

Around Main Bazaar are some other important buildings dating from the Brooke era; most of them are closed to the public. The **Supreme Court** on Main Bazaar was built in 1874 as an administrative centre. State council meetings were held here from the 1870s until 1973, when it was converted to law courts. In front of the grand entrance is a memorial to Rajah Charles Brooke (1924) and on each corner there is a bronze relief representing the four main ethnic groups in Sarawak – Iban, Orang Ulu, Malay and

A town called Cat

There are a number of explanations as to how Sarawak's capital acquired the name 'Cat'. (Kuching means 'cat' in Malay – although today it is more commonly spelt kucing as in modern Bahasa 'c' is pronounced 'ch'.) Local legend has it that James Brooke, pointing towards the settlement across the river, enquired what it was called. Whoever he asked, mistakenly thought he was pointing at a passing cat. If that seems a little far-fetched, the Sarawak Museum offers a few more plausible alternatives. Kuching may have been named after the wild cats (*kucing hutan*) which, in the 19th century, were commonly seen along jungled banks of the Sarawak River. Another theory is that it was called after the fruit *buah mata kucing* ('cat's eyes'), which grows locally. Most likely, however, is the theory that the town may originally have been known as Cochin – port – a word commonly used across India and Indochina.

Chinese. The clock tower was built in 1883. The **Square Tower**, also on Main Bazaar, was built as an annexe to Fort Margherita in 1879 and was used as a prison. Later in the Brooke era it was used as a ballroom. The square tower marks one end of Kuching's waterfront esplanade which runs alongside the river for almost 900 m to the **Hilton**.

The **Waterfront** has been transformed into a landscaped esplanade through restoration and a land reclamation project. It has become a popular meeting place, with foodstalls, restaurants and entertainment facilities including an open-air theatre. There is a restored Chinese pavilion, an observation tower, a tea terrace and musical fountains, as well as a number of modern sculptures. During the day, the waterfront offers excellent views of the Astana, Fort Margherita and the Malay kampongs which line the north bank of the river. At night, the area comes alive as younger members of Kuching's growing middle class make their way down here to relax.

A good way to see the Sarawak River is to take a **cruise** (RM35). Tickets can be bought from tourist agencies or at the waterfront at booths around halfway down the esplanade. Day and night cruises of around 90 minutes are on offer.

The **General Post Office**, with its majestic Corinthian columns, stands in the centre of town, on Jalan Tun Haji Openg. Dating back to 1931, it was one of the few edifices built by Vyner Brooke, the last Rajah. It has been renovated and there have been long-term plans to make it the home of the **Sarawak Art Museum**.

The **Courthouse complex**, which now houses the Sarawak Tourism Board's Visitors' Centre, was built in 1871 as the seat of Sarawak's government and was used as such until 1973. It remains one of Kuching's grandest structures. The buildings have *belian* (ironwood) roofs and beautiful detailing inside and out, reflecting local art forms. It also continues to house the state's high court and magistrates' court as well as several other local government departments. The colonial-baroque **Clock Tower** was added in 1883 and the **Charles Brooke Memorial** in 1924. The complex also includes the **Pavilion Building** which was built in 1907 as a hospital. During the Japanese occupation it was used as an information and propaganda centre and is now undergoing renovation with a view to making it the home of a new Textile Museum. Opposite the Courthouse is the **Indian Mosque (Mesjid India)** on Lebuh India, originally had an atap roof and *kajang* (thatch) walls; in 1876 *belian* (ironwood) walls were erected. The mosque was built by South Indians and is in the middle of an Indian quarter where spices are sold along the Main Bazaar. When the mosque was first built only Muslims from South India were permitted to worship here; even Indian Muslims from other areas of the subcontinent were excluded. In time, as Kuching's

Muslim population expanded and grew more diversified, so this rigid system was relaxed. It is hard to get to the mosque as it is surrounded by buildings. However a narrow passage leads from Lebuh India – between shop numbers 37 and 39.

The **Round Tower** on Jalan Tun Abang Haji Openg (formerly Rock Road) was originally planned as a fort (1886) but was never completed. The whole area is undergoing restoration for future art galleries and cultural exhibits. The **Steamship Building** ① *52 Main Bazaar*, was built in 1930 and was previously the offices and warehouse of the Sarawak Steamship Company. It has been extensively restored and now houses a restaurant, souvenir stalls, a handicrafts gallery and an exhibition area.

The **Bishop's House** ① *off Jl McDougall, near the Anglican Cathedral of St Thomas*, is the oldest surviving residence in Sarawak. It was built in 1849, entirely of wood, for the first Anglican Bishop of Borneo, Dr McDougall. The first mission school was started in the attic – developed into St Thomas's and St Mary's School, which is now across the road on Jalan McDougall.

Chinatown

Kuching's Chinese population, part of the town's community since its foundation, live in the shophouses lining the narrow streets around **Main Bazaar**. This street, opposite the waterfront, is the oldest in the city, dating from 1864. The Chinese families who live here still pursue traditional occupations such as tinsmithing and

Kuching

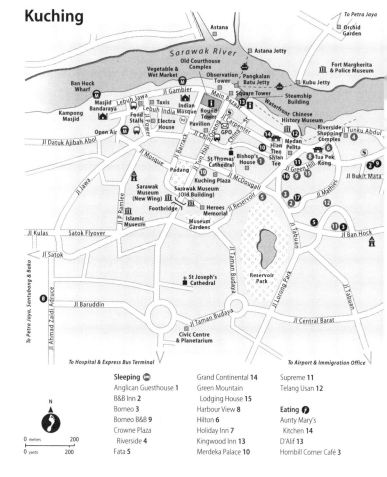

Sleeping	Grand Continental 14	Supreme 11
Anglican Guesthouse 1	Green Mountain	Telang Usan 12
B&B Inn 2	Lodging House 15	
Borneo 3	Harbour View 8	Eating
Borneo B&B 9	Hilton 6	Aunty Mary's
Crowne Plaza	Holiday Inn 7	Kitchen 14
Riverside 4	Kingwood Inn 13	D'Alif 13
Fata 5	Merdeka Palace 10	Hornbill Corner Café 3

woodworking. Kuching's highest concentration of antique and handicraft shops is to be found here. **Jalan Carpenter**, parallel to Main Bazaar, has a similar selection of small traders and coffee shops, as well as foodstalls and two small Chinese temples. Off **Lebuh China** (Upper China Street), there is a row of perfectly preserved 19th-century Chinese houses. The oldest Chinese temple in Kuching, **Tua Pek Kong** (also known as Siew San Teng), in the shadow of the Hilton on Jalan Tunku Abdul Rahman, was built in 1876, although it is now much modernized. There is evidence that the site has been in use since 1740 and a Chinese temple was certainly here as early as 1770. The first structure was erected by a group of Chinese immigrants thankful for their safe journey across the hazardous South China Sea. New immigrants still come here to give thanks for their safe arrival. The Wang Kang festival to commemorate the dead is also held here. Just to the east of here, **Jalan Padungan** has some of Kuching's finest Chinese shophouses. Most were built during the rubber boom of the 1920s and have been restored. There are also some great coffee shops in this quarter of town. Further east still, the kitsch statue of the **Great Cat of Kuching** – the sort of thing to induce nightmares in the aesthetically inclined – mews at the junction of Jalan Padungan and Jalan Central.

The **Chinese History Museum** ⓘ *daily 0900-1800, T082-231520, free,* stands on the Waterfront, opposite Tua Pek Kong temple. The building was completed in 1912 and became the court for the Chinese population of Kuching. The Third Rajah was keen that the Chinese, like other ethnic groups, should settle disputes within their community in their own way and he encouraged its establishment. From 1912 until 1921, when the Chinese court was dissolved, all cases pertaining to the Chinese were heard here in front of six judges elected from the local Chinese population. The building itself is simple, with a flat roof and shows English colonial influences. In 1993 it was handed over to the Sarawak Museum and was turned into the Chinese History Museum. The museum documents the history of the Chinese in Sarawak, from the early traders of the 10th century to the waves of Chinese immigration in the 19th century. The exhibits are now a little worse for wear.

Hian Tien Shian Tee (Hong San) temple, at the junction of Jalan Carpenter and Jalan Wayang, was built in 1897.

The Moorish, gilt-domed **Masjid Bandaraya** (Old State Mosque) is near the market, on the west side of town; it was built in 1968 on the site of an old wooden mosque dating from 1852.

Civic Centre and Planetarium

ⓘ *Jl Taman Budaya, Mon-Thu 0915-1730, Sat and Sun 0915-1800, viewing platform 0900-2100, planetarium shows RM3.*

On the south side of the river the extraordinary-looking Civic Centre is Kuching's stab at the avant garde. As well as the viewing platform for panoramas of Kuching, the Civic Centre complex houses an art gallery with temporary exhibits, mainly of Sarawakian art, a restaurant and a pub-cum-karaoke bar one floor down, together with a public library. Malaysia's first planetarium is also within the complex: **Sultan Iskandar Planetarium** has a 15-m dome and a 170-seat auditorium. To get there, take bus No 14A, 14B, 14C or 8 from Chim Lan Long Bus Station on Jalan Masjid.

Astana

ⓘ *Take a sampan across the river from the Pangkalan Batu jetty next to Square Tower on the Waterfront to the Astana and fort, less then RM1 one way, the boats can be hired quite cheaply at around RM30 per hr.*

Apart from the Sarawak Museum, the White Rajahs bequeathed several other architectural monuments to Kuching. The Astana, a variant of the usual spelling *istana* (palace), was built in 1870, two years after Charles Brooke took over from his uncle. It stands on the north bank of the river almost opposite the market on Jalan Gambier. The Astana was hurriedly completed for the arrival of Charles' new bride (and cousin), Margaret. It was originally three colonial-style bungalows, with wooden shingle roofs, the largest being the central bungalow with the reception room, dining and drawing rooms. The crenellated tower on the east end was added in the 1880s at her request. Charles Brooke is said to have cultivated betel nut in a small plantation behind the Astana, so that he could offer fresh betel nut to visiting Dayak chiefs. Today it is the official residence of the governor of Sarawak and is only open to the public on Hari Raya Puasa, a day of prayer and celebration to mark the end of Ramadan (see page 37). To the west of the Astana, in the traditionally Malay area, are many old wooden kampong houses.

Fort Margherita

ⓘ *Jl Sapi, Tue-Sun 1000-1800, closed public holidays, free.*

Not far away from the Astana, past the Kubu jetty, is this fort, now the **Police Museum**. It was also built by Rajah Charles Brooke in 1879 and named after Ranee Margaret, although there was a fort on the site from 1841 when James Brooke became Rajah. It commanded the river approach to Kuching, but was never used defensively, although its construction was prompted by a near-disastrous river-borne attack on Kuching by the Ibans of the Rejang in 1878. Even so, until the Second World War a sentry was always stationed on the lookout post on top of the fort; his job was to pace up and down all night and shout 'All's well' on the hour every hour until 0800. The news that nothing was awry was heard at the Astana and the government offices.

After 1946, Fort Margherita was first occupied by the Sarawak Rangers and was finally converted into a police museum in 1971, which is a lot more interesting than it sounds. There is a large collection of armour and weaponry on the ground floor, including weapons captured during the Indonesian *Konfrontasi* from 1963-1965 (see page 158). Up the spiral staircase there is a display of police uniforms and communications equipment used by jungle patrols. The third floor houses an exhibition on drugs, counterfeit currency and documents, supplies and weapons captured from Communist insurgents in the 1960s and 1970s. From the top, there are good views across the city and up and down the Sarawak River. En route to the courtyard at the bottom, former prison cells have been set up to recreate an opium den – complete with emaciated dummy – and to reinforce the dangers of *dadah* (drugs) the courtyard itself contains the old town gallows complete with hanging dummy. During the rule of the White Rajahs, however, death sentences were carried out by a slash of the *kris* (traditional Malay sword) through the heart. To get to the fort, see Astana, above.

The **Malay kampongs** along the riverside next to Fort Margherita are seldom visited by tourists – however, they have some beautiful examples of traditional

⁝ A ceramic inheritance

Family wealth and status in Sarawak was traditionally measured in ceramics. In the tribal longhouses upriver, treasured heirlooms include ancient glass beads, brass gongs and cannons and Chinese ceramic pots and beads (such as those displayed in the Sarawak Museum). They were often used as currency and dowries. Spencer St John, the British consul in Brunei, mentions using beads as currency on his 1858 expedition to Gunung Mulu. Jars (*pesaka*) had more practical applications; they were (and still are) used for storing rice, brewing *tuak* (rice wine) or for keeping medicines.

Their value was dependent on their rarity: brown jars, emblazoned with dragon motifs, are more recent and quite common while olive-glazed dusun jars, dating from the 15th-17th centuries are rare. The Kelabit people, who live in the highlands around Bario, treasure the dragon jars in particular. Although some of the more valuable antique jars have found their way to the Sarawak Museum, many magnificent jars remain in the Iban and other tribal longhouses along

the Skrang, Rejang and Baram rivers. Many are covered by decoratively carved wooden lids.

Chinese contact and trade with the north coast of Borneo has gone on for at least a millennium, possibly two. Chinese Han pottery fragments and coins have been discovered near the estuary of the Sarawak River and, from the seventh century, China is known to have been importing birds' nests and jungle produce from Brunei (which then encompassed all of north Borneo), in exchange for ceramic wares. Chinese traders arrived in the Nanyang (South Seas) in force from the 11th century, particularly during the Sung and Yuan dynasties. Some Chinese pottery and porcelain even bore Arabic and Koranic inscriptions – the earliest such dish is thought to have been produced in the mid-14th century. In the 1500s, as China's trade with the Middle East grew, many such Islamic wares were traded and the Chinese emperors presented them as gifts to seal friendships with the Muslim world, including Malay and Indonesian kingdoms.

and modern Malay architecture. The **Kuching Orchid Garden** ⓘ *T082-446688, Tue-Sun 1000-1800, free*, was redeveloped close to Fort Margherita and opened in 2000. The park is divided into two; the Orchid Nursery and a garden, with more than 100 species of orchids.

Petra Jaya

The new **State Mosque**, is situated across the river at Petra Jaya and was completed in 1968. It stands on the site of an older mosque dating from the mid-19th century. Its interior is of Italian marble.

Kuching's architectural heritage did not end with the White Rajahs; the town's modern buildings are often based on local styles. The new administration centre is in Petra Jaya: the **Bapak** (father) **Malaysia** building is named after the first prime minister of Malaysia and houses government offices; the **Dewan Undangan Negeri** (State Legislative Assembly of Sarawak) next door, is based on the Minangkabau style. Kuching's latest building is the ostentatious **Masjid Jamek**. Also in Petra Jaya, like a space launch overlooking the road to Damai Peninsula, is the **Cat Museum** ⓘ *daily 0900-1700 (closed public holidays), free, camera RM3*, which houses everything you ever wanted to know about cats. To get there, take Petra Jaya Transport No 2B or 6.

Nearby, the **Timber Museum** ⓘ *Wisma Sumber Alam (next to the stadium) Mon-Thu 0830-1600, Fri 0830-1130, 1430-1630, Sat 0830-1230, closed Sun and public holidays*, is meant to look like a log. It was built in the mid-1980s to try to engender a better understanding of Sarawak's timber industry. The museum, which has many excellent exhibits and displays, toes the official line about forest management and presents facts and figures on the timber trade, along with a detailed history of its development in Sarawak. The exhibition provides an insight into all the different forest types. It has background information on and examples of important commercial tree species, jungle produce and many traditional wooden implements. The final touch is an air-conditioned forest and wildlife diorama, complete with leaf litter; all the trees come from the Rejang River area. A research library is attached to the museum. While it sidesteps the more delicate moral issues involved in the modern logging business, its detractors might do worse than to brush up on some of the less emotive aspects of Sarawak's most important industry. To get there, take a taxi, RM15 as there is no bus.

Around Kuching ●❀ ›› *pp101-111. Colour map 1, C2.*

Semenggoh Orang-Utan Sanctuary
ⓘ *Daily 0800-1245, 1400-1615, RM3.*

Semenggoh, 32 km from Kuching, on the road to Serian, became the first forest reserve in Sarawak when the 800 ha of jungle were set aside by Rajah Vyner Brooke in 1920. They were turned into a wildlife rehabilitation centre for monkeys, orang-utans, honey bears and hornbills in 1975. All were either orphaned as a result of logging or were confiscated, having been kept illegally as pets. The aim has been to reintroduce as many of the animals as possible to their natural habitat. In late 1998 many of the functions which previously attracted visitors to Semenggoh were transferred to the Matang Wildlife Centre (see page 96). However, there are a few trails around the park including a plankwalk and a botanical research centre, dedicated to jungle plants with medicinal applications, and orang-utans still visit the centre for food handouts. Even when Semenggoh was operating as an orang-utan rehabilitation centre, it did not compare with Sepilok in Sabah, which is an altogether more sophisticated affair.

To get to the sanctuary, take **Sarawak Transport Co** bus No 6 from Ban Hock Wharf, Jawa Street or from the stop opposite the post office on Jalan Tun Haji Openg (RM2). There's approximately one bus every hour. Tell the bus conductor you want to go to Semenggoh and you'll be dropped off just outside the main entrance. It's a pleasant 20-minute walk through the park to the centre. The last bus back to Kuching leaves the main entrance just before 1600. Tour operators also run trips here, but you'll have more time to explore if you make your own trip. A taxi one-way costs RM25.

Gunung Penrissen ›› *Altitude: 1329 m.*
This is the highest peak in the mountain range south of Kuching running along the Kalimantan border. The mountain was visited by naturalist Alfred Wallace in 1855. Just over 100 years later the mountain assumed a strategic role in Malaysia's *Konfrontasi* with Indonesia (see page 158) – there is a Malaysian military post on the summit. Gunung Penrissen is accessible from Kampong Padawan; it lies a few kilometres south of Anna Rais, right on the border with Kalimantan. It is a difficult mountain to climb requiring two long days, but affords views over Kalimantan to the south and Kuching and the South China Sea to the north. Prospective climbers are advised to consult the detailed trail-guide in John Briggs' *Mountains of Malaysia*. The book is usually obtainable in the Sarawak Museum bookshop.

❣ *Guides – some of whom were former border scouts during the Konfrontasi – can be hired through the headman at Kampong Padawan.*

It is 100 km from Kuching to Anna Rais. To get there, take an STC bus No 9 from Kuching's Lebuh Jawa. There are two buses a day.

Gunung Gading National Park

ⓘ *T082-735714, RM10.*

Gunung Gading National Park was constituted in 1983 and covers 411,1060 ha either side of Sungai Lundu, 65 km northwest of Kuching. There are some marked trails, the shortest of which takes about two hours and leads to a series of waterfalls on the Sungai Lundu. Gunung Gading and Gunung Perigi summit treks take seven to eight hours; it is possible to camp at the summit. The park is made up of a complex of mountains with several dominant peaks including Gunung Gading (906 m). The rafflesia,

‼ *National park accommodation booking: Sarawak Tourist Information Centre, T082-248088, or the NP office in Petra Jaya, Wisma Sumber Alam, T082-442180.*

the largest flower in the world, is found in the park but if you are keen to see one in bloom, it might be worth phoning the Park HQ first, since it has a very short flowering period. The park is five minutes' drive from Lundu; taxis charge RM5. From Kuching take STC Bus No EP07 to Lundu from the Express Bus Terminal outside of town.

Lundu and Sematan

These villages have beautiful, lonely beaches and there is a collection of deserted islands off Sematan. One of the islands, **Talang Talang**, is a turtle sanctuary and permission to visit it must be obtained from the **Forest Department** ⓘ *Wisma Sumba Alam, Jl Stadium, Petra Jaya, Kuching, T082-442180, www.forestry.sarawak.gov.my/forweb/homepage/contact.html*. To get there, bus 2B goes from Kuching to Lundu via Bau (two hours).

Around Kuching

Sleeping 😴
Damai Rainforest Resort (Camp Permai) **1**   Holiday Inn Resort Damai Lagoon **3**
Holiday Inn Resort Damai Beach **2**   Santubong Kuching Resort **4**

Bau

About 60 km from Kuching is **Bau**, which had its five minutes of fame during the 19th century as a small mining town. Today, it is a market town and administrative centre. There are several caves close by; the **Wind Cave** is a popular picnic spot. The **Fairy Cave**, about 10 km from Bau, is larger and more impressive, with a small Chinese shrine in the main chamber and varied vegetation at the entrance. A torch is essential. Another reason to go to Bau is to see the Bindayuh celebrating their Gawai Padi, a festival with animistic roots that thanks the gods for an abundant rice harvest. Singing, dancing, massive consumption of *tuak* (rice wine) and colourful shamans make this a highlight. Held end of May/beginning of June. Ask at the tourist office in Kuching for exact details. To get to Bau, take bus No 2B from the Chin Lan Long bus station; the journey takes around an hour. Tour companies also organize trips.

Kubah National Park

ⓘ *T082-225003, but the National Parks and Wildlife Booking Office in Kuching, see page 87, is likely to be more helpful, RM10.*

This is a mainly sandstone, siltstone and shale area, 20 km west of Kuching, covering some 2230 ha with three mountains: **Gunung Serapi**, **Gunung Selang** and **Gunung Sendok**; there are at least seven waterfalls and bathing pools. Flora include mixed dipterocarp and kerangas (heath) forest; the park is also rich in palms (93 species) and wild orchids. Wildlife includes bearded pig, mouse deer and hornbills and numerous species of amphibians and reptiles. Unfortunately for visitors, Kubah's wildlife tends to stay hidden; it's not really a park for 'wildlife encounters'. There are four marked trails, ranging from 30 minutes to three hours; one, the **Rayu Trail**, passes through rainforest that contains a number of bintangor trees (believed to contain two chemicals which have showed some evidence of being effective against HIV). Visitors may be able to see some trees which have been tapped for this potential rainforest remedy. The park is easy to visit in a daytrip. Take the Matang Transport Company bus No 11 that departs from outside the Saujana car park (first bus departs at 0630 and last return bus at 1640). Buses no longer drop off at the Matang Wildlife Centre; ask to be dropped off at the Park HQ. Travel agents also arrange tours.

The **Matang Wildlife Centre** ⓘ *T082-225012; animal feeding times: orang-utans, daily 0900 and 1500; hornbills, daily 0830 and 1500; sambar deer, daily 0900 and 1500; crocodiles, 1430 Sun only,* is part of the Kubah National Park. It houses endangered wildlife in spacious enclosures which are purposefully placed in the rainforest. The key attraction are the orang-utans which are rehabilitated for release back into the wild. Other animals include sambar deer, sun bears, civets and bear cats. There is an Information Centre and education programmes, which enable visitors to learn more about the conservation of Sarawak's wildlife. The centre has also established a series of trails.

To get there, Matang Transport Company bus No 11 departs infrequently from outside the Saujana car park (see Kubah National Park, above, for details). However this bus does not go all the way to the Matang Wildlife Centre; ask to be deposited at the turning for the Polytechnic and wait for a lift. Alternatively take a taxi from Kuching, RM35 one-way, and ask the taxi to wait; travel agents also arrange tours to the park.

Pulau Satang Besar

ⓘ *Ask at the Visitor Information Centre, overlooking the Padang, Kuching, T082-410942, for departures from Santubong or Kampong Telaga Air.*

North of Kampong Telaga Air, Pulau Satang Besar has been designated a **Turtle Sanctuary** to protect the green turtles which come ashore here to lay their eggs.

Tanjung Datu National Park

This is the newest and smallest park in Sarawak, first gazetted in 1994, at the westernmost tip, 100 km from Kuching. It is covered with mixed dipterocarp forest, rich flora and fauna, and beautiful beaches with crystal-clear seas and coral reefs. To get there, take a bus to Lundu (see Gunung Gading National Park, page 95) and on to Sematan. At the jetty in Sematan, hire a boat (40 minutes, RM100 to hire the whole boat; there is no scheduled service); the seas are too rough for the journey October to February. The boat will drop you off at the park headquarter's jetty. You can also jump in a boat to Teluk Melano (more regular) from Sematan (about 40 minutes), and then hire a 10-minute boat trip to the park.

Damai Peninsula 🚌🏄🏔️🅿️ ▸▸ *pp101-111. Colour map 1, C2.*

The peninsula, 35 km north of Kuching, is located at the west mouth of the Santubong River and extends northwards as far as **Mount Santubong**, a majestic peak of 810 m. Its attractions include the **Sarawak Cultural Village**, trekking up Mount Santubong, sandy beaches, a golf course, adventure camp and three resorts which are particularly good value off season when promotional rates are available.

From Kuching, it's a 40-minute bus ride north to **Buntal**. Take bus No 26 from the Petra Jaya terminal. Buses depart every 40 minutes throughout the day. From here, they wind through the foothills to Santubong.

Santubong and Buntal

The village of Santubong itself, located at the mouth of the Santubong River, is small and quiet. Formerly a fishing village, most of the villagers now work in one of the nearby resorts. However, some fishing still goes on, and the daily catch is still sold every morning at the quayside. Nearby are two or three Chinese-run grocery stores and a coffee shop. The rest of the village is made up of small houses strung out along the road, built in the Malay tradition on stilts – many are wooden and painted in bright colours. Another village here is Buntal, which is just off the Kuching-Santubong road and is popular with local Kuchingites who visit at the weekends for the seafood restaurants.

Sarawak Cultural Village

ⓘ *T082-846411, www.sarawakculturalvillage.com, daily 0900-1730, cultural show 1130-1215 and 1630-1715, RM45, children (6-12 years) RM22.50, prices include cultural show.*

The Sarawak Cultural Village (Kampong Budaya Sarawak) was the brainchild of the **Sarawak Development Corporation** which built Sarawak's 'living museum' at a cost of RM9.5 million to promote and preserve Sarawak's cultural heritage. With increasing numbers of young tribal people being tempted from their longhouses into the modern sectors of the economy, many of Sarawak's traditional crafts have begun to die out. The Cultural Village set out to teach the old arts and crafts to new generations. For the State Development Corporation, the concept had the added appeal of creating a money-spinning 'Instant Sarawak' for the benefit of tourists lacking the time or inclination to head into the jungle. While it is rather contrived, the Cultural Village has been a great success and contains some superb examples of traditional architecture. It should be on the sightseeing agenda of every visitor to Kuching, if only to provide an introduction to the cultural traditions of all the main ethnic groups in Sarawak.

Each tribal group is represented by craftsmen and women who produce handicrafts and practise traditional skills in houses built to carefully researched design specifications. Many authentic everyday articles have been collected from longhouses all over Sarawak. In one case the village has served to preserve a culture – pickled – that is already effectively dead: today the Melanau people all live in

The Penan – museum pieces for the 21st century?

Economic progress has altered many Sarawakians' lifestyles in recent years; the oil and natural gas sector now offers many employment prospects and upriver tribespeople have been drawn into the logging industry. But it is logging that has directly threatened the 9000-strong Penan tribe's traditional way of life.

Sarawak's nomadic hunter-gatherers have emerged as 'the noble savages' of the late 20th century, as their blockades of logging roads drew world attention to their plight. In 1990, Britain's Prince Charles' remarks about Malaysia's "collective genocide" against the Penan prompted an angry letter of protest from former Prime Minister Dr Mahathir Mohamad. He is particularly irked by western environmentalists – especially Bruno Manser, who lived with the Penan in the late 1980s. "We don't need any more Europeans who think they have a white man's burden to shoulder", Dr Mahathir said.

Malaysia wants to integrate the Penan into mainstream society, on the grounds that it is morally wrong to condemn them to a life expectancy of 40 years, when the average Malaysian lives to well over 60. "There is nothing romantic about these helpless, half-starved, disease-ridden people", Dr Mahathir said. The government has launched resettlement programmes to transform the Penan from hunters into fishermen and farmers. One of these new longhouses can be visited in Mulu (see page 145); it has failed to engender much enthusiasm from the Penan, although 4000 to 5000 Penan have now been resettled. Environmentalists countered that the Penan should be given the choice, but, the government asks, what choice do they have if they have only lived in the jungle?

The Cultural Village, opened by Dr Mahathir in 1990, offered a compromise of sorts – but the Penan had the last laugh. One tribal elder, called Apau Madang, and his grandson were paid to parade in loincloths and make blowpipes at the Penan hut while tourists took their snapshots. The arrangement did not last long as they did not like posing as artefacts in Sarawak's 'living museum'. They soon complained of boredom and within months had wandered back to the jungle where they could at least wear jeans and T-shirts. Today, the Penan hut is staffed by other Orang Ulu. There are thought to be only 400 Penan still following their traditional nomadic way of life.

Malay-style kampongs, but a magnificent traditional wooden Melanau house has been built at the Cultural Village and is now the only such building in Sarawak. Alongside it there is a demonstration of traditional sago processing. A resident Melanau craftsman makes sickness images (*blum*) – each representing the spirit of an illness, which were floated downriver in tiny boats as part of the healing ritual.

There are also Bidayuh, Iban and Orang Ulu longhouses, depicting the lifestyles of each group. In each there are textile or basket-weavers, woodcarvers or sword-makers. There are exhibits of beadwork, bark clothing, and *tuak* (rice wine) brewing. At the Penan hut there is a demonstration of blowpipe making and visitors are invited to test their hunting skills. There is a Malay house and even a Chinese farmhouse with a pepper garden alongside. The tour of the houses, seven in all (you can collect a stamp from each one for your passport!) is capped by an Andrew Lloyd Webber-style cultural show which is expertly choreographed, if rather ersatz. It is held in the on-site theatre which is fully air conditioned.

Special application must be made to attend heritage centre workshops where courses can be requested in various crafts such as woodcarving, mat-weaving or batik-painting; they also run intensive one-day and three- to four-day courses. There is a restaurant and craft shop, **Sarakraf**, at the village.

A regular shuttle bus service operates from the **Holiday Inn** in Kuching to resort hotels and the Cultural Village (RM10, first bus at 0730, last bus 2200, last bus back from Damai is at 2100).

The Cultural Village is also the venue for the fabulous annual **Rainforest Music Festival** ① *www.rainforestmusic-borneo.com*, which takes place sometime between June and August. Food stalls are laid on, jamming sessions are held in the different sections culminating in a great stage show in the grounds for the evening.

The Cultural Village employs 140 people, including dancers, who earn around RM300 a month and take home the profits from handicraft and *tuak* sales.

Gunung Santubong » *Altitude: 810 m.*

Situated on the Santubong Peninsula, Gunung Santubong's precipitous south-western side provides a moody backdrop to Damai Beach. The distinctive mountain is most accessible from the east side, where there is a clear ridge trail to the top. There are two trails to the summit, one begins opposite the **Palm Beach Seafood Restaurant and Resort**, about 2.5 km before the **Holiday Inn Damai Beach**. The conical peak – from which there are spectacular views – can be reached in seven to nine hours (the last stretch is a tough scramble). Take your own food and water supplies. Guides are not necessary (but can be provided), check with hotel recreation counters or at the **Santubong Mountain Trek Canteen** ① *To82-846153*. The official Damai guide provides a more detailed description of the trek.

There is a bus to Damai Beach. Alternatively take No 2b (more regular) from Petra Jaya terminal to Santubong (RM3.30, 40-minute journey, first bus 0700, last one 1800), but this will not go unless there are enough passengers. A taxi to Damai should cost around RM35 one-way.

Salak River

Trips up the Salak River depart from the terminal at Santubong village, a 10-minute drive from the resort hotels. River tours last three hours. The journey goes into smaller rivers and a creek and it is a good introduction to the mangrove forest ecosystem. Contact hotel recreation counters or tour operators for details.

Bako National Park 🏠🚻🏕 » *pp101-111. Colour map 1, C2.*

Bako is situated on the beautiful Muara Tebas Peninsula, a former river delta which has been thrust above sea level. Its sandstone cliffs, which are patterned and streaked with iron deposits, have been eroded to produce a dramatic coastline with secluded coves and beaches and rocky headlands. Millions of years of erosion by the sea has resulted in the formation of wave-cut platforms, honeycomb weathering, solution pans, arches and sea stacks. Bako's most distinctive feature is the westernmost headland – **Tanjung Sapi** – a 100-m high sandstone plateau, which is unique in Borneo. Established in 1957, Bako was Sarawak's first national park. It is a very small park (2742 ha) but it has an exceptional variety of flora and guaranteed wildlife spotting! Its beaches and accessible trails make it a wonderful place to chill out for a few days.

Ins and outs

Bako lies 37 km north of Kuching, an hour's bus journey from Petra Jaya terminal; a longboat needs to be rented to reach Park HQ. Travelling by car, the drive from Kuching takes about 40 minutes; parking is safe at Kampong Bako (from where you rent a boat). It is possible to hire boats around the park: speed boats charge RM40 and can accommodate five or six passengers. On arrival visitors are required to register at the Park HQ; the information centre, next door, has a small exhibition on geology, flora and fauna within the park. Visitors can request to see a 40-minute introductory video to Bako National Park. The Park HQ has a canteen.

To obtain the necessary permits, contact **National Parks and Wildlife Booking Office** ① *c/o Visitors' Information Centre, Sarawak Tourism Complex, Kuching, T082-248088, F082-248087, daily 0800-1245 (0800-1100 on Fri) 1400-1615, RM10 per adult, RM5 per child or student, photography permit RM5, video camera RM10, professional camera RM200.*

Flora and fauna

There are seven separate types of vegetation in Bako. These include mangroves (*bakau* is the most common stilt-rooted mangrove species), swamp forest and heath forest – known as *kerangas*, an Iban word meaning 'land on which rice cannot grow'. Pitcher plants (*Nepenthes ampullaria*) do however grow in profusion on the sandy soil. There is also mixed dipterocarp rainforest (the most widespread forest type in Sarawak, characterized by its 30- to 40-m-high canopy), beach forest, and padang vegetation, comprising scrub and bare rock from which there are magnificent views of the coast. The rare *daun payang* (umbrella palm) is also found in Bako Park; it is a litter-trapping plant as its large fronds catch falling leaves from the trees above and funnel them downwards where they eventually form a thick organic mulch enabling the plant to survive on otherwise infertile soil. There are also wild durian trees in the forest, which can take up to 60 years to bear fruit.

Bako is one of the few areas in Sarawak inhabited by the rare proboscis monkey (Nasalis larvatus), known by Malays as 'Orang Belanda', or Dutchmen, or even 'Pinocchio of the jungle', because of their long noses (see page 331). Bako is home to approximately 150 proboscis monkeys. They are most often seen in the early morning or at dusk in the Teluk Assam and Teluk Delima areas (at the far west side of the park, closest to the headquarters) or around Teluk Paku (a 45-minute walk from the Park HQ). The park also has resident populations of squirrels, mouse deer, sambar deer, wild

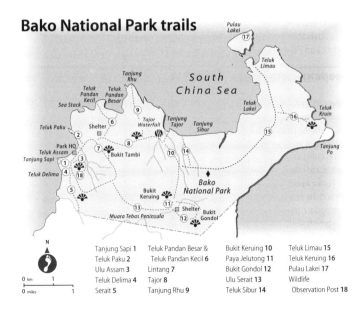

Bako National Park trails

Pulau Lakei 17

South China Sea

Teluk Limau

Tanjung Rhu

Teluk Pandan Kecil Teluk Pandan Besar

Sea Stack

Teluk Paku

Shelter 6

Tajor Waterfall

9

Tanjung Tajor

Tanjung Sibur

Teluk Lakei

Teluk Kruin

16

Park HQ 7

Teluk Assam Bukit Tambi

Tanjung Sapi 1

Teluk Delima 4

2 3

1

18

8

10 14

15

Tanjung Po

5

Bukit Keruing

Bako National Park

13

11

Shelter Bukit Gondol

Muara Tebas Peninsula

12

N

0 km   1
0 miles   1

Tanjung Sapi 1	Teluk Pandan Besar &	Bukit Keruing 10	Teluk Limau 15
Teluk Paku 2	Teluk Pandan Kecil 6	Paya Jelutong 11	Teluk Keruing 16
Ulu Assam 3	Lintang 7	Bukit Gondol 12	Pulau Lakei 17
Teluk Delima 4	Tajor 8	Ulu Serait 13	Wildlife
Serait 5	Tanjung Rhu 9	Teluk Sibur 14	Observation Post 18

pigs, long-tailed macaques, flying lemur, silver leaf monkeys and palm civet cats. Teluk Assam, in the area around the Park HQ, is one of the best places for birdwatching: over 150 species have been recorded in the park, including pied and black hornbills. Large numbers of migratory birds come to Bako between September and November. Other inhabitants of the park are the blue fiddler crab, which has one big claw and is forever challenging others to a fight, and mudskippers, evolutionary throw-backs (half-fish, half-frog), which are common in mangrove areas. Also in the park there are two species of otter: the oriental small-clawed otter and the hairy-nosed otter (the best area to see them is at Teluk Assam). The Bornean bearded pig is the largest mammal found Bako and is usually seen snuffling around the Park HQ. There are many lizards too, the largest being the water monitor which is often found near the accommodation. The only poisonous snake occasionally seen is the Wagler's pit viper. Nocturnal animals include flying lemur, pangolin, mouse deer, bats, tarsier, slow loris and palm civet (the beach by the Park HQ is a great place for a night-time stroll).

Treks

There is a good range of well-marked trails throughout the park – over 30 km in total; all paths are colour coded, corresponding to the map available from Park HQ. The shortest trek is the steep climb to the top of **Tanjong Sapi**, overlooking Teluk Assam, with good views of Gunung Santubong, on the opposite peninsula, across Tanjong Sipang, to the west. The 3.5-km trek to Tajor Waterfall is among the most popular, with varied walking – some steep climbs – spectacular views and a chance of a refreshing swim at the waterfall. The longest trek is to Teluk Limau; a five- to seven-hour walk through a variety of terrain. You can arrange with Park HQ to lay on a boat to bring you back (around RM200). Some trails are temporarily closed – check with Park HQ. Full-day treks and overnight camping expeditions can be arranged. There are plank walkways with shelters at intervals to provide quiet watching spots particularly required for viewing the proboscis monkey in the early morning.

Beaches

There are seven beaches around the park, but some are rather inaccessible, with steep paths down to the cliffs. The best swimming beach is at **Teluk Pandan Kecil**, about 1½ hours' walk, northeast from the Park HQ. It is also possible to swim at **Teluk Assam** and **Teluk Paku**. Enquire about jellyfish at the Park HQ before swimming in the sea; it is advisable not to swim in March and April. In the monsoon season, between November and February, the sea can be rough.

◉ Sleeping

Kuching *p86, map p90*
It is possible to negotiate over room rates and many of the hotels offer special deals. There is a good choice of international- standard hotels in Kuching including **Crowne Plaza**, **Holiday Inn** and **Hilton**. Most of them are along **Jl Tunku Abdul Rahman** with views of the river and the Astana and Fort Margherita on the opposite bank. For a listing of hotels and resorts with websites see the Sarawak Tourism Board site (www.sarawak tourism.com). The choice at the lower end of the market is limited, except for the **Anglican Guesthouse**; the cheaper hotels and lodging houses are concentrated around **Jl Green Hill**,

near the Tua Pek Kong temple. Some newer, mid-range accommodation has grown up in the area around **Jl Ban Hock**.

For an alternative to the usual hotels and guesthouses, you could try the **Homestay programme**, see page 103.
L-AL Harbour View Hotel, Lorong Temple, T082-274666, www.harbourview.com.my/. Good position overlooking the Waterfront next to Tua Pek Kong Temple. Business centre and in-room internet port, café and bar with live entertainment.
AL-A Grand Continental, Jl Ban Hock, T082-230399, www.grandhotels international.com.my/. Small pool and

business centre. Rooms have TV, IDD, minibar, and tea- and coffee-making facilities.

AL-A Merdeka Palace, Jl Tun Haji Openg, T082-258000, www.merdekapalace.com. Central location overlooking playing field. Pool, health club and business facilities, and broadband in every room. The 214 rooms have minibar, satellite TV. 6 bars, restaurants on site. Great value. Recommended.

A-B Borneo, 30 Jl Tabuan, T082-244122, F082-254848. Chinese atmosphere in this hotel located about a 10-min walk from the centre of town. Rooms with a/c and bath. Good-value restaurant, breakfast included. Has old world charm.

A-B Kingwood Inn, Jl Padungan, T082-330888, kingwd@po.jaring.my. Rooms have TV. Facilities include a pool, coffee house and bar. Late checkout available. Out of town but pleasant.

A-B Telang Usan, Jl Ban Hock (next to Supreme), T082-415588, tusan@po.jaring.my. The better of these 2 hotels located in an untidy area of town. A/c, TV, bath, restaurant, in-house travel agent. Orang Ulu-owned and managed hotel, friendly with traditional kenyah decor, karaoke and bar. Conference rooms, smart and comfortable, quiet location, excellent value.

B-C Fata, Jl McDougall, T082-248111, F082-428987. Clean hotel with a 1970s feel. A/c, restaurant, rooms in the older part are cheaper and better value for money.

B-C Supreme, Jl Ban Hock, T082-255155, F082-252522. 74 rooms, a/c, en suite bath or shower, minibar, TV, in-house videos. Evening entertainment; bands or karaoke. A little run down.

C-D Green Mountain Lodging House, 1 Jl Green Hill, T082-416320, F082-412457. The best and cleanest of the groups of hotels located in the Jl Green Hill area. Friendly management, hot water, secure atmosphere, and rooms on the 3rd floor have nice views onto a small wooded hill. Rooms have a/c, TVs, are airy and clean.

C-E B&B Inn, Jl Tabuan (next to the Borneo Hotel), T082-237366, gohyp@pb.jaring.my. Although popular and central, not particularly cheap. Tours organized, clean and safe, dorms beds available, although recent rumours of bed bugs.

C-E Borneo Bed & Breakfast, 2/F, 3 Jl Green Hill, T082-246292/T013-8434200, borneobed breakfast@yahoo.com. Kuching's newest one-stop backpacker guesthouse run by the friendly Mr Buan. 16 rooms ranging from doubles and triples to dorms. All rooms have shared bathroom. There's laundry, breakfast included in room rate and a lounge. Lots of travel information. Phone and book ahead as this place is always packed out. Recommended.

D-E Anglican Guesthouse, back of St Thomas' Cathedral (path from Jl Carpenter), T082-414027. Old building set in beautiful gardens on top of the hill, spacious, pleasantly furnished rooms, with basic facilities, fans, easily the best of the cheaper accommodation in town. More expensive family rooms are big with sitting room and attached bathroom. Best to book in advance. Recommended.

Gunung Penrissen *p94*

L-AL Hornbill Golf & Jungle Club, Borneo Highlands Resort, Jl Borneo Heights, Padawan, T082-790800, www.hornbill golf.com. As its name suggests, this is a mountain hideaway for golf fanatics. There are luxurious chalets and suites beautifully furnished with golfing touches like paintings of greens. The resort lies at an altitude of 1000 m and so the weather is cooler and more spring-like. Apart from golf, jungle treks are organized as well as tours of a longhouse, a rabbit farm, spas and flower gardens.

Gunung Gading National Park *p95*
A-E National park accommodation
Bookings taken through the National Parks and Wildlife Booking Office, Kuching, T082-248088. 2, 3-bedroom chalets and a hostel (RM15/person) are available.

Lundu and Sematan *p95*
A Ocean Resort, 176 Siar Beach, Jl Pandan, Sematan, T082-452245 (Kuching office) or T011-225001 (resort). Some rooms in hostel, 2-bedroom chalets with attached kitchen also available. The plushest place to stay in Sematan.

C Lundu Gadung Hotel, Lot 174 Lundu Town District, T082-735199. A/c but shared bathroom.

Kubah National Park p96

A-F National park accommodation.
Bookable through the National Parks and
Wildlife Booking Office inside the Visitors'
Information Centre in Kuching, Old Courthouse, T082-248088. There are chalets and
an 8-room hostel block and 5 huge
bungalows at the park HQ with full kitchen
facilities, 4 beds (2 rooms), a/c, hot water, TV
and veranda.

Damai Peninsula p97, map p95

The Damai Peninsula has no fewer than 2
Holiday Inns, www.holidayinn-sarawak.com:
one superbly located at the foot of Mount
Santubong on a small, well-kept, sandy
beach; the other, at Damai Beach, just below
a mansion belonging to the Sultan of Brunei.
A Santubong Kuching Resort, Jl
Santubong, PO Box 2364, T082-846888,
F082-846666. Surrounded by the Damai
Golf Course, 380 rooms all with a/c,
restaurant, large pool, chalets with jacuzzis,
tennis, basketball, volleyball, gym,
mountain biking, etc. Nestling beneath
Mount Santubong, a low-rise resort popular
with golfers, it also has the largest
conference and banquet facilities in
Sarawak. Price includes breakfast.
**A-B Damai Rainforest Resort (Camp
Permai)**, Pantai Damai, Santubong, PO Box
B91, Satok Post Office, T082-321498,
F082-321500. Located at the foot of Mount
Santubong, near the **Holiday Inn Damai
Lagoon Resort**, this is an outward-bound
centre which offers a number of courses
including adventure training and leadership
development. Other facilities include an
artificial climbing wall, obstacle course,
abseiling, sailing, canoeing and paintball
competitions. Sleeping is in 10 a/c tree
houses or log cabins, cafeteria, tents and
camping equipment for hire.

Bako National Park p99, map p100

All bookings to be made at the National
Parks and Wildlife Booking Office, Kuching,
T082-248088 (see page 87). The **hostels** are
equipped with mattresses, kerosene stoves
and cutlery; **lodges** have electricity until
2400 and refrigerators. Both have fans. The
recommended length of stay is 2 days/1
night. Accommodation is always booked
out, so you should reserve several days

before you want to go. Bako can be visited
in a day trip although an overnight stay
is preferable. **Lodge**, RM157 per house ,
RM105 per room. **Hostel**, RM42 per room,
RM15.75 per person, check-out time 1200.

   Camping   Unless you are intending to
trek to the other side of the park, it is not
worth camping as monkeys steal anything
left lying around and macaques can be
aggressive. In addition, the smallest
amount of rain turns the campsite into a
swimming pool. It is, however, necessary to
camp if you go to the beaches on the
northeast peninsula. Tents can be hired for
RM8 (sleeps 4); campsite RM5.

Homestay programmes

Borneo Inbound Tours, 98 Main Bazaar,
T082-711152, arrange all homestay
programmes. These cover not just fishing
villages in the vicinity of Kuching but also a
number of up-country communities. The
host families are chosen so that at least one
member speaks English and they are also
suitable for families.

🍴 Eating

Kuching p86, map p90

Kuching, with all its old buildings and
godowns along the river, seems made for
open-air restaurants and cafés – but good
ones are notably absent. However, the town
is not short of hawker centres. Local dishes
worth looking out for include *umai* – a spicy
salad of raw marinated fish with limes and
shallots. Other distinctive Sarawakian
ingredients are *midin* and *paku* – jungle
fern shoots. See Food glossaries, page 338.

Chinese

All the major hotels have Chinese
restaurants; most open for lunch and dinner,
closing in between.
¶¶ Hornbill Corner Café, 85 Jl Ban Hock.
All-you-can-eat steamboat and barbecue,
popular.
¶¶ Red Eastern Café, Jl Ban Hock. Specializes
in steamboat.
¶¶ River Palace, Crowne Plaza Majestic
Hotel. First-class Chinese restaurant, offers
regular food promotions.
¶ Hot and Spicy House, Lot 303, Section 10,
Rubber Rd, just outside the city centre,

T082-250873. Wed-Mon. Chinese cooking with West Malaysian influence. Speciality is Ipoh-style *yong tau hoo* (vegetables stuffed with beancurd).

¶ **Lan Ya Keng**, Jl Carpenter, opposite old temple. Specializes in pepperfish steak.

¶ **Lok Thian**, 1st floor, Bangunan Beesan, Jl Padungan, T082-331310. Good food, pleasant surroundings and excellent service, booking advisable, especially at the weekends.

¶ **Meisan**, Holiday Inn, Jl Tunku Abdul Rahman. Dim sum, set lunch; Sun all-you-can-eat dim sum special, also Sichuan cuisine. Recommended.

¶ **Min Kong Kee**, 157 Jl Pandungan. A good selection of dishes and authentic Chinese and Malay breakfasts.

¶ **Minsion Canteen**, end of Jl Chan Chin Ann, on right. Speciality is *daud special* (noodles in herbal soup with chunks of chicken).

¶ **Perfect Vegetarian Food Centre**, Jl Green Hill. Great inexpensive canteen serving Malay and Chinese food and Western breakfasts, all meatless. Tables outside. Fantastic noodle in pumpkin sauce dish. Highly recommended.

¶ **Tsui Hua Lau**, Lot 321-324, Jl Ban Hock, T082-414560. Shanghai-style dishes.

Indian

There are several cheap Indian Muslim restaurants along Lebuh India.

¶¶¶ **Serapi**, Holiday Inn, Jl Tunku Abdul Rahman. Specializes in North Indian tandoori, good vegetable dishes, excellent selection of grills and seafood, imported steak, elegant surroundings. Recommended.

¶¶ **Banana Leaf**, 7G Lorong Rubber 1, T082-239404. Open all day, specializes in Indian banana-leaf meals.

¶¶ **Bismillah**, Lebuh Khoo Hun Reang (near Central Police Station). North Indian Muslim food, good tandoori chicken.

¶¶ **Lyn's Tandoori**, Lot 62, 10G Lg 4, Jl Nanas. A worthwhile taxi-ride from the centre – genuine North Indian tandoori cuisine, excellent naan, locals recommend it, closed Sun evenings.

¶¶ **Pots 'n' Buns**, Taman Sri Sarawak Mall, opposite rear store entrance. Good *roti canai*, *murtabak*, plus usual hawker stall food.

¶¶ **Rahamath Café**, 19 Jl Padungan, good *roti canai*.

Indonesian

¶¶ **Minangkabau Nasi Padang**, 168 Jl Chan Chin Ann. Spicy Padang food including such classics as beef rendang, lunchtime only.

International

¶¶ **Hani's Bistro**, Jl Chan Chin Ann (near Holiday Inn). Reasonably priced café, good mix of Eastern and Western cuisine, generous helpings, tasty haricot oxtail, good background music. Recommended.

¶¶ **The Junk Restaurant**, 80 Jl Wayang, T082-259450. Closed Tue. Intimate little gem of a restaurant filled with crazy antiques like old cash registers and lit by lanterns. Serves good but not fantastic pasta, steaks and other Western and Asian dishes. Recommended.

¶¶ **Orchid Garden**, Holiday Inn, Jl Tunku Abdul Rahman. Good breakfast and evening buffets, international and local cuisine. Recommended.

¶¶ **San Francisco Grill**, 76 Jl Ban Hock. Steak house, cosy atmosphere, live piano, largely Chinese clientele which means steak is seasoned with 5 spices. Meat is air-freighted, chips mediocre, but nice atmosphere.

¶¶ **The Tapanga Tree**, Taman Letak Kereta, Jl Padungan (off Jl Tunku), T082-248773. Very funky place with open-air seating and cosy indoor restaurant on the 4th floor of this block. Very friendly staff and cute gecko logo. Cuisine is described as fusion – there's lamb kebab, grilled seafood and plenty of Asian choices. Nice use of local woodcrafts. Mon-Sat live music. The outdoor terrace has no view, but a pleasant place nonetheless.

¶¶ **Waterfront**, Hilton Hotel, Jl Tunku Abdul Rahman. Reasonably priced for the venue. The best pizzas and a family brunch buffet on Sun which is very popular.

¶ **Dulit Coffee House**, Telang Usan Hotel, Jl Ban Hock. Pleasant terrace café, mix of Western and Eastern food, specializes in French oxtail stew and the only genuine chicken kebabs in Kuching.

● *For an explanation of the sleeping and eating price codes used in this guide, see inside the* ● *front cover. Other relevant information is found in Essentials, pages 31-35.*

Japanese

Kikyo-Tei, Jl Crookshank, in front of Government Resthouse. Also some Chinese and Western dishes. Large main room with separate Teppanyaki and Tatami rooms. The set lunch is a good deal. Recommended by locals.

Minoru, Lot 493, Section 10, Rubber Rd, T082-251021. Set lunch and dinner as well as an extensive menu and good service.

Malay

Sarawak specialities available include *laksa* (spicy noodles – a Malaysia-wide dish, but especially good here) and *umai*.

Sri Sarawak, Crowne Plaza Riverside Hotel. Gourmet food, good views.

D'Alif, Waterfront, just in front of the Steamship. Big airy restaurant with riverside seats, specializing in Malay seafood, no alcohol. Very popular with locals.

Home Cook, Jl Song Thian Cheok. Clean and good value, speciality Assam fish.

Khatulistiwa Café, Waterfront. In a circular pavilion-style building. Great views from this café open 24 hrs serving Malay and international dishes. There's an R&B music café on the 2nd floor open at 2300.

Suan Chicken Rice, Jl Tunku Abdul Rahman, next to **Sarawak Plaza**. Steamed or curried chicken.

Aunty Mary's Kitchen, 2 and 4 Bishopsgate St (just off Main Bazaar before China St). Sells the perfect Malay breakfast, *Laksa Mee*. Good and cheap. Closed Sun.

Seafood

Excellent seafood is to be found in Kuching. On Kampong Buntal are several seafood restaurants on stilts over the sea, 25 km north of Kuching, very popular with Kuchingites.

Ah Leong, Lot 72, Jl Pandungan, near **Kingwood Inn**. Good choice of seafood.

Benson Seafood, Lot 122/3, Section 49, Jl Abell, T082-255262. Full range of Sarawak seafood.

KTS Seafood Canteen, 157 Jl Chan Chin Ann. Excellent butter prawns and grilled stingray.

See Good, Jl Bukit Mata Kuching, behind MAS office. Extensive range of seafood. Recommended by locals. Strong-flavoured sauces, lots of herbs, extensive and exotic menu, unlimited free bananas, closed 4th and 18th of every month.

Thai

Bangkok Thai Seafood Restaurant, 318-319 Jl Padungan, T082-335043. In a complex with Japanese and Chinese restaurants. Fine dining. Booking advisable for weekends.

Coffee shops

There are several Malay/Indian coffee shops on Lebuh India including **Madinah Café**, **Jubilee** and **Malaysia Restaurant**. Many Chinese coffee shops serve excellent *laksa* (breakfast) of curried coconut milk with a side plate of *sambal belacan* (chillied prawn paste).

Coffee Master, 13 China St, T082-250958. Western snacks and iced Sarawak coffee. A trendy modern drinking place in a quiet street off the waterfront. Try a hot cup of Dong Ding Ooolong tea.

Cozy Corner Cafe, Borneo Hotel, Jl Tabuan. A selection of coffees, teas, cakes and pastries in a relaxing atmosphere.

Fook Hoi, Jl Padungan. Old-fashioned coffee shop, famous for its *sio bee* and *ha kau* (pork dumpling).

Life Café, 108 Ewe Hai St (near Carpenter St, behind Main Bazaar), T082-411954. Closed Tue. Attractive café serving mostly vegetarian food plus a good range of teas and coffees (including Sarawak tea). Friendly staff and pleasant atmosphere.

Foodstalls and food centres

There are great open-air informal places along the waterfront selling everything from kebabs to *ais cream goreng* (fried ice cream) that start opening towards the evening. It makes a great place for an evening meal. Most of the foodstalls are clustered around the **Hilton** end of the promenade selling Malay dishes and fruit juices (no alcohol). There are beautiful views of the river, accompanied by popular Malay love songs.

Some of the best food centres are located in the suburbs; a taxi is essential.

Batu Lintang Open-Air Market, Jl Rock (to the south of town, past the hospital).

Chinese Food Centre, Jl Carpenter (opposite temple). Chinese foodstalls offering hot and sour soups, fish balls and more.

Hock Hong Garden, Jl Ban Hock, opposite **Grand Continental**. Finest hawker stall food in Kuching, little English spoken but definitely worth trying to be understood.

Jl Palm Open-Air Market, Lau Ya Keng, Jl Carpenter, opposite temple. Specializes in Chinese dishes.

King's Centre, Jl Simpang Tiga (bus No 11 to get there). Large range of foodstalls, busy and not many tourists.

Kubah Ria Hawker stalls, Jl Tunku Abdul Rahman (on the road out of town towards Damai Beach, next to Satok Suspension Bridge). Specialities include *sop kambling* (mutton soup).

Permata Food Centre, behind MAS office. A purpose-built alternative to the central market, prices are higher but the choice is better, bird-singing contests (mainly red-whiskered bulbuls and white-rumped sharmas) every Sun morning, excellent range of fresh seafood. Recommended.

Petanak Central Market, Jl Petanak, above Kuching's early morning wet market. Light snacks, full seafood selection, good atmosphere, especially early in the morning.

Rex Cinema Hawker Centre, Jl Wayang/Jl Temple, squashed down an alleyway. Good satay; recommended.

Satok Bridge, under the suspension bridge. Very good barbecued chicken and seafood.

Saujana Food Centre, 5th floor of the car park near the mosque (take the lift). Mostly Malay food but also seafood.

Song Thieng Hai Food Centre, between Jl Padungan and Jl Ban Hock. Every type of noodle available.

Top Spot Food Court, Jl Bukit Mata Kuching, top floor of a car park. Wide range of stalls, popular.

Damai Peninsula *p97, map p95*

New Dolphin Seafood Restaurant, Kampong Buntal, T082-846441. Great position on the coast, about 5 km east of Santubon, good food, above-average prices.

Santubong Mountain Trek Canteen, 5 mins' walk from hotels, T082-846153. Rice and noodle dishes, in nearby Buntal village there are excellent seafood restaurants.

Bako National Park *p99, map p100*

The canteen is open 0700-2100. It serves local food at reasonable prices and sells tinned foods and drinks. No need to take food, there is a good seafood restaurant near the jetty.

Bars and clubs

Kuching *p86, map p90*

There are enough clubs, pubs and bars to keep most people reasonably happy. Clubs and discos usually have a cover charge although there is often a drink or 2 thrown in with the price. Expect to pay around RM10-15 for a beer and RM20-25 for spirits. Most places have happy hours, and 2-for-1 offers. Bars tend to close around 0100-0200, a little later in hotels. Most bars are centered along Bukit Mata off Jl Pandungan and along Jl Borneo next to the **Hilton**.

The main centres of evening entertainment are **Jl Tunku Abdul Rahman**, **Jl Mendu**, **Jl Padungan** and **Jl Borneo**.

Casablanca Lounge, Crowne Plaza Riverside Hotel. Cocktail lounge and karaoke.

Cat City, Jl Chan Chin Ann (turn left at **Pizza Hut**). Happy hour 2030-2215, followed by live bands (usually Filipino) playing a mixture of Western rock covers and Malay and Chinese ballads, open late.

De Tavern, Taman Sri Sarawak Mall (facing **Hilton** car park). Friendly Kayan-run corner pub, serves good rice wine, open 1630-0130, happy hour until 2030.

Eagle's Nest & The Cottage, 16-20 Jl Bukit Mata. Great selection of wines, good party atmosphere, occasional karaoke nights which should probably be avoided.

Earthquake, 21 & 22 Jl Bukit Mata. Silver spaceship interior, looks like a thumping Asian club joint.

Hornbill's Corner Café, Jl Ban Hock. Breezy open-air pub.

Margherita Lounge, Hilton Hotel, the best cocktails and good live music.

Marina Fun Pub and Disco, Jl Ban Hock. Live band until 0200, then a DJ until 0330, crowded at weekends.

Monsoon, Riverside Complex, Jl Tunku Abdul Rahman. Balcony jutting out over the river. Nice local and tourist mix.

Rejang Lobby Lounge, Holiday Inn. Small but popular.

The Fisherman's Pub, 1st floor, Taman Sri Sarawak Mall. Karaoke, friendly staff and a pleasant crowd of regulars.

Tribes, downstairs at **Holiday Inn**. Ethnic food, tribal decor and a variety of live music, open 1600-0100.

Tropical Pub & Bar, Jl Abell. The place to go for a lively local disco (Malaysian music).
Jupiters, Jl Ban Hock. Only open on Fri, Sat and eve of public holidays. Top 40 hits played.

Damai Peninsula *p97, map p95*
PV The Fun Pub at Holiday Inn, Damai Beach. Damai's main night spot and very popular – an open-air pub with pool, karaoke and live bands.

⊕ Entertainment

Kuching *p86, map p90*
Cinemas
Riverside Cineplex, Riverside Complex, Jl Tunku Abdul Rahman, in the base of the Crowne Plaza Hotel, T082-427061, check local press for details of programme.
Star Cineplex, Level 9, Medan Pelita, top floor of car park on Temple St.

Cultural shows
Cultural Village, Damai Beach. Cultural shows, with stylized and expertly choreographed tribal dance routines, daily 1130 and 1630.

⊕ Festivals and events

Bau *p96*
May-Jun The Bindayuh celebrate **gawai padi**, a festival with animistic roots that thanks the gods for an abundant rice harvest. Ask at the tourist office in Kuching for exact details.

◐ Shopping

Kuching *p86, map p90*
When it comes to choice, Kuching is the best place in Malaysia to buy tribal handicrafts, textiles and other artefacts, but they are not cheap. In some of Sarawak's smaller coastal and upriver towns, you are more likely to find a better bargain, although the selection is not as good. If buying several items, it is a good idea to find one shop which sells the lot, as good discounts can be negotiated. It is essential to shop around: the best-stocked handicraft and antique shops in and near the big hotels are usually the most expensive. It is possible to bargain everywhere. Most shops are closed Sun.

It is illegal to export any antiquity without a licence from the curator of the Sarawak Museum. An antiquity is defined as any object made before 1850. Most things sold as antiquities are not; some very convincing weathering and ageing processes are employed.

Antiques, art and handicrafts
Most handicraft and antique shops are along **Main Bazaar**, **Lebuh Temple** and **Lebuh Wayang**, with a few in the Padungan area. There is a **Sun market** (which starts on Sat afternoon) on Jl Satok, to the southwest of town, with a few handicraft stalls. Sat evening or early Sun morning are the best times to visit. There are rows of pottery stalls along **Jl Penrissen**, out of town, take a bus (No 3, 3A, 9A or 9B) or taxi to Ng Hua Seng Pottery bus stop. Antique shops sell this pottery too.
Art Gallery, 5 Wayang St. Designer T-shirts with Sarawak motifs amongst other crafts.
Artrageouslyramsayong, 94 Main Bazaar, T082-424346, www.artrageouslyasia.com. Art gallery of Sarawak artiste extraordinaire **Ramsay Ong** who made fame with his tree bark works. Now showing an eclectic collection of contemporary Malaysian art. Recommended.
Arts of Asia, 68 Main Bazaar.
Atelier Gallery, 104 Main Bazaar.
Bong & Co, 78 Main Bazaar.
Borneo Art Gallery, Sarawak Plaza, Jl Tunku Abdul Rahman.
Borneo Arts & Crafts, 56 Main Bazaar.
Eeze Trading, Lot 250, Section 49, Ground floor, Jl Tunku Abdul Rahman.
Fabriko, Main Bazaar in beautifully restored Chinese shophouse, interesting souvenirs and gallery.
Galleri M, Hilton lobby, 26 Main Bazaar. Exclusive jewellery, bead necklaces and antiques, best available Iban hornbill carvings. Also paintings from a wide range of Sarawakian artists.
Karyaneka (handicrafts) Centre, Cawangan Kuching, Lot 324 Bangunan Bina, Jl Satok.
Loo Pan Arts, 83 Jl Ban Hock.
Native Arts, 94 Main Bazaar.
Sarakraf, Upper ground floor, Sarawak Plaza Shopping Complex, sarakraf@tm.net.my. Wide range of souvenirs and handicrafts with outlets in major hotels in Kuching,

Damai, Sarawak Cultural Village and Miri airport (chain set up by the Sarawak Economic Development Corporation).
Sarawak Batik Art Shop, 1 Lebuh Temple.
Sarawak House, 67 Main Bazaar. More expensive but better quality crafts, carvings, fabrics and pots.
Syarikat Pemasarah Karyaneka, Lot 87, Jl Rubber.
Tan & Sons, 54 Jl Padungan.
Telang Usan Hotel, Jl Ban Hock. Some Orang Ulu and Penan crafts, including good modern beadwork and traditional headgear.
Thian Seng, 48 Main Bazaar. Good for *pua kumbu*.

Birds' nests
Mostly exported to China. **Teo Hoe Hin Enterprise** (next to McDonalds) is worth visiting to view the delicacies.

Books and maps
Berita Book Centre, Jl Haji Taha, has a good selection of English-language books.
HN Mohd Yahia & Sons, Holiday Inn, Jl Tunku Abdul Rahman, and in the basement of the Sarawak Shopping Plaza, sells a 1:500,000 map of Sarawak.
Times Books, 1st floor, Riverside Shopping Complex, Jl Tunku Abdul Rahman, best and biggest bookshop for foreign-language books.

Markets
Vegetable and Wet markets are on the riverside on Jl Gambier; further up is the **Ban Hock Wharf market**, now full of cheap imported clothes. The **Sunday Market** on Jl Satok sells jungle produce, fruit and vegetables (there are a few handicraft stalls) and all sorts of intriguing merchandise; it starts on Sat night and runs through Sun morning and is well worth visiting. There is a jungle produce market, **Pasar Tani**, on Fri and Sat at Kampong Pinang Jawa in Petra Jaya.

Shopping malls
Sarawak Plaza, next to the Holiday Inn, Jl Tunku Abdul Rahman.
Riverside Shopping Complex, next to Crowne Plaza Riverside Hotel, best complex in Kuching, has **Parkson Department Store** and good supermarket in basement.

▲ Activities and tours

Kuching *p86, map p90*
Diving
Borneo Inbound Tours, 98 Main Bazaar. Scuba trips to the Tanjung Datu National Park from Teluk Melano. There are dive sites at Batu Mandi and artificial reefs off Talang Talang islands. Only available from Apr-Sep because of the monsoon. The package includes a homestay with a Malay family in the traditional fishing village of Teluk Melano (RM650, 2 days, 1 night) which includes transport there and back.

Fishing
Offshore from Santubong or deep-sea game fishing at Tanjung Datu (near Indonesian border), contact Mr Johnson, **Fui Lip Marketing**, 15 Ground floor, Wisma Phoenix, Jl Song Thian Cheok.

Golf
Damai Golf Course, Jl Santubong, T082-846088, F082-846044. Due to its popularity bookings should be made 3 days in advance. See Damai Peninsula, page 109.
Hornbill Golf & Jungle Club, Borneo Highlands Resort, Padawan, T082-790800. 18-hole golf course at 1000 m altitude.
Kelab Golf Course, Petra Jaya, 18 holes, T082-440966.
Sarawak Golf and Country Club, Petra Jaya, T082-440966.

Mountain biking
Good trails from **Kamppung Singgai**, about 30 mins from Kuching (across the Batu Kawa bridge). Beginners to intermediate – good trail near **Kampong Apar**. Advanced trail – **Batang Ai**. Alternatively, hire a bike from Kuching and tour the Malay villages adjacent to the Astana and Fort Margherita. Cross the Sarawak River by sampan (around RM1 for you and your bike) and then follow the small road that runs parallel to the river.
Borneo Adventure, Main Bazaar, T082-245175. Rents mountain bikes and can arrange specialized tours.
Power Action Cycles, 64 Carpenter St, T082-421387. Rents mountain bikes for RM30 a day.

Outward bound
Camp Permai Sarawak, PO Box 891, Satok Post Office, T082-321497, F082-321500. An 18-ha site of tropical rainforest including its own beach. It is aimed at families with kayaking, windsurfing, sailing, rafting, and trekking.
Batman Wall, Rock Climbing at the Fairy Caves outside Bau, has 20 routes and rises to 40 m.

Spectator sports
Malaysia Cup football matches are held in the **Stadium Negeri Sarawak**, Petra Jaya. The **Turf Club**, Serian Rd, is the biggest in Borneo (see newspapers for details of meetings).

Swimming
Kuching Municipal Swimming Pool, next to Kuching Turf Club, Serian Rd. Open mornings only.

Tour operators
Most tour companies offer city tours as well as trips around Sarawak to **Semenggoh**, **Bako**, **Niah**, **Lambir Hills**, **Miri**, **Mulu** and **Bario**. There are also competitively priced packages to longhouses (mostly up the Skrang River – see page 112). It is cheaper and easier to take organized tours to Mulu, but these should be arranged in Miri (see page 134) as they are much more expensive if arranged from Kuching. Other areas are easy enough to get to independently.
Borneo Adventure, No 55 Main Bazaar, T082-245175, www.borneoadventure.com. Known for its environmentally friendly approach to tourism. Offers tours all over Sarawak. Recommended.
Borneo Exploration, 76 Jl Wayang, T082-252137, ckkc@tm.net.
Borneo Fairyland, 18 Main Bazaar, T082-420194. Aimed at backpackers.
Borneo Inbound Tours & Travel, 98 Main Bazaar, T082-237287. The only agency currently organizing scuba diving around Kuching and the only agency for homestay programs. Call Mr Abang Zainudin (T013 8273711), manager of Borneo Inbound to arrange a homestay in the Kuching area.
Borneo Interland Travel, 63 Main Bazaar, T082-413595, www.bitravelcom.my. Helpful staff. The only agency licensed to sell bus

and boat tickets in town. There's another branch in the **Merdeka Palace Hotel**.
Borneo Transverse, Ground floor, 16 Jl Green Hill, T082-257784, bttt@po.jaring.my.
Gaya Holidays, 37 Main Bazaar, T082-415476, sales@interworld-borneo.com, for river cruises (RM30/person/hr).
Harrisons Travel, 28 Jl Green Hill, T082-240977. Advice on tours as well as air, bus and boat tickets.
Ibanika Expeditions, Lot 435, Ground floor, Jl Ang Cheng Ho, T082-424022, ibanika@po. jaring.my. Long-established company offering longhouse and more general tours, also offers French and German-speaking guides.
Interworld, 1st floor, 161/162 Jl Temple, T082-252344, F082-424515.
Journey Travel Agency, Hilton lobby, Jl Borneo, T082-424934, dolores@pd.jaring.my.
Pan Asia Travel, 2nd floor, Unit 217-218, Sarawak Plaza, Jl Tunku Abdul Rahman, T082-419754, half-day excursions from Kuching.
Saga Travel, Level 1, Taman Sri Sarawak Mall, Jl Tunku Abdul Rahman, T082-418705, F082-426299.
Tropical Adventure, 1st floor, 17 Main Bazaar, T082-413088, F082-413104.

Damai Peninsula *p97, map p95*
Golf
Damai Golf Course, Jl Santubong, PO Box 400, T082-846088, F082-846044. International standard, 18-hole golf course designed by Arnold Palmer, laid out over approximately 6.5 km, 10-bay driving range right on the sea. A very long 18 holes, with electric buggies to prevent your expiring through perspiring. Caddies, clubs and shoes for hire, spacious club house, restaurant, bar, pro shop, tennis, squash and pool are also available.

Mountain biking
Damai Cross-Country Track. Close to the Damai Rainforest Resort, this is a purpose-built track where visitors can get very hot, sweaty and dirty as they career around the 3.5-km track; bikes can be hired from hotels.

Watersports
Holiday Inn Resort Damai Beach and the **Holiday Inn Resort Damai Lagoon** both offer a range of watersports from jet-skiing to sailing. Snorkelling trips also arranged. The

Damai Rainforest Resort has a slightly more restricted range of watersports on offer.

⊖ Transport

Kuching *p86, map p90*
Air
Airport information: T082-457373.
Transport to town: Green bus **Sarawak Transport Co**, 12A (RM1) to **Lebuh Jawa** (45-min journey, departing every 50 mins) which operates between 0710 (0630 from Kuching) and 2000, or taxi to town (RM17.50 – buy a coupon from the counter in the arrivals lounge).

Regular connections with **KL** (8-10 flights daily), **KK**, and **Brunei**. AirAsia flies between Kuching and KL; it doesn't fly between KK and Kuching. **MAS Rural Air Service** operates Twin Otters to a large number of airfields across the state including Miri-Bario (for the **Kelabit Highlands**), Miri-Mulu (for **Gunung Mulu**) and Sibu-Kapit-Belaga (for the **Rejang River**). MAS has direct flights to **Singapore**, **Perth** and **Pontianak** (Indonesia) and via Kota Kinabalu, to **Hong Kong**, **Taipei**, **Manila**, **Seoul** and **Tokyo**.

Airline offices Air Asia, Wisma Ho Ho Lim, Ground floor, 291 Jl Abell, T082-283222. MAS, Lot 215, Jl Song Thian Cheok, T082-246622, F082-244563. **Royal Brunei**, 1st floor, Rugayah Building, Jl Song Thian Cheok, T082-243344, F082-244563. **Sin Hwa Travel Service**, 8 Lebuh Temple, T082-246688.

Boat
Local Sampans cross the Sarawak River from next to the Square Tower on Main Bazaar to **Fort Margherita** and the **Astana** on the north bank for less then RM1. Small boats and some express boats connect with outlying kampongs on the river. Sampans can also be hired by the hr (RM30 per hr) for a tour up and down the river.

International Express boats leave from the Sin Kheng Hong Wharf, 6 km out of town. Take a taxi (RM8). Tickets for **Kuching-Sibu** are only for sale at 2 places in town; Borneo Interland, 63 Main Bazaar, T082-413595 and Lim Magazine bookshop, 19 Ban Hock Lane T082-410076. Otherwise turn up 30 mins at the ferry before departure to get a ticket. 2 daily departures for **Sibu** via Sarakei at 0830 and 1230 (4 hrs, RM30).

Bus
Local There are 2 bus companies around town: blue and white **Chin Lian Long** buses serve the city and its suburbs. Major bus stops are at Jl Mosque and opposite the post office. The green and yellow **Sarawak Transport Company** (STC) buses leave from the end of Lebuh Jawa, next to Ban Hock Wharf and the market. STC buses operate on regional routes; bus 12A (RM1) airport service starts at 0630, departs every 40 mins until 1915.

Buses depart from the **Regional Express Bus Terminal** on Jl Penrissen at Mile 3.5 (a taxi ride costs around RM10). You either have to buy tickets at the bus station itself a few kilometres outside of the centre, or from **Borneo Interland** (63 Main Bazaar, T082-413595, closed Sun). Buses to **Sibu** (7 hrs, RM40, first departure 0645, last 2200) **Bintulu** (RM60) and **Miri** (15 hrs, RM80, first 0100 last 2100).

International connections There are express bus departures to **Pontianak** in Kalimantan, Indonesia, 8 hrs (first at 0730, last at 2300, RM45, bus only departs if full). It is necessary to have a valid Indonesian visa (see Embassies and consulates below). Buses leave from the **Regional Express Bus Terminal**. There are several departures daily from Kuching via Miri and Kuala Belait to **Bandar Seri Begawan** (Brunei, RM130). It is possible to enter Sarawak from Kalimantan driving a private vehicle (including rental vehicles) so long as it has international insurance cover.

Car hire
Cat City Holidays, Lot 2537, 1st floor, Central Park, Commercial Centre, T082-412500, www.catcityholidays.com. They also have a counter at the airport. **Pronto Car Rental**, 1st floor, 98 Jl Padungan, T/F082-236889. **Mayflower Car Rental**, Lot 4, 24A, 4th floor, Bangunan Satok, Jl Satok, T082-410110. **Wah Tung Travel Service**, counter at Kuching International Airport, T082-616900.

Taxi
Local taxis congregate at the taxi stand on Jl Market, or outside the big hotels; they do not use meters so agree a price before setting off. 24-hr radio taxi service T082-480000. Short distances around town should cost RM5-8.

Damai Peninsula *p97, map p95*
Bus
There are shuttle buses from the **Holiday Inn** in **Kuching** (RM10, RM5 for children, 40 mins, first bus at 0730 from Kuching, last return bus at 2200) or take the public bus No 2B, operated by **Petra Jaya Transport** (yellow buses with black and red stripes) to **Santubong** at a fraction of the price (RM3.30) from the market place at the end of JI Gambier. Tour companies offer packages for various prices including transport, entrance to the Sarawak Cultural Village and lunch.

Taxi
From **Kuching** costs RM35.

Bako National Park *p99, map p100*
Bus and boat
Petra Jaya (yellow/red/black stripes) bus No 6 or 2B every hr from Electra House on Lebuh Market to Kampong Bako, 45 mins (RM3.50); also minibuses (no fixed schedule) from Lebuh Market RM3. The last buses returning to **Kuching** depart around 1800. From **Kampong Bako**, charter a private boat to **Sungai Assam** (30 mins) which is a short walk from park HQ, RM40 per boat each way – ask price before boarding (up to 5 people).

● Directory

Kuching *p86, map p90*
Banks
Money changers in the main shopping complexes usually give a much better rate for cash than the banks – although if changing TCs the rates are much the same. ATMs are two-a-penny. Note that the 1st and 3rd Sat of every month is a bank holiday. **Standard Chartered**, Wisma Bukit Mata Kuching (opposite Holiday Inn), JI Tunku Abdul Rahman; **HSBC**, Bangunan Binamas (near Cat Statue);l **American Express**, 70 JI Padungan (assistance with Amex traveller's cheques) T082-252600; **Majid & Sons Money Changer**, 45 JI India; **Mohamed Yahia & Sons** (money changer), GF3, Sarawak Plaza – some of the best rates in Kuching.

Embassies and consulates
Indonesian Consulate, 111 JI Tun Haji Openg, T082-241734; **Australian Honorary Consul**, T082-233350; **British Honorary Representative**, T012 3220011; **French Honorary Consul**, c/o Telong Usan Hotel, T082-415588; **New Zealand Honorary Consul**, T082-482177.

Immigration
1st floor, Bangunan Sultan Iskandar (Federal Complex) JI Simpang Tiga, T082-245661.

Internet
Cyber City, Taman Sri Sarawak (opposite the Hilton, open 1000-2200 (RM4 per hr); **Waterfront Cyber Cafe**, Steamship Building, open 0900-2100 (RM4 per hr); **Dot.com**, Wayang St (next to Ting & Ting supermarket and Borneo Hotel) open 0900-2100, RM2 per hr. International calls can also be made from most public cardphones. Major hotels all have cardphones in their lobbies.

Medical services
Hospitals and clinics Sarawak General Hospital, JI Tan Sri Ong Kee Hui, off JI Tun Haji Openg, T082-257555; **Normah Medical Centre**, across the river on JI Tun Datuk Patinggi Hj; **Abdul Rahman Yakub**, T082-440055, private hospital with good reputation; **Doctor's Clinic**, Main Bazaar, opposite Chinese History Museum is said to be excellent and is used to treating travellers' more minor ailments (RM20 for consultation); **Timberland Medical Centre**, Rock Rd, T082-234991. Recommended. **Pharmacies** **Apex Pharmacy**, 125 1st floor, Sarawak Plaza, open 1000-2100; **YK Farmasi**, 22 Main Bazaar, open 0830-1700; **UMH**, Ban Hock Rd, Mon-Fri 0900-2030, Sat 0900-1800.

Police
Tourist Police T082-241222. Office located opposite Padang Merdeka.

Post
General Post Office, JI Tun Haji Openg, Mon-Sat 0800-1800, Sun 1000-1300. Operates a poste restante service.

Bandar Sri Aman and around

→ Colour map 1, C3.
Previously called Simmanggang, Bandar Sri Aman lies on the Batang Lupar, a three-to four-hour journey from Kuching, and is the administrative capital of the Second Division. The river is famous for its tidal bore; several times a year, a wall of water rushes upstream wreaking havoc with boats and divides into several tributaries: the Skrang River is one of these. It is possible to spend the night in longhouse homestays on the river. The Batang Ai National Park is home to hornbills, orang-utan and gibbons. → For Sleeping, Eating and other listings, see page 116.

Ins and outs

Bandar Sri Aman is accessible from Kuching and Sibu by bus. To reach the Skrang longhouses, buses and then chartered boats must be arranged. There is one hotel in Batang Ai National Park. It arranges transport for its guests. Trips to longhouses and the national park can be organized through **Borneo Adventure Travel Company**, see page 116.

Sights

The major sight in Bandar is the defensive Fort Alice. Most tourists do not stop in Bandar but pass through on day trips from Kuching to visit the traditional Iban longhouses sited along the Skrang River.The route to Bandar goes through pepper plantations and many 'new' villages. During Communist guerrilla activity in the 1960s (see page 158), whole settlements were uprooted in this area and placed in guarded camps.

Fort Alice was constructed in 1864. It has small turrets, a central courtyard, a medieval-looking drawbridge, and is surrounded by a fence of iron spikes. Rajah Charles Brooke lived in the Batang Lupar district for about 10 years, using this fort – and another downriver at Lingga – as bases for his punitive expeditions against pirates and Ibans in the interior. The fort is the only one of its type in Sarawak and was built commanding this stretch of the Batang Lupar River as protection against Iban raids. The original fort here was built in 1849 and named Fort James; the current fort was constructed using much of the original material. It was renamed Alice in honour of Ranee Margaret Brooke (it was her second name). It is said that every evening, until the practice was ended in 1964, a policeman would call from the fort (in Iban): "Oh ha! Oh ha! The time is now eight o'clock. The steps have been drawn up. The door is closed. People from upriver, people from downriver are not allowed to come to the fort anymore." (It probably sounded better in Iban.)

Skrang longhouses 🖐🖐 *→ p116. Colour map 1, C3.*

The Skrang River, was one of the first areas settled by Iban immigrants in the 16th to 18th centuries. The slash-and-burn agriculturalists originally came from the Kapual River basin in Kalimantan. They later joined forces with Malay chiefs in the coastal areas and terrorized the Borneo coasts; the first Europeans to encounter these pirates called them 'Sea Dayaks' (see page 161). The Ibans took many heads. Blackened skulls – which local headmen say date back to those days – hang in some of the Skrang longhouses. In 1849, more than 800 Iban pirates from the Batang Lupar and Skrang River were massacred by Rajah James Brooke's forces in the notorious Battle of Beting Marau. Four years later the Sultan of Brunei agreed to cede these troublesome districts to Brooke; they became the Second Division of Sarawak.

The longhouse – prime-site apartments with river views

Most longhouses are built on stilts, high on the riverbank, on prime real estate. They are 'prestigious properties' with 'lots of character', and with their 'commanding views of the river', they are the condominiums of the jungle. They are long-rise rather than high-rise, however, and the average longhouse has 20-25 'doors' (although there can be as many as 60). Each represents one family. The word long in a settlement's name – as in Long Liput or Long Terawan – means 'confluence' (the equivalent of kuala in Malay), and does not refer to the length of the longhouse.

Behind each of the doors – which even today, are rarely locked – is a *bilik* (apartment), which includes the family living room and a loft, where paddy and tools are stored. In Kenyah and Kayan longhouses, paddy (which can be stored for years until it is milled) is kept in elaborate barns, built on stilts away from the longhouse, in case of fire. In traditional long-houses, the living rooms are simple atap-roofed, bamboo-floored rooms; in modern longhouses – which are designed on exactly the same principles – the living rooms are commonly furnished with sofas, lino floors, a television and an en suite bathroom.

At the front of the *bilik* is the *dapur*, where the cooking takes place. All *biliks* face out onto the *ruai* (gallery), which is the focus of communal life, and is where visitors are usually entertained. The width of the wall which faces onto the *ruai* indicates the status of that family. Attached to the *ruai* there is usually a *tanju* (open veranda), running the full length of the house – where rice and other agricultural products are dried. Long ladders – notched hardwood trunks – lead up to the *tanju*; they can get very slippery and do not always come with handrails.

❗ Visiting longhouses: house rules

There are more than 1500 longhouses in Sarawak. They are usually situated along the big rivers and their tributaries, notably the Skrang (see page 112), the Rejang (see page 120) and the Baram (see page 134). The Iban, who are characteristically extrovert and hospitable to visitors, live on the lower reaches of the rivers. The Orang Ulu tribes – mainly Kayan and Kenyah – live further upriver, and are generally less outgoing than the Iban. The Bidayuh live mainly around Bau and Serian, near Kuching. Their longhouses are usually more modern than those of the Iban and Orang Ulu, and are less often visited for that reason. The Kelabit people live in the remote plateau country near the Kalimantan border around Bario (see page 150).

The most important ground rule is not to visit a longhouse without an invitation. People who arrive unannounced may get an embarrassingly frosty reception. Tour companies offer the only exception to this rule, as most have tribal connections. Upriver, particularly at Kapit, on the Rejang (see page 120), such 'invitations' are not hard to come by; it is good to ensure your host actually comes from the longhouse he is inviting you to. The best time to visit Iban longhouses is during the gawai harvest festival at the beginning of June, when communities throw an open house and everyone is invited to join the festivities.

On arrival, visitors should pay an immediate courtesy call on the headman (the *tuai rumah* in Iban longhouses). It is normal to bring him gifts; those staying overnight should offer the headman between RM10 and RM20/head. The money is kept in a central fund and saved for use by the whole community during festivals. Small gifts such as beer, coffee, biscuits, whisky, batik and food (especially rice and chicken) go down well. It is best to arrive at a longhouse during late afternoon after people have returned from the fields. Visitors who have time to stay the night generally have a much more enjoyable experience than those who pay fleeting visits. They can share the evening meal and have time to talk and drink.

If you go beyond the limits of the express boats, it is necessary to charter a longboat. Petrol costs RM2-4/litre, depending on how far upriver you are. Guides charge approx RM40-80 a day and sometimes it is necessary to hire a boatman or front-man as well. Prices increase in the dry season when boats have to be lifted over shallow rapids. Permits are required for most upriver areas; these can be obtained at the residents' or district office in the nearest town.

Visitors should note the following:

- On entering a longhouse, take off your shoes.
- Accept food and drink with both hands. If you do not want to eat or drink, the accepted custom is to touch the brim of the glass or the plate and then touch your lips as a symbolic gesture. Sit cross-legged when eating.
- When washing in the river, women should wear a sarong and men, shorts.
- Ask permission to take photographs. It is not unusual to be asked for a small fee.
- Do not enter a longhouse during *pantang* (taboo), a period of misfortune – usually following a death. There is normally a white (leaf) flag hanging near the longhouse as a warning to visitors. During this period (normally one week) there is no singing, dancing or music, and no jewellery is worn.
- Bow your head when walking past people older than you.

66 99 The first Europeans to encounter the Iban pirates called them 'Sea Dyaks'. The Ibans took many heads. Blackened skulls – which local headmen say date back to those days – hang in some of the Skrang longhouses...

There are many traditional Iban longhouses along the Skrang River, although those closer to **Pias** and **Lamanak** (the embarkation points on the Skrang) tend to be very touristy – they are visited by tour groups almost every day. **Long Mujang**, the first Iban longhouse, is an hour upriver. Pias and Lamanak are within five hours' drive of Kuching. Jungle trekking is available (approximately two hours). The guide provides an educational tour of the flora and fauna. ▸▸ *See Sleeping, page 116.*

Batang Ai and Batang Ai National Park

The Batang Ai River, a tributary of the Batang Lupar, has been dammed to form Sarawak's first hydroelectric plant, which came into service in 1985; it provides 60% of Sarawak's electricity supply, transmitting as far as Limbang. The area was slowly flooded over a period of six months to give animals and wildlife a chance to escape, but it has affected no fewer than 29 longhouses, 10 of which are now completely submerged. The rehousing of the longhouse community has been the topic of fierce controversial debate. The communities were moved into modern longhouses and given work opportunities in local palmeries. However, it now seems that the housing loans that were initially given are not commensurate with local wages and will be very difficult for the longhouse communities to pay off. In addition, the modern longhouses were not provided with farmland, so many local people have returned to settle on the banks of the reservoir. Near the dam there is a freshwater fish nursery. These fish are exported to South Korea, Japan and Europe. Those families displaced by the flooding of the dam largely work here and many of the longhouses surrounding the dam depend upon this fishery for their own fish supply.

The Batang Ai dam has created a vast and very picturesque man-made lake which covers an area of some 90 sq km, stretching up the Engkari and Ai rivers. Beyond the lake, more than an hour's boat ride upriver from the dam, it is possible to see beautiful lowland mixed dipterocarp forest.

The **Batang Ai National Park**, 250 km from Kuching and two hours from the jetty by boat, covers an area of over 24,040 ha and was inaugurated in 1991. It protects the much-endangered orang-utan, and is home to a wide variety of other wildlife, including hornbills and gibbons. As yet there are no visitor facilities, but four walking trails have been created, one of which takes in an ancient burial ground. Trips to one of the 29 longhouses surrounding the dam and to Batang Ai National Park are organized by the **Borneo Adventure Travel Company**, see Activitives and tours, below.

● The Batang Lupar River provided Somerset Maugham with the inspiration for his short story 'Yellow Streak' in Borneo Tales. It was one of the few stories he wrote from personal experience: he nearly drowned after being caught by the bore in 1929.

Sarawak Bandar Sri Aman & around

● Sleeping

Bandar Sri Aman and around *p112*
B Bukit Saban Resort, on the rarely visited
Paku River, just north of the Skrang and
Lemnak rivers, about 4½ hrs from Kuching,
T082-477145, F082-477103 (Kuching sales
office), T083-648949 (at the resort). 50 rooms
in longhouse style with traditional sago palm
thatch, restaurant, a/c, TV, hot water,
seminar facilities.
B Champion, 1248 Main Bazaar, T082-320140.
A small but central establishment.

Skrang longhouses *p112*
All longhouses along the Skrang River are
controlled by the Ministry of Tourism so all
rates are the same – RM40 inclusive of all
meals. Resthouses at most of the longhouses
can accommodate 20-40 people; mattresses
and mosquito nets are provided in a
communal sleeping area with few partitions.
Basic conditions, with flush toilet, shower,
local food (visitors are sometimes allowed to
sleep on the communal area), phone
available and clinic nearby. If the stay is 3
days/2 nights, on the 2nd night it is possible
to camp in the jungle and then get a return
boatride to the longhouse.

Batang Ai and Batang Ai National
Park *p115*
**A Hilton International Batang Ai
Longhouse Resort**, T083-584388,
www.hilton.com. On the eastern shore of the
lake. Opened in 1995, the resort is made up of
11 longhouses, built of the local *belian*
(ironwood) to traditional designs. Despite its
lakeside location there are no views, except
from the walkways, as longhouses are built,
for purposes of defence, to face landwards –
in this case over the buggy track. However,
compromises to modern comforts have been
made; the rooms are cluttered with furniture
and TV sets. 100 rooms all with a/c, fan, TV,
shower room, minibar. Other facilities include
a pool and paddling pool, restaurant, 18-km
jogging track, shuttle from **Kuching Hilton
International**, tour desk. If the **Hilton** is not
your style, there is, unfortunately, not much
else. The hotel arranges transport.

Private tour companies provide
accommodation in the longhouses here, in a
much more central location within the park
than the **Hilton**.

● Eating

Bandar Sri Aman and around *p112*
*† **Alison Café & Restaurant**, 4 Jl Council,
Chinese cuisine.
*† **Chuan Hong**, 1 Jl Council, Chinese coffee
shop, also serves Muslim food.
*† **Melody**, 432 Jl Hospital, Chinese and
Muslim food.

▲ Activities and tours

Bandar Sri Aman and around *p112*
Borneo Adventure Travel Company,
55 Main Bazaar, Kuching, T082-410569,
F082-422626 and at the **Hilton Batang Ai
Longhouse Resort**. Many of the restaurant
staff in the resort are locals and discreet
enquiries may get you a trip to a longhouse
and/or Batang Ai National Park for
considerably less than the **Borneo
Adventure Travel Company** charge.

● Transport

Bandar Sri Aman and around *p112*
Bus
Regular connections with **Kuching**, RM15
(135 km to Kuching) and **Sibu** (via Sarikei).

Skrang longhouses *p112*
Bus
Buses No 14 and 19 to **Pias** and bus No 9 to
Lemanak. Self-drive car rental (return) or
minibus (8-10 people, return) from
Kuching to **Entaban**. From these points it
is necessary to charter a boat to reach the
nearest longhouses. Many of the
Kuching-based tour agencies offer cut-price
deals for 1- to 2-day excursions to Skrang
(see page 109). Unless you are already part
of a small group, these tours work out
cheaper because of the boat costs.

Sibu, Kapit and Belaga

The third largest town in Sarawak, Sibu is sited at the confluence of the Rejang and the Igan rivers 60 km upstream from the sea. It is the starting point for trips up the Rejang to the towns of Kapit and Belaga. The Rejang is an important thoroughfare and Malaysia's longest river at 563 km. Tours to upriver longhouses can be organized from Sibu, or more cheaply from Kapit and Belaga. ▶▶ *For Sleeping, Eating and other listings, see pages 123-128.*

Sibu ⬛🚋🚍▲🚌🚢 ▶▶ *pp123-128. Colour map 1, C3.*

Ins and outs
The airport is 25 km from Sibu and there are flights to KL, Kuching and KK. The new bus station is about 3 km out of town (take a taxi – RM10 – or a Lorong Road bus (no number) or Sungei Merah bus No 12 or 17 from the local bus station just outside the ferry terminal. There are daily connections with Bintulu and Miri, and Kuching via Sarikei. Boats for Kuching and Sarikei dock at two wharves close to the centre of town. Although Sarawak's third largest town, it is still possible to see most of Sibu's sights on foot.

The **Visitors' Information Centre** ⓘ *Ground floor, 32 Jl Tukang Besi (around the corner from the Methodist Church), T084-340980, www.sarawaktourism.com, Mon-Fri 0800-1700, Sat 0800-1250, closed 1st and 3rd Sat of the month*, is very friendly and helpful. As well as information on Sibu they can advise for trips onwards to Kapit and Belaga. ▶▶ *See also Transport, page 127.*

Background
Thanks to the discovery of the Kuala Paloh channel in 1961, Sibu is accessible to boats with a sizeable draft. Sibu is a busy Chinese trading town – the majority of the population came originally from China's Foochow Province – and is the main port on the Rejang (also spelt 'Rajang'). In 1899, Rajah Charles Brooke agreed with Wong Nai Siong, a Chinese scholar from Fukien, to allow settlers to Sibu. Brooke had reportedly been impressed with the industriousness of the Chinese: he saw the women toiling in the paddy fields from dawn to dusk and commented to an aide: "If the women work like that, what on earth must the men be like?"

The Kuching administration provided these early agricultural pioneers with temporary housing on arrival, a steamer between Sibu and Kuching, rice rations for the first year and tuition in Malay and Iban. The town grew rapidly (its expansion is documented in a photographic exhibition in the Civic Centre) but was razed to the ground in the great fire of 1828. The first shophouses to be constructed after the fire are the three-storey ones still standing on Jalan Channel. At the beginning of the 20th century, Sibu became the springboard for Foochow migration to the rest of Sarawak. Today it is an industrial and trading centre for timber, pepper and rubber, and home to some of Sarawak's wealthiest families, mostly timber *towkays* (merchants).

Sights
The old trading port has now been graced with a pagoda, a couple of big hotels and a smart esplanade. The 1929 **shophouses** along the river are virtually all that remains of the old town. The seven-storey **pagoda**, adjacent to Tua Pek Kong Temple, cost RM1.5 million to build; there are good views over the town from the top, you'll need to ask for the key. The pagoda and temple are well worth visiting for the caretaker, Tan Teck Chiang, alone. Chiang speaks great English and gives impromptu animated lectures filled with unique interpretations and humour on the temple, Chinese culture

Sarawak Sibu, Kapit & Belaga

118 and Taoism. Just turn up and ask for Chiang. In the **Sibu Civic Centre** ⓘ *2.5 km out of town on Jl Tun Abang Haji Openg, Tue-Sun 1030-1730; take Sungei Merah bus No 4 from the bus terminal and ask for the Civic Centre.* There is an exhibition of old photographs of Sibu and a mediocre tribal display. This serves as Sibu's municipal museum. Five aerial photographs of the town, taken every five years or so since 1947, chart the town's explosive growth.

Kapit ⬤⬤⬤▲⬤⬤ ⇢ *pp123-128. Colour map 1, C4. Population: 100,000.*

Kapit, which means 'twin' in local dialect, is the capital of Sarawak's Seventh Division, through which flows the Rejang River and its main tributaries, the Batang Balleh, Batang Katibas, Batang Balui and Sungai Belaga. In a treaty with the Sultan of Brunei, Rajah James Brooke acquired the Rejang Basin for Sarawak in 1853. Kapit is the last big town on the Rejang and styles itself as the gateway to 'the heart of Borneo' – after Redmond O'Hanlon's book (*Into the Heart of Borneo*) which describes his adventure up the Batang Balleh in the 1980s. Kapit is full of people who claim to be characters in this book.

The main sights in the town are Fort Sylvia and the Kapit Museum but, like O'Hanlon and his journalist companion James Fenton, most visitors coming to Belaga venture into the interior to explore the upper Rejang and its tributaries, where there

Sibu

Sleeping	Li Hua 7	Ria 12
Eden Inn 1	Mandarin 8	Sarawak 13
Emas 4	New World 9	Sentosa Inn 14
Garden 5	Paramount 18	Tanahmas 15
Hoover House 17	Phoenix 10	Villa 16
Kingwood 6	Premier 11	

0 metres 100
0 yards 100

are many Iban and Orang Ulu longhouses. Maps of the Kapit Division and other parts of Sarawak are avilable from the **Land Survey Department** ① *Jl Beletik on Jl Airport*. Permits for upriver trips are available from the **Residents' Office** ① *1st floor State Government Complex (opposite the lily pond), T084-796963/796445, Mon-Fri 0800-1200, 1400-1600*. Tourists going to Baleh or Upper Rejang areas must sign a form saying they fully understand they are travelling at their own risk.

Background

There are only a few tens of kilometres of metalled road in and around Kapit, but the little town has a disproportionate number of cars. It is a trading centre for the tribespeople upriver and has grown enormously in recent years with the expansion of the logging industry upstream. Logs come in two varieties – 'floaters' and 'sinkers'. Floaters are pulled downstream by tugs in huge chevron formations. Sinkers – like *belian* (ironwood) – are transported in the Chinese-owned dry bulk carriers which line up along the wharves at Kapit. When the river is high these timber ships are able to go upstream, past the Pelagus Rapids. The Rejang at Kapit is normally 500 m wide and, in the dry season, the riverbank slopes steeply down to the water. When it floods, however, the water level rises more than 10 m, as is testified by the high-water marks on Fort Sylvia.

Sarawak Sibu, Kapit & Belaga

Sights

Fort Sylvia near the wharves was built of *belian* by Rajah Charles Brooke in 1880, and is now occupied by government offices. It was originally called Kapit Fort but was renamed in 1925 after Rajah Vyner Brooke's wife. Most of the forts built during this time were designed to prevent the Orang Ulu going downriver; Fort Sylvia was built to stop the belligerent Iban headhunters from attacking Kenyah and Kayan settlements upstream.

The other main sight is the **Kapit Museum** ① *Mon-Fri 0900-1200, 1400-1600, Sat and Sun 0900-1200 (if closed at these times search for the curator to open it), all exhibits are labelled in English*. The museum was enlarged in the 1990s, and moved to Fort Sylvia. It has exhibits on Rejang tribes and the local economy. Set up by the Sarawak Museum in Kuching, it includes a section of an Iban longhouse and several Iban artefacts including a wooden hornbill. The Orang Ulu section has a reconstruction of a longhouse and a mural painted by local tribespeople. An Orang Ulu *salong* (burial hut), totem pole and other woodcarvings are also on display. The museum also has representative exhibits from the small Malay community and the Chinese. Hokkien traders settled at Kapit and Belaga and traded salt, sugar and

Rejang River

Eating ❶
Blue Splendour **4**
Esplanade Seafood
  & Café **5**
New Capital **3**
Metropol **1**
Rex Food Court **6**
Sri Meranti **2**

ceramics for pepper, rotan and rubber; they were followed by Foochow traders. Appropriately, the Chinese exhibit is a shop. In addition, there are also displays on the natural history of the upper Rejang and modern industries such as mining, logging and tourism.

Kapit has a particularly colourful daily **market** in the centre of town. Tribeswomen bring in fruit, vegetables and animals to sell; it is quite normal to see everything from turtles, frogs, birds and catfish to monkeys, wild boar and even pangolin and pythons.

Pelagus Rapids

Forty-five minutes upstream from Kapit on the Rejang River, this 2.5-km-long series of cataracts and whirlpools is the result of a sudden drop in the riverbed, caused by a geological fault-line. Express boats can make it up the Pelagus to Belaga in the wet season (September-April), but the rapids are still regarded with some trepidation by the pilots. When the water is low (May-August), they can only be negotiated by the smallest longboats. There are seven rapids in total, each with local names such as 'The Python', 'The Knife' and one, more ominously, called 'The Grave'.

Longhouses

ⓘ *To go upriver beyond Kapit it is necessary to get a permit (no charge) from the offices in the State Government Complex; the permit is valid for travel up the Rejang as far as Belaga and for an unspecified distance up the Balleh. for upriver trips beyond Belaga another permit must be obtained there; however, these trips tend to be expensive and dangerous.*

Some longhouses are accessible by road and several others are within an hour's longboat ride from town. In Kapit you are likely to be invited to visit one of these. Visitors are strongly advised not to visit a longhouse without an invitation, ideally from someone who lives in it. As a general rule, the further from town a longhouse is, the more likely it is to conform with the image of what a traditional longhouse should be like. That said, there are some beautiful traditional longhouses nearby, mainly Iban. One of the most accessible, for example, is **Rumah Seligi**, about 30 minutes' drive from Kapit. Cars or vans can be hired by the half-day. Only a handful of longhouses IS more than 500 m from the riverbanks of the Rejang and its tributaries. Most longhouses still practise shifting cultivation; rice is the main crop but under government aid programmes many are now growing cash crops such as

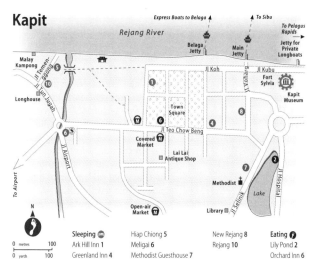

Kapit

Build and be (Bakun) Dammed: an ecological time bomb

The Bakun Dam Scheme, upriver from Belaga on the upper Rejang and 400 km east of Kuching, has had more twists and turns than the river on which it may be built.

The RM9.12 billion project, one of the largest in Southeast Asia, will flood a tract of virgin rainforest that supports at least 43 species of endangered mammals and birds. It will also displace thousands of longhouse-dwelling tribespeople.

The dam is going to be twice the height of the Aswan Dam in Egypt and will flood 69,000 ha – an area bigger than Singapore. Environmentalists say it will be an ecological time bomb in the heart of Borneo.

The project has been on and off the books countless times. In 1990 it was scrapped for environmental reasons, but was back on again in 1993. Again, in late 1997, in the midst of Malaysia's economic crisis, when money was scarce, it was shelved only to be restarted in 2001. In 2004, with the government struggling to find buyers for the dam's electricity, it was rumoured that the project would again be scrapped or postponed. But Prime Minister Badawi says he is determined to see the project through, although its original completion date of 2003 has been pushed back to 2007, a date which observers say is also unlikely to be met. Even during the hiatus preparations for the eventual flooding went on. Thousands of locals were moved from their villages and jungle longhouses and rehoused elsewhere.

The plan is for Bakun to generate 2400 MW of electricity. The power will be consumed within Sabah and Sarawak, and possibly Brunei and Kalimantan, and will involve the construction of 800 km of high-voltage power lines. Plans for an undersea cable more than 600 km long have been shelved. The cable was to pipe power to Peninsular Malaysia where energy needs are increasing, unlike Borneo where there does not seem to be the growth in demand to warrant the dam's construction.

Roads need to be carved through dense jungle to bring building materials and engineering equipment to the remote site above the Bakun Rapids. Malaysian lobby groups such as the Environmental Protection Society predict the project will cause severe soil erosion in an area already suffering from the effects of logging. In the early 1990s the river water was clear and fish abundant; now the river is a muddy brown and water levels fluctuate wildly. Nor is the project a long-term one: even the government admits its productive life is likely to be in the region of 25 years before it silts up. Friends of the Earth Malaysia say: "This project is going to have a tremendous effect on the lives of natives, plants and animals and on the biodiversity of the pristine forests where it is going to be built".

The local tribespeople, whose ancestors battled for decades against the White Rajahs, have, it seems, finally met their match, in Malaysia's relentless thrust towards modernity. See www.irn.org/programs/bakun, homepage of the International Rivers Network – for more information on the dam.

cocoa. Longhouses are also referred to as *Uma* (*Sumah*) and the name of the headman, ie Long Segaham is known locally as *Uma Lasah* (Lasah being the chief).

Longhouses between Kapit and Belaga are accessible by the normal passenger boats, but these boats only go as far as Sungai Bena on the Balleh River (2½ hours).

To go further upriver it is necessary to take a tour or organize your own guides and boatmen. The sort of trip taken by Redmond O'Hanlon and James Fenton (as described in O'Hanlon's book *Into the Heart of Borneo*) would cost more than RM1500 a head. ⏵ *For further information, see Activities and tours, page 126.*

The vast majority of the population, about 68%, in Sarawak's Seventh Division is Iban. They inhabit the Rejang up to and a little beyond Kapit, as well as the lower reaches of the Balleh and its tributaries. The Iban people are traditionally the most hospitable to visitors but, as a result, their longhouses are the most frequently visited by tourists. Malays and Chinese account for 3.4% and 7% of the population respectively. The Orang Ulu live further upriver; the main tribes are the Kayan and the Kenyah (12%) and a long list of sub-groups such as the Kejaman, Beketan, Sekapan, Lahanan, Seping, and Tanjong. In addition there are the nomadic and semi-nomadic Penan, Punan and Ukit. Many tribal people are employed in the logging industry and, with their paid jobs, have brought the trappings of modernity to even the remotest longhouses.

Rumah Tuan Lepong Balleh Only enter this longhouse with the local policeman, Selvat Anu, who lives there; ask for him at Kapit Police Station. During the day Selvat and some members of the longhouse can take visitors on various adventure tours: river trips, visiting longhouses, jungle treks, fishing, pig-hunting, camping in the jungle, trips up to logging areas, swimming in rivers, mountain trekking. Selvat is very knowledgeable and has good relations with the longhouse communities. Visitors can eat with the family and occasionally have the chance to experience a traditional Iban ceremony. ⏵ *See Sleeping, page 123.*

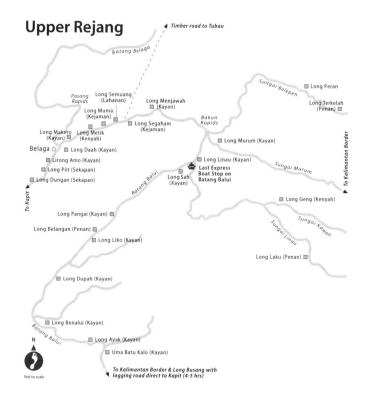

Upper Rejang

Belaga ⬤🍴🅿️🔺🅱️🅲 ▸▸ *pp123-128. Colour map 1, C5.*

This is the archetypal sleepy little town; most people while away their lifetime in coffee shops. They are the best places to watch life go by, and there are always interesting visitors in town, from itinerant wild-honey collectors from Kalimantan to Orang Ulu who have brought their jungle produce downriver to the Belaga bazaar, or those who are heading to the metropolis of Kapit for medical treatment. At night, when the neon lights flicker on, Belaga's coffee shops are invaded by thousands of cicadas, beetles and moths.

A few Chinese traders set up shop in Belaga in the early 1900s, and traded with the tribespeople upriver, supplying essentials such as kerosene, cooking oil and shotgun cartridges. The Orang Ulu brought their beadwork and mats as well as jungle produce such as beeswax, ebony, *gutta-percha* (rubbery tree gum) and, most prized of all, bezoar stones. These are gall-stones found in certain monkeys (the wah-wahs, jelu-merahs and jelu-jankits) and porcupines. To the Chinese, they have much the same properties as rhinoceros horn (mainly aphrodisiacal) and, even today, they are exported from Sarawak to Singapore where they fetch S$300 per kilogram.

Belaga serves as a small government administration centre for the remoter parts of the Seventh Division as it is the last settlement of any size as you venture up the Rejang. It is also a good place to arrange visits to the Kayan and Kenyah longhouses on the Linnau River. There is a very pretty **Malay kampong** (Kampong Bharu) along the esplanade downriver from the Belaga Bazaar. The **Kejaman burial pole** on display outside the Sarawak Museum in Kuching was brought from the Belaga area in 1902.

The **District Office** (for upriver permits) is on the far side of the basketball courts.

Upriver from Belaga

ⓘ *To go upriver beyond Belaga it is necessary to obtain a permit from the Residents' Office, T084-321963, and permission from the police station.*

When the river is high, express boats go upstream as far as **Rumah Belor** on the Batang Balui, but for the purpose of visiting longhouses in the Belaga area, it is best to hire a boat in Belaga. Many of the longhouses around Belaga are quite modern, although several of the Kenyah and Kayan settlements have beautifully carved wooden *salongs* (tombstones) nearby. All the longhouses beyond Belaga are Orang Ulu. Even longhouses which would appear appear very remote (such as Long Busang) are now connected by logging roads from Kapit, only four hours' drive away. To get well off the beaten track, into Penan country, it is possible to organize treks from Belaga towards the Kalimantan border, staying in longhouses en route.

About 2 km up the Batang Belaga from Belaga are the **Pasang Rapids** (hire a boat from Belaga), which are certainly the biggest in Sarawak. It appears that no one has purposely tried to shoot them as they are too dangerous. Boats can get reasonably close, however, and in the dry season it is possible to climb up to a picnic area overlooking the white water.

🛏️ Sleeping

Sibu *p117, map p118*

Cheaper hotels tend to be around the night-market in Chinatown but there is also a selection within walking distance of the jetty.

A Kingwood, 12 Lorong Lanang 4, T084-335888, kingwood@tm.net.my. Largest hotel in Sibu with 168 rooms, more expensive ones have views of the Rejang River. All rooms with a/c, TV, minibar. Riverfront Cafe, Chinese restaurant, pool, health centre.

A Paramount, 3 Lorong 9A, Jl Kampong Dato, T084-331122, paramounthtlrsv@myjaring.net. Sibu's newest high-end hotel a little bit out of town on the western edge facing the river. A/c, TV, kettle and other 2-star room amenities, but little atmosphere.

A **Premier**, Jl Kampong Nyabor, T084-323222, F084-323399. Restaurant, clean rooms with a/c, TV, own bath, some with river view. Helpful staff, adjoins the Sarawak House Shopping Centre, discounts often available. Recommended.

A **Tanahmas**, Jl Kampong Nyabor, T084-333188, www.tanahmas.com.my. A/c, very high-standard restaurant, well-appointed modern hotel with swimming pool, **Blowpipe Lounge bar** and conference facilities. Recommended.

B **Garden**, 1 Jl Hua Ping, T084-317888, F084-330999. A/c, restaurant, well-kept and efficiently run with a good central location and a serviceable coffee shop.

B **Li Hua**, Long Bridge Commercial Centre, T084-324000, F084-326272. Slightly out of town, but located along the river. TV, a/c, restaurant, coffee house and roof-top swimming pool. Good value.

C **Phoenix**, 1 & 3 Jl Kai Peng (off Jl Kampong Nyabor), T084-313877, F084-320392. TV, a/c. A very well-run hotel with spacious rooms and decent bathrooms.

C **Sarawak**, 34 Jl Cross, T084-333455, F084-320536. A/c, attached bathroom, TV. Centrally located and a well-furnished place, good value.

C-D **Eden Inn**, 1 Jl Lanang, T084-337277. Opposite the Sacred Heart Catholic Church. Massive rooms in a big solid building. TV and a/c make this place excellent value. Recommended.

C-D **Sentosa Inn**, 12 Jl Pulau, T084-349875, F084-311706. A/c, TV, run of the mill but clean and quiet. Military-style beds but nice extras like toilet paper, towel and soap.

D **Emas**, 3A Foochow Lane, T084-310877, F320848. Some a/c, clean.

D **Hoover House**, Methodist Church, Jl Pulau, T084-332491 or call Tony T016 869 2491. 6 rooms attached to the Methodist Church with attached bathroom. Must book ahead as almost always full. Safe and recommended.

D **Mandarin**, 183 Jl Kampong Nyabor, T084-339177, F084-333425. A/c, standard rooms, cheap.

D **New World**, 1 Jl Wong Nai Siong, T084-310311. A/c, clean rooms with attached bathrooms.

D **Ria**, 21 Jl Channel, T084-326622. A/c, reasonable value.

D **Villa**, 2-4 Lebuh Central, T084-337833. Good location next to travel agencies. Threadbare rooms, a little shabby, but clean and cheap.

Kapit *p118, map p120*
All hotels are within walking distance of the wharf.

B **Greenland Inn**, 463 Jl Teo Chow Beng, T084-796388, F084-797989. A/c, well-maintained small hotel with good rooms. Although it charges an inflated rate for what is offered, it is comfortably the smartest hotel in town. Recommended.

B-C **New Rejang Hotel**, clean rooms in a modern mid-range hotel. Rooms with a/c, desk and satellite TV, bathroom with fantastic showers. This is where you can find Joshua Muda, who can help arrange longhouse tours.

C **Meligai**, 334 Jl Airport, T084-796817. Full range of accommodation from VIP suite to dingy standard rooms, has some of the trappings of a city hotel but rooms are generally poor. Also home to a cheap restaurant and the **Meligai** pub.

D **Ark Hill Inn**, near Town Square, T084-796168, F084-796337. A/c, bathroom, friendly, clean rooms. It is also situated on the river and there are great views from some of the rooms. Recommended.

D **Hiap Chiong**, 33 Jl Temenggong Jugah, T084-796314. Some a/c, no attached bath, top floor best bet.

D **Rejang**, 28 New Bazaar, T084-796709. Some a/c, basic but clean – if you can afford the extra cash its slightly newer sister hotel is a better option.

E **Methodist Guesthouse**, Jl Selinik. Sometimes budget rooms available here.

Pelagus Rapids *p120*
A-B **Pelagus Resort**, set on the banks of the Rejang overlooking the rapids,T084-799050, www.theregencyhotel.com.my/pelagus/. 40 longhouse-style rooms, with restaurant, pool, bar and sun-deck, deluxe rooms have a/c, otherwise there are fans. Trips organized from resort to longhouses, nature treks and river safaris, whitewater rafting on the rapids. Regular express boats pass through the rapids upstream.

Longhouses *p120*
D Rumah Tuan Lepong Balleh You can stay in this longhouse, RM30 inclusive of meals, generator until 2300, basic. It is about 1 hr's drive from Kapit; take a minibus and ask for 'Selvat and Friends Traditional Hostel and Longhouse'.

Belaga *p123*
C-D Belaga Hotel, 14 Belaga Bazaar, T086-461244. Some a/c, restaurant, no hot water, particularly friendly proprietor, good coffee shop downstairs, in-house video and cicadas. Best option.
D Bee Lian Hotel, 11 Belaga Bazaar, T086-461439. A/c, rooms are fine, 9 rooms.
D Belaga Budget Hotel, 4 Belaga Bazaar (upstairs from **MAS** office), T086-461512. Just 4 rooms in this place with fan or a/c. Restaurant and internet.

⦿ Eating

Sibu *p117, map p118*
Chinese
❤❤ Jhong Kuo, 13 Jl Wong Nai Siong, Foochow.
❤❤ New Capital, 46 Jl Kampong Nyabor. You can tell this place is something fancy in Sibu with its pink tablecloths, lazy susans and faux chandeliers. Extensive menu.
❤❤ Sri Meranti, 1A Jl Hardin. Friendly staff, good seafood, nice sitting-out area with cold beer and tablecloths.
❤ Blue Splendour, 1st floor, 60-62 Jl Kampong Nyabor (opposite **Premier Hotel**), recommended by locals.
❤ Esplanade Seafood & Café, on the Rejang esplanade. Great al fresco dining, with tables facing the river. Open evening only when the place is strung with red lanterns. Excellent Chinese food and Western dishes including fish'n'chips, barbecued meats, burgers and omelettes. Recommended, best in town.
❤ Golden Palace, Tanahmas Hotel, Jl Kampong Nyabor, Cantonese and Sichuan.

International
❤ Peppers Café, Tanahmas Hotel, Jl Kampong Nyabor, Western and local food, curries particularly recommended, popular.

Malay
❤ Metropol, 1st floor, 20 Jl Morshidi Sidek, also serves Melanau curries.
❤ Sheraton, Delta Estate (out of town), Malay (and some Chinese), fish-head curries recommended by locals.

Foodstalls
There is a hawker centre on Jl Market, in the centre of town.
Rex Food Court, 28 Jl Cross, is new and clean.

Kapit *p118, map p120*
Chinese
❤ 99, Jl Pedral, fresh air, clean, local and Chinese food.
❤ Hua Hua, Jl Airport/Jl Court, Chinese food.
❤ Jade Garden, Jl Pedral, local and Chinese food, smart.
❤ Lily Pond, in the middle of the lily pond, off Jl Hospital, pleasant setting, plenty of mosquitoes and an unimaginative menu.
❤ S'ng Ee Ho Restaurant, next to Metox supermarket, happy to cook anything you ask for.

International
❤❤ Orchard Inn, Jl Teo Chow Beng, T084-796325. The most upmarket restaurant in Kapit, food well presented but no better thab the coffee shops, disco from 2200-0100.

Malay
❤ MI, Jl Pedral, Malay Muslim food.

Bakeries and breakfast
Ung Tong Bakery, opposite the market, bakery and café, good continental-style breakfasts – big selection of rolls and good coffee, fresh bread baked twice daily (0600 and 1100). Recommended.
Chuong Hin, opposite the Sibu wharf, best-stocked coffee shop in town.

Foodstalls
Stalls at the top end of the road opposite the market (dead-end road; brightly painted on the outside). Good satay stall on Jl Hospital, next to the lily pond.

Belaga *p123*
Several small, cheap coffee shops along Belaga Bazaar and Main Bazaar.

☉ Shopping

Sibu *p117, map p118*
Handicrafts
Stalls along express-boat wharves at Jl
Channel, mainly selling basketware.
Chop Kion Huat, Jl Market, just behind the
tourist information office has Sarawak
handicrafts including batik, basketware,
T-shirts and carvings.

Markets
Pasar Malam (night market), High St, Jl
Market and Lembangan Lane, Chinatown.
Native market (Lembangan market),
Lembangan River between Jl Mission and
Jl Channel, sells jungle produce.

Pottery
2 potteries at Km 7 and 12 Ulu Oya Rd.

Supermarket
Sarawak House Shopping Complex, Jl
Kampong Nyabor, has Premier Department
Store. There's a good minimarket opposite
Chop Kion Huat handicraft shop on Jl
Market that has fruit juice, wine, spirits,
Marmite and is a good place to stock up on
shampoo and shower gel. There's a book
and magazine shop on the ground floor of
Sarawak House Complex that sells English
magazines.

Kapit *p118, map p120*
Handicrafts
Lai Lai Antique Shop, next road along on
the right from the Putena Jaya, small
selection of woven rugs/sarongs, prices are
high but they are similar to the starting
prices at the longhouses.
Din Chu Café, next to Methodist
Guesthouse, sells antiques and handicrafts.

Belaga *p123*
Handicrafts
Chop Teck Hua, Belaga Bazaar, has an
intriguing selection of tribal jewellery, old
coins, beads, feathers, woodcarvings,
blowpipes, parangs, tattoo boards and
other curios buried under cobwebs and
gekko droppings at the back of the shop;
the owner is noticeably uninformed about
the objects he sells.

▲ Activities and tours

Sibu *p117, map p118*
Golf
Sibu Golf Club, Km 17 Ulu Oya Rd.

Tour operators
Most companies run city tours plus tours
of longhouses, Mulu National Park and
Niah Caves. It is cheaper to organize
upriver trips from Kapit or Belaga than
from Sibu.
Equatorial Tour & Travel Centre, 11
Raminway, T084-331599, F084-330250.
Golden Horse Travel, 62 Jl Kampong
Nyabor, T084-323288, F084-310600.
Metropolitan Travel, 72-74 Jl Market,
T084-313155, F084-345486.
RH Tours & Travel, 11 Jl Mission,
T084-316767, F084-316185.
Sazhong Trading & Travel, 4 Jl Central,
T084-336017, www.geocities.com/sazhong.
Director Frankie Ting can arrange budget
stays for groups in a longhouse in Kapit and
beyond. Recommended.
Sibu Golden Tours, 1D, Lorong Foochow
T084-316861, F084-318606.
Sitt Travel, 147 Ground floor, Jl Kampong
Nyabor, T084-320168.
Travel Consortium, 14 Jl Central,
T084-334455, F084-330589. Good for air
ticketing.
WTK Travel, Ground floor, Bangunan Hung
Ann, 1 Jl Bujang Suntong, T084-319393,
F084-319933.

Kapit *p118, map p120*
Tour operators
Sibu's tourist office and travellers
recommend local expert **Joshua Muda**,
T084-796600, joshuamuda@hotmail.com,
who can usually be found in the **New Rejang
Inn**. He arranges sensitive and authentic
longhouse trips. Some hotels will help
organize trips, or ask at the police station.
There are some guides in Kapit who
overcharge for very unsatisfactory tours.

Belaga *p123*
Tour operators
The **Belaga Hotel** will contact guides for
upriver trips and the district office can also
recommend a handful of experienced

guides. In this part of Sarawak, guides are particularly expensive – sometimes up to RM80 a day, mainly because there are not enough tourists to justify full-time work. It is necessary to hire experienced boatmen too, because of the numerous rapids. Guides recommended by Sarawak Tourism include **John Belakirk**, T086-461512, T013 6331527, johneddie1@hotmail.com; **Hamdani Louis**, T086-461039, T013 8365850, hamdani@hotmail.com. Prices for trips to longhouses upriver vary according to distance and the water level, but are similar to those in Kapit. English is not widely spoken upriver, basic Bahasa comes in handy.

⊖ Transport

Sibu *p117, map p118*
Air
The airport is 25 km north of town. **Sibu airport information centre**, T084-307755. To get to the airport take a taxi (RM26) or Lanang Bus No 3A which leaves every 2 hrs between 0630 and 1600. From the airport to Sibu you need to buy a taxi coupon (RM28). Regular connections with **Kuching** (RM86, around 10 flights a day), **Bintulu** (RM78, 4 flights a day), **Miri** (RM126, up to 4 flights a day), **Belaga** (RM49, 1 flight only on Wed and Sat), **KK** (RM194, 3 flights a day) and **KL** (MAS fly once a day for RM334, as do **AirAsia**, for as little as RM100.

Airline offices MAS, 61 Jl Tunku Osman, T084-326166. AirAsia, Jl Kai Peng.

Boat
All boats leave from the wharf. The time of the next departure is shown by big clockfaces on whiteboards; just buy the ticket at the jetty. There are 2 express boats a day between Sibu and **Kuching**. Sejahtera Pertama (T084-321424) boats leave at 0730. Ekspress Bahagia (T084-319228) leave at 1130. These boats stop off at **Sarekei**. There are regular express boats to **Kapit**, 2-3 hrs, and in the wet season, when the river is high enough, they continue to **Belaga**, 5-6 hrs. If travelling from Sibu through Kapit to Belaga, take one of the early-morning boats (the first

leaves at 0530) which connects all the way through. The last Sibu-Kapit boat departs at around 1300. In the dry season passengers change onto smaller launches to get upriver to Belaga (see below). Some of the Sibu-Kapit boats stop off at **Kanowit** and **Song** on their journey upriver.

Bus
Local Buses leave from Jl Khoo Peng Loong.
Long distance Buses leave from the new Sibu bus terminal at Jl Pahlawan. To get there take a taxi (RM10), or bus No 12 or No 17 from the local bus station. There are 3 main long-distance bus companies: **Biaramas Express**, **Borneo Highway Express** and **Suria Express** which all have routes from Sibu to **Bintulu**, **Miri** and **Kuching**. Regular connections with **Bintulu**, RM20, 3-4 hrs, and Miri RM40, 6-7 hrs, along a surfaced road. First bus leaves around 0630, and last bus at 0100, departures every hr or more. Best to purchase tickets the day before departure – there are ticket offices for the different companies around the jetty or else buy from the bus station. The early-morning buses to Bintulu connect with the buses direct to **Batu Niah** (see Bintulu). There are also daily connections with **Kuching** via **Sarikei** (8 hrs to Kuching, RM40, 2 hrs to Sarikei, RM8). There are around 10 daily departures 0700-2400.

Kapit *p118, map p120*
Boat
All 3 wharves are close together. Regular connections with **Sibu** 0500-1500, 2-3 hrs. **Belaga** is not accessible by large express boats during the dry season. Prices for the express boats start at RM15. In the dry season smaller speed boats sometimes go upriver (RM60-RM100 per person).

Belaga *p123*
At the moment Belaga is comparatively isolated and overland links are poor. During the dry season it is possible to travel by 4WD overland to **Bintulu** (see below), but it is drawn out and expensive. It is likely that road links will improve, particularly with the controversial Bakun Dam project underway

● *For an explanation of the sleeping and eating price codes used in this guide, see inside the*
● *front cover. Other relevant information is found in Essentials, pages 31-35.*

(due to be finished in 2007, see box, page 121). The road between Bakun and Bintulu has been gradually upgraded and is now surfaced along almost its full length. To charter a 4WD for the whole journey to Bintulu costs RM400 for 5 people and the journey takes 5 hrs. The **Belaga Hotel** can help with 4WD or try Peter Ho at **Soon Soon Café**, T086-461085). He has a car that leaves Belaga for Bintulu at 0800, and back to Belaga at 1500.

Air
Connections on Wed and Sat only to **Bintulu** (RM40). The airport can be reached by boat (RM8, 30 mins). Contact **Hasbee Enterprise** (near the jetty), 4 Belaga Bazaar, T086-461240, for help with flights and getting to the airport.
Airline offices MAS, c/o Lau Chun Kiat, Main Bazaar.

Boat
There is a daily boat from **Kapit** leaving early in the morning, which costs RM25-RM30, only in the wet season, the journey takes around 5 hrs. In the dry season speedboats leave from Kapit at RM60 upwards per person. When the river is very low the only option is to fly or drive to Belaga from **Bintulu**.

To **Tabau** and on to **Bintulu**: it is possible to hire a boat from Belaga to Kestima Kem (logging camp) near Rumah Lahanan Laseh (RM60 per person in a group or RM260 for 2-3 people); from there logging trucks go to Tabau on the Kemena River. Logging trucks leave irregularly and you can get stuck in logging camps. It is a 3-hr drive to Tabau; this trip is not possible in the wet season. There are regular express boats from Tabau

to Bintulu (RM12). This is the fastest and cheapest route to Bintulu, but not the most reliable. It is necessary to obtain permission from the Residents' Office and the police station in Belaga to take this route.

❶ Directory

Sibu *p117, map p118*
Banks Standard Chartered, Jl Cross. HSBC, 17 Jl Wong Nai Siong Hock Hua, Jl Pulau. Apart from the banks, cash can be exchanged at good rates at goldsmiths around town. **Internet** PCShop, Sarawak House Complex, Ground floor. Fast connection. **Police** Jl Kampong Nyabor, T084-322222.
Post General Post Office, Jl Kampong Nyabor. **Residents' Office** T084-321963.

Kapit *p118, map p120*
Banks There are 2 banks which will accept traveller's cheques, 1 in the New Bazaar and the other on Jl Airport, but it is easier to change money in Sibu. **Libraries** On the other side of the road from 1st-floor State Government Complex. Good selection of books on history and natural history of Borneo. There's also reportedly internet access here. Mon-Sat 1615-2030, Sat 0900-1115, 1400-1630, closed Sun.

Belaga *p123*
Internet Hasbee Enterprises, 4 Belaga Bazaar (RM6 per hr), open 0700-1900.
Post In the District Office building.

North coast

The north coast of Sarawak is fairly remote with Bintulu, Miri and Marudi being the only significant towns. Close to Bintulu is Similajau National Park where green turtles lay their eggs. Niah National Park boasts famous limestone caves and is home to jungle birds and primates. Miri is the launch pad for river trips into the interior and Marudi is an upriver trading post and the start of a cross-border trek. Bintulu is accessible by air, boat and bus. Miri is accessible by air and bus and Marudi by air and boat. ➤ *For Sleeping, Eating and other listings, see pages 137-143.*

Bintulu ▣🏠🅿🔺🅰🛈 ⤻ pp137-143. Colour map 1, B4.

The word Bintulu is thought to be a corruption of Mentu Ulau, which translates as 'the place for gathering heads'. Bintulu, on the Kemena River, is in the heart of Melinau country and was traditionally a fishing and farming centre until the largest natural gas reserve in Malaysia was discovered offshore in the late 1970s, making Bintulu a boom town overnight. **Shell, Petronas** and **Mitsubishi** moved to the town in force.

Few tourists stay long in Bintulu, although it is the jumping-off point for the Similajau National Park and the Niah Caves. The longhouses on the Kemena River are accessible, but tend not to be as interesting as those further up the Rejang and Baram rivers. The Penan and Kayan tribes are very hospitable and eager to show off their longhouses and traditions to tourists.

For **tourist information**, the **Sarawak Forestry Department** ⓘ www.sarawak. forestry.gov.my, will provide a (rose-tinted) view of it all.You can contact the National Parks Booking Office ⓘ T086-331117, ext 50, F086-331923.

Bintulu

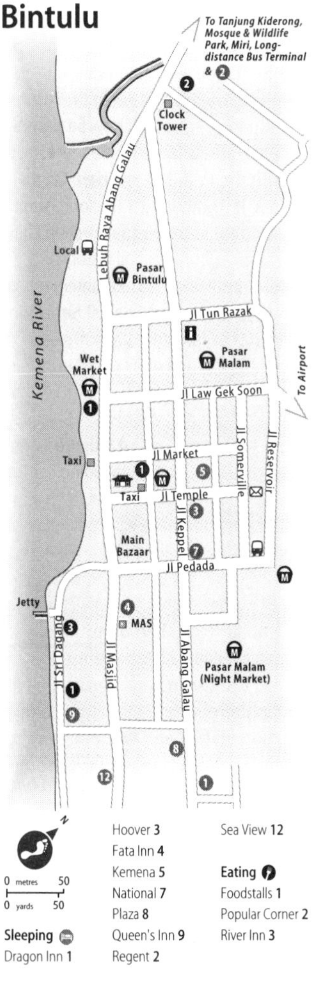

Sarawak North coast (side margin)

Background

The remnants of the old fishing village at Kampong Jepak are on the opposite bank of the Kemena River. During the Brooke era the town was a small administrative centre. The **clock tower** commemorates the meeting of five representatives from the Brooke government and 16 local chieftains, creating Council Negeri, the state legislative body.

The first project to break ground in Bintulu was the RM100-million crude oil terminal at Tanjong Kidurong from which 45,000 barrels of petroleum are exported daily. A deep-water port was built and the liquefied natural gas (LNG) plant started operating in 1982. The abundant supply of natural gas also created investment in related downstream projects. The main industrial area at Tanjong Kidurong is 20 km from Bintulu. The **viewing tower** at Tanjong Kidurong gives a panoramic view of the new-look Bintulu and out to the timber ships on the horizon. They anchor 15 km offshore to avoid port duties and the timber is taken out on barges.

Sights

Bintulu has a modern Moorish-style mosque called the **Masjid Assyakirin**; visitors may be allowed in when it is not prayer time. There is a new, colourful, centrally located Chinese temple called **Tua Pek Kong**. **Pasar Bintulu** is also an

	Hoover 3	Sea View 12
	Fata Inn 4	
	Kemena 5	**Eating** 🍴
	National 7	Foodstalls 1
	Plaza 8	Popular Corner 2
Sleeping 🛏	Queen's Inn 9	River Inn 3
Dragon Inn 1	Regent 2	

0 metres 50
0 yards 50

impressive recently constructed building in the centre of town, built to house a local jungle produce market, foodstalls and limited handicrafts stalls. A landscaped wildlife park, **Taman Tumbina** ⓘ *Mon-Sun 0800-1800, www.bda.gov.my/taman tumbina.htm, RM2*, has been developed on the outskirts of town, on the way to Tanjong Batu. It is a local recreational area and contains a small zoo and a botanic garden (the only one in Sarawak) and a newly opened **Butterfly World**.

Longhouses

Trips to the longhouses on the Kemena River (rarely visited) can be organized from Bintulu. More than 20 Kemena River longhouses can be reached by road or river within 30 minutes of Bintulu. Iban longhouses are the closest; further upriver are the more traditional Kayan and Kenyah longhouses. Overpriced tours are organized by **Similajau Adventure Tours** or hire a boat from the wharf.

Similajau National Park ⬤⬤ ▸▸ *pp137-143. Colour map 1, B4.*

Lying 20 km northeast of Bintulu, Similajau is a coastal park with sandy beaches, broken by rocky headlands. It is Sarawak's most unusually shaped national park being more than 32 km long and only 1.5 km wide. Similajau was demarcated in 1978, but has only really been open to tourists since the construction of decent facilities in 1991. **Pasir Mas** (Golden Sands) is a beautiful 3.5-km-long stretch of coarse beach, to the north of the Likau River, where green turtles come ashore to lay their eggs between July and September. A few kilometres from the Park HQ at **Kuala Likau** is a small coral reef, known as **Batu Mandi**. The area is renowned for birdwatching. Bintulu is not on the main tourist track and so the park is very quiet. Its seclusion makes it a perfect escape.

The beaches are backed by primary rainforest: peat swamp, *kerangas* (heath forest), mixed dipterocarp and mangrove (along Sungai Likau and Sungai Sebubong). There are small rapids on the Sebulong River. Sadly, the rivers, particularly the beautiful **Sungai Likau**, have been polluted by indiscriminate logging activities upstream.

Ins and outs

Permits are available from the **Bintulu Development Authority**. The **information centre** ⓘ *T086-332011*, is at Park HQ, at the mouth of Sungai Likau, across the river from the park. A boat is needed to cross the 5 m of crocodile-infested river. Because the park facilities are actually outside the park boundaries, visitors do not need a permit to stay there. This has led to the 'park' becoming very popular with Bintulites at the weekend.

Flora and fauna

One of the first things visitors notice on arrival at Kuala Likau is the prominent sign advising against swimming in the river, and to watch your feet around the Park HQ area: Similajau is well known for its saltwater crocodiles (*Crocodylus perosus*). It also has 24 resident species of mammal (including gibbons, Hose's langurs, banded langurs, long-tailed macaques, civets, wild boar, porcupines and squirrels) and 185 species of birds (including many migratory species). There are some good coral reefs to the north and marine life includes dolphins, porpoises and turtles. Pitcher plants grow in the *kerangas* forest and along the beach.

Treks

Several longish but not-too-difficult trails have been cut from the Park HQ by park rangers. One path follows undulating terrain, parallel to the coast. It is possible to cut to the left, through the jungle, to the coast, and walk back to Kuala Likau along the beach. The main trail to **Golden Beach** is a three- to four-hour walk crossing several

streams and rivers where estuarine crocodiles are reputed to lurk. Most of these 131
crossings are on 'bridges', which are usually just felled trees with no attempt made to
assist walkers (some 'bridges' have drops of around 5 m) – a good sense of balance is
required. Another enjoyable and rewarding walk is the trail to **Selansur Rapids**,
around 2½ hours in total. Start off by following the trail to Golden Beach; after about
an hour a marked trail leads off into the forest. The walk ends at the rapids where it is
possible to take a dip and cool off.

Niah National Park ●❶● ➤ *pp137-143. Colour map 1, B5.*

Niah's famous caves, tucked into a limestone massif called Gunung Subis, made
world headlines in 1958, when they were confirmed as the most important
archaeological site in Asia. The park is one of the most popular tourist attractions in
Sarawak and more than 15,000 visitors come here every year. The caves were
declared a national historic monument in 1958, but it was not until 1974 that the 3000
ha of jungle surrounding the caves were turned into a national park to protect the area
from logging.

The Niah National Park primarily comprises alluvial or peat swamp as well as
some mixed dipterocarp forest. Long-tailed macaques, hornbills, squirrels, flying
lizards and crocodiles have all been recorded in the park. There are also bat hawks
which provide an impressive spectacle when they home in on one of the millions of
bats which pour out of the caves at dusk.

Ins and outs
Getting there The nearest town to the park is Batu Niah. There are regular bus
connections with Miri (just under two hours), Bintulu (two hours) and Sibu. From Batu
Niah it is around 3 km to the Park HQ and the caves. Either walk through the forest (45
minutes), take a longboat, or catch a taxi. ➤ *For further details, see page 142.*

Getting around From Park HQ there are well-marked trails to the caves. Longboats
can be chartered for upriver trips.

Niah National Park

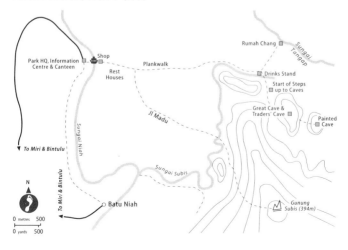

Sarawak North coast

Tourist information Park HQ ① *Pangkalan Lubang next to Sungai Niah, park daily 0800-1700, caves daily 0800-1630, entry RM10, children RM5 (camera RM5, video RM10, professional photography RM200); for more information on the park, contact Deputy Park Warden, Niah National Park, PO Box 81, Miri Post Office, Batu Niah, T085-737454.* Guides are not essential but they provide information and can relate legends about the paintings. Even with a guide, visitors cannot cross the barrier 3 m in front of the cave wall. Guides charge RM35 for groups of up to 20 and can be hired from the Park HQ. Longboats can be hired from Park HQ for upriver trips (maximum of eight people per boat). Visitors are advised to bring a powerful torch for the caves. Walking boots are advisable during the wet season as the plankwalk can get very slippery.

Background

About 40,000 years ago, when the Gulf of Thailand and the Sunda Shelf were still dry ground, and a land bridge connected the Philippines and Borneo, Niah was home to *Homo sapiens*. It was the most exciting archaeological discovery since Java man (*Homo erectus*).

Scientist and explorer A Hart Everett led expeditions to Niah Caves in 1873 and 1879, after which he pronounced that they justified no further work. Seventy-nine years later, Tom Harrisson, ethnologist, explorer, conservationist and curator of the Sarawak Museum, confirmed the most important archaeological find at that time in Southeast Asia at Niah. He unearthed fragments of a 37,000-year-old human skull – the earliest evidence of *Homo sapiens* in the region – at the west mouth of the Niah Great Cave itself. The skull was buried under 2.4 m of guano. His find debunked and prompted a radical reappraisal of popular theories about where modern man's ancestors had sprung from. A wide range of palaeolithic and neolithic tools, pottery, ornaments and beads was also found at the site. Anthropologists believe Niah's caves may have been permanently inhabited until around AD 1400. Harrisson's excavation site, office and house have been left intact in the mouth of the Great Cave. A total of 166 burial sites have been excavated, 38 of which are mesolithic (up to 20,000 years ago) and the remainder neolithic (4000 years ago). Some of the finds are now in the Sarawak Museum in Kuching.

Park Information Centre

① *Mon-Fri 0800-1230, 1400-1615, Sat 0800-1245, Sun 0800-1200.*

At the Park HQ is this centre, with displays on birds' nests and flora and fauna. The exhibition includes the 37,000-year-old human skull which drew world attention to Niah in 1958. Also on display are 35,000-year-old oyster shells, as well as palaeolithic pig bones, monkey bones, turtle shells and crabs which were found littering the cave floor. There are also burial vessels dating from 1600 BC and carved seashell jewellery from around 400 BC.

The caves

To reach the caves, take a longboat across the river from Park HQ at Pangkalan Lubang to the start of the 4-km *belian* (ironwood) plankwalk to the entrance of the **Great Cave**. Take the right fork 1 km from the entrance. The remains of a small kampong, formerly inhabited by birds' nest collectors (see below) and guano collectors, is just before the entrance, in the shelter of overhanging rocks. It is known as **Traders' Cave**. Beware of voracious insects; wear long trousers and plenty of repellent. There are no lights in the Great Cave, so torches are needed.

The **Painted Cave** is beyond the Great Cave. Prehistoric wall paintings – the only ones in Borneo – stretch for about 32 m along the cave wall. Most of the drawings are of dancing human figures and boats, thought to be associated with a death ritual. On the floor of the cave, several 'death-ships' were found with some Chinese stoneware, shell ornaments and ancient glass beads. These death-ships served as coffins and

How to make a swift buck

The Malay name for Niah's Painted Cave is Kain Hitam – or 'black cloth' – because the profitable rights to the birds' nests were traditionally exchanged for bolts of black cloth.

The Chinese have had a taste for swiftlets' nests for well over 1000 years, and the business of collecting them from 60 m up in the cavernous chamber of the Great Cave is as lucrative – and as hazardous – a profession now as it was then. The nests are used to prepare birds' nest soup – blended with chicken stock and rock salt – which is a famous Chinese delicacy, prized as an aphrodisiac and for its supposed remedial properties for asthma and rheumatism.

Birds' nests are one of the most expensive foods in the world: they sell for up to US$500 per kg in Hong Kong, where about 100 tonnes of them (worth US$40 million) are consumed annually. The Chinese communities of North America import 30 tonnes of birds' nests a year. Locally, they fetch RM150-600 per kg, depending on the grade.

Hundreds of thousands – possibly millions – of swiftlets (of the *Collocalia* swift family) live in the caves. Unlike other parts of Southeast Asia, where collectors use rotan ladders to reach the nests (see Gomantong Caves, Sabah, page 224), Niah's collectors scale *belian* (ironwood) poles to heights of more than 60 m. They use bamboo sticks with a scraper attached to one end (called *penyulok*) to pick the nests off the cave roof. The nests are harvested three times each season (the seasons run from August to December and January to March). On the first two occasions, the nests are removed before the

eggs are laid and a third are left until the nestlings are fledged. Nest collectors are now all supposed to have licences but, in reality, no one does. Although the birds' nests are supposed to be protected by the national park in the off-season, wardens turn a blind eye to illegal harvesting – the collectors also know many secret entrances to the caves. Officially, people caught harvesting out of season can be fined RM2000 or sent to jail for a year, but no one's ever caught. Despite being a dangerous operation (there are usually several fatal accidents at Niah each year), collecting has become so popular that harvesters have to reserve their spot with a lamp. Nest collecting is run on a first-come, first-served basis. Nests of the white-nest swiftlets and the black-nest swiftlets are collected – the nests of the mossy-nest and white-bellied swiftlets require too much effort to clean. The nests are built by the male swiftlets using a glutinous substance produced by the salivary glands under the tongue which is regurgitated in long threads; the saliva sets like cement producing a rounded cup which sticks to the cave wall. In the swifts' nest market, price is dictated by colour: the best are the white nests which are without any plant material or feathers. Most of the uncleaned nests are bought up by middle-men, agents of traders in Kuching, but locals at Batu Niah also do some of the cleaning. The nests are first soaked in water for about three hours and, when softened, feathers and dirt are laboriously removed with tweezers. The 'cakes' of nests are dried over-night: if left in the sun they turn yellow.

! Niah's guano collectors: scraping the bottom

Eight bat species live in the Niah Caves, some are quite common such as the horseshoe bat and fruit bats. Other more exotic varieties include the bearded tomb bat, Cantor's roundleaf horseshoe bat and the lesser bent-winged bat.

The ammonia-stench of bat guano permeates the humid air. People began collecting guano in 1929 and it is used as a fertilizer and to prevent pepper vines from rotting. Guano collectors pay a licence fee for the privilege of sweeping up *tahi sapu* (fresh guano) and digging up *tahi timbang* (mature guano) which they sell to the Bat Guano Cooperative at the end of the plankwalk.

have been carbon-dated to between AD 1 and AD 780. By around AD 700 there is thought to have been a flourishing community based in the caves, trading hornbill ivory and birds' nests with the Chinese in exchange for porcelain and beads. But then it seems the caves were suddenly deserted in about 1400. In Penan folklore there are references to 'the ancestors who lived in the big caves' and tribal elders are said to be able to recall funeral rites using death boats similar to those found at Niah.

Treks

A lowland trail called **Jalan Madu** (Honey Road), traverses the peat swamp forest and ascends Gunung Subis; it is not well marked. Return trips need a full day. The trail leads off the plankwalk to the right, about 1 km from Pangkalan Lubang (Park HQ). The left fork on the plankwalk, before the gate to the caves, goes to an Iban longhouse, Rumah Chang (40 minutes' walk), where cold drinks can be bought.

Miri and the Baram River ⬤🏵🔘🔺🏢🌑 » *pp137-143.*
Colour map 1, B5.

Miri is the starting point for adventurous trips up the Barani River to Marudi, Bario and the Kelabit Highlands. Also accessible from Miri and Marudi is the incomparable Gunung Mulu National Park with the biggest limestone cave system in the world and one of the richest assemblages of plants and animals. The capital of Sarawak's Fourth Division is a busy, prosperous town, with more than half its population Chinese. One new project is a waterfront development with a marina – there is a pleasant walk on the peninsula here across the Miri River, and some good fishing.

Ins and outs

Tourist information Tourist Information Centre ① *Jl Malay (next to bus station and just across from the Park Hotel), T085-434181 (accommodation booking, T085-434184), www.sarawaktourism.com, Mon-Fri 0800-1800, Sat 0800-1600 (closed 1st and 3rd Sat of each month), Sun 0900-1500.*

Permits are now only required for travel to Bario. Apply at the **Residents' Office** ① *Jl Kwantung, T085-433202/03,* with passport photocopy. After acquiring a permit, the police station will need to stamp it. If travelling with a tour company, the bureaucracy will be taken care of for you. You can also contact the **National Parks and Wildlife Office** ① *Jl Puchong, T085-432277, F085-431975 (closed every 1st and 3rd Sat of the month).* » *For information on tours see Activities and tours, page 141.*

History

In the latter years of the 19th century, a small trading company set up in Sarawak to import kerosene and export polished shells and pepper. In 1910, when 'earth oil' was first struck on the hill overlooking Miri, the little trading company took the plunge and diversified into the new commodity – making, in the process, Sarawak's first oil town. The company's name was **Shell**. Together with the Malaysian national oil company, **Petronas**, Shell has been responsible for discovering, producing and refining Sarawak's offshore oil deposits. Oil is a key contributor to Malaysia's export earnings and Miri has been a beneficiary of the boom. There is a big refinery at Lutong to the north, which is connected by pipeline with Seria in Brunei. Lutong is the next town on the Miri River and the main headquarters for Shell.

The oil boom in this area began on Canada Hill, behind the town (incidentally, this limestone ridge provides excellent views). **Oil Well No 1** was built by Shell and was the first oil well in Malaysia, spudded on 10 August 1910. The well was still yielding oil 62 years later, but its productivity began to slump. It is estimated that a total of 600,000 barrels were extracted from Well No 1 during its operational life. It was shut off in 1972. There are now 624 oil wells in the Miri Field, producing 80 million barrels of oil a year.

Sights

Juxtaposed against Miri's modern boom-town image is **Tamu Muhibba**, the native jungle produce market ① *open 24 hrs*, opposite the **Park Hotel** in a purpose-built concrete structure with pointed roofs on the roundabout connecting Jalan Malay and Jalan Padang. The Orang Ulu come downriver to sell their produce, and a walk around the market provides an illuminating lesson in jungle nutrition. Colourful characters run impromptu stalls from rattan mats, selling yellow cucumbers that look like mangoes, mangoes that look like turnips, huge crimson durians, tiny loofah sponges, sackfuls of fragrant Bario rice (brown and white), every shape, size and hue of banana, *tuak* (rice wine) in old Heineken bottles and a menagerie of jungle fauna – including mouse deer, falcons, pangolins and the apparently delicious long-snouted *tupai* (jungle squirrel). There is a large selection of dried and fresh seafood – fish and *bubok* (tiny prawns) and big buckets boiling with catfish or stacked with turtles – and there are some handicrafts.

Taman Bulatan is a scenic, centrally located park with foodstalls and boats for hire on the manmade lake.

Around Miri

Hawaii Beach is a pristine, palm-fringed beach, popular for picnics and barbecues. It is a 15-minute taxi ride from Miri (RM15-20) or else take bus No 13 (RM2).

Lambir Hills National Park ① *T085-491030, RM10, children RM5, photography RM5, video camera RM10, professional camera RM200*, mainly consists of a chain of sandstone hills bounded by rugged cliffs, 19 km south of Miri and just visible from the town; the main attractions are the beautiful waterfalls. *Kerangas* (heath forest) covers the higher ridges and hills while the lowland areas are mixed dipterocarp forest. Bornean gibbons, bearded pigs, barking deer and over 100 species of bird have been recorded in the park. There is only one path across a rickety suspension bridge at present, but there are numerous waterfalls and tree towers for birdwatching, and several trails which lead to enticing pools for swimming. The park attracts hordes of day trippers from Miri at weekends. It is possible to stay overnight, see Sleeping, below. The Park HQ is close to the Miri-Niah road, there is an audio-visual room with seating for 30. To get there, take Bintulu or Bakong bus from **Park Hotel** (RM3, 40 minutes) or go by taxi (RM40, 30 minutes).

Loagan Bunut National Park ① *T085-779410*, is located in the upper reaches of the Sungai Bunut and contains Sarawak's largest natural lake at approximately 650

> ♣ The National Parks Office and Visitor Information Centre are closed on the 1st and 3rd Saturday of the month.

Sarawak North coast

ha. The water level in the lake is totally dependent on the water level of the rivers Bunut, Tinjar and Baram. The level is at its lowest in the months of February, May and June and sometimes, for a period of about two to three weeks, the lake becomes an expanse of dry cracked mud. The main cultural attraction at the lake is the traditional method of fishing (*selambau*), which has been retained by the Berawan fishermen. The surrounding area is covered with peat swamp forest. The common larger birds found here are the darters, egrets, herons, bittern, hornbill and kites. Gibbons are also common.

Luconia Island is surrounded by a pristine coral reef. The Luconia Shoals are approximately 150 nautical miles north of Miri and it is only possible to dive here from a live-aboard boat. The reef covers more than 300 sq km and is said to be untouched, with large pelagics from mantas and tuna to black-tip sharks. The best months for diving are between April and August. Some dive sites are easy while others, with strong currents and deep walls, require experience and care. The better-known sites are Hayes Reef (excellent wall diving) and Atken Reef (very good drift diving with large pelagics). Night diving, with many large morays, is reported to be excellent.

✎ Trips can be organized through tour operators in Miri. For details of dive spots, see www.borneo.com.au/diving/

Marudi

Four major tribal groups – Iban, Kelabit, Kayan and Penan – come to Marudi to do business with the Chinese, Indian and Malay merchants. Marudi is the furthest upriver trading post on the Baram and services all the longhouses in the Tutoh, Tinjar

Miri

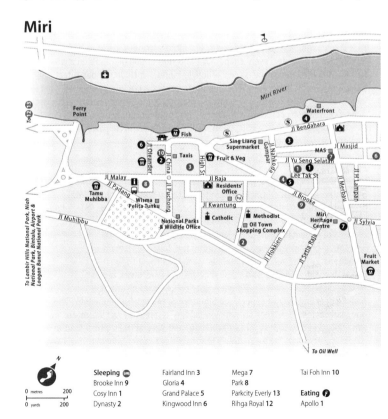

0 metres 200
0 yards 200

Sleeping 🛌
Brooke Inn **9**
Cosy Inn **1**
Dynasty **2**

Fairland Inn **3**
Gloria **4**
Grand Palace **5**
Kingwood Inn **6**

Mega **7**
Park **8**
Parkcity Everly **13**
Rihga Royal **12**

Tai Foh Inn **10**

Eating 🍴
Apollo **1**

and Baram river basins. Most tourists only stop long enough in Marudi to down a cold drink before catching the next express boat upriver; as the trip to Mulu National Park can now be done in a day, not many have to spend the night here. Because it is a major trading post, however, there are a lot of hotels, and the standards are reasonably good.

Fort Hose was built in 1901, when Marudi was still called Claudetown, and has good views of the river. It is named after the last of the Rajah's residents, the anthropologist, geographer and natural historian Dr Charles Hose. The fort is now used as administrative offices. Also of note is the intricately carved **Thaw Peh Kong Chinese Temple** (diagonally opposite the express boat jetty), also known as Siew San Teen. The temple was shipped from China and erected in Sarawak in the early 1900s, although it was probably already 100 years old by the time it began life in its new location.

The **Marudi Kampong Teraja log walk** is normally done from the Brunei end, as the return trek, across the Sarawak/Brunei border, takes a full day, dawn to dusk. It is, however, possible to reach an Iban longhouse inside Brunei without going the full distance to Kampong Teraja. The longhouse is on the Sungai Ridan, about 2½ hours down the jungle trail. The trail starts 3 km from Marudi, on the airport road. There is no customs post on the border; the trail is not an official route into Brunei. Trekkers are advised to take their passports in the unlikely event of being stopped by police, who will probably turn a blind eye. Kampong Teraja in Brunei is the furthest accessible point which can be reached by road from Labi.

Three **longhouses**, Long Seleban, Long Moh and Leo Mato, are accessible by 4WD vehicle from Marudi.

Aseanika **2**
Bilal **3**
Café Bavaria **4**
Gerai Makan **6**
Nyonya's Family Café **5**
Taman Seroja **7**

⊜ Sleeping

Bintulu *p128, map p129*
B Hoover, 92 Jl Keppel, T086-337166. Restaurant, cable TV, smallish rooms, but well-kept place. A great deal better than the slightly cheaper hotels nearby.
B Plaza, Jl Abang Galau, T086-335111, F086-332742. A/c, restaurant, pool, very smart hotel and, compared with other upmarket hotels in Sarawak, excellent value for money. Recommended. Very popular, so worth booking.
B Regent, Kemena Commercial Complex, Jl Tanjong Batu, T086-335511, F086-333770. 47 rooms with a/c, TV, minibar, restaurant, coffee house.
C Fata Inn, Jl Masjid, T086-332998. A/c, TV, bathroom. Reasonable.
C Kemena, 78 Jl Keppel, T086-331533. A/c, refurbished and on a quiet street, good quality room with TV, fridge. Recommended.
C National, 2nd floor, 5 Jl Temple, T086-337222, F086-334304. A/c, clean and well kept. Recommended.
C Queen's Inn, 238 Taman Sri Dagang, T086-338922. This hotel and its sister, the **King's Inn**, are carbon copies from the receptions to the rooms. Both

charge a reasonable rate and have small, clean, carpeted a/c rooms with cramped bathroom. OK for a night.

C Sea View, 254 Jl Masjid, T086-339118. A/c, shower, TV, spacious rooms with views over the river. Good value for Bintulu.

D Dragon Inn, Jl Abang Galau. Some a/c, a reasonable place to stay and the a/c rooms are good value.

Similajau National Park *p130*

To book accommodation contact Similajau National Park, T086-391284.

C National park accommodation, 2 chalets, 2 hostels and a 'mega' hostel – with 27 4-bed rooms. The latter has attractive polished hardwood decor. It can get block-booked. There is 24-hr electricity. The canteen at Park HQ serves basic food. There are picnic shelters at Park HQ.

Niah National Park *p131, map p131*

It's advisable to book accommodation at least 2-3 days in advance. Do this through the National Parks Office, not through the tourist information office. **Niah National Park**, T085-737454, **National Parks Booking Office**, T085-434184, www.forestry.sarawak. gov.my (click on online services, and then booking of national park). Also npbooking@ sarawak.net.gov.my. All accommodation has 24-hr electricity and treated water.

Family chalet, similar to hostel but with cooker and a/c, 2 rooms with 4 beds in each, RM157.50 per chalet. **Hostels** 5 hostels each with 4 rooms of 4 beds each, all rooms have private bathrooms, clean and Western-style with shower, toilet, electric fans, fridges, large sitting area and kitchen. No cooking facilities but kettle, crockery and cutlery can be provided on request. RM42 for 1 room, 4 beds, or RM15.75 for 1 bed. **VIP Resthouse**, RM236.25 per room, a/c, TV, hi-fi.

C Niah Caves Inn, T085-737333, F085-737332. A/c, shower, spacious, fully carpeted rooms. Reasonable value.

C Park View Hotel, T085-737023. Range of comfortable rooms with TV, a/c, bath but no shower. Some rooms face inwards, discounts often available.

D Niah Caves Hotel, T085-737726. Some a/c, shared facilities, 6 rooms (singles, doubles and triples available). Basic, but light and clean, next to the river. A fair budget option.

There are also 4 small hotels in Batu Niah (4 km from Park HQ).

Camping

Tents can be hired from Park HQ (RM8) or from the site (RM5).

Miri and the Baram River

p134, map p136

Most people going to Mulu will have to spend at least a night in Miri. The town has a growing selection of mid-to-upmarket hotels with discounts of 30-40% off quoted prices as a matter of course. Many of the mid-range hotels are around Jl Yu Seng Selatan. Being an oil town, and close to Brunei, Miri has a booming prostitution industry.

A Dynasty, Jl Miri-Pujut, T085-421111, dyhlmyy@ po.jaring.my. A/c, restaurants, pool, health centre, next to Oil Town Shopping Complex.

A Grand Palace, 2 km Jl Miri-Pujut, Pelita Commercial Centre, T085-428888, jrobson@ pc.jaring.my. Imposing peach and pastel building on town outskirts next to Miri Plaza Shopping Centre. 125 comfortable, carpeted rooms with a/c, TV, bathroom, minibar, pool, fitness centre, karaoke, restaurant.

A Mega, Jl Merbau, T085-432432, www.megahotel.net. The tallest and largest hotel in Miri town centre, 228 rooms with a/c, TV, bathroom, Chinese restaurant, coffee house, swimming pool with jacuzzi, health centre, business centre, internet, shopping mall attached.

A Rihga Royal, Jl Temenggong Datuk Oyong Lawai, T085-421121, F085-425057. Japanese- managed hotel on coast south of Miri, 5-star comforts, 225 rooms, all rooms with a/c, minibar, TV, Japanese restaurant, Chinese restaurant and coffee house, pool, tennis, health centre.

A-B Parkcity Everly, Jl Temenggong Oyong Lawai, T085-418888, F085-419999. Formerly **Holiday Inn**, situated 2 km from town centre, at mouth of the Miri River, this 5-storey, modern, white block curves around the South China Sea, very popular with families at weekends (check for special weekend rates. 168 rooms all with a/c, TV, bathroom, minibar, balcony, thick carpets and comfy beds. Sunsets over sea, colourful but noisy river traffic, free-form pool, pleasantly surrounded by plants and palms with swim-up bar in form of traditional boat (popular with kids), jacuzzi and baby pool, sandy area for kids to play. Beach too near town to be clean and sea not safe for swimming but pleasant for sunset strolls. Coffee house, Chinese restaurant, bar and bakery/delicatessen, fitness centre, sauna. Recommended.

B Gloria, 27 Jl Brooke, T085-416699, F085-418866. A/c, restaurant, 42 rooms, better than it looks from outside, although the economy rooms are windowless, comparatively expensive.

B Kingwood Inn, Jl Yu Seng Utara, T085-415888, F085-415009. A/c, restaurant, one of the smaller mid-range places to stay.

C Brooke Inn, 14 Jl Brooke, T085-412881, brookeinn@hotmail.com. Big. Clean carpeted rooms in a lazy motel-style block. Rooms have a/c, TV and big windows. Good value.

C Cosy Inn, 545-547 Jl Yu Seng Selatan, T085-415522, F085-415155. A/c, restaurant. Looks better from the outside than it is, nevertheless better than others in its class.

C Park, Jl Raja, T085-414555, F085-414488. A/c, Chinese restaurant. Ranked a 3-star hotel, although now rather run down, it isn't bad value for money and is convenient for the bus station. The place has shabby charm.

C-D Fairland Inn, Jl Raja, T085-413981. Something of a favourite among Borneo travellers, this place offers tiny dirty rooms with dribbling cold-water showers and a guaranteed bad night of sleep with the warblings and gigglings from the karaoke girls in neighbouring buildings. It does however have a veneer of cleanliness, just don't look underneath the beds. The place appears safe and the owner is used to travellers. Perhaps the best of a bad bunch.

C-D Tai Foh Inn, 19 Jl China, T012-8700530. Arriving by plane, the taxi coupon service will direct you to this establishment if you ask for budget accommodation. While budget it certainly is, whether it fulfils the definition of accommodation is debatable. Dorms and rooms are a mess, with dripping taps, malfunctioning toilets and mattresses long past their expiry date. They do appear, though, to cater for tourists, with TV, bag storage, travel info and laundry. Anyway, it's cheap.

Book accommodation through the **National Parks Booking Office**, T085-434184 for Lambir Hills.

A-C Lambir Hills. If you want to stay overnight there are chalets, 1 unit with 2 rooms and 3 beds, 4 units with 2 rooms and 2 beds, RM100 per room or RM150 per house; a/c chalet, 2 rooms with 3 beds, RM50 per room or RM75 per house.

D Loagan Bunut National Park accommodation. To book accommodation call the **National Parks Booking Office**, T085-434184. There is 1 forest hostel with 4 rooms each with 7 double bunk beds with fan and own toilet. RM15 per bed. The park has a canteen.

Marudi *p136*

A-C Grand, Lot 350 Backlane, T085-755711, F085-775293. Some a/c, large but good hotel, restaurant, 30 clean rooms with cable TV, close to jetty and plenty of information on upriver trips.

B Mount Mulu Hotel, Lot 80 & Lot 90, Marudi Town District, T085-756671, F085-756670. A/c, discounts are available making this place very good value.

C Victoria, Lot 961-963 Jl Merdeka, T085-756067, T085-7556864. All 21 rooms have cable TV.

D Mayland, 347 Mayland Building, T085-755106, F085-755333. A/c, 41 rooms, slightly run down but a good range of accommodation.

◉ Eating

Bintulu *p128, map p129*
Umai, raw fish pickled with lime or the fruit of wild palms (*assam*) and mixed with salted vegetables, onions and chillies is a Melanau speciality. Bintulu is famed for its *belacan* – prawn paste – and in the local dialect, prawns are *urang*, not *udang*.

♥♥ Marco Polo, on the waterfront on the edge of town. Locals recommend pepper steak.

♥ Fook Lu Shou, Plaza Hotel, Jl Abang Galau. Seafood and Chinese cuisine, including birds' nest soup, boiled in rock sugar.

♥ Kemena Coffee House, Western, Malay and Chinese, open 24 hrs.

♥ Popular Corner, opposite hospital. Chinese.

¶ **River Inn**, opposite wharf. Western and local food.
¶ **Sarawak**, 160 Taman Sri Dagang (near Plaza Hotel). Cheap Malay food.

Foodstalls
Pantai Ria, near Tanjong Batu, mainly seafood, only open in the evenings. Recommended. **Chinese stalls** behind the Chinese temple on Jl Temple. Stalls at both markets.

Niah National Park *p131, map p131*
Emergency rations recommended. The **Guano Collectors' Cooperative** shop at the beginning of the plankwalk sells basic food and cold drinks and camera film. There is another basic **shop/restaurant** just outside the park gates. There is a **canteen** at Park HQ, which serves good local food and full Western breakfast, good value, barbecue site provided, the canteen is supposed to be open 0700-2300, but is a little erratic.

Miri and the Baram River
p134, map p136
Chinese
¶ **Apollo**, Lot 394 Jl Yu Seng Selatan (close to Gloria Hotel). Good seafood, very popular.

Indian
¶ **Bilal**, Jl Persiaran Kabor. Excellent curries and rotis, coffee house.

International
¶¶ **Café Bavaria**, Miri Waterfront, T085-4294959. Pricey German dishes, cheaper Malay food. Run by Monikka from Germany, this place is a quaint slice of Bavaria pasted into Miri. Unfortunately, despite being close to the river, there are no views. But it's open-walled which makes it a pleasant place for an iced coffee.
¶¶ **Park View Restaurant** (coffee house of Park Hotel), Jl Malay. Most sophisticated menu in town, jellyfish, good selection of seafood and grill, but gloomy surroundings.
¶ **Bonzer Garden Steak House**, Jl Yu Seng Utara. Local dishes much cheaper than burgers.
¶ **Cosy Garden** (in Mega Hotel block). Pleasant restaurant, but the a/c inhibits any cosiness, limited menu but reasonable prices, steak.

Malay
¶ **Aseanika**, Jl China. Also serves good Indian and Indonesian food.
¶ **Nabila's**, 1st floor, 441 DUBS Building, Jl Bendahara. Also serves Indonesian and Oriental, curries, good *rendang*.
¶ **Nyonya's Family Café**, 21 Jl Brooke, T085-429727. Cheap Nyonya fare in a traditional-style coffee house with marble-topped tables, curtained dividers and Sarawak noodles. Busy at lunchtimes. Recommended. Closed Sun.

Foodstalls
Gerai Makan, near Chinese temple at end of Jl Oleander, Malay food. **Taman Seroja**, Jl Brooke, Malay food, best in the evenings. **Tamu Muhibba** (Native Market), opposite Park Hotel on roundabout connecting Jl Malay and Jl Padang, best during the day. **Tanjong Seafood stalls**, Tanjung Lobung (south of Miri), best in evening.

Marudi *p136*
There are several coffee shops in town. **Rose Garden**, opposite Alisan Hotel, a/c coffee shop serving mainly Chinese dishes.

O Shopping

Bintulu *p128, map p129*
Handicrafts
Dyang Enterprise, Plaza Hotel, lobby floor, Jl Abang Galau. Rather overpriced because of the Plaza's more upmarket clientele.
Li Hua Plaza, near the Plaza Hotel, in a 4-storey building. The best place for handicrafts.

Miri and the Baram River
p134, map p136
Books
Parksons Department Store, Bintang Plaza; **Pelita Book Centre**, 1st floor, Wisma Pelita Tunku.

Handicrafts
Borneo Arts, Jl Yu Seng Selatan (next to Cosy Inn), daily 0900-2100. T-shirts, handicrafts, wood carvings, pottery, Chinese porcelain, batik, Iban textiles, kris daggers, Dayak warrior swords and shields. **Joy Art and Fashion House**, M floor, Wisma Pelita Tunku. **Longhouse**, 2nd floor, Imperial Mall, the best

in town. Miri's council has recently built a small centre on Jl Brooke (about 15 mins' walk from the local bus station) with space for stalls and a café, and slapped the label **Miri Heritage Centre** on its side. There's a small stage for dance performances (rare) and local artists have space to sell their work including batik, beads, basketry, musical instruments and inevitably some tourist tack. **Morsjaya Commercial Centre**, Jl Miri; **Royal Selangor**, 28F, High St; **Sarawak Arts**, Level 3, Miri Sq Shopping Complex; **Sarawak Handicrafts**, 2nd floor, Soon Hup Centre; **Syarikat Unique Arts and Handicrafts centre**, Lot 2994.

Shopping malls
Boulevard (BSC), Jl Pujut Lutong, Miri's largest shopping complex, food court on the top floor, supermarket, department store and boutiques; **Soon Hup Tower**, next to Mega Hotel with **Parkwell's** supermarket and department store; **Wisma Pelita Tunku**, near bus station, department store.

Supermarkets
Parkson Grand, Bintang Plaza; **Pelita**, Ground floor, Wisma Pelita Tunku, useful for supplies for upriver expeditions; **Sing Liang Supermarket** on Jl Nakhoda Gampar – Chinese store; **Ngiukee**, moving from Pelita to Imperial Mall.

▲ Activities and tours

Bintulu *p128, map p129*
Golf
Tanjong Kidurong, 18-hole course, north of town, by the sea (regular buses from town).

Sports complex
Swimming pool (RM2), tennis, football. To get there, fork right from the Miri road at the Chinese temple, about 1 km from town centre.

Tour operators
Deluxe Travel, 30 Jl Law Gek Soon, T086-331293, F086-334995; **Hunda Travel Services**, 8 Jl Somerville, T086-331339, F086-330445. There are half a dozen other agents in town; **Similajau Travel and Tours**, Plaza Hotel, Jl Abang Galau offers tours around the city, to the Niah caves, longhouses and Similajau National Park.

p134, map p136
Golf
Miri Golf Club, Jl Datuk Patinggi, T085-416787, F085-417848, by the sea. Because this is the only golf course in this area of Sarawak, with a large membership, it is worth phoning beforehand to book a tee-off slot.

Swimming
Public pool off Jl Bintang, close to the Civic Centre, RM1.

Tours operators
Although most tour companies specialize in trips up the Baram River to Mulu National Park, some are much better than others – in terms of facilities and services offered. Every agency in Miri has a Mulu National Park itinerary covering the caves, pinnacles and summits. It is also possible to trek to Bario and Mount Murud, as well as to Limbang from Mulu. Most of the agencies employ experienced guides who will be able to advise on longer, more ambitious treks. The Mulu National Park is one destination where it is usually cheaper to go through a tour company than to try to do it independently. Costs vary considerably according to the number of people in a group. For a 3-day Mulu trip, a single tourist can expect to pay RM500; this drops to RM400 a head for a group of 4 and about RM350 each for a group of 10, all accommodation, food, travel and guide costs included. An 8-day tour of Ulu Baram longhouses would cost RM1800 for 1 person and RM1200 per person in a group of 10. A 20-day trek will cost 2 people (minimum number) around RM2000 each, and a group of 6-10, RM1300 a head. For those who want to visit remote longhouses, tour companies present by far the best option. Tour fees cover 'gifts' and all payments to longhouse headmen for food, accommodation and entertainment.
Borneo Mainland, Jl Merpati, T085-433511, F085-434289. **JJ Tour Travel**, Lot 231, Jl Maju Taman, Jade Centre, T085-418690, F085-413308, ticketing agents. **KKM Travel & Tours**, 236 Jl Maju, T085-417899, F085-414629. **Limbang Travel Service**, 1G Park Arcade (Near Park Hotel), T085-413228, efficient ticketing service. **Seridan Mulu**,

Parkcity Everly Hotel lobby arcade, T085-414300, F085-416066, private accommodation within park, recommended by National Parks Office. Can also do diving trips. **Transworld Travel Service**, 2nd floor Wisma Pelita Tunku, T085-422226, F085-415277. **Tropical Adventure**, Ground floor, **Mega Hotel**, Jl Merbau, T085-19337, F085-414503. Recommended.

⊖ Transport

Bintulu *p128, map p129*
Air
The airport is in the centre of town. Regular connections with **Kuching, Miri, Sibu**. There are also some connections with **Kota Kinabalu**. Twice weekly flights to **Belaga**.
  Airline offices MAS, Jl Masjid, T086-331554.

Boat
Enquire at the wharf for times and prices. Regular connections with **Tabau**, 2½-3 hrs, last boat at 1400 (RM18). Connections with **Belaga**, via logging road, see page 128; this route is popular with people in Belaga as it is much cheaper than going from Sibu.

Bus
There are 2 stations in town. The terminal for local buses is in the centre of town. The long-distance Medan Jaya station is 10 mins by taxi from the centre, on the road towards Miri (RM8). Regular connections with **Miri** (RM18), **Sarikei** (RM32), **Batu Niah** (RM10) and **Sibu** (RM16). There are several bus companies but the main one is the **Syarikat Bas Suria**, T086-334914.

Taxi
For **Miri** and **Sibu**, taxis leave from Jl Masjid. Because of the regular bus services and the poor state of the roads, most taxis are for local use only and chartering them is expensive.

Similaju National Park *p130*
There is no regular bus service to the park. Taxis travel the route (30 mins), Rm 40 Bintulu-Similajau trip, RM 60 for a return trip. Bintulu taxi station, T086-332009. Boats are available from the wharf or arrange through **Similajau Travel and Tours** in Bintulu (see Tour operators, above).

Niah National Park *p131, map p131*
From Batu Niah (near the market) to Park HQ at Pangkalan Lubang, Niah National Park by boat (RM10 per person or if more than 5 people, RM2 per person) or 45 mins' walk.

Bus
Every 2 hrs for a connection with **Miri** (RM10), 2 hrs; 6 buses a day to **Bintulu** and Sibu via Bintulu to Batu Niah.

Taxi
From **Miri** to Park HQ, will only leave when there are 4 passengers. From **Bintulu** to Batu Niah (RM30). RM10 to Park HQ, however the riverboat is far more scenic.

Miri and the Baram River
p134, map p136
Air
Airport information, T085-615433. Regular connections on MAS with **Kuching** (5 flights daily, RM164), **Sibu, Marudi** (RM29, 18-passenger plane), **Bario** (1 flight daily at 0930, usually full, book ahead), **Bintulu** (RM70), **Limbang, Mulu** (RM58, 2 flights daily) and **Labuan**. Also connections with **Kota Kinabalu** (3 direct flights daily, RM118). Both MAS and AirAsia have 3 flights daily to KL. There are no flights between Miri and Brunei. You need to fly first to Kuching or KK.
  Transport to town Taxi coupon from airport into town costs RM14. Bus No 30 and 28 roughly every hr go to the airport. You need to ask the driver to drop you off outside the airport, otherwise you will be dropped off on the highway, requiring a 10-min trek to the terminal.
  Airline offices MAS, 239 Halaman Kabor, off Jl Yu Seng Selatan, T085-414144. AirAsia, T085-438022.

Bus
The new bus terminal at Pujuk Padang Kerbau, Jl Padang is around 4 km from the town centre. A taxi to the terminal should cost around RM10 – watch out for inflated pricing! Or take bus No 33 from outside the tourist centre. Regular connections from early morning to early/mid-afternoon with **Batu Niah** 2-3 hrs, **Bintulu** 4 hrs, **Sibu** 7 hrs, and **Kuching** 13 hrs. There are ticket booths for the long-distance buses next to the Park Hotel.

Regular bus connections with **Kuala Baram** and the express boat upriver to Marudi.; there are also taxis to Kuala Baram, either private or shared. Express boats upriver to **Marudi** from Kuala Baram, 3 hrs. Roughly 1 boat every hr from 0715. Last boat 1430. This is the 1st leg of the journey to Mulu and the interior.

Several departures a day to **Kuala Belait** in **Brunei**, 2 hrs, RM12, via Sungai Tujuh checkpoint, with onward connections to Bandar Seri Begawan. From the checkpoint you need to change buses at Kuala Belait for Seria (B$1) and then onwards to Bandar Seri Begawan (B$6). You can use Singapore dollars in Brunei – at the exchange rate of one to one. Note the last bus from Seria leaves at 1520 which means you need to catch a morning bus from Miri (0700, 0900 or 1030) to make the connection, or you will need to stay the night in Kuala Belait or Seria. Biaramas have a direct service to Brunei's capital which is rumoured to depart Miri at 1000. Travelling by your own means of transport from Miri it is necessary to take the car ferry across the Baram River, then pass through immigration, before another ferry across the Belait River. At weekends and public holidays there are long queues for the ferries as well as at immigration – so be prepared for a long, hot wait. Be warned also that the ferry across the Belait River takes an unscheduled 1-hr break for lunch. Distance itself is nothing – the ferry crossings take no more than 10 mins each and Miri to Kuala Belait is just 27 km. Bus passengers bypass the queues because they board the ferry as foot passengers and then hop on another bus the other side of the river. From Kuala Belait regular connections with Seria, 1 hr and from Seria regular connections with Bandar Seri Begawan (B$1), 1-2 hrs. It takes at least 5 hrs to reach Bandar Seri Begawan.

Car
Car hire Avis, Permaisuri Rd, T085-430222; Lee Brothers, 17 River Rd, T085-410606; Mega, No 3, Lorong 1, Sungai Krokop, T085-431885, fleet of Proton Sagas available, RM120-150 per day.

Taxi
T085-432277.

Marudi *p136*
Air
The airport is 5 km from town. Connections with **Miri** (RM29), **Bario**, **Sibu**.

Boat
These leave from opposite the Chinese temple. Connections with **Kuala Baram**, 8 boats a day from 0700-1500 (RM18); **Tutoh**, for longboats to Long Terawan, 1 boat at 1100 (RM22 express boat or RM32 speed boat); **Long Lama**, for longboats to **Bario**, 1 boat every hr 0730-1400. From Long Terawan the longboat journey takes up to 2 hrs (RM45 per person for group of 5 or more). From Miri to Kuala Baram take Bus No 1 (RM2.50, 1st bus 0530) or a shared taxi (RM22).

Directory

Bintulu *p128, map p129*
Banks Bank Bumiputra and Bank Utama on Jl Somerville; **Standard Chartered**, Jl Keppel. **Post** General Post Office, far side of the airport near the Residents' Office, 2 km from town centre – called Pos Laju.

Miri and the Baram River
p134, map p136
Banks All major banks are represented in Miri. **Immigration Office** Jl Unus, T085-442105. **Internet** Cyberworld, 1st floor Wisma Pelita Tunku (RM3 per hr); **Cyber Corner**, Wisma Pelita Tunku (RM3 per hr); **Planet Café**, 1st floor, Bintang Plaza (RM4 per hr) open 1000-2200 daily. **Medical services** Hospital, opposite Ferry Point, T085-420033. **Police** Police Station, Jl Kingsway, T085-432533. **Post** General Post Office, just off Jl Gartak. **Telephone** Telecom Office, Jl Gartak, daily 0730-2200.

Marudi *p136*
Banks There are 2 local banks with foreign exchange facilities. **Police** Police station, Airport Rd. **Post** Post Office, Airport Rd.

Northern Sarawak

The impressive peak of Gunung Mulu is the centrepiece of the eponymous national park. The luscious jungle, home to orchids and hornbills, also boasts the largest limestone cave system on the planet. The cooler climes of the Kelabit Highlands provide good walking opportunities around Bario. Limbang is frontier country and the start of a cross-border trek. ▸▸ *For Sleeping, Eating, and other listings, see pages 151-153.*

Gunung Mulu National Park ⊜🏊▲🚌

▸▸ *pp151-153. Colour map 1, B6.*

Tucked in behind Brunei, this 52,866-ha park lays claim to **Gunung Mulu**, which at 2376 m is the second highest mountain in Sarawak, and the biggest limestone cave system in the world. In short, Mulu is essentially a huge hollow mountain range, sitting on top of 180-million-year-old rainforest. Its primary jungle contains astonishing biological diversity.

Just outside the national park boundary on the Tutoh River there are rapids which it is possible to shoot; this can be arranged through tour agencies.

Ins and outs

Park essentials RM10 (children RM5), camera RM5, video RM10, professional filming RM200.

Equipment There is a small store at the Park HQ that sells basic necessities; there is also a small shop just outside the park boundary, at Long Pala. A sleeping bag is essential for Gunung Mulu trips; other essential equipment includes good insect repellent, wet weather gear and a powerful torch.

Guides No visitors are permitted to travel in the park without an authorized guide; guides can be arranged from Park HQ or booked in advance from the national parks office in Miri. Most of the Mulu Park guides are very well informed about flora and fauna, geology and tribal customs. Tour agencies organize guides as part of their fee. Guide fees: RM20 per cave (or per day) and an extra RM10 per night. Mulu summit trips, around RM1000 for a group of five (four days, three nights); Melinau Gorge and Pinnacles; minimum RM400 for five people (three days, two nights). Ornithological guides cost an additional RM10 a day. Porterage: max 10 kg and RM30 per day, RM1 for each extra kilogramme. Mulu summit, minimum RM90; Melinau Gorge (Camp 5), minimum RM65. It is usual to tip guides and porters.

‼ *It is illegal to fish at Clearwater, although it is possible to fish anywhere else in park waters with a hook and line.*

Tourist information For up-to-date information on Mulu see www.mulupark.com. For cavers wishing to explore caves not open to the public (those open to visitors are known as 'show' caves) there are designated 'adventure caves' within an hour of Park HQ. Experienced cave guides can be organized from headquarters. The most accessible adventure cave is the one-hour trek following the river course through **Clearwater Cave**. Cavers should bring their own equipment.

Best time to visit It is best to avoid visiting the park during school and public holidays. In December the park is closed to locals, but remains open to tourists.

Background

In Robin Hanbury-Tenison's book *The Rain Forest*, he says of Mulu: "All sense of time and direction is lost." Every scientific expedition that has visited Mulu's forests has encountered plant and animal species unknown to science. In 1990, five years after it was officially opened to the public, the park was handling an average of 400 visitors a month. Numbers have increased markedly since then – the area is now attracting more than 12,000 tourists a year – and as the eco-tourism industry has extended its foothold, local tribespeople have been drawn into confrontation with the authorities. In the early 1990s, a series of sabotage incidents was blamed on the Berawan tribe, who claim the caves and the surrounding jungle are a sacred site.

In 1974, three years after Mulu was gazetted as a national park, the first of a succession of joint expeditions led by the British Royal Geographical Society (RGS) and the Sarawak government began to make the discoveries that put Mulu on the map. In 1980 a cave passage over 50 km long was surveyed for the first time. Since then, a further 137 km of passages have been discovered. Altogether 27 major caves have now been found – speleologists believe they probably represent a tiny fraction of what is actually there. The world's biggest cave, the **Sarawak Chamber**, was not discovered until 1984.

The first attempt on Gunung Mulu was made by Spencer St John, the British consul in Brunei, in 1856 (see also his attempts on Gunung Kinabalu, Sabah, page 207). His efforts were thwarted by "limestone cliffs, dense jungle and sharp pinnacles of rock". Dr Charles Hose, Resident of Marudi, led a 25-day expedition to Gunung Mulu in 1893, but also found his path blocked by 600-m-high cliffs. Nearly 50 years later, in 1932, a Berawan rhinoceros hunter called Tama Nilong guided Edward Shackleton's Oxford University expedition to the summit. One of the young Oxford undergraduates on that expedition was Tom Harrisson, who later made the Niah archaeological discoveries, see page 132. Tama Nilong, the hunter from Long Terawan, had previously reached the main southwest ridge of Mulu while tracking a rhinoceros. The cliffs of the Melinau Gorge rise a sheer 600 m, and are the highest limestone rock faces between north Thailand and Papua New Guinea

The limestone massifs of Gunung Api and Gunung Benarat were originally at the same elevation as Gunung Mulu, but their limestone outcrops were more prone to erosion than the Mulu's sandstone. Northwest of the gorge lies a large, undisturbed alluvial plain which is rich in flora and fauna. Penan tribespeople (see page 98) are permitted to maintain their lifestyle of fishing, hunting and gathering in the park. At no small expense, the Malaysian government has encouraged them to settle at a purpose-built longhouse at **Batu Bungan**, just a few minutes upriver from the Park HQ, but its efforts have met with limited success because of the desire of many Penan to maintain their travelling lifestyle. Penan shelters can often be found by river banks.

Reeling from international criticism, the Sarawak state government set aside 66,000 ha of rainforest as what it called 'biosphere', a reserve where indigenous people could practise their traditional lifestyle. Part of this lies within the park. In Baram and Limbang districts, the remaining 300 Penan will have a reserve in which they can continue their nomadic way of life. A further 23,000 ha has reportedly been set aside for 'semi-nomadic' Penan.

In 1961 geologist Dr G Wilford first surveyed Deer Cave and parts of the Cave of the Winds. But Mulu's biggest subterranean secrets were not revealed until the 1980s.

Flora and fauna

In the 1960s and 1970s, botanical expeditions were beginning to shed more light on the Mulu area's flora and fauna: 100 new plant species were discovered between 1960 and 1973 alone. Mulu Park encompasses an area of diverse altitudes and soil types – it includes all the forest types found in Borneo except mangrove. About 20,000 animal species have been recorded in Mulu Park, as well as 3500 plant species and 8000 varieties of fungi (more than 100 of these are endemic to the Mulu area). Mulu's ecological statistics are astounding: it is home to 1500 species of flowering plant, 170 species of orchid and 109 varieties of palm. More than 280 butterfly species have been recorded. Within the park boundaries, 262 species of bird (including all eight varieties of hornbill), 67 mammalian species, 50 species of reptile and 75 amphibian species have been recorded.

Mulu's caves contain an unusual array of flora and fauna too. There are three species of swiftlet, 12 species of bat and nine species of fish, including the cave flying fish (*Nemaaramis everetti*) and blind catfish (*Silurus furnessi*). Cave scorpions (*Chaerilus chapmani*) – which are poisonous but not deadly – are not uncommon. Other subterranean species include albino crabs, huntsman spiders, cave crickets, centipedes and snakes (which dine on swiftlets and bats). These creatures have been described as "living fossils... [which are] isolated survivors of ancient groups long since disappeared from Southeast Asia."

Gunung Mulu

The minimum time to allow for the climb is four days, three nights; tents are not required if you stay at Camps 1 and 2. The main summit route starts from the plankwalk at Park HQ heading towards Deer Cave. The Mulu walkway forks left after about 1 km. From the headquarters it is an easy four- to five-hour trek to Camp 1 at 150 m, where there is a shelter, built by the RGS/Sarawak government expedition in 1978. The second day is a long uphill slog (eight to 10 hours) to Camp 4 (1800 m), where there is also a shelter. Past Camp 3, the trail climbs steeply up Bukit Tumau, which affords good views over the park, and above which the last wild rhinoceros in Sarawak was shot in the mid-1940s. There are many pitcher plants (*Nepenthes lowii*) along this stretch of trail. From Camp 4, known as 'The Summit Camp', the path passes the helicopter pad, from where there are magnificent views of Gunung Benarat, the Melinau Gorge and Gunung Api. The final haul to the summit is steep; there are fixed ropes. Around the summit area, the *Nepenthes muluensis* pitcher plant is common – it is endemic to Mulu. From Camp 4 it takes 1½ hours to reach the summit, and a further seven hours back down the mountain to Camp 1.

❧ The views from the summit are best during April and May.

Equipment Camp 1 has water, as does Camp 4 if it has been raining. Water should be boiled before drinking. It is necessary to bring your own food; in the rainy season it is wise to bring a gas cooking stove. A sleeping bag and waterproofs are also necessary and spare clothes, wrapped in a plastic bag, are a good idea.

Treks from Camp 5

For a three-day trip, a longboat will cost about RM400. It takes two to three hours, depending on the river level, from Park HQ to Kuala Berar; it is then a two- to three-hour trek (8 km) to Camp 5. Visitors to the Camp 5 area are also advised to plan their itinerary carefully as it is necessary to calculate how much food will be required and to carry it up there. There is a basic shelter which can house about 30 people. The camp is next to the Melinau River; river water should be boiled before drinking.

Camp 5 is located in the Melinau Gorge, facing Gunung Benarat, about four to six hours upstream from the Park HQ. From the camp it is possible to trek up the gorge as well as to the Pinnacles on Gunung Api. It is advisable to hire a longboat for the duration of your time at and around Camp 5. The boat has to be abandoned at Kuala Berar, at the confluence of the Melinau and Berar rivers. It is only used for the first and last hours of the trip, but in the event of an emergency, there are no trails leading back to the Park HQ and there are stories of fever-stricken people being stuck in the jungle.

Melinau Gorge

Camp 5 nestles at the end of the gorge, across a fast-flowing section of the Melinau River and opposite the unclimbed 1580-m Gunung Benarat's stark, sheer limestone cliffs. The steep limestone ridges, that lead eventually to Gunung Api, comprise the east wall of the gorge. Heading out from Camp 5, the trail fizzles out after a few minutes. It takes an arduous two to three hours of endless river crossings and scrambles to reach a narrow chute of whitewater, under which is a large, deep and clear jungle pool with a convenient sandbank and plenty of large boulders to perch on. Alfred Russel Wallace's *Troides brookiana* – the majestic Rajah Brooke's birdwing – is particularly common at this little oasis, deep in undisturbed jungle. The walk

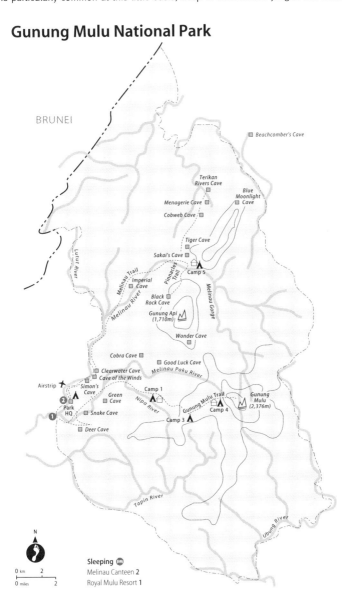

Gunung Mulu National Park

Sleeping 🛏
Melinau Canteen **2**
Royal Mulu Resort **1**

involves criss-crossing through waist-deep, fast-flowing water and over stones that have been smoothed to a high polish over centuries: strong shoes are recommended – as is a walking stick. Only occasionally in the walk upstream is it possible to glimpse the towering 600 m cliffs. Mulu can also be climbed from the south ridge of Melinau Gorge – it is three hours to Camp 1, five hours to Camp 3, a steep four- to five-hour climb to Camp 4, and finally two hours to the top.

The Pinnacles

The Pinnacles are a forest of sharp limestone needles three-quarters of the way up Gunung Api. Some of the pinnacles rise above treetops to heights of 45 m. The trail leaves from Camp 5, at the base of the Melinau Gorge. It is a very steep climb all the way and a maximum time of three to four hours is allowed to reach the pinnacles (1200 m); otherwise you must return. There is no source of water en route. It is not possible to reach Gunung Api from the pinnacles. It is strongly recommended that climbers wear gloves as well as long-sleeved shirts, trousers and strong boots to protect themselves against cuts from the razor-sharp rocks. Explorers on Spenser St John's expedition to Mulu in 1856 were cut to shreds on the pinnacles: "three of our men had already been sent back with severe wounds, whilst several of those left were much injured," he wrote, concluding that it was "the world's most nightmarish surface to travel over".

Gunung Api (Fire Mountain)

The vegetation is so dry at the summit that it is often set ablaze by lightning in the dry season. The story goes that the fires were so big that locals once thought the mountains were volcanoes. Some of the fires could be seen as far away as the Brunei coast. The summit trek takes a minimum of three days. At 1710 m, it is the tallest limestone outcrop in Borneo and, other than Gunung Benarat (on the other side of the gorge), it is probably the most difficult mountain to climb in Borneo. Many attempts to climb it ended in failure; two Berawans from Long Terawan finally made it to the top in 1978, one of them the grandson of Tama Nilong, the rhinoceros-hunter who had climbed Gunung Mulu in 1932. It is impossible to proceed upwards beyond the Pinnacles.

From Camp 5, cross the Melinau River and head down the **Limbang Trail** towards Lubang Cina. Less than 30 minutes down the trail, fork left along a new trail which leads along a ridge to the south of Gunung Benarat. Climbing higher, after about 40 minutes, the trail passes into an area of leached sandy soils called *kerangas* (heath) forest. This little patch of thinner jungle is a tangle of many varieties of pitcher plants.

It is possible to trek from Camp 5 to **Limbang**, although it is easier to do it the other way (see page 150).

Clearwater Cave

This part of the Clearwater System, on a small tributary of the Melinau River, is 107 km long. The cave passage – 75 km of which has been explored – links Clearwater Cave (Gua Ayer Jernih) with the **Cave of the Winds** (Lubang Angin), to the south. It was discovered in 1988. Clearwater is named after the jungle pool at the foot of the steps leading up to the cave mouth, where the longboats moor. Two species of monophytes – single-leafed plants – grow in the sunlight at the mouth of the cave. They only grow on limestone.

This is the longest underground cavity in Southeast Asia and the seventh longest in the world.

A lighting system has been installed down the path to **Young Lady's Cave**, which ends in a 60-m-deep pothole.

On the cave walls are some helictites – coral-like lateral formations – and, even more dramatic, are the photokarsts, tiny needles of rock, all pointing towards the light. These are formed in much the same way as their monstrous cousins, the pinnacles (see above), by vegetation, in this case algae, eating into and eroding the softer rock, leaving sharp points of harder rock which 'grow' at about half a millimetre a year. Inside Clearwater it is possible to hire a rowing boat for RM10 – the river can be followed for about 1.5 km upstream, although the current is strong.

Clearwater can be reached by a 30-minute longboat ride from the Park HQ. Individual travellers must charter a boat for a return trip. Tour agents build the cost of this trip into their package, which works out considerably cheaper.

Deer Cave
ⓘ *An hour's trek along a plank walk from Park HQ.*
This is another of Mulu's record-breakers: it has the world's biggest cave mouth and the biggest cave passage, which is 2.2 km long and 220 m high at its highest point. Before its inclusion in the park, the cave had been a well-known hunting ground for deer attracted to the pools of salty water running off the guano. The silhouettes of some of the cave's limestone formations have been creatively interpreted; notably the profile of Abraham Lincoln. Adam's and Eve's Showers, at the east end of the cave, are hollow stalactites; water pressure increases when it rains. This darker section at the east end of Deer Cave is the preferred habitat of the naked bat. Albino earwigs live on the bats' oily skin and regularly drop off. The cave's east entrance opens onto 'The Garden of Eden' – a luxuriant patch of jungle, which was once part of the cave system until the roof collapsed. This separated Deer Cave and Green Cave, which lies adjacent to the east mouth; it is open only to caving expeditions.

The west end of the cave is home to several million wrinkle-lipped and horseshoe bats. Hundreds of thousands of these bats pour out of the cave at dusk. Bat hawks can often be seen swooping in for spectacular kills. The helipad, about 500 m south of the cave mouth, provides excellent vantage points. VIPs' helicopters, arriving for the show, are said to have disturbed the bats in recent years. From the analysis of the tonnes of saline bat guano, scientists conclude that they make an 80-km dash to the coast for meals of insects washed down with seawater. Cave cockroaches eat the guano, ensuring that the cavern does not become choked with what locals call 'black snow'.

Lang's Cave
Part of the same hollow mountain as Deer Cave, Lang's Cave is less well known but its formations are more beautiful, and it contains impressive curtain stalactites and intricate coral-like helictites. The cave is well lit and protected by bus-stop-style plastic tunnels.

The Sarawak Chamber
Discovered in 1984, this chamber is 600 m long, 450 m wide and 100 m high – big enough, it is said, to accommodate 40 jumbo jets wing-tip to wing-tip and eight nose-to-tail. It is the largest natural chamber in the world. Unfortunately it is not open to the public as it is considered too dangerous.

Bario and the Kelabit Highlands
🛏️🍽️ ⏵ *pp151-153. Colour map 1, B6.*

Bario (Bareo) lies in the Kelabit Highlands, a plateau 1000 m above sea level close to the Kalimantan border (Indonesia). The undulating Bario valley is surrounded by mountains and fed by countless small streams which in turn feed into a maze of irrigation canals.

Ins and outs
Bario is only accessible by air or via a seven-day trek from Marudi. For information on Bario and the Kelabits, www.kelabit.net. The best time to visit the area is between March and October.

The local Kelabits' skill in harnessing water has allowed them to practise wet rice cultivation rather than the more common slash-and-burn hill rice techniques. Fragrant Bario rice is prized in Sarawak and commands a premium in the coastal markets. The Kelabit Highlands' more temperate climate also allows the cultivation of a wide range of fruit and vegetables.

The plateau's near-impregnable ring of mountains effectively cut the Kelabit off from the outside world: it is the only area in Borneo which was never penetrated by Islam. In 1911 the Resident of Baram mounted an expedition which ventured into the mountains to ask the Kelabit to stop raiding the Brooke Government's subjects. It took the expedition 17 days to cross the Tamu Abu mountain range, to the west of Bario. The Kelabit were then brought under the control of the Sarawak government.

The most impressive mountain in the Bario area is the distinctive twin peak of the sheer-faced 2043 m **Bukit Batu Lawi** to the northwest of Bario. The Kelabit traditionally believed the mountain had an evil spirit and so never went near it. Today such superstitions are a thing of the past since locals are mostly evangelical Christians.

In 1945, the plateau was selected as the only possible parachute drop zone in North Borneo not captured by the Japanese. The Allied Special Forces which parachuted into Bario were led by Tom Harrisson, who later became curator of the Sarawak Museum and made the famous archaeological discoveries at Niah Caves (see page 131). His expedition formed an irregular tribal army against the Japanese, which gained control over large areas of North Borneo in the following months.

Treks around Bario

Because of the rugged terrain surrounding the plateau, the area mainly attracts serious mountaineers. There are many trails to the longhouses around the plateau area, however. Treks to Bario can be organized through travel agents in Miri, see page 134. Guides can also be hired in Bario and surrounding longhouses for RM30-40 per day. It is best to go through the Penghulu, Ngiap Ayu, the Kelabit chief. He goes round visiting many of the longhouses in the area once a month. It is recommended that visitors to Bario come equipped with sleeping bags and camping equipment. There are no formal facilities for tourists and provisions should be brought from Miri or Marudi. There are no banks or money changers in Bario.

It is necessary to have a permit to visit the Bario area, obtainable from the Residents' offices in Miri or Marudi.

Several of the surrounding mountains can be climbed from Bario, but they are, without exception, difficult climbs. Even on walks just around the Bario area, guides are essential as trails are poorly marked. The lower ('female') peak of **Bukit Batu Lawi** can be climbed without equipment, but the sheer sided 'male' peak requires proper rock-climbing equipment – it was first scaled in 1986. **Gunung Murudi** (2423 m) is the highest mountain in Sarawak; it is a very tough climb.

Limbang ⬤🖉✳🔺⊖ ➠ *pp151-153. Colour map 1, B6.*

Limbang is the administrative centre for the Fifth Division and was ceded to the Brooke government by the Sultan of Brunei in 1890. The Trusan Valley, to the east of the wedge of Brunei, had been ceded to Sarawak in 1884. Very few tourists reach Limbang or Lawas but they are good stopping-off points for more adventurous routes to **Sabah** and **Brunei**. Limbang is the finger of Sarawak territory which splits Brunei in two. To contact the **Residents' Office** ① *T085-21960*.

Sights

Limbang's **Old Fort** was built in 1897, renovated in 1966, and was used as the administrative centre. During the Brooke era half the ground floor was used as a jail. It is now a centre of religious instruction, Majlis Islam. Limbang is famous for its **Pasar Tamu** every Friday, where jungle and native produce is sold. Limbang also has an attractive small museum, **Muzium Wilayah** ⓘ *400 m south of the centre along Jl Kubu, Tue-Sun 0900-1800*. Housed in a wooden villa, painted beige and white, the museum has a collection of ethnic artefacts from the region, including basketry, musical instruments and weapons. To the right of the museum, a small road climbs the hill to a park with a man-made lake.

To trek to the **Gunung Mulu National Park** (see page 144), take a car south to Medamit; from there hire a longboat upriver to Mulu Madang, an Iban longhouse (three hours, depending on water level). Alternatively, go further upriver to Kuala Terikan (six to seven hours when the water's low, four hours when it's high) where there is a simple zinc-roofed camp. From there take a longboat one hour up the Terikan River to Lubang China, which is the start of a two-hour trek along a well used trail to Camp 5. There is a park rangers' camp about 20 minutes out of Kuala Terikan where it is possible to obtain permits and arrange for a guide to meet you at Camp 5. The longboats are cheaper to hire in the wet season.

Lawas

Lawas District was ceded to Sarawak in 1905. The Limbang River, which cuts through the town, is the main transport route. It is possible to travel from Miri to Bandar Seri Begawan (Brunei) by road, then on to Limbang and Lawas. From Lawas there are direct buses to Kota Kinabalu in Sabah.

● Sleeping

Gunung Mulu National Park
p144, map p147
Park chalets must be booked in advance at the **National Parks and Wildlife Office Forest Department** in Miri or Kuching or through **Borsarmulu Park Management**, T085-424561, www.mulupark.com. Booking fee is RM20 per party (maximum 10 people). Bookings must be confirmed 5 days before visit.
AL Royal Mulu Resort, Sungai Melinau, Muku, Miri, a 20-min (RM5) boat ride downstream from Park HQ, T085-790100, www.royalmuluresort.com. A/c, restaurants, owned by Japan's **Royal Hotel Group Rihga** the resort currently has 188 rooms from chalets to executive suites. The resort has sparked much resentment among local tribespeople. The Berawan claim the resort's land as theirs by customary right.
B-E Park HQ. The park also has its own accommodation at headquarters. Top of the range are the **longhouses (B)** which have attached bathroom, a/c, and 4 single beds, or a twin share. For 4 people sharing, it works out to be RM30 per person. Then, the **Rainforest Rooms (C)** have fans and

attached bathroom, sleeping up to 4 people, working out to be just over RM20 per person. There is also a **hostel (E)** with 18 dorm beds, fan and shared toilet for RM18 per person. At Camp 5, the park has an **open-air hostel (E)** with mats for sleeping and shared bathrooms. There are also simple wooden shelters for sleeping on the summit trail. For both of these, bring your own sleeping bag.
D Melinau Canteen, T085-657884. One of several hostels just outside the park. Privately owned hostel with dorm beds about 5 mins' walk downstream from the Park HQ, on the other bank of the river.

Camping
F Camping is only allowed at the campsite at Park HQ (RM5) – bring your own sleeping bag.

Bario and the Kelabit Highlands *p149*
D De Plateau Lodge. Pretty wooden house, offering forest guides at RM65 per day.
D JR Lodge (Barview Lodge), T085-791038. Well set up for travellers, with airport transfer, restaurant, electricity in the evening, Western toilets, board games, motorbike,

4WD, bike rental and trekking offered. Rooms are simple but cheery.

D Tarawe. A well-run place to stay with a good source of information. Most visitors camp. Recommended.

Limbang *p150*

Limbang has become a sex stop for Bruneians, whose government takes a more hardline attitude to such moral transgressions, and consequently many hotels and guesthouses have a fair share of short-time guests.

B Centre Point Hotel, T085-212922. Newish place with a/c and restaurant which tops Limbang's limited bill of hotels.

B-C Metro, Lot 781, Jl Bangkita, T085-211133, F085-211051. A fairly new addition to Limbang's mid-range accommodation, fewer than 30 rooms, all with a/c, TV, fridge, good-quality beds, small but clean rooms. Recommended.

B-C Muhibbah, Lot T790, Bank St, T085-213705, F085-212153. Located in town centre, has seen better days, but rooms are fairly clean with a/c, TV and bathroom.

B-C National Inn, 62a Jl Buangsiol, T085-212922, F085-212282. Probably the best of the 3 hotels along the river here, comfortable a/c rooms with TV, minibar, higher rates for river view.

Lawas *p151*

A-B Country Park Hotel, Lot 235, Jl Trusan, T085-85522. A/c, restaurant.

C Lawas Federal, 8 Jl Masjid Baru, T085-85115. A/c, restaurant.

D Hup Guan Lodging House, T085-85362. Some a/c, above a pool hall so can be noisy, but the rooms are clean and spacious and reasonable value for money.

❼ Eating

Gunung Mulu National Park
p144, map p147

There are stoves and cooking utensils available and the small store at Park HQ also sells basic supplies. There is a small canteen at Park HQ but the menu is limited and the food rather boring. As an alternative, cross the suspension bridge and walk alongside the road to the first house on the left; down the bank from here is the **Mulu Canteen**, which fronts onto the river (so there is no

sign on the road). There is also the **Melinau Canteen**, just downriver from the Park HQ. There is a small shop with basic supplies at Long Pala. All tour companies with their own accommodation offer food.

Limbang *p150*

♩♩ **Tong Lok**. A/c Chinese restaurant next to National Inn, gruesome pink tablecloths and fluorescent lighting, but good-quality Chinese food.

♩ **Hai Hong**, 1 block south of **Maggie's**. A simple coffee shop – good for breakfast with fried egg and chips on the menu.

♩ **Maggie's Café** on the riverside near National Inn. Chinese coffee shop, pleasant location, tables outside next to river in the evening – braziers set up in evening for good grilled fish on banana leaf. Recommended.

❀ Festivals and events

Limbang *p150*

May The movable **Buffalo Racing Festival** marks the end of the harvesting season.

▲ Activities and tours

Gunung Mulu National Park *p144, map p147*

Visitors are recommended to go through one of the Miri-based travel agents (see page 143). The average cost of a Mulu package (per person) is RM350-400 (4 days/3 nights) or RM500 (6 days/5 nights). Independent travellers will find it more expensive arranging the trip on their own.

Limbang *p150*

Sitt Travel, T085-420567, specializes in treks in this area and is the ticketing agent for Miri tour operators.

❺ Transport

Gunung Mulu National Park
p144, map p147

Within the park Longboats can be chartered privately from Park HQ (maximum 10 people per boat). The cost is calculated on a rather complicated system which includes a rate for the boat, a charge for the engine based on its horsepower, a separate payment for the driver and front-man, and then fuel on top of that. The total cost can be more than RM100. How far these boats can actually get upriver depends on the season. They often have to be hauled over rapids, whatever the time of year.

Air
Daily flights from **Miri** to Mulu, 20 mins. The airstrip is just downriver from Park HQ. Currently 2 flights per day from Miri, and from **Marudi** and **Limbang**. The price of a flight is only marginally more expensive than taking the bus and boat from Miri and is infinitely faster.

Bus/taxi/boat
Bus or taxi from Miri to Marudi express boat jetty near Kuala Baram at mouth of the Baram River (see page 143). Regular express boats from **Kuala Baram** to **Marudi**, 3 hrs (RM18) from 0700 until about 1500. One express boat per day (leaves at 1100) from Marudi to **Long Terawan** on the Tutoh River (tributary of the Baram), via Long Apoh. During the dry season express boats cannot reach Long Terawan and terminate at Long Panai on the Tutoh River, where longboats continue to Long Terawan (RM20). Longboats leave Long Terawan for Mulu Park HQ: this used to be regular and comparatively cheap; now that most people travel to Mulu by air, longboats are less frequent and sometimes need to be privately chartered – an expensive business. Mulu Park HQ is 1½ hrs up the Melinau River (a tributary of the Tutoh) (RM45). As you approach the park from Long Terawan the Tutoh River narrows and becomes shallower; there are 14 rapids before the Melinau River, which forms the park boundary. When the water is low, the trip can be very slow and involve pulling the boat over the shallows; this accounts for high charter rates. For a group of 9 or 10 it is cheaper to charter a boat (RM250 one way). The first jetty on the Melinau River is Long Pala, where most of the tour companies have accommodation. The Park HQ is another 15 mins upriver. Longboats returning to Long Terawan leave the headquarters at dawn each day, calling at jetties en route.

Bario and the Kelabit Highlands *p149*
Air
The only access to Bario is by air on **MAS**. Bario's airstrip is very small and because of its position, flights are often cancelled due to mist and clouds. Flights are always booked up. There is 1 flight a day on **MAS** from **Miri** at 0930. There is also one connection a day via **Marudi**.

Foot
It is a 7-day trek from **Marudi** to Bario, sleeping in longhouses en route. This trip should be organized through a Miri travel agent (see page 141).

Limbang *p150*
Air
Daily connections with **Miri, Mulu** and **Lawas**, weekly flights to **Labuan** and twice-weekly connections with **KK**. The airport is about 5 km from town and taxis ferry passengers in.

Boat
Regular connections with **Lawas**, depart early in the morning (2 hrs, RM15). There is also an early morning express departure to **Labuan**. Regular boat connections with **Bandar Seri Begawan**, Brunei (30 mins, RM15).

Lawas *p151*
Air
Connections with **Miri**, **Limbang**, **Kuching**, **Labuan** and **KK**.

Boat
Regular connections to **Limbang**, 2 hrs. Daily morning boat departures for **Brunei**.

Bus
Connections with **Merapok** on the Sarawak/Sabah border (RM5). From here there are connections to **Beaufort** in Sabah. Twice-daily connections with **KK**, 4 hrs (RM20).

● *For an explanation of the sleeping and eating price codes used in this guide, see inside the*
● *front cover. Other relevant information is found in Essentials, pages 31-35.*

Background

History

Sarawak earned its place in the archaeological textbooks when a 37,000-year-old human skull belonging to a boy of about 15 was unearthed in the Niah Caves in 1958 (see page 132), predating the earliest relics found on the Malay Peninsula by about 30,000 years. The caves were continuously inhabited for tens of thousands of years and many shards of palaeolithic and neolithic pottery, tools and jewellery as well as carved burial boats have been excavated at the site. There are also prehistoric cave paintings. In the first millennium AD, the Niah Caves were home to a prosperous community, which traded birds' nests, hornbill ivory, bezoar stones, rhinoceros horns and other jungle produce with Chinese traders in exchange for porcelain and beads.

Some of Sarawak's tribes may be descended from these cave people, although others, notably the Iban shifting cultivators, migrated from Kalimantan's Kapuas River valley from the 16th to 19th centuries. Malay Orang Laut, sea people, migrated to Sarawak's coasts and made a living from fishing, trading and piracy. At the height of Sumatra's Srivijayan Empire in the 11th and 12th centuries, many Sumatran Malays migrated to north Borneo. Chinese traders were active along the Sarawak coast from as early as the seventh century: Chinese coins and Han pottery have been discovered at the mouth of the Sarawak River.

From the 14th century right up to the 20th century, Sarawak's history was inextricably intertwined with that of the neighbouring Sultanate of Brunei, which, until the arrival of the White Rajahs of Sarawak, held sway over the coastal areas of north Borneo. For a more detailed account of how Sarawak's White Rajahs came to whittle away the sultan's territory and expand into the vacuum of his receding empire, see Robert Payne's *The White Rajahs of Sarawak.*

Enter James Brooke

As the Sultanate of Brunei began to decline around the beginning of the 18th century, the Malays of coastal Sarawak attempted to break free from their tributary overlord. They claimed an independent ancestry from Brunei and exercised firm control over the Dayak tribes inland and upriver. But in the early 19th century Brunei started to reassert its power over them, dispatching Pangiran Mahkota from the Brunei court in 1827 to govern Sarawak and supervise the mining of high-grade antimony ore, which was exported to Singapore to be used in medicine and as an alloy. The name 'Sarawak' comes from the Malay word serawak, meaning 'antimony'.

Mahkota founded Kuching, but relations with the local Malays became strained and Mahkota's problems were compounded by the marauding Ibans of the Saribas and Skrang rivers who raided coastal communities. In 1836 the local Malay chiefs, led by Datu Patinggi Ali, rebelled against Governor Mahkota, prompting the Sultan of Brunei to send his uncle, Rajah Muda Hashim to suppress the uprising. But Hashim failed to quell the disturbances and the situation deteriorated when the rebels approached the Sultan of Sambas, now in northwest Kalimantan, for help from the Dutch. Then, in 1839, James Brooke sailed up the Sarawak River to Kuching.

Hashim was desperate to regain control and Brooke, in the knowledge that the British would support any action that countered the threat of Dutch influence, struck a deal with him. He pressed Hashim to grant him the governorship of Sarawak in exchange for suppressing the rebellion, which he duly did. In 1842 Brooke became Rajah of Sarawak. Pangiran Mahkota – the now disenfranchised former governor of Sarawak – formed an alliance with an Iban pirate chief on the Skrang River, while

J Kathirithamby-Wells wrote: "..piracy and politics became irrevocably linked and Brooke's battle against his political opponents became advertised as a morally justified war against the pirate communities of the coast."

The suppression of piracy in the 19th century became a full-time occupation for the rulers of Sarawak and Brunei – although the court of Brunei was well known to have derived a substantial chunk of its income from piracy. Rajah James Brooke believed that as long as pirates remained free to pillage the coasts, commerce would not pick up and his kingdom would never develop; ridding Sarawak's estuaries of pirates – both Iban (Sea Dayaks) and Illanun – became an act of political survival. In his *The White Rajahs of Sarawak*, Robert Payne wrote: "Nearly every day people came to Kuching with tales about the pirates: how they had landed in a small creek, spread out, made their way to a village, looted everything in sight, murdered everyone they could lay their hands on, and then vanished as swiftly as they came. The Sultan of Brunei was begging for help against them."

Anti-piracy missions afforded James Brooke an excuse to extend his kingdom, as he worked his way up the coasts, 'pacifying' the Sea Dayak pirates. Brooke declared war on them and with the help of Royal Naval Captain Henry Keppel (of latter-day Singapore's Keppel Shipyard fame), he led a number of punitive raids against the Iban Sea Dayaks in 1833, 1834 and 1849. "The assaults", wrote DJM Tate in *Rajah Brooke's Borneo*, "largely achieved their purpose, and were applauded in the Straits, but the appalling loss of life incurred upset many drawing-room humanitarians in Britain." There were an estimated 25,000 pirates living along the North Borneo coast when Brooke became Rajah. He led many expeditions against them, culminating in his notorious battle against the Saribas pirate fleet in 1849.

In that incident, Brooke ambushed and killed hundreds of Saribas Dayaks at Batang Maru. The barbarity of the ambush (which was reported in the *Illustrated London News*) outraged public opinion in Britain and in Singapore – a commission of inquiry in Singapore acquitted Brooke, but badly damaged his prestige. In the British parliament, he was cast as a 'mad despot' who had to be prevented from committing further massacres. But the action led the Sultan of Brunei to grant him the Saribas and Skrang districts (now Sarawak's Second Division) in 1853, marking the beginning of the Brooke dynasty's relentless expansionist drive. Eight years later, James Brooke persuaded the sultan to give him what became Sarawak's Third Division, after he drove out the Illanun pirates who had disrupted the sago trade from Mukah and Oya, around Bintulu.

In 1857, James Brooke ran into more trouble. Chinese Hakka goldminers, who had been in Bau (further up the Sarawak River) longer than he had been in Kuching, had grown resentful of his attempts to stamp out the opium trade and their secret societies. They attacked Kuching, set the Malay kampongs ablaze and killed several European officials; Brooke escaped by swimming across the river from his astana. His nephew, Charles, led a group of Skrang Dayaks in persuit of the Hakka invaders, who fled across the border into Dutch Borneo; about 1000 were killed by the Ibans on the way; 2500 survived. Historian Robert Payne writes: "The fighting lasted for more than a month. From time to time Dayaks would return with strings of heads, which they cleaned and smoked over slow fires, especially happy when they could do this in full view of the Chinese in the bazaars who sometimes recognized people they had known." Payne says Brooke was plagued by guilt over how he handled the Chinese rebellion, for so many deaths could not easily be explained away. Neither James nor Charles ever fully trusted the Chinese again, although the Teochew, Cantonese and Hokkien merchants in Kuching never caused them any trouble.

The second generation: Rajah Charles Brooke

Charles Johnson (who changed his name to Brooke after his elder brother, Brooke Johnson, had been disinherited by James for insubordination) became the second Rajah of Sarawak in 1863. He ruled for nearly 50 years. Charles did not have James Brooke's forceful personality, and was much more reclusive – probably as a result of working in remote jungle outposts for 10 years in government service. Historian Robert Payne noted that "in James Brooke there was something of the knight errant at the mercy of his dream. Charles was the pure professional, a stern soldier who thought dreaming was the occupation of fools. There was no nonsense about him." Despite this he engendered great loyalty in his administrators, who worked hard for little reward.

Charles maintained his uncle's consultative system of government and formed a Council Negeri, or national council, comprising his top government officials, Malay leaders and tribal headmen, which met every couple of years to hammer out policy changes. His frugal financial management meant that by 1877 Sarawak was no longer in debt and the economy gradually expanded. The country was not a wealthy one, however, and had very few natural resources – its soils proved unsuitable for agriculture. In the 1880s, Charles' faith in the Chinese community was sufficiently restored to allow Chinese immigration, and the government subsidized the new settlers. By using 'friendly' downriver Dayak groups to subdue belligerent tribes upriver, Charles managed to pacify the interior by 1880.

When Charles took over from his ailing uncle in 1863 he proved to be even more of an expansionist. In 1868 he tried to take control of the Baram River valley, but London did not approve secession of the territory until 1882, when it became the Fourth Division. In 1884, Charles acquired the Trusan Valley from the Sultan of Brunei, and in 1890, he annexed Limbang ending a six-year rebellion by local chiefs against the sultan. The two territories were united to form the Fifth Division, after which Sarawak completely surrounded Brunei. In 1905, the British North Borneo Chartered Company gave up the Lawas Valley to Sarawak too. "By 1890," writes Robert Payne, "Charles was ruling over a country as large as England and Scotland with the help of about 20 European officers." When the First World War broke out in 1914, Charles was in England and he ruled Sarawak from Cirencester.

The third generation: Charles Vyner Brooke

In 1916, at the age of 86, Charles handed the reins to his eldest son, Charles Vyner Brooke, and he died the following year. Vyner was 42 when he became Rajah and had already served his father's government for nearly 20 years. "Vyner was a man of peace, who took no delight in bloodshed and ruled with humanity and compassion," wrote Robert Payne. He was a delegator by nature, and under him the old paternalistic style of government gave way to a more professional bureaucracy. On the centenary of the Brooke administration in September 1941, Vyner promulgated a written constitution, and renounced his autocratic powers in favour of working in cooperation with a Supreme Council. This was opposed by his nephew and heir, Anthony Brooke, who saw it as a move to undermine his succession. To protest against this, and his uncle's decision to appoint a mentally deranged Muslim Englishman as his Chief Secretary, Anthony left for Singapore. The Rajah dismissed him from the service in September 1941. Three months later the Japanese Imperial Army invaded; Vyner Brooke was in Australia at the time, and his younger brother, Bertram, was ill in London.

Japanese troops took Kuching on Christmas Day 1941 having captured the Miri oilfield a few days earlier. European administrators were interned and many later died. A Kuching-born Chinese, Albert Kwok, led an armed resistance against the Japanese in neighbouring British North Borneo (Sabah) – see page 242 – but in Sarawak, there was no organized guerrilla movement. Iban tribespeople instilled fear into the occupying forces, however, by roaming the jungle taking Japanese heads, which were proudly added to much older longhouse head galleries. Despite

⁝ Tom Harrisson: life in the fast lane

Reputed to be one of the most important figures in the development of archaeology in Southeast Asia, Tom Harrisson, the charismatic 'egomaniac', put Borneo and Sarawak on the map.

Tom Harrisson loved Sarawak and, it would seem, Sarawak loved him. It was only appropriate that when he was killed in a traffic accident in 1976 it was in Thailand and not in Malaysia.

He first visited Sarawak in 1932 as part of a Royal Geographical Expedition sent, along with around 150 kg of Cadbury's chocolate, to collect flora and fauna from one of the world's great natural treasure stores. Instead Harrisson found himself entranced by the territory's human populations and so the love affair began.

By all accounts, Harrisson was a difficult fellow – the sort that imperial Britain produced in very large numbers indeed. He was a womanizer with a particular penchant for other people's spouses, he could be horribly abusive to his fellow workers and he apparently revelled in putting down uppity academics. But he was also instrumental in putting Sarawak, and Borneo more generally, on the map and in raising awareness of the ways in which economic and social change was impacting on Sarawak's tribal peoples.

Before taking up the curatorship of the Sarawak Museum in 1947 Harrisson also distinguished himself as a war hero, parachuting into the jungle and organizing around 1000 headhunters to terrorize the Japanese. All in all, Tom Harrisson led life in the fast lane.

Those wanting to read a good biography of Harrisson should get hold of *The most offending soul alive* by Judith M Heimann, Honolulu, Hawaii University Press, 1998.

the Brooke regime's century-long effort to stamp out headhunting, the practice was encouraged by Tom Harrisson (one of Sarawak's most famous adopted sons) who parachuted into the Kelabit Highlands towards the end of the Second World War and put together an irregular army of upriver tribesmen to fight the Japanese. He offered them 'ten-bob-a-nob' for Japanese heads. Australian forces liberated Kuching on September 11 1945 and Sarawak was placed under Australian military administration for seven months.

After the war, the Colonial Office in London decided the time had come to bring Sarawak into the modern era, replacing the anachronistic White Rajahs, introducing an education system and building a rudimentary infrastructure. The Brookes had become an embarrassment to the British government as they continued to squabble among themselves. Anthony Brooke desperately wanted to claim what he felt was his, while the Colonial Office wanted Sarawak to become a crown colony or revert to Malay rule. No one was sure whether Sarawak wanted the Brookes back or not.

The end of empire

In February 1946 the ageing Vyner shocked his brother Bertram and his nephew Anthony, the Rajah Muda (or heir apparent), by issuing a proclamation urging the people of Sarawak to accept the King of England as their ruler. In doing so he effectively handed the country over to Britain. Vyner thought the continued existence of Sarawak as the private domain of the Brooke family an anachronism; but Anthony thought it a betrayal. The British government sent a commission to Sarawak to ascertain what the people wanted. In May 1946, the Council Negeri agreed – by a 19-16 majority – to transfer power to Britain, provoking protests and demonstrations and resulting in the assassination of the British governor by a Malay in Sibu in 1949. He and three other anti-cessionists were sentenced to death. Two years later, Anthony Brooke, who remained deeply resentful about the demise of the Brooke Dynasty, abandoned his claim and urged his supporters to end their campaign.

As a British colony, Sarawak's economy expanded and oil and timber production increased, which funded the much-needed expansion of education and health services. As with British North Borneo (Sabah), Britain was keen to give Sarawak political independence and, following Malaysian independence in 1957, saw the best means to this end as being through the proposal of Malaysian Prime Minister Tunku Abdul Rahman. The prime minister suggested the formation of a federation to include Singapore, Sarawak, Sabah and Brunei as well as the peninsula. In the end, Brunei opted out, Singapore left after two years, but Sarawak and Sabah joined the federation, having accepted the recommendations of the British government. Indonesia's President Sukarno denounced the move, claiming it was all part of a neo-colonialist conspiracy. He declared a policy of confrontation – *Konfrontasi*. A United Nations commission which was sent to ensure that the people of Sabah and Sarawak wanted to be part of Malaysia reported that Indonesia's objections were unfounded.

Communists had been active in Sarawak since the 1930s. The *Konfrontasi* afforded the Sarawak Communist Organization (SCO) Jakarta's support against the Malaysian government. The SCO joined forces with the North Kalimantan Communist Party (NKCP) and were trained and equipped by Indonesia's President Sukarno. But following Jakarta's brutal suppression of the Indonesian Communists, the Partai Komunis Indonesia (PKI), in the wake of the attempted coup in 1965, Sarawak's Communists fled back across the Indonesian border, along with their Kalimantan comrades. There they continued to wage guerrilla war against the Malaysian government throughout the 1970s. The Sarawak state government offered amnesties to guerrillas wanting to come out of hiding. In 1973 the NKCP leader surrendered along with 482 other guerrillas. A handful remained in the jungle, most of them in the hills around Kuching. The last surrendered in 1990.

Politics and modern Sarawak

In 1957 Kuala Lumpur was keen to have Sarawak and Sabah in the Federation of Malaysia and offered the two states a degree of autonomy, allowing their local governments control over state finances, agriculture and forestry. Sarawak's racial mix was reflected in its chaotic state politics. The Ibans dominated the Sarawak National Party (SNAP), which provided the first Chief Minister, Datuk Stephen Kalong Ningkan. He raised a storm over Kuala Lumpur's introduction of Bahasa Malaysia in schools and complained bitterly about the federal government's policy of filling the Sarawakian civil service with Malays from the peninsula. An 'us' and 'them' mentality developed: in Sarawak, the Malay word *semenanjung* (peninsula) was used to label the newcomers. To many, *semenanjung* was Malaysia, Sarawak was Sarawak.

In 1966 the federal government ousted the SNAP, and a new Muslim-dominated government led by the Sarawak Alliance took over in Kuching. But there was still strong political opposition to federal encroachment. Throughout the 1970s, as in Sabah, Sarawak's strongly Muslim government drew the state closer and closer to the peninsula: it supported *Rukunegara* – the policy of Islamization – and promoted the use of Bahasa Malaysia. Muslims make up less than one-third of the population of Sarawak. The Malays, Melanaus and Chinese communities grew rich from the timber industry; the Ibans and the Orang Ulu (the upriver tribespeople) saw little in the way of development. They did not reap the benefits of the expansion of education and social services, they were unable to get public sector jobs and, to make matters worse, logging firms were encroaching on their native lands and threatening their traditional lifestyles.

been heard at all. In 1983, Iban members of SNAP – which was a part of former Prime Minister Dr Mahathir Mohamad's ruling Barisan Nasional (National Front) coalition – split to form the Party Bansa Dayak Sarawak (PBDS), which, although it initially remained in the coalition, became more outspoken on native affairs. At about the same time, international outrage was sparked over the exploitation of Sarawak's tribespeople by politicians and businessmen involved in the logging industry. The plight of the Penan hunter-gatherers came to world attention due to their blockades of logging roads and the resulting publicity highlighted the rampant corruption and greed that characterized modern Sarawak's political economy.

The National Front remain firmly in control in Sarawak. But unlike neighbouring Sabah, Sarawak's politicians are not dominated by the centre. The chief minister of Sarawak is Taib Mahmud, a Melanau, and his Parti Pesaka Bumiputra Bersatu is a member of the UMNO-dominated (United Malays National Organisation) National Front. But in Sarawak itself UMNO wields little power.

The ruling National Front easily won the 1999 election in Sarawak, successfully playing on voters' local concerns and grievances. The problem for the opposition is that local people think it is the state legislature which can help, not the federal parliament in KL which seems distant and ineffective. For this reason, UMNO does not have a presence and it is the Parti Pesaka Bumiputra Bersatu which represents Sarawak in the National Front.

The challenge of getting the voters out in the most remote areas of the country was clearly shown in Long Lidom. There it cost the government RM65,000 to provide a helicopter to poll just seven Punan Busang in a longhouse on the Upper Kajang, close to the border with Indonesia. Datuk Omar of the Election Commission said that mounting the general election in Sarawak, with its 28 parliamentary seats, was a "logistical nightmare". Along with a small air force of helicopters, the Commission used 1032 long boats, 15 speed boats and 3054 land cruisers. The Commission's workforce numbered a cool 13,788 workers in a state with a population of just two million.

Today there are many in Sarawak as well as in Sabah, who wish their governments had opted out of the Federation, as did Brunei. Sarawak is of great economic importance to Malaysia, thanks to its oil, gas and timber. The state now accounts for more than one-third of Malaysia's petroleum production (worth more than US$800 million per year) and more than half of its natural gas. As with neighbouring Sabah however, 95% of Sarawak's oil and gas revenues go directly into federal coffers.

Culture

People

About a third of the population is made up of Iban tribespeople – who used to be known as the 'Sea Dayaks' – former headhunters, who live in longhouses on the lower reaches of the rivers. Chinese immigrants, whose forebears arrived during the 19th century, make up another third. A fifth of the population is Malay; most are native Sarawakians, but some came from the peninsula after the state joined the Malaysian Federation in 1963. The rest of Sarawak's inhabitants are indigenous tribal groups, of which the main ones are the Melanau, the Bidayuh and upriver Orang Ulu such as the Kenyah, Kayan and Kelabits; the Penan are among

: In upriver Dayak communities, both men and women traditionally distend their earlobes with brass weights – long earlobes are considered a beauty feature – and practise extensive body tattooing.

Southeast Asia's few remaining hunter-gatherers. The total population of the state is almost 2.2 million. The people of the interior are classified as Proto-Malays and Deutero-Malays and are divided into at least 12 distinct tribal groups including Iban, Murut (see page 248), Melanau, Bidayuh, Kenyah, Kayan, Kelabit and Penan.

⦂ Skulls in the longhouse

Although headhunting has been largely stamped out in Borneo, there is still the odd reported case, once every few years. But until the early 20th century, headhunting was commonplace among many Dayak tribes and the Iban were the most fearsome of all.

Following a headhunting expedition, the freshly taken heads were skinned, placed in rattan nets and smoked over a fire, or sometimes boiled. The skulls were then hung from the rafters of the longhouse and they possessed the most powerful form of magic.

The skulls were considered trophies of manhood (they increased a young bachelor's eligibility), symbols of bravery and they testified to the unity of a longhouse. The longhouse had to hold festivals – or gawai – to appease the spirits of the skulls. Once placated, the heads were believed to bring great blessing – they could ward off evil spirits, save villages from epidemics, produce rain and increase the yield of rice harvests. Heads that were insulted or ignored were capable of wreaking havoc in the form of bad dreams, plagues, floods and fires. To keep the spirits of the skulls happy, they would be offered food and cigarettes and made to feel welcome in their new home. Because the magical powers of a skull faded with time, fresh heads were always in demand. Tribes without heads were considered spiritually weak.

Today, young Dayak men no longer have to take heads to gain respect. They are, however, expected to go on long journeys (the equivalent of the Australian aborigines' Walkabout), or *bejalai* in Iban. The one unspoken rule is that they should come back with plenty of good stories, and, these days, as most *bejalai* expeditions translate into stints at timber camps or on oil rigs, they are expected to come home bearing video recorders, TV sets and motorbikes.

Many Dayak tribes continue to celebrate their headhunting ceremonies. In Kalimantan, for example, the Adat Ngayau ceremony uses coconut shells, wrapped in leaves, as substitutes for freshly cut heads.

Bidayuh In the 19th century, Sarawak's European community called the Bidayuh Land Dayaks, mainly to distinguish them from the Iban Sea Dayak pirates. The Bidayuh make up 8.4% of the population and are concentrated to the west of the Kuching area, towards the Kalimantan border. There are also related groups living in west Kalimantan. They were virtually saved from extinction by the White Rajahs, because the Bidayuh were quiet, mild-mannered people, they were at the mercy of the Iban headhunters and the Brunei Malays who taxed and enslaved them. The Brookes afforded them protection from both groups.

Most live in modern longhouses and are dry-rice farmers. Their traditional longhouses are exactly like Iban ones, but without the tanju veranda. The Bidayuh tribe comprises five sub-groups: the Jagoi, Biatah, Bukar-Sadong, Selakau and Lara, all of whom live in far west Sarawak. They are the state's best traditional plumbers, and are known for their ingenious gravity-fed bamboo water-supply systems. They are bamboo specialists, making it into everything from cooking pots and utensils to finely carved musical instruments (see page 168). Among other tribal groups, the Bidayuh are renowned for their rice wine and sugar-cane toddy. Henry Keppel, who with Rajah James Brooke fought the Bidayuh's dreaded enemies, the Sea Dayaks, described an evening spent with the Land Dayaks thus: "They ate and drank, and asked for everything, but stole nothing."

Chinese Hakka goldminers had already settled at Bau, upriver from Kuching, long
before James Brooke arrived in 1839. Cantonese, Teochew and Hokkien merchants
also set up in Kuching, but the Brookes did not warm to the Chinese community,
believing the traders would exploit the Dayak communities if they were allowed to
venture upriver. In the 1880s, however, Rajah Charles Brooke allowed the
immigration of large numbers of Chinese – mainly Foochow – who settled in coastal
towns like Sibu. Many became farmers and ran rubber smallholdings. The Sarawak
government subsidized the immigrants for the first year. During the Brooke era, the
only government-funded schools were for Malays and few tribal people ever received
a formal education. The Chinese, however, set up and funded their own private
schools and many attended Christian missionary schools, leading to the formation of
a relatively prosperous, educated élite. Now the Chinese comprise nearly a third of
the state's population and are almost as numerous as the Iban; they are the middle-
men, traders, shopkeepers, timber towkays (magnates) and express-boat owners.

Iban Sarawak's best-known erstwhile headhunters make up ❂ *If you intend to visit any of Sarawak's tribal peoples, see page 114.*
nearly a third of the state's population and while some have
moved to coastal towns for work, many remain in their
traditional longhouses. But with Iban men now earning good
money in the timber and oil industries, it is increasingly common to see longhouses
bristling with television aerials, equipped with fridges, self-cleaning ovens and flush
toilets, and with Land Cruisers in the car park. Even modern longhouses retain the
traditional features of gallery, veranda and doors. The Iban are an outgoing people
and usually extend a warm welcome to visitors. Iban women are skilled weavers;
even today a girl is not considered eligible until she has proven her skills at the loom
by weaving a ceremonial textile, the *pua kumbu* (see page 167). The Ibans love to
party and, during the harvest festival in June, visitors are particularly welcome to drink
copious amounts of *tuak* (rice wine) and dance through the night.

The Iban are shifting cultivators who originated in the Kapuas River basin of west
Kalimantan and migrated into Sarawak's Second Division in the early 16th century,
settling along the Batang Lupar, Skrang and Saribas rivers. By the early 19th century,
they had begun to spill into the Rejang River valley. It was this growing pressure on
land as more and more migrants settled in the river valleys that led to fighting and
headhunting (see page 160). Probably because they were shifting cultivators, the
Iban remained in closely bonded family groups and were a classless society.
Historian Mary Turnbull said "they retained their pioneer social organization of
nuclear family groups living together in longhouses and did not evolve more
sophisticated political institutions. Long-settled families acquired prestige, but the
Ibans did not merge into tribes and had neither chiefs, rakyat class, nor slaves".

The Iban joined local Malay chiefs and turned to piracy – which is how Europeans
first came into contact with them. They were dubbed Sea Dayaks as a result – which is
really a misnomer as they are an inland people. The name stuck, however, and in the
eyes of Westerners, it distinguished them from Land Dayaks, who were the Bidayuh
people from the Sarawak River area (see page 160). While Rajah James Brooke only won
the Iban's loyalty after he had crushed them in battle (see page 155), he had great
admiration for them, and they bore no bitterness towards him. He once described them
as "good-looking a set of men, or devils, as one could cast eye on. Their wiry and supple
limbs might have been compared to the troops of wild horses that followed Mazeppa in
his perilous flight." The Iban have a very easygoing attitude to love and sex, which is
best explained in Redmond O'Hanlon's book *Into the Heart of Borneo*. Free love is the
general rule among Iban communities which have not become evangelical Christians
although, once married, the Iban divorce rate is low and they are monogamous.

Kelabit The Kelabit, who live in the highlands at the headwaters of the Baram River, are closely related to the Murut (see page 248) and the Lun Dayeh of Kalimantan. It was into Kelabit territory that Tom Harrisson parachuted with Allied Special Forces towards the end of the Second World War. The Kelabit Highlands around Bario were chosen because they were so remote. Of all the tribes in Sarawak, the Kelabit have the sturdiest, strongest builds, which is usually ascribed to the cool and invigorating mountain climate. They are skilled hill-rice farmers and their fragrant Bario rice is prized throughout Sarawak. The climate also allows them to cultivate vegetables. Kelabit parties are also famed as boisterous occasions, and large quantities of *borak* (rice beer) are consumed – despite the fact that the majority of Kelabit has converted to Christianity. They are regarded as among the most hospitable people in Borneo.

Kenyah and Kayan These two closely related groups were the traditional rivals of the Iban and were notorious for their warlike ways. Historian Robert Payne, in his history *The White Rajahs of Sarawak* described the Kayan of the upper Rejang as "a treacherous tribe, [who] like nothing better than putting out the eyes and cutting the throats of prisoners, or burning them alive". They probably originally migrated into Sarawak from the Apo Kayan district in east Kalimantan. Kenyah and Kayan raids on downriver people were greatly feared, but their power was broken by Charles Brooke, just before he became the second White Rajah, in 1863. The Kayan had retreated upstream above the Pelagus Rapids on the Rejang River (see page 120), to an area they considered out of reach of their Iban enemies. In 1862 they killed two government officers at Kanowit and went on a killing spree. Charles Brooke led 15,000 Iban past the Pelagus Rapids, beyond Belaga and attacked the Kayan in their heartland. Many hundreds were killed. In November 1924, Rajah Vyner Brooke presided over a peace-making ceremony between the Orang Ulu and the Iban in Kapit (there is a photograph of the ceremony on display in the Kapit Museum).

The Kenyah and Kayan in Sarawak live in pleasant upriver valleys and are settled rice farmers. They are very different from other tribal groups, have a completely different language (which has ancient Malayo-Polynesian roots) and are class-conscious, with a well-defined social hierarchy. Traditionally their society was composed of aristocrats, noblemen, commoners and slaves (who were snatched during raids on other tribes). One of the few things the Kayan and Kenyah have in common with other Dayak groups is the fact that they live in longhouses, although even these are of a different design, and are much more carefully constructed, in ironwood. Subgroups include the Kejaman, Skapan, Berawan and Sebop. Many have now been converted to Christianity.

In contrast to their belligerent history, the Kenyahs and Kayans are much more introverted than the Ibans; they are slow and deliberate in their ways, and are very artistic and musical. They are also renowned for their parties; visitors recovering from drinking *borak* rice beer have their faces covered in soot before being thrown in the river. This is to test the strength of the newly forged friendship with visitors, who are ill-advised to lose their sense of humour on such occasions.

Their artwork is made from wood, antlers, metal and beads. They use a lot of wooden statues and masks to scare evil spirits at the entrances to their homes.

Malay About half of Sarawak's 300,000-strong Malay community lives around the state capital; most of the other half lives in the Limbang Division, near Brunei. The Malays traditionally live near the coast, although today there are small communities far upriver. There are some old wooden Malay houses with carved façades in the kampongs along the banks of the Sarawak River in Kuching. In all Malay communities, the mosque is the centre of the village, but while their faith is important to them, the strictures of Islam are generally less rigorously enforced in Sarawak than on the peninsula. During the days of the White Rajahs, the Malays were recruited into

❡ Tribal tattoos

Tattooing is practised by many indigenous groups in Borneo, but the most intricate designs are those of the upriver Orang Ulu tribes.

Designs vary from group to group and for different parts of the body. Circular designs are mostly used for the shoulder, chest or wrists, while stylized dragon-dogs (*aso*), scorpions and dragons are used on the thigh and, for the Iban, on the throat.

Tattoos can mean different things; for the man it is a symbol of bravery and for women, a good tattoo is a beauty feature. More elaborate designs often denote high social status in Orang Ulu communities – the Kayan, for example, reserved the *aso* design for the upper classes and slaves were barred from tattooing themselves at all. In these Orang Ulu groups, the women have the most impressive tattoos; the headman's daughter has her hands, arms and legs completely covered in a finely patterned tattoo.

Designs are first carved on a block of wood, which is then smeared with ink. The design is printed on the body and then punctured into the skin with needles dipped in ink, usually made from a mixture of sugar, water and soot. Rice is smeared over the inflamed area to prevent infection, but it usually swells up for some time.

government service, as they were on the Malay peninsula. They were renowned as good administrators and the men were mostly literate in Jawi script. Over the years there has been much intermarriage between the Malay and Melanau communities. Traditionally, the Malays were fishermen and farmers.

Melanau The Melanau are a relaxed and humorous people. Rajah James Brooke, like generations of men before and after him, thought the Melanau girls particularly pretty. He said that they had "agreeable countenances, with the dark, rolling, open eye of the Italians, and nearly as fair as most of that race". The Melanau live along the coast between the Baram and Rejang rivers; originally they lived in magnificent communal houses built high off the ground, like the one that has been reconstructed at the Cultural Village in Kuching, but these have long since disappeared. The houses were designed to afford protection from incessant pirate raids (see page 155), for the Melanau were easy pickings, being coastal people. Their stilt-houses were often up to 12 m off the ground. Today most Melanau live in Malay-style pile-houses facing the river. Hedda Morrison, in her classic 1957 book *Sarawak*, wrote: "As a result of living along the rivers in swamp country, the Melanaus are an exceptionally amphibious people. The children learn to swim almost before they can walk. Nearly all progress is by canoe, sometimes even to visit the house next door."

The traditional Melanau fishing boat is called a *barong*. Melanau fishermen employed a unique fishing technique. They would anchor palm leaves at sea as they discovered that shoals of fish would seek refuge under them. After rowing out to the leaves, one fisherman would dive off his *barong* and chase the fish into the nets which his colleague hung over the side. The Melanaus were also noted for their sago production – which they ate instead of rice. At Kuching's Cultural Village there is a demonstration of traditional sago production, showing how the starch-bearing pith is removed, mashed, dried and ground into flour. Most Melanau are now Muslim and have assimilated with the Malays through intermarriage. Originally, however, they were animists (animist Melanau are called Likaus) and were particularly famed for their elaborately carved 'sickness images', which represented the form of spirits which caused specific illnesses (see page 167).

The palang

One of the more exotic features of upriver sexuality is the *palang* (penis pin), which is the versatile jungle version of the French tickler.

Traditionally, women suffer heavy weights being attached to their earlobes to enhance their sex appeal. In turn, men are expected to enhance their physical attributes and entertain their womenfolk by drilling a hole in their organs, into which they insert a range of items, aimed at heightening their partner's pleasure on the rattan mat.

Tom Harrisson, a former curator of the Sarawak Museum, was intrigued by the *palang*; some suspect his authority on the subject stemmed from first-hand experience. He wrote: "When the device is put into use, the owner adds whatever he prefers to elaborate and accentuate its intention. A lively range of objects can so be employed – from pigs' bristles and bamboo shavings to pieces of metal, seeds, beads and broken glass. The effect, of course, is to enlarge the diameter of the male organ inside the female."

It is said that many Dayak men, even today, have the tattoo man come and drill a hole in them as they stand in the river. As the practice has gone on for centuries, one can only assume that its continued popularity proves it is worth the agony.

Orang Ulu The jungle, or upriver, people comprise a range of different small tribal groups. Orang Ulu longhouses are usually made of *belian* (ironwood) and are built to last. They are well-known swordsmiths, forging lethal parangs from any piece of scrap metal they can lay their hands on. They are also very artistic people – skilled carvers and painters and famed for their beadwork – taking great care decorating even simple household utensils. Most Orang Ulu are decorated with traditional tattoos (see box, page 163).

Penan Perhaps Southeast Asia's only remaining true hunter-gatherers live mainly in the upper Rejang area and Limbang. They are nomads and are related, linguistically at least, to the Punan, former nomadic forest dwellers who are now settled in longhouses along the upper Rejang. The Malaysian government has long wanted the Penan to settle too, but has had limited success in attracting them to expensive new longhouses. Groups of Penan hunter-gatherers still wander through the forest in groups to hunt wild pigs, birds and monkeys and search for sago palms from which they make their staple food, sago flour. The Penan are considered to be the jungle experts by all the other inland tribes. Because they live in the shade of the forest, their skin is relatively fair. They have a great affection for the coolness of the forest and until the 1960s were rarely seen by the outside world. For them sunlight is extremely unpleasant. They are broad and much more stocky than other river people and are extremely shy, having had little contact with the outside world. Most of their trade is conducted with remote Kayan, Kenyah and Kelabit longhouse communities on the edge of the forest.

In the eyes of the West, the Penan have emerged as the 'noble savages' of the late 20th century for their spirited defence of their lands against encroachment by logging companies. But it is not just recently that they have been cheated: they have long been the victims of other upriver tribes. A Penan, bringing baskets full of rotan to a Kenyah or Kayan longhouse to sell may end up exchanging his produce for one bullet or shotgun cartridge. In his way of thinking, a bullet will kill one wild boar which will last his family 10 days. In turn, the buyer knows he can sell the same rotan downstream for RM50-100. Penan still use the blowpipe for small game, but shotguns for wild pig. If they buy the shotgun cartridges for themselves, they have to exchange empties first. Some of their shotguns date back to the Second World War, when the British supplied them to upriver tribespeople to fight the Japanese. During the Brooke era, a large annual market would be held which both Chinese traders and Orang Ulu (including Penan) used to attend; the district officer would have to act as judge to ensure the Penan did not get cheated.

Those wishing to learn more about the Penan should refer to Denis Lau's *The Vanishing Nomads of Borneo* (Interstate Publishing, 1987). Lau has lived among the Penan and has photographed them for many years; his photographs appear in *Malaysia – Heart of Southeast Asia* (published by Archipelago Press, 1991).

Dance

Dayak tribes are renowned for their singing and dancing, most famously for the hornbill dance. In her book *Sarawak*, Hedda Morrison wrote: "The Kayans are probably the originators of the stylized war dance which is now common among the Ibans but the girls are also extremely talented and graceful dancers. One of their most delightful dances is the hornbill dance, when they tie hornbill feathers to the ends of their fingers which accentuate their slow and graceful movements. For party purposes everyone in the longhouse joins in and parades up and down the communal room led by one or two musicians and a group of girls who sing." On these occasions, drink flows freely. With the Ibans, it is *tuak* (rice wine), with the Kayan and Kenyah it is *borak*, a bitter rice beer. After being entertained by dancers, a visitor must drink a large glassful, before bursting into song and doing a dance routine themselves. The best guideline for visitors on how to handle such occasions is provided by Redmond O'Hanlon in his book *Into the Heart of Borneo*. The general rule of thumb is to be prepared to make an absolute fool of yourself, throwing all inhibition to the wind. This will immediately endear you to your hosts.

The following are the most common dances in Sarawak. **Kanjet Ngeleput** (Orang Ulu) dance performed in full warrior regalia, traditionally celebrating the return of a hunter or headhunters. **Mengarang Menyak** (Melanau) dance depicting the processing of sago from the cutting of the tree to the production of the sago pearls or pellets. **Ngajat Bebunuh** (Iban) war dance, performed in full battledress and armed with sword and shield. **Ngajat Induk** (Iban) performed as a welcome dance for those visiting longhouses. Ngajat Lesong (Iban) dance of the *lesong* or mortar, performed during gawai. **Tarian Kris** (Malay) dance of the *kris*, the Malay dagger, which symbolizes power, courage and strength. **Tarian Rajang Beuh** (Bidayuh) dance performed after the harvesting season as entertainment for guests to the longhouse. **Tarian Saga Lupa** (Orang Ulu) performed by women to welcome guests to the longhouse, accompanied by the *sape* (see Music, below). **Ule Nugan** (Orang Ulu) dance to the sound of the *kerebo bulo*, or bamboo slates. The music is designed to inspire the spirit of the paddy seeds to flourish. The male dancers hold a dibbling stick used in the planting of hill rice.

Music

Gongs range from the single large gong, the *tawak*, to the *engkerumong*, a set of small gongs, arranged on a horizontal rack, with five players. An *engkerumong* ensemble usually involves five to seven drums, which include two suspended gongs (*tawak* and *bendai*) and five hour-glass drums (*ketebong*). They are used to celebrate victory in battle or to welcome home a successful headhunting expedition. Sarawak's Bidayuh also make a bamboo gong called a *pirunchong*. The *jatang uton* is a wooden xylophone which can be rolled up like a rope ladder; the keys are struck with hardwood sticks.

The Bidayuh, Sarawak's bamboo specialists, make two main stringed instruments: a three-stringed cylindrical bamboo harp called a *tinton* and the *rabup*, a rotan-stringed fiddle with a bamboo cup. The Orang Ulu (Kenyah and Kayan tribes) play a four-stringed guitar called a *sape*, which is also common on the Kalimantan side of the border. It is the most common and popular lute-type instrument, whose body, neck and board are cut from one piece of softwood. It is used in Orang Ulu

Sarawak Background

dances and by witch doctors. It is usually played by two musicians, one keeping the rhythm, the other the melody. Traditional *sapes* had rotan strings, today they use wire guitar strings and electric pick-ups. Another stringed instrument, more usually found in Kalimantan, or deep in Sarawak's interior, is the *satang*, a bamboo tube with strings around the outside, cut from the bamboo and tightened with pegs.

One of the best-known instruments is the *engkerurai* (or *keluri*), the bagpipes of Borneo, which is usually linked with the Kenyah and Kayan, but is also found in Sabah (where it is called a *sompoton*). It is a hand-held organ in which four bamboo pan-pipes of different lengths are fixed to a gourd, which acts as the wind chamber. Simple *engkerurai* can only play one chord; more sophisticated ones allow the player to use two pipes for the melody, while the others provide a harmonic drone. The Bidayuh are specialists in bamboo instruments and make flutes of various sizes; big thick ones are called *branchi*, long ones with five holes are *kroto* and small ones are called *nchiyo*.

Arts and crafts

Bamboo carving The Bidayuh (Land Dayaks) are best known for their bamboo carving. The bamboo is usually carved in shallow relief and then stained with dye, which leaves a pattern in the areas which have been scraped out. The Bidayuh carve utilitarian objects as well as ceremonial shields, musical instruments and spirit images used to guard the longhouse. The Cultural Village (Kampong Budaya) in Kuching is one of the best places to see demonstrations of Bidayuh carving.

Basketry A wide variety of household items are woven from rotan, bamboo, bemban reed as well as nipah and pandanus palms. Malaysia supplies 30% of the world's demand for *manau rotan* (rattan). Basketry is practised by nearly all the ethnic groups in Sarawak and they are among the most popular handicrafts in the state. A variety of baskets are made for harvesting, storing and winnowing paddy as well as for collecting and storing other items. The Penan are reputed to produce the finest rattan sleeping mats – closely plaited and pliable – as well as the *ajat* and *ambong* baskets (all-purpose jungle rucksacks, also produced by the Kayan and Kenyah). Many of the native patterns used in basketry are derived from Chinese patterns and take the form of geometrical shapes and stylized birds. The Bidayuh also make baskets from either rotan or sago bark strips. The most common Bidayuh basket is the *tambok*, which is simply patterned and has bands of colour; it also has thin wooden supports on each side.

Beadwork Among many Kenyah, Kayan, Bidayuh, and Kelabit groups, beads have long been symbols of status and wealth; necklaces, skull caps and girdles are handed down from generation to generation. Smaller glass or plastic beads, usually imported from Europe, are used to decorate baby carriers, baskets, headbands, jackets, hats, sheaths for knives, tobacco boxes and handbags. Beaded baby carriers are mainly used by the Kelabit, Kenyah and Kayan and often have shells and animals' teeth attached, which make a rattling sound to frighten away evil spirits. Rounded patterns require more skill than geometric patterns; the quality of the pattern is used to reflect the status of the owner. Only upper classes are permitted to have beadwork depicting 'high-class' motifs such as human faces or figures. Early beads were made from clay, metal, glass, bone or shell (the earliest have been found in the Niah Caves). Later on, many of the beads that found their way upriver were from Venice, Greece, India and China – even Roman and Alexandrian beads have made their way into Borneo's jungle. Orang Ulu traded them for jungle produce. Tribes attach different values to particular types of beads.

Blowpipes Blowpipes are made by several Orang Ulu tribes in Sarawak and are usually carved from hardwood – normally *belian* (ironwood). The first step is to make

a rough cylinder about 10 cm wide and 2.5 m long. This is tied to a platform, from
which a hole is bored through the rod. The bore is skilfully chiselled by an iron rod
with a pointed end. The rod is then sanded down to about 5 cm in diameter.
Traditionally, the sanding was done using the rough underside of macaranga leaves.
The darts are made from the nibong and wild sago palms and the poison itself is the
sap of the upas (Ipoh) tree (*Antiaris toxicari*) into which the point is dipped.

Hats The Melanau people living around Bintulu make a big colourful conical hat
from nipah leaves called a *terindak*. Orang Ulu hats are wide-brimmed and are often
decorated with beadwork or cloth appliqué. Kelabit and Lun Bawan women wear
skullcaps made entirely of beads, which are heavy and extremely valuable.

Pottery Malaysia's most distinctive ceramic designs are found in Sarawak where
Iban potters reproduce shapes and patterns of Chinese porcelain which was
originally brought to Borneo by traders centuries ago (see page 93). Copies of these
old Chinese jars are mostly used for brewing *tuak (*rice wine).

Sickness images The coastal Melanau, who have now converted to Islam, but used to
be animists, have a tradition of carving sickness images (*blum*). They are usually carved
from sago or other softwoods. The image is believed to take the form of the evil spirit
causing a specific illness. They are carved in different forms according to the ailment.
The Melanau developed elaborate healing ceremonies; if someone was struck down by
a serious illness, the spirit medium would perform the berayun ceremony, using the
blum to extract the illness from the victim's body. Usually, the image is in a half-seated
position, with the hands crossed over the part of the body which is affected. During the
ceremony, the medium tries to draw the spirit from the sick person into the image, after
which it is set adrift on a river in a tiny purpose-made boat or hidden in the jungle. These
images are roughly carved and can, from time to time, be found in antique shops.

Textiles The weaving of cotton *pua kumbu*, literally 'blanket' or 'cover', is one of the
oldest Iban traditions, and . Iban legend recounts that 24 generations ago the God of
War, Singalang Burong, taught his son how to weave the most precious of all *pua*, the
lebor api. Dyed deep red, this cloth was traditionally used to wrap heads taken in battle.
    The weaving of *pua kumbu* is done by the women and is a vital skill for a would-be
bride to acquire. There are two main methods employed in making and decorating *pua
kumbu*: the more common is the ikat tie-dyeing technique, known as *ngebat* by the
Iban. The other method is the *pileh*, or floating weft. The Iban use a warp-beam loom
which is tied to two posts, to which the threads are attached. There is a breast-beam at
the weaving end, secured by a back strap to the weaver. A pedal, beneath the threads,
lowers and raises the alternate threads which are separated by rods. The woven
material is tightly packed by a beater. The material is tie-dyed in the warp.
    Because the *pua kumbu* is made by the warp-tie-dyeing method, the number of
colours is limited. The most common are a rich browny-brick-red colour and black, as
well as the undyed white sections; blues and greens are used in more modern
materials. Traditionally, *pua kumbu* were hung in longhouses during ceremonies and
were used to cover images during rituals. The designs and patterns are representations
of deities which figure in Iban myths and are believed to protect individuals from harm;
they are passed down from generation to generation. Such designs, with deep spiritual
significance, can only be woven by wives and daughters of chiefs. Other designs and
patterns are representations of birds and animals, including hornbills, crocodiles,
monitor lizards and shrimps, which are either associated with worship or are sources of
food. Symbolic representations of trees, plants and fruits are also included in the
designs as well as the events of everyday life. A typical example is the zigzag pattern
which represents the act of crossing a river – the zigzag course is explained by the

canoe's attempts to avoid strong currents. Many of the symbolic representations are highly stylized and can be difficult to pick out.

Malay women in Sarawak are traditionally renowned for their *kain songket*, sarongs woven with silver and gold thread.

Woodcarvings Many of Sarawak's tribal groups are skilled carvers, producing everything from huge burial poles (like the Kejaman pole outside the Sarawak Museum in Kuching) to small statues, masks and other decorative items and utensils. The Kenyah's traditional masks, which are used during festivals, are elaborately carved and often have large protruding eyes. Eyes are always emphasized, as they are to frighten the enemy. Other typical items carved by tribal groups include spoons, stools, doors, walking sticks, *sapes* (guitars), ceremonial shields, tops of water containers, tattoo plaques, and the hilts of *parang ilang* (ceremonial knives). The most popular Iban motif is the hornbill, which holds an honoured place in Iban folklore (see page 332), being the messenger for the sacred Brahminy kite, the ancestor of the Iban. Another famous Iban carving is the sacred measuring stick called the *tuntun peti*, used to trap deer and wild boar; it is carved to represent a forest spirit. The Kayan and Kenyah's most common motif is the *aso*, a dragon-like dog with a long snout. It also has religious and mythical significance. The Kenyah and Kayan carve huge burial structures (*salong*), as well as small ear pendants made of hornbill ivory. The elaborately carved masks used for their harvest ceremony are unique.

⁛ Footprint features

Introduction

Sabah may not have the colourful history of neighbouring
Sarawak, but there is still a great deal to entice the visitor.
It is the second largest Malaysian state after Sarawak, covering
72,500 sq km, making it about the size of Ireland. Occupying
the northeast corner of Borneo, it is shaped like a dog's head,
the jaws reaching out in the Sulu and Celebes seas, and the
back of the head facing onto the South China Sea.

The highlights of Sabah are natural and cultural, from
caves, reefs, forests and mountains to tribal peoples. The
Gunung Kinabulu National Park is named after Sabah's
(and Malaysia's) highest peak and is one of the state's most
popular destinations. Also popular is the Sepilok Orang-Utan
Rehabilitation Sanctuary outside Sandakan. Marine sights
include the Turtle Islands National Park and Sipadan Island,
one of Asia's finest dive sites. While Sabah's indigenous tribes
were not cherished as they were in Sarawak by the White
Rajahs, areas around towns such as Kudat, Tenom, Keningau
and Kota Belud still provide memorable insights into the
peoples of the region.

★ Don't miss ...

1 **Seafood** Have a beach barbecue on the sands of Manukan Island off Kota Kinabalu, page 189.

2 **Rafflesia** Stroke the fleshy red petals of the world's largest (and stinkiest) flower at the Tambunan Rafflesia Reserve, page 194.

3 **Murut villages** Watch blowpipes being made while toasting the locals with *tapai* – a fiery cassava wine – in kampongs around Tenom, page 196.

4 **Gunung Kinabalu** Catch sunrise on the summit of Malaysia's tallest peak, page 212.

5 **Sungai Kinabatangan** A guided river cruise is your best chance to spot orang-utans in the wild, page 225.

6 **Sipadan** Snorkel with turtles at this world-class diving site, page 229.

Sabah

0 km 30
0 miles 30

South China Sea

Sulu Sea

Celebes Sea

SABAH
MALAYSIA

INDONESIA

KALIMANTAN

SARAWAK

BRUNEI

LABUAN

Kota Kinabalu ▶ *Colour map 2, A1. Population: 354,000.*

KK is most people's introduction to Sabah for the simple reason that it is the only town with extensive air links to other parts of the country as well as a handful of regional destinations. KK is a modern state capital with little that can be dated back more than 50 years. Highlights include the State Museum and the town's markets. Out of town, within a day's excursion, are beaches such as Tanjung Aru and those near Tuaran, as well as a number of Kadazan and Bajau districts, with their distinctive markets. While it is necessary to go further afield to get a real view of tribal life, this is better than nothing.

The city is strung out along the coast, with jungle-clad hills as a backdrop. Two-thirds of the town is built on land reclaimed from the shallow Gaya Bay, and at spring tides it is possible to walk across to Gaya Island. Jalan Pantai, or Beach Road, is now in the centre of town. Successive land reclamation projects have meant that many of the original stilt villages, such as Kampong Ayer, have been cut off from the sea and some now stand in stinking, stagnant lagoons. The government is cleaning up and reclaiming these areas and the inhabitants of the water villages are being rehoused.

▶▶ *For Sleeping, Eating and other listings, see pages 180-188.*

Sabah Kota Kinabalu

Ins and outs

Getting there

KK's airport is 6 km from town. There are connections with other towns in East Malaysia and the Peninsula as well as with various destinations in the Asian region. For buses into town, there is a bus stop five minutes' walk from the airport, RM1 to city centre. Taxis from the airport cost RM13.50 to the city centre. There is a limited railway service with trains to Beaufort and Tenom and an extensive network of bus, minibus and taxi links to destinations in Sabah. Ferries leave throughout the day for Labuan. Getting to Brunei overland takes around five hours and two ferry crossings at Temburong and Terusan (in Brunei), or a 45-minute flight. ▶▶ *For further details, see Transport, page 187.*

Getting around

City buses and minibuses provide a service around town and to destinations in the vicinity of KK. The bus system is being overhauled and a temporary local bus station is now in front of the post office and next to the city park. Buses to destinations slightly further afield but still in the KK region leave from next to Plaza Wawasan, while long-distance buses wait in the scruffy car park at the base of Signal Hill. Red taxis are unmetered, dark blue taxis have a meter. There are plenty of car hire firms.

Best time to visit

Sabah's equatorial climate means that temperatures rarely exceed 32°C or fall below 21°C, making it fairly pleasant year-round. However, October to March is the rainy season which pretty much spoils any plans for the beach and makes climbing Mount Kinabalu or trekking in Sabah's national parks an unpleasant and slippery experience. If you plan on heading to the islands of the east coast to spot turtles, your best chance is between May and September. Sabah Fest, a big carnival of dancing, music and cow races takes place in May, when the Kadazun/Dusun celebrate their harvest festival. ▶▶ *See Festivals and events, page 36.*

Tourist information

Sabah Tourism Board ⓘ *51 Jl Gaya, T088-212121, www.sabahtourism.com, Mon-Fri 0800-1700, Sat 0800-1400, closed Sun*, is a great first point for help when arriving in

KK. It is well stocked with leaflets and information and has very courteous and helpful staff. **Tourism Malaysia** ⓘ *Ground floor, Uni Asia Building, 1 Jl Sagunting, T088-211732, mtpbki@tourism.gov.my*, is not as useful for Sabah, but still does its best. A great tourist website for Sabah is at www.sabahtravelguide.com.

Tours that are widely available include: Kota Belud *tamu* (Sunday market), Gunung Kinabalu Park (including Poring Hot Springs), Sandakan's Sepilok Orang-Utan Rehabilitation Centre, train trips to Tenom through the Padas Gorge and tours of the islands in the Tunku Abdul Rahman National Park. Several companies specialize in scuba-diving tours. ⏵ *For further information see Activities and tours, page 185.*

Parks offices All accommodation and trekking at Mount Kinabalu and Poring Hot Springs is now organized through **Sutera Sanctuary Lodges** ⓘ *Ground floor, Wisma Sabah, KK, T088-243629, www.suterasanctuarylodges.com, Mon-Fri 0900-1830, Sat 0900-1630, Sun 0900-1500*. For Danum Valley and Maliau Basin, contact **Sabah Foundation** ⓘ *Likas Bay, T088-326327, rosejkj@icsb-sabah.com.my*, or **Sabah Parks** ⓘ *Lot 3, Block K, Sinsuran Complex, T088-211881, www.sabahparks.com.*

History

Kota Kinabalu started life as a trading post, established in 1881 by the **British North Borneo Chartered Company** under the directorship of William C Cowie (see page 217); not on the mainland, but on Gaya Island, opposite the present town, where a Filipino shanty town is today. On 9 July 1897 rebel leader Mat Salleh (see page 176), who engaged in a series of hit-and-run raids against the British North Borneo

Kota Kinabalu

Sabah Port / To Sabah Foundation & ❸

South China Sea

Likas Stadium

Jl Tuaran

Jl Damai

A

Sutera Harbour ❶ Sutera Harbour Golf & Country Club

❷

Jl Kolam

Sabah Golf & Country Club

Related map
A Kota Kinabalu centre, page 174

Masjid Sabah

Sabah State Museum & Science Museum

Jl Mat Balleh

Queen Elizabeth

Jl Bunda Ulam Raya

Tanjung Aru Marina

❻

TANJUNG ARU

Jl Penampang

Jl Putatan

Tanjung Aru Beach

N

To Monsopiad Cultural Village

0 metres 800
0 yards 800

Sleeping
Farida's Bed & Breakfast **3**
Magellan Sutera **1**

Pacific Sutera **2**
Shangri-La Tanjung Aru
Resort **6**

Kota Kinabalu centre

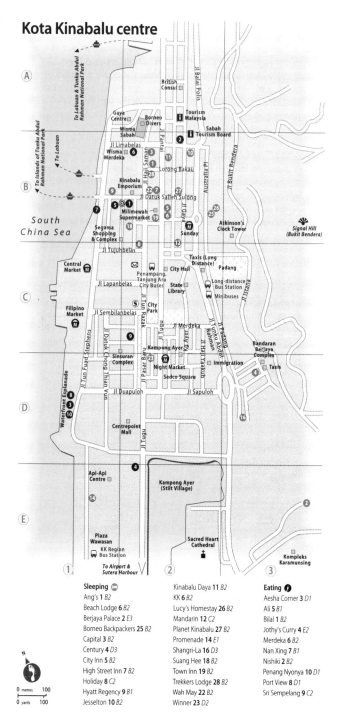

Sleeping
Ang's **1** *B2*
Beach Lodge **6** *B2*
Berjaya Palace **2** *E3*
Borneo Backpackers **25** *B2*
Capital **3** *B2*
Century **4** *D3*
City Inn **5** *B2*
High Street Inn **7** *B2*
Holiday **8** *C2*
Hyatt Regency **9** *B1*
Jesselton **10** *B2*

Kinabalu Daya **11** *B2*
KK **6** *B2*
Lucy's Homestay **26** *B2*
Mandarin **12** *C2*
Planet Kinabalu **27** *B2*
Promenade **14** *E1*
Shangri-La **16** *D3*
Suang Hee **18** *B2*
Town Inn **19** *B2*
Trekkers Lodge **28** *B2*
Wah May **22** *B2*
Winner **23** *D2*

Eating
Aesha Corner **3** *D1*
Ali **5** *B1*
Bilal **1** *B2*
Jothy's Curry **4** *E2*
Merdeka **6** *B2*
Nan Xing **7** *B1*
Nishiki **2** *B2*
Penang Nyonya **10** *D1*
Port View **8** *D1*
Sri Sempelang **9** *C2*

Chartered Company's administration, landed on Pulau Gaya. His men looted and sacked the settlement and Gaya township was abandoned.

Two years later the Europeans established another township but this time located on the mainland, opposite Pulau Gaya, adjacent to a Bajau stilt village. The kampong was called 'Api Api' – meaning 'Fire! Fire!' – because it had been repeatedly torched by pirates over the years. After the Gaya experience, it was an inauspicious name. The Chartered Company rechristened it Jesselton, after Sir Charles Jessel, one of the company directors. However, for years, only the Europeans called it Jesselton; locals preferred the old name, and even today Sabahans sometimes refer to their state capital as 'Api'.

Jesselton owed its raison d'être to a plan that backfired. William C Cowie, formerly a gun-runner for the Sultan of Sulu, became managing director of the Chartered Company in 1894. He wanted to build a trans-Borneo railway and the narrow strip of land just north of Tanjung Aru and opposite Pulau Gaya, with its sheltered anchorage, was selected as a terminus.

Photographs in the Sabah State Museum chart the town's development from 1899, when work on the North Borneo Railway terminus began in earnest. By 1905, Jesselton was linked to Beaufort by a 92-km narrow-gauge track. By 1911 it had a population of 2686, half of whom were Chinese and the remainder Kadazans and Dusuns; there were 33 European residents. Jesselton was of little importance in comparison to Sandakan, the capital of north Borneo.

When the Japanese Imperial Army invaded Borneo in 1942, Jesselton's harbour gave the town strategic significance and it was consequently completely flattened by the Allies during the Second World War. Jesselton followed Kudat and Sandakan as the administrative centre of north Borneo at the end of the Second World War, and the city was rebuilt from scratch. In September 1967 Jesselton was renamed Kota Kinabalu after the mountain; its name is usually shortened to KK.

Sights

Only three buildings remain of the old town: the old **General Post Office** on Jalan Gaya, **Atkinson's Clock Tower** (built in 1905 and named after Jesselton's first district officer) and the old red-roofed **Lands and Surveys building**. The renovated post office now houses the **Sabah Tourism Board.**

Masjid Sabah and Sabah State Museum

The golden dome of **Masjid Sabah** ① *Jl Tunku Abdul Rahman*, is visible from most areas, although it is actually about 3 km out of town. Regular minibuses connect it with the town centre. Completed in 1975, it is the second biggest mosque in Malaysia and, like the Federal Mosque in Kuala Lumpur, a fine example of contemporary Islamic architecture. It can accommodate 5000 worshippers.

Perched on a small hill overlooking the mosque is the relatively new purpose-built **Sabah State Museum (and State Archives)** ① *Jl Mat Salleh/Bukit Istana Lama (Old Palace Hill), www.mzm.sabah.gov.my, Sat-Thu 0900-1700, RM5, guided tours available*, designed to resemble a Rungus longhouse. The museum is divided into ethnography, natural history, ceramics, history and archaeology. The ethnographic section includes an excellent exhibition on the uses of bamboo. Tribal brassware, silverware, musical instruments, basketry and pottery are also on display. On the same floor is a collection of costumes and artefacts from Sabah tribes like the Kadazan/Dusun, Bajau, Murut and Rungus.

One of the most interesting items in this collection is a *sininggazanak* – a sort of totem pole. If a Kadazan man died without an heir, it was the custom to erect a *sininggazanak* – a wooden statue supposedly resembling the deceased – on his

Mat Salleh – fort-builder and folk hero

Mat Salleh was a Bajau, and son of a Sulu chief, born in the court of the Sultan of Sulu. He was the only native leader to stand up against the increasingly autocratic whims of the north Borneo government as it sequestrated land traditionally belonging to tribal chiefs. Under the **British North Borneo Chartered Company** and the subsequent colonial administration, generations of school children were taught that Mat Salleh was a rabble-rouser and troublemaker. Now Sabahans regard him as a nationalist hero.

In the British North Borneo Herald of 16 February 1899, it was reported that when he spoke, flames leapt from his mouth; lightning flashed with each stroke of his parang (cutlass) and when he scattered rice, the grains became wasps. He was said to have been endowed with 'special knowledge' by the spirits of his ancestors and was also reported to have been able to throw a buffalo by its horns.

In 1897 Mat Salleh raided and set fire to the first British settlement on Pulau Gaya (off modern-day Kota Kinabalu). For this, and other acts of sabotage, he was declared an outlaw by the governor. A price tag of 700 Straits dollars was put on his head and an administrative officer, Raffles Flint, was assigned the unenviable task of tracking him down. Flint failed to catch him and Mat Salleh gained a reputation as a military genius. Finally, the managing director of the Chartered Company, Scottish adventurer and former gun-runner William C Cowie, struck a deal with Mat Salleh and promised that his people would be allowed to settle

peacefully in Tambunan, which at that time was not under Chartered Company control.

Half the north Borneo administration resigned as they considered Cowie's concessions outrageous. With it looking less and less likely that the terms of his agreement with Cowie would be respected, Mat Salleh retreated to Tambunan where he started building his fort; he had already gained a fearsome reputation for these stockades. West coast resident G Hewett described it as "the most extraordinary place and without [our] guns it would have been absolutely impregnable". Rifle fire could not penetrate it and Hewett blasted 200 shells into the fort with no noticeable effect. The stone walls were 2.5 m thick and were surrounded by three bamboo fences, the ground in front of which was studded with row upon row of sharpened bamboo spikes. Hewett's party retreated, having suffered four dead and nine wounded.

Mat Salleh had built similar forts all over Sabah, and the hearts of the protectorate's administrators must have sunk when they heard he was building one at Tambunan. A government expedition arrived in the Tambunan Valley on the last day of 1899. There was intensive fighting throughout January, with the government taking village after village, until at last the North Borneo Constabulary came within 50 m of Mat Salleh's fort. Its water supply had been cut off and the fort had been shelled incessantly for 10 days. Mat Salleh was trapped. On 31 January 1900 he was killed by a stray bullet which hit him in the left temple.

land. There is also a collection of human skulls – called a *bangkaran* – which before the tribe's wholesale conversion to Christianity, would have been suspended from the rafters of Kadazan longhouses. Every five years a *magang* feast was held to appease the spirits of the skulls.

The museum's archaeological section contains a magnificently carved coffin found in a limestone cave in the Madai area. Upstairs, the natural history section provides a good introduction to Sabah's flora and fauna. Next door is a collection of jars, called *pusaka*, which are tribal heirlooms. They were originally exchanged by the Chinese for jungle produce, such as beeswax, camphor and birds' nests.

Next door to the State Museum is the **Science Museum**, containing an exhibition on Shell's offshore activities. The **Art Gallery and Multivision Theatre**, within the same complex, are also worth a browse. The art gallery is small and mainly exhibits works by local artists; among the more interesting items on display are those of Suzie Mojikol, a Kadazan artist, Bakri Dani, who adapts Bajau designs, and Philip Biji, who specializes in burning Murut designs onto chunks of wood with a soldering iron. The ethnobotanical gardens are on the hillside below the museum complex. There is a cafeteria at the base of the main building.

Sabah has a large Christian population and the **Sacred Heart Cathedral** has a striking pyramidal roof which is clearly visible from the Sabah State Museum complex.

To get to Masjid Sabah and the Sabah State Museum complex there are minibuses which stop near Wisma Kewangan on the Kota Kinabalu to Tanjung Aru road and near Queen Elizabeth Hospital on the Kota Kinabalu to Penampang road.

Viewpoints

Further into town and nearer the coast are a series of water villages, including **Kampong Ayer**, although it has shrunk in recent years. **Signal Hill** (Bukit Bendera), just southeast of the central area, gives a panoramic view of the town and islands. In the past, the hill was used as a vantage point for signalling to ships approaching the harbour.

Likas Bay

There is an even better view of the coastline from the top of the **Sabah Foundation (Yayasan Sabah) Complex**, 4 km northeast of town, overlooking Likas Bay. This surreal glass sculpture houses the Chief Minister's office. The Sabah Foundation was set up in 1966 to help improve Sabahans' quality of life. The foundation has a 972,800-ha timber concession, which it claims to manage on a sustainable-yield basis (achievement of a high-level annual output without impairing the long-term productivity of the land). Two-thirds of this concession has already been logged. Profits from the timber go towards loans and scholarships for Sabahan students, funding the construction of hospitals and schools and supplying milk, textbooks and uniforms to school children. The Foundation also operates a 24-hour flying ambulance service to remote parts of the interior. See also www.ysnet.org.my.

The fact that between the Yayasan Sabah and the core of the city is one of Borneo's largest squatter communities visibly demonstrates that not everyone is sharing equally in the timber boom.

Over in Likas Bay is the new **Kota Kinabalu City Bird Sanctuary** ① *Tue-Sun 0800-1800, RM10 adults, RM5 children*, a 24-ha spread of mangrove forest with a 1.5-km boardwalk that snakes inside. Possible sightings include egrets, kingfishers, green pigeons, purple herons, plover and redshanks. A pair of binoculars is recommended.

Markets

Gaya street market ① *Sun from 0800*, sells a vast range of goods from jungle produce and handicrafts to pots and pans. The market almost opposite the main minibus station on Jalan Tun Fuad Stephens is known as the **Filipino market** (Pasar Kraftangan), as most of the stalls are run by Filipino immigrants. A variety of Filipino and local handicrafts are sold in the hundreds of cramped stalls, along winding

● The federal government has viewed the spread of Christianity in Sabah with some
● displeasure and there are financial incentives for anyone converting back to Islam.

Sabah Kota Kinabalu

alleyways which are strung with low-slung curtains of shells, baskets and bags. The Filipino market is a good place to buy cultured pearls (about RM5 each) and has everything from fake gemstones to camagong-wood salad bowls, fibre shirts and traditional Indonesian medicines. Further into town, on the waterfront, is the **central market** selling mainly fish, fruit and vegetables. The daily fishing catch is unloaded on the wharf near the market. There is a lively **evening market** selling cheap T-shirts and jewellery just in front of the City Park.

Around Kota Kinabalu ⬤ ⇥ pp180-188.

Tanjung Aru Beach

This is the best beach near KK, after those in Tunku Abdul Rahman National Park, and is close to Tanjung Aru Resort, 5 km south of KK (see page 182). It is particularly popular at weekends and there is a good open-air food court that looks onto the beach. To get there take the Tanjung Aru (beach) bus from the station in front of City Hall.

Penampang

The old town of Donggongon, 13 km southeast of KK, was demolished in the early 1980s and the new township built in 1982. The population is mainly Kadazan or Sino-Kadazan and about 90% Christian. The oldest church in Sabah, **St Michael's** Roman Catholic church, is on a steep hill on the far side of the new town. Turn left just before the bridge – and after the turn-off to the new town – through the kampong and turn left again after the school. It's a 20-minute walk. A granite building with a red roof, it was originally built in 1897 but is not dramatic to look at and has been much renovated over the years. Services are conducted in Kadazan but are fascinating to attend and visitors are warmly welcomed; hymns are sung in Kadazan and Malay. The social focus of the week is the **market** every Sunday. To get to Penampang, take a green and white **Union Transport** bus from just in front of City Hall.

There are many **megaliths** in the Penampang area which are thought to be associated with property claims, particularly when a landowner died without a direct heir. Some solitary stones, which can be seen standing in the middle of paddy fields, are more than 2 m tall. The age of the megaliths has not been determined. Wooden figures, called *sininggazanak* can also be seen in the ricefields (see page 175). **Yun Chuan**, Penampang New Town (also known as Donggongon Township), specializes in Kadazan dishes such as *hinava* – or raw fish – the Kadazan equivalent of sushi. *Tapai* chicken is also recommended.

The Monsopiad Cultural Village

ⓘ *Daily 0900-1700, cultural shows at 1100, 1400 and 1600, RM50.*

This is in Kampong Monsopiad (named after a fearsome Kadazan warrior-cum-headhunter, Siou do Mohoing, the so-called Hercules of Sabah) just outside Penampang. There are 42 fragile human skulls in the collection, some of which are said to be 300 years old and possess spiritual powers. They are laced together with leaves of the hisad palm, which represents the hair of the victims. For those who have already visited longhouses in Sarawak, this collection of skulls, in the rafters of an ordinary little kampong house overlooking the village and the Penampang River, is a bit of an anticlimax. But Dousia Moujing and his son Wennedy are very hospitable and know much about local history and culture. They preside over their ancestor's dreaded sword (although Wennedy reckons it's not the original, even though there are strands of human hair hanging off it). A three-day, three-night feast is held at the house in May, in the run-up to the harvest festival. Visitors should remove footwear and not touch the skulls or disturb the rituals or ceremonies in progress. A reconstruction of the original Monsopiad main house gives the visitor an insight into the life and times of the warrior and his descendants. There is a good restaurant here serving traditional dishes; the *kadazandusun hinara* is recommended. It consists of fresh sliced raw fish marinated in lime juice and mixed with finely sliced chilli, garlic, gourd and shallots.

For more information, contact **Borneo Legends and Myths** ⓘ *5 km Ramaya/ Putaton Rd, Penampang, T088-761336, mcv@tm.net.my*, who manage the village, The house is hard to find; from the new town take the main road east past the Shell station and turn right at sign to Jabatan Air; past St Aloysus Church, the house is on the left about 1.5 km from the turn-off. Minibuses run from Donggongon Township, 10 km south of KK, to Kampong Monsopiad. Take a bus to Donggongon Town and then change to bus for Monsopiad Cultural Village. A taxi from KK should charge about RM20. For RM65 you can catch a shuttle bus from the Sutera Magellan and back, and get entrance to the village. Buses leave for the village from Sutera Magellan on Monday, Wednesday, Friday and Sunday at 0930 and 1400, and on Tuesday, Thursday and Saturday at 0900 and 1400.

Tamparuli

This popular stop for tour buses is 32 km north of KK at the junction of the roads north and east. It has a suspension bridge straddling the Tuaran River, which was built by the British Army in 1922. There is a good handicraft shopping centre here. Buses marked Tamparuli leave from the long-distance bus station at the bottom of Signal Hill.

Around Kota Kinabalu

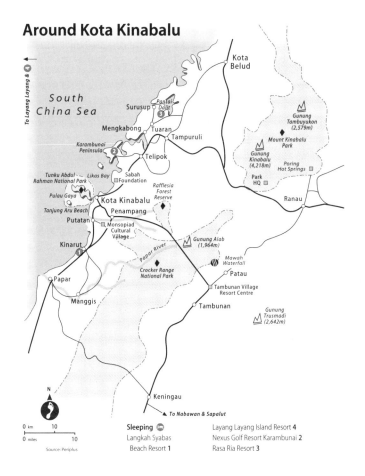

South China Sea

Kota Belud

Gunung Tambuyukon (2,579m)

Surusup — Pantai Dalit
Mengkabong — Tuaran — Tampuruli
Mount Kinabalu Park
Karambunai Peninsula
Telipok
Gunung Kinabalu (4,218m)
Poring Hot Springs
Park HQ

Tunku Abdul Rahman National Park — Likas Bay — Sabah Foundation
Pulau Gaya
Rafflesia Forest Reserve
Ranau

Tanjung Aru Beach
Kota Kinabalu
Penampang
Putatan
Monsopiad Cultural Village
Kinarut
Popar River
Gunung Alab (1,964m)
Mawah Waterfall
Papar
Crocker Range National Park
Patau
Tambunan Village Resort Centre
Manggis
Tambunan
Gunung Trusmadi (2,642m)

N

Keningau

▲ To Nabawan & Sapalut

To Layang Layang & ...

0 km 10
0 miles 10
Source: Periplus

Sleeping 🛏
Langkah Syabas Beach Resort **1**

Layang Layang Island Resort **4**
Nexus Golf Resort Karambunai **2**
Rasa Ria Resort **3**

Mengkabong Water Village and Tuaran

This Baja (sea gypsy) fishing stilt village is within easy reach of KK and is likened to an Asian Venice. The village is particularly photogenic in the early morning, before Mount Kinabalu – which serves as a dramatic backdrop – is obscured by cloud. The fishermen leave Mengkabong at high tide and arrive back with their catch at the next high tide. They use sampan canoes, hollowed out of a single tree trunk, which are crafted in huts around the village. Some of the waterways and fields around Mengkabong are choked by water hyacinth, an ornamental plant that was originally introduced by Chinese farmers as pig-fodder from South America.

For visitors wanting to escape the popular beaches close to KK, **Tuaran**, 45 minutes north of KK, offers a quieter alternative and is a good access point for several different destinations including Mengkabong. To get there, take a Tuaran bus from the long-distance bus station at the foot of Signal Hill, then change to a local minibus to Mengkabong Water Village. Taxis charge about RM30, or else you can take a tour.

The nearby **Karambunai Beach** has a good picnic area, clean beach and sea. Close by is the **Mimpian Jadi Resort**, see Sleeping, below.

Karambunai Peninsula

The scenic Karambunai Peninsula 30 km north of KK has been transformed by a sprawling multi-million-dollar golf and beach resort complex. See Sleeping, below.

Layang Layang

Layang Layang (Swallow Reef) is a man-made atoll (originally built for the Malaysian navy), some 300 km northwest of KK in the South China Sea, which has become a famous, albeit expensive, dive site. There is one resort on the island that caters solely to divers. You need to book a flight through the resort; there are flights every Tuesday, Thursday, Friday and Sunday leaving KK at 0630 (1 hour, RM770). ►► *See Sleeping, below; see also Diving, page 40.*

● Sleeping

Kota Kinabulu *p172, maps p173 and p174*
Well-heeled tourists will seek the more refined out-of-town resorts; but in KK itself, mid-range hotels have improved immeasurably in recent years. The best bets, offering good value for money, are those catering for itinerant Malaysian businessmen, such as the **Mandarin** and **Shangri-La**.
AL Sutera Harbour Resort,1 Sutera Harbour Blvd, T088-318888, www.suteraharbour.com. 156-ha resort created out of reclaimed land which was previously the South China Sea, it lies to the south of the city centre. Opened in July 2000, the **Harbour** consists of 2 hotels, the **Magellan Sutera**, and the **Pacific Sutera**, The **Magellan Sutera** offers the more relaxed resort, with much in the way of sporting activities, including 27 holes of golf and a spa. The **Pacific Sutera** is more focused towards businessmen, providing excellent conference facilities. Together, they offer almost 1000 rooms.

A Berjaya Palace, 1 Jl Tangki, Karamunsing, T088-211911, www.berjayaresorts.com.my. 160 rooms, pool, sauna and gym, conference rooms. This distinctive, castellated hotel stands on a hill south of KK. The proprietor James Sheng has a small resort, with chalets, on Pulau Gaya, at Maluham Bay, east of Police Bay, enquire at hotel.
A Hyatt Regency, Jl Datuk Salleh Sulong, T088-221134, http://kinabalu.regency.hyatt. com. A/c, 288 rooms, 3 restaurants, pool and small children's pool, good central location, rooms vary in standard, business centre, live entertainment (**Shenanigan's Fun Pub**). Tours and treks organized. Good value.
A Jesselton, 69 Jl Gaya, T088-223333, www.jesseltonhotel.com. The first to open in KK, this classic hotel dates from 1954. With just 32 rooms, it was upgraded in the mid-1990s and is now considered KK's premier boutique-style hotel. It's an old establishment, with everything from a London taxi to shoe-shining at your service.

A **Langkah Syabas Beach Resort**, Kinarut, 21 km south of KK, T088-752000, lsr@po.jaring.my. A resort with 16 detached and semi-detached chalets encircling the swimming pool. A/c, fans, TVs, tennis and riding centre close by, attractive garden.

A **Promenade**, 4 Lorong Api-Api 3, Api-Api Centre, T088-265555, www.promenade.com. my/. Attractive seafront position. Several restaurants, business facilities, gym with good range of equipment, pool.

B **Capital**, 23 Jl Haji Saman, T088-231999, F088-237222. A/c, TV, 102 rooms, coffee shop, central position. Newly renovated in 2004.

B **Century**, Jl Masjid Lama, T088-242222, F088-242929. A/c, 54 rooms, good seafood restaurant.

B **Holiday**, Block F, Segama Shopping Complex, off Jl Tun Razak, T088-213116, F088-215576. A/c, quite good with central location, but overpriced.

B **Kinabalu Daya**, 9 Jl Pantai, T088-240000, F088-263909. 68 rooms, a/c, top-floor restaurant serves Asian and Western food, seminar room. Breakfast included.

B **Mandarin**, 138 Jl Gaya, T088-225222, F088-225481. A/c, restaurant, marble floors, well-fitted rooms, excellent central location, friendly staff, 6th-floor rooms with good view over town, deluxe and super-deluxe particularly spacious. Recommended.

B **Shangri-La**, 75 Bandaran Berjaya, T088-212800, kkshang@po.jaring.my. A/c, restaurant, not in the international Shangri-La group; reasonable hotel though, and the haunt of business visitors.

C **Ang's**, 28 Lorong Bakau, off Jl Pantai, T088-234999, F088-217867. A/c, 35 rather threadbare rooms, try to get a room at the front with windows or else you'll be stuck in a windowless box. Not bad value for money, rooms are clean and there's satellite TV but don't expect anything fancy. Central location.

C **City Inn**, 41 Jl Pantai, T088-218933, F088-218937. A/c, bathroom and TV; good for the price, often full.

C **High Street Inn**, 38 Jl Pantai, T088-218111, F088-219111. A/c, TV, in-house films, hot water, small but comfortable rooms – very typical of the characterless hotels in this price range.

C **Suang Hee**, Block F, 7 Segama Shopping Centre, T088-254168, F088-217234. Clean Chinese hotel, reasonable value for money. A/c, restaurant, 24 rooms, TV and bathroom.

C **Town Inn**, 31-33 Jl Pantai, T088-225823, F088-217762. A/c, 24 rooms, clean with excellent facilities, central location, good for the price. Recommended.

C **Wah May**, 36 Jl Haji Saman, T088-266118, F088-266122. Modern Chinese hotel, 36 clean rooms kitted out with a/c, TV, fridge. Tight security with CCTV in operation.

C **Winner**, 9 & 10 Jl Pasar Baru, Kampong Ayer, T088-243222, F088-217345. A/c, 36 rooms, restaurant, pleasant central hotel, friendly staff, good restaurant.

C-E **Beach Lodge**, 46 Jl Pantai, T088-213888, beach_lodge@hotmail.com. Cute little guesthouse with friendly staff, if a little laid back. Only has a handful of double rooms, all with shared hot water showers, so you need to book about a week in advance. Also 2 8-bed dorms available. Breakfast included, and free airport pickup. Lots of tour information and little breakfast/lounge area. Very clean with tiled floors. Recommended.

C-E **Farida's Bed & Breakfast**, 413 Jl Saga, Mile 4.5 Jl Tuaran, Likas, T088-428733, www.homeaway.com.my/farida.htm. A friendly, whitewashed lodge with 12 rooms, from dorms to doubles with attached bathroom. They offer internet, kitchen, laundry and free breakfast. It's a 10-min drive from KK to the B&B in Likas. They may be able to offer free pick-up, phone in advance, else take a Likas bus from Plaza Wawasan and get off before the mosque. It's a 5-min walk from there. The place is run by **Home Away from Home**, a tour company.

C-E **Trekkers Lodge**, 30 Jl Haji Saman, T088-252263, www.trekkerslodge.com. Very popular place, so need to book ahead by several days to get a/c or fan double room. Rooms with attached bathroom are in the B category, not good value. Well set up for travellers, with helpful staff, sitting-out area, library, tour information (they can do good deals with **Borneo Divers**). But because it's so popular it feels cramped and can get a bit grubby, particularly the dorms.

D **Borneo Backpackers**, 24 Lorong Dewan, at the foot of Signal Hill on the corner with the roundabout, T088-234 009, www.borneo backpackers.com. This is a new concept backpackers opened in Jan 2005 in a renovated 3-storey building that dates back to the 1950s, when it was used as a printing works. 50 beds, internet, laundry, lounge, roof garden, and tourist information. The ground floor houses a post-war era coffee shop stacked with wartime photos and antique-style furniture.

D KK, 46 Jl Pantai, 1st floor, T088-248587. Just 2 floors down from **Beach Lodge**, this place has cheap doubles with shared bathroom, but is not set up for travellers. There's no travel information or communal lounge, simply a cheap, basic place to stay if all the guesthouses are full.

D-E Lucy's Homestay (Backpacker Lodge), Australia Pl, 25 Lorong Dewan, T088-261495, welcome.to/backpackerkk. Friendly, clean dorms and doubles with a good breakfast included in the room rate. In a quiet location near Signal Hill, this is the nicest and most relaxed of all the backpacker places. Lucy is friendly and offers tour info, simple kitchen, library and little balcony. Due to its popularity you will need to book some days in advance. Recommended.

E Planet Kinabalu, 98 & 100 Jl Gaya, T088-319168, planetkinabalu@hotmail.com. Dormitory-only place well set up for travellers. Lots of facilities, smartcard entry, laundry, TV and video, tour information and free breakfast at the Malay café downstairs (best free budget breakfast in KK). Nice, casual place.

Homestays
Homestays in Sabah are now organized through **Nature Heritage Travel and Tours**, ground floor, Wisma Sabah, T088-318747, nhtt@nature-heritage.com.

Tanjung Aru Beach *p178*
AL Shangri-La Tanjung Aru Resort, Tanjung Aru, T088-225800, www.shangri-la.com. A/c, 500 rooms, pool, one of the best hotels in Sabah, along with its sister hotel, the **Rasa Ria** at Tuaran. Tanjung Aru is a public beach, frequented by kite- flyers, swimmers, joggers and lovers; the hotel is noticeably on the European honeymoon circuit. Recommended.

Mengkabong Water Village and Tuaran *p180*
AL Rasa Ria Resort, overlooking Pantai Dalit Beach, near Tuaran, T088-792888, www.shangri-la.com/eng/hotel/23/. Top-class **Shangri-La** resort with 330 rooms, free-form pool, watersports, 18-hole golf course, driving range, spacious gardens, conference facilities, horse riding, cultural events, several restaurants including an Italian and a seafood beach-front restaurant, torch-lighting ceremony, and 30 ha of forest nature reserve with semi-tame orang-utans. There have been some complaints about the integrity of an orang-utan fostering programme run by the resort and the cleanliness of the surrounding beach away from the resort. To get there, take a local bus to Tuaran. Recommended.

A-B Mimpian Jadi Resort, No 1 Kuala Matinggi, Kampong Pulau, Simpangan, Karambunai Beach, T088-787799, F088-787775. It has chalets, a private beach, watersports, fishing, mini zoo, karaoke bar, horse riding, volleyball, children's playground, Malay/Chinese and Western food. To get there, take a bus to Menggatal, then change to a bus to Karambunai. Surusup is 10-15 mins beyond Tuaran. Ask at the store in Surusup for Haji Abdul Saman, who will take visitors by boat to the lesser-known Bajau fishing village, Kampong Penambawan, also likened to an Asian Venice, on the north bank of the river. Nearby there is a suspension bridge and rapids where it is possible to swim.

Karambunai Peninsula *p180*
LL-A The Nexus Golf Resort Karambunai, Menggatal, T088-411222, www.nexus resort.com. The complex is built on 1350 ha of land sprawling along the coast and has 490 ocean-view rooms, along with all the usual facilities including an 18-hole golf course, 3 swimming pools and a host of other sporting activities. It is popular for conferences and is patronized by businessmen from the region.

Layang Layang *p180*
AL Layang Layang Island Resort, T088-709121/141, www.layanglayang.com. This 3-star resort has 76 rather plain rooms and 10 suites, with a movie room, swimming pool, bar and restaurant. Apart from the resort the atoll is rather bleak with only an airstrip.

🍽 Eating

Kota Kinabulu *p172, maps p173 and p174*
The new waterfront has a whole range of
restaurants with outdoor seating facing the
South China Sea. Seafood is seasonally prone to
red tide. Locals will know when it's prevalent.
Avoid all shellfish if there is any suspicion.

Chinese
Hyatt Poolside Hawker Centre, Hyatt
Hotel, Jl Datuk Salleh Sulong. Steamboat
(minimum 2 people).
Aesha Corner, Anjung Perdana (the
Waterfront). Cheap Malay canteen
facing the sea.
Avasi Cafeteria & Garden Restaurant,
EG 11 Kompleks Kowasa. Steamboat and
seafood.
Nan Xing, Jl Datuk Salleh Sulong, opposite
the **Hyatt** and **Emporium**. Dim sum and
Cantonese specialities.
Phoenix Court, Hyatt Hotel, Jl Datuk
Salleh Sulong. Dim sum, 0700-1400.
Sri Sempelang, Sinsuran 2 (on the corner
with Jl Pasar Baru). Great Malay canteen
with enormous fruit juices and tables
outside. Locals recommend it.
Tioman, Lot 56 Bandaran Berjaya, good
claypot and lemon chicken.

Malay
Copelia, Jl Gaya. *Nasi lemak* for breakfast,
also does takeaway.
Restoran Ali, Segama Complex, opposite
Hyatt Hotel. Best in a string of coffee shops,
all of which are good value for money.

Nyonya
Penang Nyonya, Anjung Perdana (the
Waterfront). Good, fair-priced Nyonya dishes
as spicy as you like.
Sri Melaka Restoran, 9 Jl Laiman Diki,
Kampong Ayer (Sedco Complex, near Shiraz).
Popular with the fashionable KK set, serves
great Malay and Nyonya food.

Other Asian cuisine
Jaws, 4th floor, Gaya Centre, Jl Tun Fuad
Stephens. Thai/Chinese cuisine, such as *tom
yam* steamboat.
Nagisa, Hyatt Hotel, Jl Datuk Salleh
Sulong, T088-221234. Fancy Japanese place

with tables facing the South China Sea. Open
kitchen, sushi bar, teppanyaki counters and
a tatami room for the rich and private.
Nishiki, Jl Gaya (opposite Wing On Life
Building). Japanese. Friendly staff and
good-sized portions.
Bilal, Block B, Lot 1 Segama Complex.
Indian Muslim food, rotis, chapatis,
curries. Recommended.
Islamic Restoran, Kampong Ayer.
The best roti in town.
Jothy's Curry Restaurant, Api-Api
Centre. 1000-2200. Giant curries and
banana leaf offerings.
Korean, Jl Bandaran Berjaya, next to
Asia Hotel. Large selection, barbecues
are a speciality.
Shiraz, Lot 5, Block B, Sedco Sq, Kampong
Ayer. Indian. Recommended.
Sri Sakthi, Mile 4.5, Jl Penampeng (opposite
Towering Heights Industrial Estate). South
Indian banana-leaf, good value.

International
Fat Cat, Jl Haji Saman. Cheap slap-
up breakfasts.
Gardenia Grill Room, Jesselton Hotel,
69 Jl Gaya, T088-223333. Elegant dining.
Little Italy, Ground floor, **Hotel Capital**,
23 Jl Haji Saman, T088-232231. Award-
winning pizza and pasta place with Italian
chef. If you're craving for some European
food, this is the place to come. Open for
lunch and dinner. Recommended.
Peppino, Tanjung Aru Resort,
T088-225800. Tasty but expensive, Italian,
good Filipino cover band.

Seafood
Garden Terrace, Tanjung Aru Resort,
T088-225800, 0600-2300. Asian and Western
buffet (dim sum available) and à la carte,
with tables facing pretty gardens.
**Kampong Nelayan Floating Seafood
Market**, Taman Tun Fuad, Bukit Padang,
T088-269991. Popular with tour groups.
Chinese and Malay dishes accompanied
by traditional dancing.
Merdeka, 11th floor, Wisma Merdeka.
Reasonably good seafood, but the view is
better, in this restaurant which offers
'karaoke at no extra charge'.

Port View, the Waterfront, T088-221753. Huge selection of fresh seafood and delicious chilli crab. Massive clattering restaurant, very popular.

Seafood Market, Tanjung Aru Beach, T088-238313. Pick your own fresh seafood and get advice on how to have it cooked.

Golf Field Seafood, 0858 Jl Ranca-Ranca (better known by taxi drivers as **Ahban's Place**), excellent marine cuisine, local favourite. Recommended.

Foodstalls

Stalls above central market. **Sedco Square**, Kampong Ayer, large square filled with stalls, great atmosphere in the evenings, ubiquitous *ikan panggang* and satay. Night market on Jl Tugu, on the Waterfront at the **Sinsuran Food Centre** and at the **Merdeka Foodstall Centre**, Wisma Merdeka. **Tanjung Aru Beach**, mainly seafood – recommended for *ikan panggang* – and satay stalls: very busy at weekends, but on weekdays it is rather quiet, with only a few stalls to choose from.

Bars and clubs

Kota Kinabalu *p172, maps p173 and p174*

Bars

Many of the more popular bars are along the **Waterfront**. **Beach St** is a pedestrianized lane between Jl Pantai and Jl Gaya with restaurants and bars, all with outdoor seating.

Shamrock Irish Bar (there has to be an Irish bar!) has a ladies' night on Thu. A popular late-night club is **The Beach Club** at the end of the Waterfront, with a big dance floor, a bear theme, DJ, quite funky for KK. **Café Upperstar**, Segama Complex (opposite **Hotel Hyatt**) has fried food and sandwiches, and jugs of Long Island Iced Tea for RM45. There's the rough and ready **BB Café** on Beach St, which has cheap beer, a pool table and closes at 0300.

Clubs

Shennanigan's, Hyatt Hotel, Jl Datuk Salleh Sulong, is the smartest disco in town. **Next Door**, Tanjung Aru Resort. **Tiffiny**, Tanjung Aru, opposite Sacred Heart Church. **Rockies**, Promenade Hotel.

Karaoke is very popular in KK; found in Damai, Foh Sang and KK centre.

Entertainment

Kota Kinabalu *p172, maps p173 and p174*

Cinemas

Cinema in Centrepoint Mall.

Cultural shows

Kadazan-Dusun Cultural Centre (Hongkod Koisaan), KDCA Building, Mile 4.5, Jl Penampang. Restaurant open year-round, but at the end of May, during the harvest festival, the cultural association comes into its own, with dances, feasts and shows and lots of *tapai* (RM15). **Tanjung Aru Resort**, Wed and Sat 2000. **Cultural Palace Theatre Restaurant**, Jl Tanjung Lipat, T088-251844. Dance shows by Kadazan-Dusun, Bajau and Murut. Dinner and show RM42 (from 1845, closed Mon). You'll need a taxi to get there. **Kampong Nelayan** (see Eating, page 183) also has dance shows during dinner.

Festivals and events

Kota Kinabalu *p172, maps p173 and p174*

May Magavau (see page 36), a post-harvest celebration, is carried out at Hongkod Koisaan (cultural centre), Mile 4.5, Jl Penampang. To get there, take a green and white bus from the MPKK Building, next to state library.

Shopping

Kota Kinabalu *p172, maps p173 and p174*

Antiques

There's a good antiques shop at the bottom of the Chun Eng Building on Jl Tun Razak, and a couple on Jl Gaya. **Merdeka Complex** and **Wisma Wawasan 2020** hold a number of antiques shops. It is necessary to have an export licence from the Sabah State Museum if you intend to export rare antiques.

Books

Arena Book Centre, Lot 2, Ground floor, Block 1, Sinsuran Kompleks. **Borneo Books**, Wisma Merdeka, eco-friendly books on Borneo. Wisma Merdeka is the best place to go for the widest range of books. **Borneo Crafts**, Ground floor, Wisma Merdeka, T088-233757, selection of English-language books and magazines. **Rahmant**

Bookstore, Hyatt Hotel, Jl Datuk Salleh Sulong. **Zenithway**, 29 Jl Pantai. Some English books and magazines, also stocks Penguin books.

Clothes

The House of Borneo Vou'tique, Lot 12A, 1st floor, Lorong Bernam 3, Taman Saon Kiong, Jl Kolam, T088-268398, for that ethnic, exotic and exclusive look for men and women – corporate uniforms, souvenir items, tablecloths, cushion covers, etc. **Centrepoint Mall** provides the biggest selection of 'designer' clothing.

Electronic goods

VCDs, DVDs and stereo equipment are considered the cheapest in the country here. Both **Karamunsing Kompleks** and **Centrepoint** are the places to go.

Handicrafts

Mainly baskets, mats, tribal clothing, beadwork and pottery. **Api Tours**, Lot 49, Bandaran Berjaya, has a small selection of handicrafts. **Borneo Gifts**, Ground floor, Wisma Sabah. **Borneo Handicraft**, 1st floor, Wisma Merdeka, local pottery and material made up into clothes. **Elegance Souvenir**, 1st floor, Wisma Merdeka, lots of beads of local interest (another branch on ground floor of Centrepoint). **Kaandaman Handicraft Centre** below Seafood Market Restaurant, Tanjung Aru Beach. **Kampong Ayer Night Market**, mainly Filipino handicrafts. **Kraftangan Kompleks/ Filipino Market**, Jl Tun Fuad Stephens (see page 177). **Malaysian Handicraft**, Cawangan Sabah, No 1, Lorong 14, Kg Sembulau, T088-234471, Mon-Sat 0815-1230, Fri 0815-1600. **Sabah Art and Handicraft Centre**, 1st foor, Block B, Segama Complex (opposite **New Sabah Hotel**). **Sabah Handicraft Centre**, Lot 49 Bandaran Berjaya (next to **Shangri-La**), good selection (also has branches at the museum and the airport). **The Crafts**, Lot AG10, Ground floor, Wisma Merdeka, T088-252413. There are also several handicraft shops in the arcade at the **Tanjung Aru Resort** and one at the airport.

Jewellery

Most shops in Wisma Merdeka.

Shopping complexes

Kinabalu Emporium, Wisma Yakim, Jl Daruk Salleh Sulong is the main department store. **Likas Square**, Likas, pink monstrosity with 2 floors of shopping malls, foodstalls and restaurants. Cultural shows in central lobby. **Segama**, Jl Tun Fuad Stephens and **Sinsuran**. Beware of pickpocketing during the day and more particularly at night.

▲ Activities and tours

Kota Kinabalu *p172, maps p173 and p174*
The sports complex at Likas is open to the general public. It provides volleyball, tennis, basketball, a gym, badminton, squash, aerobics and a swimming pool. To get there take a Likas-bound minibus from Plaza Wawasan. Likas Square, the monstrous pink shopping complex north of Likas Sports Complex, has a recreation club within it providing tennis, squash, jogging, golf, driving range, a pool and a children's playground.

Bowling

Merdeka Bowl, 11th floor, Wisma Merdeka.

Diving

Do not believe dive shops when they say you must book diving through their KK office. It is cheaper to book your dive or dive courses through dive shops in Semporna. Snorkelling and scuba diving in Tunku Abdul Rahman National Park. Tour operators specializing in dive trips also organize dives all over Sabah; their offices are mostly in Wisma Sabah.

Golf

Green fees are considerably higher over the weekend – as much as double the weekday rate. Fees range from about RM50 during the week at the cheaper courses, to RM200 or more over the weekend at flasher clubs. **Golf Booking Centre Malaysia** provides escorted golf tours, nbtt@tm.net.my.
Sabah Golf and Country Club, Bukit Padang, T088-247533. The oldest course in the state, this 18-hole championship course affords magnificent views of Mt Kinabalu.
Sutera Harbour Golf and Country Club, on reclaimed land just to south of the city. A 27-hole layout with great views across to the islands of Tunku Abdul Rahman Park.

Horse riding

Kindawan Riding Centre, 21 km south of KK at Kinarut, www.kindawan.com. Call Dale Sinidal, an Australian who has run this school for over 10 years, T088-225525. There are trail rides of approximately 2 hrs through villages and paddy fields or along the beach and across to an island at low tide. The surroundings are stunning and the horses are well kept and good tempered. It is RM50 for 1 hr. Call Ms Sinidal and she will organize transport from KK. For places to stay near Kinarut, see the Papar entry on page 193.

Roller blading

Centrepoint, 3rd floor, Jl Gaya.

Sailing and watersports

Tanjung Aru Marina, snorkelling RM10 per day, waterskiing RM120 per hr, fishing RM12-25 per day, sailing RM20-40 per hr, water scooter RM60 per hr.
Yacht club, Tanjung Aru, next to the hotel.

Whitewater rafting

Papar River (Grades I & II), Kadamaian River (Grades II & III), Padas River (Grade IV). Usually requires a minimum of 3 people. Main operators include Api Tours, Diethelm Borneo Expeditions and Discovery Tours (see below).

Tour operators

The Sabah Tourism Board has a full list of tour agents operating in the state, and also on its website, www.sabahtourism.com.
Adventure Journey World Travel, Ground floor, Lot 5, Block A, Taman Fortuna Shoplots, Jl Penampang, T088-223918, www.borneo.org.
Api Tours (Borneo), No 13 Jl Punai Dekut, Mile 5, Jl Tuaran, PO Box 12851, T088-424156, www.jaring.my/apitours. Offers a wide variety of tours, including some more unusual ones such as overnight stays in longhouses. Recommended.
Borneo Divers, Ground floor, Wisma Sabag, T088-222227, www.borneo divers.info. Operates exotic scuba-diving trips all over Borneo including around Sipadan, has accommodation on Mamutik Island (Tunku Abdul Rahman), see page 229, they also have an office in Tawau,

T089761214. Dive trips are well organized but expensive, it's possible to bargain.
Trekker's Lodge can sometimes help with good deals with this dive shop.
Borneo Eco Tours, Lot 1, Pusat Perindustrian, Kolombong Jaya, 88450, T088-438300, www.borneoecotours.com. Specializes in environmentally aware tours. Their **Sukau Rainforest Lodge** on the Kinabatangan River is highly recommended.
Borneo Sea Adventurs, 1st floor, 8a Karamunsing Warehouse, T088-230000, www.bornsea.com. Also conducts scuba-diving courses and runs diving and fishing trips all around Sabah (see page 229).
Borneo Ultimate, Ground floor, Wisma Sabah, www.borneoultimate.com. Hard adventure tours including whitewater rafting, mountain biking, jungle trekking, and sea kayaking.
Borneo Wildlife Adventures, Lot F, 1st floor, General Post Office building, T088-213668, www.borneo-wildlife.com. Specializing in nature tours, wildlife and cultural activities.
Diethelm Borneo Expeditions, Suite 303, 2nd floor, EON-CMG Life Building, 1 Jl Sagunting, T088-222271, dbex@tm.net.my.
Discovery Tours, Ground floor, Wisma Sabah, Jl Haji Saman, T088-221244, www.infosabah.com.my/discovery/. Run by experienced tour operator Terry Lim. Recommended.
Exotic Borneo, Likas Post Office, Likas, T088-245920, www.exborneo.com/. Organizes well-run theme tours including culture, adventure and nature, at a price.
Pan Borneo Tours & Travel, 1st floor, Lot 127, Wisma Sabah, T088-221221, www.jaring.my/panborn. Sightseeing, diving, wildlife tours.
Sipadan Dive Centre, 11th floor, Wisma Merdeka, Jl Tun Razak, T088-240584, www.sipadandivers.com. Experienced tour outfit, running dives and courses at Sipadan and Tunku Abdul Rahman Park. They also own the new **Proboscis Lodge** at Sukau.
Tanjung Aru Tours, The Marina, Tanjung Aru Resort, T088-214215, F088-240966. Fishing and island tours – particularly to Tunku Abdul Rahman National Park.

⊙ Transport

Kota Kinabulu *p172, maps p173 and p174*

Air

The airport is 6 km from town, T088-238555. Air is the most widely used form of transportation between the major towns of Sabah (**Sandakan**, **Tawau** and **Lahad Datu**), and it's cheap. Taxi RM13.50 to town centre; coupon can be purchased in advance from the booths outside the arrivals hall. Regular connections with **KL**. There are also connections from KK with **Bintulu**, **Johor Bahru**, **Kuching**, **Labuan**, **Miri** and **Sibu**. International connections are with **Singapore**, **Brunei**, **Hong Kong**, **Philippines**, **South Korea**, **Japan**, various cities in China including **Shanghai** and **Taiwan**. AirAsia now have cheap fares between KK and Bangkok.

   Airline offices AirAsia, office on Jl Gaya, T088-438222. **British Airways**, Jl Haji Saman, T088-428057/428292. **Cathay Pacific**, Ground floor, Block C, Lot CG, Kompleks Kowasa, 49 Jl Karamunsing, T088-428733. **Dragonair**, T088-254733. **Garuda Airways**, Wisma Sabah. **MAS**, Ground floor, Karamunsing Kompleks (off Jl Tunku Abdul Rahman, south of Kampong Ayer), Jl Kemajuan, T088-213555, F088-240135, also have an office at the airport. **Philippine Airlines**, 3rd floor, Karamunsing Kompleks, Jl Kemajuan, T088-239600. **Qantas**, T088-216998. **Royal Brunei Airlines**, Ground floor, Kompleks Kowasa, T088-242193, **Sabah Air**, KK Airport, T088-256733. **Singapore Airlines**, Ground floor, Block C, Kompleks Kowasa, T088-255444. **Thai Airways**, T088-232896, Lot CG14, Block C, Ground floor, Kompleks Kowasa.

Boat

There is a ferry service between KK and **Labuan** every day between 0800 and 1500, the journey takes 2 hrs (RM31 one way). Ferries to **Serasa Muara** (Brunei) leave from the Labuan jetty between 0830 and 1630 (RM24), the trip takes 1 hr.

Bus

There is no central bus station in KK. The bus system is being overhauled and a temporary local bus station is now in front of the post office and next to the city park. Buses slightly further afield but still in the KK region leave from next to Plaza Wawasan, while long-distance buses wait in the scruffy car park at the base of Signal Hill. Buses around the state are cheaper than minibuses but not as regular or efficient. The large buses go mainly to destinations in and around KK itself.

   There are lots of bus companies and when you arrive at the bus station touts will try to get you to use their company. All the prices should be the same, and it's advisable to buy your ticket the day before. The time on the ticket is a rough guide only. Get there 10 mins before to guarantee your seat, but you may have to wait until the bus is full. Buses to **Tenom** (0800, 1200, 1600, RM16), **Keningau** (7 departures daily, RM12.15), **Beaufort** (more than 10 every day, RM7), **Tawau** (0730, 0800, RM45), **Sandakan** (0730, 0930, 1300, 2000, RM29.25), **Semporna** (0730, RM45), **Lahud Datu** (0730, RM13.50).

   Minibuses and taxis All minibuses have their destinations on the windscreen, most rides in town are less than RM1 and they will leave when full. You can get off wherever you like.

   Taxis and minibuses bound north for **Kota Belud**, **Tamparuli** and **Kudat** and those going south to **Papar**, **Beaufort**, **Keningau** and **Tenom** leave from Bandar Berjaya opposite the Padang and clock tower. Taxis and minibuses going west to **Kinabalu National Park**, **Ranau** and **Sandakan** leave from Jl Tunku Abdul Rahman, next to the Padang and opposite the State Library. Tampuruli, a few kilometres east of Tuaran, serves as a mini-terminus for minibuses heading to **Kinabalu National Park**. Minibuses leave when full and those for long-distance destinations leave in the early morning. Long-distance taxis also leave when full from in front of the clock tower on Jl Tunku Abdul Rahman. Minibus services from KK to **Tuaran** 45 mins, **Kota Belud** 2 hrs, **Kudat** 4-5 hrs, **Beaufort** 2-3 hrs, **Keningau** 2-3 hrs, **Tenom** 4 hrs, **Kinabalu National Park** 1½ hrs, **Ranau** 2 hrs, **Sandakan** 8-10 hrs.

Car

Car hire Not all roads in the interior of Sabah are paved and a 4WD vehicle is advisable for some journeys. Car hire is expensive (RM30-80 per hr) and rates often increase for use outside a 50-km radius of KK. All vehicles have to be returned to KK as there are no agency offices outside KK, although local car hire is usually available. Drivers must be between the ages of 22 and 60 and be in possession of an international driving licence. **ABAN-D Rent a Car**, Lot 22, 1st floor, Taman Victory, Mile 4.5, Jl Penampang, T088-722300, F088-721959. **Adaras Rent-a-Car**, Lot G03, Ground floor, Wisma Sabah, T088-2166671, F088-216010. **Hertz**, Level 1, Lot 39, Kota Kinabalu airport, T088-317740. **Kinabalu Rent-a-Car**, Lot 3.61, 3rd floor, Karamunsing Kompleks, T088-232602, www.kinabalurac.com/. **Samzain Rent a Car**, Lot 10, Tingkat 2 Putatan Point, Putatan 88200, Penampang, T088-765805.

Taxis

There are taxi stands outside most of the bigger hotels and outside the General Post Office, the Segama complex, the Sinsuran complex, next to the DPKK building, the Milemewah supermarket, the Capitol cinema and in front of the clock tower (for taxis to **Ranau**, **Keningau** and **Kudat**). Approximate fares from town: RM10 to **Tanjung Aru Resort**, RM10 to **Sabah Foundation**, RM8 to the museum, RM14 to the airport. See also minibuses and taxis, above.

Train

The station is 5 km out of town in Tanjung Aru. There is only 1 train line in Sabah, and rolling stock dates from the colonial era. Diesel trains run 3 times daily to **Beaufort**,

2 hrs and on to **Tenom**, a further 3 hrs. Departure times are subject to change, T088-254611. There is also a steam train which operates along this same line. For transport from the railway station to town, long-distance buses stop near the station.

⊙ Directory

Kota Kinabalu *p172, maps p173 and p174*
Banks There are money changers in main shopping complexes: HSBC, 56 Jl Gaya; Maybank, Jl Kemajuan/ Jl Pantai; Sabah Bank, Wisma Tun Fuad Stephens, Jl Tuaran; Standard Chartered, 20 Jl Haji Saman.
Embassies and consulates British Consul, Hong Kong Bank Building, 56 Jl Gaya; Indonesian Consulate, Jl Karamunsing, T088-428100; Japanese Consulate, Wisma Yakim, T088-428169. **Immigration** 4th floor Government Building, Jl Haji Yaakub, visas can be renewed at this office, without having to leave the country. **Internet** Touch Surf, 1/F Segama Complex (opposite Burger King), fast and cheap, 0900-2400, RM2 per hr; City Internet Cafe, Ground floor, Centrepoint (entrance outside), slow connection, there's also a traveller's internet café on Jl Pantai next door to Beach Lodge. **Medical services** One of the better private clinics is the Damai Specialist Centre. **Post** General Post Office, Jl Tun Razak, Segama Quarter (poste restante facilities). **Telephone** Telekom Block C, Kompleks Kuwaus, Jl Tunku Abdul Rahman, international calls as well as local, fax service.

Off the coast and south of Kota Kinabalu

West of KK is the Tunku Abdul Rahman Park, a reef and coral marine park. Travelling south from KK, the route crosses the Crocker Range to Tambunan. Continuing south the road passes through the logging town of Keningau and on to Tenom, where it is possible to take the North Borneo railway, which snakes down the Padas Gorge to Beaufort. The Padas River is the best place to go whitewater rafting in Sabah. Few towns are worth staying in for long on this route but it is a scenic journey.

Pulau Tiga National Park is a forest reserve where the pied hornbill can be spotted and Pulau Labuan is a tax-free haven off the coast. »» *For Sleeping, Eating and other listings, see pages 197-203.*

Tunku Abdul Rahman National Park ●●●

▶▶ *pp197-203. Colour map 2, A1.*

The five islands in Gaya Bay, which make up Tunku Abdul Rahman Park (TAR), lie 3-8 km offshore. Coral reefs fringe all the islands in the park. The best reefs are between **Pulau Sapi** and **Pulau Gaya**, although there is also reasonable coral around **Manukan**, **Mamutik** and **Sulug**. Named after Malaysia's first Prime Minister, they became Sabah's first national park in 1923 and were gazetted in 1974 in an effort to protect their coral reefs and sandy beaches. Geologically, the islands are part of the Crocker Range formation, but as sea levels rose after the last ice age, they became isolated from the massif. The islands can be visited all year round.

Ins and outs

Getting there Boats for the park leave from the main ferry terminal, 10 minutes' walk north of the town. Ferries to Labuan leave from here too. There are also frequent boats from the Tanjung Aru Resort.

Tourist information Park HQ is on Pulau Manukan; there are ranger stations on Gaya, Sapi and Mamutik.

Flora and fauna

Some of the only undisturbed coastal dipterocarp forest left in Sabah is on Pulau Gaya. On the other islands most of the original vegetation has been destroyed and established secondary vegetation predominates, such as ferns, orchids, palms, casuarina, coconut trees and tropical fruit trees. Mangrove forests can be found at two locations on Pulau Gaya. Animal and bird life includes long-tailed macaques, bearded pig and pangolin (on Pulau Gaya), white-bellied sea eagle, pied hornbill, green heron, sandpipers, flycatchers and sunbirds.

There is a magnificent range of marine life because of the variety of the reefs surrounding the islands. The coral reefs are teeming with exotica such as butterfly fish, Moorish idols, parrot fish, bat fish, razor fish, lion fish and stone fish, in stark contrast to the areas which have been depth-charged by Gaya's notorious dynamite fishermen.

The islands

By far the largest island, **Pulau Gaya** was the site of the first British North Borneo Chartered Company settlement in the area in 1881; the settlment lasted only 15 years before being destroyed in a pirate attack. There is still a large community on the island on the promontory facing KK – but today it is a shanty town, populated mainly by Filipino immigrants. On Pulau Gaya there are 20 km of marked trails including a plank walk across a mangrove swamp and many beautiful little secluded bays. Police Bay is a popular, shaded beach. **Gayana Island EcoResort** is a big chalet development on the island with its own ferry from the KK jetty. **Pulau Sapi**, the most popular of the islands for weekenders, also has good beaches and trails. It is connected to Pulau Gaya at low tide by a sandbar. Good day-use facilities but no accommodation available here, although there are camping facilities.

Pulau Mamutik, closer to the mainland, is the smallest island but has a well-preserved reef off the northeast tip. **Pulau Manukan** is the site of the Park HQ and most of the park accommodation. It has good snorkelling to the south and east and a particularly good beach on the east tip. It is probably the best of all the islands but is heavily frequented by day trippers and rubbish is sometimes a problem. There is accommodation here, book through **Sutera Sanctuary Lodges**, see page 173. Marine sports facilities stretch to the hire of mask, snorkel and fins (RM15 plus RM50 deposit for the day), but no sub-aqua gear is available. There's a swimming pool, watersports

Sabah Off the coast & south of Kota Kinabalu

centre for sailing, banana boat and windsurfing. Glass-bottom boat trips are available. Fish feeding off the jetty attracts large shoals of fish, making it a good place for snorkelling. The best reefs are off **Pulau Sulug**, which is less developed being a bit further away. This small island has a sand spit, making it good for swimming. There are dive facilities and a restaurant here now. You can also camp here.

Pulau Tiga National Park ⊜ ›› *pp197-203. Colour map 2, A1.*

Pulau Tiga National Park is 48 km south of KK. Declared a forest reserve in 1933, the 15,864 ha park is made up of three islands: Pulau Tiga, Kalampunian Damit and Kalampunian Besar.

Ins and outs

Getting there and around Drive 140 km to Kuala Penyu at the tip of the Klias Peninsula (two hours, you can travel by minibus from KK to Beaufort and then change to another minibus for Kuala Penyu, each trip roughly RM7), and then take a 30-minute boat ride (scheduled departure at 1000 and 1500 from Kuala Penyu). Alternatively charter a speedboat from KK; contact **Sipadan Dive Centre** ① *11th floor, Wisma Merdeka, Jalan Tun Razak, KK, T088-240584*, who run the island's resort, to organize transport to the island. **Sabah Parks Office** can help arrange the boat trip, or else contact **Pulau Tiga Resort**, see Sleeping, page 197. Speedboats cost RM350 for 10 people, but possible to bargain down to RM250 for the boat if fewer people.

Tourist information The Park HQ, on the south side of Pulau Tiga, is mainly used as a botanical and marine research centre and tourism is not vigorously promoted; as a result there are no special facilities for tourists. The best time to visit is between February and April, when it is slightly drier and the seas are calmer.

National park

Pulau Tiga has achieved notoriety as the location for the reality TV series *Survivor*, chosen for its unspoilt natural landscape. Pulau Tiga's three low hills were all formed by mud volcanoes. The last big eruption, in 1941, was heard 160 km away and covered the island in a layer of boiling mud. The dipterocarp forests on the islands are virtually untouched and they contain species not found on other west coast islands, such as a poisonous amphibious sea snake (*Laticauda colubrina*), which comes ashore on Pulau Kalampunian Damit to lay its eggs. Rare birds such as the pied hornbill (*Anthracoceros convexus*) and the megapode (*Megapodus freycinet*) are found here, as well as flying foxes, monitor lizards, wild fruit trees and mangrove forest. A network of trails, marked at 50-m intervals, leads to various points of interest.

Pulau Labuan ⊜⊘⊙▲⊜⊙⊜ ›› *pp197-203. Colour map 1, A6.*

Labuan is one of the historically stranger pieces of the Bornean jigsaw. Originally part of the Sultanate of Brunei, the 92-sq-km island, 8 km off the coast of Sabah, was ceded in 1846 to the British who were enticed to take it on by the discovery of rich coal deposits. It joined the Malaysian Federation in 1963, along with Sabah and Sarawak. In 1984 it was declared a tax-free haven – or an 'International offshore financial centre' – and hence this small tropical island with just 80,000-odd inhabitants has a plethora of name-plate banks and investment companies. For the casual visitor – rather than someone wanting to salt away their million – it offers some attractions, but not many. There are good hotels, lots of duty-free shopping, a golf course, sport fishing and diving, plus a handful of historic and cultural sights.

Ins and outs

Getting there and around From the airport, 5 km from town, there are flights to KK, Miri, Kuching and KL (both **MAS** and **AirAsia** have daily flights between KL and Labuan). There are regular speedboats to KK and Menumbok (used by those who want to take their car onto Labuan, an hour's drive from KK) and several daily boat connections with Lawas and Limbang (Sarawak) and Sipitang. There's also a regular ferry service with Brunei.

Once on the island, there is a reasonable island bus network , a few car hire firms and a small number of taxis.

Tourist information Tourist Information Office ① *Lot 4260, Jl Dewan/Jl Berjaya, T087-423445.* For more information on Pulau Labuan go to www.labuan tourism.com.my.

History

With a superb deep-water harbour, Labuan promised an excellent location from which the British could engage the pirates who were terrorizing the northwest Borneo coast. Labuan also had coal, which could be used to service steamships. Sarawak's Rajah James Brooke became the island's first governor in 1846 and two years later it was declared a free port. It also became a penal colony: long-sentence convicts from Hong Kong were put to work on the coal face and in the jungle, clearing roads. The island was little more than a malarial swamp and its inept colonial administration was perpetually plagued by fever and liver disorders. Its nine drunken civil servants provided a gold mine of eccentricity for the novelists Joseph Conrad and Somerset Maugham. In *The Outstation*, Maugham describes the desperate attempt by the resident Mr Warburton to keep a grip on civilization in the wilds of Malaysia: "The only concession he made to the climate was to wear a white dinner jacket; but otherwise, in a boiled shirt and high collar, silk socks and patent leather shoes, he dressed as formally as though he was dining at his club in Pall Mall. A careful host, he went into the dining room to see that the table was properly laid. It was gay with orchids, and the silver shone brightly... Mr Warbuton smiled his approval...."

By the 1880s ships were already bypassing the island and the tiny colony began to disintegrate. In 1881 William Hood Treacher moved the capital of the new territory of British North Borneo from Labuan to Kudat and eight years later the Chartered Company was asked to take over the administration of the island. In 1907 it became part of the Straits Settlements, along with Singapore, Malacca (Melaka) and Penang.

Modern Labuan

In 1946 Labuan became a part of British North Borneo and was later incorporated into Sabah as part of the Federation of Malaysia in 1963. Datuk Harris is thought to own half the island (including the **Hotel Labuan**). As chief minister, he offered the island as a gift to the federal government in 1984 in exchange for a government undertaking to bail out his industrial projects and build up the island's flagging economy. The election of a Christian government in Sabah in 1986, making it Malaysia's only non-Muslim-ruled state, proved an embarrassment to the then prime minister Doctor Mahathir Mohamad. Labuan has assumed strategic importance as a federal territory, wedged between Sabah and Sarawak. It is used as a staging post for large garrisons of the Malaysian army, navy and air force.

In declaring Labuan a tax haven the Malaysian government set out its vision of Labuan becoming the Bermuda of the Asia-Pacific for the 21st century; 4065 offshore firms had set up on the island by the end of 2003, and in 2000, the **Labuan International Financial Exchange** (LFX), a wholly owned subsidiary of the Kuala Lumpur Stock Exchange, was established on the island. This, together with several five-star hotels such as the **Sheraton** and the **Waterfront**, makes it seem that Labuan's days of being a sleepy rural backwater are over.

Sabah Off the coast & south of Kota Kinabalu

Included in the island's population of about 80,000 are 10,000 Filipino refugees, with about 21 different ethnic groups. The island is the centre of a booming 'barter' trade with the South Philippines; Labuan is home to a clutch of so-called string vest millionaires, who have grown rich on the trade. In Labuan, 'barter' is the name given to smuggling. The Filipino traders leaving the Philippines simply over-declare their exports (usually copra, hardwood, rotan and San Miguel beer) and under-declare the imports (Shogun jeeps, Japanese hi-fi and motorbikes), all ordered through duty-free Labuan. With such valuable cargoes, the traders are at the mercy of pirates in the South China Sea. To get round this, they arm themselves with M-16s, bazookas and shoulder-launched missiles. This ammunition is confiscated on their arrival in Labuan, stored in a marine police warehouse, and given back to them for the return trip.

Sights

Away from the busy barter jetty, Labuan Town, a name largely superseded by its name of **Port Victoria**, is a dozy, unremarkable Chinese-Malaysian mix of shophouses, coffee shops and karaoke bars. The **Labuan An'Nur Jamek State Mosque** is an impressive site, whilst the manicured **golf course** is popular with businessmen. Illegal cockfights are staged every Sunday afternoon. There is an old brick **chimney** at Tanjung Kubong, believed to have been built as a ventilation shaft for the short-lived coal mining industry which was established by the British in 1947 to provide fuel for their steamships on the Far Eastern trade route. Remnants of the industry, which had petered out by 1911, are to be found in the shape of a maze of **tunnels** in this area. Near to Tanjung Kubong is a **Bird Park**.

On the west coast there are pleasant beaches, mostly lined with kampongs. There is a large **Japanese war memorial** on the east coast and a vast, well tended, **Allied war cemetery** between the town and the airport with over 3000 graves, most of which are unknown soldiers. The **Peace Park** at Layang Layangan marks the Japanese surrender point on 9 September 1945, which brought the Second World War to an end in Borneo.

Labuan Town (Port Victoria)

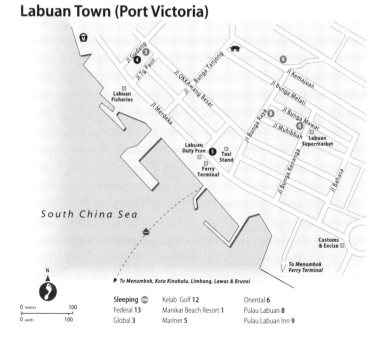

South China Sea

To Menumbok, Kota Kinabalu, Limbang, Lawas & Brunei

N

0 metres 100
0 yards 100

Sleeping
Federal **13**
Global **3**
Kelab Golf **12**
Manikar Beach Resort **1**
Mariner **5**
Oriental **6**
Pulau Labuan **8**
Pulau Labuan Inn **9**

Boat trips can be made to the small islands around Labuan, although only by chartering a fishing vessel. The main islands are **Pulau Papan** (an uninspiring island between Labuan and the mainland), **Pulau Kuraman**, **Pulau Rusukan Kecil** (known locally as 'the floating lady') and **Pulau Rusukan Besar** ('floating man'). These last three have good beaches and coral reefs but none have any facilities.

Off the south coast of the island is the **Marine Park**; a great place to dive, especially as there are four shipwrecks scattered in these waters. The park has 20 dive sites. *» See Activities and tours, page 202.*

South of Kota Kinabalu ⬛🏃🚲⛰️🏨🎭🚌 *» pp197-203*

Papar *» Colour map 2, A1.*

Formerly a sleepy Kadazan village, about 40 km south of KK, Papar is developing fast. In *bandar lama* (the old town) there are several rows of quaint wooden shophouses, painted blue and laid out along spacious boulevards lined with travellers' palms. There is a large market in the centre of town. The Papar area is famous for its fruit and there is a good *tamu* every Sunday.

There is a scenic drive between Papar and KK, with paddy fields and jungle lining the roadside. Nearby, **Pantai Manis**, a 3-km stretch of goldern sand with a deep lagoon good for swimming, can be reached easily from Papar. It is also possible to make boat trips up the Papar River, which offers gentle rapids for less-energetic whitewater rafters. Rafting trips can be organized through tour agents in KK (see page 186).

The **Klias Wetlands** is a new destination being promoted by **Sabah Tourism**, popular with visitors who do not have time to visit the east coast of Sabah. It provides the experience of taking a boat through a mangrove swamp. As boats take visitors down the Klias River, wildlife on offer include the proboscis monkey,

Sabah Off the coast & south of Kota Kinabalu

Sheraton Labuan 10 Victoria 11 **Eating** Seri Malindo 6
Sri Mutiara 2 Waterfront Labuan Café Imperial 3 Wong Kee 2
Tiara Labuan 7 Financial 4 New Sung Hwa Seafood 4 Zainab 5

long-tailed macaques, silver languor monkeys and an abundance of birdlife. The Klias Peninsula lies 120 km south of KK; trips down the Klias River depart from the Kota Klias jetty. Engaging a tour operator is recommended (**Beringgis Marina and Tours, Comfort Paradise, Diethelm Borneo Expeditions** or **Suniland Travel and Tours**, all in KK, see page 185).

Tambunan ➤ *Colour map 2, A1. Population: 28,000.*

The twisting mountain road that cuts across the **Crocker Range National Park** (see page 195) and over the Sinsuran Pass at 1649 m is very beautiful. There are dramatic views down over Kota Kinabalu and the islands beyond and glimpses of Mount Kinabalu to the northeast. The road itself, from KK to Tambunan, was the old bridleway that linked the west coast to the interior. Inland communities traded their tobacco, rattan and other jungle produce for salt and iron at the coastal markets. The road passes through Penampang. Scattered farming communities raise hill rice, pineapples, bananas, mushrooms and other vegetables which are sold at roadside stalls, where wild and cultivated orchids can also be found. After descending from the hills the road enters the sprawling flood plain of Tambunan – the Pegalam River runs through the plain – which, at the height of the paddy season, is a magnificent patchwork of greens.

The Tambunan area is largely Kadazan/Dusun, Sabah's largest ethnic group, and the whole area explodes into life each May during the harvest festival when copious quantities of *lihing*, the famed local rice wine, are consumed and the Bobolians (high priestesses) are still called upon to conduct various rituals (see page 245). There is a *lihing* brewery inside the Tambunan Village Resort Centre. The Tambunan District covers an area of 134,540 ha. At an altitude of 650 m to 900 m, it enjoys a spring-like climate during much of the year.

Tambunan (Valley of the Bamboo), so-called as there are at least 12 varieties of bamboo to be found here, also lays claim to the Kitingan family. Joseph was Sabah's first Christian chief minister until deposed in March 1994. His brother, Jeffrey, was formerly head of the Sabah Foundation. He entered politics in 1994 on his release from detention on the Malaysian peninsula. He had been charged under Malaysia's internal security act of being a secessionist conspirator.

A concrete structure at Tibabar, just outside Tambunan, situated amongst the rice fields and surrounded by peaceful kampong houses, commemorates the site of **Mat Salleh's fort** ① *Sat-Thu 0900-1700, free*, and the place of his death. Mat Salleh, now a nationalist folk hero, led a rebellion for six years against the **Chartered Company** administration until he was killed in 1900 (see box, page 176). The memorial has been set up by the Sabah State Museum and houses some exhibits including weapons, Salleh paraphernalia and a photo of the man himself.

The Rafflesia Information Centre ① *Mon-Fri 0845-1245, 1400-1700, Sat-Sun 0800-1700, T087774691*, is located at the roadside on the edge of a forest reserve that has been set aside to conserve this remarkable flower (see box, page 195). The information centre has a comprehensive and attractive display on the rafflesia and its habitat and provides information on flowers in bloom. If trail maps are temporarily unavailable, ask the ranger to point out the sites where blooms can be seen on the large relief model of the forest reserve at the back of the information centre. The blooming period of the flower is very short so, to avoid disappointment, it may be worth phoning the centre first.

Ahir Terjan Sensuron is a waterfall 4 km from the Rafflesia Information Centre on the Tambunan-KK road (heading towards KK). From the road, it is a 45-minute walk to the waterfall. A large market is held here every Thursday morning – on sale are tobacco, local musical instruments, clothing, strange edible jungle ferns and yeast used to make fermented rice wine. There are also bundles of a fragrant herb known as *tuhau*, a member of the ginger family that is made into a spicy condiment or sambal redolent of the jungle. A smaller market is held every Sunday in Kampong Toboh, north of Tambunan.

❖ Rafflesia: the largest flower in the world

The rafflesia (*Rafflesia arnoldi*), named after Stamford Raffles, the founder of modern Singapore, is the largest flower in the world. The Swedish naturalist Eric Mjoberg wrote in 1930 on seeing the flower: "The whole phenomenon seems so amazing, so unfamiliar, so fantastic, that we are tempted to explain: such flowers cannot be real!"

Stamford Raffles, who discovered the flower for Western science 100 years earlier during his first sojourn at Bengkulu on the west coast of Sumatra, noted that it was "a full yard across, weighs 15 pounds, and contains in the nectary no less than eight pints [of nectar]…". The problem is that the rafflesia does not flower for very long – only for a couple of weeks, usually between August and December. At other times of the year there is usually nothing to see. The plant is in fact parasitic, so appropriately its scent is more akin to rotting meat than any perfume. Its natural habitat is moist, shaded areas.

Crocker Range National Park ⓘ *no visitors' facilities have yet been developed*, incorporates 139,919 ha of hill and montane forest, which includes many species endemic to Borneo. It is the largest single totally protected area in Sabah. Private development is taking place along the narrow strips of land each side of the KK-Tambunan road, which were unfortunately overlooked when the park was gazetted. To get there, see Transport, page 202 (as for Tambunan).

The **Mawah Waterfall** is reached by following the road north towards Ranau to Kampong Patau, where a sign beside the school on the left indicates a gravel road leading almost to the waterfall (Mawah Airterjun). It is 15 minutes down the road by car and between five and 10 minutes' walk along the trail.

Gunung Trusmadi, 2642 m, 70 km southeast of KK, is the second highest mountain in Malaysia, but very few people climb it: the climb is difficult and facilities, compared with Gunung Kinabalu, are few. There are two main routes to the top: the north route, which takes four days to the summit (and three days down) and the south route, which is harder but shorter; two days to the summit. Trusmadi is famous for its huge, and very rare, pitcher plant *Nepethes trusmadiensis*, which is only found on one spot on the summit ridge. It is also known for its fantastic view north, towards Gunung Kinabalu, which rises above the Tambunan Valley. There is a wide variety of vegetation on the mountain as it rises from dipterocarp primary jungle through oak montane forest with mossy forest near the summit and heath-like vegetation on top. An expedition to Trusmadi requires careful planning and should not be undertaken casually. A more detailed account of the two routes can be found in *Mountains of Malaysia – A Practical Guide and Manual*, by John Briggs.

❖ *The best time to climb is in March and it is advisable to take guides and porters for the tough ascent (ask the district officer in Tambunan).*

Keningau ↠ *Colour map 2, A1.*

The Japanese built fortifications around their base in Keningau during the Second World War. It is now rather a depressing, shabby lumber town, smothered in smoke from the sawmills. The timber business in this area turned Keningau into a boom town in the 1980s and the population virtually doubled within a decade. The felling continues, but there is not much primary forest left these days. There are huge logging camps all around the town and the hills to the west. Logging roads lead into these hills off the Keningau-Tenom road, which are accessible by 4WD vehicles. It is just possible to drive across them to Papar, which is a magnificent route. Anyone attempting the drive should be warned to steer well clear of log-laden trucks on their way down the mountain.

Sapulut is deep in Murut country and is accessible from Keningau by a rough road via Kampong Nabawan (four-wheel drive required). At Sapulut, follow the river of the same name east through Bigor and Kampong Labang to Kampong Batu Punggul at the confluence of Sungai Palangan, a 2½-hour journey. **Batu Punggul** is a limestone outcrop protruding 200 m above the surrounding forest, 30-minutes' walk from the *kampong*; it can be climbed without any equipment, but with care. It is quite a dangerous climb, but there are plenty of handholds, and the view of the surrounding forest from the top is spectacular. Both the forest and the caves in and around Batu Punggul are worth exploring. Nearby is the less impressive limestone outcrop, **Batu Tinahas**, which has huge caves with many unexplored passages. It is thought to have at least three levels of caves and tunnels. Some tour operators in KK offer trips out here.

❧ Leeches can be a problem here, so take salt.

From Sapulut, it is a fairly painless exercise to cross the border into Kalimantan. A short stretch of road leads from Sapulut to Agis which is just a four-hour boat ride from the border. There is even an immigration checkpoint at Pegalungan, a settlement en route. One particular longhouse is **Kampong Selungai**, only 30 minutes from Pegalungan. Here it is possible to see traditional boatbuilders at work, as well as weaving, mat making and beadwork. There are many rivers and longhouses worth exploring in the area. Given the luxury of time, it is a fascinating area where traditional lifestyles have not been much eroded. It is possible to charter a minibus along the Nabawan road to Sapulut, where you can hire boats upriver. At Sapulut, ask for Lantir (the headman, or *kepala*). He will arrange the trip upriver, which could take up to two days depending on conditions, and accommodation in Murut longhouses, through the gloriously named **Sapulut Adventurism Tourism Travel Company**, which he runs. As in neighbouring Sarawak, these long upriver trips can be prohibitively expensive unless you are in a decent-sized group.

Tenom ❱❱ *Colour map 2, B1.*

Situated at the end of the North Borneo Railway, southwest of Keningau on the banks of the Sungei Lapas, Tenom is a hilly inland town, with a population of about 46,000, predominantly Chinese. Although it was the centre of an administrative district under the Chartered Company from the turn of the century, most of the modern town was built during the Japanese occupation in the Second World War. It is in the heart of Murut country, but do not expect to see longhouses and Murut in traditional costume; many Murut have moved into individual houses, except in the remoter parts of the interior, and their modernized bamboo homes are often well equipped.

The surrounding area is very fertile and the main crops here are soya beans, maize and a variety of vegetables. Cocoa is also widely grown. The cocoa trees are often obscured under shade trees called *pokok belindujan*, which have bright pink flowers. The durians from Tenom (and Beaufort) are reckoned to be the best in Sabah. *Tamu* (market) is on Sunday.

There are many **Murut villages** surrounding Tenom, all with their own churches. In some villages there is also an over-sized mosque or *surau*. The **Murut Cultural Centre** lies 10 km out of town. Run by the Sabah Museum, it displays something of the material culture of the Murut people including basketry, cloth and the famous Murut trampolines of lansaran. The best local longhouses are along the Padas River towards Sarawak at Kampong Marais and Kampong Kalibatang where blowpipes are still made. At **Kemabong**, about 25 km south of Tenom, the Murut community, who are keen dancers, have a lansaran dancing trampoline; a wooden platform sprung with bamboo which can support about 10 Murut doing a jig.

Sabah Agricultural Park ⓘ *Tue-Sun 0900-1630, RM25, children RM10, 15 km northeast of Tenom*, is a research initiative developed by the Sabah State Government. This is also the site of Tenom's **orchid farm**, which has been developed into an agrotourism park.

Beaufort ▸ Colour map 2, A1.

This small, sleepy, unexciting town is named after British Governor P Beaufort of the North Borneo Company, who was a lawyer and was appointed to the post despite having no experience of the East or of administration. He was savaged by Sabahan historian KG Tregonning as "the most impotent Governor North Borneo ever acquired and who, in the manner of nonentities, had a town named after him." Beaufort is a quaint town, with riverside houses built on stilts to escape the constant flooding of the Padas River. The Tamu (market) is on Saturday.

Sipitang ▸ Colour map 1, B6.

Located on the coast, Sipitang is a sleepy town with little to offer the traveller apart from a supermarket and a few hotels (see Sleeping, below). Sipitang is south of Beaufort and the closest town in Sabah to the Sarawak border. It is possible to take minibuses from Beaufort to Sipitang and on to Sindumin, where you can connect with buses bound for Lawas in Sarawak by walking across the border to Merapok. There is an immigration checkpoint here and month-long permits are given for visitors to Sarawak.

● Sleeping

Tunku Abdul Rahman Park p189
Rooms are significantly discounted during the week.
A Gayana Island EcoResort , Lot 16, Ground floor, Wisma Sabah, Jl Tun Razak, Pulau Gaya, T088-245158, www.gayana-ecoresort.com. Set on the east coast of the island, 44 a/c chalets, restaurant (serves Asian and Western food, T088-245158), barbecue site, private beach, activities include diving, snorkelling, windsurfing, trekking in the jungle, fishing, yachting and a reef rehabilitation research centre. Some reports of dirty water around the resort from nearby shanty town.
A-B Chalets, Pulau Manukan, restaurant, pool, facilities including tennis and squash courts, football field, 1500-m jogging track and a diving centre. Contact **Sutera Sanctuary Lodges**, Ground floor, Wisma Sabah, T088-243629, www.suterasanctuary lodges.com, for bookings on Manukan.

Camping
It is possible to camp on any of the islands. Obtain permission from the Sabah Parks Office in KK, Lot 3, Block K, Sinsuran Complex, T088-211881, www.sabahparks.com. The island gets packed with tourists during the day, but if you camp you can enjoy a practically deserted island after 1700 when the rabble departs. Beware of leaving your clothing unattended at the edge of the forest, as monkeys have been known to run off with it!

Pulau Tiga National Park p190
A-D Pulau Tiga Resort, T088-240584, www.pulau-tiga.com. Wholly owned by **Sipadan Dive Centre**. There are standard chalets and more budget triples in a longhouse. As well as diving, the resort organizes watersports, treks, and trips to nearby islands. There's a games room, 'Survivor Bar' and a restaurant. There is also a hostel that can accommodate 32 people (RM30 per night). Accommodation must be booked in advance through the Sabah Parks Office in KK; there is also an attached canteen. It is possible to camp here.

Pulau Labuan p 190, map p192
There is plenty of choice here, but very little at budget level.
AL Sheraton Labuan, Lot TL 462, Jl Merdeka, T087-422000, www.sheraton.com/labuan. Situated opposite the Financial Park complex, this de luxe city hotel has 183 rooms and suites, all with spacious bathrooms and all the trimmings you would expect. Facilities include pool with whirlpool and swim-up bar, business centre (in-room personal computer also available). Decor has all the opulence of a **Sheraton** with a vast lobby, clad in marble and dripping with chandeliers, and classy food outlets including **Victoria's Brasserie** for European fare and **The Emperor Chinese Restaurant** which specializes in Cantonese food. Staff are professional and offer top service with a smile. Recommended.

A **Manikar Beach Resort**, Jl Batu Manikar, T087-418700, manikar@tm.net.my. On the northwest tip of Labuan, 20 mins from town centre (complimentary shuttle). A stylish resort built with polished wood (the owner is a timber tycoon), set in 15 ha of gardens dotted with tall palms which reach down to the beach. The 250 rooms, all sea-facing with generous balconies, are very spacious, paved with stone, tastefully furnished, complete with a/c, minibar, TV, in-house video. Large pool set at sea level with swim-up bar, separate children's pool, fitness centre, tennis, playroom, business centre, duty-free shop. The beach is regularly cleaned and sprayed so sandflies are not a problem, but the sea is not recommended for swimming due to jellyfish. Restaurant with indoor and outdoor dining areas, excellent quality food, good value theme buffet nights.

A **Tiara Labuan**, Jl Tanjung Batu, T087-414300, F087-410195. On the west coast next to the golf course, 5-min taxi ride from town centre. Beautiful hotel and serviced apartments surrounding a large lotus pond and deep blue pool complete with jacuzzi. Built onto Adnan Kashoggi's old mansion, the property has an Italian feel with terracotta tiles, putty pink stone, a glorious gilt fountain and long shady arcades. The original mansion now holds the reception, restaurant (food mediocre) and acres of opulent lounge including an Arab section which has low sofas, hubbly-bubbly pipes and a marble fountain. All 25 rooms, and also the 48 serviced apartments (1 or 2 bedroom) are complete with a/c, TV, minibar, electric hob, cooker hood and sink, and a living room. The Tanjung Batu beach, just across the road, is rather muddy, but good for walks when the tide is out. The **Labuan Beach Restaurant** is here too. On the whole, holidaymakers, especially families, opt for the larger hotels as the **Tiara** has no organized activities or kiddy pool, but this is partly what makes it a haven of tranquillity. Recommended.

A **Waterfront Labuan Financial Hotel**, 1 Jl Wawasan, T087-418111, F087-413468. This property, overlooking the new yacht marina (and also an industrial seascape) has cultivated a marina-look combined with the atmosphere of being on a luxury cruise. It has over 200 rooms, all with a/c, minibar, TV and opulent fittings. The main restaurant, in seafaring spirit, called the **Clipper**, serves Western and local food. There is also a bar, the **Anchorage**, which has live entertainment nearly every evening. Other facilities include pool, tennis and health centre. The hotel also manages the marina with its total of 50 berthing spaces, each of which has internationally rated facilities. The harbour master also organizes yacht charters and luxury cruises. Recommended.

B **Global**, U0017, Jl OKK Awang Besar (near market), T087-425201, F087-425180. Best value for money in town, a/c, minibar, TV, in-house video, complimentary shuttle to ferry and airport. Recommended.

B **Mariner**, Jl Tg Purun (on crossroads opposite police HQ), T087-418822, F087-418811. A/c, restaurant, rooms well-equipped including mini fridge, a/c, TV, in-house video and attached bathroom, good coffee house. Generous discounts available on request.

B **Sri Mutiara**, Jl Dewan, T087-417811, F087-417996. Smart hotel, clean and reasonable, 39 rooms with a/c, attached bathroom, TV, in-house video and minibar.

B **Oriental**, U0123-4, Lot 33 and 34, Jl Bunga Mawar, T087-419019, F087-419408. Reception on 1st floor, clean, tiled rooms with a/c, TV, private bathroom.

B **Pulau Labuan**, 27-28 Jl Muhibbah, T087-416288, F087-416255. A/c, restaurant (**Golden Palace Restaurant** downstairs).

B-C **Pulau Labuan Inn**, Lot 8, Jl Bunga Dahlia, T087-416833, F087-441750. The downmarket sister of the **Pulau Labuan**, spotlessly clean but small a/c rooms.

C **Federal Hotel**, Jl Bunga Kesuma, T087-411711, F087-411337. A/c, restaurant, all rooms have a/c, TV, in-house video, minibar fridge, pink and pastels colour scheme, Chinese-run, catering mainly for business people, clean, good value, run by same management as **Sri Mutiara** (see above).

C **Kelab Golf**, Jl Tanjung Batu. A/c, restaurant, 6 simple but pleasant rooms in the clubhouse, 3 have a view down the manicured fairways.

C **Victoria Hotel**, Jl Tun Mustapha, T087-218511, F087-218077. One of the oldest hotels in Labuan, pale pink exterior with white stucco-decorated lobby, 46 rooms, a/c, private bath. Recommended.

Papar *p193*

A KRK 'Mai Aman Country Rest House, Km 35, off Old Papar Rd, Kinarut, T088-912580, verus@pc.jaring.my. 6-room country resthouse and 12-room bush hostel. Luxurious place, with fishing on site in spacious grounds with an orchard.

B Beringgis Beach Resort, Km 26, Jl Papar, Kampong Beringgis, Kinarut, T088-752333, ketlee@bigfoot.com. A/c, hot baths, car rental, conference halls, private beach, pool, watersports, tours and sports facilities.

B-E Seaside Travellers Inn, Km 20 Papar-KK Highway, Kinarut, T088-750555, www.info sabah.com.my/seaside. Restaurant, range of a/c or fan accommodation from dorm to detached bungalows, breakfast included, pleasant location off the beach. Tennis court, pool. Horse riding and tours can be organized.

Tambunan *p194*

The area is renowned for its rice wine (*lihing*) – watch it being brewed at the TVRC factory.

C Tambunan Village Resort Centre (TVRC), signposted off the main road before the town, located on both sides of the Pegalam River, T088-774076, F088-774205. Collection of chalets and a 'longhouse' dormitory made of split bamboo. Restaurant, motel and entertainment centre (with karaoke and slot machines), hall and sports field. There are also a couple of retreat centres located about 10 mins' walk away.

C-E Gunung Emas Highlands Resort, Km 52 (about 7 km from the **Rafflesia Centre**). Also some dormitory rooms, some very basic tree houses, a fresh climate and good views. Mini zoo and restaurant serving local food. To get there take the Rabunan or the Keningau minibus and then another bus from Tambunan.

Keningau *p195*

A-L Juta, T087-337888, www.sabah. com.my/juta. Marble-lobbied business tower, de luxe rooms have minibar and circular beds. Nice wooden theme throughout. Bar with live crooners and restaurant. Without a doubt, the swankiest pad in town.

B Hillview Garden Resort, PO Box 210, T087-333678 hillview@tm.net.my. New place with 25 rooms. Good option.

B Perkasa, Jl Kampong Keningau, T088-331045, www.perkasahotel.com.my. On the edge of town, a/c, Chinese restaurant, coffee house, health centre, comfortable rooms.

C Kristal Hotel, Pegalan Shopping Complex, T088-338888, F088-736134. Reasonable place, void of any real character, but a relatively cheap option in a town short on decent cheap accommodation.

Tenom *p196*

Orchid Hotel and Sri Jaya Hotel are both within walking distance of the bus stop.

AL-B Perkasa, top of the hill above the town, PO Box 225, T087-735811, F087-736134. A/c, restaurant, the **Tenom Perkasa** (one of a chain of 3 – the others are at Keningau and Ranau) – is a large, modern hotel, 7 storeys high, commanding superb views over Tenom and surrounding countryside. Rooms are spacious, carpeted, attractively furnished, with a/c, en suite bathroom, TV. As guests are few and far between, the restaurant has a limited but well-priced selection of Chinese and Western dishes. Staff are friendly and helpful in organizing local sightseeing. Recommended.

C Orchid Hotel, Block K, Jl Tun Mustapha, T087-737600, excelng@tm.net.my. Small but friendly with clean, well-maintained rooms.

C-D Hotel Sri Perdana, Lot 71, Jl Tun Mustapha, T087-734001, cheap, standard rooms.

D Hotel Sri Jaya, PO Box 47, T087-735007. The cheapest option in town, with 12 a/c rooms, shared bathroom, basic but clean.

E Rumah Rehat Lagud Sebren (Orchid Research Station Resthouse) is 5 km from the agricultural park and has a/c. Take a minibus from the main road. If driving, take the road over the railway tracks next to the station and head down the valley.

Beaufort *p197*

A poor selection of hotels, all roughly the same and slightly overpriced. Rooms have a/c and bathrooms.

C Beaufort Hotel, Lot 19-20, Lochung Park, T087-211911, F087-212590. Centre of town, a/c, 25 rooms.

D Mandarin Inn, Lot 38, Jl Beaufort Jaya, T087-212800. A/c rooms and garners better reviews than the **Beaufort**.

Sipitang *p197*
B-C **Hotel Asanol**, T087-821506. Offers value-for-money rooms with bathrooms.
B-C **Shangsan Hotel**, T088-821800, which has fairly comfortable rooms with a/c and TV. There is the ubiquitous coffee shop in the same street as the Shangsan.

❻ Eating

Tunku Abdul Rahman Park *p189*
Excellent restaurant on Pulau Manukan. Pulau Mamutik and Pulau Sapi each have a small shop selling a limited range of very expensive food and drink, and Sapi has some hawker-style food. For Pulau Sulug, Sapi and Mamutik take all the water you need – there is no drinkable water supply here – shower and toilet water is only provided if there has been sufficient rain.

Pulau Labuan *p190, map p192*
Chinese
Several basic places to be found along Jl Merdeka and Jl OKK Awang Besar.
❦❦❦ **The Emperor Chinese Restaurant**, Sheraton Labuan, top-class Chinese cuisine, Cantonese specialities, fresh seafood, special dim sum on Sun and public holidays. Recommended.
❦❦ **Wong Kee**, Lot 5 and 6, Jl Kemuning, large, brightly lit restaurant with a/c, good steamboat. Recommended.
❦ **Café Imperial**, Chinese coffee shop behind Federal Hotel, better than average fare.

International
❦❦ **Country Deli Restaurant and Wine Bar**, Lot 25, Block D, Jati Commercial Centre, T087-410410. Malaysian pizza, takeaways possible.
❦❦ **Labuan Beach**, Jl Tanjung Batu, T087-415611. International and local cuisine, breezy location on seashore, food not special but ambience makes up for it, as does very well chilled draft Carlsberg. Recommended.
❦❦ **The Clipper**, Waterfront Labuan Financial Hotel, 24-hr upmarket coffee shop with local and Western cuisine. Recommended.
❦❦ **Victoria's Brasserie**, Sheraton Labuan, European brasserie-style, good theme buffets as well as à la carte, prides itself on its 'show kitchen concept'. Recommended.

Malay
❦ **Restoran Zainab**, Jl Merdeka (opposite duty-free shop), Indian/Muslim.
❦ **Seri Malindo**, next to Hotel Sri Mutiara, mixture of Malay and Western food.

Seafood
❦❦❦ **Restaurant Pulau Labuan**, Lot 27-28, Jl Muhibbah, smart interior complete with chandeliers, a/c, fresh fish sold by weight – good tiger prawns). Recommended.
❦ **New Sung Hwa Seafood**, Jl Ujong Pasir, PCK Building, amongst best-value seafood restaurants in Malaysia, chilli prawns, grilled stingray steak recommended, no menu. Recommended.

Foodstalls
Above wet market and at the other end of town, along the beach next to the Island Club. There is an area of stalls on Jl Muhibbah opposite the end of Jl Bahasa, west of the cinema, and there are a few hawker stalls behind Hotel Pulau Labuan.

Papar *p193*
There are several run-of-the-mill coffee shops and restaurants in the old town.
❦ **Seri Takis**, New Town (below the lodging house). Padang food.
❦ **Sugar Buns Bakery**, Old Town. Sweet bread and thick coffee.

Keningau *p195*
❦ **Seri Wah Coffee Shop**, on the corner of the central square and a near selection of foodstalls.

Tenom *p196*
❦ **Jolly**, near the station, serves Western food (including lamb chops), karaoke.
❦ **Restaurant Curry Emas**, specializes in monitor lizard claypot curries, dog meat and wild cat.
❦ **Restoran Chi Hin**, another Chinese coffee shop.
❦ **Sabah**, Jl Datuk Yaseen, Muslim Indian food, clean and friendly.
❦ **Sapong**, Perkasa Hotel, local and Western.
❦ **Y&L (Young & Lovely) Food & Entertainment**, Jl Sapong (2 km out of town). Noisy but easily the best restaurant in Tenom. It serves mainly Chinese food: freshwater fish (steamed *sun hok* – also known as *ikan hantu*) and

❖ Tamus – Sabah's markets and trade fairs

In Sabah, an open trade fair is called a *tamu*. Locals gather to buy and sell jungle produce, handicrafts and traditional wares. *Tamu* comes from the Malay word *tetamu*, to meet, and the biggest and most famous is held at Kota Belud, north of Kota Kinabalu in Bajau country.

Tamus were fostered by the pre-war British North Borneo Chartered Company, when district officers would encourage villagers from miles around to trade among themselves. It was also a convenient opportunity for officials to meet with village headmen. They used to be strictly Kadazan affairs, but today *tamu* are multiracial events. Sometimes public auctions of water buffalo and cattle are held. Some of the biggest *tamus* around the state are:

Monday: Tandek
Tuesday: Kiulu, Topokan
Wednesday: Tampuruli
Thursday: Keningau, Tambunan, Sipitang, Telipok, Simpangan
Friday: Sinsuran, Weston
Saturday: Penampang, Beaufort, Sindumin, Matunggong, Kinarut
Sunday: Tambunan, Tenom, Kota Belud, Papar, Gaya Street (KK)

---

venison; these can be washed down with the local version of *air limau* (or *kitchai*) which comes with dried plums. There is a giant screen which was shipped in to allow Tenomese to enjoy the 1990 Football World Cup. Recommended.
❢ **Yong Lee Restaurant**, coffee shop serving cheap Chinese fare in town centre.

Beaufort *p197*
❢ **Beaufort Bakery**, behind **Beaufort Hotel**, 'freshness with every bite'.
❢ **Ching Chin Restaurant**, Chinese coffee shop in town centre.
❢ **Jin Jin Restaurant**, behind **Beaufort Hotel**, Chinese, popular with locals.

⭘ Shopping

Pulau Labuan *p190, map p192*
Duty free
If you plan to take duty-free goods into Sabah or Sarawak, you have to stay on Labuan for a minimum of 72 hrs. **Labuan Duty Free**, Bangunan Terminal, Jl Merdeka, T087-411573. This opened in Oct 1990, 142 years after Rajah James Brooke first declared Labuan a free port. The island's original duty-free concession did not include alcohol or cigarettes, but the new shop was given special dispensation to sell them. 2 months later the government extended the privilege to all shops on the island, which explains the absurd existence of a duty-free shop on a duty-free island. The shop claims to be the cheapest duty-free in the world, however you will find competitively priced shops in town too. **Monegain**, for example, can undercut most other outlets on the island due to the volume of merchandise it turns over: more than RM1 million a month. The shop owes its success to Filipino 'barter traders' who place bulk purchase orders for electronic goods or cigarettes. These are smuggled back to Zamboanga and Jolo and find their way onto Manila's streets within a week. Brunei's alcohol-free citizens also keep the shop in business – they brought nearly RM2-million of liquor from Labuan into Brunei within the first 3 months of trading.

Handicrafts
Behind Jl Merdeka and before the fish market, there is a congregation of tin-roofed shacks which houses a Filipino textile and handicrafts market and an interesting 'wet' market.

Supermarkets
Milimewah, Lot 22-27, Lazenda Commercial Centre, Phase II, Jl Tun Mustapha, department store with supermarket on ground floor. **Financial Park**, Jl Merdeka, shopping complex with Milimewah supermarket. **Thye Ann Supermarket**, central position below Sri Mutiara. Labuan Supermarket, Jl Bunga Kenanga, centre of town.

Handicrafts

There is a *tamu* on Thu. The **Handicraft Centre**, just before the Shell petrol station, sells traditional local weaving and basketry.

▲ Activities and tours

Pulau Labuan *p190, map p192*
Diving

There are at least 10 popular dive sites around the TAR islands, with reef depths ranging from 3-21 m, providing a great variety of experiences. It is possible to dive throughout the year with an average visibility of about 12 m. The water is cooler from Nov to Feb, when visibility is not as good. For extensive information on the various coral/fish/dive sites, contact **Borneo Divers** (see below).
Borneo Divers, 1 Jl Wawasan, **Waterfront Labuan Financial Hotel**, T087-415867, www.borneodivers.info. Specializes in 2-day packages diving on shipwrecks off Labuan for certified scuba divers, there are 4 wrecks in total, each wreck costs about RM100.

Fishing

Fishing with a hook and line is permitted but the use of spearguns and nets is not. Permits are not necessary.

Golf
Kelab Golf, Jl Tanjung Batu, T087-421810. Magnificent 9-hole golf course. Visitors may be asked for proof of handicap or a membership card from your own club. There is also tennis and swimming.

Horse riding
Labuan Horse Riding Centre, T087-466828. for a different way to sightsee. It offers beach and paddock rides plus lessons.

Snorkelling

Snorkel, mask and fins can be rented from boatmen at the KK jetty beforehand (although snorkelling equipment is for hire on Sapi and Manukan).

Sipitang *p197*
Tour operators
Sipitang Tours & Services, Lot 5, Tingkat 1, Kedai SEDCO, T6013-8691570, T6019-8809492.

❂ Transport

Tunku Abdul Rahman Park *p189*
Boat

All boats leave from the main jetty 10 mins' walk north of town. Small boats carry 6 people and will leave for any of the islands (RM15 per person fixed price) when full, but everyone needs to agree a destination and a return time. It will cost an extra RM10 if you want to return the next day. There's a regular service for **Gayana** between 0800 and 2300, roughly every 2 hrs, RM10 return fare), 38 km. If you want to visit more than 1 island, a boat needs to be chartered, at a cost of about RM280 for a 3-island tour or RM360 for a 5-island tour, taking 12 passengers. It is possible to negotiate trips with local fishermen. Boats also leave from **Tanjung Aru Beach Hotel**.

Pulau Labuan *p190, map p192*
Air

The airport is 5 km from town. Regular connections with **KK**, **Miri**, **Kuching** and **Kuala Lumpur**.
    Airline offices MAS, airport, T087-412263. **AirAsia**, c/o HMD Tours & Travel, T087-416117.

Boat

From the Bangunan Terminal Feri Penumpang next to the duty-free shop on Jl Merdeka. All times are subject to change, tickets are sold at arrival points at the ferry terminal, but can be bought in town at **Duta Muhibbah Agency** , T087-413827. 2 connections a day with **Menumbok** (RM10, the nearest mainland point) by speedboat (30 mins) or car ferry. It's a 2-hr bus ride from here to **KK**. At present there are 7 boats a day to **Kota Kinabalu**, 2½ hrs, RM31, 1st boat at 0830, last at 1500. There are 2 daily boats to **Limbang** at 1230 and 1400 (1½ hrs, RM20) and 1 to **Lawas** (both Sarawak), at 1230 (1½ hrs, RM20).
    To Brunei On weekends and public holidays in Brunei the ferries are packed out and it is a scramble to get a ticket. It is possible to reserve tickets to Brunei at the following agents: **Victoria Agency House**, T087-412332 (next to the Federal Hotel in Wisma Kee Chia), **Borneo Leisure Travel**, T087-410251, F087-419989 (opposite

Standard Chartered) and the booking office at the back of the Sports Toto on Jl Merdeka. 7 boats leave Labuan for Brunei (**Serasa Muara**) daily, 1st departure at 0830, last at 1630, 1½ hrs, RM24.

Bus
Local buses around the island leave from Jl Bunga Raya.

Car
Car hire Adaras Rent-a-Car, T087-421590. Travel Rent-a-Car, T087-423600.

Taxi
Old Singapore NTUC cabs are not in abundant supply, but are easy enough to get at the airport and around hotels. It is impossible to get a taxi after 1900 but minibuses abound.

Papar *p193*
Minibus
Leaves from Bandar Lama area. Regular connections with **KK**, 1 hr, **Beaufort**, 1 hr.

Tambunan *p194*
Minibus
Buses marked Tambunan go from the long-distance bus station at the bottom of Signal Hill in **KK** (1½ hrs).

Taxi
To **KK** for RM100.

Keningau *p195*
Air Connections with **KK**.
Minibus Minibuses leave from the centre of town, by the market. Regular connections with **KK** and **Tenom**.
Taxi KK costs around RM180.

Tenom *p196*
Minibus
Minibuses leave from centre of town on Jl Padas. Regular connections with **Keningau** and **KK** 4 hrs. Minibuses to **Keningau** leave from rail station after a train has arrived.

Taxi
To **KK** costs around RM200 or shared taxis are available for a fraction of the price; they leave from the main street (Jl Padas).

Train
The journey through the **Padas River** gorge is particularly spectacular. Leaves 4 times a day and takes about 3 hrs to **Beaufort** and another 2½ hrs to **Tanjung Aru**, T087-735514.

Beaufort *p197*
Minibus
Minibuses meet the train, otherwise leave from centre of town. Regular connections with **KK**, 2 hrs.

Train
The KK-Tenom line passes through Beaufort: **Tenom**, 2½ hrs, **KK**, 3 hrs.

Sipitang *p197*
There is a line of minibuses and taxis along the waterfront. The jetty for ferries to **Labuan** (daily departures) is a 10-min walk from the centre.

⊙ Directory

Pulau Labuan *p190, map p192*
Banks HSBC, Jl Merdeka; Standard Chartered, Jl Tanjung Kubang (next to Victoria Hotel); Syarikat K Abdul Kader, money changer. **Post** General Post Office Jl Merdeka.

Beaufort *p197*
Banks HSBC and Standard Chartered in centre of town. **Post** General Post Office & Telekom, next to Hong Kong Bank.

North of Kota Kinabalu

From KK, the route heads north to the sleepy Bajau town of Kota Belud which wakes up on Sunday for its colourful tamu (market). Near the northernmost tip of the state is Kudat, the former state capital. The region north of KK is a more interesting area with Gunung Kinabalu always in sight. From Kota Belud, the mountain looks completely different. It is possible to see its tail, sweeping away to the east and its western flanks, which rise out of the rolling coastal lowlands. ▶▶ *For Sleeping, Eating and other listings, see pages 206-207.*

Kota Belud ⊜❼❇⬒⊜❽ ▶▶ *pp206-207. Colour map 2, A1.*

This busy little town is in a beautiful location, nestling in the foothills of Mount Kinabalu on the banks of the Tempasuk River, but has little to recommend it save its market. It is the heart of Bajau country – the so-called 'cowboys of the East' – but is of little obvious interest to most tourists.

The first Bajau to migrate to Sabah were pushed into the interior, around Kota Belud. They were originally a seafaring people but then settled as farmers in this area. The famed Bajau horsemen wear jewelled costumes, carry spears and ride bareback on ceremonial occasions. The ceremonial headdresses worn by the horsemen, called *dastars*, are woven on backstrap looms by the womenfolk of Kota Belud. Each piece takes four to six weeks to complete. Traditionally, the points of the headdress were stiffened using wax; these days, strips of cardboard are inserted into the points.

The largest **market** (*tamu*) in Sabah is held every Sunday in Kota Belud behind the mosque, starting at 0600. A mix of races, Bajau, Kadazan/Dusun, Rungus, Chinese, Indian and Malay, come to sell their goods and it is a social occasion as much as it is a market. Aside from the wide variety of food and fresh produce on sale, there is a weekly water-buffalo auction at the entrance to the *tamu*. Visitors are strongly recommended to get there early, but don't expect to find souvenirs at these markets. However the *tamu besar* (big market) is held in November, when cultural performances take place and handicrafts are on sale.

This is the account of a civil servant, posted to the KB district office in 1915: "The tamu itself is a babel and buzz of excitement; in little groups the natives sit and spread their wares out on the ground before them; bananas, langsats, pines and bread-fruit; and, in season, that much beloved but foul-smelling fruit the durian. Mats and straw-hats and ropes; fowls, ducks, goats and buffaloes; pepper, gambia sirih and vegetables; rice (*padi*), sweet potatoes, *ubi kayu* and indian-corn; *dastars* and handkerchiefs, silver and brassware. In little booths, made of wood, with open sides and floors of split bamboos and roofs of *atap* (sago palm-leaf) squat the Chinese traders along one side of the Tamu. For cash or barter they will sell; and many a wrangle, haggle and bargain is driven and fought before the goods change hands, or money parted with."

Tempasuk River has a wide variety of migrating birds and is a proposed conservation area. More than 127 species of bird have been recorded along this area of the coastal plain and over half a million birds flock to the area every year, many migrating from northern latitudes in winter. These include 300,000 swallows, 50,000 yellow longtails and 5000 water birds. The best period for birdwatching is from October to March. Between Kota Belud and the sea, there are mangrove swamps with colonies of proboscis monkeys. You can hire small fishing boats in town to go down the Tempasuk River (RM10 per hour).

⁝ Tamus (markets) in Kota Belud District

Monday and Saturday: Kota Belud. Market time is 0600-1200. All *tamus* provide many places to eat.
Tuesday: Pandasan (along the Kota Belud to Kudat road).
Wednesday: Keelawat (along the Kota Belud to KK road).
Thursday: Pekan Nabalu (along the Kota Belud to Ranau road).
Friday: Taginambur (along the Kota Belud to Ranau road, 16 km from Kota Belud).

Kudat ⊜⊖🛌🛈 ▸▸ *pp206-207. Colour map 2, A1.*

Kudat town, surrounded by coconut groves, is right on the northern tip of Sabah, 160 km from KK. The local people here are the Rungus, members of the Kadazan tribe. Gentle, warm and friendly, Rungus have clung to their traditions more than other Sabahan tribes and some still live in longhouses, although many are now building their own houses. Rungus longhouses are built in a distinctive style with outward-leaning walls; the Sabah State Museum incorporates many of the design features of a Rungus longhouse. The Rungus used to wear coils of copper and brass round their arms and legs and today the older generation still dress in black. They are renowned for their fine beadwork and weaving. A handful of Rungus longhouses are dotted around the peninsula, away from Kudat town.

The East India Company first realized the potential of the Kudat Peninsula and set up a trading station on Balambanganan Island, to the north of Kudat. The settlement was finally abandoned after countless pirate raids. Kudat became the first administrative capital of Sabah in 1881, when it was founded by a Briton, AH Everett. William Hood Fletcher, the protectorate's first governor, first tried to administer the territory from Labuan, which proved impossible, so he moved to the newly founded town of Kudat which was nothing more than a handful of atap houses built out into the sea on stilts. It was a promising location, however, situated on an inlet of Marudu Bay, and it had a good harbour. Kudat's glory years were shortlived; it was displaced as the capital of North Borneo by Sandakan in 1883.

Today it is a busy town dominated by Chinese and Filipino traders (legal and illegal) on the coast, and prostitutes trading downtown. Kudat was one of the main centres of Chinese and European migration at the end of the 19th century. Most of the Chinese who came to Kudat were Christian Hakka vegetable farmers: 96 of them arrived in April 1883, and they were followed by others, given free passages by the Chartered Company. More Europeans, especially the British, began to arrive on Kudat's shores with the discovery of oil in 1880. Frequent pirate attacks and an inadequate supply of drinking water forced the British to move their main administrative offices to Sandakan in 1883.

Sights

Kudat is dotted with numerous family farms cultivating coconut trees, maize, ground nuts and keeping bees. Being surrounded by the sea, seafood is also a staple element in the diet and fisheries an important industry. Kudat is inhabited by many other ethnic groups: Bonggi, Bajau, Bugis, Kadazandusun, Obian, Orang Sungai and Suluk. The market is on Mondays.

There are some beautiful and extensive unspoilt white-sand beaches north of town, the best known is **Bak-Bak**, 11 km north of Kudat. This beach, however, can get crowded at weekends and there are plans to transform it into a resort. It is signposted off the Kota Belud-Kudat road. You can take a minibus, but they are irregular; the best option is a taxi but this is expensive.

Sikuati, 23 km west of Kudat on the northwest side of the Kudat peninsula, has a good beach. Every Sunday (0800) the Rungus come to the market in this village. Local handicrafts are sold. You can get there by minibus.

Between Kota Belud and Kudat there is a marsh and coastal area with an abundance of birds. Costumed Bajau horsemen can sometimes be seen here.

The **'Longhouse Experience'** is possibly the most memorable thing to do in Kudat. A stay at a longhouse enables visitors to observe, enjoy and take part in the Rungus' unique lifestyle. There are two Baranggaxo longhouses with 10 units. Nearby are the village's only modern amenities, toilets and showers. During the day, the longhouse corridor is busy with Rungus womenfolk at work stringing elaborate beadworks, weaving baskets and their traditional cloth. Visitors can experience and participate in these activities. Longhouse meals are homegrown; fish and seafood come from nearby fishing villages, drinks are young coconuts and local rice wine. Evening festivities consist of the playing of gongs with dancers dressed in traditional Rungus costume. Tour companies organize trips for visistors. (See box, page 114, for advice on visiting longhouses; for more information, enquire at **Sabah Tourism,** T088-212121, www.sabahtourism.com).

Matunggong is a less toursity area found on the road south of Kudat best known for its longhouses, though they are rather dilapidated now.

At **Kampong Gombizau,** visitors get to see bee-keeping and the process of harvesting beeswax, honey and royal jelly, while at **Kampong Sumangkap,** an enterprising little village, visitors can learn about traditional gong- and handicraft-making.

⊜ Sleeping

Kota Belud *p204*
C-D **Impian Siu Motel**, Kg Sempirai, Jl Kuala Abai, T088-976617. Just 10 rooms in this reasonable place. You get what you pay for.

Homestay
There is no limit to your length of stay. Live with and be treated as part of the family, getting invited to celebrations such as weddings. Activities include buffalo riding, jungle trekking, river swimming, cultural dancing, visits to local *tamus*, padi planting. Contact **Nature Heritage Travel and Tours**, Ground floor, Wisma Sabah, KK, T088-318747, nhtt@nature-heritage.com, or **Taginambur Homestay**, T088-423993, T013-8528753, hopfans@tm.net.my. Very affordable for young travellers and an excellent way to learn the language and gain an in-depth knowledge of the culture.

Kudat *p205*
The **Sunrise** and **Oriental** hotels are within walking distance of the bus stop.
A-B **Kudat Golf & Marina Resort**, off Jl Urus Setia, T088-611211, www.kudatgolfmarina resort.com. A spanking-new orange monster next to a marina. Main attraction is the 18-hole championship golf course.

C **Greenland**, Lot 9/10, Block E, Sedco Shophouse (new town), T088-613211, F088-611854. A/c, standard rooms, shared bath.
C **Kinabalu**, Kudat Old Town, Jl Melor, T088-613888, F088-615388. A/c, clean enough, average value.
D **Southern Hotel**, Kudat Old Town, T088-613133. Only 10 rooms, but quite cheap and represents reasonable value in comparison with its competitors.

✷ Eating

Kota Belud *p204*
There are several Indian coffee shops around the main square.
† **Bismillah Restoran**, 35 Jl Keruak (main square), excellent *roti telur*.
† **Indonesia Restoran**, next to the car park behind the **Kota Belud Hotel**.

❀ Festivals and events

Kota Belud *p204*
Nov The annual **Tamu Besar** includes a parade and equestrian games by the Bajau horsemen, a very colourful event. Contact Sabah Tourism for more information.

○ Shopping

Kota Belud *p204*
Market in main square every day, fish market to the south of the main market. Large *tamu* every Sun and an annual *tamu besar* provides a wide variety of local handicrafts amongst the day-to-day items.

○ Transport

Kota Belud *p204*
Minibus
Leaves from main square. Regular connections with **KK**, **Kudat** and **Ranau**. It takes 90 mins for **KK** to **Kudat** and Kota Belud could be a stop along the way, as connections are easy.

Kudat *p205*
Air
Connections with **KK**, **Sandakan**.

Minibus
Minibuses leave from Jl Lo Thien Hock. Regular connections with **KK**, 4 hrs.

○ Directory

Kota Belud *p204*
Banks Public Bank Berhad, Jl Kota Kinabalu; Sabah Finance, Jl Ranau; Bank Pertanian, Jl Kudat.

Kudat *p205*
Banks Standard Chartered, Jl Lo Thien Hock.

Gunung Kinabalu National Park

▸▸ *Colour map 2, A1.*
Gunung Kinabalu is the pride of Sabah, the focal point of the national park and probably the most magnificent sight in Borneo. In recognition of this, the park was declared a World Heritage Site by UNESCO in 2000 – a first for Malaysia. Although Gunung Kinabalu has foothills, its dramatic rockfaces, with cloud swirling around them, loom starkly out of the jungle. The view from the top is unsurpassed and on a clear day you can see the shadow of the mountain in the South China Sea, over 50 km away. ▸▸ *For Sleeping, Eating and other listings, see pages 214-216.*

Best time to visit
The average rainfall is 400 cm a year, with an average temperature of 20°C at Park HQ but at Panar Laban it can drop below freezing at night. With the wind chill factor on the summit, it feels very cold. The best time to climb Gunung Kinabalu is in the dry season between March and April when views are clearest. The worst time has traditionally been November to December during the monsoon, although wet or dry periods can occur at any time of the year. Avoid weekends, school and public holidays if at all possible.

The park is occasionally closed to climbers. Contact the **Sutera Sanctuary Lodges**, see below, to check the mountain is open for climbing at the time of your visit.

Permits, entrance fees and accommodation
It costs RM100 per person to climb Gunung Kinabalu; a RM15 entry fee must be paid on arrival by all park visitors and compulsory insurance costs RM3.50. The park is run by **Sutera Sanctuary Lodges** ① *Ground floor of Wisma Sabah, KK, To88-242629, www.suterasanctuarylodges,com, Mon-Fri 0900-1830, Sat 0900-1630, Sun 0900-1500.* All accommodation in the park must be booked in advance through its office. ▸▸ *See also Sleeping, page 214.*

Sabah Gunung Kinabalu National Park

Equipment

A thick jacket is recommended, but at the very least you should have a light waterproof or windcheater to beat the wind chill on the summit. You can hire jackets from Laban Rata but you need to book ahead as there are limited numbers. Carry a dry sweater and socks in your backpack and change just before you get to the peak – if it's raining the damp chill is worse than the actual cold. There are small shops at Park HQ and Laban Rata that sell gloves, hats, raincoats, torches and food for the climb (but it's cheaper if you stock up in KK). It is also best to bring a sweater or thick shirts; the shops in Wisma Merdeka sell cheap woollies. Walking boots are recommended, but not essential – many people climb the mountain in trainers. Stock up on food, chocolate and drinking water in KK the day before. Essential items include a torch, toilet paper, water bottle, plasters, headache tablets and suntan lotion. A hat is also a good idea – to guard against the sun and the cold. Lockers are available, RM1 per item, at the Park HQ reception office. Sleeping bags are provided free of charge in the **Laban Rata Resthouse; essential for a good night's sleep.** The Laban Rata Resthouse has hot-water showers, but soap and towels are not provided. Some of the rooms are well heated, cheaper ones leave you to freeze.

Guides

Hiring a guide is compulsory: RM70 for the round trip (one to three people), RM80 for the Mesilau trail. Porters are available at a charge of RM60 (for 10 kg carried). Guides and porters should be reserved at least a day in advance at the Park HQ or at at **Sutera Sanctuary Lodges**. On the morning of your climb, go to the HQ and a guide will be assigned to you. While a tour will cost around RM500 each, a group of you can hire a taxi, book heated accommodation, and share a guide for the climb for less than RM250 each including all the fees. If you are doing it by yourselves it is best to get to the park a day in advance, and stay at Park HQ to get up early for the first part of the climb to Laban Rata. Alternatively you can scramble out of bed at 0600 and make a dash from KK to the Park HQ to arrive before 0900 to be sure of finding a guide.

✴ Mount Kinabalu is a tough, steep climb but requires no special skills or equipment.

If you are desperate to go, short of time, and have been informed that there is no accommodation available on the mountain in the next few days (as can happen during busy periods such as school holidays), it might still be worth turning up in person to enquire. A bus to the park leaves KK at 0700, and will drop you outside Park HQ around 0900 – arrive no later if you are hoping to climb the mountain that day. You may still be able to pick up a guide if you are there before 1000, although you will be unlikely to find anyone else to share with; the climb should begin around 1100, allowing enough time to reach Laban Rata. Reports suggest that beds/mattresses up the mountain can sometimes be found if someone turns up in person. This method should be an absolute last resort, and it is by no means guaranteed to work. If things don't work out, accommodation will probably be available at Park HQ, or there are a number of good places within 2 km of the park.

Park headquarters

Located a short walk from the main Ranau-KK road and all the accommodation and restaurants are within 15 minutes' walk from the main compound. There is a shop selling books next to the Park HQ which has good books on the mountain and its flora and fauna. Slide and film shows are held in the mini-theatre in the administration building at 1400 during the week and at 1930 on weekends and public holidays, while naturalists give escorted trail walks every morning. The museum displays information on local flora and fauna, beetles "as large as [Sir] Tom Jones' medallions" and foot-long stick insects.

Treks

A small colour pamphlet, *Mount Kinabalu/A Guide to the Summit Trail*, published by Sabah Parks, serves as a good guide to the wildlife and the trail itself. Most treks are well used and are easy walks, but the **Liwagu Trail** is a good three- to four-hour trek up to where it joins the summit trail and is very steep and slippery in places; not advised as a solo trip. There is a daily guided trail walk at 1100, from the park administration building. This is a gentle walk with a knowledgeable guide, although the number of participants tends to be large. The climb to the summit of Mount Kinabalu is not something which should be undertaken lightly. It can be perishingly cold on the summit and altitude sickness is a problem. Some points of the trail are steep and require adequate footware. Changeable weather conditions add to the hazards.

Gunung Kinabalu Trail

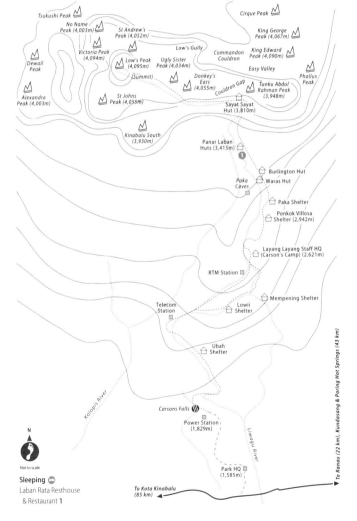

In the first written mention of the mountain, in 1769, Captain Alexander Dalrymple of the East India Company, wrote from his ship in the South China Sea: "Though perhaps not the highest mountain in the world, it is of immense height." During the Second World War Kinabalu was used as a navigational aid by Allied bombers – one of whom was quoted as saying "That thing must be near as high as Mount Everest". It's not, but at 4095 m, Gunung Kinabalu is the highest peak between the Himalayas and New Guinea. It is not the highest mountain in Southeast Asia: peaks in Northern Burma and the Indonesian province of Irian Jaya are higher.

There are a number of theories about the derivation of its name. The most convincing is the corruption of the Kadazan Aki Nabulu – 'the revered place of the spirits'. For the Kadazan, the mountain is sacred as they consider it to be the last resting place of the dead, and the summit was believed to be inhabited by their ghosts. In the past the Kadazan are said to have carried out human sacrifices on Mount Kinabalu, carrying their captives to the summit in bamboo cages, where they would be speared to death. The Kadazan guides still perform an annual sacrifice to appease the spirits. Today they make do with chickens, eggs, cigars, betel nuts and rice, on the rock plateau below the Panar Laban rockface.

The Chinese also lay claim to a theory. According to this legend, a Chinese prince arrived on the shores of northern Borneo and went in search of a huge pearl on the top of the mountain, which was guarded by a dragon. He duly slew the dragon, grabbed the pearl and married a beautiful Kadazan girl. After a while he grew homesick, and took the boat back to China, promising his wife that he would return. She climbed the mountain every day for years on end to watch for her husband's boat. He never came and in desperation and depression, she lay down and died and was turned to stone. The mountain was then christened China Balu – or Chinaman's widow.

In 1851, Sir Hugh Low, the British colonial secretary in Labuan, made the first unsuccessful attempt at the summit. Seven years later he returned with Spencer St John, the British consul in Brunei. Low's feet were in bad shape after the long walk to the base of the mountain, so St John went on without him, with a handful of reluctant Kadazan porters. He made it to the top of the conical southern peak, but was "mortified to find that the most westerly [peak] and another to the east appeared higher than where I sat." He retreated, and returned three months later with Low, but again failed to reach the summit, now called Low's Peak (standing at 4095 m above sea level). It remained unconquered for another 30 years. The first to reach the summit was John Whitehead, a zoologist, in 1888. Whitehead spent several months on the mountain collecting birds and mammals and many of the more spectacular species bear either Low's or Whitehead's name. More scientists followed and then a trickle of tourists, but it was not until 1964, when Kinabalu Park (encompassing 75,000 ha) was gazetted, that the 8.5-km trail to the summit was opened. Today the mountain lures around 200,000 visitors a year. Although the majority are day visitors who do not climb the peak, the number of climbers is steadily increasing, with around 30,000 making the attempt each year.

Gunung Kinabalu is an important watershed with eight major rivers originating on its slopes. It has been gazetted to protect the mountain and its remarkably diverse flora and fauna.

In plan, the top of the mountain is U-shaped, with bare rock plateaux. Several peaks stand proud of these plateaux, around the edge of the U; the space between the western and eastern arms is the spectacular gully known as Low's Gully. No one has ever scaled its precipitous walls, nor has anyone climbed the Northern Ridge (an extension of the eastern arm) from the back of the mountain. From Low's Peak, the eastern peaks, just 1.5 km away, look within easy reach. As John Briggs points out in his book *Mountains of Malaysia*, "It seems so close, yet it is one of the most difficult places to get to in the whole of Borneo".

The range of climatic zones on the mountain has led to the incredible diversity of plant and animal life. Kinabalu Park is the meeting point of plants from Asia and Australasia. There are thought to be more than 1200 species of orchid alone, and this does not include the innumerable mosses, ferns and fungi. These flowering plants of Kinabalu are said to represent more than half the families of flowering plants in the world. Within the space of 3 km, the vegetation changes from lowland tropical rainforest to alpine meadow and cloud forest. The jungle reaches up to 1300 m; above that, to a height of 1800 m, is the lower montane zone, dominated by 60 species of oak and chestnut; above 2000 m is the upper montane zone with true cloud forest, orchids, rhododendrons and pitcher plants. Above 2600 m, growing among the crags and crevices of the summit rock plateau are gnarled tea trees (*Leptospermums*) and stunted rhododendrons. Above 3300 m, the soil disappears, leaving only club mosses, sedges and Low's buttercups (*Ranunculus lowii*), which are alpine meadow flowers.

Among the most unusual of Kinabalu's flora is the world's largest flower, the rust-coloured rafflesia (see box on page 195). It can usually only be found in the section of the park closest to Poring Hot Springs. Rafflesia are hard to find as they only flower for a couple of weeks between August and December.

Kinabalu is also famous for the carnivorous pitcher plants, which grow to varying sizes on the mountain. A detailed guide to the pitcher plants of Kinabalu can be bought in the shop at Park HQ. Nine different species have been recorded on Kinabalu. The largest is the giant Rajah Brooke's pitcher plant; Spencer St John claimed to have found one of these containing a drowned rat floating in four litres of water. Insects are attracted by the scent and, when they settle on the lip of the plant, they cannot maintain a foothold on the waxy, ribbed surface. At the base of the pitcher is an enzymic fluid which digests the 'catch'.

Rhododendrons line the trail throughout the mossy forest (there are 29 species in the park), especially above the Paka Cave area. One of the most beautiful is the copper-leafed rhododendron, with orange flowers and leaves with coppery scales underneath. There are an estimated 1000 species of orchid in the park, along with 621 species of fern and 52 palm species.

It is difficult to see wildlife on the climb to the summit as the trail is well used, although tree shrews and squirrels are common on the lower trails. There are, however, more than 100 species of mammal living in the park. The Kinabalu summit rats, which are always on cue to welcome climbers to Low's Peak at dawn, and nocturnal ferret badgers are the only true montane mammals in Sabah. As the trees thin with altitude, it is often possible to see tree shrews and squirrels, of which there are more than 28 species in the park. Large mammals, such as flying lemurs, red-leaf monkeys, wild pigs, orang-utan and deer, are lowland forest dwellers. Nocturnal species include the slow loris (*Nycticebus coucang*) and the mischievous-looking bug-eyed tarsier (*Tarsius bancanus*).

More than half of Borneo's 518 species of bird have also been recorded in Kinabalu Park, but the variety of species decreases with height. Two of the species living above 2500 m are endemic to the mountain: the Kinabalu friendly warbler and the Kinabalu mountain blackbird.

More than 61 species of frog and toad and 100 species of reptile live in the park. Perhaps the most interesting frog in residence is the horned frog, which is virtually impossible to spot thanks to its mastery of the art of camouflage. The giant toad is common at lower altitudes; he is covered with warts, which are poisonous glands. When disturbed, these squirt a stinking, toxic liquid. Other frogs found in the park include the big-headed leaf-litter frog, whose head is bigger than the rest of its body, and the green stream shrub frog, who has a magnificent metallic green body, but is deadly if swallowed by any predator.

The famous flying tree snake has been seen in the park. It spreads its skin flaps, which act as a parachute when the snake leaps blindly from one tree to another.

There are nearly 30 species of fish in the park's rivers, including the unusual Borneo sucker fish (*Gastomyzon borneensis*), which attaches itself to rocks in fast-flowing streams. One Sabah Parks publication likens them to 'underwater cows', grazing on algae as they move slowly over the rocks.

Walkers and climbers are more likely to come across the park's abundant insect life than anything else. Examples include pill millipedes, rhinoceros beetles, the emerald green and turquoise jewel beetles, stick insects, 'flying peapods', cicadas, and a vast array of moths (including the giant atlas moth) and butterflies (including the magnificent emerald green and black Rajah Brooke's birdwing).

Gunung Kinabalu

The climb to the summit and back should take two days; four to six hours from Park HQ at 1585 m to the **Laban Rata Resthouse** (3550 m) on the first day (note a second slightly tougher trail has opened from Mesilau which takes two to three hours longer to get to Laban Rata, but which has far less tourists) and then three hours to the summit for dawn, returning to the Park HQ at around 1200 hours on the second day. Gurkha soldiers and others have made it to the summit and back in well under three hours. For the really keen, or the really foolhardy, depending on one's perspective and inclination, there is also the annual Kinabalu Climbathon which is held in early October. Having said that the climb to the top 'requires no special skills', the death of a British teenage girl on the mountain in 2001 highlights the hazards of climbing an unfamiliar mountain where changes in the weather can be sudden and dramatic. Keep to the trails and avoid parting company with your group.

A minibus for 12 people can take groups from headquarters to the power station at 1829 m where the trail starts (RM5 per person). It is a 25-minute walk from the power station to the first shelter. The trail splits in two soon afterwards, the left goes to the radio station and the helipad and the right towards the summit. The next stop is **Layang Layang staff headquarters** (drinking water, cooking facilities, accommodation) – also known as **Carson's Camp** (2621 m), named after the first warden of the park. There is one more shelter, **Ponkok Villosa** (2942 m, and about 45 minutes from Carson's Camp) before the stop at the path to **Paka Caves** – really an overhanging rock on the side of a stream. Paka is a 10-minute detour to the left, where Low and St John made their camps.

From the cave/fifth shelter the vegetation thins out and it is a steep climb to **Panar Laban huts** – which includes the well-equipped **Laban Rata Resthouse** – affording magnificent views at sunset and in the early morning. The name Panar Laban is derived from Kadazan words meaning 'place of sacrifice': early explorers had to make a sacrifice here to appease the spirits and this ritual is still performed by the Kadazan once a year. **Sayat Sayat** (3810 m) hut – named after the ubiquitous shrubby tea tree – is an hour further on, above the Panar Laban rockface. Most climbers reach Panar Laban (or the other huts) in the early afternoon in order to rest up for a 0300 start the next morning to reach the summit by sunrise. This second part of the trail – 3 km long – is more demanding technically, but the trail is well laid out with regular 500-m resting points. Ladders, hand-rails and ropes are provided for the steeper parts (essential in the wet, as the granite slabs can be very slippery). The final 1 km has no hand rails or ropes but is less steep. The first two hours after dawn are the most likely to be cloud-free. For enthusiasts interested in alternative routes to the summit, John Briggs's *Mountains of Malaysia* provides a detailed guide to the climb.

Mountain Garden

ⓘ *Tours leave at 0900, 1200, 1500 and cost RM4 – the garden is closed at other times.*
Situated behind the park administration building, this landscaped garden has species from the mid-levels of the mountain, which have been planted in natural surroundings.

Mesilau Nature Resort

This rainforest resort nestles at the foot of Mount Kinabalu at 2000 m. The main attractions are the cool climate and the superb views up the mountain and across the plains toward Ranau and the sea. It is possible to scale the peaks of the mountain using the resort as a base, providing an alternative route from which to launch any assault on Low's Peak. Taking this new trail, one would join the main trail at Layang Layang. Alternatively there are a number of walks to be made around the reserve, in this secluded location.

Poring Hot Springs ₩ *Colour map 2, A1.*

ⓘ *If you've already paid the entrance fee to the national park keep your ticket for entrance to the hot springs; if staying at Poring there is no charge, and the baths can be used all night long; permits not necessary.*

Poring lies 43 km from Gunung Kinabalu Park HQ and is actually part of the national park. The **hot sulphur baths** ⓘ *sulphur bath, RM15 per hr, sulphur bath and jacuzzi, RM20 per hr*, were installed during the Japanese occupation of the Second World War, for the jungle-weary Japanese troops. There are individual concrete pools which can fit two people, with taps for hot- and cold-spring mineral water; once in your bath you are in complete privacy. However, many visitors now complain that the water is no longer hot, more like lukewarm. The springs are on the other side of the Mamut River from the entrance, over a suspension bridge. They are a fantastic antidote to tiredness after a tough climb up Gunung Kinabalu. There is also a cold water rock pool. The pools are in a beautiful garden setting of hibiscus and other tropical flowers, trees and thousands of butterflies. There are some quite luxurious private cabin baths available and also large baths which hold up to eight people. The de luxe cabins have lounge areas and jacuzzis. The Kadazans named the area Poring after the towering bamboos of that name nearby.

The **jungle canopy walk** ⓘ *daily 0900-1600, RM5, camera RM5, video RM30*, guides are available, at Poring is a rope walkway 35 m above the ground, which provides a monkey's-eye view of the jungle; springy but quite safe. The entrance is five minutes' walk from the hot springs and the canopy walkway is 15 minutes' walk from the entrance. The canopy walkway at Danum Valley is far more exciting. If the weather is clear at Ranau, it is generally safe to assume that the canopy walk will also be clear.

Kipungit Falls are only about 10 minutes' walk from Poring and swimming is possible here. Follow the trail further up the hill and after 15 minutes you come to bat caves; a large overhanging boulder provides shelter and a home for the bats.

The **Langanan Waterfall** trail takes 90 minutes one way, is uphill, but worth it. There is another hard, 90-minute trail to **Bat Cave** (inhabited by what seems to be a truly stupendous number of bats) and a waterfall. The **Butterfly Farm** ⓘ *Tue-Sun 0900-1600, RM5*, was established, close to the springs, by a Japanese-backed firm in 1992 and is very educational in the descriptions of butterflies and other insects.

There is also an Information Centre, a rafflesia centre, orchid centre, aviary and tropical garden at Poring. It is better not to visit the hot springs at the weekend or on public holidays, if you want to relax in a peaceful atmosphere. Minibuses to the springs leave Park HQ at 0900, 1300, 1600; alternatively flag down a bus/minibus to Ranau on the main road a two-minute walk from HQ and take a taxi from there to Poring.

Ranau and Kundasang ₩ *Colour map 2, A1.*

The Ranau plateau, surrounding the Kinabalu massif, is one of the richest farming areas in Sabah and much of the forest not in the park has now been devastated by market gardeners. Even within the national park's boundaries, on the lower slopes of Mount Kinabalu itself, shifting cultivators have clear-felled tracts of jungle and planted their patches. More than 1000 ha are now planted out with spinach, cabbage, cauliflower, asparagus, broccoli and tomatoes, supplying much of Borneo.

Kundasang and Ranau are unremarkable towns a few kilometres apart; the latter is bigger. The **war memorial**, behind Kundasang, which unfortunately looks like Colditz, is in memory of those who died in the 'death march' in the Second World War (see page 220). In September 1944, the Japanese marched 2400 Allied prisoners of war through the jungle from Sandakan to Kundasang. The march took 11 months and only six men survived to tell the tale. The walled gardens represent the national gardens of Borneo, Australia and Britain.

Mentapok and Monkobo are southwest of Ranau. Both are rarely climbed. Mentapok, 1581 m, can be reached in 1½ days from Kampong Mireru, a village at the base of the mountain. A logging track provides easy access halfway up the south side of the mountain. Monkobo is most easily climbed from the northwest, a logging track from Telupid goes up to 900 m and from here it is a two-hour trek to the top. It is advisable to take guides, organized from Ranau or one of the nearby villages.

● Sleeping

Gunung Kinabalu Park *p207, map p209*
Management of the park is privatized. It is currently being managed by **Sutera Sanctuary Lodges**, all accommodation in the park must be booked in advance through its office: Ground floor, Wisma Sabah, KK, T088-242629, www.suterasanctuarylodges.com, Mon-Fri 0900-1830, Sat 0900-1630, Sun 0900-1500.

Park HQ
Each cabin is provided with a fireplace, kitchen, shower, gas cooker, refrigerator and cooking and eating utensils. Electricity, piped water and firewood are all provided free of charge. The rates quoted below are reduced on weekdays. The most expensive option at the Park HQ is the **Rajah Lodge**, sleeping 10 people (RM1,150 for the whole lodge). **Kinabalu Lodge**, 8 people, RM414 per night. **Nepenthes Lodge**, 4 people, RM288 per night. **Twin-bedded cabins**, 2 people, RM92 per night, great views. **Four-person chalets**, RM230 per night. There are also unheated dormitory rooms with shared bathroom for RM12 per bed.

Gunung Kinabalu
Laban Rata Resthouse, Panar Laban, 54 rooms (space is often made for extra bodies by laying out matresses on the restaurant floor), a good-quality though pricey canteen (but sometimes rather limited food – it all has to be walked up the mountain) and hot-water shower facilities, plus electricity and heated rooms, bedding provided. Most expensive rooms are the heated de luxe Buttercup rooms at RM230 or RM115 per room, heated dormitory rooms for RM34 per bed, while chilly unheated dorms are RM17 per bed.

Close to Park HQ
A Haleluyah Retreat Centre, Jl Linouh, Km 61, Tuaran-Ranau Highway, T088-423993, kandiu@tm.net.my. This Christian centre is open to all and is located at 1500 m close to the foot of Mount Kinabalu. It makes a good stop-off point before climbing the mountain. Set amidst natural jungle and approximately 15 mins' walk from the Park HQ, it is isolated but safe, clean, friendly and with a relaxing atmosphere. Cooking and washing facilities, camping area, multi- purpose hall and meeting rooms make it a suitable venue for seminars, meetings, youth camps or family holidays. Food is available at a reasonable price from a canteen, dormitory beds also available.
A-C Sonny's Cottage, T088-750555, T088-750479. 6 bedrooms with spectacular views.
A-E Rina Ria Lodge, Batu 36, Jl Tinompok, Ranau, T088-889282. About 1 km from the Kinabalu National Park, rooms have attached kitchen and basic bathroom, armchairs and beautiful views. There is also a shop. Prices increase at weekends. Dormitories also available.
B Kinabalu Rose Cabin, Km18, Ranau-Kinasaraban Rd, Kundasang, T088-889233 F088-889800. A/c, restaurant, 2 km from the park, towards golf course (30% discount to golfers); range of rooms, suites.
C Mountain View Motel, 5 km east of Kinabalu National Park on the Ranau-Tamparuli Highway, T088-875389,

bbmtkinabalu@hotmail.com. Price includes breakfast, hot water, restaurant, laundry facilitites, local tours, climbing gear available for hire. The corrugated-iron roof can be loud when it rains.

E Mountain Resthouse and Restaurant, T088-771109. Located just outside the park, this has small 4-person dormitories that are cheaper, newer, cleaner and warmer than the park dormitories. Spectacular views. This is arguably preferable to the park accomodation.

Mesilau Nature Resort *p213*

L-C Mesilau Nature Resort, managed by Sutera Sanctuary Lodges, T088-871733, www.suterasanctuarylodges.com. Mesilau provides a range of tasteful wooden chalets that blend neatly into the environment, housing groups of up to 6 people (RM400 per room). There is also more budget accommodation provided in dormitories in the hostel (RM30 per bed).

Other services available include laundry, gift shop and regular educational talks. The nature reserve is situated close to the Mt Kinabalu Golf Club, just a few mins' drive away.

Poring *p213*

Booking is recommended. Camping is also available, RM6.

E Serindit hostel, 24-person dormitories, RM12 per adult; **Tempua Lodge**, 4 people, RM92 per chalet; **Enggang Lodge**, 6 people, RM115 per night; **Rajawali Lodge**, 6 people, RM288 per night.

Ranau and Kundasang *p213*

L-B Zen Garden Resorts, Km 2, Jl Mohimboyan Kibas, T088-889242, F088-889251, cable TV, hot showers and pleasant restaurant.

A-B Perkasa, visible on the hill above Kundasang (a further 1 km down the road from Kinabalu Pine), T088-889511, www.perkasahotel.com.my. A/c, terrace restaurant, slightly run down but a good view of the mountain, organizes tours to Kinabalu National Park and surrounding area. Oriented towards business travellers.

B Kinabalu Pine Resort, Kampong Kundasang, T088-889388, F088-889288. A/c, great views in this attractive but isolated area, 6 km from the national park. Great value.

🍴 Eating

Gunung Kinabalu Park *p207*

The best places to stay are at Park HQ but the restaurants are rather spread out requiring a walk between buffet and bed.

🍴 **Liwagu restaurant**, 0600-2200, has beer, chips and curries.

🍴 **Balsam Cafeteria**, 0600-1800, is the cheaper option for Malay staples.
Both open early for climbers to stock up on high-carb breakfasts.

There are cooking facilites at the hostels plus **Rajah Lodge**, **Nepenthes Lodge** and **Kinabalu Lodge**.

Mesilau Nature Resort *p213*

🍴 **The Kedamaian Restaurant** will provide the 3 main meals.

🍴 **Malaxi Café** has a stunning veranda offering great views of the mountain.

Poring *p213*

🍴 **Restaurant**, quite good Chinese and Malay food at the springs and stalls outside the park.

Ranau and Kundasang *p213*

There are several restaurants along the roads serving simple food in Kundasang, open 0600-2100.

🍴 **Perkasa Hotel Restaurant**, Kundasang. Local and Western dishes, service good and food excellent.

🍴 **Five Star Seafood Restaurant**, Ranau. Chinese, opposite the market

🍴 **Sin Mui Mui**, top side of the square near the market. Closed Fri afternoons.

🛍 Shopping

Ranau and Kundasang *p213*

Cheap sweaters and waterproofs for the climb from **Kedai Kien Hin**, Ranau. A *tamu* is held near Ranau on the 1st of each month and every Sat. Kundasang *tamu* is held on the 20th of every month and also every Fri.

● For an explanation of the sleeping and eating price codes used in this guide, see inside the
● front cover. Other relevant information is found in Essentials, pages 31-35.

⛰ Activities and tours

Ranau and Kundasang *p213*
Golf
Kundasang Golf Course, 3 km behind Kundasang, one of the most beautiful courses in the region. Club hire from the **Perkasa Hotel**, Kundasang. The **Perkasa** offers golfing packages which include golf fees, accommodation, breakfast and lunch, and transfer from hotel to course.

⊖ Transport

Gunung Kinabalu Park *p207*
Bus
All buses heading to **Sandakan** and **Ranau** will drop you off at the turn-off to the park.

Minibus
Regular connections from **KK** to **Ranau**, ask to be dropped at the park, 2 hrs. Return minibus (roughly every hr) must be waved down from the main road.

Taxi
RM60 fixed price, taxi from long-distance bus station in **Kota Kinabalu**.

Poring *p213*
Minibuses can be shared from **Ranau** for RM5. Buses running between **KK** and **Sandakan** stop in town on Jl Kibarambang. Taxis are also available.

Ranau and Kundasang *p213*
Minibus
Minibuses leave from the market place. Regular connections to **Park HQ**, **KK** and **Sandakan** (8 hrs).

East coast

From Ranau it is possible to reach Sandakan by road. Several key sights are within reach of Sandakan: the Turtle Islands National Park, 40 km north in the Sulu Sea, Sepilok Orang-Utan Rehabilitation Centre and the Kinabatangan Basin, to the southeast. From Sandakan, the route continues south to the wilds of Lahad Datu and Danum Valley and on to Semporna, the jumping off point for Pulau Sipadan (an island which has achieved legendary status among snorkellers and scuba divers). Tawau Hills State Park has some unusual natural features which draw visitors at weekends. ▸▸ *For Sleeping, Eating and other listings, see pages 231-241.*

Sandakan ⊟⊘⊕⊙⛰⊖⊙ ▸▸ *pp231-241. Colour map 2, A2.*

Sandakan is at the neck of a bay on the northeast coast of Sabah and looks out to the Sulu Sea. It is a post-war town, much of it rebuilt on reclaimed land and is Malaysia's biggest fishing port; it even exports some of its catch to Singapore. Sandakan is often dubbed 'mini Hong Kong' because of its Cantonese influence; its occupants are well-heeled and the town sustains many prosperous businesses, despite being rather scruffy as a whole. It is now also home to a large Filipino community, mostly traders from Mindanao and the Sulu Islands. Manila still officially claims Sabah in its entirety – Sandakan is only 28 km from Philippines' territorial waters.

Ins and outs
Getting there The airport is around 10 km north of town. There are daily connections with KK and several lesser destinations in Sabah. Mminibuses travel from the airport to the station at the southern end of Jl Pelabuhan. From the long-distance bus terminal 5 km to the west of town, there are connections with KK, Tawau, Ranau, Lahad Datu, Semporna and several other destinations. ▸▸ *See also Transport, page 239.*

Sandakan is not a large town and it is easy enough to explore the
central area on foot – although it does stretch some way along the coast. Minibuses
provide links with out-of-town places of interest.

Tourist information The privately run **Tourist Information Centre** ⓘ *To89-22975,
Mon-Fri 0800-1230, 1330-1630, Sat 0800-1230 (closed 1st and 3rd Sat every month)*,
next to the municipal council building opposite Lebuh Empat is staffed by the
enthusiastic Elvina who does her best to answer all questions with limited resources.
The centre was opened by the owner of the **Sepilok Jungle Resort** but it provides
impartial advice.

History

The Sandakan area was an important source of beeswax for the Sulu traders, and
came under the sway of the Sultans of Sulu. William Clarke Cowie, a Scotsman with a
carefully waxed handlebar moustache who ran guns for the Sultan of Sulu across the
Spanish blockade of Sulu (and was later to become the managing director of the
North Borneo Chartered Company), first set up camp in Sandakan Bay in the early
1870s. He called his camp; which was on Pulau Timbang, 'Sandakan', which had
been the Sulu name for the area for about 200 years, but it became known as
Kampong German as there were several German traders living there, and early
gun-runners tended to be German. The power of the Sulu sultanate was already on
the wane when Cowie set up. In its early trading days, there were many nationalities
living in Sandakan: Europeans, Africans, Arabs, Chinese, Indians, Javanese, Dusun
and Japanese. It was an important gateway to the interior and used to be a trading
centre for forest produce like rhinoceros horn, beeswax and hornbill ivory, along with
marine products like pearls and sea cucumbers (*tripang*, valued for their medicinal
properties). In 1812, an English visitor, John Hunt, estimated that the Sandakan/
Kinabatangan area produced an astonishing 37,000 kg of wild beeswax and 23,000
kg of birds' nests each year.

The modern town of Sandakan was founded by an Englishman, William Pryer, in
1879. Baron von Overbeck, the Austrian consul from Hong Kong who founded the
Chartered Company with businessman Alfred Dent, had signed a leasing agreement for
the territory with the Sultan of Brunei, only to discover that large tracts on the east side
of modern-day Sabah actually belonged to the Sultan of Sulu. Overbeck sailed to Sulu
in January 1878 and on obtaining the cession rights from the Sultan, dropped William
Pryer off at Kampong German to make the British presence felt. Pryer's wife Ada later
described the scene: "He had with him a West Indian black named Anderson, a
half-caste Hindoo named Abdul, a couple of China boys. For food they had a barrel of
flour and 17 fowls and the artillery was half a dozen sinder rifles." Pryer set about
organizing the three existing villages in the area, cultivating friendly relations with the
local tribespeople and fending off pirates. He raised the Union Jack on 11 February 1878.

Cowie tried to do a deal with the Sultan of Sulu to wrest control of Sandakan back
from Pryer, but Dent and Overbeck finally bought him off. A few months later Cowie's
Kampong German burned to the ground, so Pryer went in search of a new site, which
he found at Buli Sim Sim. He called his new settlement Elopura, meaning 'beautiful
city', but the name did not catch on. By the mid-1880s it was renamed Sandakan and,
in 1884, became the capital of North Borneo when the title was transferred from
Kudat. In 1891 the town had 20 Chinese-run brothels and 71 Japanese prostitutes;
according to the 1891 census there were three men for every one woman. The town
quickly established itself as the source of birds' nests harvested from the caves at
Gomantong and shipped directly to Hong Kong, as they are today.

Timber was first exported from this area in 1885 and was used to construct
Beijing's Temple of Heaven. Sandakan was, until the 1980s, the main east-coast port
for timber and it became a wealthy town. In its heyday, the town is said to have boasted

Sabah East coast

one of the greatest concentrations of millionaires in the world. The timber-boom days are over: the primary jungle has gone, and so has the big money. In the mid-1990s the state government adopted a strict policy restricting the export of raw, unprocessed timber. The hinterland is now dominated by cocoa and oil palm plantations.

Following the Japanese invasion in 1942, Sandakan was devastated by Allied bombing. In 1946 North Borneo became a British colony and the new colonial government moved the capital to Jesselton (later to become Kota Kinabalu).

Sights

Sandakan is strung out along the coast but in the centre of town is the riotous **daily fish market**, which is the biggest and best in Sabah. The best time to visit is at 0600 when the boats unload their catch. The **Central Market** along the waterfront, near the local bus station, sells such things as fruit, vegetables, sarongs, seashells, spices and sticky rice cakes.

The **Australian war memorial** ① *take Labuk bus service Nos 19, 30 and 32*, near the government building at Mile Seven on Labuk Rd, between Sandakan and Sepilok, stands on the site of a Japanese prison camp and commemorates Allied soldiers who lost their lives during the Japanese occupation. The Japanese invaded North Borneo in 1942 and many Japanese also died in the area. In 1989 a new **Japanese war memorial** – walk 20 minutes up Red Hill (Bukit Berenda) – was built in the Japanese cemetery, financed by the families of the deceased soldiers.

St Michael's Anglican church is one of the very few stone churches in Sabah and is an attractive building, designed by a New Zealander in 1893. Most of Sandakan's stone churches were levelled in the war and, indeed, St Michael's is one of the few colonial-era buildings still standing. It is just off Jalan Singapura, on

Sandakan

To Goddess of Mercy Temple

To Trig Hill & 8 6

St Michael's

Sam Sing Kung Temple

Jl Puncak

Three Saints Temple

Jl Tokong

BUKIT ELTON

Jl Singapura

Jl Utara

To Long-distance Bus Terminal, Tanah Merah Town, Pertubuhan Ugama Buddhist & 9 10 11 12 3 5 6 7 8

Padang

Night

Jl Leila

Tun Razak Park

Community Centre

Minibuses

Lebuh Tiga (3rd Av)

Jl Dua (2nd Av)

Jl Europa

Minibuses

Centre Point Plaza

Local Bus Station

MAS

Jl Pelabuhan

Fisherman's

N

0 metres (approx) 100
0 yards (approx) 100

Sleeping 😴
City View **1**
Hung Wing **2**
Hsiang Garden **5**
London **3**

Mayfair **4**
Ramai **10**
Sabah **8**
Sanbay **11**
Sandakan **6**

Sepilok Inn **7**
Travellers Rest
Hostel **12**
Uncle Tan's **13**

Sabah East coast

the hill at the south end of town. In 1988 a big new **mosque** was built for the burgeoning Muslim population at the mouth of Sandakan Bay. The main Filipino settlements are in this area of town. The mosque is outside Sandakan, on Jalan Buli Sim Sim where the town began in 1879, just after the jetty for Turtle Islands National Park and is an imposing landmark. There is also a large water village here.

There are a couple of other notable Chinese temples in Sandakan. The oldest one, the **Goddess of Mercy Temple** is just off Jalan Singapura, on the hillside. Originally built in the early 1880s, it has been expanded over the years. Nearby is **Sam Sing Kung Temple** which becomes a particular focus of devotion during exam periods since one of its deities is reputed to assist those attempting examinations. The **Three Saints Temple**, further down the hill at the end of the padang, was completed in 1887. The three saints are Kwan Woon Cheung, a Kwan clan ancestor, the goddess Tien Hou (or Tin Hau, worshipped by seafarers) and the Min Cheong Emperor.

Sabah's only **Crocodile Farm** ① *daily 0800-1730, RM2, weekday showtimes at 1145 and 1600, feeding times throughout the day*, is a commercial licensed enterprise, set up in 1982 when the government made the estuarine crocodile a protected species. The original stock was drawn from a population of wild crocodiles found in the Kinabatangan River. Visitors can see around 2000 crocs at all stages of maturity waiting in concrete pools for the day when their skins are turned into bags and wallets and their meat is sold to local butchers. The farm, at Mile 8, Labuk Road, has about 200 residents. To get there take the Labuk Road bus.

The **Forest Headquarters** (Ibu Pejabat Jabatan Perhutanan) ① *Mile 6 Labuk Rd, T089-660811*, next to the Sandakan Golf Course, contain an exhibition centre and a well-laid-out and interesting mini- museum showing past and present forestry practice.

Sabah East coast

The **Sandakan Heritage Trail** is a loop which supposedly takes in the historical gems of this scruffy town (the walk should take a leisurely 90 minutes) including a good lookout point. The tourist office has trail maps. It starts off at the town mosque, nips up the 'stairs with 100 steps' a nice shady climb with good views from the top. However, in summer 2004, the tourist office warned that several visitors had been mugged on the steps and so it is advisable not to climb them alone. From here the trail passes through the newly opened **Agnes Keith House** ① *Sat-Thu 0900-1700, RM5* (see box, page 221), the restored British colonial government quarters built on the site of her home. Inside the grounds, there's an **English Tea House** serving scones and pastries on manicured lawns. From here the trail takes in the Goddess of Mercy Temple, St Michael's Anglican Church and ends up at the **Sandakan Heritage Museum** ① *next to the tourist office, Sat-Thu 0900-1700, free*, a rather slipshod affair with some early photos of the town and an unexplained mannequin dressed in a kilt. There is, however, a good wall photo of Sandakan razed to the ground taken in 1945.

To Airport, Australian & Japanese War Memorials, Crocodile Farm, Labuk Road, Sepilok, Forest HQ & ⑬

Agnes Keith House ❶

100 steps

Sandakan Heritage Museum 🏛

Lebuh Empat

Town Mosque

Jl Empat

Wisma Sandakan ❷

Wisma Khoo Siak Chiew ❸

To Jln Buli Sim Sim, New Mosque & Turtle Islands Jetty

ℹ

❻

Lebuh Tiga

$

$

❶

Jl Empat (4th St)

Jl Tiga (3rd St)

❷

Air Asia

Jl Dua

Jl Lima (5th St)

❹

Jl Pryer

Fish Market

Central Market 🅼

❹

🅼

Wharf

To Turtle Islands ➚

Eating ❼

English Tea House 1
Golden Palace 6
Jiaman 2
New Bangsawan 8

Ocean King Seafood 3
Penang Curry House 4
Seoul Garden 7
XO Steak House 5

⦂ The Borneo Death March

The four years of Japanese occupation ended when the Australian ninth division liberated British North Borneo. Sandakan was chosen by the Japanese as a regional centre for holding Allied prisoners. In 1942 the Japanese shipped 2750 prisoners of war (2000 of whom were Australian and 750 British) to Sandakan from Changi Prison, Singapore. A further 800 British and 500 Australian POWs arrived in 1944. They were ordered to build an airfield (on the site of the present airport) and were forced to work from dawn to dusk. Many died, but in September 1944 2400 POWs were force-marched to Ranau, a 240-km trek through the jungle which only six Australians survived. This 'Death March', although not widely reported in Second World War literature, claimed more Australian lives than any other single event during the war in Asia, including the building of the notorious Burma-Siam railway.

Tanah Merah

Pertubuhan Ugama Buddhist (Puu Jih Shih Buddhist temple) overlooks Tanah Merah town. The US$2 million temple was completed in 1987 and stands at the top of the hill, accessible by a twisting road which hairpins its way up the hillside. The temple is very gaudy, contains three large Buddha images and is nothing special, although the 34 teakwood supporting pillars, made in Macau, are quite a feature. There is a good view of Sandakan from the top, with Tanah Merah and the log ponds directly below, in Sandakan Bay. The names of local donors are inscribed on the walls of the walkway.

Pulau Lankayan

Pulau Lankayan is a fairly new dive resort on a virtually uninhabited island, 90-minutes' boat trip from Sandakan in the Sulu Sea. The resort, **Lankayan Island Dive Resort**, see Sleeping, offers more than 40 dive sites including a couple of wrecks. Sightings of whale sharks are said to be common here in April and May.

Pulau Berhala

ⓘ *To get to the beach charter a boat from the fish market. You can camp on the island.* This island is ideal for picnicking and swimming. It has 200-m rust-coloured sandstone cliffs on the south end, with a beach at the foot, within easy reach by boat. The island was used as a leper colony before the Second World War and as a prisoner of war camp by the Japanese. Agnes Keith was interned on the island during the war.

Turtle Islands National Park 🅿🔺🅖 ▸▸ *pp231-241. Colour map 2, A2.*

Forty kilometres north of Sandakan, the Turtle Islands are at the south entrance to Labuk Bay. The park is separated from the Philippine island of Bakkungan Kecil by a narrow stretch of water. These eight tiny islands in the Sulu Sea are among the most important turtle-breeding spots in all Southeast Asia. The turtle sanctuary is made up of three tiny islands (**Pulau Selingan**, **Pulau Bakkungan Kecil** and **Pulau Gulisan**) and also encompasses the surrounding coral reefs and sea, covering 1700 ha. On Pulau Bakkungan Kecil there is a small mud volcano.

⁝ Agnes Keith's house

American authoress Agnes Keith lived with her English husband in Sandakan from 1934 to 1952. He was the conservator of forests in North Borneo and she wrote three books about her time in the colony. *The Land Below the Wind* tells stories of dinner parties and tiffins in pre-war days. *Three Came Home* is about her three years in a Japanese internment camp during the war on Pulau Berhala, off Sandakan, and in Kuching and was made into a film. *White Man Returns* tells the story of their time in British North Borneo. The Keiths' rambling wooden house on the hill above the town was destroyed during the war, but was rebuilt by the government to exactly the same design when Harry Keith returned to his job when the war ended.

Ins and outs

Best time to visit The driest months and the calmest seas are between March and July. The egg-laying season is between July and October. Seas are rough between October and February.

Tourist information The number of visitors is restricted to 50 per night in an effort to protect the female turtles, which are easily alarmed by noise and light when laying. Visitors are asked not to build campfires, shine bright torches or make noise at night on the beach. The turtles should be watched from a distance to avoid upsetting the nesting process. The park is managed by **Sabah Parks** ⓘ *Sabah Parks Office Room 906, 9th floor, Wisma Khoo, Lebuh Tiga, T089-273453, entrance fee, RM10*. All accommodation must be booked through **Crystal Quest** (see Sleeping). This is booked up weeks, sometimes months in advance.

The islands

The islands are famous for their green turtles (*Chelonia mydas*), which make up about four-fifths of the turtles in the park, and hawksbill turtles (*Eretmochelys imbricata*), known locally as *sisik*. Most green turtles lay their eggs on Pulau Selingan. The green turtles copulate 50-200 m off Pulau Selingan and can be seen during the day, their heads popping up like submarine periscopes. Hawksbills prefer to nest on Pulau Gulisan.

Both species come ashore, year-round, to lay their eggs, although the peak season is between July and October. Even during the off-season between four and 10 turtles come up the beach each night to lay their eggs. Pulau Bakkungan Kecil and Pulau Gulisan can only be visited during the day but visitors can stay overnight on Pulau Selingan to watch the green turtles.

Only the females come ashore; the male waits in the sea nearby for his mate. The females cautiously crawl up to nest after 2000 or with the high tide. The nesting site is above the high-tide mark and is cleared by the female's front and hind flippers to make a 'body pit', just under a metre deep. She then digs an egg chamber with her powerful rear flippers after which she proceeds to lay her eggs. The clutch size can be anything between 40 and 200; batches of 50-80 are most common.

When all the eggs have been laid, she covers them with sand and laboriously fills the body pit to conceal the site of the nest, after which the exhausted turtle struggles back to the sea, leaving her Range Rover-like tracks in the sand. The egg-laying process can take about an hour or two to complete. Some say the temperature of the sand affects the sex of the young: if it is warm the batch will be mostly female and if cold, mostly male. After laying her eggs, a tag reading "If found, return to Turtle Island Park, Sabah, East Malaysia" is attached to each turtle by the rangers, who are stationed on each island. Over 27,000 have been tagged since 1970; the measurements of each turtle are recorded and the clutches of eggs are removed and transplanted to the hatchery where they are protected from natural predators – such as monitor lizards, birds and snakes.

The golf ball-sized eggs are placed by hand into 80 cm-deep pits, covered in sand and surrounded by wire. They take up to 60 days to hatch. The hatchlings mostly emerge at night when the temperature is cooler, breaking their shells with their one sharp tooth. There are hatcheries on all three islands and nearly every night a batch is released into the sea. Millions of hatchlings have been released since 1977. They are released at different points on the island to protect them from predators: they are a favoured snack for white-bellied gulls and sadly only about 1% survive to become teenage turtles.

Sepilok Orang-Utan Sanctuary and Rehabilitation Centre 🖰🌴🚌🏨 ➤ *pp231-241. Colour map 2, A2.*

Sepilok, a reserve of 43 sq km of lowland primary rainforest and mangrove, was set up in 1964 to protect the orang-utan (*Pongo pygmaeus*), from extinction. It is the first and largest of only four orang-utan sanctuaries in the world and now welcomes around 40,000 visitors a year. Logging has seriously threatened Sabah's population of wild orang-utan, as has their capture for zoos and as pets. The orang-utan (see page 331) lives on the islands of Borneo and Sumatra and there are estimated to be perhaps as few as 10,000 still in the wild. In Sabah there are populations of orang-utan in the Kinabatangan basin region (see page 225) and in the Danum Valley Conservation Area as well as in a few other isolated tracts of jungle.

Ins and outs

Getting there There are several buses a day from Sandakan.

Park information The park is open 0900-1230, 1400-1630, RM30, camera RM10. It is worth getting to the park early. The **Information Centre**, next to the Park HQ, runs a nature education exhibition with replicas of jungle mammals and educational videos. Video viewing times are at 1100, 1200 and 1530. If you want to do the walks you'll need to arrive at the centre in the morning so you can get a permit. The pass is valid all day so you can see both feeds if you arrive early enough. Feeding times: Platform A, 1000 and 1500. Note, the morning feed is packed with tour groups, the afternoon feed is generally calmer. Further information about Sepilok can be obtained from the co-ordinator, Sepilok Orang-Utan Rehabilitation Centre, Sabah Wildlife Department, WDT 200, 95000 Sandakan, T089-531180, F089-531189.

Sandakan Bay

PHILIPPINES

Sulu Sea

Pulau Selingan
Pulau Gulisan
Turtle Islands National Park ♦
Pulau Libaran
Pulau Bakkungan Kecil

Tanjung Pisau

Tanjung Lari Lari

MALAYSIA

Samawang

Pulau Berhala

Sandakan

Tanjung Aru

Sepilok Orang-utan Rehabilitation Centre

Sandakan Harbour

Segaliud

Sandakan Bay

Sekong River

Suan Lamba

Sukau

Lamag   Batangan   Malapi

Gomantong Caves   Bilit

Kinabatangan River

Batu Tulug

▼ To Lahad Datu

N

0 km   10
0 miles   10

⁞ Small and hairy: the Sumatran rhinoceros

Although not as rare as its Javan brother, the Sumatran, or Asian two-horned rhinoceros (*Didermoceros sumatrensis*) is severely endangered. It was once widespread through mainland and island Southeast Asia but has now been hunted to the point of extinction; there are probably less than 1000 in the wild, mostly in Sumatra but with small populations in Borneo, Peninsular Malaysia and Vietnam. It is now a protected species. Only on Sumatra does it seem to have a chance of surviving. The situation has become so serious that naturalists have established a captive breeding programme as a precaution against extinction in the wild. Unfortunately this has been spectacularly unsuccessful. Around one-third of animals have died during capture or shortly thereafter

and, according to naturalists Tony and Jane Whitten, the only recorded birth was in captivity in Calcutta in 1872. The species has suffered from the destruction of its natural habitat, and the price placed on its head by the value that the Chinese attach to its grated horn as a cure-all. Should the Sumatran rhino disappear so, too, it is thought, will a number of plants whose seeds will only germinate after passing through the animal's intestines.

The Sumatran rhino is the smallest of all the family, and is a shy, retiring creature, inhabiting thick forest. Tracks have been discovered as high as 3300 m in the Mount Leuser National Park in Sumatra. It lacks the 'armoured' skin of other species and has a soft, hairy hide. It also has an acute sense of smell and hearing, but poor eyesight.

The sanctuary

Sepilok is an old forest reserve that was gazetted as a forestry experimentation centre as long ago as 1931, and by 1957 logging had been phased out. Orphaned or captured orang-utans which have become too dependent on humans through captivity are rehabilitated and protected under the Fauna Conservation Ordinance and eventually returned to their natural home. Many, for example, may have been captured by the oil-palm planters because they eat the young oil palm trees. Initially, the animals at the centre and in the surrounding area are fed every day but, as they acclimatize, they are sent further and further away or are re-released into the Tabin Wildlife Reserve near Lahad Datu. In 1996, researchers placed microchip collars on the orang-utans enabling them to be tracked over a distance of up to 150 km so that a better understanding of their migratory habits and other behaviour could be acquired.

After an initial period of quarantine at Sepilok, newly arrived orang-utans are moved to Platform A and taught necessary survival skills by the rangers. At the age of seven they are moved deeper into the forest to Platform B, about half an hour's walk from Platform A and not open to the public. At Platform B, they are encouraged to forage for themselves. Other animals brought to Sepilok include Malay sun bears, wild cats and baby elephants.

Sepilok also has a rare Sumatran rhinoceros (*Didermoceros sumatrensis*), also known as the Asian two-horned rhinoceros, see box page 223. This enclosure is sometimes closed to the public.

The **Mangrove Forest Trail** takes two to three hours one way. The walk takes in transitional forest, pristine lowland rainforest, a boardwalk into a mangrove forest, water holes and a wildlife track. The visitors' reception centre will provide other information.

Rainforest Interpretation Centre
Mon-Thu 0815-1215, 1400-1600, Fri 0815-1135, 1400-1600, Sat 0815-1215, free; a free booklet is available; for more information contact the Forest Research Centre, PO Box 14-07, T089-531522, F089-531068.

The Rainforest Interpretation Centre on the road to Sepilok provides detailed and informative displays about the vegetation in the area. It is run by the **Forest Research Centre,** which is also found on this road. Great emphasis is given to participation, with questionnaires, games and so on; it offers a wide range of information about all aspects of tropical rainforests and the need for their conservation. The centre is located in the Forest Research Centre's arboretum and in addition to the exhibits there is an 800-m rainforest walk around the lake.

Gomantong Caves ▲ ⇥ *pp231-241.*

The Gomantong Caves are 32 km south of Sandakan Bay, between the road to Sukau and the Kinabatangan River, or 110 km overland on the Sandakan-Sukau road. The name Gomantong means 'tie it up tightly' in the local language and the caves represent the largest system in Sabah. They are contained within the 3924-ha Gomantong Forest Reserve.

Ins and outs
At the Park HQ there is an information centre, a small cafeteria where drinks and simple dishes are sold, and a pit latrine. Good walking shoes are essential, as is a torch. If you're squeamish about cockroaches give this cave a miss. If you arrive independently then one of the nest workers, a person from the information centre, or a ranger will show you around. The bats can be seen exiting from the caves between 1800 and 1830; to request to see this it is necessary to ask at the **Gomantong Wildlife Department** *T011-817529,* at the information centre.

The caves and reserve
Daily 0800-1600, RM30.
There are sometimes orang-utan, mouse deer and many others, wild boar and wild buffalo in the reserve, which was logged in the 1950s. There are several cave chambers. The main limestone cave is called Simud Hitam, or the Black Cave. This cave, with its ceiling soaring up to 90 m overhead, is just a five-minute walk from the registration centre and picnic area. The smaller and more complex White Cave (or Simud Putih) is above. It is quite dangerous climbing up as there is no ladder to reach the caves and the rocks are slippery. Two to three hundred thousand bats of two different species are thought to live in the caves: at sunset they swarm out to feed. Sixty-four species of bat have been recorded in Sabah, most in these caves are fruit- and wrinkled-lipped bats whose guano is a breeding ground for cockroaches. The squirming larvae make the floor of the cave seethe. The guano can cause an itchy skin irritation. The bats are preyed upon by birds like the bat hawk, peregrine falcon and buffy fish owl.

There are also an estimated one million swiftlets which swarm into the cave to roost at sunset, the birds of bird's nest soup fame (see box). The swiftlets of Gomantong have been a focus of commercial enterprise for perhaps 400 or 500 years. However, it was not until 1870 that harvesting birds' nests became a serious industry here. The caves are divided into five pitches and each is allocated to a team of 10-15 people. Harvesting periods last 10 days and there are two each year (February-April and July-September). Collecting the nests from hundreds of feet above the ground is a dangerous business and deaths are not uncommon. Before each harvesting period a chicken or goat is sacrificed to the cave spirit; it is thought that deaths are not the result of human error, but an angry spirit. The birdlife around the caves is particularly rich, with crested serpent eagles, kingfishers, Asian fairy bluebirds, and leafbirds often sighted. Large groups of richly coloured butterflies are also frequently seen drinking from pools along the track leading from the forest into the caves.

Sungai Kinabatangan 🖼🔺 ›› *pp231-241*

At 560 km, this river is Sabah's longest. Much of the lower basin is gazetted under the Kinabatangan Wildlife Sanctuary and meanders through a flood plain, creating numerous ox-bow lakes and an ideal environment for some of the best wildlife in Borneo.

Ins and outs

Visitors who prefer an in-depth look at the area's wildlife can stay overnight at Sukau, two hours by road from Sandakan, where accommodation is provided by local tour operators (see Sleeping). Tour operators take visitors by boat in the late afternoon through the freshwater swamp forest to see proboscis monkeys and other wildlife. There are also walks through the jungle. Because of the lack of public transport to Sukau, the only way to visit the area is with a tour; all tours must be booked in Sandakan or KK. ›› *See Sleeping, page 231.*

Kinabatangan Riverine Forest area

One of the principal reasons why the Kinabatangan has remained relatively unscathed by Sabah's rapacious logging is because much of the land is permanently waterlogged and the forest contains only a small number of commercially valuable trees. Just some of the animals include: tree snake, crocodile, civet cat, otter, monitor lizard, long-tailed and pig-tailed macaque, silver-, red- and grey-leaf monkey and proboscis monkey. It is the most accessible area in Borneo to see proboscis monkeys, which are best viewed from a boat in the late afternoon, when they converge on tree tops by the river banks to settle for the night. Sumatran rhinoceros have also been spotted (see box page 223) and herds of wild elephant often pass through the park. The birdlife is particularly good and includes oriental darter, egret, storm's stork, osprey, coucal owl, frogmouth, bulbul, spiderhunter, oriole, flowerpecker and several species of hornbill.

Because of the diversity of its wildlife, the Kinabatangan Riverine Forest area has been proposed as a forest reserve. In addition, there has been little disturbance from human settlements: the Kinabatangan basin has always been sparsely inhabited because of flooding and the threat posed by pirates. The inhabitants of the Kinabatangan region are mostly Orang Sungai or people of mixed ancestry including Tambanua, Idahan, Dusun, Suluk, Bugis, Brunei and Chinese. The best destination for a jungle river safari is not on the Kinabatangan itself, but on the narrow, winding Sungai Menanggol tributary, about 6 km from Sukau. The Kinabatangan estuary, largely mangrove, is also rich in wildlife, and is a haven for migratory birds. Boats can be chartered from Sandakan to Abai (at the mouth of the river).

The Kinabatangan River is one of the best places to see orang-utans in the wild.

Batu Tulug, also known as Batu Putih (white stone), on the Kinabatangan River 100 km upstream from Sukau, is a cave containing wooden coffins dating back several hundred years. Some of the better examples have been removed to the Sabah State Museum in KK. The caves are about 1 km north of the Kinabatangan Bridge, on the east side of the Sandakan-Lahad Datu road.

Lahad Datu and around 🖂🕿🅾🔺🚻🔔

↪ *pp231-241. Colour map 2, B3.*

Lahad Datu is Malaysia's 'wild East' at its wildest, and its recent history testifies to its reputation as the capital of cowboy country. The population is an intriguing mixture of Filipinos, Sulu islanders, migrants from Kalimantan, Orang Bugis, Timorese and a few Malays. Most came to work on the oil palm plantations. Nowadays there are so many migrants few can find employment in this grubby and uninteresting town. There are reckoned to be more illegal Filipino immigrants in Lahad Datu than the whole official population put together. Piracy in the Sulu Sea and the offshore islands in Kennedy Bay is rife; local fishermen live in terror. In October 2003, a band of Abu Sayyaf rebels grabbed six Filipino and Indonesian workers from the **Borneo Paradise Resort** near Kunak. Eight months later, four of the hostages were freed. It was thought a Malaysian businessman had paid a ransom.

During the Second World War, the Japanese made Lahad Datu their naval headquarters for east Borneo. After the war, the timber companies moved in: the **British Kennedy Bay Timber Company** built Lahad Datu's first plywood mill in the early 1950s. Oil palm plantations grew up in the hinterland after the timber boom finished in the 1970s. As for the town, what it lacks in aesthetic appeal is made up for by its colourful recent history.

Kampong Panji is a water village with a small market at the end of Jalan Teratai, where many of the poorer immigrant families live.

The only good beaches are on the road to Tungku; Pantai Perkapi and Pantai Tungku. They can be reached by minibus from Lahad Datu or by boat from the old wharf. It is possible to get to the nearby islands from the old wharf behind the Mido Hotel, but because of lawlessness in the area, particularly at sea, a trip is not advisable. In April 2000, the Philippines-based radical Islamic group Abu Sayyaf kidnapped 21 people from Sipadan (see page 229).

Madai Caves, are about 2 km off the Tawau-Lahad Datu road, near Kunak. The caves are an important archaeological site; there is evidence they were inhabited over 15,500 years ago. Birds' nests are harvested from the caves three times a year by local Idahan people whose lean-to kampong goes right up to the cave mouth. Your own transport is required for this trip as it's not catered for by tour operators.

Another 15 km west of Madai is **Baturong**, another limestone massif and cave system in the middle of what was originally Tingkayu Lake. The route is not obvious, so it is advisable to take a local guide. Stone tools, wooden coffins and rock paintings have been found there. Evidence of humans dating from 16,000 years ago, after the lake drained away, can be found at the huge rock overhang (take a torch; it is possible to camp here). To get to Baturong, take a minibus from Lahad Datu.

At **Gunung Silam**, 8 km from Lahad Datu on the Tawau road, a track leads up the mountain to a Telekom station at 620 m and from there, a jungle trail to the summit. There are good views over the bay, when it isn't misty, and out to the islands beyond. It is advisable to take a guide. You can stay at the **Silam Lodge** (see Sleeping, below).

Gazetted in 1984 as a protected forest area, **Tabin Wildlife Reserve**, according to the WWF, is one of the last reserves for the critically endangered Sumatran rhino. It's also home to the Borneo pygmy elephant. The reserve is about 50 km or an hour's drive from Lahad Datu. Since 2002, it's been possible to stay inside the privately run reserve at the **Tabin Jungle Resort** (see Sleeping). There are several huge bubbling mud volcanoes an easy trek from the resort.

⁝ The gentler beast of Borneo

It was dung that eventually solved the mystery surrounding Borneo's rare elephants. For a long time scientists couldn't decide whether the animals were native to the island, or introduced by human settlers. One argument suggested that the British East India Company gave the beasts as gifts to the Sultan of Sulu in the 17th century.

Using evidence gleaned from DNA analysis of the mucus which sticks to elephant droppings, scientists from Columbia University in the United States discovered the pachyderm is indeed indigenous. From genetic data they concluded the Borneo variety is a distinct sub-species

of Asian elephant having been isolated from its cousins 300,000 years ago. In recognition of its new status, the animal was rechristened the Borneo Pygmy Elephant in 2003.

The animals are smaller than the Asian elephant, with larger ears, longer tails and straighter tusks. They are also said to be gentler in temper. Scientists believe elephants trooped across swampy land joining Borneo with Sumatra when sea levels were lower during the ice ages.

Conservation groups estimate there are only around 2000 of the endangered elephants left, which are threatened by ivory poachers and loss of habitat.

Danum Valley Conservation Area ⬤⬤

▸▸ *pp231-241. Colour map 2, B2.*

Danum Valley's 438 sq km of virgin jungle is the largest expanse of undisturbed lowland dipterocarp forest in Sabah. The Segama River runs through the conservation area and past the field centre. The Danum River is a tributary of the Segama joining it 9 km downstream of the field centre. Gunung Danum (1093 m) is the highest peak, 13 km southwest of the field centre. Within the area is a Yayasan Sabah timber concession, which is tightly controlled.

Ins and outs

The field centre, which is 65 km west of Lahad Datu and 40 km from the nearest habitation, was set up by the Sabah Foundation (Yayasan) in 1985 for forest research, nature education and recreation; the centre is not open for tourists, but does accept visiting scientists and researchers. If you are a biologist or an educator you may be able to get permission to visit the centre contact the **Sabah Foundation** ⓘ *Likas Bay, To88-326327, www.ysnet.org.my,* for permission. Guides charge RM5 per hour. Tourists are allowed to visit only through the **Borneo Rainforest Lodge**, see Sleeping and Transport, pages 231 and 239.

The valley

This area has never really been inhabited, although there is evidence of a burial site which is thought to be for the Dusun people who lived here about 300 years ago. There is also growing evidence of prehistoric cave dwellers in the Segama River area. Not far downstream from the field centre, in a riverside cave, two wooden coffins have been found, together with a copper bracelet and a *tapai* jar, all of uncertain date. There is evidence of some settlement during the Japanese occupation; townspeople came upstream to escape from the Japanese troops. The area was first recommended as a national park by the **World Wide Fund for Nature's** Malaysia Expedition in 1975 and designated a conservation area in 1981. The field centre was officially opened in 1986.

The main purposes of this large conservation area are to undertake research into the impact of logging on flora and fauna and to try and improve forest management, to understand processes which maintain tropical rainforest and to provide wildlife management and training opportunities for Sabahans. Many are collaborative projects between Malaysian and foreign scientists.

Flora and fauna

Because of its size and remoteness, Danum Valley is home to some of Sabah's rarest animals and plants. The dipterocarp forest is some of the oldest, tallest and most diverse in the world, with 200 species of tree per hectare; there are over 300 labelled trees. The conservation area is teeming with wildlife: Sumatran rhinoceros have been recorded, as have elephant, clouded leopards, orang-utans, proboscis monkeys, crimson langur, pig-tailed macaques, sambar deer, bearded pigs, western tarsier, sunbears and 275 species of bird including hornbills, rufous picolet, flowerpeckers and kingfishers. A species of monkey, which looks like an albino version of the red-leaf monkey, was first seen on the road to Danum in 1988, and appears to be unique to this area. There are guided nature walks on an extensive trail system. Features include a canopy walkway, a heart-stoppingly springy platform, 107 m long and 27 m above the ground, ancient Dusun burial site, waterfalls and a self-guided trail.

Semporna 🏨🍴🛍️🏔️🚌☕ ⟩⟩ pp231-241. Colour map 2, B3.

Semporna is a small fishing town at the end of the peninsula and is the main departure point for Sipadan Island. Semporna has a lively and very photogenic market, spilling out onto piers over the water. It is a Bajau town and is known for its seafood. There are scores of small fishing boats, many with outriggers and square sails. There is a regatta of these traditional boats every March. The town is built on an old coral reef, said to be 35,000 years old, which was exposed by the uplift of the seabed. Many illegal Filipino immigrants pass through Semporna, as it is only two hours from the nearest Philippine island, which gives the place quite a different feel from that of other Malay towns.

The islands off Semporna stand along the edge of the continental shelf, which drops away to a depth of 200 m to the south and east of Pulau Ligitan, the outermost island in the group. Darvel Bay, and the adjacent waters, are dotted with small, mainly volcanic islands, which are all part of the 9300-ha **Semporna Marine Park**. The bigger ones are Pulau Mabul, Pulau Kapalai, Pulau Si Amil, Pulau Danawan and Pulau Sipadan. The reefs surrounding these islands have around 70 genera of coral, placing them, in terms of their diversity, on a par with Australia's Great Barrier Reef. More than 200 species of fish have also been recorded in these waters.

Locals live in traditional boats called *lipa-lipa* or in pilehouses at the water's edge, and survive by fishing. In the shallow channels off Semporna, there are three fishing villages built on stilts: Kampong Potok Satu, Kampong Potok Dua and Kampong Larus. There are many more islands than are marked on the map; most are hilly, uninhabited and have beautiful white sandy beaches.

Reefs in Semporna Marine Park include Bohey Dulang, Sibuan Ulaiga, Tetugan, Mantabuan Bodgaya, Sibuan, Maigu, Selakan and Sebangkat. Pulau Bohey Dulang is a volcanic island with a Japanese-run pearl culture station. Visitors can only visit if there is a boat from the pearl culture station going out. The **Kaya Pearl Company** leases part of the lagoon and Japanese pearl oysters are artificially implanted with a core material to induce pearl growth. The oysters are attached to rafts moored in the lagoon. The pearls are harvested and exported direct to Japan. Some of the islands can be reached by local fishing boats from the main jetty by the market, including Sibuan, Sebangkat, Maigu and Selakan.

Sipadan Island Marine Reserve 🅿🔺🚌

⏭ *pp231-241. Colour map 2, B3.*

The venerable French marine biologist Jacques Cousteau 'discovered' Sipadan in 1989 and after spending three months diving around the island from his research vessel *Calypso* had this to say: "I have seen other places like Sipadan 45 years ago, but now no more. Now we have found an untouched piece of art." Since then Sipadan has become a sub-aqua shangri-la for serious divers. It is regularly voted one of the top dive destinations in the world by leading scuba magazines. The reef is without parallel in Malaysia. But Sipadan Island is not just for scuba divers: it is a magnificent, tiny tropical island with pristine beaches and crystal-clear water and its coral can be enjoyed by even the most amateur of snorkellers.

❧ Since the end of 2004, resorts on Sipadan have been closed for environmental reasons.

Ins and outs

The island's tourist facilities are run by four tour companies, who control everything (see Activities and tours, page 185). In 2004, after much legal wrangling, the tour operators agreed to close all resort facilities on the island to protect the environment; although dive boats can still take visitors around the island, numbers will be limited. Tourists can still stay on Mabul, Kapalai and Mataking. It's expected that other islands will soon be developed.

Best time to visit The best diving season is from mid-February to mid-December when visibility is greater (20-60 m); most of the dives involve drift diving; the night diving is said to be absolutely spectacular.

Background

While Sipadan may win lots of points from dive enthusiasts, it has also been in the news for less savoury reasons. In April 2000 Abu Sayyaf, a separatist group in the Philippines, kidnapped 21 people including 10 foreign tourists from the island. Abu Sayyaf, linked to Osama bin Laden's al-Qaeda, spirited the hostages to the Philippine island of Jolo. Here they remained under guard and threat of execution while the armed forces of the Philippines tried, sometimes incompetently, to rescue them. The hostages were freed in dribs and drabs with the final batch being released in September 2000, but it wasn't the sort of publicity that Sipadan was looking for. There is a heavy Malaysian navy presence on the island and around Semporna.

The island is disputed by the Indonesian and Malaysian governments. Indonesia has asked Malaysia to stop developing marine tourism facilities on Sipadan. Malaysia's claim to the island rests on historical documents signed by the British and Dutch colonial administrations. Periodically the two sides get around the negotiating table, but it appears that neither is prepared to make a big issue of Sipadan. Occasionally guests on the island see Indonesian or Malaysian warships just offshore. A third party also contests ownership of Sipadan: a Malaysian who claims his grandfather, Abdul Hamid Haji, was given the island by the Sultan of Sulu. He has the customary rights to collect turtles eggs on the island, although the Malaysian government disputes this.

Pulau Sipadan

Pulau Sipadan is the only oceanic island in Malaysia; it is not attached to the continental shelf, and stands on a limestone and coral stalk, rising 200 m from the bed of the Celebes Sea. The limestone pinnacle mushrooms out near the surface, but a few metres offshore drops off in a sheer underwater cliff to the seabed. The

Sabah East coast

reef comes right into the island's small pier, allowing snorkellers to swim along the edge of the coral cliff, while remaining close to the coral-sand beach. The edge is much further out around the rest of the island. The tiny island has a cool, forested interior and it is common to see flying foxes and monitor lizards. It is also a stopover point for migratory birds, and was originally declared a bird sanctuary in 1933. It has been a marine reserve since 1981 and three Wildlife Department officials are now permanently stationed on the island. In addition, the island is also a breeding ground for the green turtle; August and September are the main egg-laying months.

Sipadan is known for its underwater overhangs and caverns, funnels and ledges, all covered in coral. Five metres down from the edge of the precipice there is a coral overhang known as the Hanging Gardens, where coral dangles from the underside of the reef. The cavern is located on the cliff right in front of the island's accommodation area. Its mouth is 24-m wide and the cave, which has fine formations of stalactites and stalagmites, goes back almost 100 m, sometimes less than 4 m below the surface. Visibility blurs where fresh water mixes with sea water. Inside, there are catacombs of underwater passages.

Mabul Island

Located between Semporna and Sipadan, this island of 21 ha is considerably larger than Sipadan and is partly home to Bajau fishermen who live in traditional, palm-thatched houses. In contrast to Sipadan's untouched forest, the island is predominantly planted with coconut trees. Diving has been the most recent discovery; an Australian diver claims it is "one of the richest single destinations for exotic small marine life anywhere in the world". It has already become known as the world's best 'muck diving' – so called because of the silt-filled waters and poor visibility (usually around 12 m, which is quite reasonable compared with many other places in the area). The island is surrounded by gentle sloping reefs with depths from 3-35 m and a wall housing numerous species of hard corals.

Mataking and Kapalai

Mataking has only been open as a dive-resort spot for a few years, but with the closure of Sipadan its popularity is almost guaranteed to rocket. There are about 30 good dive sites around the island including various reefs (plenty of good shallow ones making it an ideal spot for beginner divers), a sea fan garden, a 100-m crevice called Alice Channel which runs to Pulau Sipadan and Sweet Lips rock, a good night-diving spot. Accommodation is provided by the upmarket **Mataking Island Reef Dive Resort**. See Sleeping, page 231.

Kapalai is basically a sandbar, heavily eroded and sat on top of the Litigan Reefs between Sipadan and Mabul islands. **Uncle Chang's** will take guests diving around Sipadan as well as the shallow waters around Kapalai.

Tawau 🌐🎉🍴🏛️🔺🍷🎭 ▸▸ *pp231-241. Colour map 2, B2.*

Tawau is a timber port in Sabah's southeastern corner. It is a busy commercial centre and the main channel for the entry of Indonesian workers into Sabah. Kalimantan is visible, just across the bay.

The town was developed in the early 19th century by the British who planted hemp. The British also developed the logging industry in Sabah, using elephants from Burma. The **Bombay Burma Timber Company** became the **North Borneo Timber Company** in 1950, a joint British and Sabah government venture.

Tawau is surrounded by plantations and smallholdings of rubber, copra, cocoa and palm oil. The local soils are volcanic and very fertile and palm oil has recently taken over from cocoa as the predominant crop. Malaysian cocoa prices dropped

66 99 The limestone pinnacle mushrooms out near the surface, but a few metres offshore drops off in a sheer underwater cliff to the seabed...

when its quality proved to be 20% poorer than cocoa produced in Nigeria and the Ivory Coast and this, coupled with disease outbreaks in the crop, caused many of the cocoa growers emigrated to the Ivory Coast. KL is now an established research centre for palm oil where there are studies on using palm oil as a fuel.

Now that the Sandakan area has been almost completely logged, Tawau has taken over as the main logging centre on the east coast. The forest is disappearing fast but there are ongoing reforestation programmes. At **Kalabakan** west of Tawau there is a well-established, large-scale reforestation project with experiments on fast-growing trees such as *Albizzia falcataria*, which is said to grow 30 m in five years. There are now large plantation areas. The tree is processed into, among other things, paper for paper money.

Tawau Hills State Park

① *RM2, for more information, contact Ranger Office, Tawau Hills Park, T089-810676, F011-884917.*

Tawau Hills State Park, 24 km northwest of Tawau, protects Tawau's water catchment area. The Tawau River flows through the middle of the 27,972-ha park and forms a natural deep-water pool, at Table Waterfall, which is good for swimming. There is a trail from there to some hot-water springs and another to the top of Bombalai Hill, an extinct volcano. Most of the forest in the park below 500 m has been logged; only the forest on the central hills and ridges is untouched. The park is popular with locals at weekends. Camping is possible but bring your own equipment. Access to the park is via a maze of rough roads through the **Borneo Abaca Limited** agricultural estates. It is advisable to hire a taxi.

● Sleeping

Sandakan *p216, map p218*

A **Hotel Sandakan**, 4th Av, T089-221122, tengis@tm.net.my. A/c, coffee house, Cantonese restaurants, bar with live music, business centre (has a lot of business clients). Centrally located, this is not cheap but provides excellent service.

A **Sabah Hotel**, Km 1, Jl Utara, T089-213299, www.sabahhotel.com.my. With a/c, restaurants, attractive pool, Sandakan's only 4-star hotel, with 108 rooms, fitness centre, tennis, pool and squash courts.

A **Sanbay**, Mile 1.25, Jl Leila, T089-275000, F089-275575. Spacious rooms with bathrooms in this 3-star hotel.

B **City View**, Lot 1, Block 23, 3rd Av, T089-271122, F089-273112. Restaurant, bath and shower, TV, fridge, a/c. For a little more

than the price of standard guesthouses this is a considerable step up. Recommended.

B **Hsiang Garden**, Km 1, T089-273122, F089-273127. A/c, restaurant, all facilities, good bar.

B **Ramai**, Km 1.5, Jl Leila, T089-273222, F089-271884. A/c, restaurant, all 44 rooms are a good size, with bathrooms. Recommended.

B **Sepilok Inn**, Block 46, Lot 9, Tingkat 1,2,3, Jl Sekolah, T089-271222, F089-273231. A/c, clean rooms with attached bathrooms and TVs, good value.

C **Hung Wing**, Lot 4, Block 13, Jl Tiga, T089-218855, F089-271240. Some a/c, shower, a wide variety of rooms and prices available. Rooms are spacious, clean and light with bathrooms. The owner is very helpful and speaks excellent English. Probably the best of the mid-range hotels.

C **London**, Lot D1, Block 10, Jl Empat, T089-216366. A/c, shower and bath, TV, light rooms although not large.

C **Mayfair**, 24 Jl Pryer, T089-219855. A/c, shower, each room has a TV, and the owner has a vast collection of DVDs free to watch. As there's little to do in Sandakan after 2100, the Mayfair offers some welcome entertainment. The decor leaves something to be desired but there's a very friendly atmosphere and it's in a central location with views of the market and the sea, good value. Recommended, but book ahead as often full.

D **B&B**, T089-218328. A simple guesthouse at the bus station if you get stuck here overnight or if you need to be up very early for a connection. RM20 for a dormitory bed.

D **Uncle Tan's**, Mile 16, Jl Gum Gum (5 km beyond Sepilok junction), T089-531639, www.uncletan.com. A simple bed and breakfast usually catering for those heading for **Uncle Tan's Wildlife Adventure Camp** in the Kinabatangan area (see Tour operators, below). Very cheap but not very clean and, being on the main road, it's noisy from the logging trucks which thunder past all night long. A popular stop for travellers.

D-E **Travellers Rest Hostel**, 2nd floor, Apt 2, Block E, Jl Leila, Bandar Ramai-Ramai, T089-221460. Some a/c, no attached bathrooms and limited toilet facilities, friendly with lots of travel information. Cooking and washing facilities.

Pulau Lankayan *p220*

AL **Lankayan Island Dive Resort**, run by **Pulau Sipadan Resort & Tours**, 1st floor, Bandar Sabindo, Tawau, T089-765200, www.lankayan-island.com. The resort offers quiet chalets by the beach and more than 40 dive sites including a couple of wrecks. Sightings of whale sharks are said to be common here in Apr and May.

Turtle Islands National Park *p220*

The number of visitors to the islands is restricted, even at peak season. There are 3 chalets (1 with 2 double bedrooms, 2 with 6 double bedrooms) on Pulau Selingan (RM255-370 per person). You have to book in advance through **Crystal Quest** (Sabah Park Jetty, Jl Buli Sim Sim, T089-212711, cquest@tm.net.my). Tour agencies can also organize trips to the island.

Sepilok Orang-Utan Sanctuary and Rehabilitation Centre *p222*

B-D **Sepilok Jungle Resort (and Wildlife Lodge)**, KM22 Labuk Rd, Sepilok Orang-Utan Sanctuary, 100 m behind the government resthouse, T089-533031, www.borneo-online.com.my/sjungleresort. This resort is the realization of a dream for John and Judy Lim, who have gradually purchased all the land on the edge of the forest, landscaped the area surrounding 3 man-made lakes and cleared the fruit orchards they inherited. They have planted lots of flowering and fruiting trees, attracting butterflies and birds in the process. Pleasant restaurant, great setting, clean and comfortable, boats for fishing available. Recommended. The resort is split into 2: the **Wildlife Lodge** is the older part with more budget accommodation offering 6-bed dormitories RM18 per bed, and plain doubles with own hot-water showers and a/c. More luxurious wood-panelled rooms with TV, a/c are in the **Jungle Resort** next door. The owners are actively involved in Sandakan tourism and opened the tourist information office in the town.

They are due to open **Bilit Adventure Camp** in 2005, which will offer mid-range rooms along the Kinabantangan River.

B-D **Sepilok Resthouse**, Mile 14 Labuk Rd, T089-534900. Nice wooden house next to the Orang-Utan Sanctuary. Government-owned, although now privately run. Big rooms, with bathtub and balcony. Clean dormitories for RM20 per bed.

C **Sepilok B&B**, Jl Sepilok, Mile 14, PO Box 155, T089-532288, F089-217668. Breakfast included. Around 1 km from the Orang-Utan Sanctuary. Fairly good value although there is no hot water.

Camping

F There's a campsite at **Sepilok Jungle Resort**, but you must bring your own gear.

Kinabatangan River *p225*

Most companies running tours to the Kinabatangan put their guests up in Sukau or in camps along the river.

A **Sukau Rainforest Lodge** (Borneo Eco-Tours, 2nd floor, Lorong Bernam, Taman Soon Kiong, Kota Kinabalu, T088-234009, www.borneoecotours.com)

accessible by boat from Sukau, provides eco-friendly accommodation for 40 visitors in traditional Malaysian-style chalets on stilts. All 20 rooms have solar-powered fans, twin beds, mosquito netting, and attached tiled bathroom with hot water. Other facilities include an open dining and lounge area (good restaurant), garden and sundeck overlooking the rainforest, and gift shop. Friendly and efficient service. All in all, a shining example of eco-tourism at its best. Highly recommended.

D Proboscis Lodge, run by **Sipadan Dive Centre**, 10th floor, Wisma Merdeka, Kota Kinabalu, T088-240584. A more upmarket Kinabatangan experience. The resort is located near Sukau, not in the heart of the jungle like the jungle camps. Accommodation is in chalets with hot-water showers and windows, transport in landcruisers.

E Uncle Tan Wildlife Adventures, Mile 16, Jl Gum Gum, T089-531639, www.uncletan.com. A long-established budget option for exploring the lower Kinabatangan Valley. Accommodation is in simple 3-sided huts with a floor mattress, mosquito net and shared cold water bucket showers. A 3-day, 2-night package which includes van transport to the river from the B&B on Jl Gum Gum, several river cruises including an amazing night cruise, jungle treks and all meals (simple but hearty) costs RM240 (extra nights can be bought for RM20 each). Prepare to get very muddy, wellington boots are available. The camp is on the edge of an ox-bow lake and very remote in the middle of the jungle. It is run by enthusiastic young locals who speak pretty good English, love to mix with the guests and, while not expert naturalists, are very knowledgeable about the wildlife. Some of the staff have been working there for more than 5 years. The camp was started by Uncle Tan, who began taking tourists out to the jungle in 1988. A colourful character, he fought stridently for conservation issues in the region. He died of a heart attack in 2002, and the running of the resort has been taken over by his brother who is based in Singapore. This place is deservedly very popular, so book ahead. Bring raincoat and torch. Very common to see proboscis monkeys and wild orang-utan sightings are not rare. Perhaps your best chance of seeing Sabah's wildlife. Recommended.

Lahad Datu and around *p226*

Lahad Datu is not a popular tourist spot and accommodation is poor and expensive. Avoid the **Perdana** and **Venus** hotels on Jl Seroja.

A-D Tabin Jungle Resort, Tabin Wildlife Reserve. Book through **Intra Travel Services**, T088-264071, www.tabinwildlife.com.my. Has lodges and chalets with a/c and hot showers or more budget-priced tented platforms.

B Silam Lodge, Gunung Silam, T088-243245, F088-254227. Owned by the **Borneo Rainforest Lodge** and mostly used by people in transit to the Danum Valley. Minibuses run from Lahad Datu.

B-C Jagokota, Jl Kampong Panji, T089-882000, F089-881526. A well-furnished establishment.

C Mido, 94 Jl Main, T089-881800, F089-881487. A/c, restaurant, the façade (facing the **Standard Chartered Bank**) is pock-marked with M-16 bullet holes, the result of over-curious residents watching the 1986 pirate raid on the bank; the **Mido** comes with all the sleaze of the 'wild East' and fails miserably to live up to its reputation as the best hotel in town.

C Permaisaba, Block 1, Lot 3, 1/4 Jl Tengah Nipah, T089-883800, F089-883681. 5 mins' drive from the airport and town, seafood restaurant, Malaysian and Indian food, conference hall, free transfers to/from the airport and town. Big rooms with bathroom attached and hot water, information on the Danum Valley, characterless but convenient.

Danum Valley Conservation Area *p227*

AL Borneo Rainforest Lodge, c/o Borneo Nature Tours, Block 3, Ground floor, Fajar Centre, Lahad Datu, T089-880207, F089885051. KK office: Block D, Lot 10, 3rd floor, Sadong Jaya Complex, T088-243245, ijl@po.jaring.my. One of the finest tourism developments in Sabah. 18 bungalows in a magnificent setting beside the river, built on stilts from *belian* (ironwood) and based on traditional Kadazan design with connecting wooden walkways. There are 28 rooms, each with private bathroom and balcony overlooking the Danum River, good restaurant, jacuzzi (solar-heated water). Designed by naturalists, the centre aims to combine a wildlife experience in a remote primary rainforest with comfort and privacy and provide high-quality natural history information. There is a conference hall, excellent guides (who pre-plan their routes so that visitors don't bump into each other while thinking they are latter-day Indiana Jones); day visits to a forest management centre, an adequate library of resource books, after-dinner slide shows and a gift shop. Rafting is available and night drives can be organized. Mountain bikes, fishing rods and river tubes are all available for hire. Electricity is available all day. Expensive but well worth it. Price includes meals and guided jungle excursions.

If you get permission to stay at the centre, the **Sabah Foundation** has dormitory rooms for 45RM per night, or RM80 for a single room.

Semporna *p228*
A-B Seafest Hotel, Jl Kastam, T089-782333, www.seafesthotel.com. 6-storey monster on the waterfront. The only real hotel in Semporna, which markets itself as a business establishment. Characterless 2-star hotel rooms with a/c, TV, bathroom, kettle. Facilities include in-house tour office, gym (for which guests need to pay RM5 for each use) and restaurant. Front-facing rooms will have great views of the bay.
C Arung Hayat Resort, Jl Pinggir Bakau, T/F089-782526. A traditional Bajau home, a 10-min trek from town in quiet countryside. Rooms are rickety and simple with lino floors and ill-fitting doors, but the place has charm and the staff are very friendly. They organize snorkelling trips to Sipadan and have a homestay on Mabul Island. The resort might need to relocate as there are plans to build a road through the current site.
C Lee's Resthouse and Cafe, Pekau Baru, Semporna New Town, T/F089-784491, leesrest@tm.net.my. Some rooms are without windows but appear clean and fresh with nice attached shower. Great value but poor location in the scruffy town. Helpful staff.
C Seafest Inn, Jl Kastam, T089-782399, F089-781282. Big comfortable rooms although rather plain. Rooms at the front will have views of the bay.
C-D Damai Traveller's Lodge, TL 89, 3rd floor, town centre, T089-782011, F089-781525. Recently refurbished budget hostel with big clean rooms, some with

views of the market and ocean. More expensive rooms have TV and hot water. Stuck in town, but not a bad choice.
C-E Dragon Inn, Jl Kastam (next to the jetty), T089-781088, F089-781099. Stands out as the hotel built on stilts over the sea, a/c, restaurant, quite a novel setting and great value. Family rooms, doubles with attached bathroom, hot water, a/c, TV. Very rustic. Budget longhouse dormitory beds for RM15 a night. Great experience to have a shower and look down at the green ocean through the wooden slatted floor. You can get a discount if you stop off at **Uncle Chang's dive shop** at the entrance and get a voucher. Recommended.
D Semporna Lodging House, Lot 33, Seafront, T019-8233564. Not really facing the sea, but a concrete car park at right angles to the bay. It's a 5-min walk to the jetty. Staff here do not speak English and rooms are hot little hutches with brightly painted doors, with shared toilet and shower. Cheap but very simple.

Mabul *p230*
For people diving off Sipadan, Mabul is a convenient place to stay. There are 2 resorts on the island.
AL Sipadan Water Village, for reservation PO Box 62156, T089-751777, swvill@ tm.net.my. Constructed on several wharves in Bajau, water-village-style on ironwood stilts over the water. 35 chalets with private balconies, hot-water showers, restaurant serving good range of cuisine, dive shop and centre, deep-sea fishing tours available. Budget or student travellers are sometimes given large discounts. Prices range from RM470 for divers, including equipment, to RM370 for non-divers.
L Sipadan Mabul Resort, located at the southern tip of the island, overlooking Sipadan, PO Box 14125, T088-8823000, mabul@po.jaring.my. 25 beach chalets with a/c, hot-water showers, balcony, pool and jacuzzi, restaurant serving Chinese and Western food in buffet style, all-inclusive price, PADI diving courses, snorkelling, windsurfing, deep-sea fishing, volleyball, private diving boats.

Just offshore is a dilapidated sea platform (some flotsam from an oil rig apparently) which is run as a resort by **Sea Ventures**

Dives, T088-261669, F088-251667, 4th floor, Wisma Sabah, Kota Kinabalu. It appears to be abandoned but with the closure of Sipadan this may well open up again.

Homestay
B Arung Hayat Resort Homestay, T089-782526. Mabul's only budget option is a 'homestay' run by this resort. Simple mattresses in a hut with 3 meals for RM70.

Mataking and Kapalai *p230*
L Mataking Island Reef Dive Resort. Bookings through 193-195 Jl Bakau, Tawau, T089-770022, F089-763270, or Ground floor, Wisma Sabah, KK, T/F088-318022, www.mataking.com. It also has a counter in Semporna at the jetty on Jl Kastam. The resort has 3 daily speedboats from Semporna jetty, and the journey takes 45 mins. The resort has chalets and de luxe rooms, some with sea view and balcony, all with a/c. Facilities at the resort include a spa, satellite TV, internet, bar and restaurant.
AL Sipadan-Kapalai Dive Resort, run by Pulau Sipadan Resort & Tours, 1st floor, Bandar Sabindo, Tawau, T089-765200, www.sipadan-kapalai.com. This resort straddles Kapalai's sandback on stilts. The sand spit has no shelter. The resort, modelled as a water village, has twin-sharing chalets,with attached bathrooms, balconies and amazing sea views all round, connected by a network of wooden platforms.

Tawau *p230*
Hotels here are not great value for money. Avoid the cheaper lodging houses around Jl Stephen Tan, Jl Chester and Jl Cole Adams.
A Belmont Marco Polo, Jl Abaca/Jl Clinic, T089-777988, F089-763739. A/c, restaurant, best hotel in Tawau although considerably more expensive than the competition.
B Emas, Jl Utara, T089-762000, F089-763569. A/c, restaurant.
B Merdeka, Jl Masjid, T089-776655, F089-761743. A/c, restaurant.
B Millennium, 561 Jl Bakau, T089-771155, F089-755511. A/c, spacious rooms. Considerably cheaper than the **Marco Polo** and very acceptable.
B North Borneo, 52-53 Dunlop St, T089-763060, F089-773066. A/c, TV, hot shower, reasonable but expensive for Tawau.

C Loong, Jl Abaca, T089-765308. A/c, fully carpeted, clean and light.
C Pan Sabah, Jl Stephen Tan, behind local minibus station, T089-762488. A/c, TV, attached bathrooms, clean rooms and very good value compared to other options in town.
C Sanctuary, Jl Chester, T089-751155. A/c, clean, central and spacious, but sterile and characterless.

❼ Eating

Sandakan *p216, map p218*
Sandakan is justifiably renowned for its inexpensive and delicious seafood.

Chinese
¶¶ **Golden Palace**, Trig Hill (2 km out of town). Fresh seafood, specializes in drunken prawns, crab and lobster, and steamboats. Owners will provide transport back to Sandakan if there are no taxis available. Recommended.
¶¶ **Japanese Corner**, Hsiang Garden Hotel , Jl Leila, Hsiang Garden Estate, T089-273122. Lobster and tiger prawns, good value and a popular local lunch venue.
¶¶ **See Lok Yum**, next door to **Sea View Garden**, also very popular with locals.
¶¶ **Trig Hill Ming Restaurant**, Sabah Hotel, Km 1, Jl Utara, T089-213299. Cantonese and Szechuan cuisine, particularly renowned for dim sum (breakfast).

Fast food
¶ **Fairwood Restaurant**, Jl Tiga, an inexpensive, a/c fast-food place with all the local favourites, situated in the centre of town.

Indian
¶ **Penang Curry House**, 15 Jl Dua. Fabulous Indian food for rock-bottom prices. Simple canteen with friendly Filipino waitresses but a real gem in Sandakan. Try their *dosa masala*. Recommended.

International
¶¶ **English Tea House & Restaurant**, Agnes Keith House, T089-222544, www.englishteahouse.org. Indoor and outdoor seating with crisp white tablecloths, pots of tea and scones.

There's also a weekend barbecue. Good views of the town nearby.

ŤŤ XO Steak House, Lot 16, Hsiang Garden Estate (opposite the **Hsiang Garden Hotel**), Mile 1.5, Jl Leila. Lobster and tiger prawns and a good choice of fresh fish as well as Australian steaks, buffet barbecue on Fri nights. Recommended.

Ť Apple Fast Food, Lorong Edinburgh. Good spot for breakfasts.

Ť Fat Cat, 206 Wisma Sandakan, 18 Jl Haji Saman. Several branches around town, breakfasts recommended.

Ť Hawaii, **City View Hotel**, Lot 1, Block 23, 3rd Av. Western and local food, set lunch. Recommended.

Ť Seoul Garden, Hsiang Garden Estate, Mile 1.5, Leila Rd. Korean food.

Malay
Ť Jiaman, 1st floor, Wisma Khoo Siak Chiew. Serves an interesting selection of Malay and Bajau dishes, no alcohol.

Ť Perwira, **Hotel Ramai**, Jl Leila. Malay and Indonesian food, good value. Recommended.

Seafood
In the semi-outdoor restaurants situated at the top of Trig (Trigonometry) Hill. See Chinese food section, above.

ŤŤ Ocean King Seafood, Mile 2.5, Jl Batu Sapi, T089-618111. Great seafood place built on stilts over the water. Big, over-the-top statues of lobster and marine life Disney-up the place. But unbeatable for a relaxing sunset meal, great views.

ŤŤ Pesah Putih Baru, on the coast, nearly at the end of Sandakan Bay, about 5 km from the port. Great views of Sandakan and good food. Recommended.

Vegetarian
Ť Supreme Garden Vegetarian Restaurant, Block 30, Bandar Ramai Ramai, Jl Leila (west of town). Well priced and excellent range of dishes, open for lunch and dinner.

Coffee shops
New Bangsawan, next to New Bangsawan cinema, just off Jl Leila, Tanah Merah. No great shakes, but best restaurant in Tanah Merah (where there are stacks of coffee shops). **Silver Star Ice Cream and Café**, 3rd Av, popular coffee shop with on-site satay

stall in the evenings, particularly friendly and helpful management. Recommended. **Union Coffee Shop**, 2nd floor Hakka Association Building, 3rd Av. Budget.

Foodstalls
Next to minibus station, just before the community centre on the road to Ramai Ramai, also at summit of Trig Hill.

Sepilok Orang-Utan Sanctuary and Rehabilitation Centre *p222*
By far the best place to eat is the veranda restaurant at the **Sepilok Jungle Resort** which serves international and Malaysian food. The food is merely okay but the setting is lovely.

Lahad Datu and around *p226*
Indian
Ť Restoran Ali, opposite **Hotel New Sabah**. Indian, good roti.

Seafood
ŤŤ Melawar, 2nd floor, Block 47, off Jl Teratai (around the corner from the **Mido Hotel**). Seafood restaurant, popular with locals.

ŤŤ Ping Foong, 1.5 km out of Lahad Datu, on Sandakan Rd. Open-air seafood restaurant, highly recommended by locals.

Ť Evergreen Snack Bar and Pub, on 2nd floor, Jl Teratai, opposite the Hap Seng Building. A/c, excellent fish and chips and best known for its tuna steaks. Recommended.

Ť Golden Key, on stilts over the sea opposite the end of Jl Teratai. It is really just a tumbledown wooden coffee shop, but is well known for its seafood.

Ť Good View, just over 500 m out of town on Tengku Rd. Recommended by locals.

Ť Seng Kee, Block 39, opposite **Mido Hotel** and next to **Standard Chartered Bank**. Cheap and good.

Foodstalls
Pasar Malam behind **Mido Hotel** on Jl Kastam Lama. Spicy barbecued fish (*ikan panggang*) and skewered chicken wings recommended.

The new market has foodstalls upstairs with attractive views out to sea.

Semporna *p228*

Anjung Paghalian, next to police station near bridge to jetty. Simple outdoor place with good cheap seafood and giant iced avocado juices. Recommended.

Pearl City Restaurant, attached to Dragon Inn. Pile house with good seafood, verify prices before ordering. Great setting.

Seafest Restaurant, next to the Seafest Inn. Malay food predominantly with some excellent fish dishes. Good standard for very reasonable prices.

Tawau *p230*

Chinese

Dragon Court, 1st floor, Lot 15, Block 37 Jl Haji Karim. Chinese, popular with locals, lots of seafood.

Kublai Khan, Marco Polo Hotel, Jl Abaca/Jl Clinic. Cantonese food in cavernous dining hall.

International

Dreamland, 541 Jl Haji Karim. Good local selection.

The Hut, Block 29, Lot 5, Fajar Complex, Town Extension II. Western, Malay and Chinese, large menu.

Malay

Asnur, 325B, Block 41, Fajar Complex. Thai and Malay, large choice.

Venice Coffee House, Marco Polo Hotel, Jl Abaca/Jl Clinic. Hawker centre for late-night eating, Malay and Chinese.

Yun Lo, Jl Abaca (below the **Hotel Loong**), good Malay and Chinese. A popular spot with the locals, this has a good atmosphere. Recommended.

Seafood

May Garden, 1 km outside town on road to Semporna. Outside seating.

Maxims, Block 30, Lot 6 Jl Haji Karim.

Foodstalls

Along the seafront.

● Entertainment

Sandakan *p216, map p218*

There is a karaoke parlour on just about every street. **Tiffany Discotheatre and Karaoke**, Block C, 7-10, Jl Leila, Bandar Ramai-Ramai.

Tawau *p230*

Cinema, Jl Stephen Tan, next to central market. There are **karaoke** bars on every street corner. Several of the hotels have nightclubs and bars.

○ Shopping

Sandakan *p216, map p218*

Almost everything in Sandakan is imported. There are some inexpensive batik shops and some good tailors. **Wisma Sandakan**, next to the town mosque offers 3 floors of dimly lit shopping. **Centre Point**, near the bus station, is even more down at heel. **Handicrafts Sabakraf**, opposite **Hotel Sandakan** has basketry, pearls, and souvenirs.

Lahad Datu and around *p226*

The central market is on Jl Bungaraya and there is a spice market off Jl Teratai where Indonesian smugglers tout Gudang Garam cigarettes and itinerant dentists and *bumohs* (witchdoctors) draw large crowds.

Semporna *p228*

Cultured pearls are sold by traders in town. Filipino handicrafts.

Tawau *p230*

General and fish market at the west end of Jl Dunlop, near the customs wharf.

▲ Activities and tours

Sandakan *p216, map p218*
Bowling

Champion Bowl, Jl Leila, Bandar Ramai Ramai. Jl Leila is the main road that heads out of Sandakan, Champion Bowl is just out of town at Mile 1¼, T089-211396.

Sabah East coast Listings

● *For an explanation of the sleeping and eating price codes used in this guide, see inside the*
● *front cover. Other relevant information is found in Essentials, pages 31-35.*

Sandakan Golf Club, Jl Kolam, Bukit Padang, T088-247533, 10 km out of town, open to non-members.

Recreation clubs
Sepilok Recreation Club, Bandar Ramai Ramai, with snooker, sauna and darts as well as karaoke.

Tour operators
Many tour operators have their offices in Wisma Khoo Siak Chiew.
Borneo Ecotours, c/o **Hotel Hsiang Garden**, PO Box 82, Jl Leila, T089-220210, F089-213614. **Crystal Quest**, Sabah Park Jetty, Jl Buli Sim Sim, T089-212711, cquest@tm.net.my, the only company running accommodation on Pulau Selingan, Turtle Islands National Park.
Capac Travel Service, Ground floor, Rural District Building, Jl Tiga, T089-217288. Ticketing, tour and hotel services.
Discovery Tours, Room 908 10th floor, Wisma Khoo Siak Chiew, T089-274106, F089-274107. **SI Tours**, 1st floor, Wisma Khoo Siak Chiew, T089-213501, www.sitours.com.my. Well-established company running tours to Gomantong Caves, Kinabatangan and Turtle Islands National Park. Recommended. **Wildlife Expeditions**, Room 903, 9th floor, Wisma Khoo Siak Chiew, Lebuh Tiga, Jl Buli Sim-Sim, T089-219616, F089-214570 (branch in **Sabah Hotel**). The most expensive, but also the most efficient, with the best facilities and guides.

Turtle Islands National Park *p220*
The average cost of a 1-night tour including 1 night's accommodation and boat transfer is RM360 or more. An expedition to the islands needs to be well planned; the vagaries such as bad weather, which can prevent you from leaving the islands as planned, can mess up itineraries. Most visitors book their trips well in advance.

Gomantong Caves *p224*
It is easiest to visit the caves on a tour, see under Sandakan, above. They are accessible by an old logging road, which can be reached by bus from the main Sandakan-Sukau Rd. The timing of the bus is inconvenient for those wishing to visit the caves. Alternatively take a taxi (around RM150 from Sandakan). It is a good idea to visit the caves on the way to Sukau, where you can stay overnight.

Kinabatangan River *p225*
Tour operators will transport their guests to the lodge or camp as part of the package, some of them offer tours of Gomantong and/or Sepilok en route. **Uncle Tan's** take you from B&Bs just outside Sandakan (buses from KK and Lahad Datu stop outside). The others have transport from Sandakan, Tawau, Danum Valley and Semporna.

Lahad Datu and around *p226*
Tour operators
Borneo Nature Tours, Block 3, Fajar Centre, T089-880207, F089-885051.

Semporna *p228*
Tour operators
Today Travel Services, No 90, Lot 2, Tingkat Bawah, T089-781112. Sells **AirAsia** and MAS flights to KK and KL from Tawau, the nearest airport. Book well in advance.

Sipadan Island Marine Reserve *p229*
Tour operators
Most dive centres here offer PADI courses. Each operator rents out equipment (RM75-100 per day) and provides all food and accommodation. Pre-arranged packages operated by the companies sometimes include air transfer to and from Kota Kinabalu. Walk-in rates are cheaper.
Borneo Divers, Rooms 401-412, 4th floor, Wisma Sabah, KK, T088-222226, bdivers@ po.jaring.my. Major Sipadan player, it organizes trips from KK to Sipadan with accommodation on Mabul. However, some tourists complain the operation has gone downhill. 3-day package with 10 dives and stay on Mabul around RM1200.
Pulau Sipadan Resort, 484, Block P, Bandar Sabindo, Tawau, T089-765200, www.sipadan-resort.com. Organizes dive tours, food and lodging and diving instruction, snorkelling equipment is also available, maximum of 30 divers at any one time. It also runs accommodation on Pulau Kapalai.
Sipadan Dive Centre, A1103, 11th floor, Wisma Merdeka, Jl Tun Razak, KK,

T088-240584, sipadan@po.jaring.my.
Packages (all in) approximately US$740
(5 days/4 nights). Recommended.
Uncle Chang's, entrance to **Dragon Inn**,
Semporna, T019 8030988/89-781002.
Uncle Chang, entrepreneur extraordinaire,
offers the budget traveller everything. He
can get discount bus tickets, offers shuttle
service to the airport, gets discounts for
the **Dragon Inn**, has an efficient laundry
service and runs some great dive trips
out to Sipadan including courses. 3 boat
dives including all equipment hire and
lunch for RM270.

Tawau *p230*
Diving
Borneo Divers, 46, 1st floor, Jl Dunlop,
T089-762259, F089-761691.
Pulau Sipadan Resort & Tours, 1st floor,
Bandar Sabindo, Tawau, T089-765200,
F089-763563.

Golf
9-hole golf course, modest green fees, even
cheaper during the week.

Tour operators
GSU, T089-772531, booking agent for
Kalimantan.

⊖ Transport

Sandakan *p216, map p218*
Air
The airport is 10 km north of the town centre
(RM15 by taxi into town). Early morning
flights from **KK** to Sandakan allow
breathtaking close-up views of Mt Kinabalu
as the sun rises. Connections with **Lahad
Datu**, **Kudat**, **Tawau** (RM87) and **KK** (RM96).
There are also connections between **KL** and
Sandakan by **MAS** and **AirAsia**.
   Airline offices MAS, Ground floor,
Sabah Building, Jl Pelabuhan, T089-273966;
AirAsia office on Jl Dua.

Boat
There's a ferry service to **Zamboanga** in the
southern **Philippines**. The journey takes 8 hrs
and leaves at 1700 on Tue and Thu from
Sandakan (RM58-RM150 for a suite).

Local minibuses from the bus stop between
the Esso and Shell stations on on Jl Pryer.
   Sandakan's a/c long-distance buses leave
from the bus station at Mile 2.5. Some buses
and all minibuses don't leave until they are
full, so be prepared for a long wait. Regular
connections with most towns in Sabah
including **Kota Kinabalu**, 8 hrs (RM29.25),
Ranau, 3½ hrs, **Lahad Datu** (RM15, 3-4 hrs).
Buses start at 0715, and then several
departures until 1100. After this you will
have to take a Tawau bus, get off at Simpang
Assam and take a minibus into Lahad Datu
(RM0.50) **Tawau** (RM28.05, 6 hrs): buses
from 0630, every 30 mins until 1100. Also 1
bus at 1400. **Semporna** (RM30), departure
around 0800.

Turtle Islands National Park *p220*
Boat
Daily speedboat at 0930, returning 1900,
RM100, 40 km northeast of Sandakan at
Sabah Parks Jetty. Tour operators have their
own boats and the fee is included with the
package price, so times will vary.

Sepilok Orang-Utan Sanctuary and
Rehabilitation Centre *p222*
Bus
8 daily public buses from **Sandakan**, from
the central minibus terminal in front of **Nak
Hotel**. Ask for the Sepilok Batu 14 line. From
the airport, the most convenient way to
reach Sepilok is by taxi. Sepilok is 1.9 km
from the main road. A taxi should cost
around RM25 into Sandakan. You can
charter a car for RM30 into Sandakan from
the **Sepilok Jungle Resort**.

Lahad Datu *p226*
Air
Connections with **Tawau**, **Sandakan**,
Semporna, **KK** and **Kudat**.
   Airline offices MAS, Ground floor, **Mido
Hotel**, Jl Main, T089-881707.

Boat
Fishing boats take paying passengers from
the old wharf (end of Jl Kastam Lama) to
Tawau and **Semporna**, although time-wise
(and, more to the point, safety-wise) it makes
much more sense to go by road or air.

Minibus

Minibuses and what are locally known as wagons (basically 7-seater, 4WD Mitsubishis) leave from the bus station on Jl Bunga Raya (behind Bangunan Hap Seng at the mosque end of Jl Teratai) and from opposite the Shell station. Regular connections with **Tawau**, 2½ hrs, **Semporna**, **Sandakan**, **Madai**.

Danum Valley Conservation Area *p227*
From Lahad Datu, turn left along the logging road at Km 15 on the Lahad Datu-Tawau road to Taliwas and then left again to field centre, 85 km west of Lahad Datu. The **Borneo Rainforest Lodge** is 97 km (not an easy trip) from **Lahad Datu**; it provides a transfer service (2 hrs), telephone the lodge for details.

Semporna *p228*
Minibus and bus
Minibus station in front of USNO headquarters. Regular connections with **Tawau** (RM5, 1½ hrs) and **Lahad Datu**, most departures are in the morning. Minibus to **Tawau airport**. One daily bus to **KK** (1930, RM48, 10 hrs).

Mataking and Kapalai *p230*
Air and sea
Flight to Tawau, minibus, taxi or resort van to Semporna (1½ hrs), from where speed boats depart for the islands (30-60 mins). Boats to the islands are taken either with dive companies or as a transfer to a resort. Lots of boats leave daily but generally only in the morning between 0700-1000 for day-trips.

Tawau *p230*
Air
The airport is 2 km from town centre. Regular connections with **KK**, **Lahad Datu** and **Sandakan**. AirAsia and MAS both run daily flights between Tawau and **KL**.

For flights to **Tarakan, Indonesia**, it is necessary to obtain a visa in advance. You can try your luck at the Indonesian consulate in Tawau and in KK. **Indonesian Bouraq** and MAS operate flights.

Airline offices MAS, Lot 1A, Wisma SASCO, Fajar Complex, T089-765533. **Merdeka Travel**, 41 Jl Dunlop, T089-772534/1, booking agents for **Bouraq**

(Indonesian airline). **Merpati**, 47A Jl Dunlop, 1st floor, next to Borneo Divers, T089-752323. **Sabah Air**, Tawau airport, T089-774005. **AirAsia** office at the airport.

Boat
Packed boats leave Tawau's customs wharf (behind Pasar Ikan) twice daily at 0800 and 1600 for **Pulau Nunukan Timur** in **Kalimantan**, 2 hrs. It is no longer possible to get a direct boat from Tawau to **Tarakan, Indonesia**; travellers must stop over at **Nunukan**. All visitors need to get a visa before arriving in Indonesia. Tickets available from the offices opposite Pasar Ikan. From there you can get a boat to Tarakan the next day, or a direct boat to **Pare Pare** (**Sulawesi**), 48 hrs.

Bus
Station on Jl Wing Lock (west end of town). Minibus station on Jl Dunlop (centre of town). Direct service from Tawau to **Kota Kinabalu** leaving at 2000 to arrive 0500 in KK.

It's possible to drive from **Sapulut** (south of **Keningau**) across the interior to Tawau on logging roads (4WD vehicle is required).

❶ Directory

Sandakan *p216, map p218*
Banks Most around Lebuh Tiga and Jl Pelabuhan. HSBC, Jl Pelabuhan/Lebuh Tiga; **Standard Chartered**, Sabah Building, Jl Pelabuhan. **Immigration** Federal Building, Jl Leila. **Internet** Sandakan Cybercafe, 2nd floor, Wisma Sandakan; also in Centre Point mall. **Parks Office** Sabah Parks Office, Room 906, 9th floor, Wisma Khoo, Lebuh Tiga, T089-273453. Bookings for Turtle Islands National Park. **Post** General Post Office, Jl Leila, to the west of town; parcel post off Lebuh Tiga. **Telephone** Telecom Office, 6th floor, Wisma Khoo Siak Chiew, Jl Buli Sim-Sim.

Lahad Datu *p226*
Banks Standard Chartered, in front of Mido Hotel. **Post** Post office, Jl Kenanga, next to the Lacin cinema.

Semporna *p228*
Internet Several places in town. **Cyber Planet** (opposite Damai), 1st floor, open 0800-2200, RM3 per hr; **Zanna Computer**, next to Maybank, 1st floor; **@DCCN** opposite

the bus station, RM2 per hr (this place is often closed). **Post** **General Post Office** next to minibus station.

Tawau *p230*
Banks Bumiputra, Jl Nusantor, on seafront; HSBC, 210 Jl Utara, opposite the padang;

Standard Chartered, 518 Jl Habib Husein (behind HSBC); **exchange kiosk** at wharf. **Embassies and consulates** Indonesian Consulate, Jl Apas, Mile 1.5. **Immigration office** Jl Stephen. **Post** Post Office off Jl Nusantor, behind the fish market.

Background

The name Sabah probably derives from the Arabic Zir-e Bad, meaning 'the land below the wind'. Appropriately, as the state lies just to the south of the typhoon belt. Officially, the territory has only been called Sabah since 1963, when it joined the Malay federation, but the name appears to have been in use long before that. When Baron Gustav Von Overbeck was awarded the cession rights to North Borneo by the Sultan of Brunei in 1877, one of the titles conferred on him was 'Maharajah of Sabah'. In the *Handbook of British North Borneo*, published in 1890, it says: "In Darvel Bay there are the remnants of a tribe which seems to have been much more plentiful in bygone days – the Sabahans". From the founding of the Chartered Company until 1963, Sabah was known as British North Borneo.

Sabah has a population of almost 2.5 million, and a good number of illegal immigrants on top of that. The inhabitants of Sabah can be divided into four main groups: the Murut, the Kadazan, the Bajau and the Chinese, as well as a small Malay population. These main groups are subdivided into several different tribes (see page 245).

History

Prehistoric stone tools have been found in eastern Sabah, suggesting that people were living in limestone caves in the Madai area 17,000-20,000 years ago. The caves were periodically settled from then on; pottery dating from the late neolithic period has been found, and by the early years of the first millennium AD, Madai's inhabitants were making iron spears and decorated pottery. The Madai and Baturong caves were lived in continuously until about the 16th century, and several carved stone coffins and burial jars have been discovered in the jungle caves, one of which is exhibited in the Sabah State Museum. The caves were also known for their birds' nests; Chinese traders were buying the nests from Borneo as far back as AD 700. In addition, they exported camphor wood, pepper and other forest products to Imperial China.

There are very few archaeological records indicating Sabah's early history, although there is documentary evidence of links between a long-lost kingdom, based in the area of the Kinabatangan River, and the Sultanate of Brunei, whose suzerainty was once most of North Borneo. By the start of the 18th century, Brunei's power had begun to wane in the face of European expansionism. To counter the economic decline, it is thought the sultan increased taxation, which led to civil unrest. In 1704 the Sultan of Brunei had to ask the Sultan of Sulu's help in putting down a rebellion in Sabah and, in return, the Sultan of Sulu received most of what is now Sabah.

The would-be White Rajahs of Sabah

It was not until 1846 that the British entered into a treaty with the Sultan of Brunei and took possession of the island of Labuan, in part to counter the growing influence of the Rajah of Sarawak, James Brooke. The British were also wary of the Americans; the US Navy signed a trade treaty with the Sultan of Brunei in 1845 and in 1860 Claude Lee

Moses was appointed American consul-general in Brunei Town. He was only interested in making a personal fortune and quickly persuaded the sultan to cede him land in Sabah. He sold these rights to two Hong Kong-based American businessmen who formed the American Trading Company of Borneo. They styled themselves as rajahs and set up a base at Kimanis, just south of Papar. It was a disaster. One of them died of malaria, the Chinese labourers they imported from Hong Kong began to starve and the settlement was abandoned in 1866.

The idea of a trading colony on the North Borneo coast interested the Austrian consul in Hong Kong, Baron Gustav von Overbeck, who, in turn, sold the concept to Alfred Dent, a wealthy English businessman also based in Hong Kong. With Dent's money, Overbeck bought the Americans' cession from the Sultan of Brunei, and extended the territory to cover most of modern-day Sabah. The deal was clinched on 29 December 1877, and Overbeck agreed to pay the sultan 15,000 Straits dollars a year. A few days later Overbeck discovered that the entire area had already been ceded to the Sultan of Sulu 173 years earlier, so he immediately sailed to Sulu and offered the sultan an annual payment of 5000 Straits dollars for the territory. On his return, he dropped three Englishmen off along the coast to set up trading posts; one of them was William Pryer, who founded Sandakan (see page 217). Three years later, Queen Victoria granted Dent a royal charter and, to the chagrin of the Dutch, the Spanish and the Americans, the British North Borneo Company was formed. London insisted that it was to be a British-only enterprise however, and Overbeck was forced to sell out. The first managing director of the company was the Scottish adventurer and former gun-runner William C Cowie. He was in charge of the day-to-day running of the territory, while the British government supplied a governor.

The new chartered company, with its headquarters in the City of London, was given sovereignty over Sabah and a free hand to develop it. The British administrators soon began to collect taxes from local people and quickly clashed with members of the Brunei nobility. John Whitehead, a British administrator, wrote: "I must say, it seemed rather hard on these people that they should be allowed to surrender up their goods and chattels to swell even indirectly the revenue of the company". The administration levied poll tax, boat tax, land tax, fishing tax, rice tax, *tapai* (rice wine) tax and a 10% tax on proceeds from the sale of birds' nests. Resentment against these taxes sparked the six-year Mat Salleh rebellion (see page 176) and the Rundum Rebellion, which peaked in 1915, during which hundreds of Muruts were killed by the British.

Relations were not helped by colonial attitudes towards the local Malays and tribal people. One particularly arrogant district officer, Charles Bruce, wrote: "The mind of the average native is equivalent to that of a child of four. So long as one remembers that the native is essentially a child and treats him accordingly he is really tractable." Most recruits to the chartered company administration were fresh-faced graduates from British universities, mainly Oxford and Cambridge. For much of the time there were only 40-50 officials running the country. Besides the government officials, there were planters and businessmen: tobacco, rubber and timber became the most important exports. There were also Anglican and Roman Catholic missionaries. British North Borneo was never much of a money-spinner – the economy suffered whenever commodity prices slumped – but it mostly managed to pay for itself until the Second World War.

The Japanese interregnum

Sabah became part of Dai Nippon, or Greater Japan, on New Year's Day 1942, when the Japanese took Labuan. On the mainland, the Japanese Imperial Army and Kempetai (military police) were faced with the might of the North Borneo Armed Constabulary, about 650 men. Jesselton (Kota Kinabalu) was occupied on 9 January and Sandakan 10 days later. All Europeans were interned and when Singapore fell in 1942, 2740 prisoners of war were moved to Sandakan, most of whom were

Australian, where they were forced to build an airstrip. On its completion, the POWs were ordered to march to Ranau, 240 km through the jungle. This became known as The Borneo Death March and only six men survived (see page 220).

The Japanese were hated in Sabah and the Chinese mounted a resistance movement which was led by the Kuching-born Albert Kwok Hing Nam. He also recruited Bajaus and Sulus to join his guerrilla force which launched the Double Tenth Rebellion (the attacks took place on 10 October 1943). The guerrillas took Tuaran, Jesselton and Kota Belud, killing many Japanese and sending others fleeing into the jungle. But the following day the Japanese bombed the towns and troops quickly retook them and captured the rebels. A mass execution followed in which 175 rebels were decapitated. On 10 June 1945 Australian forces landed at Labuan, under the command of American General MacArthur. Allied planes bombed the main towns and virtually obliterated Jesselton and Sandakan. Sabah was liberated on 9 September, and thousands of the remaining 21,000 Japanese troops were killed in retaliation, many by Muruts.

A British military administration governed Sabah in the immediate aftermath of the war, and the cash-strapped chartered company sold the territory to the British crown for £1.4 million in mid-1946. The new crown colony was modelled on the chartered company's administration and set about rebuilding the main towns and war-shattered infrastructure. In May 1961, following Malaysian independence, Prime Minister Tunku Abdul Rahman proposed the formation of a federation incorporating Malaya (ie Peninsular Malaysia), Singapore, Brunei, Sabah and Sarawak. Later that same year, Tun Fuad Stephens, a timber magnate and newspaper publisher formed Sabah's first-ever political party, the United National Kadazan Organisation (UNKO). Two other parties were founded shortly afterwards – the Sabah Chinese Association and the United Sabah National Organization (USNO). The British were keen to leave the colony and the Sabahan parties thrashed out the pros and cons of joining the proposed federation. Elections were held in late 1962 in which a UNKO-USNO alliance (the Sabah Alliance) swept to power and ,the following August, Sabah became an independent country... for 16 days. Like Singapore and Sarawak, Sabah opted to join the federation, to the indignation of the Philippines and Indonesia which both had claims on the territory. Jakarta's objections resulted in the *Konfrontasi* – an undeclared war with Malaysia (see page 158) which was not settled until 1966.

Modern Sabah

Politics

Sabah's political scene has always been lively and never more so than in 1994 when the then Malaysian Prime Minister, Doctor Mahathir Mohamad, pulled off what commentators described as a democratic coup d'état. With great political dexterity, he out-manoeuvered his rebellious rivals and managed to dislodge the opposition state government, despite the fact that it had just won a state election.

Following Sabah's first state election in 1967, the Sabah Alliance ruled until 1975 when the newly formed multi-racial party, Berjaya, swept the polls. Berjaya had been set up with the financial backing of the United Malays National Organization (UMNO), the mainstay of the ruling Barisan Nasional (National Front) coalition on the Peninsula. Over the following decade that corrupt administration crumbled and in 1985 the opposition Sabah United Party (PBS), led by the Christian Kadazan Datuk Joseph Pairin Kitingan, won a landslide victory and became the only state government in Malaysia that did not belong to the UMNO-led coalition. It became an obvious embarrassment to then Prime Minister Doctor Mahathir Mohamad to have a rebel Christian state in his predominantly Muslim federation. Nonetheless, the PBS eventually joined Barisan Nasional, believing its partnership in the coalition would help iron things out. It did not.

When the PBS came to power, the federal government and Sabahan opposition parties openly courted Filipino and Indonesian immigrants in the state, almost all of whom are Muslim, and secured identity cards for many of them, enabling them to vote. Doctor Mahathir has made no secret of his preference for a Muslim government in Sabah. Nothing, however, was able to dislodge the PBS, which was resoundingly returned to power in 1990. The federal government had long been suspicious of Sabahan politicians, particularly following the PBS's defection from Doctor Mahathir's coalition in the run-up to the 1990 general election, a move which bolstered the opposition alliance. Doctor Mahathir described this as "a stab in the back", and referred to Sabah as "a thorn in the flesh of the Malaysian federation". But in the event, the prime minister won the national election convincingly without PBS help, prompting fears of political retaliation. Those fears proved justified in the wake of the election.

Sabah paid heavily for its 'disloyalty'; prominent Sabahans were arrested as secessionist conspirators under Malaysia's Internal Security Act, which provides for indefinite detention without trial. Among them was Jeffrey Kitingan, brother of the chief minister and head of the Yayasan Sabah, or Sabah Foundation (see page 177). At the same time, Joseph Pairin Kitingan was charged with corruption. The feeling in Sabah was that the men were bearing the brunt of Doctor Mahathir's personal political vendetta.

As the political feud worsened, the federal government added to the fray by failing to promote Sabah to foreign investors. As investment money dried up, so did federal development funds; big road and housing projects were left unfinished for years. Many in Sabah felt their state was being short-changed by the federal government. The political instability had a detrimental effect on the state economy and the business community felt that continued feuding would be economic lunacy. Politicians in the Christian-led PBS, however, continued to claim that Sabah wasn't getting its fair share of Malaysia's economic boom. They said that the agreement which enshrined a measure of autonomy for Sabah when it joined the Malaysian federation had been eroded.

The main bone of contention was the state's oil revenues, worth around US$852 million a year, of which 95% disappeared into federal coffers. There were many other causes of dissatisfaction, too, and as the list of grievances grew longer, the state government exploited them to the full. By 1994, anti-federal feelings were running high. The PBS continued to promote the idea of 'Sabah for Sabahans', a defiant slogan in a country where the federal government was working to centralize power. Because Doctor Mahathir likes to be in control, the idea of granting greater autonomy to a distant, opposition-held state was not on his agenda. A showdown was inevitable.

It began in January 1994. As Datuk Pairin's corruption trial drew to a close, he dissolved the state assembly, paving the way for fresh elections. He did this to cover the eventuality of his being disqualified from office through a 'guilty' verdict: he wanted to have his own team in place to take over from him. He was convicted of corruption but the fine imposed on him was just under the disqualifying threshold and, to the prime minister's fury, he led the PBS into the election. Doctor Mahathir put his newly appointed deputy, Anwar Ibrahim, in charge of the National Front alliance campaign.

Datuk Pairin won the election, but by a much narrower margin than before. He alleged vote-buying and ballot rigging. He accused Doctor Mahathir's allies of whipping up the issue of religion. He spoke of financial inducements being offered to Sabah's Muslim voters, some of whom are Malay, but most of whom are Bajau tribespeople and Filipino immigrants. His swearing-in ceremony was delayed for 36 hours; the governor said he was sick; Datuk Parin said his political enemies were trying to woo defectors from the ranks of the PBS to overturn his small majority. He was proved right.

Three weeks later, he was forced to resign; his fractious party had virtually collapsed in disarray and a stream of defections robbed him of his majority. Datuk Parin's protestations that his assemblymen had been bribed to switch sides were ignored. The local leader of Doctor Mahathir's ruling party, Tan Sri Sakaran Dandai, was swiftly sworn in as the new chief minister.

In the 1995 general election the PBS did remarkably well, holding onto eight seats and defeating a number of Front candidates who had defected from the PBS the previous year. Sabah was one area, along with the east coast state of Kelantan, which resisted the Mahathir/BN electoral steamroller.

The March 1999 state elections pitted UMNO against Pairin's PBS. Again the issues were local autonomy, vote rigging, the role of national politics and political parties in state elections, and money. A new element was the role that Anwar Ibrahim's trial might play in the campaign but otherwise it was old wine in mostly old bottles.

The outcome was a convincing win for Mahathir and the ruling National Front who gathered 31 of the 48 state assembly seats – three more than the prime minister forecast. Mahathir once again used the lure of development funds from KL to convince local Sabahans where their best interests might lie. "We are not being unfair" Mahathir said. "We are more than fair, but we cannot be generous to the opposition. We can be generous to a National Front government in Sabah. That I can promise."

But, worryingly for the National Front, the opposition Parti Bersatu Sabah (PBS) still managed to garner the great bulk of the Kadazan vote and in so doing won 17 seats. As in Sarawak, the election, in the end, was more about local politics than about the economic crisis and the Anwar trial.

However, in the 2004 state and federal elections, the PBS rejoined the National Front and, faced only with the disunity of opposition parties, the BN-PBS coalition won resounding victories in both polls. A legitimate alternative to KL's ruling steamroller has all but died. The BN gave itself half the seats, one third to non-Malays, and distributed the rest between Chinese representatives. The message is that Sabahans accept dominance by the Malay minority from KL in return for money and development.

Sabah Background

Culture

People

Sabah's main tribal communities comprise the Kadazan, who mostly live on the west coast, the Murut, who inhabit the southern interior, and the Bajau, who are mainly settled around Gunung Kinabalu. There are more than 30 tribes, more than 50 different languages and about 100 dialects. Sabah also has a large Chinese population and many illegal Filipino immigrants.

Kadazan The Kadazan are the largest ethnic group in Sabah comprising about a third of the population and are a peaceful agrarian people with a strong cultural identity. Until Sabah joined the Malaysian Federation in 1963, they were known as Dusuns, meaning 'peasants' or 'orchard people'. This name was given to them by outsiders, and picked up by the British. It became, in effect, a residual category including all those people who were not Muslim or Chinese. Most Kadazans call themselves after their tribal names. They can be divided into several tribes including the Lotud of Tuaran, the Rungus of the Kudat and Bengkoka peninsulas, the Tempasuk, the Tambanuo, the Kimarangan and the Sanayo. Minokok and Tengara Kadazans live in the upper Kinabatangan River basin while those living near other big rivers are just known as Orang Sungai, or 'river people'. Most Kadazans used to live in longhouses; these are virtually all gone now. The greatest chance of coming across a longhouse in Sabah is in the Rungus area of the Kudat Peninsula; even there, former

⦂ Sabah's ethnic breakdown

	Population	%
Kadazan/Dusun	561,000	17.8%
Other Muslim	415,400	13.2%
Bajau	353,200	11.3%
Chinese	327,900	10.5%
Others	275,600	8.8%
Malay	204,700	6.5%
Murut	92,000	2.9%
Non-Malay	906,800	28.9%

Total population (Malay and non-Malay – Filipino and Indonesian, etc)
3.14 million.
Source: July 2000 estimates from Monthly Statistical Bulletin, Sabah.

longhouse residents are moving into detached, kampong-style houses while one or two stay for the use of tourists.

But Kadazan identity is not that simple. The 1991 census lists both Kadazan (110,866) and Dusun (229,194). The 1970 census listed all as Kadazan, while the 1960 census listed all as Dusun. In 1995 the Malaysian government agreed to add the common language of these people(s) to the national repertoire to be taught in schools. This they named Kadazandusun. The others are Malay, Chinese, Tamil and Iban.

All the Kadazan groups had similar customs and modes of dress (see below). Up to the Second World War, many Kadazan men wore the *chawat* loin cloth. The Kadazans used to hunt with blowpipes and in the 19th century were still headhunting. Today, however, they are known for their gentleness and honesty; their produce can often be seen sitting unattended at roadside stalls, and passing motorists are expected to pay what they think fair. The Kadazans traditionally traded their agricultural produce at large markets, held at meeting points, called *tamus* (see box, page 201). The Kadazan are farmers, and the main rice-producers of Sabah. They used to be animists, and were said to live in great fear of evil spirits; most of their ceremonies were rituals aimed at driving out these spirits. The job of communicating with the spirits of the dead, the *tombiivo*, was done by priestesses, called *bobohizan*. They are the only ones who can speak the ancient Kadazan language, using a completely different vocabulary from modern Kadazan. Most converted to Christianity, mainly Roman Catholicism, during the 1930s, although there are also some Muslim Kadazan.

The big cultural event in the Kadazan year is the harvest festival which takes place in May. The ceremony, known as the Magavau ritual, is officiated by a high priestess. These elderly women, who wear black costumes and colourful headgear with feathers and beads, are now rarely seen. The ceremony ends with offerings to the *Bambaazon* (rice spirit). After the ceremonies Catholic, Muslim and animist Kadazan all come together to play traditional sports such as wrestling and buffalo racing. This is about the only occasion when visitors are likely to see Kadazan in their traditional costumes. In the Penampang area a woman's costume consists of a fitted, sleeveless tunic and ankle-length skirt of black velvet. Belts of silver coins (*himpogot*) and brass rings are worn round the waist; a colourful sash is also worn. Men dress in a black, long-sleeved jacket over black trousers; they also wear a *siga*, colourful woven headgear. These costumes have become more decorative in recent years, with colourful embroidery. Villages send the finalists of local beauty contests

● Tapai – Sabah's rice wine

Tapai, the fiery Sabahan rice wine, is much loved by the Kadazan and the Murut people of Borneo. It was even more popular before the two tribal groups converted to Christianity in the 1930s. Writer Hedda Morrison noted in 1957 that "The squalor and wretchedness arising from [their] continual drunkenness made the Murut a particularly useful object of missionary endeavour... they grasped at this new faith as the drowning man is said to grasp at a straw."

In the Sabah State Museum there is a recipe for *tapai*, which reads: "Boil 12 lbs of the best glutinous rice until well done. In a wide-mouthed jar, lay the rice in layers of no more than two fingers deep, and between layers, place a total of about 20½-oz yeast cakes. Add two cups of water, tinctured with the juice of six beetroots. Cover jar with muslin and leave to ferment. Each day, uncover it and remove dew which forms on the muslin. On the fifth day, stir the mixture vigorously and leave for four weeks. Store for one full year, after which it shall be full of virtue and potence and most smooth upon the palate."

Oscar Cook, a former district officer in the North Borneo civil service, noted in his 1923 book Borneo: the Stealer of Hearts: "As an alternative occupation to head-hunting, the Murut possess a fondness for getting drunk, indulged in on every possible occasion...Births, marriages, deaths, sowing, harvesting and any occasion that comes to mind is made the excuse for a debauch. It is customary for Murut to show respect to the white man by producing their very best *tapai*, and pitting the oldest and ugliest women of the village against him in a drinking competition." Cook admits that all this proved too much for him and when he was transferred to Keningau, he had to employ an 'official drinker'. "The applicants to

to the grand final of the Unduk Ngadau harvest festival queen competition in Penampang, near Kota Kinabalu.It is the Kadazans who dominate the Pasti Bersatu Sabah (PBS), the critical piece in Sabah's political jigsaw.

Bajau The Bajau, the famous cowboys of the Wild East, came from the south Philippines during the 18th and 19th centuries and settled in the coastal area around Kota Belud, Papar and Kudat, where they made a handsome living from piracy. The Bajau who came to Sabah joined forces with the notorious Illanun and Balinini pirates. They are natural seafarers and were dubbed 'sea gypsies'; today they form the second largest indigenous group in Sabah and are divided into subgroups, notably the Binadan, Suluk and Obian. They call themselves 'Samah'; it was the Brunei Malays who first called them Bajau. They are strict Muslims and the famous Sabahan folk hero, Mat Salleh, who led a rebellion in the 1890s against British Chartered Company rule, was a Bajau (see page 176). Despite their seafaring credentials, they are also renowned horsemen and (very occasionally) still put in an appearance at Kota Belud's tamu (see page 205). Bajau women are known for their brightly coloured basketry – *tudong saji*. The Bajau build their atap houses on stilts over the water and these are interconnected by a network of narrow wooden planks. The price of a Bajau bride was traditionally assessed in stilts, shaped from the trunks of bakau mangrove trees. A father erected one under his house on the day a daughter was born and replaced it whenever it wore out. The longer the daughter remained at home, the more stilts he got through and the more water buffalo he demanded from a prospective husband.

⁞ Dance

Sumazau Penampang (Kadazan/Dusun – Penampang, west coast) Performed during annual harvest Penampang Festival (Pesta Kaamatan) to honour the rice spirit (Bambaazon). *Sumazau* means dancing.

Angalang (Murut – Pensiangan and Tenom, interior and south) A solo warrior dance, accompanied by a group of women dancers (*angalong*). Originally performed after a victorious battle or headhunting trip.

Mangiluk (Suluk – east coast) Performed at weddings and social events.

Magunatip (Murut and Kwijau Dusun – interior and south) These dancers need skill and agility to dance among bamboo poles which are hit together to produce the rhythm of the dance.

Adai Adai (Brunei Malay – Sipitang and Membakut) Evolved from a song; it tells of the activities of the local fishermen and farmers southwest of Sabah.

Mongigol Sumundai (Rungus – Kudat and Pitas, north of Sabah) Can be performed as part of certain ritual festivals; for instance, thanksgiving to the rice spirit for a bountiful harvest or when moving into a new house.

Limbai (Bajau – Kota Belud, west coast) Performed at weddings, characterized by graceful wrist rotations. Accompanying music is called *bertitik*.

Dansa (Cocos – Lahad Datu, east coast) Performed at weddings. It features energetic foot stomping.

Bolak Bolak (Bajau – Semporna, east coast) *Bolak Bolak* is Malay for castanets. The dancers hold the castanets and create the rhythm of the music.

Mongigol Sumayan (Lotud – Tuaran, west coast) Ritual dance performed during *Rumaha* ceremony to honour spirits of skulls, or the *Mangahau* ceremony for the spirits of sacred jars.

Umang-Umang Ting-Ting (Brunei Malay – Bongawan, west coast) Celebrates the birth of a child.

Daling-Daling (Suluk – east coast) A courting dance said to be derived from the English 'darling'. Usually accompanied by a love song.

Sumazau Papar (Kadazan/Dusun – Papar, west coast) Performed at similar occasions to Sumazau Penampang. Distinctive footwork.

Titikas (Orang Sungai – Kinabatangan, east coast) *Titikas* is based on the Ingki-Ingki game, similar to hopscotch.

Liliput (Bisaya – Beaufort, west coast) *Liliput* means 'go around'. A dance to banish evil spirits from a possessed person.

Kuda Pasu (Bajau – Kota Belud, west coast) Originally performed by horsemen to escort a bridegroom and his entourage to the bride's home. The female dancers hold handkerchieves as a sign of welcome.

Murut The Murut live around Tenom and Pensiangan in the lowland and hilly parts of the interior, in the southwest of Sabah and in the Trusan Valley of north Sarawak. Some of those in more remote jungle areas retain their traditional longhouse way of life, but many Murut have opted for detached kampong-style houses. Murut means 'hill people' and is not the term used by the people themselves. They refer to themselves by individual tribal names. The Nabai, Bokan and Timogun Murut live in the lowlands and are wet-rice farmers, while the Peluan, Bokan and Tagul Murut live in the hills and are mainly shifting cultivators. They are thought to be related to Sarawak's Kelabit and Kalimantan's Lun Dayeh people, although some of the tribes in the south Philippines have similar characteristics. The Murut staples are rice and tapioca; they are known for their weaving and basketry and have a penchant for drinking *tapai* (rice wine – see page 247). They are also enthusiastic dancers and devised the *lansaran*, a sprung dance floor like a trampoline. The Murut are a mixture of animists, Christians and Muslims and were the last tribe in Sabah to give up headhunting, a practice stopped by the British North Borneo Chartered Company.

Chinese The Chinese accounted for nearly a third of Sabah's population in 1960; today they make up just a tenth. Unlike Sarawak, however, where the Chinese were a well-established community in the early 1800s, Sabah's Chinese came as a result of the British North Borneo Chartered Company's immigration policy, designed to ease a labour shortage. About 70% of Sabah's Chinese are Christian Hakka, who first began arriving at the end of the 19th century, under the supervision of the company. They were given free passage from China and most settled in the Jesselton and Kudat areas; today most Hakka are farmers. There are also large Teochew and Hokkien communities in Tawau, Kota Kinabalu and Labuan while Sandakan is mainly Cantonese, originating from Hong Kong.

Filipinos Immigration from the Philippines started in the 1950s and refugees began flooding into Sabah when the separatist war erupted in Mindanao in the 1970s. Today there are believed to be upwards of 700,000 illegal Filipino immigrants in Sabah (although their migration has been undocumented for so long that no one is certain), and the state government fears they could soon outnumber locals. There are many in Kota Kinabalu, the state capital, and a large community – mainly women and children – in Labuan, but the bulk of the Filipino population is in Semporna, Lahad Datu, Tawau and Kunak (on the east coast) where they already outnumber locals by a majorioty of three to one. One Sabah government minister, referring to the long-running territorial dispute between Malaysia and the Philippines, was quoted as saying "We do not require a strong military presence at the border any more: the aliens have already landed".

Although the federal government has talked of its intention to deport illegal aliens, it is mindful of the political reality: the majority of the Filipinos are Muslim, and making them legal Malaysian citizens could ruin Sabah's predominantly Christian, Kadazan-led state government. The Filipino community is also a thorn in Sabah's flesh because of the crime wave associated with their arrival: the Sabah police claim 65% of crime is committed by Filipinos. The police do not ask questions when dealing with Filipino criminal suspects; about 40-50 are shot every year. Another local politician was quoted as saying: "The immigrants take away our jobs, cause political instability and pose a health hazard because of the appalling conditions in which some of them live".

There are six different Filipino groups in Sabah: the Visayas and Ilocano are Christian as are the Ilongo (Ilo Ilo), from Zamboanga. The Suluks are Muslim; they come from south Mindanao and have the advantage of speaking a dialect of Bahasa Malaysia. Many Filipinos were born in Sabah and all second generation immigrants are fluent in Bahasa. Migration first accelerated in the 1950s during the logging boom, and continued when the oil palm plantation economy took off; the biggest plantation is at Tungku, east of Lahad Datu. Many migrants have settled along the roadsides on the way to the Danum Valley; it is easy to claim land since all they have to do is simply clear a plot and plant a few fruit trees.

Sabah Background

Arts and crafts

Compared with neighbouring Sarawak and Kalimantan, Sabah's handicraft industry is rather impoverished. Sabah's tribal groups were less protected from Western influences than Sarawak's, and traditional skills quickly began to die out as the state modernized and the economy grew. In Kota Kinabalu today, the markets are full of Filipino handicrafts and shell products; local arts and crafts are largely confined to basketry, mats, hats, beadwork, musical instruments and pottery.

The elongated Kadazan backpack baskets found around Mount Kinabalu National Park are called *wakids* and are made from bamboo, rattan and bark. Woven food covers, or *tudong saji*, are often mistaken for hats, and are made by the Bajau of Kota Belud. Hats, made from nipah palm or rattan, and whose shape varies markedly from place to place, are decorated with traditional motifs. One of the most common motifs is the *nantuapan*, or 'meeting', which represents four people all drinking out of the same *tapai* (rice wine) jar. The Rungus people from the Kudat peninsula also make linago basketware from a strong wild grass; it is tightly woven and not decorated. At *tamus*, Sabah's big open-air markets (see box on page 201), there are usually some handicrafts for sale. The Kota Belud *tamu* is the best place to find the Bajau horseman's embroidered turban, the *destar*. Traditionally, the Rungus people, who live on the Kudat Peninsula, were renowned as fine weavers, and detailed patterns were woven into their ceremonial skirts (*tinugupan*). These patterns all had different names but, like the ingredients of the traditional dyes, many have now been forgotten.

Brunei

⚑ Footprint features

Introduction

Brunei is a one-off; a tiny oil-rich sultanate on the north coast of Borneo, cornered and split in two by the Malaysian state of Sarawak. Barely a third of a million Bruneians are ruled over by one of the world's wealthiest men – the living link in a dynasty of sultans stretching back 600 years. At one time, Brunei was the driving seat of Borneo, but its territories were whittled away piece by piece, first by the Sulu kings, then by the British. Today Brunei is a peculiar mix of material wealth and Malay tradition. Affluence has numbed Sultan Bolkiah's subjects into acquiescence with the political system – a monarchical autocracy, to all intents and purposes (albeit a benevolent one). Bruneians see no reason to complain: they pay no taxes, and the purchase of cars and houses is heavily subsidized. Healthcare and education are free and trips to Mecca are a snip. Politics, it seems, is not their business. This climate of benign affluence, combined with the prohibition of alcohol and the complete lack of nightlife, makes Brunei's tagline – 'The Abode of Peace' – ring perfectly true.

Still, change is in the air. For the first time since independence, Brunei is turning its back on the introspection that has kept it largely hidden from the world. The Asian financial crisis of 1997 hit Brunei hard, cutting GDP almost in two, and, with oil reserves expected to dry up by 2020, the economy needs to diversify. The sultan's latest plan is to transform his realm into an offshore tax haven. But Brunei holds another trump card for the future: ecotourism. One of the happy consequences of its dependence on oil is the amount of rainforest left intact. With three-quarters of its landmass beneath virgin rainforest, Brunei can claim the highest proportion of primary forest of any country in the world. Brunei is the easy way in to Borneo. You get *kampong* culture, pristine jungle, endangered wildlife and all the creature comforts you could hope for. Just don't expect to rough it.

Brunei

★ Don't miss...

1 Kampong Ayer Wander the endless boardwalks of Kampong Ayer, Brunei's huge water village; or take a tour by water taxi, page 256.

2 Omar Ali Saifuddien Mosque Brunei's definitive monument, an elegant lakeside mosque in the heart of the capital, page 258.

3 Night market in Gadong Taste the full range of local Malay food at this friendly night market on the outskirts of Bandar Seri Begawan, pages 261 and 271.

4 Ulu Temburong National Park Brave the canopy walkway for magnificent views over Brunei's interior rainforest, page 263.

5 Tasek Merimbun Head inland to Brunei's largest lake, a magnificent peat-black body of water surrounded by dense jungle, page 266.

6 Brunei River safari Scream upriver in a *temuai* (longboat), then paddle into the mangroves for a close encounter with rare proboscis monkeys, page 273.

Bandar Seri Begawan ›› *Colour map 1, B6.*

Bandar Seri Begawan, more commonly referred to simply as Bandar ('sea port' in Malay), is the capital of Brunei and the only place of any real size. Even so, Bandar's population is barely 80,000, and with most people living in the suburbs or among the stilted homes of the water village, downtown Bandar feels decidedly sleepy. This is no bad thing for the visitor; traffic and crowds are restricted to the suburbs, where most of the shops are located, leaving the centre in relative peace and quiet. The streets are clean and spacious, and the only persistent noise is the whirr of outboards, as water taxis (tambang) ferry people to and from the water village.

Bandar sits on a bend of the Sungai Brunei, with the stilted homes of Kampong Ayer ('water village') reaching out across the river from the opposite bank. Back on dry land, the dominant feature is the impressive Omar Ali Saifuddien Mosque – though the primary point of reference nowadays seems to be the Yayasan Complex, a smart shopping mall whose two wings are aligned to provide a colonnaded vista of both the mosque and the river. ›› *For Sleeping, Eating and other listings, see pages 269-275.*

Ins and outs

Getting there
Brunei International Airport is situated 11 km outside Bandar Seri Begawan. Between 0630-1800, there are regular buses from the airport to the bus station on Jalan Cator, in downtown Bandar. Buses from Sarawak and other parts of Brunei also terminate here. A taxi from the airport costs about B$20, or B$30 after 1800. ›› *For further information, see Airport information, page 25.*

Getting around
Downtown Bandar is tiny and easy to negotiate on foot. Water taxis are the major form of public transport here, with hundreds flying back and forth across the river, ferrying people to and from their stilted homes in Kampong Ayer. A short hop should cost no more than about B$2, while a 45-minute tour of the water village will cost around B$20 (less if you barter hard). The Brunei Museum, the Malay Technology Museum and the suburb of Gadong are all accessible on Central Line buses (daily 0630-1800), which pass through the bus station on Jalan Cator. Metered taxis take people around Bandar and its suburbs: B$3 for the first kilometre (B$4.50 between 2100-0600) and B$1 for every subsequent kilometre. ›› *For further information, see Transport, page 274.*

Tourist information
The **Tourist Information Centre** ⓘ *General Post Office Building, corner of Jl Sultan and Jl Elizabeth Dua, T2223734, Mon-Sat 0800-1200 and 1400-1630*, is a helpful resource, with brochures, lists of hotels, car rental companies and tour operators. You can also pick up the useful *Explore Brunei* visitors' guide. Other than this, you could try the out-of-town headquarters of **Brunei Tourism** ⓘ *Ministry of Industry and Primary Resources, Jl Menteri Besar, T2382822, www.tourismbrunei.com.*

Background

Bandar Seri Begawan has a history that can be traced back as far as the 7th century, by which time a water village was already well established on the banks of the Sungai Brunei. The original site of the village was Kota Batu, several kilometres to the east of

today's capital (close to the Brunei Museum). Brunei's history is bound closely to the
development of Kampong Ayer, which moved to its present-day location sometime
before the 15th century.

By the time Portuguese explorer Ferdinand Magellan passed by on his
round-the-world voyage in 1521, Kampong Ayer had developed from a small trading
base and fishing settlement into a powerful entrepôt. The Spanish crew were
astounded to find a sprawling water village of some 100,000 people – much larger
than today's capital – complete with the trappings of great wealth (see page 256). The
settlement flourished as a collecting point for much-coveted jungle products such as
sandalwood, beeswax, birds' nests, turtle shells, sago and camphor. Along with the
trade in commodities came the blending of cultures and ideologies, with Islam first
establishing a foothold in the late 14th century. Kampong Ayer went on to become the
centre of a small empire whose sphere of influence extended across much of Borneo
and the Philippines.

Bandar Seri Begawan – known as Brunei Town until 1970 – only established itself
as a land-based settlement under the influence of the British. It was in 1904 that
Stewart McArthur, the first British Resident, encouraged inhabitants to move onto
reclaimed land beside the water village. One of the first buildings to appear was the
British Residency, set in the wooden building known now as Bubongan Dua Belas
(see page 259). The sultan himself followed in 1909, moving the *istana* (palace) onto
land for the first time in 500 years.

It was not until the discovery of oil in 1929 that Brunei Town really began to
develop, with the first grid of shophouses appearing and a new set of government
buildings. The capital's modern landmarks – the Omar Ali Saifuddien Mosque and
the Istana Nurul Iman – were built in the 1950s, after exports of oil and natural gas
had begun to take off. But the capital never expanded beyond the dimensions of a
small town. The centre of Bandar has remained a quiet, almost sleepy, place with
development limited mainly to the suburbs. Kampong Ayer, meanwhile, is gradually
dwindling in size, thanks to government initiatives to encourage its inhabitants to
move inland. The water village, it seems, doesn't fit with the sultan's progressive
vision of a modern Brunei.

Sights

The main entry point to Bandar is via Jalan Tutong, which crosses the Sungai Kedayan
tributary at Edinburgh Bridge, providing the first views of Kampong Ayer and the
golden dome of the mosque. The road becomes Jalan Sultan, which cuts past a
handful of museums and a small grid of shophouses, before hitting the waterfront.
The city centre is bordered to the west by Sungai Kedayan, and, barely half a kilometre
to the east, by the narrow Sungai Kianggeh tributary. Along its banks is the Tamu
Kianggeh, an open-air market.

A number of the city's more interesting sights are located along the picturesque
road which follows the course of the river east out of town. Jalan Residency runs past
the Arts and Handicrafts Centre and the old British Residency itself, before becoming
Jalan Kota Batu and bypassing the tombs of two sultans, the Brunei Museum and the
Malay Technology Museum.

The suburbs of Kampong Kiarong and Gadong lie several kilometres to the
northwest of the city centre. The former is a residential quarter, home to the enormous
Kiarong Mosque, while Gadong is the main commercial centre, full of department
stores and restaurants, and home, too, to an excellent pasar malam (night market).
North of town, near the airport, are the government offices and the impressive but
ghostly-quiet National Stadium.

Kampong Ayer

When people think of Bandar Seri Begawan, they think of Kampong Ayer, the stretch of stilted homes that extends for more than 3 km along the banks of Sungai Brunei. Officially, Kampong Ayer is not part of the municipality of Bandar – a reflection, perhaps, of the government's long-term aim to rehouse the villagers on dry land. It qualifies merely as a suburb. Not so long ago, however, Kampong Ayer was all there was of Bandar; it was the British who began to develop the town on land, starting with construction of the Residency in 1906 (see Bubongan Dua Belas, page 259).

With its wonky walkways and ramshackle appearance, Kampong Ayer may look like a bit of a slum. Adventurer James Brooke made this mistake when he visited Brunei in the 1840s; he described Kampong Ayer as a 'Venice of hovels, fit only for frogs'. Antonio Pigafetta, the diarist aboard the Magellan voyage of 1521, saw the village from a different perspective, describing it as the 'Venice of the East'.

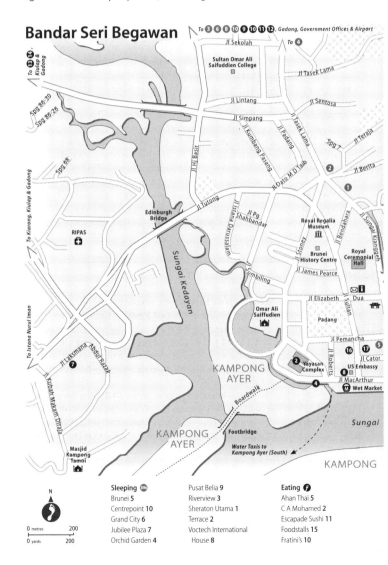

Bandar Seri Begawan

Sleeping
Brunei 5
Centrepoint 10
Grand City 6
Jubilee Plaza 7
Orchid Garden 4

Pusat Belia 9
Riverview 3
Sheraton Utama 1
Terrace 2
Voctech International
 House 8

Eating
Ahan Thai 5
C A Mohamed 2
Escapade Sushi 11
Foodstalls 15
Fratini's 10

The truth is that the architecture of Kampong Ayer is perfectly suited to the tropical environment, making use of local materials and allowing for excellent ventilation. The oldest houses stand on mangrove and ironwood posts, with walls of woven nipa palm. The modern buildings stand on reinforced concrete piles, which allow for double-storey structures to be built. Many of the houses are painted in a profusion of colours, with pot plants and bougainvillea spilling from covered verandas. It may look primitive, but take a closer look and you notice the trappings of wealth; all houses have electricity and a piped water supply; many have satellite dishes and internet access.

Records of Kampong Ayer go back 14 centuries. In its 16th-century heyday, the 'village' had a population of 100,000 and was the centre of an empire stretching across most of Borneo, Mindanao and the Sulu archipelago. Though it still claims to be the world's largest water village, today's population is a mere 25,000 to 30,000. The village is separated into 42 different units, each governed by a *tua kampong* (headman). These units are grouped into *mukims* (wards). The community is self-sufficient, with mosques, shops, schools, medical clinics, the odd karaoke lounge, even fire stations and floating petrol stations.

The future of Kampong Ayer looks somewhat uncertain. Many villagers have taken up the government's offer of free plots of land and subsidized housing and have moved on land. Meanwhile, the traditional cottage industries associated with each of the village units are giving way to new professions (today's young Bruneians aspire to become lawyers or computer programmers rather than blacksmiths or boat builders). Still, there are plenty of artisans left, and some are will open their doors to passing visitors.

To visit Kampong Ayer, jump aboard any of the water taxis (*tambang*) which race back and forth across the river. The main pick-up point is just south of the Yayasan Complex. The boatmen will compete raucously for your attention, then haggle with you over a price. The going rate is about B$20 for a 45-minute tour. Most boatmen are happy to pass by the Istana (the best views are from the river); you may want to combine the tour with a trip downriver to spot proboscis monkeys (see box, page 262).

It is also possible to access part of the water village by foot: set off along the boardwalk that runs west from the Yayasan Complex and you soon come to a bridge across the Sungai Kedayan tributary. From here there are good views across the maze of stilted homes as far as the copper-domed Masjid Kampong Tamoi, an elegant new mosque built on the water's edge.

Brunei Bandar Seri Begawan

Tasek Recreational Park

Spg 39

Spg 67

Jl Kampong Barangan

Spg 14

Spg 2

9

Jl Kampong Kianggeh

7 5

Tamu Kianggeh

Bukit Subok Recreational Park

Sungai Kianggeh

To Bubongan Dua Belas, Brunei Museum &Malay Technology Museum

Jl Residency

15

Temburong Jetty

Brunei

Arts & Handicraft Centre

AYER

Omar Ali Saifuddien Mosque

ⓘ *The compound is open daily 0800-2030; visiting hours for non-Muslims: Sat-Wed 0800-1200, 1400-1500 and 1700-1800; visitors must leave shoes outside and dress conservatively; ccasionally, the lift that runs to the top of the 44-m minaret is in operation.*

The Omar Ali Saifuddien Mosque, built by and named after the 28th sultan (1950-1967), has become the symbol of Brunei, the nation's definitive monument. It is certainly one of Asia's finest-looking mosques, elegant and somehow modest, despite its great golden dome, its setting beside an artificial lake and its nightly illumination in unearthly green light.

Built in 1958 in classical Islamic style, the architecture is not overstated though, along with the sultan's hugely extravagant palace, the mosque was one of the first obvious signs of Brunei's oil wealth. When flakes of gold began falling from the central dome, due to contraction and expansion in the searing heat, the mosque quickly became something of a wonder to the villagers of Kampong Ayer (whose boardwalks run tight up to the edge of the mosque). Novelist Anthony Burgess' arrival as a teacher in Brunei coincided with the ceremonial opening of the mosque, and in his autobiography he recounts how this falling gold was "taken by the fisherfolk to be a gift from Allah".

The materials used to build and furnish the mosque came from right across the globe: carpets from Belgium and Arabia; chandeliers and stained glass from England; marble from Italy; granite from Shanghai; and, topping the central onion dome, a mosaic of more than three million pieces of gold-leafed Venetian glass. In the middle of the lake, which envelops the mosque on three sides, is a replica of a 16th-century *mahligai* (royal barge), used on special occasions and for Koran recital competitions.

Brunei Museum

ⓘ *About 4 km east of downtown Bandar along Jl Kota Batu, Sat-Thu 0900-1700, Fri 0900-1130 and 1430-1700, free admission.*

Brunei's national museum holds a mixed bag of galleries, although it's certainly worth a visit. If you have limited time, be sure to head straight for the **Islamic Gallery**, an outstanding collection of artwork and artefacts from the sultan's personal collection. In pride of place – on a marble pedestal in the centre of the gallery – is a page of ornate calligraphy written by the sultan himself, in which he encourages his subjects to memorize the Koran. Around the pedestal, in Rooms 1 and 2, are the real McCoy – Korans and beautifully preserved pieces of calligraphy dating from as early as the 9th century. Across one wall is a talismanic banner from 18th-century India, on which the whole Koran is transcribed in tiny script. Further rooms hold collections of pottery and ceramics from the Islamic world; gold and silver jewellery and coins dating back to AD 661; delicate perfume bottles alongside a collection of Indian and Ottoman sabres; and several oddities, such as a decorative wooden boot with compass, inlaid with mother-of-pearl.

Also on the ground floor is the mediocre **Natural History Gallery** – full of awkward-looking stuffed animals, birds and insects – and the obligatory **Petroleum Gallery**, which charts the discovery and extraction methods of Brunei's black gold. Upstairs, in Gallery 4, is the **Traditional Culture Gallery**, with examples of *keris* (ceremonial daggers), *bedok* (call-to-prayer drums), *gasing* (spinning tops), traditional dress, hand-crafted kites and board games such as *congkak* and *pasang*. Traditional customs are explained, too (after birth, a date is placed on the tongue of a newborn and the placenta is either hung from a tree, buried or floated downriver). Next door, the **Archaeology and History Gallery** (Gallery 5) provides a thorough introduction to the history of the region from neolithic times. Gallery 6 is reserved for temporary exhibitions.

⦂ Estranged brothers

Prince Jefri's playboy lifestyle and his long-term embezzlement of government funds would have caused a scandal in any country. In the context of Brunei's modesty, the prince's behaviour stands out as plain shocking. He is the thorn in the side of his more conservative brother, the Sultan of Brunei.

In 1997 – year of the Asian Economic Crisis – Prince Jefri's company **Amedeo Development Corporation** collapsed under the weight of US$3.5 billion of debts. Its legacy is the area around Jerudong, where the prince built the world's most extravagant polo ground, the theme park and the **Empire Hotel & Country Club** (complete with a Jack Nicklaus golf course). The hotel alone was said to have cost an astonishing US$800 million.

Surprisingly, Bruneians seem to have a soft spot for Prince Jefri. Over the years, his ambitious projects have provided many jobs. But this doesn't hide his playboy tendencies; and when you have billions to play with, the sky is the limit. The name of his 165-ft yacht? *Tits*. And its two tenders? *Nipple 1* and *Nipple 2*. Why ever not?

Prince Jefri has four wives, 17 (official) children, and a penchant for Filipino and American beauty queens, who he used to fly in for his own pleasure – until one of them sued him in the US, claiming she had been lured to Brunei to become a 'sex slave'.

In 2001, the sultan himself sued his brother for embezzling billions from the **Brunei Investment Agency**, for which the prince had served as chairman. The brothers eventually settled out of court, but the publicity has had lasting consequences – not least in light of Brunei's attempts to establish itself as an 'Offshore Financial Haven' (in the vein of Bermuda or the Isle of Man).

The greatest publicity surrounded the auction (in August 2001) of many of Prince Jefri's personal possessions – items removed from his palaces by Amedeo's liquidator in attempts to appease out-of-pocket creditors. Does Princess Caroline of Monaco have her own set of gold-plated toilet brushes? Does Prince Charles have an F1 racing-car simulator to play with? No, but Prince Jefri once did. Alas, even his favourite plaything, *Tits*, is now in someone else's hands.

A staircase leads down the hill from the back of the Brunei Museum to the **Malay Technology Museum** (same opening hours), where a series of dioramas explain the development of fishing techniques, boatmaking, stilt-house construction, metalwork and *songkok* (hats worn by Muslim men) weaving. The top floor of the museum includes examples of indigenous dwellings (from the Murut, Kedayan and Dusun tribes of the interior), along with tools such as blowpipes and fishing traps.

Along the road between the museum and the centre of town, look out for the tombs of two of Brunei's greatest sultans. **Sultan Syarif Ali** (1426-1432) was the founder of Islamic rule in Brunei, while **Sultan Bolkiah** (1485-1524) presided over the 'golden age' of Brunei, conquering Sulu and the Philippines.

To get there, Eastern Line buses (Nos 11 and 39) run every half hour from the main bus terminal (or wait at the stop opposite the Arts and Handicraft Centre).

Bubongan Dua Belas

ⓘ *Jl Residency, 1 km or so east of the town centre, Sat-Thu 0900-1630, Fri 0900-1130 and 1430-1630, free admission.*

Bubongan Dua Belas, which means 'Twelve Roofs', served as the British Residency until Brunei's independence in 1984. It was built on the side of a hill overlooking

Kampong Ayer in 1906, and is one of Brunei's oldest surviving buildings, with traditional wood shingle roofing and hardwood floors. The building now hosts a small 'Relationship Exhibition', celebrating the ties between Brunei and the United Kingdom. There are charts and maps of the Kampong Ayer area dating from the time of the first British contact in 1764. There is also a fascinating report on Brunei, penned by the acting Consul Stewart McArthur, which led to the appointment of the first British Resident in 1904. He describes the 'strange and picturesque' ceremony of the mengalei padi harvest festival: "Everyone was feasting and I regret to say that, when I left, nearly everyone was overcome by *borak*, an extremely nauseous drink made locally from *padi* and of which I was forced to partake."

Arts and Handicraft Centre

ⓘ *Jl Residency, Sat-Thu 0745-1215 and 1330-1615, free admission.*

The Arts and Handicraft Centre was established as a means of preserving traditional skills, such as weaving, brass casting and *keris* making. The centre is focused more on workshops for young Bruneians than attracting tourists, though there is a handicraft shop selling hand-crafted jewellery, basketry, *keris* (ceremonial daggers), *songket* (traditional fabric woven with gold thread), *songkok* (hats worn by Muslim men) and other gifts.

Round the other side of the handicraft centre, past one of the most enormous strangler figs you're ever likely to see, is a small **Art Gallery** ⓘ *Sat-Thu 0830-1630, Fri 0830-1130 and 1400-1630*, with exhibits by local artists.

Royal Regalia Museum

ⓘ *Jl Sultan, Sat-Thu 0900-1630, Fri 1430-1630, free admission.*

Dedicated almost exclusively to the present sultan's life, this is (predictably) the flashiest of all Brunei's museums, set in an extravagant domed building in the centre of town. Bring an extra top – the main galleries are air-conditioned to fridge temperatures – and try not to take too much notice of the guards, who are armed to the hilt (literally), each with truncheon, dagger and gun.

The museum's opening in 1992 coincided with the sultan's Silver Jubilee celebrations, and many of the exhibits relate to this event. The Royal Chariot – an enormous gold-winged thing that looks like a movie prop – is the largest exhibit, while the strangest is probably the creepy golden hand and forearm, used to support the chin of the sultan during the coronation. There are hundreds of photos, too, and a mass of ceremonial costumes, armoury and other items of regalia. The **Constitutional Gallery** charts Brunei's recent history.

Next door is the **Brunei History Centre** ⓘ *Sat-Thu 0745-1215, 1330-1630, admission free*, which serves as a centre of research for documenting the history and genealogy of the royal family. The centre is open to the public, but there's not much to see.

The enormous building across the road is the **Lapau Di Raja** (**Royal Ceremonial Hall**), where the coronation ceremony took place back in 1968. The hall is closed to the public.

Parks and green spaces

For the best vantage points above Bandar and Kampong Ayer, head for the **Bukit Subok Recreational Park**, which rises steeply off Jalan Residency. The entrance to the park is just before Bubongan Dua Belas (the old Residency building). A boardwalk loops through the forest between a series of viewing towers. The going in steep, so avoid visiting during the middle part of the day.

The **Tasek Recreational Park** is a more sedate option, with a picnic area, small waterfall and reservoir. It is situated about 1 km north of the centre. To get there, head north along Jalan Tasek Lama and turn right opposite the Sultan Omar Ali Saifuddien College. From the park gates, it's another 500 m or so to the waterfall.

Bandar's suburbs

The increasingly busy suburbs of Bandar lie a few kilometres to the northwest of the centre, across Edinburgh Bridge. **Gadong** is the commercial centre and primary suburb of Bandar Seri Begawan. It's not pretty on the eyes in the way that Bandar is (Gadong is a traffic-clogged grid of modern shophouses and department stores), but this is the modern-day heart and soul of the capital. It is where Bruneians come to shop and to eat – either in the local restaurants and international franchises or at the food stalls of the excellent *pasar malam* (night market), which serves up (mainly) Malay food seven days a week. **Kiulap**, a little closer to the city centre, is really an extension of Gadong, with more shops and offices. Just south of Kiulap is Kampong Kiarong, home to the striking **Kiarong Mosque** ① *Sat-Wed 0800-1200, 1400-1500, 1700-1800 and 2000-2130; sometimes closed to the public on Sat*. Known officially as Masjid Jame'Asr Hassanal Bolkiah, the mosque was built in 1992 to commemorate the sultan's Silver Jubilee. Though it supplanted Masjid Omar Ali Saifuddien (see above) as Brunei's national mosque, there seem to be mixed opinions as to which is superior. The older mosque conforms more to classical convention and forms the focal point of Bandar itself. The Kiarong Mosque, meanwhile, is bigger and brasher – set in landscaped gardens and immense in size, with a quartet of intricate minarets and 29 gilded cupolas. Around 5 km north of the city centre, meanwhile, are the government offices, scattered widely around a leafy grid of streets close by to the Brunei International Airport.

Around Brunei

The capital, Bandar Seri Begawan, makes the ideal base for forays deeper into Brunei. Most of the following sights and destinations can be visited on day trips from the capital – either on guided tours or with the use of a hire car. Of Brunei's four districts, Temburong is the least populated and, for many people, the most appealing, thanks to the Ulu Temburong National Park. Each of the remaining districts offers its own diversions, with the interior of Belait providing the most challenging itineraries. ➤ For *Sleeping, Eating and other listings, see pages 269-275.*

Brunei Muara District ●● ➤ pp269-275. Colour map 1, B6.

Brunei Muara is the smallest of Brunei's four districts, with Bandar Seri Begawan at its heart. As well as several notable sights on the outskirts of Bandar, there are a few minor places of interest further afield, including sandy beaches, forest reserves and a theme park.

Istana Nurul Iman

The Istana Nurul Iman, official residence of the sultan, is situated several kilometres upriver from the capital, its twin gold cupolas clearly visible from the river. It is the largest residential palace in the world, and must surely count as one of the most extravagant, too. Beneath the curving Minangkabau-style roofs lie a staggering 1778 rooms (including 257 toilets), which makes the Istana bigger than the Vatican and on a par with Versailles. The banquet hall seats 5000, and there's an underground parking lot to house the sultan's extensive collection of cars (which runs into three figures). Needless to say, the palace is not open to the public. For the best views, catch a water taxi from Bandar Seri Begawan. You'll pass by the royal jetty, where guests of the sultan (including Queen Elizabeth II on her last visit) are welcomed.

⁞ Proboscis monkeys

Proboscis monkeys are not pretty to look at. At least, they're an acquired taste. With their pendulous noses, pot bellies and hooded eyes, they look more like caricatures than bona fide monkeys. The Malays had a special name for them – not orang-utan ('man of the forest'), but *orang belanda*, meaning 'Dutchman' (more a snipe at their would-be oppressors than a simian insult).

It is one of Brunei's great secrets that it holds the world's largest population of proboscis monkeys. With an estimated 10,000 of them living along the banks of Sungai Brunei, this is more than the rest of their scattered populations put together. The Kinabatangan Wetlands of Sabah are widely thought to be the best place to spot proboscis monkeys. Not so; just minutes from Brunei's capital, by tambang, plentiful troops of proboscis monkeys feed peacefully among the mangrove trees. Proboscis monkeys are unique to Borneo. They are the world's largest monkeys, with adult males often exceeding 25 kg. They are great swimmers, too, with their long noses serving well as snorkels. Scientists, however, point to sex rather than swimming as the reason for the unusual hooter. Having a big nose is a matter of pride for a male proboscis (who, incidentally, sports a permanent erection). It's all to do with Darwinian 'sexual selection': the bigger the nose, the bigger the harem (proboscis monkeys live in troops of 10-30 animals with a single adult male at the helm). In common with most of Borneo's larger mammals, the proboscis monkey is a seriously threatened species – though you might not think so from their numbers on the Brunei River. It is thought that no more than 20,000 proboscis monkeys survive in the wild.

Alternatively, make your way to the **Taman Persiaran Damuan**, a kilometre-long park which runs along the riverside just beyond the palace. Within the park are sculptures from each of the 10 ASEAN nations.

If you're lucky, and you visit the park at dusk, you may spot proboscis monkeys (see box, page 262) on **Pulau Ranggu**, the small island opposite the park. Proboscis monkeys, an endangered species endemic to Borneo, are the world's largest monkeys, with males often exceeding 25 kg in weight. Surprisingly, Brunei holds the healthiest population in Borneo (around 10,000). To guarantee sightings, take a proboscis tour by tambang along the Sungai Damuan tributary – it's one of the highlights of a trip to Brunei for any nature enthusiast. Look out for monkeys crossing the river (they swim doggy-style, their bulbous noses raised above the water like snorkels). ›› *For further details, see Activities and tours, page 273.*

Jerudong Park Playground
ⓘ *Kampong Jerudong (along the Muara-Tutong highway northwest of Bandar Seri Begawan), Wed-Sat 1700-2400, Sat 1700-0200, Sun 1600-2400, admission B$15 adults, B$5 children.*
This peculiar theme park opened in 1994 to coincide with the sultan's 48th birthday. By Western standards, it's nothing special, although there are plenty of rides, including a decent rollercoaster and an excellent log ride (expect to get wet). Today it has a slightly jaded feel and, thanks to Brunei's tiny population, it is probably the quietest theme park in the world – on some days you'll have the park more or less to yourself. Beware, many of the rides are often out of action (ask before handing over the entry fee).

Just along the coast from Jerudong Park is the extravagant **Empire Hotel & Country Club** (see page 269), which is worth a look for its towering, gold-adorned atrium; at 80 m it is said to be the tallest in the world. Both hotel and theme park were built by Prince Jefri, brother to the sultan and an endless source of scandal (see box, page 259).

Muara and around ↦ *Colour map 1, B6.*

At Brunei's northeast tip is the port of Muara, a non-descript place with a single sleepy grid of shophouses and nothing much to draw the visitor. There are several nearby beaches that are pleasant enough, if you can bear the heat. Pantai Muara is a 4-km stretch of sand north of Muara, with a kids' playground and picnic shelters among the casuarinas, while to the south, at the end of a road lined with mansions, is a sandy spit known as Pantai Serasa, home to a fleet of traditional fishing boats and the Serasa Watersports Complex.

There are two forest reserves worth visiting along the main Muara-Tutong highway, which runs beside Brunei's north-facing coastline. **Bukit Shahbandar Reserve** (just east of Kampong Jerudong) is a popular spot with joggers and cyclists, with narrow roads and trails running up and down seven hills. At the highest point, there's a wooden observation tower. The **Hutan Berakas Forest Reserve** (directly north of the airport) is wilder, with trails weaving through casuarina forests and kerangas (heath forest), the favoured habitat of carnivorous pitcher plants. There are paved trails here, a popular picnic area and a lovely long beach used by Bruneians for swimming.

Out in Brunei Bay itself is **Pulau Selirong**, an uninhabited island covered in mangrove forest. The island has recently been designated a forest reserve and 2 km of elevated walkways have been installed. Monitor lizards, crabs, mud skippers and wading birds can be viewed, along with the occasional mangrove snake and saltwater crocodile. Tours can be arranged with many of the Bandar-based tour operators (see page 273).

Temburong District 🖻 ↦ *pp269-275. Colour map 1, B6.*

Temburong is the forested finger of land set adrift from the rest of Brunei by the Malaysian district of Limbang, which was snatched from Brunei's control in 1890 by Raja Brooke of Sarawak. The population of Temburong is barely 10,000, with Malays living alongside a scattered population of Iban, Murut and Kadazan tribespeople. The whole district has something of a village atmosphere; wherever you go in Temburong, it seems that everybody knows one another.

Speedboats for Temburong leave regularly from the jetty on Jalan Residency in Bandar Seri Begawan. They roar downriver, passing briefly into Brunei Bay, before weaving through the mangrove channels as far as Bangar, Temburong's main town. The journey is an adventure in itself: look out for proboscis monkeys swimming doggy-style across the narrow channels.

Bangar (not to be confused with Bandar) is a quiet place with a single row of shophouses and a sultry, sleepy air. There's a mosque, a few government offices, a resthouse and two or three coffee shops for passing the time of day – otherwise there's no particular reason to linger. Most people carry straight on in the direction of the Ulu Temburong National Park, the principal attraction for visitors to the district.

Ulu Temburong National Park

ⓘ *Entry fee B$5. Be sure to get hold of an entry permit in advance from the Forestry Department Ministry of Industry and Primary Resources, Bandar Seri Begawan BB3910, T2381687, forestrybrunei@hotmail.com.*

ǃ *The penalty for entering the park without a permit is two years' imprisonment!*

The 50,000-ha Ulu Temburong National Park is the jewel in the crown of Brunei's ecotourism push. It sits in the remote southern portion of Temburong, in the heart of the **Batu Apoi Forest Reserve**. The region has never been settled or logged, so there are no roads, and access to the park is by *temuai* (traditional longboat). Getting there is half the fun; the journey begins at Bandar Seri Begawan with a ride in a 'flying coffin', a wooden speedboat so called because of its shape (though, when you see the speed with which these things hurtle through the mangroves, you may suspect the name is fitting for other reasons). The speedboat passes briefly into the Malaysian territory of Limbang, before turning into the mouth of Sungai Temburong and speeding upriver as far as Bangar. A short car journey follows, bypassing a series of picturesque *kampongs* and longhouses, before the final leg of the trip by longboat from Batang Duri to the park headquarters, with towering dipterocarps climbing the river banks.

Despite being relatively unknown, Ulu Temburong compares favourably with the jungle reserves of neighbouring Malaysia. Work carried out at the **Belalong Rainforest Field Studies Centre** confirms the unusual biodiversity of Ulu Temburong; many species new to science have been found here, and one scientist was reported to have identified more then 400 separate species of beetle on a single tree. The main attraction for visitors, however, is the towering canopy walkway, which stands 50 m tall and provides unbeatable views of the surrounding forest.

The fact that few people visit is also part of the appeal – the park remains virtually unscathed by tourism, despite being easily accessible. There can't be many places in the world where you can leave the city mid-morning, have a picnic lunch deep in pristine rainforest, and be back at your hotel by late afternoon.

Though it is possible to visit Ulu Temburong independently, most people find it simpler to use one of the Bandar-based tour operators (see page 273); they'll make all travel arrangements for you and provide guides and entry permits (with everything paid upfront). It is perfectly possible to visit the park as a day trip, though there is accommodation at park headquarters for longer stays (see Sleeping, below).

The journey to Ulu Temburong involves two boat journeys and a taxi ride. Bangar-bound speedboats leave regularly from the jetty on Jalan Residency in Bandar Seri Begawan (daily every 30 minutes 0745-1600; 45 minutes journey time; B$6 one-way). From the Bangar jetty, there are taxis to take visitors south along a sealed road to **Batang Duri** (literally 'Spiky Hamlet'), a small settlement on the banks of Sungai Temburong. From here, visitors need to charter a longboat for the final leg of the journey upriver to the park headquarters (90 minutes, B$50-60 per boat). During dry season (July and August) water levels can be low and passengers may have to get out and help push the boat.

At park headquarters, visitors need to sign a register and pay the entry fee before heading into the park proper. There's a small information centre here with displays, and a series of chalets and dormitories, linked by plankwalks.

Flora and fauna Borneo's rainforests are among the most biodiverse places on Earth and Ulu Temburong is no exception. More species of tree can be found in a single hectare here than in the entirety of North America. Animal life is abundant too, though hard to spot. Some of the more conspicuous creatures include flying lizards, Wallace's flying frog, pygmy squirrels, wild boar, mousedeer, gibbons (more often heard than seen), various species of hornbill (the biggest being the majestic rhinoceros hornbill, frequently seen gliding across the river), and of course myriad weird and wonderful insects, from the peculiar lantern beetle to the Rajah Brooke birdwing butterfly. The canopy walkway provides the opportunity to look directly down upon the jungle canopy, home to the greatest density of life. Notice the abundance of epiphytes – plants which survive at this height by clinging on to host trees. From the walkway, it is sometimes possible to see tiger orchids, one of the largest of their species.

Treks With 7 km of wooden walkways, few visitors stray off the main trail, though there is unlimited scope for serious trekking in the vicinity (either using park headquarters as a base, or camping out in the forest). The terrain here is steep and rugged, and not suited to those without a moderate level of fitness. Wherever you go, take plenty of water. Falling trees and landslides often lay waste to sections of the boardwalk, making it unlikely that the whole trail will be open at any one time.

The boardwalk begins at park headquarters and leads across the Sungai Temburong via a footbridge to the foot of a towering hill, upon which stands the canopy walkway. The climb is steep and sweaty, with almost a thousand steps. Once you've conquered the hill, reaching the canopy walkway itself is no easy matter either – the walkway is suspended in sections between 50-m-tall aluminium towers built around a seemingly endless series of step ladders. The views from the top are truly magnificent – though vertigo sufferers will find it living hell. Standing on the walkway, above the jungle canopy, on top of a hill, you can see for many miles around, with the confluence of Sungai Temburong and Sungai Belalong at your feet. Gaze for long enough, and you'll probably spot the black and white backs of hornbills as they glide from tree to tree along the riverbank.

From the walkway, the trail continues for several kilometres along a steeply descending boardwalk in the direction of a second suspension bridge across Sungai Temburong. The boardwalk ends at Sungai Apan, a narrow stream. By following the course of the stream upriver, you soon come to a picturesque waterfall, with a plunge pool deep enough for swimming (outside dry season). A steep trail traverses the hillside with the aid of ropes to a second waterfall.

Most people make their way back to park headquarters by longboat from the confluence of Sungai Apan and Sungai Temburong (returning on foot would mean retracing your steps along the boardwalk). You may cross tracks with local Iban, who fish this stretch of the river with traps and nets. They'll probably wave you over and offer you a swig of grog – rice wine, or more likely, Bacardi rum.

Those looking for the chance to explore largely uncharted rainforest may be interested in tackling the strenuous week-long trek to the summit of **Bukit Pagon** (1843 m), which is situated near the border with Sarawak in the southernmost corner of Temburong. Contact the tourist office, or one of the Bandar-based tour operators, for help with arrangements.

Elsewhere in Temburong

If time is very limited, you may consider skipping Ulu Temburong and heading instead for the **Peradayan Forest Reserve**, which is just 20 minutes east of Bangar by road (taxis cost around B$15 one-way). Within the reserve is a small forest recreation park with picnic tables and trails, one of which climbs to the summit of **Bukit Patoi** (310 m), passing caves along the way. The summit of the hill is a bare patch of stone, allowing wide views across the forest north to Brunei Bay and east to Sarawak. A tougher and less distinct trail continues from here to the summit of **Bukit Peradayan** (410 m).

Though the majority of Temburong's indigenous inhabitants have taken the opportunity to move into detached homes, plenty still live in longhouses. In theory, unannounced visits are welcome at any longhouse, but a handful have established formal arrangements with tour operators for receiving guests. The largest is a '16-door' Iban longhouse (home to 16 families) situated along the road to Batang Duri, at **Kampong Sembiling**. Various guides and tour operators will stop off here, allowing visitors to meet the inhabitants and try a glass or two of *tuak* (rice wine). If it's daytime, there won't be many people around, but you'll get a chance to see inside a modern Iban longhouse, complete with satellite TV and parking bays for cars. Another longhouse offering 'homestays' is the curiously named five-door **Amo C**, located just north of **Batang Duri** itself. Overnight guests are set up with mattresses on the *ruai* (communal veranda), and guided treks along hunting trails can be arranged for a fee.

Tutong District 🖥 ⟩⟩ *pp269-275. Colour map 1, B5.*

The central district of Tutong is wedged between Belait District to the west and Limbang (Malaysia) to the east, following the flood plain of Sungai Tutong. Recent growth in agriculture has seen the introduction of small-scale plantations in areas of Tutong, though most of the district is sparsely populated and covered by rainforest.

The coastal highway passes by the district capital, Tutong, a small and pleasant town on the banks of the river. There's nothing much for the visitor to do here, other than stop by the small wet market or the nearby *tamu* (the regional open-air market, held every Thursday afternoon through to Friday morning). The *tamu* draws Tutong's indigenous inhabitants – Kedayan, Dusun and Iban tribespeople – who come down from the interior to sell their produce. It is mainly a food market, though there are handicrafts on sale, too. A kilometre to the north of Tutong is the **Taman Rekreasi Sungai Basong**, a small recreation park with a pond, a stream and picnic tables. Meanwhile, just west of town is **Pantai Seri Kenangan** (Unforgettable Beach) – a largely forgettable spit of sand dividing Sungai Tutong from the sea. Still, the beach is kept clean and the sea here is calm. Every July a local festival is held on the beach, with Malay games such as top-spinning and kite-flying.

The road continues along the spit as far as **Kampong Kuala Tutong**, a sleepy place among the coconut palms. There's a small boatyard here called Marine Yard, where river trips can sometimes be organized. The arrangement is pretty informal, and you'll have to just turn up and hope there's someone around. The boat weaves upriver through mangrove-lined swampland, past Dusun and Malay *kampongs*. Look out for monkeys and estuarine crocodiles, which can sometimes be seen basking on the sandbanks. River tours along Sungai Tutong can be arranged through **Ilufah Leisure Tours** (see page 273).

Tasek Merimbun

There is no public transport to Tasek Merimbun, Brunei's largest lake. If you've rented a car, head west from Bandar Seri Begawan on the old Tutong Road (rather than the coastal highway). At Mile 18, take the left fork for Lamunin. Beyond Kampong Lamunin itself, follow signs for Tasek Merimbun. The journey takes up to one hour 30 minutes.

Tasek Merimbun is a beautiful and remote spot rich in wildlife. The lake and its environs are home to Dusun tribespeople, who for many centuries took advantage of the abundance of fish and wildlife. Now that the lake has been set aside as a nature reserve, only a handful of Dusun people remain. Merimbun is becoming increasingly popular as a weekend escape for well-heeled Bruneians. The setting is magnificent: an S-shaped, peat-black body of water surrounded by dense jungle. In the centre of the lake is tiny island, accessible by boardwalk. The **Tasek Merimbun Heritage Park** encompasses the lake, plus wetlands, peat-swamp forest and lowland dipterocarp rainforest. The area is home to a great diversity of wildlife, including crocodile and clouded leopard (Borneo's biggest cat). The most important scientific discovery has been the white-collared fruit bat, which appears to be unique to Tasek Merimbun.

On the banks of the lake is a small visitor centre with a few fish tanks, plus chalets for accommodation. Local Dusun have kayaks for rent, too. Opposite the chalets is a 2-km botanical trail through the rainforest. Guides can be hired for longer treks in the area.

Belait District ⟩⟩ *pp269-275. Colour map 1, B5.*

Belait wears two faces. On the one hand it is oil country, the driving force behind Brunei's economy and home to a large expatriate population of British and Dutch. On the other, it is the best example of 'old' Brunei – Brunei before oil.

When oil was first discovered at Seria in 1929, the whole region was largely uninhabited, the lowlands dominated by peat swamps, mangroves and rainforest, with indigenous Iban and Dusun tribespeople sticking largely to the valley of Sungai Belait. Though the coastal strip has developed beyond recognition, the interior remains largely unscathed.

Aside from Temburong, Belait District is the best place to explore Brunei's rainforest and visit indigenous longhouses. Most visitors are unaware of this: the tourism infrastructure here remains underdeveloped, so few people visit. Nevertheless, the interior of Belait is ear-marked as an important ecotourism destination for the future, and tour operators are beginning to put together itineraries into the region.

Seria

Seria is a surreal place. Once open swampland, Seria is now dominated by level fields full of lawn-mowing tractors, egrets and 'nodding donkeys' – small land-based oil wells that nod back and forth as they pump oil to the surface. There is no real centre of town to speak of; row upon row of neat bungalows line the roads – home, presumably to Chinese and expatriate oil workers, whose wives ride about town in land cruisers. It is a strange, functional place with an odd mix of inhabitants that includes indigenous tribespeople and a garrison of Gurkhas.

The town straggles along the coastal strip between Seria and Kuala Belait, which serves as the centre of Brunei's oil production. On the edge of Seria is the **Billionth Barrel Monument**, commemorating the obscene productivity of Brunei's first oil field. For those who want to delve deeper into the history and technicalities of oil production, there is the **Oil & Gas Discovery Centre** (**OGDC**) ⓘ *F20 Seria, T3377200; Tue-Thu 0900-1700, Fri 1000-1200, 1400-1800, Sat-Sun 1000-1800; admission B$5*, set in a building that resembles an oil drum. It's a fun place for kids, with a gyroscope, a bed of nails and a fish pond.

Kuala Belait

Though it all started at Seria, Kuala Belait (known locally as 'KB') is the district's principal town. It also serves as the border town with nearby Sarawak. Like Seria, Kuala Belait is a purely functional place which has developed over time to serve the needs of the oil workers. The centre of town comprises a large grid of streets with Chinese shophouses alongside familiar outlets such as **Body Shop** and **KFC**.

Kuala Belait sits on the east bank of the Sungai Belait, and it is possible to hire a boat upriver as far as Kuala Balai (see below). Boats leave from behind the market building on Jalan Pasar, at the southern end of Jalan McKerron (sometimes it is spelled Mackeron).

Belait Interior

Kuala Balai

Before the oil boom, the main settlement in this part of Brunei was the riverine village of Kuala Balai, situated about an hour upriver from Kuala Belait. Between 1930 and 1980 the population slowly dwindled, until the village virtually ceased to exist. Today just a handful of permanent inhabitants remain.

The people from these parts are known as the Belait Malays, and they have a lot in common with the Melanau people of coastal Sarawak, including their Muslim faith, their traditional reliance on sago processing and their stilted longhouses. Despite the fact that Kuala Balai is now little more than a ghost town, it is still possible to get a sense of how things once looked; the old longhouse, which deteriorated many years ago, has been rebuilt as part of a **Raleigh International** project. And there are still one or two old sago processors around, though they use light machinery now, rather than trampling the sago scrapings underfoot, as was once the way. Just downriver from the longhouse is a small wooden box on stilts by the riverside. Inside are 20 human skulls, victims of headhunters from as long ago as the 17th century.

As is the case across Belait District, tourism hasn't yet taken off and few people visit the longhouse. Whether or not the building is maintained remains to be seen, but at the time of writing there were plans to market Kuala Balai more actively as a tourist destination.

Jalan Labi

The other route into the interior of Belait is via Jalan Labi, a decent road which turns south off the coastal highway at Kampong Lumut, near the border with Tutong District. A little way along the road is Brunei's oldest forest reserve, the **Sungai Liang Forest Reserve**, with ponds, picnic shelters and various well-maintained paths into the surrounding forest. One climbs a steep hill as far as a treehouse (closed for renovation at the time of writing). Close by is the **Forestry Department** building, set back from the road, with a small 'Palmetum' leading up to the offices. There's a tiny forestry museum here, too – the **Muzium Perhutanan** ① *Mon-Thu and Sat 0800-1215 and 1330-1630*, with two rooms of displays that aren't worth going out of your way for.

The Labi road continues south through undulating rainforest as far as the village of Kampong Labi itself, passing another forest reserve along the way – the **Labi Hills Forest Reserve**. Within its boundaries is the 270-ha **Luagan Lalak Recreation Park**, covering an area of alluvial swampland, which floods to become a lake during the monsoon rains. The lake (or swamp, depending on the season) is accessible via a 200-m-long boardwalk.

Kampong Labi, some 40 km south of the coastal highway, is a small settlement that has served for years as a base for speculative (and unsuccessful) oil drilling in the surrounding hills. Tropical fruits, such as rambutan, durian, cempedak and jackfruit, are grown in the area. Beyond Labi, the road turns into a dirt track which serves as an access route to a number of Iban longhouses. The largest of these is the 12-door **Rumah Panjang Mendaram Besar**, home to 100 or so people. Like most of the longhouses in Brunei, this one has piped water and electricity, with the men commuting to the towns to work for either **Shell** or the government. A nearby trail leads to the **Wasai Mendaram**, a large waterfall with plunge pool for bathing.

At the end of the 12-km track is **Rumah Panjang Teraja**. The inhabitants of this six-door longhouse cultivate paddy, rear pigs and chickens, and grow their own fruit and vegetables. From the longhouse, a well-marked trail leads to the summit of Bukit Teraja, from where there are magnificent views as far as Gunung Mulu (see page 144) in Sarawak. Walking the trail to the summit takes about an hour and a half. Reported wildlife sightings along the way include orang-utans, Borneo bearded pigs, barking deer, macaques and hornbills.

Ulu Belait

Further longhouses can be found deep in the interior, along the upper reaches of Sungai Belait. These are accessible by longboat from Kampong Sungai Mau, which is situated halfway along the Jalan Labi. Of course, it is possible to begin the journey in Kuala Belait, passing Kuala Balai along the way, but this route takes many hours.

The journey upriver into Ulu Belait (Upriver Belait) depends very much on the level of the river; in the dry season its upper reaches are barely navigable. Kampong Sukang, some two hours from Kampong Sungai Mau by longboat, is a community of Dusun and Punan tribespeople, with two longhouses and a hamlet of family homes. The Punan are nomadic hunter-gatherers by tradition, though the inhabitants of Kampong Sukang were persuaded to settle here back in the 1970s. They now farm paddy rather than relying on the old staple diet of wild sago, but they still hunt in the traditional manner – using blowpipes and poison darts.

If you're feeling still more intrepid, there is another hamlet of longhouses at **Kampong Melilas**, located between one and three hours upriver from Kampong Sukang (depending on the water level). These are home to Iban people and, like the Labi longhouses, they are upgraded versions of the traditional longhouse – though this community supports a thriving cottage industry in traditional basketry and weaving. Beyond Kampong Melilas, there are hot springs to visit and plenty of waterfalls – a guide can be arranged at the village.

● Sleeping

Bandar Seri Begawan *p254, map p256*
L The Centrepoint, Abdul Razak Complex, Gadong BE3519, T2430430, www.arhbrunei.com. This 220-room hotel matches the **Sheraton** for luxury (and beats it for marble content), though it is situated several kilometres outside the city centre in the suburb of Gadong (Bandar's main shopping district). Special discounts can see rates halved. The Executive rooms come with kitchenettes. There's a 24-hr business centre, but no swimming pool or fitness centre.
L Sheraton Utama Hotel, Jl Tasek Lama, PO Box 2203, BS8674, T2244272, www.sheraton.com/utama. Bandar's best hotel, with 149 large comfortable rooms, each with internet access (chargeable), swimming pool, 2 restaurants, health club with spa treatments, and the full range of business facilities. The centre of Bandar is within walking distance.
AL Orchid Garden Hotel, Lot 31954, Simpang 9, Kampong Anggerek Desa, Jl Berakas BB3713, T2335544, www.orchid gardenbrunei.com. A 4-star hotel located next to the National Stadium (between the airport and the government complex), several kilometres from the centre of Bandar. Comfortable rooms with high-speed internet access and all the usual amenities, plus 2 restaurants, a pool and spa. This is the closest hotel to the airport, so handy for stop-overs.
AL Riverview Hotel, Km 1, Jl Gadong, PO Box 1, BS8670, T2238238, rivview@brunet.bn. Set on its own near the suburb of Gadong, halfway between downtown Bandar and the airport. Rooms are big, if uninspiring. Facilities include swimming pool, sauna and jacuzzi.
A Brunei Hotel, 95 Jl Pemancha, T2242372, www.bruneihotel.com.bn. The most central of Bandar's hotels, adjacent to the Tamu Sungai Kianggeh (market). The 63 rooms are all spacious, with satellite TV, a/c, minibar and floral bedspreads. There's a restaurant

and function room, too.
B Grand City Hotel, Lot 25115, Block G, Kampong Pengkalan Gadong, BE3719, T2452188, grandcity@brunet.bn. A good mid-range option, if you don't mind staying out of town (in the shopping suburb of Gadong). Rooms have a/c, tea and coffee facilities, TV and phone. Airport transfer included in the price.
B Terrace Hotel, Jl Tasek Lama, PO Box 49, BS8670, T2243554, www.terracebrunei.com. 80 a/c, en-suite rooms, with TV, kettle and safe. They're a touch worn, but nevertheless good value for money. There's a pleasant little outdoor pool, a restaurant and a karaoke lounge (which can get noisy). Situated 1 km from the waterfront.
B Jubilee Plaza Hotel, Jubilee Plaza, Jl Kampong Kianggeh, BS8111, T2228070, jubilee@brunet.bn. Situated off a side road, 10 mins' walk from the waterfront, this is a functional place offering decent-sized (if plain) rooms with TV, minibar and en-suite bathrooms. Breakfast and airport transfers are included in the price.
C Voctech International House, Jl Pasar Baharu, Gadong BE1318, T2447992, voctech@brunet.bn. With spacious, clean, functional rooms, this is the best budget option, not least because it is within walking distance of the excellent *pasar malam* (the night market where you can get great, cheap local food). All rooms have TV and fridge. Several kilometres outside Bandar centre.
D Pusat Belia, Jl Sungai Kianggeh, T2223936, jbsbelia@brunet.bn. Brunei's youth hostel, 5 mins' walk from the waterfront, with clean 4-man dorms, and a swimming pool.

Muara and around *p263*
LL Empire Hotel & Country Club, Jerudong BG3122, T2418888, www.theempire hotel.com. Brunei's only beach resort, and a monument to the extravagance of the

sultan's brother, Prince Jefri (see page 259). No expense was spared in the construction of this 6-star hotel, which centres around an 80-m-high, marble-pillared atrium. The 400-plus rooms all have large balconies and huge marble-clad bathrooms, with walk-in showers and vast bath tubs. The Presidential Suite covers more than 650 sq m and has its own lavish indoor swimming pool, with attached sauna, steam room and jacuzzi. With the click of a button, a cinema screen descends from the ceiling above the pool. There are antiques everywhere and swathes of gold leaf. Facilities include an 18-hole Jack Nicklaus golf course, a separate sports club, a cinema and numerous swimming pools, including a meandering 11,000-sq-m lagoon pool with fake, sandy beach (great for kids). There is a kids' club too, with full-time staff and water slide. There are 7 dining outlets, covering the range of world cuisine. The watersports on offer include scuba diving, sailing, jet skiing, kayaking and parasailing. The hotel lays on a free shuttle service in and out of Bandar Seri Begawan, 4 times daily. It is definitely worth checking for special discounts; low occupancy means that rooms here are often excellent value for money.

Temburong District *p263*
B **Ulu Temburong National Park**, c/o Tourist Information Centre, General Post Office Building, corner of Jl Sultan and Jl Elizabeth Dua, Bandar Seri Begawan, T2223734 (Mon-Sat 0800-1200 and 1400-1630). Virtually everyone visits Ulu Temburong as part of an organized tour, with accommodation pre-arranged for longer stays. If you want to go to the trouble of arranging the trip yourself, there is plenty of basic (but clean and modern) chalet accommodation at park headquarters. Book in advance through the tourist office in Bandar.
C **Government Resthouse**, Jl Batang Duri, Bangar, T5221239. The only place to stay in Bangar, situated a short walk from the jetty along the road to Batang Duri. Simple, functional rooms, plus a few chalets for B$80.
D **Longhouses**. Visitors to Temburong District can stay at various longhouses – either informally or as part of an organized tour. Those most commonly visited are **Amo C** and the main longhouse at **Kampong**

Sembiling, both along the Batang Duri road. The **Amo C** longhouse has established an informal homestay arrangement with guests: for a small amount of money (no more than B$10), they will feed you and set you up with mattresses on the *ruai* (the common veranda). Hospitality is an important part of indigenous culture and, in theory, any longhouse will put you up for the night. In practice, this is only the case with the more traditional or remote longhouses. If you turn up at a longhouse unannounced, be sure to follow the correct etiquette. Always ask the permission of the headman, or Tuai Rumah, before heading inside. Remove shoes before entering a family room (*bilik*), or an area of the *ruai* laid with mats. More often than not, shoes are not worn at all in a longhouse and are left at the entrance to the *ruai*.

Tutong District *p266*
B **Halim Plaza Hotel**, Lot No 9003, Kampong Petani, Tutong TA1141, T4260688, halimplaza@onebrunei.com. Surprisingly attractive and good-value rooms set inside a small shopping centre in Tutong itself. Used mainly by Bruneians on business.
C **Researchers' Quarter**, Tasek Merimbun Heritage Park, c/o Director of Brunei Museum, T2222713, bmdir@bunet.bn. If available, the **Researchers' Quarter** (a new wooden chalet) at Tasek Merimbun is available to members of the public. Contact the Brunei Museum in advance.

Belait District *p266*
AL **Riviera Hotel**, Lot 106, Jl Sungai, Kuala Belait KA2331, T3335252, www.rivierakb.com. The best hotel in Kuala Belait, situated on the riverfront in the centre of town. There are 30 bedrooms and suites, all modern in design and in great nick. All rooms feature tea- and coffee-making facilities, satellite TV, minibar, shower and bath. Frequent promotions make this hotel good value.
B **Brunei Sentosa Hotel**, 92-93 Jl McKerron, PO Box 252, Kuala Belait KA1131, T3334341, www.bruneisentosahotel.com. In the heart of town. A step down from the **Riviera**, but decent nonetheless, with added features such as in-room broadband access. Rooms are spacious, though some are a little dingy.

❷ Eating

The night market (*pasar malam*) in the suburb of **Gadong** is probably the best place to sample local fare. Every evening from about 1700, hundreds of stalls turn out seemingly endless varieties of satay, curries, grilled meats and Malay coconut-based sweets. The same sort of food is available on a smaller scale at the **Tamu Kianggeh** (open-air market) in downtown Bandar.

Also worth trying are the stalls set on the waterfront near the Temburong jetty for *nasi campur* and *teh tarik*. The **Padian Foodcourt** (1st floor, Yayasan Complex; daily 0900-2200) is great for cheap local food and drink, as well as Thai and Indonesian staples. There are also larger food courts in **Gadong**, including one on the top floor of The Mall, which serves the full range of Asian cuisines – try Malay *nasi lemak* and beef *rendang*.

You'll find yourself drinking vast amounts of fruit juice in Brunei (it's served in place of alcohol). Obviously, there is no bar scene here; the closest you get are the 'mocktail' lounges in the top hotels. Still, if you have brought in your allowance of alcohol (and declared it at customs), top-end restaurants will often allow you to drink it with your meal.

Restaurants come and go with great frequency in Brunei. A selection of the current favourites is listed below.

Bandar Seri Begawan *p254, map p256*
₮₮₮ **Zaika**, G24, Block C, Yayasan Complex, T2230817. Daily 1130-1430, 1800-2000. Excellent North Indian cuisine in pleasing wood-panelled surroundings (*zaika* means 'fine dining' in Urdu). Try tandoori chicken or lamb (straight from an authentic oven) and Kashmiri *rogan josh*. Classical Indian lamps hang overhead, old Indian paintings adorn the walls, and gentle Indian music tinkles in the background. The menu is vast (12 pages).
₮₮ **Ahan Thai**, Ground floor, Jubilee Plaza, Jl Kampong Kianggeh, T2239599. Daily 0700-2400. A fast turnover of Thai food with all the usual favourites, including *tom yam* soup, chicken with cashew nuts, and chilli squid.
₮₮ **Hua Hua**, 48 Jl Sultan, T2225396. Daily 0700-2100. An attractive-looking Chinese restaurant with a wide variety of well-priced dishes, including excellent dim sum; in the heart of town.

₮₮ **RMS Portview Seafood Restaurant**, Jl MacArthur (opposite Yayasan Complex), T2231466. Daily 1000-2300. Set right on the riverfront. Cheaper café downstairs (Malay, Chinese and Western) and a more formal restaurant upstairs serving Thai, Japanese and Chinese cuisine. Excellent steamboats.
₮ **CA Mohamed**, Unit 202, Yayasan Complex, T2232999. Daily 0900-2200. Inexpensive Malay and Indian staples.
₮ **Isma Jaya**, 27 Jl Sultan, T2220229. Daily 0700-2100. A great place for Indian Muslim food, such as *roti canai*, as well as good biryani and curries.
₮ **Popular Restaurant**, Unit 5, Ground floor, Norain Complex, T2221375. Daily 0800-2200. A simple restaurant with plastic chairs serving north and south Indian cuisine: chicken masala, *roti kosong*, naan, *dosai*, chappati. All delicious.
₮ **Seri Indah**, Jl MacArthur, T2243567. A simple *mamak* (Indian Muslim) restaurant serving delicious *roti kosong* and *teh tarik*. Situated opposite the waterfront wet market.

Bandar's suburbs
₮₮₮ **I-Lotus Restaurant**, 28 Spg 12-26, Perumahan Rakyat Jati, Rimba Gadong (just past Tungku Link), T2422466. Daily 1030-1430 and 1800-2400. Serves a wide range of Chinese and Thai dishes, with frequent steamboat promotions. Specialities include coconut prawn curry and Nyonya steamed fish. Has a very good reputation.
₮₮₮ **Fratini's**, No1, Centrepoint Foodcourt, Abdul Razak Complex, Gadong, T2451300. Daily 1000-2300. An Italian restaurant next door to the **Centrepoint Hotel**, with a big range of pizza and pasta dishes (gnocchi, too), along with steaks and seafood.
₮₮ **Escapade Sushi**, Unit 4-5, Block C, Abdul Raza Complex (opposite **Centrepoint Hotel**), Gadong, T2443012. Sushi on a conveyor belt.
₮₮ **Pondok Sari Wangi**, Unit 12-13, Abdul Razak Complex, Gadong, T2445045. Daily 1000-2200. Popular Indonesian restaurant serving staples such as *crab masak* and *ikan bakar* (barbecued fish/seafood).
₮₮ **Teo Poi Hoon**, 17-18 Ground floor, Bang Hg Awang, Kiulap, T2233938. Sat-Thu 0800-2200, Fri 0800-2300. Serves traditional Taiwanese and Cantonese cuisine, with specialities that include *guisei* beancurd rice and *mamie* chicken. Very popular at lunchtime.

Brunei Listings

♥ **Le Taj Restaurant**, 2-3, 2nd Floor, Seri Kiulap Complex, Kiulap, T223 8996. Daily 0800-2300. Serves the full range of North Indian cuisine (biryani, tandoori, masala, korma, etc). Great lassis.

Muara and around *p263*
♥♥♥ **Li Gong**, Empire Hotel & Country Club, Jerudong BG3122, T2418888, ext 7329. Tue-Thu and Sun 1830-2230, Fri-Sat 1100-1500, 1830-2230. Excellent Chinese cuisine, set in a pavilion surrounded by koi ponds. The menu covers specialities from every province in China. There's an all-you-can-eat buffet on Wed and steamboat on Thu.
♥♥♥ **Spaghettini**, Empire Hotel & Country Club, Jerudong BG3122, T2418888, ext 7368. Daily 1830-2300, also Mon and Wed 1130-1430. Mimics an Italian trattoria, with its own authentic, wood-fired oven and dough-flinging chefs. Perched at the top of the towering atrium at the Empire Hotel.

✵ Festivals and events

Bandar Seri Begawan *p254, map p256*
Jan-Feb Chinese New Year: 18 Feb 2007. A 2-week celebration beginning with a family reunion dinner on the eve of the New Year.
23 Feb National Day Celebrations. Celebration of independence at the Hassanal Bolkiah National Stadium.
Mar-Apr The Prophet's Birthday, 11 Apr 2006, 31 Mar 2007. As well as religious functions, there's a procession through the streets of Bandar Seri Begawan.
31 May Royal Brunei Armed Forces Day. Celebrates the formation of the Royal Brunei Armed Forces, with military parades and displays.
15 Jul The Sultan's Birthday. One of the biggest events in the national calendar, and the only time when the grounds of the the Istana Nural Iman are open to the public. There's a royal address, too, and an investiture ceremony.
Sep-Oct Ramadan. Starts 24 Sep 2006, 13 Sep 2007. The holy month, when Muslims abstain from eating and drinking between dawn and dusk. During fasting hours it is considered ill-mannered to eat, drink or smoke openly in public. The end of Ramadan is marked by the Hari Raya Puasa celebration, when families gather for a feast.

☻ Entertainment

Bandar Seri Begawan *p254, map p256*
In a dry country like Brunei, you might expect there to be some form of replacement entertainment. But, no, come evening time, everything quietens down yet another gear. The centre of Bandar Seri Begawan itself is more or less deserted after dark. The suburb of Gadong is probably the busiest place in the evenings, its lively *pasar malam* churning out local food until late at night to an endless stream of Bruneians, who turn up in their 4x4s, pick up their food, then drive home to eat it. If there were tables and chairs laid out at the night market, it might become Brunei's prime hang-out; but then, that wouldn't be in the spirit of things.

In the top hotels, you can sip mocktails in mock bars and listen to sedate local bands. The Jerudong theme park is about as good as it gets when it comes to entertainment, and even that is deadly quiet by Western standards.

Stumble across a remote longhouse, and you enter another world. Guests are entertained with gusto and will almost certainly be offered traditional rice wine (known as *tuak* in Iban) – a drink so ingrained in indigenous heritage that the sultan has exempted it from the ban on alcohol. But in the towns of Brunei, entertainment is something that happens – if at all – behind closed doors.

Cinema
Strangely, you'll never have a problem catching the latest Hollywood blockbuster. Head for the Empire Cinema Empire Hotel & Country Club, Jerudong, T2417977, or The Mall Cineplex, The Mall, Gadong, T2422455.

✪ Shopping

Bandar Seri Begawan *p254, map p256*
Brunei's main shopping district is centred on the suburb of Gadong, 4 km from the centre of Bandar Seri Begawan. The principal shopping malls here are Gadong Centrepoint and The Mall, both on the main thoroughfare. In Bandar itself, shopping is focused on the elegant Yayasan Complex, which has everything from small boutiques and restaurants to a supermarket and an upmarket department store (Hua Ho).

Crafts

Traditional handicrafts include brassware, silverware, *keris* (ornate ceremonial daggers) and a type of *songket* known as *jong sarat* – a traditional cloth, hand woven with gold and silver thread. Bandar's **Arts and Handicraft Centre** (see page 260) sells all of these items, though the choice is limited. Each of the major shopping malls has one or two gift shops selling Southeast Asian crafts (again, prices are much higher than in Malaysia). Both the **Sheraton Utama** and the **Empire Hotel** have upmarket gift and antiques shops.

For better-priced indigenous handicrafts, you could try the weekly *tamu* (open-air market) in **Tutong** (see page 266), which starts Thu afternoon and finishes late morning on Fri. Occasionally there are handicrafts for sale at the **Tamu Kianggeh** in Bandar Seri Begawan, though this is predominantly a food market. **Kampong Ayer** is another place where it is possible to find crafts and antiques (at one time, the water village thrived as a centre for cottage industries, with silversmiths, brass-casters, blacksmiths, boat-builders and songket weavers). You won't find anything on your own; ask the boatmen.

▲▲ Activities and tours

Jungle trekking

Jungle trekking is one of the main attractions for visitors. The best place is the **Ulu Temburong National Park** (see page 263), but there are plenty of other opportunities in each of Brunei's districts. The easiest (and often the cheapest) way of organizing a trip into the rainforest is through one of the Brunei-based tour operators (see below).

River trips

No trip to Brunei is complete without a *tambang* ride along the Brunei River (Sungai Brunei). These trips can combine tours of the water village, with a water safari in search of proboscis monkeys. Any of the tour operators listed below can arrange a river trip, though only **Mona Florafauna Tours** guarantees sightings of proboscis monkeys. Once the secret location has been reached, the boatman will cut the engine and paddle quietly into the mangroves to allow for a close encounter with the monkeys.

Sports

There's a stunning 18-hole, floodlit, Jack Nicklaus golf course at the **Empire Hotel & Country Club** (see page 269). The Country Club also has facilities for tennis, squash, badminton, 10-pin bowling and snooker. As far as leisure centres go, you won't beat the **Hassanal Bolkiah National Stadium**, built to Olympic specifications, with a track-and-field complex, a tennis centre, squash courts and a swimming pool. As you might imagine, you'll have the place to yourself. The sports complex is situated close to the government offices, between the airport and the centre of Bandar Seri Begawan. Other than this, there are plenty of private sports clubs catering to the large expat population; but visitors are limited to hotel facilities.

Watersports

This isn't big in Brunei. Your best bet is to contact **Scuba-Tech International**, based at the **Empire Hotel & County Club** (see page 269). They can arrange parasailing, jetskiing, deep-sea fishing, sailing and scuba diving (there are a number of wreck sites off Brunei's coast and around Labuan).

Tour operators

Independent travel in Brunei is a little more complicated than it is in Malaysia. That's not to say that it is impossible – anyone can visit Ulu Temburong independently, for example, but it works out cheaper to go as part of an organized tour. Plus, it saves the hassle of applying for permits and organizing transport. Because Brunei is still in its infancy as a tourist destination, you're very unlikely to find yourself in a large tour group (more often than not, you'll have a guide to yourself; many of them are indigenous to the region and hugely knowledgable). The major tour operators based in Brunei are listed below.
Century Travel Centre, First Floor, Darussalam Complex, Jl Sultan, BSB, T2221747, www.centurytravelcentre.com.
Freme Travel Services, Wisma Jaya, Jl Pemancha, BSB, T2234277, www.freme.com. Recommended.
Ilufah Leisure Tours, 20A, Bangunan Awg. Hj Ahmad Awg. Hassan & Anak-Anak, Kiulap, Gadong, T2233524, ilufah_tours@brunet.bn.
Intrepid Tours, PO Box 2234, T2262676, www.bruneibay.net.

Mas Sugara Travel Services, 1st Floor, Complex Warisan, Mata Simpang 322, Jl Gadong, T2423963, www.massugara.com.
Mona Florafauna Tours, Ground floor, Yayasan Complex, T2230761, mft@brunet.bn. Recommended.
Pan Bright Travel Services, Haji Ahmad Laksamana Building, 38-39 Jl Sultan, T2240980, www.panbright.com.
Scuba-Tech Inernational, Empire Hotel & Country Club (see page 269), www.scubatechintl.com.
Sunshine Borneo Tours, No 2, Simpang 146, Jl Kiarong, T2441791, www.exploreborneo.com.

⊖ Transport

Bandar Seri Begawan *p254, map p256*
To explore Brunei in any depth, you really need to hire a car. Thanks to subsidised vehicles and cheap petrol, most Bruneians drive; as a result of this, the public transport system is far from comprehensive. There are no internal flights within Brunei (it's so small that flying would be impractical).

Air
Brunei International Airport is situated 11 km south of the capital. **Royal Brunei Airlines** is the only airline that flies direct to Brunei from the UK (daily flights to and from London Heathrow; 16 hrs, including a brief stop in Dubai for refuelling). Flights cost in the region of £450-650. Otherwise, you'll have to fly direct to Kuala Lumpur or Singapore on a different airline and transfer flights for the remainder of the journey (see page 24). **Royal Brunei Airlines** and **Malaysian Airlines** fly regularly from Kuala Lumpur (about £100 return), while **Singapore Airlines** and **Royal Brunei** fly daily from Singapore (about £90). **Royal Brunei Airlines** also fly direct to Sydney, Perth, Brisbane, Darwin and Auckland (3 flights per week to and from each city). There are no direct flights to Brunei from the USA or Canada.
Airline offices Royal Brunei Airlines, PO Box 737, BS 8671, T2212222, www.bruneiair.com.

Boat
Boats, of course, are the main form of transport around **Kampong Ayer**. Small,

speedy *tambang* depart from the jetty behind the **Yayasan Complex** from dawn until late at night. A short journey across to the water village should cost no more than a couple of Brunei dollars. Regular speedboats leave from the **Jl Residency** jetty in Bandar Seri Begawan to **Bangar**, the main town in Temburong District (hourly 0630-1630; B$6). Speedboats also depart from the main jetty to destinations in Malaysia – **Lawas**, **Labuan** and **Limbang**. Access upriver to the interior of Brunei is by indigenous longboat. Journeys need to be pre-arranged (best to speak to a tour operator, see page 273).

Bus
Fairly regular daylight buses serves Bandar Seri Begawan and the surrounding Brunei Muara district. There are 6 bus routes – the Eastern, Western, Northern, Southern, Central and Circle Lines, each of which operate buses every 20 mins from 0630-1800. The handiest route is probably the Central Line, which links the main bus station in Bandar Seri Begawan (on Jl Cator) with **Gadong** and the Brunei Museum (B$1.50). Buses for **Muara** (B$3), **Tutong** (B$4), **Seria** (B$6) and **Kuala Belait** (B$7) leave less regularly from the Jl Cator bus station.

Car
To make the most of a trip to Brunei, it is best to hire a car. The major car-hire firms operate out of the airport or Bandar Seri Begawan, and there are plenty of cheaper local firms to choose from, too.
Car hire AA Car Rental, Unti 26, Simpang 69-44, Jl Kiarong, T2427238, aacarrental@gmail.com; **Avis**, 16 Haji Daud Complex, Jl Gadong, T2426345; **Hertz**, Lot Q33, West Berakas Link, T2390300 (airport T2452244), www.hertz.com; **Qawi Enterprise**, PO Box 1322, Gadong, T2340380.

Taxi
Metered taxis ferry people about Bandar and its suburbs, with fares set at B$3 for the first kilometre (or B$4.50 between 2100-0600) and B$1 for every subsequent kilometre. For longer journeys, it makes more sense to hire a car. Taxis can be waved down. Otherwise call T2222214 (**Bandar Seri Begawan**); T3334581 (**Kuala Belait**); T3222030 (**Seria**); T2343671 (**airport**).

◐ Directory

Bandar Seri Begawan *p254, map p256*
Banks Banking hours are Mon-Fri
0900-1500, Sat 0900-1100. **Citibank NA**, Jl
Sultan, T2233233; **HSBC**, Jl Sultan, T2242305;
Malaysian Banking Berhad, Jl Pemancha,
T2242494; **Overseas Union Bank**, RBA Plaza,
Jl Sultan, T2225477; **Standard Chartered
Bank**, Jl Sultan, T2242386. **Embassies
and consulates** Australia, 4th Floor,
Teck Guan Plaza, Jl Sultan, T2229435,
ozcombrn @brunet.bn; **Canada**, 5th Floor,
1 Jl McArthur, T2220043, hicomcda
@brunet.bn; **Malaysia**, 27 Simpang 396, Lot
9075, Kampong Sungai Akar, Jl Kebangsaan,
T2345652, mwbrunei@brunet.bn; **New
Zealand**, 36A Seri Lambak Complex, Jl
Berakas, T2331612; **Singapore**, 8 Simpang
74, Jl Subok, T2262741, singa@brunet.bn;
United Kingdom, Level 2, Block D, Yayasan
Complex, T2222231, brithc@brunet.bn;
USA, 3rd Floor, Teck Guan Plaza, Jl Sultan,
T2229670, amembbsb@brunet.bn.
Emergencies Ambulance T991; Police

T993; Fire T995. **Internet** Deltech
Communications, Unit 5, Ground floor,
Bangunan Hj Mohm Salleh, Simpang 103,
Jl Gadong, T2453808, daily 0900-2300, B$5
per hr; **E-Mart Cyber Junction**, GP Properties
Building, Jl Gadong, T2426010, daily
0800-2300, B$3 per hr; **KASCO IT Centre**,
Ground floor, 5 Jl Ong Sum Ping, T2223541;
LA Ling Cyber Café, 2nd Floor, Yayasan
Complex, T2232800, daily 0930-2130, B$3
per hr. **Laundry** Superkleen, 95 Jl
Pemancha, T2242372. **Medical
services** RIPAS Hospital, Jl Putera
Al-Muhtadee Billah, T2242424; **Jerudong
Park Medical Centre**, Jerudong, T2611433.
Post office General Post Office Building,
corner of Jl Sultan and Jl Elizabeth Dua,
Mon-Thu and Sat 0745-1630, Fri 0800-1100
and 1400-1600. **Telephone** Pre-paid
phonecards called 'Hallo Kad' are widely
available and can be used with any phone
(including phone booths). Coin phones are
operable with 10- and 20-cent coins.
Directory enquiries: T113.

Background

History

Brunei's early history is obscure – but although precise dates have been muddied by time, there is no doubt that the sultanate's early prosperity was rooted in trade. As far back as the 7th century, China was importing birds' nests from Brunei, and Arab, Indian, Chinese and other Southeast Asian traders were regularly passing through. Links with Chinese merchants were strongest: they traded silk, metals, stoneware and porcelain for Brunei's jungle produce: bezoar stones, hornbill ivory, timber and birds' nests. Chinese coins dating from the 8th century have been unearthed at Kota Batu, 3 km from Bandar Seri Begawan. Large quantities of Chinese porcelain dating from the Tang, Sung and Ming dynasties have also been found. The sultanate was on the main trade route between China and the western reaches of the Malayan archipelago and by 10th to 13th centuries, trade was booming. By the turn of the 15th century there was a sizeable Chinese population settled in Brunei.

It is thought that some time around 1370 Sultan Mohammad became first Sultan. In the mid-1400s, Sultan Awang Alak ber Tabar married a Melakan princess and converted to Islam. Brunei already had trade links with Melaka and exported camphor, rice, gold and sago in exchange for Indian textiles. But it was not until an Arab, Sharif Ali, married Sultan Awang Alak's niece, that Islam spread beyond the confines of the royal court. Sharif Ali – who is said to have descended from the Prophet Mohammad – became Sultan Berkat. He consolidated Islam, converted the townspeople, built mosques and set up a legal system based on Islamic Sharia law. Trade flourished and Brunei assumed the epithet 'Darussalam' – 'the abode of peace'.

The golden years

The coastal Melanaus quickly embraced the Muslim faith, but tribal groups in the interior were largely unaffected by the spread of Islam and retained their animist beliefs. As Islam spread along the coasts of North and West Borneo, the sultanate expanded its political and commercial sphere of influence. By the 16th century, communities all along the coasts of present-day Sabah and Sarawak were paying tribute to the Sultan. The sultanate became the centre of a minor empire whose influence stretched beyond the coasts of Borneo to many surrounding islands, including the Sulu archipelago and Mindanao in the Philippines. Even Manila had to pay tribute to the Sultan's court.

On 8 July 1521 Antonio Pigafetta, an Italian historian on Portuguese explorer Ferdinand Magellan's expedition, visited the Sultanate of Brunei and described it as a rich, hospitable and powerful kingdom with an established Islamic monarchy and strong regional influence. Pigafetta published his experiences in his book, *The First Voyage Around the World*. He records the existence of a sophisticated royal court and the lavishly decorated Sultan's palace. Brunei Town was reported to be a large, wealthy city of 25,000 households. The townspeople lived in houses built on stilts over the water.

In 1526 the Portuguese set up a trading post in Brunei, and from there conducted trade with the Moluccas – the famed Spice Islands – via Brunei. At the same time, more Chinese traders immigrated to Brunei, to service the booming trade between Melaka and Macau and to trade with Pattani on the South Thai isthmus.

But relations with the Spaniards were not so warm; the King of Spain and the Sultan of Brunei had mutually exclusive interests in the Philippines. In the 1570s Spaniards attacked several important Muslim centres and in March 1578, the captain-general of the Philippines, Francesco de Sande, led a naval expedition to Brunei, demanding the Sultan pay tribute to Spain and allow Roman Catholic missionaries to proselytize. The Sultan would have none of it and a battle ensued off Muara, which the Spaniards won. They captured the city, but within days the victors were stopped in their tracks by a cholera epidemic and had to withdraw. In 1579 they returned and once again did battle off Muara, but this time they were defeated.

The sun sets on an empire

Portugal came under Spanish rule in 1580, and Brunei lost a valuable European ally: the sultanate was raided by the Spanish again in 1588 and 1645. But by then Brunei's golden age was history and the Sultan's grip on his further-flung dependencies had begun to slip.

In the 1660s, civil war erupted in Brunei due to feuding between princes and, together with additional external pressures of European expansionism, the once mighty sultanate all but collapsed. Only a handful of foreign merchants dealt with the sultanate and Chinese traders passed it by. Balanini pirates from Sulu and Illanun pirates from Mindanao posed a constant threat to the Sultan and any European traders or adventurers foolhardy enough to take them on. In return for protection from these sea-borne terrorists, the Sultan offered the British East India Company a base on the island of Labuan in Brunei Bay in the late 1600s – although the trading post failed to take off.

For 150 years, Brunei languished in obscurity. By the early 1800s, Brunei's territory did not extend much beyond the town boundaries, although the Sarawak River, and the west coastal strip of North Borneo officially remained under the Sultan's sway.

James Brooke – the man who would be king

The collection of mini-river states that made up what was left of the Sultanate were ruled by the pangeran, the lesser nobles of the Brunei court. In the 1830s Brunei chiefs had gone to the Sarawak valley to organize the mining and trade in the high-grade antimony ore which had been discovered there in 1824. They recruited

Dayaks as workers and founded Kuching. But, with the support of local Malay chiefs, the Dayaks rebelled against one of the Brunei noblemen, the corrupt, Pangeran Makota, one of the Rajah's 14 brothers. By all accounts, Makota was a nasty piece of work, known for his exquisite charm and diabolical cunning.

It was into this troubled riverine mini-state, in armed rebellion against Makota, that the English adventurer James Brooke sailed in 1839. Robert Payne, in his book *The White Rajahs of Sarawak*, describes Makota as a "princely racketeer" and "a man of satanic gifts, who practised crimes for pleasure". Makota confided to Brooke: "I was brought up to plunder the Dayaks, and it makes me laugh to think that I have fleeced a tribe down to its cooking-pots." With Brooke's arrival, Makota realized his days were numbered.

In 1837, the Sultan of Brunei, Omar Ali Saiffuddin, had dispatched his uncle, Pengiran Muda Hashim, to contain the rebellion. He failed, and turned to Brooke for help. In return for his services, Brooke demanded to be made Governor of Sarawak.

After he had been formally installed in his new role by Sultan Omar, Brooke set about building his own empire. In 1848 he said: "I am going in these revolutionary times to get up a league and covenant between all the good rivers of the coast, to the purpose that they will not pay revenue or obey the government of Brunei ..." Brooke exploited rivalries between various aristocratic factions of Brunei's royal court which climaxed in the murder of Pengiran Muda Hashim and his family.

No longer required in Sarawak, Hashim had returned to Brunei to become Chief Minister and heir apparent. He was murdered along with 11 other princes and their families, by Sultan Omar. The Sultan and his advisers had felt threatened by their presence, so they disposed of Hashim to prevent a coup. The massacre incensed Brooke. In June 1846, his British ally, Admiral Sir Thomas Cochrane bombarded Brunei Town, set it ablaze and chased the Sultan into the jungle.

Cochrane wanted to proclaim Brooke Sultan of Brunei, but decided, in the end, to offer Sultan Omar protection if he cleaned up his act and demonstrated his loyalty to Queen Victoria. After several weeks, the humiliated Sultan emerged from the jungle and swore undying loyalty to the Queen. As penance, Sultan Omar formally ceded the island of Labuan to the British crown on 18 December 1846. The brow-beaten Sultan pleaded proneness to sea sickness in an effort to avoid having to witness the hoisting of the Union Jack on Labuan Island. Although Brunei forfeited more territory in handing Labuan to the British, the Sultan calculated that he would benefit from a direct relationship with Whitehall. It seemed that London was becoming almost as concerned as he was about Brooke's expansionist instincts. A Treaty of Friendship and Commerce was signed between Britain and Brunei in 1847 in which the Sultan agreed not to cede any more territory to any power, except with the consent of the British government.

The Sultan's shrinking shadow

The treaty did not stop Brooke. His mission, since arriving in Sarawak, had been the destruction of the pirates who specialized in terrorizing Borneo's coastal communities. Because he knew the Sultan of Brunei was powerless to contain them, he calculated that their liquidation would be his best bargaining chip with the Sultan, and would enable him to prise yet more territory from the Sultan's grasp. Over the years he engaged the dreaded Balanini and Illanun pirates from Sulu and Mindanao as well as the so-called Sea-Dayaks and Brunei Malays, who regularly attacked Chinese, Bugis and other Asian trading ships off the Borneo coast. As a result, Sultan Abdul Mumin of Brunei ceded to Brooke the Saribas and Skrang districts, which became the Second Division of Sarawak in 1853 and, eight years later, he handed over the region that was to became the Third Division of Sarawak.

But by now the Sultan was as worried about territorial encroachment by the British as he was about the Brookes and as a counterweight to both, granted a 10-year concession to much of what is modern-day Sabah to the American consul in Brunei,

Charles Lee Moses. This 72,500-sq-km tract of North Borneo later became British North Borneo and is now the East Malaysian state of Sabah, see page 242.

With the emergence of British North Borneo, the British reneged on their agreement with the Sultan of Brunei again and the following year approved Brooke's annexation of the Baram river basin by Sarawak – which became its Fourth Division. The Sarawak frontier was advancing ever northwards.

In 1884 a rebellion broke out in Limbang and Rajah Charles Brooke refused to help the Sultan restore order. Sultan Hashim Jalilul Alam Aqamaddin, who acceded to the throne in 1885, wrote to Queen Victoria complaining that the British had not kept their word. Sir Frederick Weld was dispatched to mediate; he sympathized with the Sultan, and his visit resulted in the Protectorate Agreement of 1888 between Brunei and Britain, which gave London full control of the Sultanate's external affairs. When Brooke annexed Limbang in 1890 and united it with the Trusan Valley to form the Fifth Division of Sarawak, while the Queen's men looked on, the Sultan was reduced to a state of disbelief. His sultanate had now been completely surrounded by Brooke's Sarawak.

From sultanate to oilfield

In 1906 a British Resident was appointed to the Sultan's court to advise on all aspects of government except traditional customs and religion. In his book By God's Will, Lord Chalfont suggests that the British government's enthusiastic recommitment to the Sultanate through the treaty may have been motivated by Machiavellian desires. "More cynical observers have suggested that the new-found enthusiasm of the British Government may not have been entirely unconnected with the discovery of oil ... around the turn of the century." Oil exploration started in 1899, although it was not until the discovery of the Seria oilfield in 1929 that it merited commercial exploitation. Historian Mary Turnbull notes the quirk of destiny that ensured the survival of the micro-sultanate: "It was ironic that the small area left unswallowed by Sarawak and North Borneo should prove to be the most richly endowed part of the old sultanate."

The Brunei oilfield fell to the Japanese on 18 December 1942. Allied bombing and Japanese sabotage prior to the sultanate's liberation caused considerable damage to oil and port installations and urban areas, necessitating a long period of reconstruction in the late 1940s and early 1950s. Australian forces landed at Muara Beach on 10 July 1945. A British Military Administration ruled the country for a year, before Sultan Sir Ahmad Tajuddin took over.

In 1948 the Governor of Sarawak, which was by then a British crown colony, was appointed High Commissioner for Brunei, but the Sultanate remained what one commentator describes as "a constitutional anachronism". In September 1959 the UK resolved this by withdrawing the Resident and signing an agreement with the Sultan giving Whitehall responsibility for Brunei's defence and foreign affairs.

Because of his post-war influence on the development of Brunei, Sultan Omar was variously referred to as the 'father' and 'architect' of modern Brunei. He shaped his sultanate into the anti-Communist, non-democratic state it is today and, being an Anglophile, held out against independence from Britain. By the early 1960s, Whitehall was enthusiastically promoting the idea of a North Borneo Federation, encompassing Sarawak, Brunei and British North Borneo. But Sultan Omar did not want anything to do with the neighbouring territories – he felt Brunei's interests were more in keeping with those of peninsular Malaysia. The proposed federation would have been heavily dependent on Brunei's oil wealth. Kuala Lumpur did not need much persuasion that Brunei's joining the Federation of Malaysia was an excellent idea.

Democrats versus autocrat

In Brunei's first-ever general election in 1962, the left-wing Brunei People's Party (known by its Malay acronym, PRB) swept the polls. The party's election ticket had marked an end to the Sultan's autocratic rule, the formation of a democratic government and immediate independence. Aware that there was quite a lot at stake, the Sultan refused to let the PRB form a government. The Sultan's emergency powers, under which he banned the PRB, which were passed in 1962, remain in force, enabling him to rule by decree.

On 8 December 1962, the PRB, backed by the Communist North Kalimantan National Army – effectively its military wing – launched a revolt. The Sultan's insistence on British military protection paid off as the disorganized rebellion was quickly put down with the help of a Gurkha infantry brigade, and other British troops. Within four days the British troops had pushed the rebels into Limbang, where the hard core holed up. By 12 December, the revolt had been crushed and the vast majority of the rebels disappeared into the interior, pursued by the 7th Gurkha Rifles and Kelabit tribesmen.

Early in 1963, negotiations over Brunei joining the Malaysian Federation ran into trouble, to the disappointment of the British. The Malaysian Prime Minister, the late Tunku Abdul Rahman, wanted the Sultanate's oil and gas revenues to feed the federal treasury in Kuala Lumpur and made the mistake of making his intentions too obvious. The Tunku envisaged central government exercising absolute control over oil revenues – in the way it controls the oil wealth of Sabah and Sarawak today. Unhappy with this proposal and unwilling to become 'just another Malaysian sultan', Omar abandoned his intention to join the Federation.

Meanwhile, Indonesia's Sukarno was resolute in his objective of crushing the new Federation of Malaysia and launched his *Konfrontasi* between 1963 and 1966. Brunei offered itself as an operational base for the British army. But while Brunei supported Malaysia against Indonesia, relations between them became very strained following the declaration of the Federation in September 1963.

In 1975 Kuala Lumpur sponsored the visit of a PRB delegation to the UN, to propose a resolution calling on Brunei to hold elections, abolish restrictions on political parties and allow political exiles to return. In 1976 Bruneian government supporters protested against Malaysian 'interference' in Bruneian affairs. Nonetheless, the resolution was adopted by the UN in November 1977, receiving 117 votes in favour and none against. The United Kingdom abstained. Relations with Malaysia warmed after the death of Prime Minister Tun Abdul Razak in 1976, leaving the PRB weak and isolated. The party still operates in exile, although it is a spent force. Throughout the difficult years, the Sultan had used his favourite sport to conduct what was dubbed 'polo diplomacy', fostering links with like-minded Malaysian royalty despite the tensions in official bilateral relations.

By 1967, Britain's Labour government was pushing Sultan Omar to introduce a democratic system of government. Instead, however, the Sultan opted to abdicate in favour of his 21-year-old son, Hassanal Bolkiah. In November 1971, a new treaty was signed with Britain. London retained its responsibility for Brunei's external affairs, but its advisory role applied only to defence. The Sultan was given full control of all internal matters. Under a separate agreement, a battalion of British Gurkhas was stationed in the Sultanate. As Bruneians grew richer, the likelihood of another revolt receded.

Independence

Britain was keen to disentangle itself from the 1971 agreement: maintaining the protectorate relationship was expensive and left London open to criticism that it was maintaining an anachronistic colonial relationship. Brunei did not particularly relish the prospect of independence as, without British protection, it would be at the mercy of its more powerful neighbours. But in January 1979, having secured Malaysian and Indonesian assurances that they would respect its independence, the government signed another agreement with London, allowing for the Sultanate to become independent from midnight on 31 December 1983 after a century-and-a-half of close involvement with Britain and 96 years as a protectorate.

Brunei Background

In January 1984, Sultan Hassanal Bolkiah declared Brunei a 'democratic' monarchy. Three years later, he told his official biographer Lord Chalfont: "I do not believe that the time is ripe for elections and the revival of the legislature. What I would wish to see first is real evidence of an interest in politics by a responsible majority of the people... When I see some genuine interest among the citizenry, we may move towards elections." Independence changed little: absolute power is still vested in the Sultan, who mostly relies on his close family for advice. Following independence, the Sultan took up the offices of Prime Minister, Minister of Finance and Minister of Home Affairs. In 1986, he relinquished the latter two, but appointed himself Minister of Defence. He also took over responsibility for Finance on the resignation of his brother, Prince Jefri (see box, page 259).

In May 1985 the Brunei National Democratic Party (BNDP) was officially registered. Its aim was to introduce a parliamentary democracy under the Sultan. But just before the Malays-only party came into being, the government announced that government employees would not be allowed to join any other political party. In one stroke, the BNDP's potential membership was halved. In early 1986, the Brunei United National Party – an offshoot of the BNDP – was formed. Unlike its parent, its manifesto was multi-racial. The Sultan allowed these parties to exist until 27 January 1988 when he proscribed all political parties and imprisoned, without trial, two of the BNDP's leaders.

In the early 1990s, the Sultan was reported to have become increasingly worried about internal security and about Brunei's image abroad. Eight long-term political detainees, in prison since the abortive 1962 coup, were released in 1990. The last political detainee, the former deputy leader of the Brunei People's Party (PRB), Zaini Ahmad, is said to have written to the Sultan from prison following the releases. He apparently apologized for the 1962 revolt and called for the democratically elected Legislative Council – as outlined in the 1959 constitution – to be reconvened. To coincide with the Sultan's 50th birthday in 1996, Zaini Ahmad was released from prison. The exiled PRB has been greatly weakened and increasingly isolated since Brunei's relations with Malaysia became more cordial following the sultanate's accession to the Association of Southeast Asian Nations (ASEAN) in 1984 and clearly the Sultan and his adviser no longer feel threatened by the party.

Foreign relations

Brunei joined ASEAN on independence in 1984. Prince Mohammed, the foreign affairs minister, is said to be one of the brightest, more thoughtful members of the royal family, but in foreign policy, Brunei is 'timid' and goes quietly along with its ASEAN partners. Relations with Malaysia are greatly improved, but the sultanate's closest ties in the region, especially in fiscal and economic matters, are with Singapore. Their relationship was initially founded on their mutual distrust of the Malaysian Federation, which Brunei never joined and Singapore left two years after its inception in 1965. Singapore provides assistance in the training of Brunei's public servants and their currencies are linked.

As a member of ASEAN, on good terms with its neighbours, Brunei does not have many enemies to fear. But if its Scorpion tanks, Exocet rockets, Rapier ground-to-air missiles and helicopter gunships seem a little redundant, it is worth considering the recent experience of another oil-rich Islamic mini-state. As *The Economist* wrote, in October 1992, "substitute jungle for desert and Brunei is uncannily like Kuwait."

Modern Brunei

The last years of the 20th century saw Brunei's waning fortunes come to a head. By 2001, the country's per capita GDP was down almost 50% on what it had been at the time of Brunei's independence. The troubles began with the Asian Economic Crisis of 1997, and were further compounded by falling oil prices and by the collapse of the country's biggest non-oil company, Amedeo Development Corporation, which had run up debts of US$3.5 billion. Amedeo had been owned and run by the sultan's brother and Finance Minister, Prince Jefri, a man of excessive extravagance and little business acumen (see box, page 259). The prince resigned from his position as Finance Minister, and a national scandal followed, with the sultan eventually suing his brother for syphoning billions of dollars from the Brunei Investment Agency, for which the prince had served as chairman. The brothers eventually settled out of court, but the publicity has had lasting consequences, damaging Brunei's credibility with foreign investors. Brunei's shaken economy has now stabilized, but the whole episode has served to highlight just how over-dependent Brunei is on oil (at present Brunei's economy relies almost exclusively on exports of oil and LNG – liquefied natural gas). As oil prices peak and trough, so do Brunei's fortunes. More worrying, the nation's oil and gas reserves are expected to dry up in 2018 and 2033 respectively. This vulnerability has prompted the sultan to initiate reforms – both economic and political. Diversification of the economy has become a priority and the sultan has curbed government spending while encouraging the growth of privatization. One of his primary visions is to transform Brunei into an 'Offshore Financial Haven' (in the vein of Bermuda or the Isle of Man), and the government is presently putting legislation in place to this end. So-called 'Islamic Finance' is also being targeted. In 2000, the BIFC (Brunei International Finance Centre) began trading successfully. The International Brunei Exchange (IBX), established in 2002, was less successful, and has since closed down. There are also plans to take advantage of Brunei's strategic geographical position on the East-West trade route by building a huge container terminal at the Muara port. Ecotourism, meanwhile, is another of Brunei's trump cards for the future (more than 70% of the land mass remains cloaked in virgin rainforest). Still, many commentators point out that visitor figures are likely to remain low until the government eases laws on the prohibition of alcohol. Perhaps more significant has been the political fallout of Brunei's economic problems. The new-found desire to attract investors and tourists has forced the sultan to reconsider Brunei's international image. There has been a shift away from the Islamic conservatism of the 1990s – a fact underlined by the dismissal in 2005 of the Education Minister, a conservative Islamist whose introduction of a strict religious education had become increasingly unpopular. Prior to this, the first tentative move towards 21st-century democracy was instigated, with the appointment of a new legislative council. In September 2004, the country's parliament re-opened for the first time since independence. Though no political parties are allowed, a new 45-seat council was called for, with 15 elected members. To all intents and purposes, the sultan still retains authoritarian control over his kingdom – just as his ancestors have for six centuries. Nevertheless, the pending elections are being viewed as the first step towards a modern Brunei – a Brunei without oil, but with a new politics of consensus.

Population

In the days of Charles Brooke, the sultanate had a population of about 20,000. In 2005, it stood at 372,361. The city-state of Singapore has more than 10 times as many people. Today 60% of the country's population lives in towns; more than half is aged under 20, a third under 14. At 1.9% a year, Brunei has one of the fastest-growing populations in the region; it also has the region's lowest death rate and second lowest infant mortality rate after Singapore; Bruneians' average life expectancy is 75. About 67% of the population is Malay, 15% Chinese, 6% indigenous tribal groups and 12% other (see People, below); there are also some 100,000 expatriate workers – both professionals and labourers. The average density of population is low: about 64 people per sq km; most are concentrated along the narrow coastal belt.

Land and environment

Geography and geology

Brunei Darussalam lies about 400 km north of the equator, between 4° and 5° north, on the northwest coast of Borneo. The sultanate has a 160 km-long coastline, facing the South China Sea. The country is divided into four districts: Brunei/Muara, Tutong, Belait and Temburong.

Territorially, modern Brunei is the rump of what was once a sprawling empire. Today the sultanate has a land area of 5769 sq km – a pinprick on the map, about twice the size of Luxembourg. In 1981 the government bought a cattle ranch at Willeroo, in Australia's Northern Territory, which is larger than the whole of Brunei. As a country, it is a geographical absurdity; its two wedges of territory are separated by Limbang, ceded to the expansionist Charles Brooke, Rajah of Sarawak in 1890. Bruneians commute between the Temburong district and Bandar Seri Begawan in speedboats nicknamed 'flying coffins'.

Most of Brunei occupies a low alluvial coastal plain. There are four main rivers, flowing north into the South China Sea. The coastal lowlands and river valleys are characterized by a flat or gently undulating landscape, rarely rising more than 15 m above sea level. The coastline is mainly sandy except for a stretch of rocky headlands between Muara and Pekan Tutong. These cliffs rise to a height of about 30 m, where the north coastal hills meet the South China Sea. Further west, the Andulau Hills stand at the north end of a watershed separating the Belait and Tutong drainage basins.

Towards the interior of West Brunei, along the border with Sarawak and in South Temburong district, it gets much hillier. In West Brunei there are two upland areas, comprised of sandstones and shale: the Ladan Hills run north to south between the Tutong and Limbang basins. Bukit Bedawan is the highest of these, at 529 m. In Belait district, near the border with Sarawak, are the Labi Hills – the highest being Bukit Teraja at 417 m. The south half of Temburong district is much more mountainous, with deep, narrow valleys and several hills of over 600 m. The highest of these is Bukit Pagon at 1850 m, although the summit itself is actually outside Brunei.

The Seria oilfield, the source of Brunei's liquidity, lies on a narrow anticline, a quarter of which is submerged by the sea. All the oil comes from a strip just 13 km long and 2.5 km wide. The oil is in fractured blocks of sandstone between 240 m and 3000 m below the surface. Some of the oil under the sea is accessed by wells drilled from the shore which reach more than 1.5 km out to sea.

Climate

Brunei is only 5° north of the equator and so is characterized, like the rest of north and west Borneo, by consistently hot and sticky weather: uniform temperature, high humidity (average 82%) and regular rainfall.

Daily temperatures average at 28°C. Mid-day temperatures rarely exceed 35°C; at night it is unusual for the temperature to dip below 21°C. The average daily minimum temperature is 23°C, the maximum 32°C.

Rainfall is well distributed throughout the year but two seasons are distinguishable: there is less rainfall between February and August, and the rainy season sets in during September and runs through to the end of January. The northeast monsoon peaks in December and January and is characterized by short-lived, violent downpours. Even during the monsoon season, though, there is a 50% chance of it not raining each day and a daily average of seven hours of sunshine. The annual average rainfall is over 2500 mm a year, nearly five times that of London or more than double New York's annual rainfall. The south interior region, including Temburong district, is wetter, with up to 4060 mm a year. The west coast areas get between 2540 and 3300 mm of rainfall a year. In Bandar Seri Begawan, the average annual rainfall is 2921 mm.

Flora and fauna

Like much of the neighbouring Malaysian state of Sarawak, the low-lying areas of Brunei are characterized by peat swamp forest which is unsuited to agriculture. In parts the peat is up to 9 m thick and cannot support permanent agriculture. About 70% of Brunei is still covered in lush virgin jungle. If secondary forest – known as *belukar* – is included, about 80% of Brunei's land area is still forested.

Apart from the peat swamp forest, Brunei has areas of heath forest (*kerangas*) on sandy soils near the coast, and mangrove, which grows on the tidal mudflats around Brunei Bay and in the Belait and Tutong estuaries. The most common mangrove tree is the bakau, which grows to a height of about 9 m and has stilt roots to trap sediment. The *bakau* was the source of *cutch* – a dye made from boiling its bark, and used in leather-tanning – which was produced at Brunei Bay until the 1950s. Bakau wood also made useful piles for stilt-houses in Bandar Seri Begawan's Kampong Ayer as it is resistant to rotting, and excellent charcoal. Also on the coast, between Kuala Belait and Muara, are stretches of casuarina forest.

✱ For more details on jungle flora and fauna, see page 330.

Away from the coastal plain and the river valleys, the forest changes to lowland rainforest – or mixed dipterocarp forest – which supports at least eight commercial hardwood species. The *Dipterocarpacae* family forms the jungle canopy, 30-50 m above the ground. Timber from Brunei's jungle is used locally – none is exported. By 1990, logging firms were required to use sustainable management techniques and within a year, felling was cut to half the 1989 level. Forest reserves have been expanded and cover 320,000 ha. Indeed, Brunei has some of Southeast Asia finest forests – despite its small size when compared with the neighbouring Malaysian states of Sabah and Sarawak and with Indonesian Borneo (Kalimantan).

Wildlife

Brunei's jungle has been left largely intact – thanks to its oil wealth there is no need to exploit the forest. Loggers and shifting cultivators have been less active than they have in neighbouring territories and the forest fauna have been less disturbed. Their only disruptions come from a few upriver tribespeople, a handful of wandering Penan hunter-gatherers, the odd scientist and the occasional platoon of muddied soldiers enduring jungle warfare training exercises. Relatively few tourists venture into Brunei's jungle as Sarawak's nearby national parks are much more accessible and better known. 1996, however, marked the opening of the Ulu Temburong National Park with its network of wooden walkways and a fantastic canopy walkway. What is more, Brunei is the best place for spotting the rare proboscis monkey (see box, page 262). For those who have access to a car, there are also several jungle trails on Brunei's doorstep.

Brunei boasts much of Borneo's jungle exotica. For oil explorers and their families in the early 1900s, some local residents proved more daunting than others. Up until the 1960s, encounters with large crocodiles were commonplace in Brunei, and in the oil town of Seria they posed a constant menace to the local community. In August 1959 Brunei Shell Petroleum was forced to recruit a professional crocodile-catcher. Mat Yassin bin Hussin claimed to have caught and destroyed more than 700 crocodiles in a career spanning four decades, the largest being a highly unlikely 8.5-m long man-eater which had devoured 12 Ibans south of Kuala Belait.

Mat Yassin's technique was to sprinkle gold dust into the river as part of a magic ritual, then to dangle chickens over bridges on baited rattan hooks. According to GC Harper, a Seria oilfield historian, Mat Yassin would wait until a crocodile jumped for the bait and then he would "blow down its snout with the aid of a blowpipe to make the strong reptile weak. It could then be dragged up the river bank and its jaws tied before it was destroyed." Mat Yassin silenced cynics when he landed two maneaters in as many days and said he had come across an old white crocodile which was considered sacred; he refused to touch it because it "could never be destroyed either by bullets or by magic".

Culture

People

Brunei 'Malays', who make up 67% of the sultanate's population, are mostly Kedayans or Melanaus, indigenous to north Borneo. There was no great migration of Malays from the peninsula. Similarly, few Iban migrated into what is modern Brunei, although in the 19th century, they pushed up to the middle-reaches of Sarawak's rivers, which in those days came under the sultanate's ambit. Ibans, Muruts, Kedayans, Dayaks and even Dusuns are all represented in the 6% of the population labelled 'indigenous tribal groups' (for more detail on individual tribal groups, see page 323).

Today most Bruneian Malays are well off and well educated; more than half of them have secure government jobs. Car ownership in Brunei is a telling indicator of Bruneians' affluence: the country has one of the highest car population ratios in the world. Recognizing that things might get out of hand, in 1995 the authorities introduced a new car tax to try and curb Brunei's love affair with the automobile. The standard of living is high by Southeast Asian standards although there are poorer communities living in Kampong Ayer and Kampong Kianggeh (near the open market). Many of these are recent immigrants – there is a high level of illegal immigration from the neighbouring states of Sabah and Sarawak as well as from Kalimantan.

The government policy of 'Bruneization' discriminates positively in favour of the Malays and against the Chinese, who make up 30% of the population. Most of the Chinese are fairly wealthy as they account for the vast majority of Brunei's private sector businessmen. Unlike the Malays, the Chinese did not automatically become citizens of Brunei at independence – even if they could trace their ancestry back several generations. The question of citizenship is very important as only citizens of Brunei can enjoy the benefits of the welfare state – free education, health care, subsidized housing and government jobs.

Religion

Brunei is a Sunni Muslim monarchy; the state motto, 'Always render service by God's guidance', is emblazoned on the crescent on Brunei's national flag. Islam appears to have been firmly established in the Sultanate by the mid-15th century. Today it is the official religion, and a religious council advises the Sultan, who is head of the Islamic faith in Brunei, on all Islamic matters.

Arts and crafts

Brass is said to have been introduced into Brunei at the end of the 15th century, when the Sultanate became particularly famous for its brass cannon, which were used in battle and to convey messages from one village to another about deaths, births and festivities – such as the beginning and end of Ramadan. The 500 cannon and guns in the Brunei Museum are largely of local manufacture. Brass cannon and gongs were items of currency and barter and often used in dowries, particularly among the tribal Belaits and Dusuns. Brassware is a prized family heirloom, and was the basis of fines in the traditional legal system. In 1908 there were more than 200 brass workers in Brunei, but by the mid-1970s their numbers had reportedly fallen to fewer than 10. Today, traditional casting by the 'lost wax' technique is being revived. Brunei's **silversmiths** have a good reputation for their intricate designs, betelnut boxes being a speciality. **Gold jewellery**, mostly 22 and 24 carat is also reasonable.

The best known local **textile** is *Kain Jong Sarat*, a cotton sarong, usually about 2 m in length, woven with more than 1000 gold threads on a handloom. Today Jong Sarat are only used on ceremonial occasions. The *Sukma-Indera* is distinguished by its multi-coloured floral patterns, while the *Tenunan* is woven with gold thread and worn by men round the waist on Hari Raya Aidil Adha; it can cost up to B$1000.

Kalimantan

Introduction

Few tourists make it to Kalimantan: travel can be difficult and facilities, beyond the main cities, are not as well developed as elsewhere in Indonesia. But, for anyone seeking an alternative insight into the country, it offers a great deal: jungle trekking and whitewater rafting, orang-utans and proboscis monkeys, tribal villages and traditional cultures.

The island of Borneo has always held a mystical fascination for Westerners – it was a vast, isolated, jungle-covered island, where headhunters ran wild, and which, if romantic myths were to be believed, was rich in gold and diamonds. It is the third largest island in the world (after Greenland and New Guinea) and Kalimantan's 549,000 sq km (nearly 30% of Indonesia's total land area) form the major part. Most of the population is concentrated in a handful of coastal cities; the interior is populated by various Dayak tribes, whose villages are scattered along the Kalimantan's river banks.

Kalimantan

★ Don't miss...

1 Banjarmasin Charter a *klotok* and head off to the floating market and explore the waterways of Banjarmasin, page 289.

2 Martapura and Cempaka For an alternative to the usual view of Kalimantan, visit the diamond fields at Cempaka, outside Banjarmasin, and then the jewellery shops at nearby Martapura, page 291.

3 Tanjung Puting National Park Pay a visit to the orphaned and rescued animals at the Orang-Utan Rehabilitation Centre, page 293.

4 Meratus Mountains Trek in the Meratus Mountains and wildlife reserve, stay overnight in a Dayak longhouse and perhaps include rafting on the Amandit River, page 296.

5 Mahakam River Explore the river and its associated lakes and Dayak villages and even try your hand at some kayaking, page 302.

South Kalimantan (Kalsel and Kalteng)

The timber industry is an important source of revenue for Kalsel. Even with the cataclysmic fires of 1982-1983 and 1997 – which were concentrated in already logged areas rather than untouched forest – it is estimated that perhaps 40% of the province's 3,700,000 ha is still officially forested. The area between the road and the coast, the Pegunungan Meratus, the range of mountains which forms the backbone of the state, is still covered in primary forest – it is too remote even for loggers and much of the logging has been along the coast and on either side of the main road to Balikpapan.

To the west of this range is the Barito River, which has its headwaters deep in the interior. The coastal area is low lying and swampy; the name of the provincial capital, Banjarmasin, derives from the Javanese term meaning 'saline garden'. Kalsel's coasts are dominated by rice land – where high-yielding varieties have been successfully introduced. The hybrid strains have been named after Kalsel's main rivers, the Barito and Negara. Over the past 50 years most of these rice fields have been reclaimed from the tidal swamps. Paddy seedlings are planted in the swamps during the dry season, and in the wet season they flood to a depth of 2-3 m. This padi air dalam *(deep water paddy) is harvested from boats. These swamplands are also home to another oddity: the swimming buffalo of South Kalimantan. Herds of water buffalo paddle from one grazing area to another, sometimes swimming long distances. Farmers build log platforms (called* kalang*) as resting places for their buffalo (which are known as* kalang buffalo*). In recent years the unchecked spread of water hyacinth has begun to threaten their grazing grounds. The best time to visit Kalsel is during the dry season from June to September.* ▸▸ *For Sleeping, Eating and other listings, see pages 294-298.*

Background

Legend has it that a kingdom centred on the southeast corner of Borneo was founded by Ampu-jatmika, the son of a merchant from India's Coromandel coast, who settled in the area in the 12th century. He called it Negara-dipa. It became a vassal state of Java's Hindu kingdom of Majapahit in the 13th century and from then on, the city retained close cultural and trade links with Java, which led to its conversion to Islam in the 1540s. The city of Banjarmasin was founded by the Hindu ruler Pangeran Samudera (The Prince from the Sea) in 1526; it was he who first embraced Islam, changing his name to Pangeran Suriansyah in the process.

The Banjarese sultanate – which continued through a succession of 22 rulers – was the most important in Borneo (other than Brunei, on the north coast), and its tributary states included all the smaller sultanates on the west and east coasts of the island. However, in 1860, after several years of political turmoil, the Dutch abolished the sultanate altogether, and installed its administrative headquarters, for all of what is now Kalimantan, in Banjarmasin. This sparked the four years' Banjarmasin War against the Dutch occupiers; long after the uprising was put down, the Dutch presence was deeply resented. The hero of the guerrilla struggle against the Dutch was Pangeran Antasari (his name immortalized in many Kalimantan street names), who was born in the nearby city of Martapura. He unified the Banjarese, the Dayaks and the Buginese

● *A Banjar proverb goes* "Sekali jukung didayuh, haram balabuh" *(Once you start paddling,*
● *don't dock).*

against the Dutch, and had a 100,000 guilder price on his head. He died in 1862, having evaded capture, and 106 years later was proclaimed an Indonesian national hero.

South Kalimantan or Kalsel is the smallest and most densely populated of the four provinces in Indonesian Borneo: it has a population of 2,600,000. The population density is about 60 per sq km – low by Javanese standards, but high in comparison with Kalimantan's other sparsely populated provinces. Kalsel used to include all of Central Kalimantan (Kalteng), until the latter's predominantly Dayak population won administrative autonomy from the Muslim Banjarese. The Banjarese are descended from a mixture of Dayak, Sumatran Malay, Javanese and Buginese stock – although their dialect is close to classical Malay.

Banjarmasin ⬤🌙✿⬛🔺🚌🌗 ➠ *pp294-298. Colour map 4, C3.*

In 1930 the the provincial capital, Banjarmasin – the name derives from the Javanese term 'saline garden' – had a population of just 66,000, but this still made it the largest town on the island. Today the figure must be close to, or more than, 500,000. Like several other cities in Asia, Banjarmasin has been dubbed 'The Venice of the

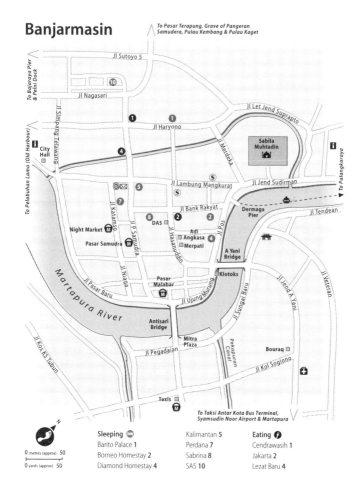

Banjarmasin

To Pasar Terapung, Grave of Pangeran Samudera, Pulau Kembang & Pulau Kaget

Sleeping 🛏
Barito Palace **1**
Borneo Homestay **2**
Diamond Homestay **4**
Kalimantan **5**
Perdana **7**
Sabrina **8**
SAS **10**

Eating 🍴
Cendrawasih **1**
Jakarta **2**
Lezat Baru **4**

0 metres (approx) 50
0 yards (approx) 50

Orient'. It might be an over-worked cliché, but if there is one city that deserves the epithet, this is it. Dominated by its waterways, most of Banjarmasin's population lives in pile houses and floating houses (*lanting*) on the sides of the Martapura, Barito, Kuin and Andai rivers, along and around which the city is built. These rivers – and the canals which link them – are the focus of day-to-day life in Banjarmasin. The waterways are alive with people bathing, swimming, fishing and washing their clothes; they clean their teeth in them, squat over them and shop on them.

Although Banjarmasin may be the largest urban centre in Borneo, it does not exude wealth in the same way that other cities do. Periodic outbreaks of cholera, and a shortage of drinking water in the dry season, means that wealthier potential inhabitants tend to live elsewhere – such as at Banjarbaru/Martapura some 40 km away.

Ins and outs

Getting there Syamsudin Noor airport is 27 km east of Banjarmasin, Kalimantan's largest city. There are flights to Balikpapan. Long-distance buses for Balikpapan, Palangkaraya and Samarinda leave from the Taksi Antar Kota terminal, 6 km from the town centre. Passenger ferries depart from Bajaraya Pier for Palangkaraya and beyond. Speedboats to Palangkaraya depart from the Dermaga pier in front of the Grand Mosque. **Pelni** (the Indonesian shipping company) ships leave from the Trisakti port.

Getting around *Bemos* (small pickups) follow fixed routes while rickety *bajajs* (three-wheeled scooters) are available for hire. *Ojeks* (motorcycle taxis), *becaks* (bicycle rickshaws) and taxis provide the full house of road-going public transport. More entertaining is to charter a *klotok* (motorized gondola) to explore Banjarmasin's waterways.

Tourist information **Dinas Pariwisata Kalimantan Selatan** ⓘ *Jl Panjaitan 34, Mon-Fri, closes at 1130 on Fri*, the Kalsel provincial tourist office, is the best organized in Kalimantan; it produces some reasonably informative literature. The **City Tourist Office** ⓘ *Jl Pasar Baru*, is next to the City Hall.

Sights

The number of tourists visiting Banjarmasin was growing fast for much of the early and mid-1990s; an estimated 30,000 every year, mostly from Java and Bali. However, this has since tailed off; the economic crisis, combined with the fires and the bad press that was generated by the communal violence of the late 1990s, understandably, directed people elsewhere. Nonetheless, there is plenty to see in Banjarmasin, and much of the sightseeing can be done from a *klotok*.

The imposing **Sabila Muhtadin Mosque** (Grand Mosque), built in 1980, dominates the city's waterfront. Every Friday, 15,000 Muslims gather for prayer in its cool marbled interior; about 98% of Banjarmasin's population is Muslim. The Banjarese became Muslims when the local prince, Pangeran Samudera, converted to Islam around 1540, after which he became known as Pangeran Suriansyah. The city has more mosques per head of population than anywhere else in Indonesia – about one for every 40 families. Mosques, and their smaller equivalent *surau*, line the city's waterways – their domes and minarets, standing out among the parabola satellite dishes and television aerials on the skyline.

Muslim sensitivities should be observed in Banjarmasin: women should dress modestly and should avoid smoking in public.

At the 1989 World Expo' in Vancouver, Canada, a Bugis schooner sailed over from Banjarmasin carrying skilled boat builders and the materials to build another one. It was completed within the year and was one of the stars of the show. The boat builders, welcomed home as national heroes, received medals from President Suharto.

The highlight of most people's visit to Banjarmasin is the **Pasar Terapung** (floating market) ⓘ *early morning only, 0400-0900 or 1000,* which lies on the western outskirts of town on the Barito River. Unlike floating markets elsewhere in the region, this is far from being a tourist showpiece. The market is big and very lively – perhaps because sellers can actively pursue buyers, paddling after them in their sampans and canoes (*jukung*) or chasing them in their *klotoks*. The market includes a floating clinic (*posyandu*) and floating pharmacy; as well as *jukung*-vendors selling rice, fish, fruit and vegetables, there are floating boutique shops, hardware shops, supermarkets, petrol stations and soup stalls. There is even a floating parking attendant, who extracts money from each of the stallholders. There are also delightful floating tea shops; these little covered sampans have their front sections covered in plates of sticky rice, doughnuts, cakes and delicacies, which customers draw up alongside and spear with a long harpoon-rod handed over by the teaman. When the sun comes up, the *tanggui* – the famous wide-brimmed Banjar hat – comes into its own as marketeers shelter from the heat under its lofty rim. The floating market starts early and finishes early, but there is little point getting there much before 0700. By 0600 it is just light enough to see, so the river trip down the canals to the market, as Banjarmasin is awakening, is fantastic.

En route to the floating market, from town, in Kuin village, is the **Grave of Pangeran Samudera** (see page 288). Next to the floating market and along the canals there are *pengger gajian* – small family-run **sawmills** – making sawn timber for the construction industry and for the building of Bugis schooners. The main schooner-building yards – in riverside dry docks called *alalak* – are just upstream from the floating market at the confluence of the Barito and Andai rivers. But the best place to see the schooners is at the **Pelabuhan Lama** (Old Harbour) on the Martapura River, not far from the town centre. The Orang Bugis, who still build their beautiful sailing ships in the traditional manner, live in little pockets along the Kalsel coast (there is another boat-building yard at Batu Licin on the coast, 225 km east of Banjarmasin). The schooners, with their sweeping bows and tall masts, are known as *perahu layar* (sailing boats). These days, most of them have powerful engines too, so they are commonly known as PLMs (*parahu layar motor*). The schooners are still in frequent use as trading vessels and most have a crew of about 30, living in quarters at the stern. On the opposite bank of the Barito River to the floating market there are several large plywood factories, some owned by the cronies of former president Suharto.

Pulau Kembang (Flower Island) ⓘ *just downriver from the floating market, in the middle of the Barito River, donation on arrival,* is better known as 'Monkey Island' because of the troops of monkeys found there. Do not touch the big, male, long-tailed macaques; they can be vicious. A trip here is often included at the end of a tour to the floating market; alternatively, take a *klotok* from under A Yani Bridge.

About 12 km further down the Barito River is **Pulau Kaget**, also in the middle of the river. The river around the island is one of the best places to observe proboscis monkeys (*Nasalis larvatus* – see page 331), which are active on the shoreline at dawn and dusk. The local name for these is the *kera Belanda* – the monkey that looks like a Dutchman. The round trip takes 1½ to two hours.

Around Banjarmasin ⇢ *Colour map 4, C3.*

Martapura and the Cempaka diamond fields
ⓘ *Martapura's diamond fields are shut on Fri, as are the stone-cutting and polishing workshops; most jewellery shops do, however, stay open. Fri, however, is the best day to see the Martapura market in full swing.*

The focus of Kalsel's gemstone mining industry, these diamond fields are near the village of **Cempaka**, 10 km from **Martapura**, about 40 km southeast of Banjarmasin.

There, labourers dig 5-m-deep shafts using techniques little changed in over a century, extending tunnels from the bottom of the shafts. The stony mud is handed to the top in bamboo baskets and then sifted and swilled in flowing water in the hope of striking lucky. If other precious stones are found in the pan, it is taken as an indication that a diamond is nearby. Many large diamonds have been unearthed at Cempaka over the past 150 years; the biggest was the 167.5-carat *Intan Trisakti* diamond, found in 1965. In 1990, a 48-carat diamond was found and was named *Intan Galuh Pampung*.

Diamonds are traditionally believed to be benevolent spirits, with characters like virtuous virgins. The miners treat them with respect, referring to them as *Galuh*, or 'Princess'. A rigorously observed code of social conduct is in force in the diamond field so that nothing is done to frighten or offend 'her' in case 'she' refuses to appear. This includes the barring of sour-tasting food (said to be craved for by pregnant women), the banning of whistling (a vulgar means of attracting a girl's attention), and smoking is also taboo in case it offends Galuh. But there is also a saying: *Siapa yang mendapat batu besar, dia pasti susah nanti* – 'Whoever finds a big stone will eventually suffer'. The problem is that large stones are so valuable that they overwhelm the local marketing system. Local traders cannot buy them, such is their value. And *orang kecil*, little people, should not hold such wealth in their hands. *Orang besar* – big men – in Banjarmasin quickly come to hear of these extraordinary finds and the miners find that wealth, if they get it, quickly turns sour. Other precious metals and stones mined at the site include gold, sapphires and amethysts. Cempaka is one of at least six diamond-mining villages in the area. Cempaka can be reached from the *bemo* terminal in Martapura (take green minibuses to the diamond fields).

Around 30,000 people are employed in the gemstone industry, both in the mines and at Martapura. The latter is the gemstone cutting and polishing centre, and there are many shops selling stones of all qualities. The best of Martapura's jewellery shops is **Kayu Tangi** ① *Jl Sukaramail 4/J*; it is the only one where stones are guaranteed. They have a good selection of precious and semi-precious stones, from diamonds to rough-cut lapis lazuli, but it is still important to bargain. Although this is the best shop in Kalsel for stones, they are not well finished and will probably require recutting and repolishing. There is a **polishing factory** ① *closed Fri*, next door, and many stalls selling semi-precious stones, beads and jewellery – including *manik manik* stone necklaces – in the **Pasar Niaga** market ① *some shops close Fri*. There is a vast and very colourful **vegetable market** ① *next to Pasar Niaga, Mon-Sun, but the Fri market is the biggest*. Behind the vegetable market is a building with shops where silversmiths make rings.

Lambung Mangkurat State Museum ① *Tue-Thu and Sun 0830-1400, Fri 0830-1100, Sat 0830-1300, 750 Rp*, housed in a dubious modern interpretation of a traditional Banjar-style building at Banjarbaru, near Martapura, has historical and cultural displays on Kalsel. On the ground floor there is a life-size, ulin-wood (*belian*/ironwood) *tambangan* boat (the traditional Banjar river boat, in use from the 17th century to the 1950s). To get to the museum, take a taxi, minibus or bus (45 minutes) from the intercity bus terminal, or a speedboat from the Dermaga Pier in front of the Grand Mosque.

Kalteng ⊜⊜ ➤ *pp294-298. Colour map 4, B2.*

The vast province of Kalteng is most easily reached from Banjarmasin, but few tourists go there; it is the domain of Dayaks and loggers. It is Borneo's Dayak heartland; the province was created in the late 1950s when the Dayak tribes sought autonomy from the Muslims of Banjarmasin. It covers nearly 154,000 sq km and has a population of 1,400,000. The north part of Kalteng is particularly remote, and is fringed by the mountains of the Schwaner and Muller ranges. The south part of the state is nearly all marshland, with virtually impenetrable mangrove swamps which reach inland as far as 100 km.

Sasirangan tie-dyes – from shaman to shop shelf

The bright Banjar cloth is called *sasirangan*, and was traditionally believed to hold magical powers capable of driving out evil spirits and curing illnesses. The cloth could be made only by shamans – it was *pamali* (taboo) for common people to make it – and was designed to cure specific medical problems, from headaches to malaria. It was tailor made by the shaman for specific customers and was known as *kain pamintan*, or 'the cloth that is made to order'. Patterns had particular significance to the spirit world, and dragons, bamboo shoots, rocks and waves, lotus and sun motifs were prescribed like drugs at a pharmacy. Colours were also important: the most common ones were yellow, green, red and purple. The afflicted person's medical prescription was then worn as a headcloth (*laung*) by men and a scarf (*serudung*) by women, who would also wear *sasirangan* blouses. Babies swung in *sasirangan* hammocks and children wore *sasirangan* sarungs to protect them from disease.

When pharmaceuticals arrived in Banjarmasin, the shamans began to go out of business, and with their demise, the *sasirangan* faded into obscurity. Realizing that the art form had all but disappeared, local women enthusiastically began to revive the dying art in the 1980s. Within a few years, hundreds of tiny cottage industries had sprung up across the town, and in a bid to popularize the material, *sasirangan* shirts and blouses were presented to celebrities. The cloth was traditionally coloured with natural dyes: yellow came from turmeric root, brown from the areca nut and red from the karabintang fruit; today, chemical dyes are used, but the tie-dye procedure is lengthy: a simple *sasirangan* with basic motifs can take four days to produce, while complex ones are said to take several months.

Palangkaraya

This provincial capital was built virtually from scratch in 1957 and in 1991, at the time of the last census, had a population of 100,000. It has little to offer the tourist. There is a small **state museum** ① *Jalan Cilik Riwut, 2 km from town, Tue-Sun 0800-1200, 1600-1800*, containing some Dayak heirlooms; mostly brass and ceramic jars. The only real tourist attraction here is the Tanjung Puting Orang-Utan Rehabilitation Centre, see below, which is still 8-10 hours by road.

Pangkalanbun

Few people bother to stay in this riverside town – or if they do, it's probably not out of choice. However, it is necessary to make a stop in Pangkalanbun to obtain a permit to visit the Tanjung Puting National Park (see below), 25 km away. Permits and guides are available from **police headquarters** ① *1 km from centre of town on Jl Diponegoro, daily 0700-1700*. To get there, take a *bemo* from the Janan Kasamayuda-Jalan Santrek intersection. If organizing this leaves enough time, most people move straight on to Kumai (see below), on the park boundary.

Tanjung Puting National Park

The 300,040-ha Tanjung Puting National Park was founded by Dr Birute Galdikas in the early 1970s, in an area with a wild population of orang-utans. The park straddles several forest types, including swamp forest, heath forest and lowland dipterocarp rainforest. The unusual heath forest is found in the northern area of the park where stunted trees, many with undersized leaves, grow on impoverished white-sand soils.

The swamp forest is concentrated in the central portion of the park and many of the trees here are adapted to periodic flooding with stilt roots. Anyone who is sick is strictly barred from entering the centre.

The **Orang-Utan Rehabilitation Centre** ① *www.orangutan.org/facts/tanjung*, is smaller and less touristy than Sepilok in Sabah (see page 222) but has the same mission: to look after and rehabilitate orang-utans orphaned by logging or rescued from captivity. In addition to the orang-utans, there is a large population of other fauna in Tanjung Puting, including proboscis monkeys (see page 331), crab-eating macaques, clouded leopards, false gharial crocodiles, monitor lizards and over 200 species of bird.

❈ Malaria is rife in this region. Anti-malarial drugs are essential, see Health, page 44.

There are two main stations in the park: **Camp Leakey**, the main research centre, and **Tanjung Harapan**, which was set up in the late 1980s as an overflow centre (it is the one visited by most tourists). At Camp Leakey, orang-utans are fed at 1500, 1600 and 1700. There is an ongoing proboscis monkey research programme at **Natai Lengknas**, within the park.

Permits A police permit must be obtained in Pangkalanbun (see above) before making the 25-km road trip to **Kumai**; here, visitors should obtain a park permit from the **Conservation Office** (**PHPA Office**) ① *T0532-61508, F61187, Mon-Thu and Sat 0700-1400, Fri 0700-1100, permits cost 2000 Rp per day, and a boat is another 2000 Rp per day, a photocopy of the police letter and a photocopy of the 1st page of your passport is required to secure the park permit.* Guides are not required for exploring the park. The boatmen know the channels well. However, guides are available from the PHPA office in Kumai or from the ranger posts at Tanjung Harapan and Podok Tanggui (15,000 Rp per day). Tours to the park can be organized from Banjarmasin.

◉ Sleeping

Banjarmasin *p289, map p289*

A Kalimantan, Jl Lambung Mangkurat, T0511-66818, F67345. Top of the range in Banjarmasin following renovation, has its own shopping centre, good sports facilities and restaurants. Popular with foreign business people.

B Barito Palace, Jl Haryono MT 16-20, T0511-67300, F52240. A/c, restaurants, large clean pool, spacious upmarket foyer, satellite TV. Clean bright rooms, beware the north-facing rooms as some are bombarded by noise coming from the nightclub and the gruesome town amusement park.

C-E Diamond Homestay, Jl Simpang Hasanuddin II, T0511-66100. Like the **Borneo Homestay**, this is a backpackers' haunt. Cheaper than the **Borneo** but less room choice. Otherwise, a good place to stay.

C-E Borneo Homestay, Jl Simpang Hasanuddin 33, T0511-66545, F57515. Run by Johan and Lina Yasin. Johan is perhaps the friendliest tour guide in Banjar, offering jungle treks, diamond mine tours, canal and floating-market cruise. This simple accommodation is set just back from the river (next to A Yani Bridge). Be sure to add your name to the thousands who've signed the walls around the rooftop veranda bar. The best-value homestay in Borneo and the only place in Banjar which is geared to foreign backpackers. Highly recommended.

D SAS, Jl Kacapiring 2, T0511-53054, 53146. Some a/c, restaurant, traditional Banjar house in very quiet location, but rooms a bit dark, breakfast included, ticketing assistance, excellent bamboo-furnished family room with fridge and separate living area for up to 3 travellers. Highly recommended.

D-E Perdana, Jl Brig Jend Katamso 8, T0511-69029, F67988. A/c extra charge, restaurant, airy, bright and clean, good range of rooms, friendly staff, eager to help with ticketing and taxis, **Merpati** (airline) office next door, room rate includes breakfast.

E Sabrina, Jl Bank Rakyat (Jalan Samudra end) 51, T0511-54442. Some a/c, 1400 checkout, clean but characterless, some rooms a bit dark and pokey, some triple rooms, all standards have basic shared bathrooms.

Palangkaraya *p293*
C-D **Dandang Tingang**, Jl Yos Sudarso 13,
T0536-21805. A/c, restaurant and bar, multi-
lingual staff. Best hotel around though a little
out of town (take taxi bus C). Recommended.
D-E **Yanti**, Jl A Yani 82A, T0536-21634. Very
clean little hotel, more expensive rooms with
a/c, attached bathrooms and hot water.
E **Mina**, Jl Nias 17, T0536-22182. Some a/c,
pleasant staff, clean rooms and a good place
to stay at this price, popular so often full.

Pangkalanbun *p293*
C **Hotel Blue Kecubung**, Jl Domba 1 (south
of town), T0532-21211, F21513. A/c, the
swishest place in town and sister hotel
to the **Rimba Lodge** in Tanjung putting
(see below). Rooms here are certainly a
notch above those anywhere else in town
but it is a lot to pay for what you get.
D **Andika**, Jl Hasanuddin, T21218. A few
kilometres from town on the road to the
airport. Simple rooms, a/c more expensive,
restaurant.

Tanjung Puting National Park *p293*
The best way to visit the park is to spend a
couple of nights on a 6-m *klotok*, sleeping
and eating afloat. National park staff can
help you to find a suitable boat. The fixed
rate of 75,000 Rp is a better deal than the
land accommodation, as the boats hold 4
plus 2 crew members. All food is bought in
Kumai, and will be cooked by the crew.
B-C **Rimba Lodge** (in the park at Tanjung
Harapan), bookable in Pangkalabun at the
Hotel Blue Kecubung (see above).
Comfortable safari-type place with restaurant
B-C **Sekonyer Ecolodge**, across the river
from PHPA cabins, F0532-22991. Bare but
comfortable, with restaurant.
E **Aloha**, Kumai, on the road from
Pangkalabun. One of several places to stay in
this sleepy port at the edge of the park. Basic
but clean.
{E} **PHPA cabins**, bookable through the park
office at Kumai. Provides basic accommodation at Tanjung Harapan, just inside the
park on the Sekonyer River. It is necessary to
bring food and water upriver. River water
must be thoroughly boiled before drinking.

🍴 Eating

Banjarmasin *p289, map p289*
🍴 **Rama Steak Corner**, Arjuna Plaza, Jl
Lambung Mangkurat 62. Very cosy
restaurant with soft lighting. Imported
Australian steaks cost double local ones.
🍴 **Cendrawasih**, Jl P Samudra 65. Simple but
excellent Indonesian Padang food, good
selection of seafood including spicy roast fish
and, unfortunately, turtle eggs
🍴 **Cherry Café**, Jl Jend A Yani 57. Serves good
European, Indonesian and Chinese dishes.
Excellent value.
🍴 **Jakarta Restaurant**, Jl Hasanuddin 1,
T0511-52488. Formerly **Corner Garden**.
Seafood speciality is fried lobster in butter
sauce, also good crab curries. Recommended.
🍴 **Lezat Baru**, Jl Pang Samudra 22. Part of a
small chain of restaurants, with branches in
Samarinda and Balikpapan, huge Chinese
menu with a good choice of seafood,
specials including excellent steamed crab
and oysters done 10 different ways (when in
season). Highly recommended.
🍴 **Warung Yana Yani**, 10-min *klotok* ride
downriver from the **Borneo Homestay** (see
Sleeping, above), ask Johan to take you. This
is the best riverside restaurant for *soto
banjar*, the famed duck egg soup. For less
than 5000 Rp you'll get a huge bowlful and
a long glass of *es teh* (iced Jasmine tea).
For really cheap food, visit the *warungs*
(foodstalls) in the night market, off **Jl Lambung**
Mangkurat, open to 0100, where you can eat
for around 1000 Rp or less. For delicious local
cakes (*kuey*) try Minseng Bakery, near the
corner of Jl Pasar Baru and Jl Samudra.

☻ Festivals and events

Banjarmasin *p289, map p289*
Mar/Apr Mappanre Tassi Buginese
Fishermens' Festival (movable), 7-day
festival on Pagatan beach (South of Batu
Licin on the southeast coast, 240 km east of
Banjarmasin) in which local Buginese
fishermen sacrifice chickens, food and flour
to the sea. Dancing and traditional songs,
boat races and tug-of-war competitions. The
festival climaxes on the last day. It is possible
to stay overnight in the village where there
are several *losmen* (cheap hotels); enquire at

the tourist office or with tour operators as to how best to get to Pagatan. The Department of Tourism will transport visitors free of charge to the festival.

Aug/Sep **Aruh Ganal** (the big feast; movable) is the Hill Dayak harvest festival. (Another smaller harvest festival, **Aruh Halus**, is held in Jun, to celebrate the 1st of the twice-yearly rice crop.) Dancing all night from 2000-0800; celebrated in the Hill Dayak longhouses in the Loksado and South Hulu Sungai districts. **Boat races** (17 Aug) where teams compete in traditional *tanabangan* rowing boats on the river in front of the mosque – the course is from the government office to the Grand Mosque.

Ramadan (movable) throughout the Islamic fasting month, when Banjaris break *puasa* after sundown, they indulge in local delicacies. Every day from 1400-1800, in front of the Grand Mosque, the Ramadan Cake Fair is held, where people come to sell cakes for the evening feast. Traditional Banjari cakes are made from rice flour, glutinous rice, cassava and sago. Most are colourful, sweet and sticky.

Traditional **Banjarese wedding ceremonies** take place on Sun, in the auspicious month before Ramadan. Tourists are always welcome at these celebrations and do not require invitations. Traditional dances (such as the *hadrah* and *rudat*, which have Middle Eastern origins) are performed during wedding festivities.

O Shopping

Banjarmasin *p289, map p289*
Hill Dayak handicrafts for sale in town include basketware and semi-precious stones from the Martapura mines. Many of the shops have good selections of Dayak knives (*mandau*) from Central Kalimantan; in South Kalimantan, these knives are just called *parang*. One of the more unusual items on sale are the Dayak war canoes/death ships, intricately carved from rubber. There are several art shops on Simpang Sudimampir and Pasar Malabar (near Antsari Bridge).

Toko Citra, Km 3.5 Jl Jend A Yani (towards the airport), is the best place in town for Sasirangan tie-dyes (see box, page 293). Also good for handicrafts are the markets,

especially **Pasar Malabar**, next to Antasari Bridge (on the opposite side of the river from Mitra Plaza), and **Pasar Samudra**, on Jl Samudra/Jl Pangeran, which is good for sarungs and mosquito nets.

▲ Activities and tours

Banjarmasin *p289, map p289*
Trekking
The best area for trekking is in the Meratus Dayak – or Hill Dayak – country around Loksado (on the Amandit River) and Mount Besar (1892 m), 190 km northeast of Banjarmasin in the **Pegunungan Muratus** range. There are more than 30 longhouses – or *balai* – in and around Loksado, where trekkers can stay overnight. There are also caves in the area. The Kalsel tourism office produces a detailed list of treks between villages, with distances and approximate timings. To the southeast of Banjarmasin, at the south end of the range, there are jungle trails around Lake Riamkanan, accessible from Martapura/Awang Bankal. It is necessary to take guides to both these areas (see Tour operators below), as few people speak English; also, take mosquito repellent, a torch and a sleeping bag (temperatures drop sharply at night). The cheapest option is to hire a local guide in Loksado.

Whitewater rafting
From Loksado, it is possible to run the rapids on the Amandit by bamboo raft – there are many stretches of whitewater, of varying grades of difficulty.

Tour operators
All in Banjarmasin.
Adi Angkasa, Jl Hasanuddin 27, T0511-53131, F66200, and **Arjuna**, Ground floor, Arjuna Plaza, Jl Lambung Mangkurat 62, T0511-65235, F64944. Run tours of the **Banjarmasin waterways**, 1½ hrs, floating market, 3 hrs, **Kaget Island**, 5 hrs, **Martapura** and **Cempaka** and the **Tanjung Puteh Orang-Utan Sanctuary** (see page 294), 3-4 days for US$350, with a minimum of 2 people (cost includes flight to Pankalanbun, Southwest Kalimantan). They also organize treks through **Hill Dayak** areas northeast of Banjarmasin involving bamboo rafting and staying overnight in longhouses (*balai*).

Indo Kalimantan Tours, run by Johan Yasin at **Borneo Homestay**, is a good source for trekking information and has a team of highly recommended guides. They will even offer to store your luggage while you take a jungle trek, and deliver it to the airport in time to meet your connecting flight (no extra charge).

⊖ Transport

Banjarmasin *p289, map p289*
Air
Syamsudin Noor Airport is 27 km east of town. Regular connections on **Garuda/Merpati, Sempati, Bouraq, Asahi** and **DAS** with most major Indonesian cities, including **Jakarta, Surabaya, Balikpapan, Palang-karaya, Yogyakarta** and **Semarang**. A taxi from the airport to town costs 15,000 Rp – coupons available after exiting through customs. Alternatively, walk the 1.5 km to the main highway and catch one of the constant colts (minibuses) that ply the road between Banjarmasin and Martapura. This will deliver you to the Km 6 terminal – where it is necessary to catch a *bemo* into the city.

Airline offices Bouraq, Jl Jend A Yani 343, 4 km out of town, T0511-52445. **DAS**, Jl Hasanuddin 6, T0511-52902. **Garuda**, at **Barito Palace Hotel**, T0511-59063, F59064. **Merpati**, Jl Hasanuddin 31, T0511-53885.

Boat
Local For travelling on the waterways, the best place to hire a *klotok* is from under A Yani Bridge or Kuin Cerucuk (also known as Kuin Pertamina), to the northwest side of town on the Kuin River. Motorized *klotoks* (which can hold up to 8 or 10 passengers) cost about 7500 Rp per hr. Speedboats are hired for around 30,000 Rp per hr and leave from the Dermaga speedboat pier near the Grand Mosque.

Long distance **Passenger boats** leave for destinations upriver from **Bajaraya Pier**, at the far west end of Jl Sutoyo. The boats are double-deckers which, for trips beyond Palangkaraya, are equipped with beds (for rent) and even *warungs*. Behind the *warungs* there is a small prayer room and toilets and *mandi*. Those travelling long distances upriver should reserve beds the day before. Boats have signs next to them indicating their

departure times. Most leave in the morning around 1100; ticket office open 0800-1400. To get to Bajaraya pier take a yellow *bemos* or *bajaj* from Pasar Malabar. **Palangkaraya** 24 hrs, **Muara Teweh** 48 hrs and **Puruk Cahu** 60 hrs. In the dry season big passenger boats cannot make it to Muara Teweh and Puruk Cahu; it is necessary to disembark at Pendang and take speedboats and motorized *klotoks* further upriver, to Muara Teweh 3 hrs and Puruk Cahu 8 hrs. **Pelni** ferries leave from Banjarmasin's Trisakti terminal for other destinations in Indonesia. You can get to **Trisakti** by bemo from Jl Antasari. The *Karakatau* leaves for **Pangkalanbun** (for Orang-Utan Sanctuary, every fortnight, 18 hrs. The **Pelni** vessel *Kelimutu* also calls here on its fortnightly circuit.

Speedboats are a quicker and easier way to get upriver to **Palangkaraya**. They leave from the **Dermaga pier** in front of the Grand Mosque. Daily departures for Palangkaraya (and other upriver destinations). Most leave from 0900 to 1100, 5 hrs.

Bugis schooner to **Java**, enquire at Kantor Syahbandar Pelabuhan I, Jl Barito Hilir at Trisakti dock. The harbour master will demand identification before allowing you to see the schooner. Primarily only available for special-interest groups, photographers and journalists. If you require assistance, contact Johan at **Borneo Homestay**.

Road
Local *Bajaj* congregate around Pasar Malabar (off Jl Samudra); they can be chartered. Yellow *bemos* leave from in front of the **Minseng Bakery** near the corner of Jl Pasar Baru and Jl Samudra. They follow fixed routes, but go all over town. *Bemos* can also be found on the corner of Jl Bank Rakyat and Jl Hasanuddin, in front of the **Corner Steak House**. *Ojeks* and *becaks* congregate around Mitra Plaza.

Taxis The city taxi terminal is on Jl Antisari, next to the main market, 5000 Rp per hr.

Bus Intercity buses leave from the **Terminal Taksi Antar Kota** at Km 6. Overnight buses (with and without a/c) to **Balikpapan** leave at 1600-1700, 12 hrs. Overnight buses direct to **Samarinda** leave at the same time, 15 hrs. With the opening of 3 new bridges it is also possible to travel upriver by road. To **Palangkaraya**, 5 hrs.

Car Vehicles can be chartered for a more comfortable overland journey upriver.

Taxis Taxis around Kalsel leave from the Terminal Taksi Antar Kota at Km 6.

Palangkaraya *p293*
Air

The airport is just outside town; taxis in cost 5000 Rp. Regular connections with **Banjarmasin**, **Sampit** and **Pangkalanbun** on Bouraq, and **Balikpapan** and **Surabaya** (Java) on Sempati. Merpati flies these routes too.

River

Canals, cut by the Dutch in the late 19th century, connect the Barito, Kapuas and Kahayan river systems. Boats travelling downstream leave from **Rambang Pier**; tickets are available from here. To **Banjarmasin**, the fast boat takes 6 hrs, the slow boat takes 18 hrs (travelling past **Pulang Pisau** and **Kuala Kapuas** en route). Boats travelling upstream to **Tewah** leave from **Dermaga Flamboyan** (or Flamboyant Pier). For journeys beyond Tewah you'll need to charter a boat.

Road

With the opening of 3 new bridges (open year round), it is now possible to travel overland between Palangkaraya and **Banjarmasin** by bus and car.

Bus Connections with **Banjarmasin**, 5 hrs (25,000 Rp), **Pulang Pisau** and **Kuala Kapuas**.

Car charter Vehicles can be chartered for a more comfortable overland journey down river to **Banjarmasin**.

Jeeps Patas Tours, Jl Yani 52, for twice daily travel to **Kuala Kapuas**, 4 hrs, or to **Sempas**, 7 hrs (in the dry season).

Pangkalanbun *p293*
Air

Regular Bouraq and DAS flights to/from **Banjarmasin**, 2 hrs. DAS also flies to **Palangkaraya** and **Pontianak**. Merpati flies daily to **Semarang** (change here, if coming from Jakarta) and **Bandung** (3¼ hrs). Transport to town by taxi or *bemo*.

Road

Local *Bemos* around town are cheap.

Long distance The road to **Palangkaraya** from Pangkalanbun is poor. *Kijang* taxis make the journey but it is long (about 10 hrs) and painful. The trip to **Tanjung Puting**, by contrast, is short and comparatively sweet. Minibuses leave from the market area, 30 mins.

Sea

Boats do leave from the dock near town for **Pontianak** and **Banjarmasin** but they are not scheduled, so you will need to ask around.

Tanjung Puting National Park *p293*
Air

The nearest airport is in **Pangkalanbun** (see above for details).

Sea

Local Speedboats can be chartered from **Kumai** to the park for about 120,000 Rp, 45 mins to Tanjung Harapan, 1½ hrs to Camp Leakey. *Klotoks* can be hired in Kumai from around 75,000 Rp per day, sleeps 4 plus 2 crew. For travelling along the **Sekonyer River**, canoes (paddle powered) can be hired from Ecolodge or Rimba – it's the best and most peaceful way to see the forest and its wildlife.

Long distance Pelni vessels from **Semarang** and **Surabaya** call at Kumai on their fortnightly circuits. The same vessels also dock at **Banjarmasin** en route.

❶ Directory

Banjarmasin *p289, map p289*
Banks BDN and BNI are both on Jl Lambung Mangkurat; **BDN** has good rates for TCs and BNI has ATM (Cirrus and MasterCard). Money changer in the back of Adi Angkasa Travel, Jl Hasanuddin 27.
Internet Facilities available at the post office (7500 Rp per hr, but very slow).
Medical services Suaka Insan Hospital, Jl Pembangunan (on the north side of town), is the best in Banjarmasin, with wards and private rooms. **Post office** On the corner of Jl Lambung Mangkurat and Jl Samudra.

East Kalimantan (Kaltim)

With its economy founded on timber (it produces 70% of Indonesia's sawn timber exports), oil, gas and coal, Kaltim is the wealthiest province in Kalimantan. Its capital is Samarinda, the launch pad for trips up the Mahakam River. Balikpapan, an ugly oil town, is bigger than Samarinda and is the provincial transport hub. The province covers an area of 211,400 sq km and has a population barely more than 2,000,000. It is the second largest province in Indonesia after Irian Jaya. ▸▸ *For Sleeping, Eating and other listings, see pages 307-314.*

Background

Archaeological digs on the East Kalimantan coast have uncovered stone *yupa* poles with Sanskrit inscriptions, suggesting Indian cultural influence possibly dating back to the fifth century or even earlier. The province's first substantial settlement was founded by refugees from Java in the 13th century, who had fled from the Majapahits. They founded the kingdom of Kertanegara ('the lawful nation' – which later became known as Kutai). This kingdom is believed to have been an important centre on the trade route between Java and China. The word *kutai* is thought to have been the term used by Chinese traders, who knew it as 'the great land'. The imaginative Chinese traders also gave the Mahakam River its name (*mahakam* means 'big river').

Following Banjarmasin's conversion to Islam, Kutai also embraced the faith in 1565 and became an Islamic sultanate. Disputes between Kutai and the Hindu kingdom of Martapura, on the Mahakam River, were settled by a royal marriage which forged an alliance between the upriver kingdom and the Islamic sultanate. In the 17th century, hostilities broke out again and Kutai was defeated and then absorbed into the Kingdom of Martapura. The first Buginese settlers arrived from Sulawesi in 1701. As piracy in the Sulu Sea grew worse, Kutai's capital moved inland and was finally transferred to Tenggarong on the Mahakam in 1781. Kutai remained intact as a sultanate until 1960.

Balikpapan ●●●●▲●● ▸▸ *pp307-314. Colour map 4, B4.*

Administrative headquarters for Kaltim's oil and gas industry, Balikpapan's population has grown from under 100,000 in 1961 to more than 300,000 in the space of a few decades. At night, from the dirty beach along Balikpapan's sea front, the clouds are periodically lit up by the orange glow of flares from the offshore rigs in the Makassar Strait. The support staff of **Pertamina**, the Indonesian national oil company, live mainly on Gunung Dubb, in Dutch colonial villas dating from the 1920s and overlooking the refinery. **Unocal** and **Total**, US and French oil companies, have their residential complexes on the opposite hill, on **Pasir Ridge**, overlooking the town. These foreign oil workers live like kings in Balikpapan, which is a soulless town, strung out untidily along several kilometres of road. It was established in the early 20th century as an oil town, and to a significant extent remains one. Some attempt has been made in recent years to create a business district and this has begun to bear fruit around the bottom of Jalan Jend A Yani, next to the smart **Altea Benakutai Hotel**. Apart from some excellent arts and crafts shops and some good restaurants and hotels, Balikpapan has little to offer tourists; it is a transit camp for visits to Samarinda and the Mahakam River, or for Banjarmasin, to the south. There is a **tourist information office** ⓘ *Seppinggang Airport, T0542-21605, unpredictable opening hours*, but **Altea Benakutai Hotel** representative office is usually staffed and can help with immediate queries. The best beaches are to the north of Balikpapan at **Tanah Merah** and **Manggar** (3 km from town). These tend to become crowded at weekends.

Samarinda 🖥️🚌🛫⛺🏔️🚍🍴 ▶ *pp307-314. Colour map 4, A5.*

Kaltim's capital, 120 km north of Balikpapan, is the gateway to the interior, up the Mahakam River and to the remote Dayak areas of the Apo Kayan, near the border with Sarawak. A bustling modern town that has grown rich from the proceeds of the timber industry, Samarinda was founded by Buginese seafarers from South Sulawesi in the early 1700s and became the capital of the Kutai sultanate. It is 40 km from the coast at the head of the splayed Mahakam estuary and the river is navigable by large ships right up to the town – only the recently built bridge across the Mahakam prevents them going further upriver.

The rapid population growth of Samarinda is based squarely on natural resource exploitation. The town produced almost three-quarters of East Kalimantan's plywood in the early 1990s and was reputed to have one of the world's highest densities of plywood factories and sawmills, although this output has since declined because of a shortage of logs and a stiff export tax on sawn timber.

Unlike some other cities in Indonesian Borneo, like Balikpapan, the Banjarese are still the largest ethnic group in Samarinda, making up perhaps 40% of the population (with 30% Javanese, 10% Bugis and 10% Chinese).

Ins and outs

Getting there and around Samarinda's airport, on the edge of town, has connections with other destinations in Kalimantan and Java. There are long-distance buses to Balikpapan, Bontang and Tenggarong. **Pelni** vessels dock here on their fortnightly circuits through the archipelago and there are also boats that venture up the Mahakam River.

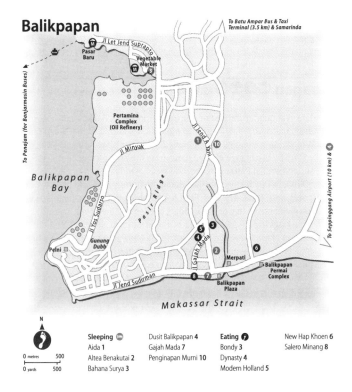

Sleeping Aida 1, Altea Benakutai 2, Bahana Surya 3, Dusit Balikpapan 4, Gajah Mada 7, Penginapan Murni 10

Eating Bondy 3, Dynasty 4, Modern Holland 5, New Hap Khoen 6, Salero Minang 8

Bemos and minibuses, which follow set routes, are the main means of transportation. There are also many *ojeks*.

Tourist information There is a poorly organized and badly informed tourist office, **Kantor Pariwisata** ① *Jl Ade Irma Suryani 1 (off Jalan Kesuma Bangsa), T41669*. You will be better off getting information from travel agents.

Sights
The only real 'sight' is the **Mahakam River** itself and it is well worth chartering a boat to cruise around for an hour. On the left bank, at the east end of town, is the harbour, where the elegant Bugis schooners dock. **Kampong Sulili**, further downriver from Samarinda, is built out over the river on stilts and backed by a steep hillside; there are lively scenes all along the riverbank. Small boats can be hired or speedboats can be chartered from any of the countless jetties behind the Pasar Pagi (morning market).

Samarinda

Sleeping ⬤	Mesra 5	Eating ⬤	Lezat Baru 4
Bumi Senyiur 2	Pirus 6	Gading Kencana 2	Mirasa 5
Hidayah I 3	Rahayu 7	Lembur Kuring 3	

0 metres 200

0 yards 200

Kalimantan East Kalimantan (Kaltim)

Kutai National Park ⊜ ↠ pp307-314. Colour map 4, A5.

Kutai National Park, 120 km north of Samarinda, is a 200,000-ha area of forest. The **World Wide Fund for Nature** (WWF) believes it contains at least 239 species of bird. It is also home to a population of wild orang-utans (around Teluk Kaba) and proboscis monkeys. The park was first gazetted as a protected area before the Second World War, but has found itself gradually diminished in size as the government has allowed portions to be logged. At the beginning of the 1980s, 60% of the remaining protected area was devastated by a vast forest fire. Kutai park is reached via **Bontang**, which lies on the equator. Bontang is the site of a large liquified natural gas plant. Nearby, at Kuala Bontang, there is a Bajau fishing kampong built out on stilts over the water.

Most people visit the park on an organized tour (see page 311). Regular buses run every three hours and there are passenger boats from Samarinda to Bontang. Tour agencies sometimes fly tourists into Bontang (45 minutes' flight from Balikpapan). From Bontang (Lok Tuan or Tanjung Limau harbours), the park can be reached by speedboat in 30 minutes. Chartering boats can be expensive for the independent traveller (around 50,000 Rp).

Permits/guides It is necessary to acquire a permit from the Conservation Office (PHPA Office) in Bontang (no charge). The office can advise independent travellers on their itinerary and organize boat trips to the park; it will also provide guides and help charter boats.

Tenggarong ⊜✸⊜ ↠ pp307-314. Colour map 4, A5.

Tenggarong was the last capital of the Sultanate of Kutai, and is the first major town (45 km) upriver from Samarinda. The highlight of a visit to the town is the **Mulawarman Museum** ① *Tue-Thu, Sat and Sun 0800-1600, Fri 0800-1100, 1330-1600, admission 500 Rp.* It is housed in the Dutch-built former sultan's palace – his old wooden one, which was exquisitely furnished, burned to the ground in the mid-1930s. The museum contains a recreation of the opulent royal bed chamber, a selection of the sultan's *krisses* (knives), clothes and other bits and pieces of royal regalia as well as his collection of Chinese ceramics. There are also replicas of the stone stelae bearing Sanskrit inscriptions, dating from the fourth or fifth centuries. The display of Dayak arts and crafts is poor, although there are some woodcarvings in the grounds – notably the tall Dayak *belawang* pole (with a carved hornbill on top) in front of the museum. A Dayak cultural show is often staged in the museum on Sunday. Near the museum is the **royal cemetery**, containing graves of the founder of Tenggarong, Sultan Muslidhuddin and his descendants.

Mahakam River ⊜▲⊜ ↠ pp307-314. Colour map 4, A2-A5.

The 920-km-long muddy Mahakam is the biggest of Kaltim's 14 large rivers and is navigable for 523 km. There are three main stretches. The Lower Mahakam runs from Samarinda, through Tenggarong to Muara Muntai and the three lakes; these lower reaches are most frequently visited by tourists. The Middle Mahakam stretches to the west from Kuara Muntai, through Long Iram to Long Bagun – where public riverboat services terminate. The Upper Mahakam, past the long stretch of rapids, runs from Long Gelat into the Muller Range; only a few adventure tours go this far. Most tours reach the Upper Mahakam by plane (**Asahi Airways** flies to Data Dawai airstrip at Long Lunuk). The Mahakam's riverbanks have been extensively logged, or turned over to

The tough life of a turtle

Historically, green and hawksbill turtles have been hunted for their meat, shells and their edible eggs (a Chinese delicacy). They were a favourite food of British and Spanish mariners for centuries. Japanese soldiers slaughtered thousands of turtles for food during the Second World War. Dynamite fishermen are also thought to have killed off many turtles in Indonesian, Malaysian and Philippines waters in recent years.

Malaysia, Hong Kong, Japan and the Philippines, where green turtle meat and eggs are much in demand, are all signatories of the Convention in International Trade in Endangered Species (CITES), and trading in sea turtles has been proscribed under Appendix 1 of the Convention since 1981.

In his book *Forest Life and Adventures in the Malay Archipelago*, the Swedish adventurer and wildlife enthusiast Eric Mjoberg documents turtle egg-hunting and shell collecting in Borneo in the 1920s. He tells of how the Bajau would lie in wait for hawksbills, grab them and put them on the fire so their horny shields could be removed.

"The poor beasts are put straight on the fire so that their shield may be more readily removed, and suffer, in the process, the tortures of the damned. They are then allowed to go alive, or perhaps half-dead into the sea, only to come back again after a few years and undergo the same cruel process."

The Bajau, he says, used an "ingenious contrivance" to hunt their prey. They would press pieces of common glass against their eyes "in a watertight fashion" and would lie face-down on a piece of floating wood, dipping their faces into the water, watching for hawksbills feeding on seaweed. They would then dive in, armed with a small harpoon, and catch them, knocking them out with a blow to the head.

cultivation. To reach less-touristed destinations along the river you need plenty of time on your hands and, if on an organized tour (see page 311), plenty of funds as well. Many tourists just enjoy relaxing on the decks of the boats as they wind their way slowly upriver: one of the most important pieces of equipment for a Mahakam trip is a good, long book.

September to October, before the rainy season starts, is the best time to visit; it coincides with rice-planting rituals and the Erau festival. Harvesting festivals are held from February to March. During the dry season (July to September), many of the smaller tributaries and shallow lakes are unnavigable except by small canoes; during the height of the wet season (November to January), many rivers are in flood and currents are often too strong for upriver trips. Most people travel up the Mahakam River on an organized tour, either from Samarinda (see page 306) or from Balikpapan (see page 311). ▸▸ See also Tours, page 306, and Activities and tours, page 311.

Background

One of the first Western explorers to venture up the Mahakam was Carl Bock (1849-1932). Though born in Oslo he went to England as a young man, and from there to the Dutch East Indies collecting biological specimens for the collection of Arthur Hay, the Marquis of Tweeddale and president of the Zoological Society. Unfortunately, while frantically pillaging the flora and fauna of Sumatra, his patron died. A stroke of good fortune gave him a new mission: in Batavia (Jakarta) he met Governor-General Van Lansberghe, who asked him to mount an expedition to 'Koetai' (Kutai) and venture up the Koetai or 'Mahakani' River. He agreed, but immediately found a problem: no one would accompany him – even when the wages were so high they "amounted to a positive bribe" – because of the fear of cannibals. But perseverance and the governor-general's deep pocket allowed him to proceed and, accompanied by the Sultan of Kutai himself, Bock ventured upstream. In a sense, the expedition was a bit of a let down: he met no headhunters in six months, nor did he find the celebrated *Orang Buntut* – the 'Tailed People' who were supposed to be the missing link between apes and humans. Nonetheless, he wrote up the account of the journey – with a literary flourish which did more for sales than his scientific credibility – that was published, in Dutch, in 1881. The book was translated into English and published as *The headhunters of Borneo* (available as a 1985 reprint from Oxford University Press).

Today, when they are taking time out from their cultural performances for tourists, the Mahakam's Dayaks are not the noble savages, dressed in loin cloths and hornbill feathers, that some of the tourist literature might paint them as. Longhouses are quite commercialized and tourists are likely to be asked for money for photographs. Most villages on the lower and middle reaches of the river have been drawn – economically and socially – into the modern world over the past century. Although the traditional Kaharingan religion is still practised in some areas, many upriver Dayak groups have been converted to Christianity. This is all in marked contrast to neighbouring Sarawak, where the upriver tribespeople maintain their traditional lifestyles to a much greater degree.

The reason for this can be traced back to the policy of Sarawak's successive Brooke governments – the White Rajahs of Sarawak who attempted to protect the Orang Ulu (the upriver tribes) from the warring Ibans and Chinese traders. Other than trying to stamp out 'social vices' such as head-hunting, they were largely left undisturbed. In Kalimantan, the Dutch colonial government did nothing to discourage the activities of Muslim and Christian missionaries, traders and administrators.

Mahakam River

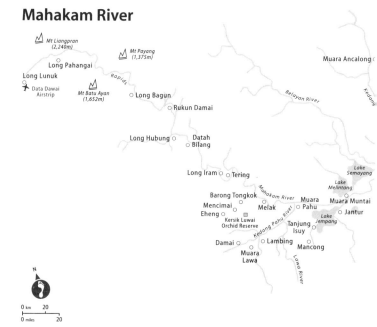

Tenggarong (see page 302) is the first major town upriver on the Mahakam from Samarinda – a trip of about 40 km. Upriver tours then pass through the villages of **Muara Kaman** and **Kota Bangun**, about six or seven hours upriver from Tenggarong. The lakes of **Semayang**, **Melintang** and **Jempang** – collectively known as the Mahakam Lakes – lie to the west and southwest of Kota Bangun. The lakes used to be known for their freshwater dolphins, which were sadly decimated during the drought and associated fire of 1982-1983. The lakes remain an important source of fish, though; it has been estimated that 30% of dried freshwater fish sold in Java come from these lakes. Other wildlife in this area of the Mahakam includes the proboscis monkeys.

Muara Muntai is the next village travelling upriver on the Mahakam, built out over the riverbank on ironwood stilts.

The Dayak village of **Tanjung Isuy** is on the Mancong River, which feeds into Lake Jempang, the most southerly of the three main lakes; it takes about 2½ hours to reach the village from Muara Muntai. Tanjung Isuy is quite touristy, being popular with tour groups. It is, however, the best place on the Mahakam to witness traditional dance performances in full costume. The villagers of Tanjung Isuy have rejected longhouse living in favour of detached *kampong* houses, strung out along the riverbank. One of these rejected longhouses contains a government craft centre, which is also a hostel (**F**), with private rooms and good beds.

A worthwhile excursion from Tanjung Isuy is to visit the **Mancong longhouse**, about 10 km away, which was built as a tourist attraction in 1987. There are sometimes weaving demonstrations and traditional dance performances. But it is worth making the effort for the trip itself, rather than the destination; the chances of seeing wildlife, including proboscis monkeys and a profusion of water birds, are good.

The Middle and Upper Mahakam

Along the Mahakam, west of Muara Muntai, are many modern Dayak villages where the traditional Kaharingan religion is still practised. Funerals are particularly interesting affairs, involving the ritual sacrifice of water buffalo. Several more traditional villages are within reach of **Melak** (all are accessible by motorcycle), the largest settlement hereabouts (for accommodation, see Sleeping, below). There is a scattering of *warungs* and Melak is also quite a good place to buy rattan goods. Guides and transport are available, but the latter tends to be expensive.

Around 15 km southwest of Melak is the **Kersik Luwai Orchid Reserve**, which is best visited in January or February. Charter an ojek for the trip there and back. Northwest of the reserve is **Barong Tongkok**, a small community lodged near the centre of this plateau. From here, travel southwest to visit **Mencimai**, where there is a great little museum showing local farming methods. Beyond here is **Eheng**, with an exceptional Banauq longhouse, and local people selling handicrafts (the last stretch of road beyond Mencimai is not made up).

Kalimantan East Kalimantan (Kaltim)

Towards **Long Bagun**, places become increasingly traditional, although some villages and tribal groups have embraced Christianity, and the long arm of the state and of modernity, reaches far into the upper stretches of the Mahakam. Only a few public river-boats go beyond **Long Iram**, partly because of a lack of demand and partly because travel in the dry season becomes difficult upriver from here. Long Iram is a small, rather pleasing little town, with a relaxed atmosphere and a few architectural hangovers from the Dutch period.

Upriver from Long Iram is the domain of the **Tunjung** and **Benuaq Dayaks**, and a substantial number of Kenyah who have spilled over from the Apo Kayan, see below. The scenery becomes increasingly dramatic towards Long Bagun; there are many villages and it is always possible to stay somewhere. Past the long stretch of rapids to the west of Long Bagun is the upper Mahakam, which runs southwest and then twists north to its headwaters in the Muller Range, on the Sarawak border. It is possible to fly from Samarinda to **Long Lunuk** (Data Dawai airstrip), well to the southwest of the rapids, and then continue upriver by longboat.

Tours

About 15,000 tourists travel up the Mahakam River annually. The vast majority go on organized tours which can be tailored to suit all budgets. Most tours are prohibitively expensive unless you are part of a group; the costs fall dramatically the more people there are. Tour agents usually require a deposit of 50% upon booking. There are some excellent tour companies in Samarinda and three major ones in Balikpapan (see page (see page 311) offering similar deals. There are also more adventurous trekking trips to the Apo Kayan (see page 306) and three- to four-day package deals to the Kutai National Park, north of Samarinda (see above).

Unlike neighbouring Sarawak, upriver tours on the Mahakam lasting less than a week will not get far enough to reach traditional longhouses; three- to four-day tours cost about US$300 per head for four to six people and travel to **Lake Jempang** and **Tanjung Isuy**; five- to nine-day tours continue upriver to **Tunjung**, **Bahau** and **Kenyah Dayak** villages west of Long Iram, costing from US$400 to US$800 per head for four to six people. A 14-day tour should reach **Long Baun** or beyond.

All tours to the **Apo Kayan** area (see page 306) include the return flight from Samarinda to Long Ampung. Few are shorter than six days, most are about nine to 10 days. Most tours involve a mixture of trekking and river trips by longboat and canoe, visiting Long Nawang and nearby longhouses and waterfalls. Some even throw in a day's hunting with local Dayaks. Tours cost around US$700-900 for groups of four to six.

Freelance guides tout around hotels looking for tourists wanting to go upriver. Some are good, others terrible: it is advisable to stick to those with tourist guide licences. (When planning a trip with a freelance guide, ask them to trace the intended route on a map; it soon becomes apparent whether they know what they are talking about.) Many of the good guides in Samarinda contract out their services to tour companies. An average daily rate for a freelance guide should be about 50,000 Rp.

The Apo Kayan 🚌🚻 ›› *pp307-314. Colour map 2, C1-2.*

This remote plateau region borders Sarawak and is the most traditional tribal area in Kalimantan. The inaccessible mountains and rapids have made the Apo Kayan non-viable from a commercial logger's point of view and the jungle is largely intact. The region has suffered from out-migration in recent decades and the tribal population has shrunk to a fraction – perhaps just a tenth – of what it was in the early 1900s. This migration has been spurred by the availability of well-paid work in the timber camps of Sarawak and East Kalimantan, combined with the prohibitive cost of ferrying and portering supplies from downriver. Since the late 1980s the airstrip at Long Ampung has been served by DAS – opening the area up and bringing the cost of freight and passenger fares down.

The Apo Kayan is divided into the **Kayan Hulu** (upriver) and **Kayan Hilir** (downriver) districts. The former has a much higher population (about 5000) and the vast majority are Kayan (see page 162), most, originally from Sarawak, driven upriver by Iban raids. Nearly all of them have converted to Christianity (most are Protestant.) Until the 1920s the Kayan were the sworn enemies of Sarawak's Iban: in 1924 the Sarawak Brooke government convened a peace conference in Kapit (on the Rejang River), which was attended by Dayak groups from both sides of the border. This formally put a stop to upriver and cross-border headhunting raids.

During the Second World War, many Europeans in the coastal towns of East Kalimantan made their way upriver to what they considered the relative safety of Long Nawang, deep in the Apo Kayan, in the face of Japanese occupation. The Japanese troops followed them upriver and many were killed, having been forced to dig their own graves. Among those shot was a group of women and children – refugees from Kapit in Sarawak.

Most tours to the Apo Kayan involve trekking and canoe trips from **Long Ampung** to **Long Nawang**, and visits to longhouses in the area, such as Nawang Baru and Long Betoah, and west of Long Ampung, along the Boh River, to Long Uro, Lidung Panau and Long Sungai Barang.

Tarakan ⊟⊘▲⊟❶ ⤍ *Phone code: 0551. Colour map 2, B2.*

The oil-rich island of Tarakan, with over 81,000 inhabitants, has little to offer the tourist, besides being a hopping-off point for neighbouring Sabah. In the closing months of the Second World War, a vicious battle was fought here as Australian forces spent several weeks trying to prise the Japanese out of their well-protected bunkers. They succeeded, but not before suffering many casualties. The legacy of the battle is still in evidence.

Nunukan ⊟⊟ ⤍ *pp307-314. Colour map 2, B2.*

Travellers making the journey between Tarakan and Tawau (in Sabah, East Malaysia) need to stop over in Nunukan as there are no longer any direct boats. Nunukan offers very little for the visitor: there are no beaches and it seems to be impossible to arrange even a canoe trip. On the plus side the people are friendly. There is one bank (**BNI**) on the main square, but it gives very poor exchange rates.

⊟ Sleeping

Balikpapan *p299, map p300*
Largely because Balikpapan is an oil town and is geared to the needs of oil men and government officials, there is woefully little accommodation for the budget traveller.
AL Altea Benakutai, Jl Jend A Yani, T0542-33022, F31823. A/c, restaurants, pool, smart, international-class hotel, mainly used by oil-industry workers. 24-hr room service, good service and wide range of facilities including fitness and business centres, helpful representative office at airport.

AL Dusit Balikpapan, Jl Jend Sudirman, T0542-420155, http://balikpapandusit.com. The most luxurious hotel in Kalimantan, set in extensive gardens overlooking the Makassar Strait. A/c, restaurants, pool, room rate includes breakfast. 191 rooms, fitness centre, business facilities, fine for those with transport or willing to use taxis, but with a 15-min drive to the centre of town a trifle inconvenient. Highly recommended, nevertheless.
A Bahana Surya (formerly **Blue Sky**), Jl Let Jend Suprapto 1, T0542-35845, www.regit.com.

5 mins' drive from major oil company offices. A/c, 3 restaurants, pool, Balikpapan's next best after the Dusit, large modern hotel with a good range of facilities including in-house videos, satellite TV, sauna, billiards and Japanese Shiatsu massage. Friendly staff. Recommended.

C Gajah Mada, Jl Jend Sudirman 14, T0542-34634, F34636. A/c, breakfast included, clean, large rooms, satellite TV, unmarried couples might be a little circumspect here (the Muslim management has been known to ask to see marriage certificates!) The rooms on the seaward side at the back of the hotel are the nicest, there is a very pleasant balcony running along the back of the hotel on both floors. Recommended.

E Penginapan Murni, Jl P Antasari 434, T0542-25290. Basic (fan only) and the location is also noisy, but a very pleasant bright blue interior with sunny sitting rooms on both floors, good value and the best of the cheaper places to stay.

E Aida, Jl Jend A Yani 1/12, T0542-21006. Sister hotel to its namesake in Samarinda. Don't be fooled by the renovated exterior – it's still grotty at the back, but the sheets are clean and it remains popular with budget travellers.

Samarinda *p300, map p301*
AL-A Hotel Bumi Senyiur, Jl Diponegoro 17-19, T0541-41443, www.senyiur.co.id. The best-value hotel in this price range, beautifully furnished, marble bathrooms, fluffy towels, soft lighting, IDD and satellite TV, huge pool, sauna and spa, restaurants and nightclub/pub. Great for post-trek recovery.
C Mesra, Jl Pahlawan 1, T0541-32772, www.mesra.com/hotel. A/c, restaurant, pool, at the top of a hill, golf course and tennis, good bar, rooms, suites and cottages, good value for money. Recommended.
D-E Hidayah I, Jl KH Mas Temenggung, T0541-31408, F37761. A/c, restaurant, next to the morning market, very friendly staff, average rooms, pleasant balcony over-looking the street.
E Pirus, Jl Pirus 30, T0541-41873, F35890. Good range of rooms, some a/c, some with own *mandis*. Good value.
E Rahayu, Jl KH Abul Hasan 17, T0541-22622. Clean and best of the budget options, shared bathroom.

Kutai National Park *p302*
E Kartika, Jl Yani 37, Bontang, T0548-21012. There are a number of rangers' posts in the park with basic accommodation and food. There is one on **Teluk Kaba** and others along the **Sengata River** (**F**, 3000 Rp per meal).

Tenggarong *p302*
There are a handful of cheap *losmen* (hotel) in town (a couple by the dock) and 1 mid-range place to stay.
C Timbau Indah, Jl Muksin 15 (on the road into town from Samarinda, on the river), T0541-61367. A/c, restaurant, good rooms but rather a trek from the town centre.
E Penginapan Anda II, Jl Sudirman 63 (over the bridge from the mosque), T0541-61409. The best bet for budget accommodation. As well as some cheap but clean fan rooms, this place also has a/c rooms with attached *mandi*.

The Lower Mahakam: Samarinda to Muara Muntai *p305, map p304*
D Sri Bangun Lodge, 10 mins' walk from Mukjizat and quite a comfortable place to stay.
E Penginapan Mukjizat, Kota Bangun, facing the mosque. A welcoming place with average to poor rooms but an above average atmosphere and position. Also good source of information on the Upper Mahakam.
F Hostel, Tanjung Isuy, in longhouse, with private rooms and good beds.

The Middle and Upper Mahakam *p305, map p304*
Several adequate places to stay in Melak.
F Losmen, Long Iram. There's also a very good small restaurant.

The Apo Kayan *p306*
It is possible to stay in the longhouses but is important to bring gifts (see box, page 114). Independent travellers should pay around 6000-8000 Rp per night to the longhouse headman. Visitors should bring a sleeping bag (it gets cold at night) and essential equipment includes insect repellent and a torch.

Tarakan *p307*
C Barito Timur, Jl Sudirman 129, T0551-21181. A/c, basic but clean.
C-D Tarakan Plaza, Jl Yos Sudarso 1, T0551-21870. A/c, hot water, restaurant, best in town, with helpful, friendly staff.

F **Jakarta**, Jl Sudirman 112, T0551-21704. Rock-bottom rates for basic but clean rooms and a friendly welcome.

F **Taufiq**, Jl Sudarso 26, T0551-21347. Some a/c, rather basic but OK and has a certain ramshackle charm.

Nunukan *p307*
E **Losmen Monaco**, 5-min walk from the port. One of several *losmen* in town. Clean and reasonable value with shared *mandis*.

🅿 Eating

Balikpapan *p299, map p300*
🍴🍴 **Bondy**, Jl Jend A Yani 7. One of the best restaurants in town, entrance through bakery with enticing smell of fresh pastries, past the fast-food area, to the rear where it opens into a large 2-storey open-air restaurant, built around an open courtyard. European and local food, mixed grill very good and local and imported steaks, vast selection of sundaes and ice creams, very popular with locals. Recommended.

🍴🍴 **Tenggarong Grill**, Altea Benakutai Hotel, Jl Jend A Yani. International food, steaks and seafood, popular with expatriates.

🍴 **Dynasty**, Jl Jend A Yani 10/7. Chinese food and seafood, huge menu, deep-fried crab claws, prawns fried with *rambutan*, shellfish, *saté*. Recommended.

🍴 **Lezat Baru**, Pasar Baru Blok A, Jl Jend Sudirman 1, Komplex Pertokoan. Part of a small chain of restaurants, huge Chinese menu with a good choice of seafood, specials include oysters done 10 different ways.

🍴 **Mahakam**, Bahana Surya Hotel, Jl Let Jend Suprapto 1. Chinese and European cuisine, seafood and steaks, popular with expatriates.

🍴 **Modern Holland**, Jl Jend A Yani 2. Bakery with small restaurant attached, serving local and imported steaks, good ice creams.

🍴 **New Hap Khoen**, Jl Jend Sudirman 19. Huge Chinese menu, good seafood selection, specialities include crab curry, chilli crab and *goreng tepung* (squid fried in batter). Recommended.

🍴 **Salero Minang**, Jl Gajah Mada 12B, fresh and tasty Padang food.

🍴 **Sampan**, Altea Benakutai Hotel, Jl Jend A Yani. Coffee shop with Chinese, Indonesian and international selection. Recommended.

Foodstalls
There are stalls in the Balikpapan Permai complex on the road to the airport, more at the vegetable market – **Kebun Sayur** – the Chinatown of Balikpapan.

Samarinda *p300, map p301*
🍴🍴 **Gading Kencana**, top floor of Hotel Gading Kencana, Jl Pulau Sulawesi 4, T0541-22456. Beautifully decorated with ikats, baskets and Dayak handicrafts, soft lighting, does not fill up until after 2000. Romantic breezy balcony available for dining, freshwater fish (*ikan mas*) and saltwater – *ikan bawal*, *terkulu*, *bandeng* and *kakap* – also Mahakam River prawns. Highly recommended.

🍴 **Gumarang**, Jl Jend Sudirman 30. Extraordinary menu which includes cow brain gravy, cow foot gravy, cow lung gravy, sliced lung, raw leaves and potatoes, spicy *tongkol* fish wrapped in banana leaf. Recommended.

🍴 **Lembur Kuring**, Jl Bhayangkara (next to cinema). Small, basic but tasty selection of curry dishes.

🍴 **Lezat Baru**, Jl Mulawarman 56. Part of a small chain of restaurants, huge Chinese menu with a good choice of seafood, specials include oysters done 10 different ways. Recommended.

🍴 **Mirasa**, Jl H Agus Salim 18/2 (opposite Andhika Hotel). Good *nasi campur* curries, specializes in grilled fish and chicken.

Tarakan *p307*
🍴 **Antara**, Jl Yos Sudarso. Good *ikan bakar* (fish).

🍴 **Bagi Alam**, Jl Yos Sudarso. Another place worth visiting for its *ikan bakar*.

🍴 **Kepeting Saos**, Jl Sudirman. Excellent crab dishes.

🅔 Entertainment

Balikpapan *p299, map p300*
Balikpapan's status as an oil town, with a good number of testosterone-charged men, means that it has a lively nightlife. The major hotels all have bars and discos and their popularity changes with the seasons.

Samarinda *p300, map p301*
Blue Pacific Disco, Kaltim Building, Citra Niaga. There are 5 discos in the building, and

this is the best of the bunch. Lively music, good atmosphere and no cover charge.
Tepian Mahakam, Jl Untung Suropati, T0541-34204. Floating disco – which plays a mixture of chart hits and traditional Indonesian love songs – is in the bowels of a barge moored next to the bridge on the Mahakam; cover charge. Restaurant on top. Recommended.

❀ Festivals and events

Tenggarong *p302*
23-28 Sep Erau Festival, traditionally celebrated at the coronation of a new Sultan of Kutai, used to go on for 40 days and nights. Today it lasts for 5 days. Festivities include traditional Dayak dances, where the different tribes dress in full costume (including the impressive Hudoq dance, designed to frighten spirits, diseases, rats, wild boar, monkeys and birds away from the rice crops), and sporting events such as *behempas* (where men fight with braided whips and rattan shields), *sepak takraw* (top spinning), *lomba perahu* (boat races) and blowpipe competitions. Following the final *ngulur naga* ceremony – in which a large colourful dragon is floated down the Mahakam – the festival degenerates into a water fight (water in which the dragon has swum is lucky water and should be shared – in bucketfuls). Dayak rituals are performed during the festival, including the *belian* healing ceremony – where shamans cast out evil spirits causing sickness – and *mamat*, the ceremony which traditionally welcomed heroes back from war and headhunting expeditions, and during which a buffalo is slaughtered.

○ Shopping

Balikpapan *p299, map p300*
Arts, crafts and antiques
Balikpapan has a vast array of arts and crafts shops, and is probably the best place in Kalimantan to buy Dayak handicrafts; 'antiques' may not, however, be as old as they first appear. A new shopping centre has been built right on the seafront, at the bottom of Jl Jend A Yani. There are lots of arts and crafts shops above the vegetable market (Kebun Sayur/Pasar Inpres) on Jl Let Jend Suprapto, at the north end of town.

Bahati Jaya Art Shop, Jl May Jen Sutoyo 9. A good range of tribal arts and crafts and antiques.
Borneo Art Shop, Jl Jend A Yani 34/03. One of the best selections of handicrafts, Dayak antiques, bone-carvings, ceramics, gemstones and coins. If needed, the manager will deliver your purchase to your hotel and complete the purchase on the premises.
Kalimantan Art Shop, Blok A1, Damai Balikpapan Permai, Jl Jend Sudirman 7. The undisputed king of Balikpapan's antiques, and Dayak arts and crafts shops, textiles, beads, porcelain, etc. Proprietor Eddy Amran is friendly and knowledgeable.
Syahda Mestika, Jl Jend A Yani 147. A vast selection of tribal arts and crafts, Chinese porcelain and antiques.
Iwan Suharto Batik Gallery, Hotel Benakutai, Jl Jend A Yani, T0542-31896. Excellent selection of very original batik paintings (traditional and modern), much of it from Java, but includes some interesting Dayak designs.

Shopping centres
Balikpapan Plaza, Jl Sudirman. 1000 until late. 3 floors of everything an expat could desire, in a/c bliss.

Samarinda *p300, map p301*
The **Pasar Pagi** (morning market) is in the middle of town and is busy most of the day; the area around the modern **Citra Niaga** shopping complex, between Jl Yos Sudarso and Jl P Batur, is particularly lively in the evenings with musicians, fortune-tellers, quack doctors and dentists.

Arts, crafts and antiques
Samarinda has many small arts and crafts shops, mostly selling Dayak bits and pieces; there are 1 or 2 good ones, but the selection is not as good as Balikpapan. Always bargain and be suspicious of 'antiques'.
Dewi Art Shop, Jl Awang Long 19, T0541-21482. Antiques, tribal arts and crafts, especially good selection of statues and sculptures.
Fatmawati, Jl Kesuma Bangsa 2. Good selection of semi-precious stones and rings.
Other art shops are located along Jl Martadinata.

▲ Activities and tours

Balikpapan *p299, map p300*
Tour operators
There are 3 big agents which operate tours, mainly up the Mahakam River, as well as more unusual treks around the Apo Kayan and trans-Borneo treks to Putussibau and Pontianak in Kalbar. On the whole these agents are more expensive than the smaller (but often equally efficient) companies at Samarinda.

Kaltim Adventure Tour, Blok C-1/1 Komplex Balikpapan Permai, Jl Jend Sudirman, T0542-31158, F33408. Have 2 houseboats at Samarinda for Mahakam trips, as well as 5 full-time guides and cooks. Tours include: 3 to 15-day Mahakam trips; Long Apung/Apo Kayan tours; Kutai Game Reserve and overland 15-day treks from Balikpapan to Pontianak. Recommended.

Musi, Jl Dondang (Antasari) 5A, T0542-24272, F24984. A variety of package tours, mainly up the Mahakam River. Recommended.

Tomaco, Hotel Benakutai, Jl Jend A Yani, T0542-22747. The biggest, most professional and most expensive tour agent in town, has a houseboat in Samarinda with a/c cabins to accommodate 12. Also several other smaller boats. Tour prices are 15% off published rates for walk-in tourists. Recommended.

Samarinda *p300, map p301*
Anggrek Hitam, Jl Yos Sudarso 21, T0541-22132, F23161; **Ayus Wisata**, Jl H Agus Salim 13B, T0541-22644, F32080; **Cisma Angkasa**, Jl Abul Hasan, T0541-42098, **Dayakindo**, Jl Bhayangkara; **Makila**, Jl Pirus 68, T0541-75121, a good source of information on visiting the Dayak.

Mahakam River *p302*
Ayus Wisata, Jakarta, T21-749155, F7491560. An adventure tourism specialist which has good boats with a/c cabins and bunks, as well as experienced guides. Recommended.

Cisma Angkasa is an experienced tour agent specializing in adventure tourism along the Mahakam River and the Apo Kayan. The company owns 4 well-fitted double-decker river boats (a/c cabins) and

supplies mosquito nets. It can arrange tours to destinations well off the beaten track (including trans-Borneo treks) and caters for all budgets (cheaper tours use public transport). Recommended.

Freelance guides
Local guides **Jailani** (who hails from Muara Muntai) and his Dayak friend **Marten** (contact them through the **Hidayah 1 Hotel**, Samarinda, above), can arrange cheaper tailor-made trips upriver to **Muara Muntai** and **Malak** over 3-5 days, via houseboat and canoe for around 150,000 Rp per day including all food, sheets, mosquito nets and guide. Also on offer are 4- to 9-day trips to **Data Dawai**, including a 7-hr longboat ride through the rapids near Long Bagun and a 1½-hr flight inland. Prices start at US$1500 for 4 people. They also run a Dayak trek (for a minimum of 2 passengers) as far as **Long Ampung** (flying on **DAS**) which is excellent value – 3 days for US$650 or 5 days for US$750 (including return airfares, food and guide).

    Suriyadi, another recommended freelance guide, can be contacted through the **Hidayah 1 Hotel** or through **Anggrek Hitam** tour company.

Tarakan *p307*
Angkasa, Jl Sebengkok 33, T0551-21130. **Wisma Murni Travel**, Hotel Wisata, T0551-21697.

⊖ Transport

Balikpapan *p299, map p300*
Air
Sepinggang Airport is 10 km from Balikpapan. Airport facilities include a post office, souvenir shop, money changer and restaurant, and an international telephone which takes major credit cards. Fixed price taxis run from the airport to town (13,000 Rp representative, less from town to the airport). The cheapest way to travel from town to the airport is to catch a yellow *bemo* No 2 and then change onto a green *bemo* No 7. Regular connections on **Garuda**, **Merpati**, **Sempati** and **Bouraq** airlines with most major cities in Indonesia, such as Samarinda, Banjarmasin, Pontianak, Tarakan, Pangkalanbun, Jakarta, Semarang,

Yogyakarta, Surabaya, Denpasar, Palu and Monado, Ujung Pandang, Maumere and Kupang. International connections with Singapore (via Pontianak).

Airline offices Bouraq, Jl Sudirman, T0542-31475. **Garuda**, Jl Jend A Yani 19, T0542-22300. **Merpati**, Jl Jend Sudirman 22, T0542-24452. **Sempati**, Altea Benakutai Hotel, Jl Jend A Yani, T0542-31612.

Boat

The **Pelni** ships *Kerinci*, *Kambuna*, *Umsini* and *Tidar* dock at the harbour to the west of the city centre, off Jl Yos Sudarso, and call at **Tarakan**, **Toli-Toli**, **Ujung Pandang**, **Surabaya** and **Tanjung Priok** (Jakarta) – among other ports – on their 2-week circuits. The **Pelni** office is at Jl Yos Sudarso 76, T0542-21402.

Road

Local *Bemos* trips around town cost 400 Rp. They take a circular route around town, down Jl Jend A Yani, Jl Jend Sudirman and past the Pertamina complex on Jl Minyak. They can be hailed at any point; shout 'Stop!' when you want to alight. *Ojeks* have a 2000 Rp minimum charge for a short journey and can also be chartered for a minimum 10,000 Rp per hr.

Bus Regular long-distance bus connections with Samarinda and Banjarmasin. **CV Gelora** express buses to **Samarinda** leave every 30 mins 0530-2000 from Batu Ampar terminal at Km 3.5 on the Samarinda road, 2 hrs. (To get to Batu Ampar terminal take a Kijang taxi to Rapak, the junction with the Samarinda Rd. From Rapak, taxis and *bemos* leave for Batu Ampar when full; alternatively take an *ojek*.) Buses to **Banjarmasin** also leave from the Batu Ampar terminal or from Penajam, on the other side of the bay. Boats cross to Penajam from Pasar Baru at the north end of town on Jl Monginsidi, 10 mins.

Taxi Saloon taxis also go to **Samarinda** from Batu Ampar bus terminal; each car takes up to 7 people. It is also possible to charter an a/c taxi to Samarinda.

Samarinda *p300, map p301*
Air

The airport is on the northeastern outskirts of town. Regular connections on **Bouraq**, **Merpati**, **Sempati**, **Garuda** and **Asahi** airlines with Balikpapan, Banjarmasin, Berau, Tarakan, Surabaya, Jakarta, Yogyakarta and Semarang. Other less regular connections include Bandung and Ujung Pandang. **Asahi** also flies to Datah Dawai on the Upper Mahakam and both **Asahi** and **Merpati** fly to Long Ampung in the Apo Kayan (see page 313). Take a taxi to town or walk out of the airport to Jl Gatot Subroto and catch a *bemo* heading for the city.

Airline offices Bouraq, Jl Mulawarman 24, T0541-41105; DAS, Jl Gatot Subroto 92, T0541-35250. MAF, Jl Ruhui Rahaya 1, T0541-43628. **Merpati**, **Garuda** and **Sempati** are all at Jl Sudirman 20, T0541-43385.

Boat

Sapulidi speedboat from end of Jl Gajah Mada (near the post office), T0541-23821. Terminal Feri, Jl Sungai Kunjang, is the launchpad for **Mahakam River tours**. To get there, take a 'taxi A' – green minibus (500 Rp). The **Pelni** vessels *Leuser* and *Binaiya* call here on their fortnightly circuit between ports in Java, Sulawesi and Kalimantan. **Pelni** office, Jl Yos Sudarso 40-56, T0541-41402.

Road

Local Minibuses: as in Balikpapan, these are called taxis. Red ones go anywhere in town and congregate around Mesra Indah Komplex, 350 Rp. Green ones go to **Sungai Kunjang** (for upriver trips and express buses to Balikpapan). *Bemos* are colour coded to different destinations. For *bemos* to the north, wait on Jl Awang Long; for those travelling west, Jl Sudirman or Jl Gajah Mada.

Ojeks congregate around the Pasar Pagi (Morning Market); 400 Rp around town (can be chartered for 3000 Rp per hr).

Bus Southbound buses arrive and depart from Seberang on the outskirts of town on the south bank of the river, **Balikpapan** 2 hrs, **Tenggarong** 1 hr. The terminal can be reached by green taxis (see above) or by boat – a pleasant trip from Pasar Pagi; the station is immediately behind the ferry terminal. Buses to **Bontang** leave from Terminal Bontang 5 km to the northeast of town.

Taxi Taxis to **Balikpapan** leave from Sungai Kunjang, and to **Bontang** leave from Terminal Segeri.

Tenggarong *p302*
Boat
Travelling by public transport (staying in *losmen* and longhouses en route) gives visitors more contact with locals and it costs a fraction of the price of a package tour. However, these boats are much less comfortable than the big houseboats operated by tour companies. There are regular connections from Sungai Kunjang in Samarinda to all settlements upriver to Long Bagun (in the wet season) and Long Iram (in the dry season). Boats leave from Sungai Kunjang in the early to mid-morning: **Kota Bangun**, 9 hrs, **Tanjung Isuy**, 14 hrs, **Muara Muntai**, 12-14 hrs, **Melak**, 24 hrs, **Long Iram**, 36 hrs, **Long Bagun**, 40 hrs. It is possible to charter a longboat anywhere along the river for a cruise.

Road
The **Petugas** terminal is outside town; *bemos* ferry passengers in to the centre. Regular connections by **Taksi kota** (colts) with **Samarinda**, 1 hr, or take the ferry (Tenggarong lies 3 hrs upstream from Samarinda).

The Lower Mahakam: Samarinda to Muara Muntai *p305, map p304*
There are daily bus connections from Kota Bangun to Samarinda. There are boat connections with Samarinda from **Muara Muntai** (12-14 hrs on the express boat), as well as public boats upriver to **Tanjung Isuy**, 2½ hrs. Boats from Samarinda to Tanjung Isuy every Mon and Thu. From Tanjung Isuy, **Mancong** is 3 hrs' walk (1-way); 2½ hrs canoe (1-way), or you can get there by hired motorcycle.

The Middle and Upper Mahakam
p305, map p304
It takes about 25 hrs from Samarinda by boat to **Melak**. Few tours make it as far as Long Iram – 1½ days from Samarinda; it is possible to go further upriver, but this usually involves chartering a longboat which is expensive.

The Apo Kayan *p306*
Air
The only realistic way of getting to the Apo Kayan is by air. Limited connections to **Long Ampung** from Samarinda on **DAS** only, 1½ hrs and only 4 passengers. Flights are booked up about 6 weeks in advance. Booking possible at the Samarinda office. Organized package tours to the Apo Kayan with big tour companies are expensive: this is because it is necessary to hire a guide (costly) from the agency, charter a longboat (also costly), in addition the lack of demand tends to inflate prices. But at least your flight out is guaranteed. **Kaltim Adventure** (based in Balikpapan) will charter a helicopter if its tourists cannot get onto a flight. **Missionary Aviation Fellowship** (MAF) also flies **Cessna** aircraft to longhouses in the interior, including Long Ampung. But **MAF** is not a commercial airline and should not be treated as one. It does not have a concession from the government to operate on a commercial basis, and also has an agreement with **Merpati** that it will not poach passengers. It is a religious, non-profitmaking organization servicing remote communities; it will only agree to fly tourists out of Long Ampung in the case of emergencies or in the unlikely event of planes being empty. Once in Long Ampung, MAF may consider requests for flights further into the interior; prices vary depending on whether they are scheduled or non-scheduled flights. MAF flies to about 5 airstrips in the remote parts of the Apo Kayan. Write in advance to **MAF**, Box No 82, Samarinda, with details of where and when you intend to go.

Tarakan *p307*
Air
Regular connections on **Bouraq, Merpati, Sempati** and DAS with **Balikpapan** and **Samarinda**. Taxis to town charge 5000 Rp or chartered *bemo* charge about 1000 Rp.

International connections with **Tawau** in Sabah, East Malaysia on **Bouraq** and MAS, 35 mins. 1-month visas are available on arrival at the airport.

Airline offices Bouraq, Jl Yos Sudarso 8, T0551-21248; **DAS**, Jl Sudirman 9, T0551-51578; **Garuda**, Jl Sebengkok 33, T0551-21130; **MAF**, Jl Sudirman 129 (Hotel

Barito Timur), T0551-51011; **Merpati**, Jl Yos Sudarso 8, T0551-21875; **Sempati**, Tarakan Plaza Hotel, Jl Yos Sudarso 8, T0551-21871.

Boat

The **Pelni** office is at the main port, at the south end of Jl Yos Sudarso. The **Pelni** ship *Leuser* calls here . Regular passenger boat connections with **Samarinda** and **Balikpapan** and daily ferries to **Nunukan**, where there are onward connections to **Tawau** in Sabah, East Malaysia. This will require a night in Nunukan (see page 307).

Road

Bemos around town charge 300 Rp.

Nunukan *p307*
Boat

Daily ferry connections (which are packed) with **Tawau** in Sabah, 2 hrs. Also daily ferries to **Tarakan**. The **Pelni** ships *Kerinci*, *Tidar*, *Awu*, *Leuser* and *Binaiya* dock here.

☉ Directory

Balikpapan *p299, map p300*
Banks BCA, Jl Jend A Yani. ATMs outside Balikpapan Plaza; **Bank Dagang Negara**, Jl Jend A Yani; **Bank Duta**, Jl Jend Sudirman 26 (near Altea Benakutai Hotel), probably the best place for foreign exchange; **Bank Negara Indonesia**, Jl Jend Sudirman 30; **Bank Rakyat**, Jl May Jend Sutoyo. **Medical services** Public Hospital, Jl Yani, T0542-34181.

Samarinda *p300, map p301*
Banks Bank Bumi Daya, Jl Irian 160; **Bank Dagang Negara**, Jl Mulawarman 66; **Bank Negara Indonesia**, Jl Pulau Sebatik 1 (corner with Jl Batur); **Bank Rakyat**, Jl Gajah Mada 1 (across from the post office). **Telephone** 24-hr telephone on Jl Awang Long; also in Citra Niaga Plaza.

Tarakan *p307*
Banks Bank Dagang Negara, Jl Yos Sudarso, for TCs and cash.

West Kalimantan (Kalbar)

Kalbar attracts few tourists because it is cut off from Kalimantan's other provinces. It occupies about a fifth of Kalimantan's land area (146,800 sq km), most of which is very flat. The Kapuas River, Indonesia's longest at 1243 km, runs through the middle of the province, east to west. Its headwaters, deep in the interior, are in the Muller range, which fringes the northeast and east borders of Kalbar.

The Kapuas River is navigable for most of its length, which – as with the Mahakam River in East Kalimantan – has allowed the penetration of the interior by merchants and missionaries over the past century. There are small towns all along the river, and the surrounding forest has been heavily logged. For tourists, the Kapuas is less interesting than the Mahakam River, and pales in comparison with the rivers in neighbouring Sarawak. Because few foreign visitors make the trip, however, the Kapuas River is certainly not 'touristy'. To the north, the province borders Sarawak, and the east end of this frontier runs along the remote Kapuas Hulu mountain range. The southeast border with Central Kalimantan province follows the Schwaner Range. About two thirds of West Kalimantan's jungle (a total of some 9,500,000 ha) is classed as 'production forest'; most of the remaining 3,000,000 ha is protected, but it is such a large area that it is impossible to guard against illegal loggers. The timber industry is the province's economic backbone, but Kalbar is also a major rubber producer.

▸▸ For Sleeping, Eating and other listings, see pages 320-322.

Background

History

At about the time Java's Hindu Majapahit Empire was disintegrating in the mid-1300s, a number of small Malay sultanates grew up along the coast of West Kalimantan. These controlled upriver trade and exploited the Dayaks of the interior. When Abdul Rahman, an Arab seafarer-cum-pirate, decided to set up a small trading settlement at Pontianak in 1770, he crossed the paths of some of these sultans. This prompted the first Dutch intervention in the affairs of West Kalimantan, but they did not stay long, and for the next 150 years their presence there was minimal: Borneo's west coast ranked low on the colonial administration's agenda. A gold rush in the 1780s brought Hakka Chinese immigrants flooding into the Sambas area. Their descendants – after several generations of intermarriage with Dayaks – make up more than 10% of West Kalimantan's population today, most living in Pontianak. In the 19th century, the Dutch were worried about the intentions of Rajah James Brooke of Sarawak as he occupied successive chunks of the Sultanate of Brunei. In response, the Dutch increased their presence but any threat that Brooke posed to Dutch territory never materialized. During the Second World War, the people of Kalbar suffered terribly at the hands of the Japanese Imperial Army, who massacred more than 21,000 people in the province, many at Mandor in June 1944.

People

West Kalimantan's 3,900,000 inhabitants are concentrated along the coasts and rivers. Malay Muslims make up about 40% of the inhabitants, Dayaks account for another 40%, Chinese 11% and the remainder include Buginese (originally from Sulawesi) and Minangkabau (originally from Sumatra). West Kalimantan has also received large numbers of transmigrants from Java. Most were originally resettled at Rasau Jaya, to the south of Pontianak, but many have come to the metropolis to find work as labourers – others have simply resorted to begging. Tribal people also come to Pontianak from settlements upriver on the Kapuas; they have usually fared better than the transmigrants and a number hold important jobs in the provincial administration.

Tourism

In 1986 only 5000 foreign tourists arrived in Kalbar; by 1990 this had quadrupled and, following the opening of the Entikong border crossing on the Sarawak frontier, the number of tourists rose again by around 50%. The vast majority of these tourists were curious Malaysians; Westerners account for less than a 10th of Pontianak's tourist arrivals – according to provincial government statistics, a maximum of around 2000 pass through a year. The main reason for this is that the province is rather lacking in tourist sites and receives little attention in the national tourism promotion literature. True, Kalbar has jungle and rivers and Dayaks and offshore islands – but these can also be found in countless other more accessible places in Indonesia.

English is not widely spoken in Kalbar: visitors are advised to learn some basic Bahasa – particularly those heading upriver. The tourist literature produced by the provincial tourism office waxes lyrical about Kalbar's many beautiful islands just offshore and the national parks. But besides being written in rather opaque English, it also fails to mention that few of these have any facilities for tourists and most are extremely difficult to get to. Visitors who want to immerse themselves in Dayak culture and visit traditional longhouses will not find much of interest in Kalbar; only a few tribal groups still live in longhouses on the uppermost reaches of the Kapuas River and its tributaries.

Pontianak ⬡🅿️❄️🗂️🔺🚌🅱️ ⟩⟩ pp320-322. Colour map 3, A4.

⟩⟩ pp320-322. Colour map 3, A4.

Living in Pontianak would be like a European living in a city called 'Dracula' – the name literally translates as 'the vampire ghost of a woman who dies in childbirth'. Apparently, hunters who first came to this area heard terrible screams in the jungle at night and were so scared by them that they dubbed the area 'the place that sounds like a *pontianak*'. But modern Pontianak is no ghost town. It is a thriving, prosperous town with a satellite dish on almost every rooftop. A third of the population of around 387,000 is Chinese. Other ethnic groups are Melayu (26%), Bugis (13%), Javanese (12%) and Dayaks (3%). While Pontianak is certainly a buzzy place, there's nothing obvious here to attract the tourist.

The confluence of the Kapuas and Landak rivers, where the Arab adventurer Abdul Rahman founded the original settlement in 1770, is a strongly Malay part of town. This area, which encompasses several older *kampongs*, is known as Kampong Bugis. The commercial heart of Pontianak is on the left bank of the Kapuas, around the old Chinese quarter. The other side of the river is called Siantan and is distinguished only by its bus terminal, a few rubber-smoking factories (whose choking smell permeates the air) and the pride of Pontianak: the Equator Monument. Like other cities in Kalimantan, Pontianak derives much of its wealth from timber – there seem to be scores of plywood factories and sawmills close to the city. The second string to Pontianak's economic bow, so to speak, is Siam orange production, of which it is Indonesia's largest grower.

Tourist offices The **Department of Posts and Telecommunications (Parpostel)**, ① *Jl Sutan Syahril 17, T0561-39444*, has information on travelling around Kalbar, not

Pontianak

To Tugu Khatulistiwa (Equator Monument) & Batu Layang Long-distance Bus Terminal

To Pasar Ikan (Fish Market)

Jl Khatulistiwa

Jl P Kasih

Kapuas River

SIANTAN

Pelni

Jl Hasanuddin

Jl Usman

Jl Mahmud

Siantan Terminal (Local Buses)

Jl Rahwal

Jl Tamar

Jl Sisingamar

Jl Putri

Kapuas Indah Market

Landak River

Landak Bridge

Jl B Barisan

Jl KHW Hasyim

Jl Merdeka

Jl Jend Urip

Jl Johar

Jl Pattimura

Jl S Muhammad

St Yosef Kathedral

Jl Cokroaminoto

Jl Diponegoro

KAMPONG BUGIS

Mesjid Jami

Anyang

Jl Teuku

Jl Setia Budi

Bugis Schooner Dock

Perintis Kemerdekaan

Jl Putri Daranante

Jl KHA Dahlan

Jl Lelanang

Jl Tanjungpura

Kadriyah Palace

Jl Cendra Wasih

Jl Gajah Mada

Kapuas Bridge

MAF

Jl Supramo

Jl Pahlawan

Kapuas Kecil River

Jl Tanjung Raya

Malaysian Consulate

Jl Jend A Yani

Jl Veteran

Jl Imam Bonjol

Immigration

Musium Negeri

To Supadio Airport

N

0 metres 500
0 yards 500

Sleeping 🛏		Eating 🍴
Kapuas Palace **2**	Mahkota **4**	Do 'n' Mi **1**
Kartika **3**	Pontianak City **5**	Hawaii **2**
	Wisma Patria **6**	

much English spoken; the **Tourist Information Office** is at the airport (and at Entikong border crossing); **Tourist Promotion Office (Kalbar)** ⓘ *Jl Achmad Sood 25, T0561-36172*, is out of town.

Sights

The **Musium Negeri** ⓘ *southern end of Jl Jend A Yani, Tue-Sun 0900-1300*, the state museum, contains good models of longhouses and a comprehensive display of Dayak household implements, including a collection of tattoo blocks, weapons from blowpipes to blunderbusses, one sad-looking skull, masks, fish traps and musical instruments. There are examples of Dayak textiles, *ikat*, *songket* and basketry. There is also a model of a Malay house and a collection of typical household implements. The Dayak and Malay communities are represented in the huge relief sculptures on the front of the museum. But there is absolutely nothing on or in it acknowledging the presence of the large Chinese population – other than some Chinese ceramics. Nor, unfortunately, are any of the objects labelled in English. To get there take an *oplet* (pick-up) from Kapuas Indah covered market. Just past the museum is the huge whitewashed West Kalimantan **governor's office**. There is a replica Dayak longhouse near the museum, off Jalan Jend A Yani, built in 1985 to stage a Koran-reading contest.

The ironwood *istana* or *kraton* – **Kadriyah Palace** ⓘ *admission by donation, open 0900-1730*, was built at the confluence of the Landak and Kapuas rivers by the town's Arab founding father, Abdul Rahman, shortly after he established the trading settlement. The palace was home to seven sultans; Sharif Yusof, son of the the seventh, looks after it today. His uncle married a Dutch woman whose marble bust is one of the eccentric collection of items which decorate the palace museum. Among the fascinating array of odds and ends are two 5 m-tall decorated French mirrors, made in 1923; these face each other across the room and Sharif's party trick is to hold a lighter up to create an endless corridor of reflected flames. There is also a selection of past sultans' *bajus* and *songkoks*, a jumble of royal regalia, including two thrones and tables of Italian marble and a photograph of the sixth sultan and his heir, who were murdered by the Japanese in a mass killing during the Second World War.

The **Mesjid Jami** (mosque), or Mesjid Abdurrahman – which is next to the palace – was built shortly after the founding of the city in the late 1700s, although it has been renovated and reconstructed over the years. It is a beautiful building with tiered roofs, standing at the confluence of the two rivers, with its lime-green turret-like minarets and its bell-shaped upper roof. The Kapuas riverbank next to the mosque is a pleasant place to sit and watch life on the river – the elegant Bugis schooners berth at the docks on the opposite bank. The sky over the mosque and palace is alive with kites flown by the children in Kampong Bugis.

Over the Landak Bridge and past the stinking Siantan rubber smokehouses, which line the right bank of the Kapuas, is the **Tugu Khatulistiwa** (Equator Monument). During the March and September equinoxes, the column's shadow disappears, which is an excuse for a party in Pontianak. In 1991, the old *belian* (ironwood) equator column was encased in a new architectural wonder, a sort of concrete mausoleum where it is intelligently hidden from the sun. There is a new 6-m column on top.

The heart of the city, around **Kapuas Indah** indoor market, is an interesting and lively part of town. There are a number of *pekong* (Taoist temples) around the market area; the oldest, **Sa Seng Keng**, contains a huge array of gods. The **Dwi Dharma Bhakti Chinese Temple** on Jalan Tanjungpura is notable for its location in the middle of the main street.

The **Pasar Ikan** (Fish Market), downriver from town on Jalan Pak Kasih, is a great place to wander in the early morning; the stallholders are just as interesting as the incredible variety of fish they sell. One of the most rewarding things to do in Pontianak is to **hire a sampan** for a couple of hours and potter along the river, taking in all the activity.

Tourist facilities are limited outside Pontianak – and so are tourist sights. Some areas along the northwest coast – including offshore islands – can be visited in day-long excursions from Pontianak, and these have been listed under the separate sections, below.

Pontianak's two main tour operators offer city tours and short package tours along the west coast to Singkawang and Sambas regencies, as well as offshore islands. Longer upriver trips on the Kapuas can be arranged, as can adventure tours with jungle trekking and whitewater rafting. **Insan** offers one particularly adventurous whitewater rafting trip to rapids on the Pinoh River.

Singkawang and the northwest coast 💻📇

➤➤ *pp320-322. Colour map 3, A4.*

Singkawang was originally settled by Hakka Chinese in the early 1800s and was the main town servicing the nearby gold rush shanty at Mantrado. It is now an important farming area and is named after a local turnip.

About 7 km south of Singkawang there is a **pottery** village, where replicas of antique Chinese ceramics are fired in a big kiln. **Pasir Panjang** beach is 17 km south of Singkawang.

Facilities are being developed on **Pulau Randayan**, a 12-ha island with good coral. It takes two hours to get there by boat from Pasir Panjang, and it is possible to stay overnight. Trips to the island are organized by Mr Sukartadji, owner of the **Palapa Hotel** in Singkawang.

Pulau Temajo, 60 km south of Singkawang (off the coast from the village of Sungai Kunyit), an island with white-sand beaches and good coral. There is some accommodation available on the island. **Ateng Tours & Travel** in Pontianak (see page 321) can advise on the best way to get there; the company also runs one-day package tours to the island, supplying food and skin-diving equipment.

Kapuas River 💻📇 ➤➤ *pp320-322. Colour map 3, A4-5.*

The first European to venture up the 1243-km-long Kapuas River was a Dutchman, Major George Muller, who reached the site of present-day Putussibau in 1822 and who lent his name to the mountains to the east. Four years later, while attempting to cross these mountains from the upper Mahakam to the Kapuas, he had his head taken by Dayaks. The Dayaks of the upper Kapuas were themselves terrorized by Iban headhunters, mostly from the Batang Lupar in Sarawak – although some Iban settled in the area to the north of the Kapuas. Few Dayak communities (except those in more remote areas) live in traditional longhouses or observe tribal rituals today. Those who did not turn to Islam (under the influence of the coastal Malays) converted to Christianity: there is a large number of Roman Catholic and Protestant evangelists working throughout the Kapuas Basin; Christians (mainly Catholics) make up about 28% of Kalbar's population.

‡ While tourists heading into remoter areas upriver are no longer shadowed by soldiers, it is necessary to report to the local police station on arrival.

There is still a lot of gold-panning along the Kapuas – using *palong dulang* pans – and larger operations have turned some areas of jungle into a moonscape. Many Dayaks are also employed in the logging industry. Although it is possible to take a *bandung* barge all the way up the river from Pontianak (four or five days to Putussibau, 40,000 Rp), most tourists opt to travel to Sintang by road, which branches off the coast road from Sungai Pinyuh, 50 km northwest of Pontianak.

Pah Auman, between Pontianak and Ngabang (120 km from Pontianak, en route to Entikong), is the nearest village to Kamung Saham longhouse (12 km by road). This 30-door Kendayang (or Kenatyan) longhouse is one of the most traditional longhouses remaining in Kalbar, despite the fact that it is not particularly remote. It is possible to ask the Kepala's (headman's) permission and stay here overnight. Tourists are under the impression that the further they go into the interior, the further they will get from civilization – but in that, Kalbar is not like neighbouring Sarawak. The area north of the Kapuas River was a focus of the *Konfrontasi* – the brief war between Indonesia and Malaysia from 1963 to 1965. The West Kalimantan Communist Party was also very active in the area in the late 1960s, before being crushed.

Sintang and further east

Sintang (245 km, eight hours, east of Pontianak) is at the confluence of the Kapuas and Melawi rivers. About 18 km from town is Mount Kelam – 'Dark Mountain' – which at 900 m affords good views of the surrounding plains and rivers. Guides can be hired in Sintang (two hours walk to the summit). Sintang is a mainly Chinese town, founded by traders dealing with the Dayaks of the interior. On the upper reaches of the Melawi – and its tributary, the Pinoh – there are some traditional Ot Danum (upriver) Dayak groups (the equivalent of Sarawak's Orang Ulu), notably the Dohoi on the upper Melawi. The two rivers begin in the Schwaner Range.

Sentarum, Luar and Sumpa lakes

From **Semitau** – halfway between Sintang and Putussibau – it is possible to visit Sentarum, Luar and Sumpa lakes. The lake area is predominantly settled by Ibans, who originally came upriver from the Batang Lupar in Sarawak; other tribal groups include the Maloh Dayaks (famed for their skill as silversmiths and goldsmiths) and the Kantuq.

Putussibau

Putussibau is the last noteworthy settlement on the Kapuas before the Muller Range, which divides the watersheds of the Kapuas and Mahakam (in East Kalimantan). In the 1800s, when Chinese traders first visited the Upper Kapuas, the settlement was frequently raided by Iban headhunters from the Batang Lupar in Sarawak. The Malays along the Upper Kapuas are mainly Dayaks who converted to Islam. Despite Putussibau's remoteness, few Dayaks in the area live in traditional longhouses, the exception being the Taman Kapuas Dayaks. Two Taman Kapuas longhouses are accessible from Putussibau: **Melapi I** and **Semangkok**, the latter being more traditional; it is possible to stay overnight at both (see House Rules, page 114). Longboats for expeditions further upriver are prohibitively expensive to charter; regular passenger boats connect main towns.

South of Pontianak ⇢ *Colour map 3, A4.*

There are few tourist attractions in the southern **Ketapang** regency, except for the 90,000-ha **Mount Palung Wildlife Reserve**, which encompasses most forest types and contains a wealth of flora and fauna, including orang-utans and proboscis monkeys. It is difficult – and expensive – to get to and is mainly a scientific research centre; there are, however, basic facilities at nine camps within the park. Permits must be obtained from the **Conservation Office (PHPA)** ① *Jl Abdurrahman Saleh 33*, in Pontianak. Tourists wishing to visit the reserve should contact Mr Tan Yong Seng, director of **Ateng Tours & Travel**, whose company can organize the tortuous travel arrangements.

🛏 Sleeping

Pontianak *p316, map p316*

A Mahkota, Jl Sidas 8, T0561-36022, F36200. The smartest hotel in Pontianak, with full range of facilities including swimming pool, tennis courts, a billiard room and a good bar and a restaurant. A/c rooms are small but well appointed, discounts available. Recommended.

B Kapuas Palace, Jl Imam Bonjol, T0561-36122, F34374. A/c, restaurant, large pool, modern low-rise hotel in spacious grounds with good range of facilities, located quite a long way from the market area. Rooms in block and cottages available.

C Kartika, Jl Rahardi Usman, T0561-34401, F38457. A/c, good location on the river, next to the docks and the market area, not as good as the **Mahkota** and **Kapuas Palace** but rooms facing the river recommended.

C Pontianak City, Jl Pak Kasih 44, T0561-32495, F33781. A/c, TV, good mid-range place, friendly staff, good value.

E Wisma Patria, Jl Hos Cokroaminoto 497 (Jl Merdeka Timur), T0561-36063. A/c, own bathroom, no restaurant, sprawling overgrown homestay, without much charm, rooms average but popular with tourists and friendly staff, automatic *teh/kopi* wake-up call at 0630.

Singkawang and the northwest coast *p318*

D Pasir Panjang, Singkawang. Cottage-style, beach-side hotel, a/c, restaurant, pool, facilities include tennis court and watersports.

F Mahkota, Jl Diponegoro 1, Singkawang, T0561-31244, F31491. A/c, restaurant, pool, sister hotel to **Mahkota** in Pontianak with equally good range of facilities.

F Wisata, Jl Diponegoro 59, Singkawang, T056131082, F32563. Clean rooms and good English-speaking receptionist.

Sintang and further east, *page 319*

E Flamboyan. Some a/c and some baths, a notch up from the Sasean.

E Sasean Hotel, Jl Brig Jend Katamso on the river. Welcoming.

🍴 Eating

Pontianak *p316, map p316*

🍴 Do 'n' Mi, Jl Pattimura. Cakes, ice creams and other delicacies served in trendy surroundings. Popular with the Pontianak middle classes. Don't go here if you're hungry – the portions are small.

🍴 Gajah Mada, Jl Gajah Mada 202. Big Chinese-run restaurant with a landscaped interior offering very high-quality food, particularly seafood and freshwater fish. Specialities include: *jelawat* (West Kalimantan river fish), *hekeng* (chopped, deep-fried shrimp), *kailan ca thik pow* (thinly sliced salted fish), crab *fu yung* and sautéed frog. Recommended.

🍴 Nikisa, Jl Sisingamangaraja 108. Sophisticated Japanese restaurant, the most upmarket in Pontianak, *shabu-shabu* buffet, *sukiyaki*, teriyaki burgers and an international selection – mainly imported steaks, set lunch/dinner. Recommended by locals.

🍴 Beringin, Jl Diponegoro 113 and 149. 2 Padang restaurants within 40 m of each other. Recommended.

🍴 Hawaii, Jl Satria 79-80 (across the road from Nusa Indah Plaza), also branch at Jl Gajah Mada 24. A/c restaurant serving Chinese dishes and seafood. Specialities include *puyung hai* (crab or prawn omelette with spicy peanut sauce) and chicken steaks. Recommended.

🍴 Pinang Merah Restoran, Disko dan Singing House, Jl Kapten Marsan 51-53 (behind Kapuas Indah), down the alleyway past the **Wijaya Kusuma Hotel**. Very cool and pleasant place for a drink in the early evening, on wooden walkway next to the river, seafood and Chinese dishes.

🍴 Warung Dangau, Jl Jend A Yani. Excellent place, not easy to find in Taman Budaya. Great Indonesian dishes with a difference.

🍴 Warung Somay Bandung, Jl Sisingamangaraja 132. Very good little place serving basic Indonesian dishes.

Foodstalls

Bobo Indah, opposite the **Wijaya Kusuma Hotel** next to the colourful cinema hoardings. There are also some stalls next to the river. In the mornings there are hawker stalls selling breakfast fishballs and *mee* *kepitang* (noodles and crab) along Jl Nusa Indah II. In the evenings, on the south side of Jl Diponegoro, there are lots of hawker stalls selling cheap Chinese, Padang and Batawi (Jakarta) food.

Fruit market At the top of Jl Nusah Indah, next to St Yosef Katholik Kathedral, excellent selection, including jeruk oranges from around Tebas, north of Singkawang. Their greeny-yellow appearance makes them look rather unappetizing, but they are very sweet. Good durians when in season in Jul and Aug.

Coffee shops
Warung kopi are the hubs of Pontianak social life. They serve not just good coffee, but also snacks such as *pisang goreng* (deep-fried banana) and local patisseries.

Around Pontianak *p318*
Sea Food Garden, Kakap. About 30-mins' drive west of Pontianak, on the coast, in a village famous for its seafood, local farm crabs, lobsters, shrimps and fish, recommended by locals.

⊛ Festivals and events

Pontianak *p316, map p316*
1 Jan West Kalimantan Anniversary, commemorating its accession to the status of an autonomous province in 1957. Folk art exhibitions and dance.
21 Sep Naik Dango Festival (rice storage), when the sun is directly overhead at noon.
Nov Trans-Equator Marathon; in the past this has been a full 42-km event; in 1992 it became a quarter marathon (10 km).

◐ Shopping

Pontianak *p316, map p316*
Due mainly to its large Chinese population, Pontianak is full of gold shops. There are a number of art and craft shops selling Dayak handicrafts, porcelain, textiles (including *ikat* and *songket*) and antiques, but the selection is limited in comparison with Balikpapan and Samarinda.
Leny Art Shop, Jl Khattulistiwa, at the roundabout opposite the Equator Monument (also branch at 1A Blok D, Jl Nusa Indah III), interesting collection of antique Dayak pieces – includes stone axes, medicine boxes,

knives, *ikat*, basketware and Chinese ceramics – and not forgetting a few model equator monuments.

▲ Activities and tours

Pontianak *p316, map p316*
Tour operators
Ateng, Jl Gajah Mada 201, T0561-32683, F36620. Recommended; **Citra Tour & Travel**, Jl Rahadi Usman, T0561-36436; **Insan Worldwide Tours & Travel (ITT)**, Jl Tanjungpura 149; **Jambore Express Tour**, Jl Pahlawan 226, T0561-36703.

⊖ Transport

Pontianak *p316, map p316*
Air
Supadio Airport is 20 km from town. Taxis to and from the airport into town cost 15,000 Rp, although ticket agents in town should be able to organize one for less. Regular connections on **Garuda**, **Merpati**, **Sempati**, **Bouraq** and **DAS** with most major destinations in Indonesia.

There are international connections with **Kuching** (Sarawak) on **MAS** (3 times a week) and **Singapore**, although it is much cheaper to fly to **Batam Island** and then take the 30-min boat trip to Singapore from **Sekupang**.

Airline offices Bouraq, Jl Pahlawan 3A, T0561-37261; **DAS**, Jl Gajah Mada 67, T0561-32313; **Garuda**, Jl Rahadi Usman 8A, T0561-78111; **MAF**, Jl Supranto 50a, T0561-30271. **Mandala**, Jl HOS Cokroaminoto 278A, T0561-35108; **Merpati**, Jl Gajah Mada 210, T0561-36568. **Sempati/Deraya**, Jl Sisingamangaraja 145, T0561-34840.

Boat
A/c express launches bought from Sibu in Sarawak leave for Ketapang (south of Pontianak) daily at 0900. Tickets for **Malindo** and **Kita** express boats sold at **Insan Worldwide Tours & Travel**. *Bandong*, Kalbar's ungainly big river cargo barges, go from near the **Hotel Wijaya Kusuma**, Pontianak, to **Putusibau** (4 days, 3 nights), from Sep-Apr when the water level is high. The **Pelni** ships *Lawit* and *Bukitraya* call at Pontianak on their fortnightly circuits through **Java**, **Sumatra**,

Sulawesi and **Kalimantan**. There are also
regular connections with **Montok**, **Kijang**,
Dumai and **Mahayati**.

Pelni office, Jl Pelabuhan 2, T0561-34133.

Road
Local Bus (*bis kota*): around the Pontianak
area leave from Sintian terminal on the north
side of the river (regular ferries cross the river
from Jl Bardan to the terminal). *Ojeks* are a
good way to see the sights; the easiest place
to pick up an *ojek* is along Jl Tanjungpura.
Oplets leave from Jl Kapten Marsan in front of
the Kapuas Indah indoor market, next to the
warungs; special demarcated routes to most
destinations around town. There are also
oplet stations on Jl Sisingamangaraja and Jl
Teuku Cik Ditiro. **Taxis** (saloons): congregate
around **Dharma Hotel** on Jl Tanjungpura.

Bus Long-distance buses (**Kirana**, **Sago** and
SJS – on Jl Sisingamangaraja – bus
companies) leave from Batu Layang terminal
at Km 8 on the Sambas road. Tickets can be
bought at the bus station. Regular buses to
Singkawang 3½ hrs, **Sambas**, **Sintang** (on
the Kapuas River) 10 hrs, **Meliau**, **Tayan**,
Sekadan and **Ngabang**. To get to the Batu
Layang terminal, take a ferry to Siantan
terminal and *bis kota* (city bus) from Siantan
terminal or *oplet*.

For international connections, the border
is open 0600-1800 West Indonesian time
(0500-1700 Malaysian time). Many buses ply
the route between Pontianak and **Kuching**,
7-10 hrs (RM 34.50). SJS Executive Bus, at
Jl Sisingamangaraja 155 (Pontianak), is
recommended. Note that this is classified as
a gateway 'port' of entry so visas are not
required for citizens of those countries which
are permitted visa-free entry, to Indonesia.
PTS SJS, Jl Sisingamangaraja 155,
T0561-34626, run several buses a day to
Kuching, **Sibu** and **Miri**.

Car Car hire is available from Citra Tour &
Travel.

Taxi Long-distance taxis are available from
the taxi office by the **Kartika Hotel**.

Singkawang and the northwest coast *p318*
Road 143 km north of Pontianak. There are
regular connections with **Pontianak**'s Batu
Layang terminal, 3½ hrs by colt.

Pah Auman and north of the river *p319*
Pah Auman can be reached on any
east-bound bus from **Pontianak**'s Batu
Layang bus station.

Sintang and further east *p319*
Regular buses from **Pontianak**'s Batu Layang
bus station. There are regular passenger
boats leaving Sintang for **Putussibau**. MAF
flies between Sintang and **Putussibau**.

❶ Directory

Pontianak *p316, map p316*
Banks There are several banks along Jl
Tanjungpura (including **Bank Dagang
Negara** and **Bank Duta**); Safari
Money-changer, Jl Tanjungpura 12 (and Jl
Nusa Indah III 57). **Consulate** Malaysia, Jl
Jend Ah Yani 42. **Immigration office** Jl
Sutoyo, T0561-34516, for Pontianak.
Internet Email at the GPO, Mon-Thu, Sat,
Sun 0800-1400, Fri 0800-1100. **Medical
services** Dr Sudarso Hospital, Jl
Adisucipto; **Sei Jawi Hospital Centre**, Jl
Merdeka Barat. **Post office** Jl Rahadi
Usman 1 and Jl Sultan Abdul Rakhman 49,
0800-2100. Poste restante available.
Telephone Department of Posts and
Telecommunications (Parpostel), Jl Sutan
Syahril 17, T0561-39444. **Telkom office**, Jl
Teuku Umar 15, open 24 hrs.

Background

History

Borneo Proper was first visited by Europeans in the early 16th century, most notably by Antonio Pigafetta, the official chronicler on the Portuguese explorer Ferdinand Magellan's expedition which called in on the Sultan of Brunei in 1521. The Ibans of Sarawak maintain that the name Borneo derives from the Malay *buah nyior*, meaning 'coconut', while the Malays had another, less well-known name for the island: Kalimantan. This appears to have been the name of a species of wild mango "and the word would simply mean 'Isle of Mangoes'". This was the name chosen by Indonesia for its section of the island; for some reason, it is generally translated as 'River of Diamonds' – probably because of the diamond fields near Martapura in the south.

The outside world may have been trading with Borneo from Roman times, and there is evidence in Kaltim (East Kalimantan) of Indian cultural influence from as early as the fourth century. Chinese traders began to visit Borneo from about the seventh century – they traded beads and porcelain in exchange for jungle produce and birds' nests. By the 14th century, this trade appears to have been flourishing, particularly with the newly formed Sultanate of Brunei. The history of the north coast of Borneo is dominated by the Sultanate of Brunei from the 14th to 19th centuries. The Europeans began arriving in the East in the early 1500s, but had little impact on North Borneo until British adventurer James Brooke arrived in Sarawak in 1839.

To the south, in what now comprises Kalimantan, a number of small coastal sultanates grew up, many of which were tributary states of Brunei, and most of which are thought to have been founded by members of the Brunei nobility. The upriver Dayaks were left largely to themselves. In the 16th century, following the conversion of Banjarmasin to Islam, the religion was embraced by these other sultanates. The Dutch, who first tried to muscle in on Banjarmasin's pepper trade in the late 1500s, were unsuccessful in establishing themselves in Kalimantan until 1817 when they struck a deal with the Sultan of Banjarmasin.

Culture

People

The vast majority of Borneo's population is concentrated in the narrow coastal belt; the more mountainous, jungled interior is sparsely populated by Dayak tribes. While Dayak communities are represented in all state and provincial governments in Borneo, they only have one province of their own – Kalimantan Tengah (Central Kalimantan), with its capital at Palangkaraya. The Dayaks lived in self-sufficient communities in the interior until they began to come under the influence of Malay coastal sultanates from the 14th and 15th centuries. Some turned to Islam, and more recently, many have converted to Christianity, as a result of the activities of both Roman Catholic and Protestant missionaries (see page 329). Few Dayaks – other than those in the remoter parts of the interior – still wear their traditional costumes.

Dayaks throughout Borneo have only been incorporated into the economic mainstream relatively recently. Relations with coastal groups were not always good, and there was also constant fighting between groups. Differences between the coastal peoples and inland tribes throughout Borneo were accentuated as competition for land increased. Today, however, Dayak groups have relatively good access to education and many now work in the timber and oil and gas industries, which has caused out-migration from their traditional homelands.

The Kalimantan Dayaks can be broadly grouped by region. Kalsel (South Kalimantan) and Kalteng (Central Kalimantan) groups are collectively known as the **Barito River Dayaks** and include the 'Hill Dayaks' of the Meratus Mountains, northeast of Banjarmasin. The **Ngaju** live in Kalteng; they were the first Dayak group in Kalimantan to assert their political rights, by lobbying (and fighting) for the creation of Kalteng in the 1950s. The province was later separated from Kalsel, which was dominated by the strictly Islamic Banjarese. Other Dayak groups in Kalteng include the **Ma'anyan** and the **Ot Danum**, who live along the rivers on either side of the Schwaner Range.

Kayan and Kenyah The main groups living in East Kalimantan are the Kayan and Kenyah, who live in the Apo Kayan region and near the Mahakam River. They are also found on the Mendalam River in West Kalimantan. Almost all Kayan and Kenyah have converted to Christianity (most are Protestant). These two closely related groups were the traditional rivals of the Ibans and were notorious for their warlike ways. Historian Robert Payne, in his history *The White Rajahs of Sarawak*, described the Kayans of the upper Rejang as "a treacherous tribe, [who] like nothing better than putting out the eyes and cutting the throats of prisoners, or burning them alive".

The Kenyahs and Kayans have a completely different language (with ancient Malayo-Polynesian roots) from other tribal groups and a well-defined social hierarchy. Traditionally their society was composed of aristocrats, noblemen, commoners and slaves (who were snatched during raids on other tribes). One of the few things they have in common with other Dayak groups is the fact that they live in longhouses, although even these are of a different design, and are much more carefully constructed, in ironwood. Many have now been converted to Christianity.

Today, the Kenyah and Kayan are renowned for their arts, their music and their parties; visitors recovering from drinking borak rice beer may have their faces covered in soot before being thrown in the river. This is to test the strength of the newly forged friendship with visitors, who are ill-advised to lose their sense of humour on such occasions.

The **Bahau**, related to the Kayan, live in the upper Mahakam region, upriver from Long Iram; the majority are Roman Catholics. The other groups living in the upper Mahakam area include the **Modang** (they are mainly Catholic and are a subgroup of the Kenyah who migrated south), the **Bentian** and the **Penihing**. **Tanjung Dayaks** live in the middle reaches of the Mahakam; some remain animist although large numbers have converted to Christianity (both Roman Catholic and Protestant). The other main group on the middle Mahakam are the **Benuaq** – Tanjung Isuy (see page 305) is a Benuaq village, for example. They are also Roman Catholic.

Murut The Murut live in Northeast Kalimantan, as well as around Tenom and Pensiangan in the southwest of Sabah and in the Trusan Valley of North Sarawak. Some of those living in more remote jungle areas retain their traditional longhouse way of life – but many Murut have now opted for detached kampong-style houses. Murut means 'hill people' and is not the term used by the people themselves. They refer to themselves by their individual tribal names. The **Nabai**, **Bokan** and **Timogun Murut** live in the lowlands and are wet-rice farmers, while the **Peluan**, **Bokan** and **Tagul Murut** live in the hills and are mainly shifting cultivators. They are related to Kalimantan's Lun Dayeh people, although some of the tribes in the South Philippines have similar characteristics too. The Murut staples are rice and tapioca, they are known for their weaving and basketry and have a penchant for drinking *tapai* (rice wine). They are also enthusiastic dancers and devised the *lansaran* – a sprung dance floor like a trapeze. The Murut are a mixture of animists, Christians and Muslims and were one of the last tribes to give up head-hunting.

Kelabit who live in the highlands at the headwaters of the Baram River, are closely related to the Kelabit-Murut and the Lun Dayeh and Lun Bawang of interior Kalimantan. The Kelabit-Murut are distinct culturally and linguistically from the Murut of Northeast Kalimantan. They are skilled hill-rice farmers and the highland climate also allows them to cultivate vegetables. Kelabit parties are also famed as boisterous occasions, and large quantities of borak rice beer are consumed. They are regarded as among the most hospitable people in Borneo.

Penan Perhaps Southeast Asia's only remaining true hunter-gatherers, the nomadic Penan live mainly in the upper Rejang and Limbang areas of Sarawak, but there is also a small population in the Apo Kayan of Kalimantan. Groups of Penan hunter-gatherers still wander through the forest in groups to hunt wild pigs, birds and monkeys, and search for sago palms from which they make their staple food, sago flour. The Penan are considered to be the jungle experts by all the other inland tribes. Because they live in the shade of the forest, their skin is relatively fair. They have a great affection for the coolness of the forest and until the 1960s were rarely seen by the outside world.

Kadazan Living in the border areas of East Kalimantan, the Kadazan are an agrarian people with a strong cultural identity. Formerly, they were known as 'Dusuns', meaning 'peasants' or 'orchard people'. This name was given to them by outsiders, and picked up by the British. Traditionally Kadazans lived in longhouses but these are rare now, and most live in Malay-style houses.

All the Kadazan groups share a common language (although dialects vary). The Kadazans traditionally traded their agricultural produce at large markets, held at meeting points called *tamus*. They used to be animists, and were said to live in great fear of evil spirits; most of their ceremonies were rituals aimed at driving out these spirits. The job of communicating with the spirits of the dead, the *tombiivo*, was done by priestesses, called *bobohizan*. But most Kadazans converted to Christianity during the 1930s, although there are also some Muslim Kadazan.

The big cultural event in the Kadazan year is the Harvest Festival which takes place in May. The ceremony, known as the Magavau ritual, is officiated by a *bobohizan*. These elderly priestesses – who wear traditional black costumes and colourful headgear with feathers and beads – are now few and far between. The ceremony culminates with offerings to the Bambaazon, or rice spirit. After the ceremonies, Catholic, Muslim and animist Kadazans all come together to play traditional sports such as wrestling and buffalo racing. This is about the only occasion when visitors are likely to see Kadazan in their traditional costumes. Belts of silver coins (*himpogot*) and brass rings are worn round the waist; a colourful sash is also worn. Men dress in a black, long-sleeved jacket over black trousers; they also wear a *siga*, colourful woven headgear. These costumes have become more decorative in recent years, with colourful embroidery.

Iban Dayak communities in Kalbar (West Kalimantan) include the Iban. But the Iban are far better known as the largest tribal group in East Malaysia than they are in Kalimantan. They are usually stereotyped as an outgoing people who extend a warm welcome to visitors. Iban women are skilled weavers; even today a girl is not considered eligible until she has proven her skills at the loom by weaving a ceremonial textile. The Ibans love to party, and during the Gawai harvest festival (June), visitors are particularly welcome to drink copious amounts of *tuak* (rice wine) and dance through the night.

Probably because they were shifting cultivators, the Iban remained in closely bonded family groups and were a classless society. Historian Mary Turnbull says "they retained their pioneer social organization of nuclear family groups living together in longhouses and did not evolve more sophisticated political institutions. Long-settled families acquired prestige, but the Ibans did not merge into tribes and had neither chiefs, rakyat class, nor slaves." The Iban have a very easy-going attitude to love and sex (best explained in Redmond O'Hanlon's book *Into the Heart of Borneo*). Free love is the general rule among Iban communities which have not become evangelical Christians, although once married, the Iban divorce rate is low and they are monogamous. Groups related to the Iban include the Seberuang, Kantuq and Mualang.

Bugis Another of the groups who live along Kalimantan's coasts are the Bugis (Sea Gypsy) people, originally from South Sulawesi. They are famous shipbuilders and their schooners are still made in Kalsel, South Kalimantaŋ (see page 291).

Dance
Dayak tribes are renowned for their singing and dancing, and the most famous is the hornbill dance. In her book, *Sarawak*, Hedda Morrison writes: "The Kayans are probably the originators of the stylized war dance which is now common among the Ibans but the girls are also extremely talented and graceful dancers. One of their most delightful dances is the hornbill dance, when they tie hornbill feathers to the ends of their fingers which accentuate their slow and graceful movements. For party purposes everyone in the longhouse joins in and parades up and down the communal room led by one or two musicians and a group of girls who sing." On these occasions, drink flows freely. With the Ibans, it is *tuak* (rice wine), with the Kayan and Kenyah it is *borak*, a bitter rice beer. After being entertained by dancers, a visitor is under compunction to drink a large glassful, before bursting into song and doing a dance routine themselves. The best guideline for visitors on how to handle such occasions is provided by Redmond O'Hanlon in his book *Into the Heart of Borneo*. The general rule of thumb is to be prepared to make an absolute fool of yourself, throwing all inhibition to the wind. This will immediately endear you to your hosts.

Music
Gongs range from the single large gong, the *tawak*, to the *engkerumong*, a set of small gongs, arranged on a horizontal rack, with five players. An *engkerumong* ensemble usually involves between five and seven drums, which include two suspended gongs (*tawak* and *bendan*) and five hour-glass drums (*ketebong*). They are used to celebrate victory in battle or to welcome home a successful head-hunting expedition. The Bidayuh also make a bamboo gong called a *pirunchong*. The *jatang uton* is a wooden xylophone which can be rolled up like a rope ladder; the keys are struck with hardwood sticks.

The Bidayuh make two main stringed instruments: a three-stringed cylindrical bamboo harp called a *tinton* and the *rabup*, a rotan-stringed fiddle with a bamboo cup. The Kenyah and Kayan play a four-stringed guitar called a *sape*. It is the most common and popular lute-type instrument, whose body, neck and board are cut from one piece of softwood. It is used in Orang Ulu dances and by witchdoctors. It is usually played by two musicians, one keeping the rhythm, the other the melody. Traditional *sapes* had rotan strings; today they use wire guitar strings and electric pick-ups. Another stringed instrument, more usually found in Kalimantan than Sarawak, is the *satang*, a bamboo tube with strings around the outside, cut from the bamboo and tightened with pegs.

One of the best-known instruments is the *engkerurai* (or *keluri*), the bagpipes of Borneo, which is usually associated with the Kenyahs and Kayans. It is a hand-held organ in which four vertical bamboo pan-pipes of different lengths are fixed to a gourd, which acts as the wind chamber. Simple *engkerurai* can only manage one chord; more sophisticated ones allow the player to use two pipes for the melody, while the others provide a harmonic drone. The Bidayuh are specialists in bamboo

Arts and crafts

Basketry A wide variety of household items are woven from rotan, bamboo and bemban reed, as well as nipah and pandanus palms. Basketry is practised by nearly all the ethnic groups in Borneo and they are among the most popular handicrafts. A variety of baskets are made for harvesting, storing and winnowing paddy, as well as for collecting and storing other items. The Penan are reputed to produce the finest rattan sleeping mats – closely plaited and pliable. The Kayan and Kenyah produce four main types of basket. The *anjat* is a finely woven jungle rucksack with two shoulder straps; the *kiang* is also a rucksack-type affair but with a rougher weave, and is stronger and used for carrying heavier loads; the *lanjung* is a large basket used for transporting rice; while the *bakul* is a container worn while harvesting rice, so that the pannicles drop in. The *bening aban* is the famous baby carrier; it is woven in fine rattan, has a wooden seat and is colourfully decorated with intricate beadwork. Many of the native patterns used in basketry come from Chinese patterns and take the form of geometrical shapes and stylized birds. The Bidayuh also make baskets from either rotan or sago bark strips. The most common Bidayuh basket is the *tambok*, which is simply patterned and has bands of colour; it also has thin wooden supports on each side.

Beadwork Among many Kenyah, Kayan, Bidayuh and Kelabit groups, beads have long been symbols of status and wealth; necklaces, skull caps and girdles are handed down from generation to generation. Smaller glass – or plastic – beads (usually imported from Europe) are used to decorate baby carriers, baskets, headbands, jackets, hats, sheaths for knives, tobacco boxes and handbags. Beaded baby carriers are mainly used by the Kelabit, Kenyah and Kayan, and often have shells and animals' teeth attached which make a rattling sound to frighten away evil spirits. Rounded patterns require more skill than geometric patterns, the quality of the pattern used to reflect the status of the owner. Only upper-classes are permitted to have beadwork depicting 'high-class' motifs such as human faces or figures. Early beads were made from clay, metal, glass, bone or shell (the earliest have been found in the Niah Caves.)

Blowpipes Blowpipes are usually carved from hardwood – normally *belian* (ironwood). The first step is to make a rough cylinder about 10 cm wide and 2.5 m long. This rod is tied to a platform, from which a hole is bored through the rod. The bore is skilfully chiselled by an iron rod with a pointed end. The rod is then sanded down to about 5 cm in diameter. Traditionally, the sanding was done using the rough underside of macaranga leaves. The darts are made from the nibong and wild sago palms, and the poison itself is the sap of the *upas* (Ipoh) tree (*Antiaris toxicari*) into which the point is dipped.

Hats Kalimantan's Dayak hats are called *seraung* and are made from biru leaves; they are conical and often have colourful *ta-ah* patchwork cloth sewn onto them, or they might be decorated with beads. The Kenyah – like their relations across the Sarawak border – wear distinctive grass-plaited caps called *tapung*.

Textiles The Benuaq Dayaks of the Mahakam are known for their *ikat* weaving, producing colourful pieces of varied designs. They are woven with thread produced from pineapple leaves. While traditional costumes are disappearing fast, it is still possible to find the *sholang*, colourful appliqué skirts, which have black human figures and dragon-dogs (*aso/asok*) sewn on top. The traditional sarong worn by Dayak women is called a *ta-ah*, which is a short, colourful, patchwork-style material.

The weaving of cotton *pua kumbu* is one of the oldest Iban traditions, and literally means 'blanket' or 'cover'. The weaving is done by the women and is a vital skill for a would-be bride to acquire. There are two main methods employed in making and decorating *pua kumbu*: the more common is the ikat tie-dyeing technique, known as *ngebat* by the Iban. The other method is the *pileh*, or floating weft. The Ibans use a warp-beam loom which is tied to two posts, to which the threads are attached. There is a breast-beam at the weaving end, secured by a back strap to the weaver. A pedal, beneath the threads, lowers and raises the alternate threads which are separated by rods. The woven material is tightly packed by a beater. The material is tie-dyed in the warp. Because the *pua kumbu* is made by the warp-tie-dyeing method, the number of colours is limited. The most common are a rich browny-brick-red colour and black, as well as the undyed white sections; blues and greens are used in more modern materials. Traditionally, *pua kumbu* were hung in longhouses during ceremonies and were used to cover images during rituals. The designs and patterns are representations of deities which figure in Iban myths and are believed to protect individuals from harm; they are passed down from generation to generation. Such designs, with deep spiritual significance, can only be woven by wives and daughters of chiefs. Other designs and patterns are representations of birds and animals, including hornbills, crocodiles, monitor lizards and shrimps, which are either associated with worship or are sources of food. Symbolic representations of trees, plants and fruits are also included in the designs as well as the events of everyday life. A typical example is the zigzag pattern which represents the act of crossing a river – the zigzag course is explained by the canoe's attempts to avoid strong currents. Many of the symbolic representations are highly stylized and can be difficult to pick out.

Weapons The traditional Dayak head-hunting knife is called a mandau. It is a multi-purpose knife with practical and ritualistic uses. The different tribes have different-shaped mandau blades, which are made of steel; their handles are carved in the shape of a hornbill's head from bone. Human hair was traditionally attached to the end of the handle. Other Dayak weapons include the tombak hunting spear, made from ironwood, with a steel tip. The sumpit, or blowpipe, was used for hunting, but now plays a largely ceremonial role during rituals and festivals. The Dayak battle shield (kelbit) is made from cork, and is shaped like an elongated diamond.

Woodcarvings Many of Borneo's tribal groups are skilled carvers, producing everything from huge burial poles to small statues, masks and other decorative items and utensils. The traditional Kenyah masks, which are used during festivals, are elaborately carved and often have large protruding eyes. Eyes are always emphasized, as they are to frighten the enemy. Other typical items carved by tribal groups include spoons, stools, doors, walking sticks, *sapes* (guitars), ceremonial shields, tops of water containers, tattoo plaques and the hilts of *parang ilang* (ceremonial knives). The most popular Iban motif is the hornbill, which holds an honoured place in Iban folklore (see page 332), being the messenger for the sacred Brahminy kite, the ancestor of the Iban. Another famous Iban carving is the sacred measuring stick called the *tuntun peti*, used to trap deer and wild boar; it is carved to represent a forest spirit. The Kayan and Kenyahs' most common motif is the *aso*, a dragon-like dog with a long snout. It also has religious and mythical significance. The Kenyah and Kayan carve huge burial structures, or *salong*, as well as small ear pendants made of hornbill ivory.

Small carved statues, or *hampatong*, are commonly found in handicraft shops. They are figures of humans, animals or mythical creatures and traditionally have ritual functions. They are often kept in Dayak homes to bring good luck, good health or good harvests. They are divided according to the Dayak cosmology: male figures (human and animal) are associated with the upper world, female figures (human and animal) with the lower world, while hermaphrodite figures symbolize the middle world. Large *hampatong* are associated either with death or headhunting, while others, usually placed as a totem outside a village, will serve as its protector. Another group of large *hampatong* are the *sapundu*, to which sacrificial victims were tied before being put to death.

Land and environment

Geography

The highest peak in Kalimantan is Gunung Rajah (2278 m) in the Schwaner Range, to the southwest; the two biggest rivers are in Kalimantan: the Kapuas, which flows west from the centre of the island, and the Mahakam, which flows east.

Kalimantan itself is divided into four provinces. South Kalimantan (or Kalimantan Selatan) is ubiquitously referred to as Kalsel and is the smallest of the four and is also the highlight of most tourists' visits to Kalimantan. To the west is Central Kalimantan (Kalimantan Tenggah), known as Kalteng, a vast province with a very small population; few foreign tourists venture here; its only real tourist attraction is a remote orang-utan rehabilitation centre near the swampy south coast. East Kalimantan (Kalimantan Timur) is known as Kaltim and is the richest of the four provinces because of its timber, oil and gas resources. Its main attraction is the Mahakam River which penetrates deep into the interior from the provincial capital, Samarinda. West Kalimantan (Kalimantan Barat) – or Kalbar – is, like neighbouring Kalteng, visited by few tourists. It is cut off from the rest of Kalimantan by the mountainous, jungled interior and can only be reached by air – although some east coast tour operators offer two-week trans-Borneo treks. The longest river in Indonesia, the 1243-km-long Kapuas, reaches far into the interior from Kalbar's capital, Pontianak.

Tourists usually come to Kalimantan in search of two things: jungle and jungle culture – the Dayak forest tribes. It sometimes comes as a shock that loggers have beaten them into the jungle, particularly in the more accessible areas along the coasts and rivers. For quite long distances on either side of the riverbanks, the primary forest has all been 'harvested'. Kalimantan's powerful rivers (the Kapuas, Mahakam and Berito) have been the arteries of commerce and 'civilization'; the riverbanks are lined with towns and villages as far as they are navigable. Missionaries and traders have also beaten tourists into the tribal interior. Many Dayak tribes have been converted to Christianity and most have completely abandoned their cultures, traditions and animist religion. The majority of upriver people – apart from those in the remoter parts of the Apo Kayan in Kaltim – prefer to wear jeans and T-shirts, and many have relatively well-paid jobs in the timber industry.

That said, it is still possible to visit traditional longhouses in Kalimantan (in the hills of Kalsel and the upper reaches of the Mahakam and Kenyah rivers in Kaltim) – and trek through tracts of virgin rainforest. But trips to these areas take time and cost money. There are several experienced adventure tourism companies in Kalimantan – mostly based in Balikpapan and Samarinda. They categorize their tours into 'comfortable', 'safari' and 'adventure'.

Climate

Borneo has a typical equatorial monsoon climate: the weather usually follows predictable patterns, although in recent years it has been less predictable. Temperatures are fairly uniform, averaging 23-33°C during the day and rarely dropping below 20°C at night, except in the mountains, where they can drop to below 10°C. Most rainfall occurs between November and January during the northeast monsoon; this causes rivers to flood, and there are many short, sharp cloudbursts. The dry season runs from May to September. It is characterized by dry southeasterly winds and is the best time to visit. Rainfall generally increases towards the interior; most of Borneo receives about 2000-3000 mm a year, although some upland areas get more than 4000 mm. Note that there are significant variations in the pattern of rainfall across Kalimantan.

Flora and fauna

Borneo's ancient rainforests are rich in flora and fauna, including between 9000 and 15,000 species of seed plant (of which almost half may be endemic), 200 species of mammal, 570 species of birds 100 species of snake, 250 species of freshwater fish and 1000 species of butterfly. Despite years of research the gaps in scientists' knowledge of the island's flora and fauna remain yawning – and if anything are becoming more so. For a significant proportion of the flora of Borneo, scientists have barely any information on their geographic distribution, let alone details of their ecology.

Borneo's forests hit the news for all the wrong reasons in 1997: a series of fires scorched millions of hectares of land and shrouded an area the size of Western Europe, with a population of around 100,000,000, in what became euphemistically termed 'the haze'.

As late as the mid-19th century, the great bulk – perhaps as much as 95% – of the land area of Borneo was forested. Alfred Russel Wallace, like other Western travellers, was enchanted by the island's natural wealth and diversity: "ranges of hill and valley everywhere", he wrote, "everywhere covered with interminable forest". But Borneo's jungle is disappearing fast and since the mid-1980s there has been a mounting international environmental campaign against deforestation.

The best known timber trees fall into three categories, all of them hardwoods. Heavy hardwoods include selangan batu and resak; medium hardwoods include kapur, keruing and keruntum; light hardwoods include madang tabak, ramin and meranti. There are both peat-swamp and hill varieties of meranti, which is one of the most valuable export logs. *Belian*, or Bornean ironwood (*Eusideroxylon zwageri*), is one of the hardest and densest timbers in the world. It is thought that the largest *belian* may be 1000 years or more old. They are so tough that when they die they continue to stand for centuries before the wood rots to the extent that the trunk falls.

The main types of forest include: lowland rainforest (mixed dipterocarp) on slopes up to 600 m. Many of the rainforest trees are an important resource for Dayak communities. The jelutong tree, for example, is tapped like a rubber tree for its sap ('jungle chewing gum'), which is used to make tar for waterproof sealants – used in boat-building. It also hardens into a tough but brittle black plastic-like substance used for parang (machette) handles. Montane forest occurs at altitudes above 600 m, although in some areas it does not replace lowland rainforest until considerably higher than this. Above 1200 m mossy forest predominates. Montane forest is denser than lowland forest, with smaller trees of narrower girth. Moreover, dipterocarps are generally not found, while flowering shrubs like magnolias and rhododendrons appear. In place of dipterocarps, tropical latitude oaks, as well as other trees that are more characteristic of temperate areas, like myrtle and laurel, make an appearance.

The low-lying river valleys are characterized by peat swamp forest – where the peat is up to 9 m thick – which makes wet-rice agriculture impossible.

Heath forest or *kerangas* – the Iban word meaning 'land on which rice cannot grow' – is found on poor, sandy soils. Although it mostly occurs near the coast, it is also sometimes found in mountain ranges, but almost always on level ground. Here trees are stunted and only the hardiest of plants can survive. Some trees have struck up symbiotic relationships with animals – like ants – so as to secure essential nutrients. Pitcher plants (*Nepenthes*) have also successfully colonized heath forest. The absence of bird calls and other animal noises make heath forest rather eerie, and it also indicates their general biological poverty.

Along beaches there are often stretches of casuarina forest; the casuarina grows up to 27 m and looks like a conifer, with needle-shaped leaves. Mangrove occupies tidal mud flats around sheltered bays and estuaries. The most common mangrove tree is the bakau (*Rhizophora*), which grows to heights of about 9 m and has stilt roots to trap sediment. Bakau wood is used for pile-house stilts and for charcoal.

Orang-utan (*Pongo pygmaeus*) Borneo's great red-haired ape is known as 'man of the jungle' after the translation from the Malay: orang (*man*), utan (*jungle*). It is endemic to the tropical forests of Sumatra and Borneo. The Sumatran animals tend to keep the reddish tinge to their fur, while the Borneo ones go darker as they mature. It is Asia's only great ape; it has four hands, rather than feet, bow-legs and has no tail. Males of over 15 years old stand up to 1.6 m tall and their arms span 2.4 m. Adult males (which make loud roars) weigh 50-100 kg – about twice that of adult females (whose call sounds like a long, unattractive belch). Orang-utans are said to have the strength of seven men but they are not aggressive; they are peaceful, gentle animals, particularly with each other.

Orang-utans mainly inhabit riverine swamp forests or lowland dipterocarp forests. They are easily detected by their nests of bent and broken twigs, which are woven together, in much the same fashion as a sun bear's, in the fork of a tree. They are solitary animals and always sleep alone. Orang-utans have a largely vegetarian diet consisting of fruit and young leaves, supplemented by termites, bark and birds' eggs. They are usually solitary, but the young remain with their mothers until they are five or six years old. Two adults will occupy an area of about 2 sq km and are territorial, protecting their territory intruders. They can live up to 30 years and a female will have an average of three to four young during her lifetime. The gestation period is nine months. After giving birth, they do not mate for around another seven years.

Estimates of the numbers of orang utan vary considerably. What is certain is that the forest is disappearing fast, and with it the orang-utan's natural habitat. Orang-utans' favoured habitat is lowland rainforest and this is particularly under threat from logging. The black market in young apes in countries like Taiwan means that they fetch relatively high returns to local hunters.

Proboscis monkey (Nasalis larvatus) The proboscis monkey is an extraordinary-looking animal, endemic to Borneo, which lives in lowland forests and mangrove swamps all around the island. Little research has been done on proboscis monkeys; they are notoriously difficult to study as they are so shy. Their fur is reddish-brown and they have white legs, arms, tail and a ruff on the neck, which gives the appearance of a pyjama-suit. Their facial skin is red and the males have grotesquely enlarged, droopy noses; females' noses are shorter and upturned. The male's nose is the subject of some debate among zoologists: whatever else it does, it apparently increases their sex-appeal. To ward off intruders, the nose is straightened out, 'like a party whoopee whistle', according to one description. Recently a theory has been advanced that the nose acts as a thermostat, helping to regulate body temperature. But it also tends to get in the way: old males often have to resort to holding their noses up with one hand while stuffing leaves into their mouths with the other.

Proboscises' penises are almost as obvious as their noses – the proboscis male glories in a permanent erection, which is probably why they are rarely displayed in zoos. The other way the males attract females is by violently shaking branches and making spectacular – and sometimes near-suicidal – leaps into the water, in which they attempt to hit as many dead branches as they can on the way down, so as to make the loudest noise possible. The monkeys organize themselves into harems, with one male and several females and young – there are sometimes up to 20 in a group. Young males leave the harem they are born into when the adult male becomes aggressive towards them, and they rove around in bachelor groups until they are in a position to form their own harem.

The proboscis is a diurnal animal, but keeps to the shade during the heat of the day. The best time to see them is very early in the morning or around dusk. They can normally be heard before they are seen; they make loud honks, rather like geese; they also groan, squeal and roar. Proboscis monkeys are good swimmers; they even swim underwater for up to 20 m – thanks to their partially webbed feet. Males are about twice the size and weight of females. They are known fairly ubiquitously (in both Malaysian and Indonesian Borneo) as *Orang Belanda*, or Dutchmen – which is not entirely complimentary. In Kalimantan they also have other local names including *Bekantan*, *Bekara*, *Kahau*, *Rasong*, *Pika* and *Batangan*.

Other monkeys Other monkeys found in Borneo include various species of leaf monkey – including the grey leaf monkey, the white-fronted leaf monkey and the red-leaf monkey. One of the most attractive members of the primate family found in Borneo is the tubby slow loris or *kongkang*. And perhaps the most difficult to pronounce – at least in Dusun – is the tarsier, which is locally known as the *tindukutrukut*.

Hornbill There are nine types of hornbill in Borneo, the most striking and biggest of which is the rhinoceros hornbill (*Buceros rhinoceros*) – or *kenyalang*. They can grow up to 1.5 m long and are mainly black, with a white belly. The long tail feathers are white too, crossed with a thick black bar near the end. They make a remarkable, resonant 'geronk' call in flight, which can be heard over long distances; they honk when resting. Hornbills are usually seen in pairs – they are believed to be monogamous. After mating, the female imprisons herself in a hole in a tree, building a sturdy wall with her own droppings. The male bird fortifies the wall from the outside, using a mulch of mud, grass, sticks and saliva, leaving only a vertical slit for her beak. She remains incarcerated in her cell for about three months, during which the male supplies her and the nestlings with food – mainly fruit, lizards, snakes and mice. Usually, only one bird is hatched and reared in the hole, and when it is old enough to fly, the female breaks out of the nest hole. Both emerge looking fat and dirty.

The 'bill' itself has no known function, but the males have been seen duelling in mid-air during the courting season. They fly straight at each other and collide head-on. The double-storeyed yellow bill has a projection, called a casque, on top, which has a bright red tip. In some species the bill develop wrinkles as the bird matures: one wrinkle for each year of its life. For this reason they are known in Dutch, and in some eastern Indonesian languages as 'year birds'.

Most Dayak groups consider the hornbill to have magical powers and the feathers are worn as symbols of heroism. In tribal mythology the bird is associated with the creation of mankind, and is a symbol of the upper world. The hornbill is also the official state emblem of Sarawak. The best place to see hornbills is near wild fig trees – they love the fruit and play an important role in seed dispersal. The helmeted hornbill's bill is heavy and solid and can be carved, like ivory. These bills were highly valued by the Dayaks, and have been traded for centuries. The third largest hornbill is the wreathed hornbill which makes a yelping call and a loud – almost mechanical – noise when it beats its wings. Others species on Borneo include the wrinkled, black, bushy-crested, white-crowned and pied hornbills.

Footnotes

Useful words and phrases

Bahasa Malaysia and Bahasa Indonesia are mutually intelligible but not the same; the list below gives the word in Malay with the Indonesian version in the third column if the difference is significant. ▸▸ *See also page 16.*

Basic phrases

Yes/No	Ya/tidak	
Thank you	Terimah kasih	
Good morning	Selamat pagi	
Good afternoon (early)	Selamat tengahari	Selamat siang
Good afternoon (late)	Selamatpetang	Selamat sore
Good evening/night	Selam at malam	
Welcome	Selamat datang	
Goodbye (said by the person leaving	Selamat tinggal	
Goodbye (said by the person staying)	Selamat jalan	
Excuse me/sorry	Ma'af saya (Ma'af)	
Where's the...?	Dimana...	
How much is this...?	Ini berapa?	Berapa harganya?
I [don't] understand	Saya [tidak] mengerti	

Sleeping

How much is a room?	Bilik berapa?	Kamar berapa harga?)
Does the room have air-conditioning?	Ada bilik yang ada air-con-kah?	Ada kamar yang ada AC-nya?
I want to see the room first please	Saya mahu lihat bilik dulu	Saya mau lihat kamar dulu
Does the room have hot water?	Ada bilik yang ada air panas?	Ada kamar yang ada air panas?
Does the room have a bathroom?	Ada bilik yang ada mandi-kah?	Ada kamar yang ada kamar mandi?

Travel

Where is the railway station?	Stesen keretapi dimana?	Dimana stasiun ketera api?
Where is the bus station?	Stesen bas dimana?	Dimana stasiun bis?
How much to go to...?	Berapa harga ke...?	
I want to buy a ticket to...	Saya mahu beli tiket ke...	Saya mahu beli karcis ke...
Is it far?	Ada jauh?	
Turn left / turn right	Belok kiri /belok kanan	
Go straight on!	Turus turus!	Terus saja

Time and days

Monday	Hari Isnin	Hari Senin
Tuesday	Hari Selasa	
Wednesday	Hari Rabu	
Thursday	Hari Khamis	
Friday	Hari Jumaat	
Saturday	Hari Sabtu	
Sunday	Hari Minggu	
Today	Hari ini	
Tomorrow	Esok	Hari besok

Numbers

1 satu	12 dua-belas...etc
2 dua	20 dua puluh
3 tiga	21 dua puluh satu...etc
4 empat	30 tiga puluh
5 lima	100 se-ratus
6 enam	101 se-ratus satu...etc
7 tujuh	150 se-ratus limah puluh
8 lapan	200 dua ratus
9 sembilan	1000 se-ribu
10 sepuluh	2000 dua ribu
11 se-belas	100,000 se-ratus ribu
	1,000,000 se-juta

Basic vocabulary

Malay, with the Indonesian version in parenthesis if the difference is significant

a little sedikit
a lot banyak
all right/good baik
bank bank
beach pantai
beautiful cantik
bed sheet cadar
big besar
boat perahu
bus bas (bis)
buy beli
can boleh
cheap murah
chemist rumah ubat (apotek)
clean bersih
closed tutup
day hari
delicious sedap (enak)
dentist doktor gigi
dirty kotor
doctor doktor
eat makan
excellent bagus
expensive mahal
food makan
hospital rumah sakit

hot (temperature) panas
hot (spicy) pedas
I/me saya
island pulau
market pasar
medicine ubat ubatan (obat)
open masuk
please sila
police polis (polisi)
police station pejabat polis (stasiun polisi)
post office pejabat pos (kantor pos)
restaurant kedai makanan (rumah makan)
room bilik (kamar)
sea laut
ship kapal
shop kedai (toko)
sick sakit
small kecil
stop berhenti
taxi teksi (taksi)
that itu
they mereka
toilet – female/male tandas – perempuan/ lelaki (WC, 'way say')
town bandar (kota)
very sangat (Sekali)
water air
what apa

Glossary

A

Adat　custom or tradition

Amitabha　the Buddha of the Past (see Avalokitsvara)

Atap　thatch

Avalokitsvara　also known as Amitabha and Lokeshvara, the name literally means 'World Lord'; he is the compassionate male Bodhisattva, the saviour of Mahayana Buddhism and represents the central force of creation in the universe; usually portrayed with a lotus and water flask

B

Bahasa　language, as in Bahasa Malaysia and Bahasa Indonesia

Bajaj　three-wheeled motorized taxi

Barisan Nasional　National Front, Malaysia's ruling coalition comprising UMNO, MCA and MIC along with seven other parties

Batik　a form of resist dyeing common in Malay areas

Becak　three-wheeled bicycle rickshaw

Bodhi　the tree under which the Buddha achieved enlightenment (Ficus religiosa)

Bodhisattva　a future Buddha. In Mahayana Buddhism, someone who has attained enlightenment, but who postpones nirvana in order to help others reach the same state

Brahma　the Creator, one of the gods of the Hindu trinity, usually represented with four faces, and often mounted on a hamsa

Brahmin　a Hindu priest

Budaya　cultural (as in Muzium Budaya)

Bumboat　small wooden lighters, now used for ferrying tourists in Singapore

C

Cap　batik stamp

Chedi　from the Sanskrit *cetiya*, meaning memorial. Usually a religious monument (often bell-shaped) containing relics of the Buddha or other holy remains. Used interchangeably with stupa

Cutch　see Gambier

D

Dalang　wayang puppet master

Dayak/Dyak　collective term for the tribal peoples of Borneo

Dharma　the Buddhist law

Dipterocarp　family of trees (*Dipterocarpaceae*) characteristic of Southeast Asia's forests

Durga　the female goddess who slays the demon Mahisa, from an Indian epic story

G

Gambier　also known as cutch, a dye derived from the bark of the bakau mangrove and used in leather tanning

Gamelan　Malay orchestra of percussion instruments

Ganesh　elephant-headed son of Siva

Garuda　mythical divine bird, with predatory beak and claws, and human body; the king of birds, enemy of naga

Gautama　the historic Buddha

Geomancy　or feng shui, the Chinese art and science of proper placement

Godown　Asian warehouse

Goporum　tower in a Hindu temple

Gunung　mountain

H

Hamsa　sacred goose, Brahma's mount; in Buddhism it represents the flight of the doctrine

Hinayana　'Lesser Vehicle', major Buddhist sect in Southeast Asia, usually termed Theravada Buddhism

I

Ikat　tie-dyeing method of patterning cloth

Indra　the Vedic god of the heavens, weather and war; usually mounted on a three-headed elephant

J

Jataka(s)　birth stories of the Buddha, of which there are 547; the last 10 are the most important

K

Kajang thatch

Kala (makara) literally, 'death' or 'black'; a demon ordered to consume itself; often sculpted over entranceways to act as a door guardian, also known as *kirtamukha*

Kampong or *kampung*, village

Kerangas from an Iban word meaning 'land on which rice will not grow'

Kinaree half-human, half-bird, usually depicted as a heavenly musician

Klotok motorized gondolas of Banjarmasin

Kongsi Chinese clan house

Kris traditional Malay sword

Krishna an incarnation of Vishnu

Kuti living quarters of Buddhist monks

L

Laterite bright red tropical soil/stone sometimes used as a building material

Linga phallic symbol and one of the forms of Siva. Embedded in a pedestal shaped to allow drainage of lustral water poured over it, the linga typically has a succession of cross sections: from square at the base through octagonal to round. These symbolize, in order, the trinity of Brahma, Vishnu and Siva

Lintel a load-bearing stone spanning a doorway; often heavily carved

Lokeshvara see Avalokitsvara

Lunggyi Indian sarong

Losmen guesthouse

M

Mahabharata a Hindu epic text written about 2000 years ago

Mahayana 'Greater Vehicle', major Buddhist sect

Mandi Indonesian/Malay bathroom with water tub and dipper

Maitreya the future Buddha

Makara a mythological aquatic reptile, somewhat like a crocodile and sometimes with an elephant's trunk; often found, along with the *kala*, framing doorways

Mandala a focus for meditation; a representation of the cosmos

MCA Malaysian Chinese Association

Meru the mountain residence of the gods; the centre of the universe, the cosmic mountain

MIC Malaysian Indian Congress

Mudra symbolic gesture of the hands of the Buddha

N

Naga benevolent mythical water serpent, enemy of Garuda

Naga makara fusion of *naga* and *makara*

Nalagiri the elephant let loose to attack the Buddha, who calmed him

Nandi/Nandin bull, mount of Siva

Negara kingdom and capital, from the Sanskrit

Negeri also negri, state

Nirvana 'enlightenment', the Buddhist ideal

O

Ojek motorcycle 'taxi'

P

Paddy/padi unhulled rice

Pantai beach

Pasar market, from the Arabic 'bazaar'

Pasar malam night market

Pelni Indonesian state shipping line

Perahu/prau boat

Peranakan mixed race, usually applied to part-Chinese and part-Malay people

Pradaksina pilgrims' clockwise circumambulation of a holy structure

Prang form of stupa built in the Khmer style, shaped rather like a corncob

Prasat residence of a king or of the gods (sanctuary tower), from the Indian *prasada*

Pribumi indigenous (as opposed to Chinese) businessmen

Pulau island

Pusaka heirloom

R

Raja/rajah ruler

Raksasa temple guardian statues

Ramayana the Indian epic tale

Ruai common gallery of an Iban longhouse, Sarawak

Rumah adat customary or traditional house

S

Sago multi-purpose palm

Sal the Indian *sal* tree (*Shorea robusta*), under which the historic Buddha was born

Sakyamuni the historic Buddha

Silat or *bersilat*, traditional Malay martial art

Singha mythical guardian lion

Siva one of the Hindu triumvirate, the god of destruction and rebirth

Songket Malay textile interwoven with supplementary gold and silver yarn

Sravasti the miracle at Sravasti when the Buddha subdues the heretics in front of a mango tree

Sri Laksmi the goddess of good fortune and Vishnu's wife

Stele inscribed stone panel or slab

Stucco plaster, often heavily moulded

Stupa see *chedi*

Sungai river

T

Tamu weekly open-air market

Tanju open gallery of an Iban longhouse, Sarawak

Tara also known as Cunda; the four-armed consort of the Bodhisattva Avalokitsvara

Tavatimsa heaven of the 33 gods at the summit of Mount Meru

Theravada 'Way of the Elders'; major Buddhism sect also known as Hinayana Buddhism ('Lesser Vehicle')

Tiffin afternoon meal – a word that was absorbed from the British Raj

Timang Iban sacred chants, Sarawak

Tong or *towkay*, a Chinese merchant

Totok 'full blooded'; usually applied to Chinese of pure blood

Towkay Chinese merchant

Triads Chinese mafia associations

Tunku also Tuanku and Tengku, prince

U

Ulama Muslim priest

Ulu jungle

UMNO United Malays National Organization

Urna the dot or curl on the Buddha's forehead, one of the distinctive physical marks of the Enlightened One

Usnisa the Buddha's top knot or 'wisdom bump', one of the physical marks of the Enlightened One

V

Vishnu the Protector, one of the gods of the Hindu trinity, generally with four arms holding the disc, the conch shell, the ball and the club

W

Waringin banyan tree

Warung a foodstall – a simple place to eat on the street – the alernative Malay name is *Kedai Makan*. The word originally comes from Indonesia.

Wayang traditional Malay shadow plays

Food glossary

For more information on cuisine, see page 33.

assam sour; tamarind

ayam chicken

babek duck

babi pork

belacan hot fermented prawn paste

buah fruit

daging meat

es krim ice cream

garam salt

gula sugar

ikan fish

kacang tanah peanut

kambing mutton

kopi coffee

lombok chilli

manis sweet

mee noodles

minum drink

nasi rice

roti bread, pancake

sayur vegetables

sejuk crab

susu milk

tahu beancurd

telur egg

udang prawn

Rice dishes

nasi campur Malay curry buffet of rice served with meat, fish, vegetables and fruit.

nasi goreng rice, meat and vegetables fried with garlic, onions and sambal.

nasi lemak a breakfast dish of rice cooked in coconut milk and served with prawn *sambal*, *ikan bilis*, a hard-boiled egg, peanuts and cucumber.

nasi puteh plain boiled rice.

nasi dagang glutinous rice cooked in coconut milk and served with fish curry, cucumber pickle and sambal.

nontong rice cakes in a spicy coconut-milk topped with grated coconut and sometimes bean curd and egg (Sarawak).

nasi biryani saffron rice flavoured with spices and garnished with cashew nuts, almonds and raisins (Sarawak).

rijsttafel Indonesian meal consisting of a selection of rice dishes, to which are added small pieces of meat, fish, fruit and pickles.

Soup

lontong cubed, compressed rice served with mixed vegetables in coconut milk. *Sambal* is the accompaniment. Popular for breakfast.

soto ayam a spicy chicken soup served with rice cubes, chicken and vegetables, popular for breakfast in Sarawak.

sup manuk on hiing chicken soup with rice wine (Sabah).

sup terjun jumping soup – salted fish, mango and ginger (Sabah).

Meat, fish and seafood

hinava marinated raw fish (Sabah).

pan suh manok chicken cooked in bamboo cup, served with *bario* (Kelabit mountain rice) (Sarawak).

satay chicken, beef or mutton marinated and skewered on a bamboo, barbecued over a brazier. Usually served with *ketupat*.

tapai chicken cooked in rice wine (Sabah).

ternbok fish, either grilled or steamed (Sarawak).

Sayur masak lemak deep-fried marinated prawns (Sarawak).

Noodles

kway teow flat noodles fried with seafood, egg, soy sauce, beansprouts and chives.

laksa johor noodles in fish curry sauce and raw vegetables.

mee goreng fried noodles.

mee jawa noodles in gravy, served with prawn fritters, potatoes, tofu and beancurd.

mee rebus noodles with beef, chicken or prawn with soybean in spicy sauce. In Sarawak, it's yellow noodles served in a thick sweet sauce made from sweet potatoes and garnished with sliced hard-boiled eggs and green chillies.

mee siam white thin noodles in a sweet and sour gravy made with tamarind (Sarawak).

Curries

longong vegetable curry made from rice cakes cooked in coconut, beans, cabbage and bamboo shoots.

Salad

gado-gado cold dish of bean sprouts, potatoes, long beans, tempeh, bean curd, rice cakes and prawn crackers, topped with a spicy peanut sauce.

rojak Malaysia's answer to Indonesia's *gado gado* – mixed vegetable salad served in peanut sauce with *ketupat*.

Vegetables

kang-kong belacan water spinach fried in chilli-shrimp paste.

pakis ferns, which are fried with mushrooms and belacan. Sometimes ferns are eaten raw, with a squeeze of lime (*sayur pakis limau*) (Sabah).

sayur manis sweet vegetables; vegetables fried with chilli, belacan and mushrooms.

Sweets (kueh)

apam steamed rice cakes.

es delima dessert of water chestnut in sago and coconut milk.

hinompula a dessert made from tapioca, sugar, coconut and the juice from screwpine leaves (Sabah).

ice kachang similar to *chendol* (see Chinese food) but with evaporated milk instead of coconut milk.

pulut inti glutinous rice served with sweetened grated coconut.

nyonya kueh Chinese *kueh*, among the most popular is *yow cha koei* – deep-fried kneaded flour.

Index

Footnotes Map index

Map index

Credits

Footprint credits

Editor: Felicity Laughton
Map editor: Sarah Sorensen
Picture editor: Claire Benison
Proofreaders: Claire Boobbyer,
Sarah Sorensen
Publisher: Patrick Dawson
Editorial: Alan Murphy, Sophie Blacksell,
Nicola Jones
Cartography: Robert Lunn, Claire Benison,
Kevin Feeney
Series development: Rachel Fielding
Cover design: Robert Lunn
Design: Mytton Williams and Rosemary
Dawson (brand)
Sales and Marketing: Andy Riddle
Advertising: Debbie Wylde
Administration: Elizabeth Taylor

Photography credits

Front cover: Alamy (young orang-utan)
Back cover: Alamy (market in
eastern Borneo)
Inside colour section: Alamy, Jamie
Marshall, Shaun Tierney, Superstock

Print

Manufactured in India by Nutech
Photolithographers, Delhi. Pulp from
sustainable forests

Footprint feedback

We try as hard as we can to make each
Footprint guide as up to date as possible
but, of course, things always change. If you
want to let us know about your experiences –
good, bad or ugly – then don't delay, go to
www.footprintbooks.com and send in
your comments.

Publishing information

Footprint Borneo
1st edition
© Footprint Handbooks Ltd
March 2006

ISBN 1 904777 60 0
CIP DATA: A catalogue record for this book is
available from the British Library

® Footprint Handbooks and the Footprint
mark are a registered trademark of
Footprint Handbooks Ltd

Published by Footprint

6 Riverside Court
Lower Bristol Road
Bath BA2 3DZ, UK
T +44 (0)1225 469141
F +44 (0)1225 469461
discover@footprintbooks.com
www.footprintbooks.com

Distributed in the USA by

Publishers Group West

Every effort has been made to ensure that
the facts in this guidebook are accurate.
However, travellers should still obtain
advice about travel and visa requirements
before travelling. Hotel and restaurant price
codes should only be taken as a guide to
the prices and facilities offered by the
establishment. It is with the discretion of
the owners to vary them from time to time.
The authors and publishers cannot accept
responsibility for any loss, injury or
inconvenience however caused.

Acknowledgements

For all their help and enthusiasm, James Alexander would like to thank Jennifer Kang and her team at the Empire Hotel & Country Club, David Coleman of Mona Florafauna Tours and Jean Christophe Robles Espinosa at Brunei Tourism.

Dinah Gardner would like to thank Pearlyn Ng for soup and support in Singapore and the following were also a massive help: in KL – Doreen Lim, David Bowden and Kevin the pixel miner; elsewhere – Jodi Smith, Chwee Sze Foong, Carey Walker, Narelle at Langkawi's Bon Ton Resort, Kieth Sarson, Mark Elliot, the crazy boys at Uncle Tan's in Sabah and, last but not least, Andrew Paterson, who knows what he did.

Footprint would also like to thank Professor Larry Goodyer, Head of the Leicester School of Pharmacy and director of Nomad Medical, for providing the health section.

And finally, thanks to Joshua Eliot, Jane Bickersteth and Liz Capaldi for all their work on earlier editions of *Footprint Malaysia* and *Footprint Indonesia*.

Map 1

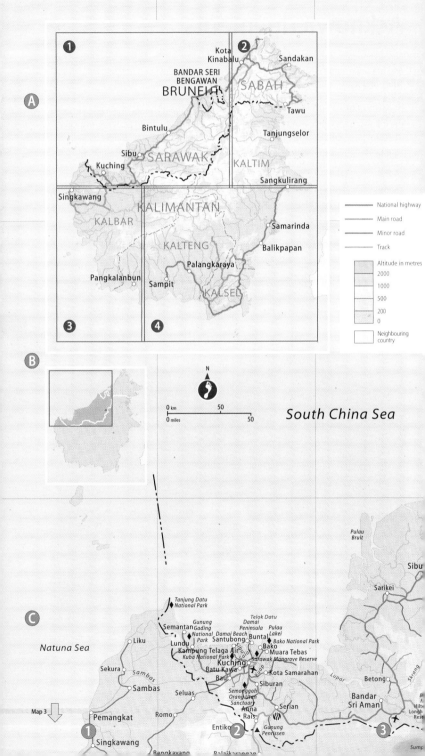

National highway
Main road
Minor road
Track

Altitude in metres
2000
1000
500
200
0

Neighbouring country

A

①
Kota Kinabalu
Sandakan
BANDAR SERI BENGAWAN
BRUNEI
SABAH
②
Tawu
Bintulu
Tanjungselor
Sibu
SARAWAK
Kuching
KALTIM
Sangkulirang

Singkawang
KALIMANTAN
Samarinda
KALBAR
KALTENG
Balikpapan
Palangkaraya
Pangkalanbun
Sampit
KALSEL
③
④

B

South China Sea

N

0 km   50
0 miles   50

C

Natuna Sea

Tanjung Datu National Park
Semantan
Gunung Gading National Park
Liku
Lundu
Kampung Telaga Air
Kuba National Park
Telok Datu
Damai Peninsula
Damai Beach
Santubong
Pulau Lakei
Buntal
Bako
Bako National Park
Muara Tebas
Sarawak Mangrove Reserve
Sekura
Sambas
Batu Kawa
Kuching
Kota Samarahan
Sambas
Bau
Seluas
Siburan
Semonggoh Orang Utan Sanctuary
Anna Rais
Serian
Pulau Bruit
Sibu
Sarikei
Betong
Bandar Sri Aman
Lupar

Map 3
Pemangkat
Singkawang
Romo
Entiko
Gunung Penrissen
Bengkayang
①
②
③

Luconia Island

A

Tunku Abdu
Rahman Nationa
Pulau
Kota Kir
Tanju
P
Pa

Pulau Tiga
National Park ◆
Kuala
Penyu

Klias Peninsula

LABUAN
Pulau ✈
Labuan
Menumbok
Beaufort

Ten
Muara   Telok Brunei   Sipitang
Sindumin
BANDAR SERI
BEGAWAN   Merapok
BRUNEI & MUA □   Lawas
Tutong   Labu
Limbang   Batang Duri   Lumaku
Bangar   ▲ (1,966m)
Kuala   Seria   Lumut
Baram   TUTONG   TEMBURONG
Kuala   Limbang
Kuala   Belait
Baram   Ulu Temburong
BRUNEI   National Park
Lutong   ✈   Labi
Miri   Teraja   Ladan   Long
Lambir Hills   ✈   Hills   Semado
National Park ◆   Marudi   BELAIT   Mulu
(2,376m)   Murudi
Niah   Gunung Mulu   ▲ (2,423m)
National   National Park   Long
Park   Seridan
Niah Caves ◆   Long   Bukit Batu Bali
Terawan   Tutoh   (2,082m)

Loagan Bunut   Bario
National Park ◆   Baram
Patah

Similajau   Kelabit Highlands
National Park
Bintulu   Kemena
✈
Tatua
R Baling   Tinjar
Skalap ▲   Long
Long   Peran
Muma   Belepeh
Belaga   Long
Lirong Amo   Sah   Long Murum
Long Dungan   Long Linau
Mersing   Long   Long Geng
Kakus   Pangai   Murum
Rejang   Balui
SARAWAK
Pelagus   Batu
Rapids   (2,012m)   Long Ayak
owit   Kapit
Rejang   ✈   Balleh

k   Mengiong   Muller Range   Map 2
an
fe   C
ary   Long Nawang
g Ai
Park   KALTIM

Map 4   Apo Kayan
4   5   6
um   Putussibau
Luar Lake

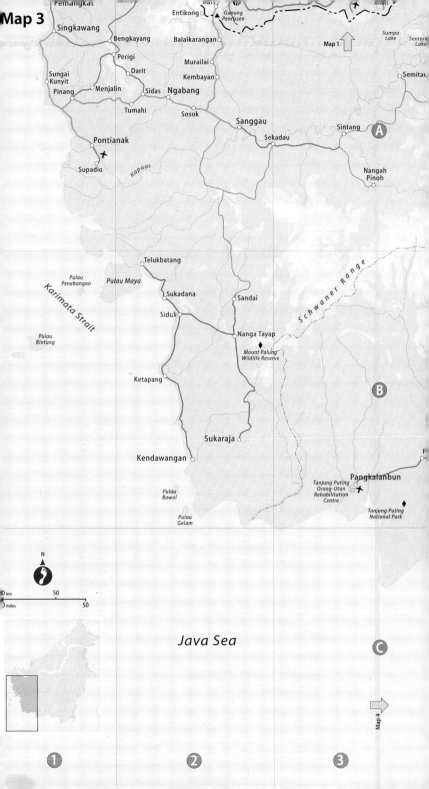

Map symbols

Administration

- □ Capital city
- ○ Other city/town
- International border
- Regional border
- Disputed border

Roads and travel

- Motorway
- Main road (National highway)
- Minor road
- ---- Track
- ...... Footpath
- Railway with station
- ✈ Airport
- ⊟ Bus station
- Ⓜ Metro station
- ---- Cable car
- ++++ Funicular
- ⛴ Ferry

Water features

- River, canal
- Lake, ocean
- Seasonal marshland
- Beach, sandbank
- Waterfall

Topographical features

- Contours (approx)
- Mountain
- Volcano
- Mountain pass
- Escarpment
- Gorge
- Glacier
- Salt flat
- Rocks

Cities and towns

- Main through route
- Main street

(continued)

- Minor street
- Pedestrianized street
-) (Tunnel
- → One way-street
- Steps
- Bridge
- Fortified wall
- Park, garden, stadium
- Sleeping
- Eating
- Bars & clubs
- Building
- Sight
- Cathedral, church
- Chinese temple
- Hindu temple
- Meru
- Mosque
- Stupa
- Synagogue
- Tourist office
- Museum
- Post office
- Police
- Bank
- Internet
- Telephone
- Market
- Medical services
- Parking
- Petrol
- Golf
- Detail map
- Related map

Other symbols

- Archaeological site
- National park, wildlife reserve
- Viewing point
- Campsite
- Refuge, lodge
- Castle
- Diving
- Deciduous/coniferous/palm trees
- Hide
- Vineyard
- Distillery
- Shipwreck
- Historic battlefield